365

Your Date with History

365

Your Date with History

W.B. Marsh and Bruce Carrick

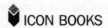

ICON BOOKS

Published in the UK in 2004
by Icon Books Ltd., The Old Dairy,
Brook Road, Thriplow,
Cambridge SG8 7RG
email: info@iconbooks.co.uk
www.iconbooks.co.uk

Reprinted 2004

Sold in the UK, Europe, South Africa
and Asia by Faber and Faber Ltd.,
3 Queen Square, London WC1N 3AU
or their agents

Distributed in the UK, Europe, South Africa
and Asia by TBS Ltd., Frating Distribution Centre,
Colchester Road, Frating Green, Colchester CO7 7DW

Published in Australia in 2004
by Allen & Unwin Pty. Ltd.,
PO Box 8500, 83 Alexander Street,
Crows Nest, NSW 2065

Distributed in Canada by
Penguin Books Canada,
10 Alcorn Avenue, Suite 300,
Toronto, Ontario M4V 3B2

ISBN 1 84046 606 5

Typesetting by Hands Fotoset

Printed and bound in the UK by Mackays of Chatham plc.

The most important date of all:
28 December 1972
W.B. Marsh

Dates worth the keeping:
23 March, 4 May, 19 October and 29 November
Bruce Carrick

Contents

CONTENTS

CONTENTS

Preface

SMALL DATES in the calendar resonate with history. Most people associate 5 November with Guy Fawkes's failed attempt to blow up Parliament, 14 July with a Paris mob storming the Bastille, and 4 July with America's declaration of its independence from Great Britain. The more historically knowledgeable might connect 15 March with the Ides of March and Julius Caesar's assassination, 30 January with the beheading of King Charles, and 18 June with the Battle of Waterloo.

But most calendar dates are not so easily linked with the past. Indeed, some dates that were once synonymous with great historical events have disappeared from our modern calendar. How many of us remember that 24 May was Queen Victoria's birthday? Nevertheless, it is our contention that something worth noting in history occurred on every day of the year. This book is based on that idea.

We attempted to go further than simply connecting events with every date in the calendar. We tried to give some background and colour to each story we selected, to say why it happened, and to describe the sometimes surprising results. Because we have concentrated on portraying the individuals involved, the articles are often as much about men and women – and sometimes children – in unusual circumstances as about the historical events themselves.

Our selection of events is inevitably arbitrary owing to the vast array of history from which to pick and to the practical limitation on the number that could appear in a printed book. The stories we relate here are drawn in the main from British, European and American history but also in smaller number from Japan, India, China, Canada and elsewhere. The article with the earliest date, 25 June 1229 BC, concerns the day the great Pharaoh Ramses II took power in Egypt. Because we decided to regard anything occurring in the past 50 years as a matter of current events rather than history, the most recent event in the book is the French defeat at Dien Bien Phu, which happened on 7 May 1954.

Whatever their dates, we selected events we thought were important, with impact on their time (and maybe on our own as well). They include births, deaths, marriages, funerals, coronations, assassinations, convocations, scandals, executions, battles, publication dates, duels and treaties. Often the events involve a famous figure, like Horatio Nelson or Lorenzo the Magnificent or Robespierre or Dante. Sometimes, however, they are simply fascinating bits of historical trivia, such as how the English dynastic name Plantagenet derived from a French noble's habit of adorning his hat with a sprig of yellow gorse, with the name *planta genista*.

Regarding historical 'truth', we have made every effort to be as accurate as possible, but we have seen that historians often disagree even about facts, let alone interpretations. And, in the spirit of offering an entertaining narrative, we have on occasion included reported historical detail that today may not seem altogether credible, such as the 'fact' that Mary, Queen of Scots' lips continued to move for ten minutes after her decapitation.

At one point in the writing we asked ourselves who we thought would constitute the audience for such a book. The response was simple: people like us, of course. That is, anyone who has even a passing interest in the events of the past, who relishes the human dramas that have shaped our civilisation, who enjoys a good tale or an ironic detail or a historical quirk, who is amused by the foibles of great people in all ages, and – above all – who wants to know what else of importance happened on his wife's birthday.

For such an audience, it seems appropriate to end this preface with the same words John Locke used to begin another in 1690:

Reader, I Here put into thy Hands, what has been the diversion of some of my idle and heavy Hours: If it has the good luck to prove so of any of thine, and thou hast but half so much Pleasure in reading, as I have had in writing it, thou wilt as little think thy Money, as I do my Pains, ill bestowed.

1 January

Samuel Pepys starts his diary

1660 'Jan. 1 (Lord's Day). This morning (we living lately in the garret) I rose, put on my suit with great skirts, having not lately worn any other clothes but them. Went to Mr. Gunning's chapel at Exeter House, where he made a very good sermon ...'

So begins the first entry of Samuel Pepys's diary, which he kept faithfully for nine years and five months. After chapel, Pepys returned to the rooms he leased in Axe Yard to dine on leftover Christmas turkey with his wife Elizabeth, who had burned her hand in the preparation of the meal. He spent the afternoon going over accounts. In the evening he and Mrs Pepys ate dinner at his father's house in Salisbury Court, 'where in came Mrs. The. Turner and Madam Morrice, and supt with us. After that my wife and I went home with them, and to our own home.'

When he began the diary, Pepys was 26, the ambitious son of a poor tailor but lucky in his influential cousins. He was also a graduate of Magdalene College, Cambridge, already married for five years, and at the beginning of what would turn out to be a long and successful career as a servant of the crown. He maintained the diary, with most of its contents obscured by his use of short-hand, until 31 May 1669, when failing eyesight forced him to desist. The diary touches on many of the great events and figures of the day – King Charles II, the Great Fire of 1666, the plague, the court, Restoration politics and the naval war against the Dutch – but these serve as background for the main subject, drawn with such remarkable candour, which is Pepys himself, 'that entrancing ego of whom alone he cared to write', in Robert Louis Stevenson's phrase.

Pepys's diary was a secret during his lifetime. After his death in 1703 its six leather-bound volumes remained unnoticed among his library and papers for over a century. It was first published in 1825, in a heavily bowdlerised version that excised many passages dealing frankly with the delicate matters of politics and Pepys's own sexual conquests. Despite the editorial damage done to it, the diary was recognised as a work of genius. Expanded editions followed, but the full diary as Pepys wrote it was not published until 1970. His biographer Claire Tomalin summed up the diarist's accomplishment this way:

> 'The most unlikely thing at the heart of his long, complex and worldly life is the secret masterpiece ... The achievement is astounding, but there is no show or pretension; and when you turn over the last page of the Diary you know you have been in the company of both the most ordinary and the most extraordinary writer you will ever meet.'

1

Lincoln frees America's slaves

1863 On this day Abraham Lincoln's Emancipation Proclamation became law, freeing the 4 million slaves living in the Confederate states. Most of these remained in bondage for another two years, until the North had finally won the Civil War.

Although Lincoln is most famous for abolishing slavery, this was not his foremost goal. Holding the United States together as a single nation was his primary reason for leading his country into war. 'If I could save the Union without freeing *any* slaves, I would do it,' Lincoln wrote, 'and if I could save it by freeing *all* the slaves I would do it; and if I could save it by freeing some and leaving others alone, I would also do that.'

By 1862 Lincoln had come to realise that the only way to save the Union was through military victory, but he knew that Emancipation would not only weaken the South economically but would also give the North a higher moral posture. What he wanted was to strike a double blow, one against the enemy's army, the other against his economy, and both with a background of high moral purpose. He therefore delayed on announcing the Proclamation until he had a major victory in hand. On 17 September, the Battle of Antietam provided him with that (although history rates it as a draw rather than a Union victory), and the Proclamation followed, to start the next year.

Also on this day

1431: Roderigo Borgia (Pope Alexander VI) is born * 1449: Lorenzo de' Medici (the Magnificent) is born * 1729: British statesman Edmund Burke is born * 1735: American revolutionary Paul Revere is born * 1901: The Australian commonwealth is established

2 January

Ferdinand and Isabella capture the last Moorish stronghold in Spain

1492 'They are yours, O King, since Allah decrees it', said Boabdil, ruler of Granada, as he handed the keys to the city to King Ferdinand of Aragon after a virtually bloodless siege that had lasted nine months.

So on this day over five centuries ago the last Moorish stronghold in Spain surrendered to the crusading might of the Catholic Monarchs, Ferdinand and Isabella. The Moors, who had arrived in Spain almost 800 years earlier in 711, were finally defeated. The gates of Granada were thrown open and Ferdinand entered, bearing the great silver cross he had carried throughout the crusade of eight years.

Mortified by his capitulation, Boabdil rode out through the gates of the city with his entourage, never to return. Reaching a lofty spur of the Alpujarras, he stopped to gaze back at the fabulous city he had lost. As he turned to his mother who rode at his side, a tear escaped him. But instead of the sympathy he expected, his mother addressed him with contempt: 'You do well to weep like a woman for what you could not defend like a man.' The rocky ridge from which Boabdil had his last look at Granada has henceforth been called El Ultimo Suspiro del Moro (The Last Sigh of the Moor).

The fall of Granada provoked intense and joyful celebration across all of Christian Europe, much as the fall of Jerusalem to Christian crusaders had almost four centuries earlier. Nowhere was the joy greater than in Spain itself, which, during the process of conquering the Moors, had at last become a truly unified nation.

Why France had kings but no queens

1322 Today died Philip V of France, who is little remembered, having left this world at the age of 28. But Philip left one enduring legacy, the law that prohibited a queen regnant in France.

Philip's older brother had been King Louis X, who had died leaving a daughter and a pregnant wife. A few months after Louis's death the Queen gave birth to a son, who also died in only five days. Philip, a man with an eye for the main chance, immediately proclaimed himself King. But what about Louis's daughter?

Philip and his advisors quickly dredged up the Salic Law, a custom of the Salian Francs not implemented in over 800 years. The 'law' simply said that land must be inherited equally by male heirs. Since the crown of France meant the ownership of land, said Philip, the crown could go only to a man. Philip won his argument – and the crown. And in all its history France has never had a reigning queen.

A Welsh buccaneer loses his treasure

1669 The Welsh pirate captain Henry Morgan was violent, cruel and so successful that he was occasionally sent on missions against the Spanish with secret backing from the English government. As he sailed off the coast of Haiti at the beginning of 1669, his ship, the 150-foot *Oxford*, was heavily laden with treasure – not only Morgan's fabulous personal collection of jewels, gold and silver but also some 200,000 pieces of eight that he had received in ransom during the sacking of Porto Bello.

But Captain Morgan was not to enjoy his treasure. While the *Oxford* was anchored near the Ile à Vache, he decided to throw a victory banquet to celebrate the capture of two French ships and unwisely ordered a pig to be barbecued on deck. Sparks from the fire flew into the powderhold and touched off a mammoth explosion that blew off the front of the ship. Morgan was propelled through a window in his cabin and escaped to raid another day, but most of his 250 sailors – and all the treasure – sank to the bottom.

Six years later Morgan returned to Haiti but failed to find his sunken booty, and for over three centuries countless treasure hunters had no more success than he had, but in April 2004 a team of professional divers finally located the wreck in only twelve feet of water. To date they have found cannon, powder barrels and musket balls, but so far the fabulous treasure has eluded them.

Also on this day

AD 17: Roman poet Ovid and Roman historian Livy die * 1635: Cardinal Richelieu establishes the Académie Française

3 January

François Villon vanishes

1463 A habitual criminal, the great French poet François Villon had been sentenced to be 'pendu et etranglé' (hanged and strangled) for participating in a bloody fracas in the streets of Paris, but today the French Parlement reduced the penalty to banishment for a period of ten years, and he hastily left the city.

Villon (whose real name was François de Montcorbier) was born in Paris in 1431, but he spent his life as a roving poet who travelled with a gang of thieves and murderers. In 1455 he was convicted of killing a priest with his sword during a drunken brawl in the cloisters of Saint-Benoît, but he was eventually pardoned by the King.

We know that Villon was imprisoned at least three times after that, but despite his unruly life, he produced some of France's most beautiful poetry, including the famous 'Ballade des Dames du Temps Jadis' (Ballad of the Ladies of Old) with its haunting refrain 'Mais où sont les neiges d'antan?' (But where are the snows of yesteryear?).

Villon's banishment from Paris on 3 January is our last glimpse of him. We do not know where or when he died.

Martin Luther is excommunicated

1521 Today that round-faced Medici pope Leo X excommunicated the Augustinian monk Martin Luther for his heretical beliefs, which he had so dramatically posted on a church door four years earlier.

The previous June, Leo had demanded that Luther submit to Rome within 60 days or face the full wrath of the Church, but Luther refused to budge.

In his zeal to strike, Leo did not even wait for Luther's trial, which started eighteen days after the excommunication, at the famous Diet of Worms, but on this day issued the *Decet Romanum pontificem* excluding him from the sacraments and formal communication with the Church.

4

106 BC: Roman statesman Marcus Tullius Cicero is born * 1777: George Washington defeats General Cornwallis's forces at the Battle of Princeton * 1833: Britain seizes control of the Falkland Islands

4 January

Birth of the father of fairytales

1785 The first of six children, Jacob Grimm was born today in Hanau. His lasting fame of course stems from a three-volume work entitled *Kinder- und Hausmärchen* that he published with his brother Wilhelm when both were still in their 20s. More familiar to us under the title of *Grimm's Fairy Tales*, literally translated it means 'Children and House Tales', suggesting that the book was intended for adults as well as children. The brothers believed that folktales were important to everyone because they expressed the universal dreams, fears and joys of mankind.

Considered the greatest anthology of fairytales ever put together, the collection includes stories not just from Germany but from all over Europe from as far south as Spain to as far north as Finland. Among the most famous are *Snow White, The Frog Prince, Hansel and Gretel, Rumpelstiltskin, The Bremen Town Musicians, Cinderella, The Brave Little Tailor, The Wolf and the Seven Little Kids* and *Sleeping Beauty*.

In his time Jacob was known for much more serious work. The master of seven languages, during his peripatetic lifetime he was secretary to the war office in Kassel, private librarian to King Jérôme of Westphalia, a librarian and lecturer at the University of Göttingen, a delegate to the Congress of Vienna and a professor in Berlin invited personally by the King of Prussia. He was a leading expert in German and wrote a book that related the early history of the German people to the growth of the language.

Of all his works, Grimm considered his major achievement to be a massive German dictionary that included the etymology of the words. Sadly, when he died at 78 he was still working on the letter F. (His brother Wilhelm had predeceased him, dying at the letter D.) The dictionary, however, was not abandoned, and was finally completed a mere 97 years later.

A queen arrives in England

1236 Eleanor was the second daughter of Raimond Berenger V, the impoverished Count of Provence, but like her older sister and her two younger ones, she was a woman of surprising beauty combined with all the charm and gaiety of her native country in the south of France. On this day she and her train landed at Dover, for she had come to England for the grandest of all reasons, to marry the King, Henry III.

Eleanor's father Raimond must have been one of history's great salesmen. He had little in the way of wealth or position with which to lure potential suitors to his daughters. Nevertheless, despite his meagre territories and air of genteel poverty, he managed to marry off his four daughters to the four most eligible bachelors in Europe.

As related, Eleanor married King Henry III of England. Her sister Sanchia wed Henry's brother Richard of Cornwall, who eventually became German Emperor. Beatrice, the youngest, captured a French prince named Charles of Anjou, who would one day be King of Sicily. And the eldest girl, Marguerite, had the greatest triumph of all, marrying Louis IX of France, who was not only king of Europe's most powerful country but a saint as well.

Three queens and an empress: not bad for daughters of a count.

Also on this day

1797: Napoleon defeats the Austrians at the Battle of Rivoli * 1809: Louis Braille, French deviser of an alphabet for the blind, is born

5 January

England's only saintly king meets his maker

1066 On this day died Edward the Confessor, the only English king who ever became a saint. Kindly and pious, he spent hours each day in prayer and was reputed to have performed miracles of healing. With his prematurely white and flowing beard, he looked more like an ascetic prophet than a ruling monarch. He reigned for 24 years.

Edward was the son of King Ethelred II (the Unready), who died when Edward was only thirteen. By this time the Danes were ruling the country, and Edward was forced to flee to Normandy with his mother Emma. Emma, however, soon returned to England and married the Danish/English King, Canute, who was anxious to consolidate his hold on his English subjects. Two years later a son arrived, whom they christened Hardecanute.

In 1035 King Canute died, and his bastard son Harold claimed the English crown because Canute's legitimate son, Edward's half-brother Hardecanute, was too busy running Denmark to move to England. Meanwhile Edward continued to live in exile in Normandy. But in 1040 Harold died and Hardecanute became English king. A year later he invited Edward to return to his native land as heir to the throne.

Edward was a weak and ineffectual king who permitted the powerful Godwine family virtually to rule in his name. He even married a Godwine daughter, but the marriage was never consummated and foundered after six years. In all his long life Edward never had a sexual relationship with a woman, but the theories explaining why are legion. Some believe that he was homosexual and others that he was impotent, while the more trusting give credence to the report that he had taken a holy vow of chastity. Unsurprisingly, he had no children.

Edward was 63 when he died, and his death let loose the rivalry between his Norman cousin William the Conqueror and his successor on the English throne, his brother-in-law Harold Godwine, who as Harold II became England's last Anglo-Saxon king.

Edward left two enduring reminders of his reign. The first is the so-called St Edward's sapphire, a rose-cut stone once in his coronet, now in the imperial state crown of England. The other is Westminster Abbey, which he founded.

Charles the Bold perishes on the snowy fields at Nancy

1477 Perhaps because he challenged the French, in English we call him Charles the Bold. But the French have always called him *Charles le Téméraire*, more properly translated as Charles the Rash. The French were closer to the mark.

Charles was a strange and moody man, with dark brown hair cut pageboy style and expressive eyes that could be soft or gay or with 'une dureté métallique' (a metallic hardness). Intelligent and hardworking, he spoke French, Dutch, English, Latin and Italian. He was also a fine musician who both composed and played the harp and may have invented counterpoint. A thoughtful man, he felt keenly the sadness and transience of life. According to his contemporary Lorenzo the Magnificent, he had 'un animo inquieto' – a troubled spirit. But most of all he was ambitious. It was a family tradition.

Just 115 years earlier Charles's great-grandfather, Duke Philip the Bold, had made Burgundy virtually independent, with only spasmodic and fiercely resisted control from France. During the intervening years the duchy had been ruled by the same talented, determined and ruthless family, father to son: Jean Sans Peur, Philip the Good and now Charles. But Charles was even more ambitious than his forefathers, for he dreamed of resurrecting the ancient kingdom of Lotharingia, one of the three parts of Charlemagne's empire. The greatest obstacle in his path was his wily enemy, King Louis XI of France.

Although King Louis could hardly match Charles on the battlefield, he was so adroit at political manoeuvring that he was known as the Universal Spider for the deceitful webs he wove. After years of inconclusive (if sometimes bloody) sparring with Charles, Louis concluded a treaty with Charles's English brother-in-law and erstwhile ally, Edward IV. Then in August 1471 he signed another with René of Lorraine, who hired scores of feared Swiss pikemen to bolster his forces.

In 1476 Charles was twice defeated by René and his Swiss auxiliaries, and by early the next year even he must have known he stood little chance, obliged to fight in the bitter cold of winter. But somehow his moody sense of destiny and his famed obstinacy prevented him from retreat.

The two forces met outside Nancy on Sunday 5 January 1477. Charles's Burgundian troops were badly routed, and for two days no one knew what had become of the great duke. But then a captured Burgundian page was led to the barren and frozen battlefield, where he identified Charles's naked body lying near the pond of St Jean. Charles's face had been opened from ear to jaw by the blow of an axe and his body was pierced by two lance thrusts. Wolves had gnawed the bloody remains.

And so died the Burgundian dream of power and with it the 43-year-old ruler, Charles by the Grace of God Duke of Burgundy, Lorraine and Brabant, of Limbourg and Luxembourg, Count of Flanders, Artois and Burgundy, Palatin of Hainaut, Holland, Zealand and Namur, Margrave of the Holy Roman Empire, Lord of Frisia, Salins and Malines.

Walter Raleigh is knighted

1585 It may be pure fiction that Walter Raleigh flung down his new cloak so that Queen Elizabeth wouldn't muddy her shoes, but the story truly represents the charming, romantic daring of the man.

Walter Raleigh: poet himself and patron of the greater poet Spenser; founder on Roanoke Island of the first American colony (which failed to survive); soldier of fortune who conquered Cadiz, fought with the Huguenots and explored the Orinoco. He was also the man who did most to popularise smoking tobacco in England, about which Queen Elizabeth observed, 'I have seen many a man turn his gold into smoke, but you are the first who has turned his smoke into gold.'

On top of this, Raleigh was a man of sophistication and wit. No wonder the Queen liked him – so much that she knighted him this day, when he was just 31 and still had most of his adventures ahead of him.

As for the tale of the cloak, it was concocted by a 17th-century historian named Thomas Fuller, who wanted to add spice to his histories. But the story really picked up steam in the 1820s when Sir Walter Scott incorporated it into his bestselling novel *Kenilworth*, and it became one of the best-loved bits of folklore about the Queen and her courtier.

Also on this day
1589: Catherine de' Medici dies * 1592: Shah Jahan, the man who built the Taj Mahal, is born

6 January

The man who would command the tides becomes king

1017 On this day Canute, the king who we all know ordered the tide not to come in, was crowned at the old St Paul's Cathedral in London.

Canute had first come to England from Denmark with his father's conquering army in 1013. Over the next three years he tricked, conquered or destroyed all local opposition and finally obtained the crown of all of England on the death of Edmund Ironside.

At first Canute ruthlessly murdered any who resisted him, but over time he came increasingly to rely on his English barons, slowly easing out his Danish ministers to replace them with English ones.

Canute's rule was fair and effective; he even became a strong supporter of the Church and made a pilgrimage to Rome. By modern standards, however, his legislation was sometimes excessively stern; his Law 53 ruled that if a woman committed adultery, her husband was entitled to all her property and 'she is to lose her nose and ears'.

But Canute never forgot his Scandinavian origins, inheriting the throne of Denmark in 1019 and that of Norway in 1028, making him King of three countries simultaneously. He was an equally just sovereign in Scandinavia, famous for instructing, 'I want no money raised from injustices.'

Canute died in 1035, and his legitimate son Hardecanute became King of Denmark while his illegitimate son Harold claimed the English throne. Five years later Harold died and Hardecanute became English King.

If you doubt that such a successful monarch would be so foolish as to command the tide, you would be correct. The true story concerns Canute's dislike of fawning courtiers ever praising his supposedly infinite powers. One day he ordered his throne brought to the seashore and then bid the sea, 'Ocean! The land where I sit is mine, and you are part of my dominion. Therefore rise not – obey my commands and do not presume to wet the edge of my robe.'

His sycophantic retainers waited for the sea to comply, but obstinately it continued to roll in. When waves had wet his shoes Canute addressed his courtiers: 'Confess ye now how frivolous and vain is the might of an earthly king compared to that great Power who rules the elements.'

Joan of Arc is born

1412 Epiphany would seem to be a suitable day for a saint to enter the world, and in the year 1412 one did, in the tiny French village of Domrémy, a hamlet some 170 miles south-east of Paris.

The saint-to-be was named Jeanne (Joan in English), daughter of humble tenant farmers Isabelle and Jacques d'Arc. Sixteen years later she achieved the inconceivable – persuading the French King to let a teenage girl lead an army against the perfidious English. Believing she was commanded by God, she routed the enemy at Orléans but was later captured and burned at the stake, condemned as a heretic.

Today her birthplace honours her with its name of Domrémy-la-Pucelle (Domrémy-the-Maiden) and the French have proclaimed a national holiday in her honour. The Church was less certain, as Joan of Arc's sainthood was a long time coming. She was not canonised until 1920, some 508 years after her birth.

Also on this day
1838: Samuel Morse gives the first public demonstration of his invention, the electric telegraph * 1919: American president Theodore Roosevelt dies

7 January

The last English stronghold in France

1558 For centuries English kings considered parts of France their own, starting with William the Conqueror, who was still Duke of Normandy after he seized the English crown.

In spite of the success of French kings like Philippe Augustus in clawing back French lands, English monarchs continued to lay claim to large tracts of France. In 1345 England's Edward III launched the Hundred Years' War to regain territory that he thought should be his, and in 1346, in an eleven-month siege, he starved the French port of Calais into submission and added it to his holdings.

And so Calais remained English for over two centuries, the last English possession in France, until King Henri II determined to throw the English out for good.

Henri selected his greatest general, François de Lorraine, second duc de Guise, and ordered him to besiege Calais. Guise was a robust and athletic warrior of 39 who had been fighting for French kings all his adult life. His face carried a deep scar from a battle wound suffered when he was 26, resulting in his nickname, *le Balafré* (Scarface).

At the beginning of January 1558 Guise and his small army launched an assault against the English garrison at Calais, and on this day, after only six days of fighting, the English were forced to yield. And so, after five centuries, England had finally been swept clean out of France.

Among the French, the region around Calais became proudly known as *le Pays Reconquis*, but back in England, bloody Queen Mary lamented the loss with the only quotable comment of her reign, 'When I am dead and opened, you shall find "Calais" lying within my heart.'

Henry VIII's first queen dies

1536 Today in East Anglia Catherine of Aragon, once Queen to Henry VIII of England, breathed her last at the age of 51.

Catherine was the daughter of Spain's Ferdinand and Isabella, and her first marriage had been to Arthur Tudor, heir to the English throne.

But Arthur had died soon after their marriage (before it had been consummated, according to Catherine's sworn testimony), and Catherine had been passed along to Arthur's younger brother Henry, whom she married just 21 days before he was crowned as King Henry VIII.

Five years older than Henry, Catherine had a youthful prettiness crowned with reddish-golden hair. But as the years passed without a male heir, Henry's ardour cooled, and he finally determined to be rid of her, come what may. First he appealed to the Pope for an annulment on the grounds that her marriage to his brother contravened strictures laid down in the Bible. When the Pope refused, Henry tore England from the bonds of Catholicism to divorce her and marry his mistress, Anne Boleyn. The fact that Anne's sister had previously been Henry's mistress, bearing him two children, hardly seemed to matter.

When Catherine died in 1536, her divorce from Henry had already been in effect for three years. On hearing the news of her demise, her husband for twenty years and his new wife Anne dressed themselves in joyous yellow and celebrated Catherine's death with a royal banquet attended by dancing and jousting.

Also on this day

1776: Thomas Paine's *Common Sense* is first published

8 January

Andrew Jackson wins a peacetime battle

1815 Today the United States badly mauled their British enemies at the Battle of New Orleans – even though, unbeknownst to the combatants, peace had been signed in December of the previous year.

The War of 1812 was the result of what Americans considered unjust and intolerable British conduct at sea during Britain's titanic struggle with Napoleon. Although France had finally agreed not to interfere with American shipping, the British, with the world's most powerful navy, had blockaded all French ports, making it difficult or impossible for Americans to trade. Worse, under the pretence that many American seamen were really disguised British deserters, the Royal Navy blithely stopped American ships and impressed their crews. In June 1812 American President James Madison declared war.

The war was a desultory affair, enlivened principally by the British burning of Washington. Weary of fighting, the two adversaries formally ended the conflict by the Treaty of Ghent signed on 24 December 1814, but communications at the time were so slow that two weeks later the two armies facing each other at New Orleans thought they were still at war.

Commanding the British was Major General Sir Edward Pakenham, the brother-in-law of the Duke of Wellington. He anticipated no trouble in taking New Orleans, as his forces outnumbered those of defender Andrew Jackson by three to one. Hoping he could frighten the Americans into submission, under flag of truce he sent in a letter threatening, 'If you do not surrender, I shall destroy your breastworks and eat breakfast in New Orleans Sunday morning.'

Enraged rather than intimidated, Jackson replied, 'If you do, you will eat supper in hell Sunday night.'

The British promptly attacked, but Jackson's men were sheltered behind bales of cotton. His Tennessee and Kentucky riflemen cut down whole ranks of the advancing enemy, while his pirate-trained cannoneers devastated the enemy with grapeshot, killing 2,000, including General Pakenham. The Americans suffered only seven killed and six wounded. The entire battle lasted only 30 minutes.

This was the last serious fighting in the War of 1812. From his victory at New Orleans Andrew Jackson became a hero, who, despite having won a battle during 'peacetime', used the fame he earned there to launch a political career that culminated in the presidency fourteen years later.

Death of a blind man who could see more than all the rest

1642 Today a blind man of just under 78 years died in the tiny Italian town of Arcetri, just a few miles from Florence, where the Inquisition had forced him to live in near seclusion for the last eight years of his long life. But during those 78 years this great genius discovered the laws of the pendulum, proved that objects of different weights fall at the same speed, found that any projectile follows the path of a parabola, confirmed Copernicus's theory that the Earth revolves around the Sun, was the first to see that the Moon is cratered and mountainous rather than smooth, and discovered that the Milky Way is composed of stars.

He was the greatest astronomer, physicist and mathematician of his century, perhaps of any century. He was of course Galileo Galilei.

The Church's stern discipline of Galileo stemmed from his validation of the Copernican view that the Earth revolves around the Sun, a theory they saw as in direct contradiction to the Scriptures. On his death Rome forbade the construction of any memorial, but the Medici family, which had long supported him, arranged for him to be buried in Santa Croce.

Also on this day

1337: Italian painter Giotto dies * 1499: Louis XII marries Anne de Bretagne, putting Brittany under the control of the French crown * 1713: Italian composer Arcangelo Corelli dies

9 January

The British abandon Gallipoli

1916 At 3.45 this morning, with a half gale blowing, boats shoved off from W Beach at Cape Helles carrying the last 200 British soldiers from the Gallipoli peninsula, south-west of Constantinople. Ten minutes later the ammunition dumps on shore erupted in a savage roar, bringing to a noisy and unhappy conclusion the greatest amphibious operation the world had ever seen. It could have been a forerunner of D-Day; instead it was the herald of Dunkirk.

In early 1915 Gallipoli had held great strategic promise: by seizing the peninsula and sending a naval force through the fortified Dardanelles straits into the Black Sea, Britain and France could have knocked Germany's war partner Turkey out of the war, opened up a critical supply line to their ally Russia, and moved up the Danube against Austria. Success might have shortened the First World War by three years.

But in ten months of struggle and at the cost of some quarter of a million casualties – British, French, Australian and New Zealand – the Allies came very close but ultimately failed either to get their warships though the straits or to advance their army up the well-defended peninsula. It was not an operation for the faint-hearted, the inconstant or the unimaginative, all of which types were well represented in the highest levels of British civilian and military leadership. Gallipoli needed a Nelson or a Lee or a Rommel.

In Parliament the setbacks at Gallipoli threatened to bring down the government. Needing a scapegoat for the failure, the Cabinet found one in Winston Churchill, a staunch supporter of the operation. He lost his job as First Lord of the Admiralty. Later, the Army commander was sacked. There were calls for reinforcements and a renewal of attacks, but by now there was a shortage of artillery shells and troops were sent to other fronts. By October the government had decided on evacuation.

The next year a Parliamentary commission investigating the failure cleared Churchill of mismanagement for his part in the operation. He took the occasion to deliver this judgement, which time has proved the right one: 'The ill-supported armies struggling on the Gallipoli peninsula, whose efforts are now viewed with so much prejudice and repugnance, were in fact within an ace of succeeding in an enterprise which would have abridged the miseries of the World … It will then seem incredible that a dozen old ships, half a dozen divisions, or a few hundred thousand shells were allowed to stand between them and success. Contemporaries have condemned the men who tried to force the Dardanelles. History will condemn those who did not aid them.'

Death of earthy Victor Emmanuel

1878 'On me dit que les danseuses françaises ne portent pas des caleçons. Si c'est comme cela, ce sera pour moi le paradis terrestre.' (They tell me that French dancers don't wear underwear. If it is really like that, for me it would be heaven on Earth.) A ribald remark by a French travelling salesman? No, a casual comment by the King of Italy, Victor Emmanuel, to the beautiful but rigid and frigid French Empress Eugénie, wife of Napoleon III.

Victor Emmanuel was squat, strong and athletic and bore an immense upturning moustache. According to an English nobleman who met him, he was 'as vulgar and coarse as possible'. He preferred peasant stews to fine cooking and pursued game and women with equal enthusiasm.

Beneath Victor Emmanuel's boorishness, however, were determination and a certain shrewdness. As the King of Sardinia-Piedmont, he recognised in Camillo di Cavour a man of political genius whose will towards a united Italy surpassed his own. During the struggle against Austrian hegemony he took command of his own armies, leading them in person at the decisive battles of Magenta and Solferino. Although a conservative monarchist, he later covertly backed the revolutionary Garibaldi in his efforts to bring together the various Italian kingdoms into a single nation.

In 1860 Victor Emmanuel became the first King of a united Italy and then transferred the capital from Turin first briefly to Florence and finally, in 1871, to the nation's ancient heart, Rome. It was there that he died on this day in 1878 at the age of 57, five years to the day after the demise of his ally at Solferino, Napoleon III.

Napoleon III passes on

1873 Death came to Louis Napoleon Bonaparte today at the age of 64. He had led a dramatic and in some senses fantastic life. Born a prince, he had been elected a president and seized power as an emperor, styling himself Napoleon III. He had also spent five and a half years in prison, from which he escaped disguised as a labourer. He spoke five languages fluently and was a great seducer of women – he once kept a circus acrobat as a mistress. His wife Eugénie had been exceptionally beautiful – and frigid.

Louis Napoleon had generalled his own armies, gloriously victorious at Solferino, disastrously defeated at Sedan. He had ruled France for 22 years, and he ended his life where most of his youth had been spent, in exile in England. He died of a stone in the bladder. His last words were addressed to his doctor, a friend of many years: 'N'est-ce pas, Conneau, que nous n'avons pas été des lâches à Sedan?' (It's true, isn't it, Conneau, that we weren't cowards at Sedan?)

Also on this day

1522: Adrian of Utrecht is elected Pope Adrian VI, the last non-Italian pope until John Paul II from Poland in 1978 * 1799: British Prime Minister William Pitt the Younger introduces income tax, at two shillings in the pound, to raise funds for the Napoleonic Wars * 1828: The Duke of Wellington becomes Prime Minister

10 January

Caesar crosses the Rubicon

49 BC Today Julius Caesar led one of his legions across a small stream called the Rubicon, thus defying the Roman Senate and breaking the *Lex Cornelia Majestatis* that forbade a general from bringing an army out of the province to which he was assigned. Turning to his lieutenants just before he crossed, Caesar remarked bitterly, 'Jacta alea est.' (The die is cast.) It was a de facto declaration of war against the Roman Republic.

The Rubicon is a narrow river south of Ravenna that marked the border between the Republic and its province of Cisalpine Gaul, now northern Italy. For the past nine years Caesar had been governor there and also of Transalpine Gaul, most of today's France and Belgium. There he had waged ferocious war on the primitive local tribes, subduing them in the name of Rome. It was said that he had conquered 800 towns while defeating enemy armies totalling 3 million men, of whom a third were killed and another third sold into slavery.

But now the Roman Senate, jealous of Caesar's success and fearful of his ambitions, were determined to bring him to heel. They demanded that he give up command of his legions and report back to Rome as an ordinary citizen. Caesar knew that, despite his enormous achievements, a small clique of senators were not willing to concede to him the honours he thought he deserved, even wanted to destroy him. He believed, almost certainly correctly, that, once he had relinquished his power, his enemies would trump up charges against him and then ruin or even execute him.

Some credit Caesar with loftier motives – the urgent need to rehabilitate the creaking Roman state that was badly misgoverned by a fractious and self-serving nobility. Most agree that he had no desire to start a war, let alone create a dictatorship, but his *amour propre* demanded that the ungrateful senators recognise his achievements and reward him as they had so many other great generals in the past.

When Caesar crossed the Rubicon, the die really was cast. Not only did his action initiate a three-year civil war but it also led to the end of the Republic and the age of Roman emperors. Many historians consider it the most extraordinary achievement in human history. One man, armed only with a few legions, his own military genius and what Pliny the Elder called 'the fiery quickness of his mind', took over the largest and most advanced empire the world had known.

A pugnacious revolutionary is born

1738 Today in Litchfield, Connecticut, was born one of colonial America's most pugnacious, irascible and determined leaders, Ethan Allen. Although he fought in the American Revolution against Great Britain, he gained his greatest fame for his political battles against other American states.

At nineteen Allen joined the militia to fight in the French and Indian War but saw no action. At its close he moved to Salisbury, Connecticut, where he and his brother built a blast furnace. This was the cause of his first contretemps with the law.

Allen wanted to sell the furnace, but in an argument over the sale he assaulted the would-be purchaser and ended up on trial. According to the court record, 'Ethan Allen did, in a tumultuous and offensive manner, with threatening words and angry looks, strip himself even to his naked body, and with force and arms, without law or right, did assail and actually strike the person of George Caldwell of Salisbury, aforesaid, in the presence and to the disturbance of His Majesty's good subjects.' Allen was fined ten shillings and soon moved to what, largely through his efforts, would one day become the state of Vermont.

Before the Revolution, land in Vermont was variously controlled by New York and New Hampshire, but Allen was determined that Vermont should have independent status. He led the patriot militia called the Green Mountain Boys that confronted a group of sheriffs from New York sent to toss out Vermont residents who had received their land grants from New Hampshire. At one stage the bellicose Allen captured two of the sheriffs and jailed them in adjoining cells. One night he hanged a human-sized dummy outside the jail, close enough so that the sheriffs would see it but far enough away so that they would think it was human, and in the morning he informed each sheriff that the other had been hanged the previous night. Then, one by one, he released his terrified captives.

During the Revolution, Allen led a group of 83 Green Mountain Boys in a joint attack with the American general Benedict Arnold on British-held Fort Ticonderoga. The Americans attacked at dawn, catching the surprised commander still in bed. Allen demanded immediate surrender, and when the British commander asked on whose authority he acted, the forceful American thundered, 'In the name of the great Jehovah and the Continental Congress!' Only four months later, however, Allen led a reckless attack on Montreal and was captured. He was imprisoned for a time in England and then paroled in New York City. In 1778 he was exchanged for a British officer and then joined Washington, who made him a colonel in the Continental Army.

After the Revolution, Allen returned to his favourite cause, the gaining of statehood for Vermont, arguing that people who had fought for independence deserved recognition by the national government. Infuriated by the reluctance of the Continental Congress, at one point he started to negotiate with Canada to absorb Vermont if the Americans wouldn't make it a state, but this was probably just a bluff to force the issue.

In spite of all his efforts, Allen must have believed he had failed, as the Continental Congress continued to deny Vermont statehood. Then in February 1789, when he was still only 51, he fell ill while returning with hay from a neighbouring farm. It was soon clear that he was dying, and the local minister was summoned to his bedside.

'The angels are waiting for you, General Allen', whispered the minister, hoping for a few last words of piety.

'They are, are they?' growled the dying man, belligerent to the end. 'Well, God damn 'em, let 'em wait!' But a few minutes later he was dead.

Two years after Allen's death, on 4 March 1791, Vermont was at last admitted into the Union as the fourteenth state.

Also on this day

1645: William Laud, Archbishop of Canterbury, is executed * 1769: French marshal Michel Ney is born

11 January

Birth of a British bastard who became an American hero

1757 Today is the birthday of Alexander Hamilton, hero of the American Revolution, member of the Continental Congress and first Secretary of the Treasury of the nation he helped found.

But before his brilliant trajectory began, he was born on the volcanic island of Nevis in the Leeward Islands in the West Indies in unpromising circumstances that might have inspired a novel by Dickens. Some years earlier, his mother, with well-to-do planter connections, had deserted an unsatisfactory marriage, abandoning an outraged husband and an infant son. She took up with James Hamilton, the feckless fourth son of a Scottish laird come to the West Indies to make his fortune. They lived together for eight years, during which she bore him two illegitimate sons – Alexander was the second – while he dissipated her money. In 1765 James Hamilton deserted the family to seek prosperity elsewhere, forcing the mother to run a store to make ends meet. Three years later she died of fever, leaving Alexander an orphan at the age of eleven.

Despite his situation, Hamilton was an outstanding youth: largely self-educated, hardworking, precocious, bold beyond his years, and absolutely determined to make his way – cut a swathe, he might have said – in the larger world. In 1769 he wrote revealingly to a friend: 'My ambition is [so] prevalent that I contemn the groveling condition of a clerk and the like, to which my fortune, etc. condemns me, and would willingly risk my life, though not my character, to exalt my station.'

Fortune smiled. In the tight island society of St Croix, his talents and potential were recognised, not only by the merchant employer for whom he clerked but also by a Scottish Presbyterian minister, educated at the College of New Jersey, who saw that the boy's future, whatever it might be, was better found in North America than in the West Indies. The Reverend Hugh Knox arranged for Hamilton's passage to New York, where he arrived, as one biographer put it, 'like a seed blown by happy chance onto perfect ground'. It was May of 1773, revolution was in the air, and Alexander Hamilton was sixteen years old.

Also on this day

1449: Italian painter Domenico Ghirlandajo is born * 1879: The Zulu War breaks out * 1891: French city designer Georges Haussman dies in Paris * 1928: British novelist Thomas Hardy dies * 1935: Amelia Earhart becomes the first woman to fly solo across the Pacific

12 January

The man who married Austria into a great power

1519 'Bella gerant fortes: tu, felix Austria, nube. Nam quae Mars aliis, dat tibi regne Venus.' (The strong make war, but you, happy Austria, make marriages. What Mars grants to others, Venus gives to you.) So wrote a 16th-century monk, and it fitted no one so well as that ebullient Austrian Habsburg, Emperor Maximilian I.

Maximilian had been born noble but poor and had himself made the first great dynastic marriage in the family, to Mary of Burgundy, heiress to the fabulous dukedom that included most of modern Belgium and Holland and bits of France. Subsequently Maximilian arranged for his son Philip to wed Juana of Spain, that insane princess who would inherit most of the Iberian Peninsula from her parents Ferdinand and Isabella. Philip died young, leaving two sons. The younger brother Ferdinand would, again through the arrangement of grandfather Maximilian, marry Princess Anne of Hungary, thus sowing the seeds for eventual Habsburg domination of the Balkans. The older brother Charles was to be the greatest emperor in history, ruling Austria, Germany, Belgium, parts of Italy, the Netherlands, Spain and all its vast territories in the New World.

The man who started it all, charming, diffident, ambitious Maximilian, died this day at the age of 60. He changed history by marrying Austria into an empire, parts of which lasted until the First World War. He also founded the Wiener Sängerknaben or Vienna Boys' Choir, which included Haydn and Schubert among its singers and which is still going strong.

A great Swiss newspaper starts publishing

1780 Frederick the Great of Prussia was the first European king to believe in freedom of the press, and his influence was felt even in Zurich, which was distant from Prussian control. But because of the spirit he engendered, a group of liberal Swiss on this day launched a new newspaper, the *Neue Zürcher Zeitung*, then and now a bastion of independent thought.

Originally it was established as a weekly entitled the *Zürcher Zeitung*, but in 1821 it started appearing twice a week and added *Neue* to its title. It became a daily in 1869.

The *Neue Zürcher Zeitung* (or NZZ as it is affectionately known) has always been admired for its painstaking reporting and scrupulous objectivity, and although a tabloid in format, it has been quite the opposite in its serious approach to the news. In fact, its dogged and sometimes plodding seriousness has also earned it the more irreverent nickname of ZZZ.

Writers such as Thomas Mann, Romain Rolland and Hermann Hesse have contributed to the *Neue Zürcher Zeitung*, and it earned a special badge of honour by being banned by Nazi Germany for claiming that Hermann Göring, and not the Communists, had started the Reichstag fire.

Also on this day

1519: Spanish conquistador Vasco Núñez de Balboa is beheaded ∗ 1625: Jan Bruegel the Elder, Flemish painter, dies ∗ 1882: Wagner's *Parsifal* is completed in Palermo, Sicily

13 January

'J'accuse'

1898 This afternoon 300,000 copies of the newspaper *L'Aurore* hit the Paris newsstands with the force of an explosion. On its front page it ran an article that was the news story of the century. Under the title 'J'accuse', the article accused the leaders of the French Army of framing an innocent Army captain on a charge of treason in 1894, and then, four years later, of covering up their misdeed by arranging the acquittal of a second officer whom they knew to have been the guilty party.

The unlucky captain was, of course, Alfred Dreyfus, the only Jew on the Army's general staff. Convicted as a spy who had passed on French artillery secrets to Germany, he had been sentenced to life imprisonment on Devil's Island. The man who joined his cause with 'J'accuse' was the great French writer Emile Zola.

The Army reacted quickly to 'J'accuse' and put Zola on trial for libel. He was found guilty, and seeing that his appeal would fail, fled to the safety of England. Zola was not the first Dreyfusard, but the Dreyfus case – *l'affaire*, as it became known in France – gained enormous publicity when he took it up so dramatically. With him were men like Georges Clemenceau, Jean Jaurès and Anatole France. Together they and the other Dreyfusards faced a public sentiment, laced with anti-Semitism, that believed in the Army's rectitude and the captain's guilt.

In a nation divided to its very core, it took a long time for justice to be done. Before it was, Zola died in 1902, asphyxiated by fumes from a faulty chimney (some maintained that anti-Dreyfusards had stuffed the flue). But by then the cause he championed had gained great strength.

Dreyfus was granted a second trial in 1899. He was pronounced guilty once again, but because of 'extenuating circumstances' he was sentenced to just ten years in prison. Many in France now understood that what was extenuating in the case was Dreyfus's innocence. In very poor health, he accepted a pardon from the President of France. In time the guilty officer confessed his role. In 1906 Dreyfus was cleared of all charges by a French court. He was restored to the Army, promoted to the rank of major and given the Legion of Honour. He served in the First World War as a lieutenant colonel.

The death of Gaius Marius, the general who saved Rome from the barbarians

86 BC Today the Roman general Gaius Marius died of a stroke in his 70th year, just three months after he had been elected consul for the seventh time. His death came none too soon because he had suffered some sort of mental collapse and was hardly sane during his final months, unleashing a reign of terror against any he felt had opposed him. Surrounded by a guard of slaves, he walked through Rome ordering instant executions.

Yet Marius had been one of Rome's very greatest generals. He had saved his country from almost certain invasion and changed the very nature of the Roman army.

Marius had been born a *novus homo* or new man, someone without senatorial forebears, in Arpinum, a provincial town 60 miles south-east of Rome. According to Plutarch, when he was a young boy Marius caught an eagle's nest falling from a tree. In it he found seven eaglets which he brought home to his parents, who consulted the augurs to find the meaning of this omen. The augurs foretold that Marius 'should become the greatest man in the world, and that the fates had decreed he should seven times be possessed of the supreme power and authority'.

Becoming a soldier, Marius became both respected and rich through his victories in Spain and North Africa, and when he was about 45 he married into the patrician Julii Caesar family. His wife Julia was Julius Caesar's aunt. Three years later he was elected consul for the first time, an enormous honour for a *novus homo*. He was subsequently elected six more times, fulfilling the augurs' prophecy.

During Marius's first consulship in 107 BC Rome found itself threatened by the Cimbri and Teutones, two fierce tribes which had descended from Germany en masse with 300,000 fighting men plus an even greater number of women and children, determined to conquer Italy. After the tribes had destroyed two Roman armies near Lake Geneva, Marius led his army against them at Aquae Sextiae (now Aix-en-Provence) and Vercellae (between Turin and Milan). He utterly routed the invaders, killing tens of thousands and selling the prisoners and their families into slavery, saving the Roman Republic.

Marius vastly improved the fighting ability of the army. He made the cohort of 600 men the standard unit, and equipped each legionnaire with the same armament, a pilum (a sort of javelin) and a sword. He trained his men ferociously, using techniques from gladiatorial schools, and had them carry their own supplies and shovels, thus eliminating slow-moving baggage trains. From this his soldiers earned the proud sobriquet 'Marius's mules'.

Even more important in the longer term was Marius's change in the way new soldiers were recruited. Previously only Romans who owned land could join, but Marius dropped all property qualifications and instead offered land as reward for faithful soldiers. The result was an influx of poorer citizens who stayed in service even after battle, thus for the first time creating something like a professional standing army. It was Marius who gave each legion a standard in the form of an eagle. Critically, the legions' first loyalty now was to their commander, who alone could reward them, rather than to the Roman state, a change exploited to the full first by Sulla and then by Pompey and ultimately by Julius Caesar.

Although a military genius, Marius was a clumsy politician who made enemies both in the Senate and among rival commanders, especially his one-time subordinate Sulla. Consequently at one point he had to flee for his life but was captured and imprisoned in a dark cell. Then a Gallic soldier was ordered in to decapitate him. According to Plutarch, 'The room itself was not very light, that part of it especially where he then lay was dark, from whence Marius's eyes, they say, seemed to [the soldier] to dart out flames at him, and a loud voice to say, out of the dark, "Fellow, darest thou kill Gaius Marius?" The barbarian hereupon immediately fled, and leaving his sword in the place, rushed out of doors, crying only this, "I cannot kill Gaius Marius."'

Marius escaped and eventually returned to Rome where he became consul for the seventh time, when he wreaked havoc among his enemies. By now he was clearly becoming unhinged, drinking heavily, suffering hallucinations and running 'into an extravagant frenzy fancying himself to be a general at war … throwing himself into such postures and motions of his body as he had formerly used when he was in battle, with frequent shouts and loud cries'. Despondent and afraid, he fell ill and died seven days later.

Also on this day

1599: English poet Edmund Spenser dies * 1625: Flemish painter Pieter Bruegel 'the Elder' dies * 1628: Charles Perrault, French author of *Mother Goose*, is born * 1898: Lewis Carroll (Charles Dodgson), writer of *Alice in Wonderland*, dies

14 January

Murder triggers the Albigensian Crusade

1208 Of all the cruel and senseless persecutions inflicted in the name of religion, few have been as ferocious as the medieval Church's crusade against the Cathars in south-west France. It was triggered today by the murder of the Pope's representative.

The word 'Cathar' comes from the Greek *katharos* (pure), which is what believers attempted to be. Cathars thought that the material world was evil and man's task was to free himself from it. The most devout renounced life's pleasures, including meat and sex, in an attempt to find communion with God.

The Church in Rome could hardly find fault with such asceticism, but other Cathar doctrines were anathema. Cathars refused to accept the divinity of Christ, and, worse, sternly criticised the Church for its nepotism, greed and corruption. Perhaps the most terrible crime of all was the Cathars' refusal to contribute financial support to Rome.

The Cathar cult was particularly strong around Toulouse and Albi (hence the name of the crusade, the Albigensian), and Count Raymond of Toulouse was such a defender of the Cathars that an investigating papal legate, Pierre de Castelnau, was sent to threaten him with excommunication for his failure to suppress the heresy. The Count quietly submitted and swore his allegiance, so, his mission accomplished, Castelnau began his journey back to Rome. But when he reached the River Rhône, a knight in the Count's service, but perhaps not on his orders, stabbed the legate to death with a hunting spear. It was a deed with terrible consequences.

Incandescent with rage when he heard the news, Pope Innocent III immediately launched the Albigensian Crusade, offering participants full absolution for all sins if they served for 40 days exterminating the heresy.

A minor French noble, Simon de Montfort, was given the task of leading the campaign, spiritually supported by another papal legate, the fanatical Arnald-Amaury, who believed in massacre in the service of God. Together they gathered an army and ravaged southern France, slaughtering and pillaging indiscriminately.

Unlike most of the crusades to the Holy Land (one of which was also launched by Pope Innocent), the Albigensian Crusade eventually succeeded in its aims by besieging and destroying city after city in southern France, among them Carcassonne, Albi, Toulouse, Mont Ségur and finally, in 1255, the very last Cathar stronghold, the Castle of Quéribus. With some poetic justice, Montfort himself was killed by a boulder thrown from a trebuchet mounted on the ramparts of Toulouse. The few surviving Cathars fled where they could – Spain, Lombardy, England and Germany – or went underground. Three centuries later, the Midi, particularly the area around Toulouse, proved fertile territory for the Protestant Reformation.

The Church's experience with the Cathars had wider repercussions. Innocent died in 1216, but his nephew gained the papal throne as Gregory IX. Fully aware of the dangers of heresy, in 1231 the new Pope launched the Inquisition, which lasted in one form or another until 1908.

Attentat *against Emperor Napoleon III*

1858 Napoleon III and Eugénie, Emperor and Empress of France, were relaxing in their closed carriage as it neared the Opera House on rue Lepelletier in Paris when suddenly an explosion shattered the calm. Then came a second explosion and then a third. Four Italian revolutionaries, led by a deranged terrorist named Felice Orsini, had hurled three bombs.

Immediately there was chaos. Gas lamps went out, shards of glass rained down from broken windows, and horses and people bolted in panic. The Emperor and Empress nursed superficial cuts on their faces, but they nonetheless left their carriage to enter the opera, she so intense and shocked that when Napoleon wished to stop to speak to the wounded she cut him short with 'Pas si bête. Assez de farces comme ça.' (Don't be stupid. There have been enough jokes like that already.)

The opera audience went into frenzied cheering at the sight of their courageous monarchs. They had survived what King Alfonso XIII of Spain would later term 'la risque du métier' (the risk of the trade).

In the street outside, 144 people were wounded and twelve lay dead. As for Felice Orsini and his fellow conspirators, they were condemned and brought to the guillotine.

Also on this day

1742: Astronomer Edmund Halley dies * 1867: French painter Jean-Auguste Ingres dies * 1875: Alsatian-German theologian, philosopher, organist and mission doctor Albert Schweitzer is born

15 January

What ever became of Emma Hamilton?

1815 History sentimentally remembers Emma Hamilton as the great love of the illustrious English Admiral Horatio Nelson, and portraits of her as a young woman show a beguiling beauty with large, luminous eyes and splendid chestnut hair.

She was born Emma Lyon on 26 April 1765, the daughter of a blacksmith who died when she was two. By all accounts a stunning beauty, her first jobs were as maids. But by age sixteen she was already a kept woman, bearing a child to Sir Harry Fetherstonhaugh. Later, after some time as a sort of *poule de luxe*, she moved in with Charles Greville, who claimed 'a cleanlier, sweeter bedfellow did not exist'. Greville subsequently passed her on to his uncle, Sir William Hamilton, the 62-year-old British minister to the Kingdom of Naples. Emma was then still only 21. After living together for five years she and Sir William married.

When Emma started her famous affair with Nelson she was already in her 30s and on the way to becoming immensely fat. Though still beautiful, she was a vain and silly woman. She seems to have been as truly besotted with Nelson as he was with her, and they lived in a *ménage à trois* with the complaisant Sir William, even when she bore Nelson a daughter.

After Sir William died in 1803, Emma and Nelson (who was still married but had left his wife) set up house in England, becoming something of a national joke and scandal. Although the public adored the admiral, his equals noted his pretensions and evident self-satisfaction. As Admiral St Vincent said of him at the time, 'Poor man, drowned with vanity, weakness and folly, strung with ribbons and medals.'

When Nelson was killed at Trafalgar, Emma was left little money by either husband or lover. She nonetheless continued her extravagant ways, forever hoping for a government pension for her daughter, the only offspring of the great admiral.

Emma moved to progressively cheaper lodgings in London and finally fled to Calais, where she spent much of each day consuming as much wine as her meagre funds could provide. It is there that she died on this day at the age of 50.

Elizabeth is crowned

1559 Over her dress of embroidered silk she wore a cloak lined with ermine, for the Queen not only would have to stand for long hours in draughty Westminster Abbey but would also ride from the Tower of London through the city so that the crowds could see her. She was 25-year-old Elizabeth Tudor, daughter of Henry VIII, and this Sunday was her coronation day, the date carefully selected by the most authoritative court astrologers.

The ceremony in the Abbey was the traditional Latin service used since medieval times, for Protestant England had not yet created its own service. When at last it was over Elizabeth moved on to Westminster Hall for her coronation banquet, which lasted from three in the afternoon until one the following morning. There, fatigued but exhilarated, she could finally go off to bed, an anointed queen who would reign for 44 years, two months and nine days.

Also on this day
1622: French playwright Molière (Jean-Baptiste Poquelin) is born * 1759: The British Museum is opened at Montague House, Bloomsbury, London

16 January

Sir John Moore falls at La Coruña

1809 Today in the Spanish port of La Coruña, in the final act of his outnumbered army's arduous retreat, the British General Sir John Moore fell from his horse, mortally wounded by a French cannonball that had shattered his left shoulder and collarbone. He died later in the day, but he had already managed to lead his command – battered but intact – to the safety of evacuation by a British fleet.

In October, Moore had taken command of Britain's only field army on the continent of Europe. He had led it out of Portugal into Spain to face an enormous invading French army now commanded by the Emperor Napoleon himself. The Spanish army was in disarray, and when the capital Madrid fell on 4 December Moore's forces were left isolated in the north-west of the country. His first instinct was to retreat to Lisbon, but after learning that Spanish resistance to French occupation had broken out in Madrid, he decided instead to move against the French line of communications.

Thus, his army became, to use Sir Charles Oman's phrase, the matador's cape that distracted the Gallic bull from its main intention of conquering the rest of Spain and then Portugal. Surprised at trouble from this quarter, Napoleon detached significant forces to pursue Moore and postponed his advances south and west. 'If the English are not already in full retreat, they are lost,' the Emperor wrote to his brother, 'and if they retire they will be pursued right up to their embarkation and at least half of them will not get away ... Put it in the newspapers and have it spread everywhere that 36,000 Englishmen are surrounded ...'

In their 250-mile retreat to La Coruña, over mountains and in fierce winter weather, the British army became a rabble. Nevertheless, with strong rear guard actions and by dint of personal leadership, Moore was able to keep his forces together and ahead of their pursuers, now commanded by Marshal Nicolas Soult. Reaching La Coruña on 11 January, Moore formed his lines of defence. Throughout the fighting, strong French attacks were unable to pierce the British positions.

At last, on the 14th the British fleet appeared, and the evacuation, starting with the sick, the artillery and the healthier horses, began. But before it was completed Moore was struck down. At dawn the next day he was buried in the central bastion of the fortress as he had ordered, wrapped in his military cloak with his sword at his side. Only a day later the last British soldier was evacuated to the waiting fleet, and the French occupied the port.

It was perhaps as well that Moore died, like Wolfe and Nelson, in the moment of victory, for when his army was returned to Britain the first public reaction was one of anger and criticism; many armchair strategists at home believed that instead of retreating, Moore should have attacked. It was many

25

years before his feat was recognised for what it accomplished: a severe disruption of Napoleon's plan to conquer Spain and Portugal and the skilful preservation of a British army that would fight the Emperor another day.

A granite monument erected on the orders of another gallant soldier, his pursuer Marshal Soult, still marks Moore's grave at La Coruña. Almost two centuries later, in January of 2004, the mayor of La Coruña dedicated a bronze bust of Moore at his burial site.

Columbus leaves a doomed colony in the New World

1493 When Christopher Columbus set sail today from Hispaniola (the current Dominican Republic) he left behind a garrison of 39 Spaniards – in effect the first true colony in the New World, predating Walter Raleigh's Roanoke by 91 years.

Like Raleigh's colony, however, Columbus's ended tragically. Indians massacred all 39 members before his return in 1496.

Also on this day

1547: Ivan the Terrible is crowned first Tsar of Russia * 1794: English historian Edward Gibbon dies * 1891: French composer Leo Delibes dies * 1920: The Eighteenth Amendment to the US Constitution is ratified, starting Prohibition

17 January

A tough-minded empress saves her husband's empire

532 Today one of the most remarkable women in history stood firm in the face of bloody insurrection and saved her husband's control of the Byzantine Empire.

The Empress Theodora was hardly born to the purple; she was a prostitute who, according to the contemporary historian Procopius, was sorry that 'God had not given her more orifices to give more pleasure to more people at the same time'.

The daughter of a bear keeper in Constantinople and by all accounts exceptionally beautiful, by her mid-teens Theodora had been kept and discarded by several lovers, by one of whom she bore an illegitimate child. Highly regarded for her voracious sexual appetite, she was an actress (virtually synonymous at the time with prostitute), famous for her role of Leda in which she lay stripped on the stage, her thighs covered with grains of barley, which a live goose playing Zeus-as-swan picked up with its bill.

But by the age of twenty Theodora had met, charmed and married Justinian, who had persuaded his uncle the Emperor Justin to change the law that

26

prohibited a noble from marrying an actress. She was, however, far more than just a superb sexual partner; she was possessed of both an acute intelligence and nerves of steel. After her husband became Emperor in 527, he treated her as a full partner in ruling his realm. An early supporter of women's rights, she also had her own agenda, backing new laws that prohibited the killing of adulterous wives, closing down Constantinople's brothels and outlawing the killing of unwanted children by exposure to the elements.

Justinian's greatest challenge came five years after his ascension, when rioting broke out between the Green and Blue factions at the chariot races in Constantinople's Hippodrome. A city prefect ordered seven hooligans hanged, but during the execution the scaffolding broke, saving two, who fled to sanctuary in a nearby church. When both Greens and Blues petitioned the Emperor for clemency, his refusal provoked a full week of chaos, the two factions combining forces under the slogan 'Nika' (Conquer), the catchword usually shouted during the races. They freed the condemned men, conducted a burning and looting spree throughout the city and demanded that the Emperor dismiss two of his senior officials.

At dawn on Sunday 17 January, Justinian publicly agreed to the rioters' conditions, but it was too late. The hostile mob continued its wanton destruction, proclaimed a noble named Hypatius as Emperor and drove Justinian into his royal palace in full retreat.

The terrified Justinian called together his panicky counsellors, who urged him to flee the city on the ship that was waiting at the garden stairs of the palace. But Theodora would have none of it, addressing her husband and his advisors with a ringing call to defy the rioters: 'If flight were the only means of safety, yet I should disdain to fly ... may I never be seen, not for a day, without my diadem and purple ... I believe in the maxim of antiquity, that kingship is a glorious shroud.'

Inspired by her courage, Justinian regained his nerve and sent his loyal general Belisarius to lead his soldiers to the Hippodrome. There he slaughtered over 30,000 rebels and executed Hypatius, whose body was thrown into the sea. Without Theodora's stirring call to action, Justinian's reign would have ended in shameful flight. As it was, he ruled for another 33 years.

During the rioting an old church had been burned to the ground. Just 45 days after the suppression of the revolt, on Justinian's orders work began on its replacement, the magnificent Hagia Sophia that stands in Istanbul to this day.

Benjamin Franklin is born

1706 It was a quiet Sunday in the Massachusetts Bay Colony town of Boston (population 6,000) when Josiah Franklin's seventeenth and last child was born in the family house on Milk Street. As the baby was a boy, perhaps Josiah thought of a famous biblical youngest son as he named the child Benjamin.

Although his formal schooling stopped at the age of ten, Benjamin Franklin would display a profound intellect and a dazzling versatility of achievement.

Most of us know Franklin as a printer, postmaster, diplomat and of course one of his nation's Founding Fathers. But he was also an inventor (of the Franklin stove, the lightning rod and bifocals), a musician (he played the harp, guitar and violin and invented a type of harmonica), a linguist (French, Italian and Spanish) and a philosopher. During his long life he raised a militia, organised a fire department and was a director of the first American fire insurance company.

Finally, of course, he was his country's great aphorist. 'Keep your eyes open before marriage, half shut afterwards', he advised, and, 'It's as plain as Euclid, that whoever was constant to several persons was more constant than he who was constant only to one.' He also believed that 'three may keep a secret, if two of them are dead'.

Three of his more famous lines are 'Fish and visitors smell after three days', 'Time is money', and 'Snug as a bug in a rug'. And as for the motto 'E Pluribus Unum' (Out of many, one) on every piece of American money, well, Franklin, er, coined that, too.

Also on this day

1377: The 'Babylonian Captivity' comes to an end, as the papacy returns to Rome from Avignon * 1751: Italian composer Tomaso Giovanni Albinoni dies * 1773: Captain Cook is the first to cross the Antarctic Circle * 1863: English Prime Minister David Lloyd George is born

18 January

Germany's first emperor is crowned in France

1871 At noon on this bitter cold day, with the smell of smoke in the air from nearby Paris, burning under the Prussian siege and bombardment, a magnificent and fateful gathering took place in the Palace of Versailles. In the Hall of Mirrors King Wilhelm of Prussia was crowned Kaiser of the Germans.

It was a moment for which the Prussian Chancellor Otto von Bismarck had devoted all his craft and considerable energies, the unification of all German states into a single empire led by Prussia. It had taken two wars over six years – first with Denmark in 1864, then with Austria in 1866 – to establish Prussia's dominant position among the German-speaking states and to bring the northern states into a confederation.

In 1870 he produced a third conflict – this one with France – by provoking Emperor Napoleon III into a declaration of war. French aggression, Bismarck calculated, and the resulting need for a collective German defence would have the salutary effect of encouraging the still-independent southern states – principally Wurtemberg and Bavaria – to join the northern confederation.

The combined German armies under Prussian leadership defeated Napoleon's forces with unexpected ease and then embarked on an invasion of France. Even as military operations dragged on longer than expected – stubborn Paris refused to capitulate and guerrilla activities mounted against the German occupation – Bismarck knew the time was right to complete an empire and crown an emperor. He made a variety of concessions to the southern states to overcome their remaining reluctance over the loss of sovereignty to the Prussian confederation. One secret arrangement involved furnishing the mentally unstable King Ludwig II of Bavaria with substantial Prussian funds to reduce the considerable debt he had amassed in his mad castle-building spree.

Standing with Bismarck in the crowded hall waiting for the coronation ceremony to commence was that other architect of victory, the great Prussian General von Moltke, the success of whose war plans had made today's event possible. Others in attendance included General von Roon, the Prussian War Minister; the Kaiser's son the crown prince of Prussia (deemed by his soldiers too tender-hearted for the enterprise of war); the crown prince's own son, almost thirteen (who as Kaiser Wilhelm II would prove far less tender-hearted than his father); and a large collection of kings, grand dukes, princes, land-graves, margraves and lesser ranks of rulers assembled from the various states of Germany.

W.H. Russell described the Kaiser Wilhelm's entrance to the Hall of Mirrors for *The Times*:

> It is twelve o'clock. The boom of a gun far away rolls above the voices in the Court hailing the Emperor King. Then there is a hush of expectation, and then rich and sonorous rise the massive strains of the chorale chanted by the men of regimental bands assembled in a choir, as the King, bearing his helmet in his hand, and dressed in full uniform as a German general, stalked slowly up the long gallery, and bowing to the clergy in front of the temporary altar opposite him, halted and dressed himself right and front, and then twirling his heavy moustache with his disengaged hand, surveyed the scene at each side of him.

Ten days after the coronation at Versailles, combat operations in the Franco-Prussian War came to an end with the capitulation of Paris. In March, Kaiser Wilhelm returned to Berlin, where standing on the royal balcony with his grandson he was hailed as the conquering hero by rapturous crowds. On 10 May 1871, the Treaty of Frankfurt was signed, by which, in addition to paying an enormous indemnity of 5 billion francs, France was required to hand over to Germany the provinces of Alsace and Lorraine. So, in military triumph, the German Empire was born. It lasted not quite a half-century, ending in 1918 with Germany's defeat in the First World War. Kaiser Wilhelm II abdicated to a modest retirement in Holland, and Germany became for the first time but not the last a republic.

Red rose marries the white

1486 Henry VII had seized the throne of England as the last representative of the Lancaster faction of the Wars of the Roses. Being a shrewd politician, however, one of his first acts as anointed King was to marry Elizabeth of York, eldest daughter of Edward IV and as such heiress to the Yorkist claims. The wedding took place only 79 days after his coronation, on 18 January 1486.

Luckily for Henry, Elizabeth offered more than just a political triumph, as she was young, blonde and beautiful. In fact, the birth of a son just eight months after the marriage ceremony suggests that perhaps Henry's passions had been even more urgent than his politics.

Although largely forgotten except by lovers of history, Elizabeth plays a more prevalent role today than you might imagine, as you see her face every time you play cards. She is said to be the model for the Queen of Hearts.

Also on this day
1778: James Cook discovers Hawaii * 1919: The Versailles Peace Conference opens

19 January

Death and the legend of Don Carlos

1568 It is difficult to separate the truth from the legend when it comes to Don Carlos, eldest son of Philip II of Spain. Some reports claim that he was warped in both body and mind, slightly hunchbacked and almost small enough to be a dwarf. Others (more probably) say that he had been a fairly normal boy until at the age of eighteen he fell down a staircase, severely cracking his head in the process. For several days he lay blind and delirious, his head swollen to enormous size, and all despaired for his life.

In a last attempt to save him, his family and doctors called on the intervention of God. In the nearby monastery of Jesús María lay the mummified body of the holy Fray Diego, who had died a century before. Fray Diego's desiccated corpse was placed beside Carlos in bed, and after one night in such company the dying boy started to recover. Soon he was physically well, but all reports agree that before long it became clear that he was mad.

The more extreme stories have him torturing horses, whipping nubile girls and cooking rabbits alive. What is certain is that during the next few years Carlos revelled in sadism and suffered periods of manic and murderous fury. He once attacked the Inquisitor General, shouting, 'A little priest dares to oppose me!' Proclaiming hatred for his father Philip, he tried to escape to Germany.

Finally Philip had no choice but to turn Carlos's room into a prison. Early on the morning of 19 January 1568, the King entered his son's chambers personally to supervise the incarceration: all doors and windows were nailed shut and no one but his jailers was allowed to speak to the Prince. Carlos was never seen again in public.

On 24 July it was announced that Carlos had died. King Philip informed his court that his son had repeatedly attempted suicide, trying everything from self-starvation to lying naked on blocks of ice, to setting his bed on fire. Philip claimed that eventually he had succumbed to fever.

In all probability Carlos died of slow poisoning on his father's orders. The more lurid accounts say that the reason was Philip's fury on learning of Carlos's passion for his Queen, young Elizabeth of Valois, a theory embraced with more gusto than historical probability by Schiller and Verdi. Others claim that Carlos had repeatedly threatened to kill his father. But in all likelihood tough-minded Philip's reason was that only mad Carlos's death could keep him from inheriting the throne of Spain.

A mad empress finally expires

1927 Today Carlota, wife of the ill-fated Mexican Emperor Maximilian, died in the 12th-century Bouchot Castle on the outskirts of Brussels. She had lived 86 years, mad for the last 60 of them.

Carlota had been born Marie Charlotte Amélie Augustine Victoire Clémentine Léopoldine, the only daughter of the Belgian King, Leopold I. At seventeen she had married Maximilian von Habsburg, the younger brother of Austrian Emperor Franz Joseph, a weak and amiable man of neither talent nor ambition. But Carlota (as she would be known when her husband became Emperor of Mexico) more than made up for her spouse's lack of drive. When reactionary Mexican aristocrats, backed by France's Napoleon III, offered Maximilian the crown of Mexico, Carlota endlessly and enthusiastically urged him to accept.

Carlota proudly accompanied her husband to Mexico in 1864, but only two years later her dream started to collapse. Pressure mounted from the United States, which was proclaiming the Monroe Doctrine, a policy that made it a hostile act against the United States for a European power to attempt to control any nation in the Western hemisphere. Napoleon III withdrew his army from Mexico, and Maximilian's regime was doomed as forces of the pre-imperial republican government of Benito Juárez smashed what remained of the Emperor's army.

On 9 July 1866 Carlota set out from Mexico City for Europe to rally support for her beleaguered husband. She was never to see him again. It was then that she showed the first signs of insanity. Stopping at the town of Puebla, at midnight she rose from bed and ordered her entourage to take her to the house where the local prefect had entertained her months before. Although the house now held only servants, she insisted on revisiting the rooms where she had once been royally fêted.

The next day she moved on to Veracruz to sail for Europe. Her first stop was Paris, where she failed to persuade Napoleon to restore his army in Mexico. In desperation, she travelled on to Rome to enlist the support of that dogmatic reactionary, Pope Pius IX. To His Holiness she begged to be allowed to spend the night in the Vatican (although no woman had even been granted that privilege) because she feared for her life: Napoleon III, she said, was trying to poison her.

The Pope granted her wish, but the next day sent her back to her hotel. There she refused all food and drink except live chickens that she kept in her hotel suite and had slaughtered and cooked by her own servants and water that she collected herself from the Trevi Fountain. She busied herself with writing letters to the court in Mexico accusing Napoleon of ordering her murder.

News of Carlota's paranoia soon reached her brother, now King Leopold II of Belgium. He brought her to Brussels and placed her in the care of an Austrian doctor who directed a lunatic asylum. Here she remained for the rest of her pitiful life, continuing to ask until she was in her 70s why Maximilian was not there. In the spring of every year she would board a tiny skiff afloat in the moat of her castle and inform her companions, 'Today we are leaving for Mexico.'

Why Carlota fell into insanity is still a mystery, although there is no lack of conjectures. Some say she was driven mad by feelings of guilt at having left Maximilian in Mexico, emotions greatly exacerbated when he was executed by firing squad less than a year after her departure; Queen Victoria blamed it on Napoleon III for having talked Maximilian into his imperial adventure and then removed his support; and modern psychiatrists see possible cause in her failure to produce an heir to the Mexican throne; but the most bizarre theory was that Benito Juárez had had a secret Indian drug administered to her during her trip to Europe.

One final mystery has outlived the deranged empress. In January of 1867, six months after Carlota had left Mexico for Europe, a baby boy was born in Brussels. For unexplained reasons he was reared in Carlota's household. He was said to be the illegitimate son of a Polish aristocrat, but rumours have continued ever since that he was in fact the lovechild of Carlota and one of Maximilian's officers. Whatever the truth of his parentage, this baby boy grew up to be Maxime Weygand, the French general who in the Second World War, as Commander in Chief of the Allied armies in France, advised the French government to capitulate to the Germans in 1940.

Also on this day

1807: Confederate general Robert E. Lee is born * 1809: American writer Edgar Allan Poe is born * 1839: French painter Paul Cézanne is born

20 January

Nice at last becomes French

1860 On this day at last, after centuries of dispute, attack, besiegement, defeat, pillage and changes of ownership, the great city of Nice finally became permanently part of France.

Today's Nice is an idyllic sweep of coastline along the Baie des Anges on the Côte d'Azur. Its most famous street, the wonderfully named Promenade des Anglais, runs for two and a half miles along the shore, embellished with palm trees and flowers. Originally built by English residents in 1822, it follows the long pebble beach where bikinied temptations loll in the sun and the chic-est hotels like the pink-roofed Négresco face the sea.

It was not always so. Archaeological remains indicate that some 40 millennia ago early man settled here, but the first true city was founded in about 350 BC by Greeks from the colony of Marseille, who called it Nikaia, a name derived from the word 'victory' (*nike* in Greek).

About four centuries later Nice was taken over by the Romans, but with the fall of the Empire, barbarians and Saracens sacked it in turn, obliterating the Roman city. By the 10th century, however, Nice had recovered its prosperity and was appropriated by the Counts of Provence. Then, in the 14th century, greed and murder led to its annexation by the House of Savoy. At that time Nice was ruled by the beautiful and kind Queen Jeanne of Provence, who had earlier made the fatal error of adopting Charles de Durazzo, Prince of Naples. Hungry to inherit the city, in 1382 Durazzo ordered his stepmother smothered. Into the ensuing chaos stepped Amadeus VII, Count of Savoy, who in 1388 fomented a rebellion and annexed the city, to the joy of the population.

For the next four centuries Nice remained part of the House of Savoy, although it was occasionally besieged, most famously in 1543 by the combined forces of France and Turkey under the generalship of that famous corsair Barbarossa.

During one assault an earthy Niçoise named Catherine Ségurane was bringing food to soldiers manning a rampart when suddenly the Turks started swarming over the walls. Grabbing her carving knife, Catherine threw several attackers into the moat, grabbed their banner and inspired her fellow defenders. As the Turks fled in panic, Catherine mounted the walls and, turning her back on the enemy with scorn, lifted her skirt in one of the first recorded incidents of mooning.

In the late 18th century during the Revolution French troops marched into Nice, and in 1793 it was incorporated into France. But when Napoleon fell in 1814, Nice once again reverted to the House of Savoy.

Finally, in 1859, French Emperor Napoleon III entered an alliance with the House of Savoy to kick the Austrians out of the north of Italy. Victorious, he received Nice as reward for his help on this day in 1860 on the signing of the

Treaty of Turin, an exchange confirmed by the Niçois in a plebiscite by 25,743 to 260.

George V is 'helped' by his doctor

1936 This evening at just past eleven o'clock England's heavy-smoking King George V died of influenza at his mansion at Sandringham, in Norfolk. To this day there remain rumours that the King's doctors, with the understanding of the government, administered a fatal dose of morphine to the dying king so that his death would come in time to be announced in the next day's *Times* rather than in the plebeian tabloids that came out a few hours later.

During his 70 years on earth George V had been a reserved and unbending monarch, bereft of imagination but determined to do his duty. After his death his own biographer wrote that the King was distinguished 'by no exercise of social gifts, by no personal magnetism, by no intellectual powers. He was neither a wit nor a brilliant raconteur, neither well read nor well educated, and he made no great contribution to enlightened social converse. He lacked intellectual curiosity and only late in life acquired some measure of artistic taste.' As such, notes historian Robert Lacey, 'he was, in other words, exactly like most of his subjects'.

By the time George had reached his Silver Jubilee in 1935, however, the British people had developed a certain admiration for him, in spite of his mundanity. As Harold Nicholson wrote, 'In those twenty-five years his subjects had come to recognise that King George represented and enhanced those domestic and public virtues that they regarded as specifically British virtues. In him they saw, reflected and magnified, what they cherished as their own individual ideals – faith, duty, honesty, courage, common sense, tolerance, decency, and truth.'

By the time George became King in 1910, English monarchs had ceded virtually all power to Parliament, in spite of the awe in which they were held by most of their subjects. Nonetheless, George's actions – or lack of them – have left some traces that remain today.

During the First World War, in a moment of high patriotism, George changed the name of the royal family from the Germanic Saxe-Coburg-Gotha to Windsor and ordered all his British relatives to adopt British-sounding names. Thus his cousin Louis of Battenberg simply translated his to Louis Mountbatten. When Germany's Kaiser Wilhelm (who was also George's first cousin) heard of the changes he ridiculed the effort by claiming that henceforth Shakespeare's *The Merry Wives of Windsor* would be known in Germany as *The Merry Wives of Saxe-Coburg-Gotha*.

A different First World War incident concerning yet another first cousin had more serious consequences. On 15 March 1917 Tsar Nicholas II of Russia had been forced to abdicate by the revolt of Petrograd's disillusioned and war-weary soldiers and workers. Although aware that Nicholas was in jeopardy,

George refused to grant him and his family asylum in Great Britain for fear of being too closely associated with the autocratic Russian regime at a time when British socialism was raising its head. The Communists subsequently shot Nicholas, his wife and their five children.

More happily, George also set a Christmas precedent that has endured to this day. On the afternoon of Christmas Day in 1932 he broadcast a short radio message to his subjects, the text carefully scripted by Rudyard Kipling (who died two days before King George). Ever since, it has become a tradition for the monarch to broadcast to the nation on Christmas afternoon, although of course now the primary medium is television.

There is still some debate concerning George's last words. According to the high-minded *Times*, as he lay in his bed surrounded by his wife and children, with his final breath he asked, 'How is the Empire?' Another story, however, insists that his last comment was to his doctor. Seven years earlier after a serious illness George had recuperated at the seaside resort of Bognor, which had re-labelled itself Bognor Regis in his honour. Now the doctor tried to soothe his patient with the thought that once again he could convalesce at the same resort, to which the King pithily responded, 'Bugger Bognor!'

Also on this day

1265: The Earl of Leicester Simon de Montfort convenes the first English parliament in Westminster Hall * 1841: Hong Kong is ceded by China and occupied by the British

21 January

Louis XVI goes to the guillotine

1793 Today the king who legalised the guillotine in France himself mounted the scaffold amid the roars of the mob in Paris's place de la Révolution, today the place de la Concorde. He was the well-meaning but fat and bumbling Louis XVI.

The guillotine had been introduced into France as an instrument of kindness and an extension of democracy. It was proposed in the States-General in 1789 by Dr Joseph-Ignace Guillotin, who saw it as a more merciful way of dispatching the condemned and even a gesture of democracy; previously only the nobility had died by decapitation. The guillotine itself was not new. Something very similar was in use in Italy, and the 'Scottish maiden' had anticipated it 200 years earlier in Scotland.

Louis had already been under virtual house arrest for almost two years, and the monarchy had been abolished five months before. Then in December of 1792 Louis had been tried for treason and he was found guilty on 18 January. On the following day the Convention had voted for the death sentence by 380 votes to 310.

And so today ex-King Louis was brought through the streets of Paris in a carriage surrounded by troops in a cavalcade that lasted two hours. At every corner were citizens armed with pikes or guns, a precaution against any demonstration in favour of the King. At last they arrived at the place of execution.

Only 38 years old, the King faced death with courage and composure. He refused to let his jailers bind him and walked resolutely across the scaffold, the surrounding crowd in total silence. Arriving at the foot of the guillotine, he turned to address the throng. His last words were 'I die innocent of the crimes laid to me. I forgive those who have caused my death, and I pray God that the blood you are about to shed may never be visited upon France.' Then the drums drowned out his words and Louis was laid on the plank of the guillotine. The blade swept down, but the King's fat neck prevented it from slicing through instantly and he screamed once before his neck was finally severed. Then, according to his priest, who was an eyewitness, 'The youngest of the guards, who seemed about eighteen, immediately seized the head, and showed it to the people as he walked round the scaffold ... At first an awful silence prevailed; at length some cries of "Vive la République!" were heard. By degrees the voices multiplied, and became the universal shout of the multitude, and every hat was in the air.'

Based on experience gained during the French Revolution, the French considered the guillotine such a success that they kept it in use until a Tunisian murderer named Hamida Djandoubi became the last person ever guillotined in France on 10 September 1977.

Also on this day

1924: Vladimir Ilyich Lenin dies * 1932: English critic and biographer Lytton Strachey dies * 1950: English writer George Orwell dies

22 January

An imprisoned emperor dies gazing at the most beautiful building in the world

1666 Today in Agra in north-central India died Shah Jahan, the most cultured and romantic of all Mughal emperors, as he gazed from his fortress prison on the fabulous Taj Mahal he had built in memory of his beloved wife.

Shah Jahan had been born to power, son of the Emperor Jahangir, but in his youth he had rebelled against his father, something his own sons were later to do. Eventually reconciled, he rushed to Agra to seize power when his father died in 1627. After a year of eradicating his rivals he became Emperor.

By this time Shah Jahan had already been married for fourteen years to the beautiful Mumtaz Mahal, whose alliterative name translates as 'Chosen One of the Palace'. Their union was a true love match in which Mumtaz Mahal played a crucial supporting role as his advisor and inseparable companion, accompanying him when he travelled around his empire, even on military operations. Together they established a brilliant court of splendid display and oriental grandeur. Shah Jahan's jewellery collection was possibly the most spectacular the world has seen.

During their years together Mumtaz Mahal bore fourteen children, but died in childbirth with the last during a military campaign when Shah Jahan was still only 38, just three years after he had seized power.

So stricken by grief was the Emperor that his hair and beard turned white in only a few months after Mumtaz Mahal's death. He determined to build in her honour a monument of eternal love, the most beautiful mausoleum in history. He called it a shortened version of her name, Taj Mahal.

Requisitioning over 1,000 elephants for transport, Shah Jahan had white marble and other construction materials brought from all over India. More than 20,000 workers laboured for 22 years to complete the building, at the staggering cost of 32 million rupees.

The Taj Mahal was completed in 1652. Legend has it, probably apocryphal, that Shah Jahan was so enamoured of its splendour that he had the thumbs of all 20,000 workers amputated to prevent them from ever creating another building so beautiful.

Five years later Shah Jahan fell ill, igniting a power struggle among his four sons. The third son Aurangzeb defeated and killed his eldest brother and, on Shah Jahan's unexpected recovery, locked his father away in his own fort within sight of the Taj Mahal. (For good measure, Aurangzeb later had his other two brothers and his nephew executed.)

For the eight years that remained to him Shah Jahan lived in opulent confinement in his fortress prison, wistfully gazing at the magnificent monument he had constructed for Mumtaz Mahal. When he died his body was laid in the vault below the building alongside that of his adored wife.

'Mysterious little Victoria is dead and fat vulgar Edward is King'

1901 After 63 years, eight months and two days on the throne of England, Queen Victoria died on this day at the age of 81. 'We all feel a bit motherless today,' wrote the American expatriate writer Henry James, 'mysterious little Victoria is dead and fat vulgar Edward is King.'

For most of her long life Victoria had enjoyed robust health, but in her last years, stricken by rheumatism, she had first used a stick and later needed a wheelchair. Nonetheless she continued to work until five days before the end. Then, in the words of British historian Lytton Strachey, 'as she lay blind and silent, [she] seemed to those who watched her to be divested of all thinking – to have glided already, unawares, into oblivion'. She died painlessly in her bedroom at Osborne House on the Isle of Wight, the royal residence designed by her husband.

Queen at eighteen on the death of her uncle William IV, Victoria had the good fortune to marry her handsome cousin Prince Albert of Saxe-Coburg-Gotha, whom she adored, and the misfortune to lose him to typhoid fever after 21 years of marriage. Not an intellectual woman herself, for the remainder of her life she based her decisions on what she believed he would have thought. Essentially conservative, she had a particular dislike of women's suffrage, writing (in the third person, as was her wont) 'The Queen is most anxious to enlist everyone who can speak or write to join in checking this mad, wicked folly of "Woman's Rights", with all its attendant horrors on which her poor feeble sex is bent, forgetting every sense of womanly feeling and propriety.'

By the time of her death Victoria had become a sort of Queen Mother of Europe. She and Albert had nine children, from whom many of Europe's royal houses were descended. Her grandsons George V of England and Kaiser Wilhelm II of Germany fought each other in the First World War, and 37 of her great-grandchildren were still living when she died.

Ironically, although Victoria spent 60 years fighting to retain the political power of the throne, during her long reign the British monarchy was gradually transformed into a predominantly ceremonial institution.

British and Americans land at Anzio

1944 All roads lead to Rome. But at the end of 1943 none seemed to. None, certainly, for the Allied armies whose advance up the Italian boot was stalemated at the chain of German fortifications known as the Gustav Line with its key stronghold, Monte Cassino. Which is why another way to Rome had to be found, and why, at 2.00 this morning, 40,000 American and British troops of the US VIth Corps made a surprise and unopposed landing at Anzio, a port on the Tyrrhenian Sea some 30 miles south of the Italian capital.

Codenamed Shingle, the amphibious end run was intended to force the Germans to abandon the Cassino front, clearing the way for the US Fifth Army to move on towards Rome, the Allies' objective. Churchill had cabled Stalin enthusiastically: 'We have launched the big attack against the German armies defending Rome which I told you about at Teheran. The weather conditions seem favourable. I hope to have good news for you before long.'

But there was no good news. Operation Shingle never got near accomplishing its goal. Intended by its planners as the strong first thrust of a two-pronged effort, the landings were carried out more like a diversion. Moreover, insufficient sea transportation – most of the tank-carrying landing craft had already been sent west for use in the invasions scheduled for Normandy and southern France – affected the size and composition of the VIth Corps, resulting in an initial deployment of only two divisions with no mechanised units.

German reaction to the landings was swift and severe. Calling Anzio 'an abscess', Hitler told General Kesselring, his military commander in Italy, that 'the Gustav Line must be held at all costs'. Eight divisions were rushed from France, Yugoslavia and northern Italy to seal off the beachhead and mount a counter-attack that would drive the VIth Corps into the sea. Perhaps a Patton or a MacArthur might have made a success of the operation with a fast strike inland, but the competent, cautious Major General John Lucas, whose advice from Fifth Army commander Mark Clark was 'Don't stick your neck out, Johnny', spent the first week ashore organising the beachhead. By 30 January, when he attempted a move north to seize the Alban Hills, the key high ground south of Rome, it was too late.

Now, the troops gathered at Anzio, instead of preparing to mount a bold, front-busting flanking movement, suddenly found themselves penned in and under savage attack by an enemy with superior numbers. To prevent their being overrun entirely, Allied forces in front of the Gustav Line resumed the costly frontal attacks that Anzio had been meant to eliminate. It was not until the middle of May, after the destruction of Monte Cassino, that the Fifth Army, now joined by the British Eighth Army, broke through in the south.

In the end, there was one prospect for redemption at Anzio. On 25 May, Fifth Army units heading north linked up at last with the VIth Corps near Valmontone, where they were in a position to cut the escape route and bag the Germans retreating up Route 6. But General Clark, intent on winning for his Fifth Army and himself the honours of reaching Rome before the British Eighth, now redirected his advance on the capital itself, allowing the Germans to dodge almost sure envelopment.

The welcome news that Allied troops had entered Rome on 4 June was soon obscured by bulletins about even greater events in Normandy. General Kesselring, interviewed after the war, called the Allied effort at Anzio, 'a halfway measure as an offensive'. Winston Churchill, who had championed the landings, called them 'a story of high opportunity and shattered hopes'.

Also on this day

1561: English writer Francis Bacon is born * 1788: English poet Lord Byron is born * 1879: Zulus massacre British troops at Isandhlwana * 1924: Ramsay MacDonald takes office as Britain's first Labour Prime Minister

23 January

William Pitt the Younger pays for his consumption of port

1806 In Parliament he was incisive, astute and forceful, a brilliant orator with a comprehensive knowledge of the issues of the day. In private he was reserved, withdrawn and arrogant, a man with few friends who never married and was apparently indifferent to women. Such was William Pitt the Younger, Britain's youngest ever Prime Minister, who gained that office at the age of 24 and who occupied it for almost nineteen years. He died today, probably of renal failure and cirrhosis of the liver exacerbated by his heavy consumption of port.

Pitt was the son of William Pitt, now called the Elder, Earl of Chatham, who had twice been Prime Minister for a total of eight years in the 1750s and 60s. The younger Pitt had early showed signs of intellectual brilliance – he had entered Cambridge at fourteen. At 21 he became a Member of Parliament, and his maiden speech was so forceful and eloquent that the British statesman Edmund Burke commented: 'He is not a chip off the old block: he is the old block itself.'

In December 1783 King George III invited Pitt to form a government. On the nineteenth he became Prime Minister but was immediately challenged the following month when his government was defeated on a virtual motion of censure. Despite this reverse, Pitt stubbornly clung to power, backed by the King, who threatened to abdicate rather than allow an opposition coalition of Lord North and Charles James Fox to take over. Although the situation was unprecedented, Pitt hung on, and in March, with the majority against him down to one vote, his government 'went to the country' and retained power, no surprise whatever in a century when no government ever lost a general election. Indeed, Pitt was hardly the people's choice; he had been put in office by King George and stayed there only as long as the King wanted him.

Although serious-minded and hard working, Pitt was extraordinarily insular. He hardly travelled in England, never went to Ireland or Scotland and visited France only once. He showed little interest in either the arts or science.

The greatest test during Pitt's time as Prime Minister was war with France. On 1 February 1793 Republican France declared war, a conflict that was to last 22 years, well beyond his lifetime. Indeed, this war consumed much of Pitt's time and most of his energy, and in spite of Nelson's brilliant victory at Trafalgar in October of 1805, within two months Napoleon had utterly crushed the Austrians at Austerlitz, prompting Pitt's despairing but accurate remark, 'Roll up that map [of Europe], it will not be wanted these ten years.'

By now hard work and too much port were taking their toll. Pitt was clearly ill and looked it. Still he continued to labour, never losing his confidence in a successful outcome to the Napoleonic Wars. 'England has saved herself by her exertions,' he said, 'and will, as I trust, save Europe by her example.' But by 16 January he was too weak to continue and took to his bed in his house in Richmond. For several days he received visits from leading politicians and generals, including the future Duke of Wellington, and made his will. He then lapsed into periods of delirium in which he imagined he was debating in Parliament. On 23 January the young starter became a young finisher at the age of 46.

Shortly after his death English hagiography established Pitt's last words to have been an anguished 'Oh, my country! How I leave my country!' But Disraeli insisted that an aged servant had once told him that his last thoughts were somewhat less high-minded. 'I think', he said, 'I could eat one of Bellamy's veal pies.'

Birth of the painter who gave birth to Impressionism

1832 A Parisian newspaper once described him: 'Yellow gloves, a crisp cravat, superb shoes, light-coloured trousers and a flower in his buttonhole, he can be found striding along the boulevard des Italiens with the hurried step of a man who is meeting a pretty woman; or one sees him at ease, smoking a good cigar, on the terrace of the Café Riche or the Café Tortoni.' Actor? Politician? Confidence man? None of these but one of Europe's greatest painters, Edouard Manet, who was born this day in Paris in 1832.

Born to wealth, Manet was expected to follow his father into law, but he was determined to become an artist. His first real fame came in 1863 when Napoleon III established the famous 'Salon of the Rejected' for paintings turned down by the prestigious but hidebound 'official' salon at the Louvre. Manet's *Le Déjeuner sur l'Herbe* shocked and titillated the public, as it showed a nude woman casually enjoying a picnic in the woods with two unconcerned but fully dressed men.

Manet rejected the idea of painting classical allusions, claiming to paint only the commonplace, showing life as it was lived. 'There is only one true thing,' he said, 'to paint spontaneously what one sees' – a comment that might have made some people wonder where he saw *Le Déjeuner sur l'Herbe*.

Although not truly an Impressionist himself, Manet is widely considered the father of Impressionism and one of the most influential painters of his century. He died of a wasting disease of the nervous system on 30 April 1883 at the age of 51.

Elected Pope but damned by Dante

1295 On this day Benedetto Caetani was elected Pope, taking the name of Boniface VIII. He was an ambitious and unscrupulous man, but he failed miserably in his self-appointed task of establishing the Augustinian ideal: a Christian world in which the Pope would be not only the spiritual ruler but the temporal one as well, whom even kings would have to obey.

Boniface's grab for absolute power placed him in direct confrontation with Europe's rulers, especially Philip the Fair of France and the anti-papal Colonna family of Rome. While Boniface won his war with the Colonnas, even his excommunication of Philip did not prevent the French King from claiming authority over the selection of French bishops and Church revenue in France.

Another Boniface opponent was Dante Alighieri, who, as a member of Florence's ruling faction, strongly resisted papal pretensions to political suzerainty. Partly through Boniface's conniving, Dante was exiled from Florence, but he triumphed poetically in the end by placing the pope in the eighth circle of hell in his *Inferno*, stuck upside-down in a narrow hole, his feet roasted by fire.

From the chaos of Boniface's reign (which lasted until he died in 1303) there was, however, one lasting achievement. He canonised King Louis IX in 1297. St Louis is the first and last French monarch ever to achieve sainthood.

Also on this day

1783: French writer Stendhal (Marie Henri Beyle) is born * 1944: Norwegian painter Edvard Munch dies * 1947: French painter Pierre Bonnard dies * 1989: Spanish painter Salvador Dalí dies

24 January

Frederick the Great is born

1712 Prussia. The word indicates a country but more strongly evokes a state of mind: stern, military, disciplined, orderly, masculine – some of the best but all of the worst of what the world thinks about Germany. Today the greatest Prussian of them all was born, the king who was one of history's generals of genius. He was Frederick II of Prussia, Frederick the Great.

Frederick's military fame comes from a lifetime of generally successful wars – defeating the Austrians and French alternately while carrying on his father's tradition of a well-trained, highly disciplined army. He had no doubts about the importance of military force; he once wrote to his younger brother, 'Don't forget your great guns, which are the most respectable arguments for the rights of kings.'

When Frederick inherited the throne the Prussian army stood at 83,000 men. When he died 46 years later the number had risen to 190,000 – an enormous force in a country whose population was only about 2,500,000, equivalent to Great Britain today having an army of over 4 million. During the Seven Years' War alone (1756–63), Prussia is believed to have suffered 180,000 casualties, almost 15 per cent of the male population.

Apart from his brilliant generalship, however, Frederick himself was hardly what we see today as 'Prussian'. He was an accomplished musician who composed, played the flute and knew Bach personally. He wrote poetry (mostly mediocre), collected art, was a passionate gardener and was probably homosexual. For a king he was a true intellectual, the author of a number of books and patron and friend of Voltaire, with whom he shared a sceptical view of life, once declaring as he looked at himself in the mirror, 'They say kings are made in the image of God. I feel sorry for God if that is what He looks like.' In stark contrast to the German government that followed him two centuries later, Frederick abolished the use of judicial torture.

Frederick was a tolerant if autocratic ruler. 'My people and I have come to a satisfactory understanding', he said. 'They say what they like and I do what I like.' Most surprising of all, he seldom spoke German but both conversed and wrote almost entirely in French.

The California Gold Rush

1848 It all started in the small Caloma Valley on this day in 1848 when a young carpenter named James Marshall spied a golden pebble in the millrace of his new saw mill. 'I reached my hand down and picked it up', he wrote. 'It made my heart thump, for I was certain it was gold. The piece was about half the size and shape of a pea. Then I saw another …' And so the California Gold Rush was on.

Within ten years of its beginnings almost a million miners would have gouged and scraped the California landscape for over $500 million in gold, and the California Gold Rush would have for ever left its legends of wild no-holds-barred frontier America, where prospectors could make a million or die in a gun fight.

Two Churchills die on the same date

1895, 1965 On this day died Randolph Churchill, once a leading British politician and Chancellor of the Exchequer, third son of the Seventh Duke of Marlborough. Although a prominent Member of Parliament, he never achieved the post of Prime Minister that he sought. He retired from politics at the end of 1886 but then slowly sunk into insanity from the tertiary syphilis that eventually killed him, a disease he contracted while still in his 20s.

Randolph's more famous son Winston was to die on the same day, exactly 70 years later. Fifteen years earlier he had famously told a friend, 'I am prepared to meet my Maker. Whether my Maker is prepared for the ordeal of meeting me is another matter.'

Edward III marries a loving queen

1328 The groom was fifteen, the bride just fourteen, but he had already been crowned Edward III, King of England, while she was Princess Philippa of Hainaut (in modern Belgium). The marriage celebrated today was to be one of the more loving ones among royalty, lasting 41 years until Philippa's death and producing twelve children, including two of England's most famous princes, Edward the Black Prince and John of Gaunt.

It seems likely that this marriage was happier for the royal couple than the years it covered were for England. It was during this time (in 1337) that England initiated the Hundred Years' War with France and that in 1348–9 the Black Death killed one third of the population. But it is to some degree thanks to Philippa that we know so much about this appalling era, for she brought her compatriot the chronicler Jean Froissart to her court in 1361, and he is history's primary source for knowledge of the period.

Philippa's father had been called William the Good, and it appears that she inherited his gentle and benevolent nature. She often tempered her husband's more draconian instincts, most famously when she convinced him to spare the lives of six burghers of Calais, when Edward had conquered the town after a prolonged siege.

Philippa has left us one lasting memorial. Queen's College, Oxford, was founded by her chaplain and named after her.

Also on this day

AD 41: Roman emperor Caligula is assassinated * AD 76: Roman emperor Hadrian is born

25 January

Al Capone, America's greatest gangster, croaks at last

1947 Today in Palm Island, Florida, Al Capone, the most notorious gangster in US history, died four days after his 48th birthday of an apoplectic stroke complicated by pneumonia. Slow of mind from the ravages of syphilis, he had lived his final eight years in retirement on his Florida estate after eight and a half years in prison.

Raised in Brooklyn of Neapolitan immigrant parents, Capone had left school when he was twelve and had soon become a violent criminal. As a teenager he had murdered at least two men, for which he was never convicted. It was during this time in Brooklyn that he gained the nickname 'Scarface' when he insulted a young woman in a bar-cum-whorehouse named the Harvard Inn and her hoodlum brother slashed his face with a razor.

At twenty Capone moved to Chicago, where he quickly moved up in the gangland hierarchy. Soon he became the city's leading mobster, controlling gambling houses, brothels and racetracks, but his most lucrative business was the illicit sale of alcohol in Prohibition-ridden America. His organisation ran a string of illegal nightclubs, speakeasies and distilleries and generated an income in excess of $100 million a year.

To gain and hold his empire, Capone ruthlessly wiped out all underworld competitors. His most infamous murder was the St Valentine's Day Massacre of 1929, when four of his henchmen, two masquerading as policemen, entered a garage at 2122 North Clark Street in Chicago where the rival bootlegger Bugs Moran kept his headquarters. There they lined up six of Moran's gang plus an unlucky garage attendant against a wall and opened fire with two shotguns and two machine guns. (Moran himself, who was probably the intended victim, was across the street and survived the day, but his rivalry with Capone was over, and he drifted into petty crime, eventually dying in Leavenworth Penitentiary.)

For years Capone seemed immune from prosecution in a city famous for the corruption of both its administration and its police force, and the federal government despaired of bringing him to justice. But finally, ignoring his murders, extortion and other more brutal crimes, the government came up with the idea of prosecuting him for tax evasion, for Capone had never filed a tax return.

In 1931 Capone was indicted for tax evasion and, along with 68 of his henchmen, for violating Prohibition laws. When the trial judge refused to do a deal, Capone tried to bribe the jury, but the judge astutely changed the jury members at the last minute.

On 17 October Capone was convicted on only five of the 23 counts against him, but that was sufficient to earn an eleven-year sentence plus a $50,000 fine.

Capone was still only 33 when he started his term at Atlanta, and he had soon become the kingpin of the prison's inmates and obtained special privileges from the warders. Determined that he should experience a more rigorous regime, the government transferred him to the notorious Alcatraz prison on an island in San Francisco Bay, where he had no contact with the outside world.

While incarcerated at Alcatraz, Capone began to show signs of the dementia caused by tertiary syphilis. He was later transferred to Terminal Island in California and then finally released on 16 November 1939. Now a free man, he moved to his estate in Florida, but his failing mind precluded further mob activity and he lived in slow-witted retirement until his unmourned death.

A marriage made in hell

1533 The bride was two months pregnant and her elder sister had once been the bridegroom's mistress. The bridegroom, on the other hand, was still married to his first wife (who previously had been married to his elder brother). No wonder the marriage didn't work. It ended dramatically three years later when the bride lost her head for another man – and then lost it for her husband.

The bride of course was Anne Boleyn, the bridegroom Henry VIII, who was still married to Catherine of Aragon when he married Anne. Catherine had previously been married to Henry's brother Arthur, who died, according to Catherine, before the marriage had been consummated. The 'other man' was, according to the charges against Anne, in fact several other men, including her own brother. And of course it was her loving husband Henry who finally made her lose her head for ever.

The only success from the wedding was the two-month old foetus that Anne carried in her womb. It turned out to be the future Queen Elizabeth.

Also on this day

1586: German painter Lucas Cranach the Younger dies * 1759: Scottish poet Robert Burns is born

26 January

Chinese Gordon goes down fighting

1885 He was of medium height with a square jaw, sandy hair and a clipped military moustache. His power of command came through his pale blue and penetrating eyes as well as his somewhat unworldly righteousness. He was Charles Gordon, a British major general known as Chinese Gordon for his daring leadership in helping to put down rebel Chinese warlords in the Taiping Rebellion twenty years earlier.

A man of iron nerve, Gordon was a classic case of Victorian complexity. When not soldiering he spent much time helping orphaned children. He meditated three hours a day with his Bible, was celibate throughout his life and looked forward to death to meet his God. Queen Victoria's secretary referred to him as 'that Christian lunatic'.

In 1884 the British government sent Gordon to the Sudan where a Muslim fanatic called the Mahdi was taking over the country with a large army and threatening British interests in Egypt. Gordon soon arrived in Khartoum where he organised the defending garrison – all Sudanese or Egyptian soldiers except for a handful of British officers.

Soon the Mahdi neared the walled city. Knowing he had no chance of defeating the Mahdi's large army, Gordon still refused to leave. In the meantime Prime Minister Gladstone had at last authorised a relief force, but it seemed beset with incessant delays.

Early on the morning of 26 January the Mahdi ordered the final assault on the doomed city. In rode his fanatical hordes, leaving the streets red with blood. Gordon pulled back to the royal palace and there on an outside staircase he awaited his enemies, unarmed. Tearing open his tunic he faced his attackers and cried out 'Strike! Strike hard!' He finally fell in a rain of spear thrusts.

The relief force arrived two days later, on what would have been Gordon's 52nd birthday, to find they had come too late. Today Chinese Gordon's effigy lies in St Paul's Cathedral in London but not his body, for it was never found.

Birth of a Romanian tyrant

1918 One of thirteen children from a peasant family, Nicolae Ceausescu was born today in Oltenia, Romania. The hard life he lived created a hard man, one who joined the Communist Party's youth organisation at fifteen, later served a prison sentence for 'agitation' and finally rose to the top Party rank at the age of 47, in effect the Romanian dictator.

Ceausescu followed three basic principles throughout his long dictatorship: independence from Russia (while still firmly in the Communist bloc), brutal repression of the Romanian people and extravagant self-aggrandisement. He razed great parts of Bucharest to build a massive presidential palace and destroyed countless villages for reconstruction along collectivist lines. His wife Elena virtually shared power with him, so great was her influence, and 38 other family members had important government posts.

The price Romania would pay for his rule was enormous in both human and economic terms. And finally, at the very close of 1989, the Romanian people decided they would no longer pay it.

In late December civil demonstrations against the government were met with gunfire and thousands were killed. But finally Ceausescu and his wife were forced to flee Bucharest by helicopter, only to be captured almost immediately by his own army, which had joined the revolt.

Quickly put on secret trial by the insurgent army, the man who had ruled with an iron hand for 25 years was condemned to die along with his wife. Unrepentant to the end, he claimed, 'The people had everything they needed.' Still rock hard, the couple's last words were 'We want to die together.' They faced a firing squad in an army barracks courtyard, refusing to be blindfolded. At four o'clock in the darkening afternoon a volley rang out. It was Christmas Day.

Also on this day

1788: The first convicts from England land in Australia * 1905: The Cullinan diamond, weighing 114 pounds, is found near Pretoria, South Africa

27 January

Trajan becomes Emperor on the death of Nerva

AD 98 The Emperor Nerva was 62 and looked older when he died of apoplexy on this day in Rome, after a reign of a mere sixteen months. His death brought to power one of Rome's greatest rulers, 44-year-old Marcus Ulpius Traianus, better known to us as Trajan.

A good administrator and 'second man' but not a leader, Nerva had been propelled to the top by the Senate when his malevolent predecessor Domitian had been assassinated. Although hated by the Senate and feared by the population, Domitian had been popular with the army, particularly his Praetorian Guard. So no sooner had Nerva become Emperor than the Guard forced him to execute Domitian's murderers, the very people to whom Nerva owed his throne.

Thus publicly humiliated, Nerva sought to re-establish his authority and regain support in the army by adopting the popular general Trajan. Consequently, when Nerva succumbed, it was Trajan who became the new Emperor.

Trajan was all that Nerva was not – tall, rugged and a first-rate commander who instinctively knew how to win public support. The first time he entered Rome as Emperor he walked among the common people and embraced each senator. But he could also be coldly authoritative; one of his first acts was to summon those guards who had threatened Nerva and order their execution.

Although Trajan came from an Umbrian family, he had been born in Italica, near modern Seville, thus becoming the first Roman emperor born outside Italy. He was to rule for nineteen years, six months and fifteen days, during which time he enlarged the Empire to its greatest extent, conquering parts of Parthia (now Iraq and Iran) and Dacia (now Romania). Even today Romanians claim descent from his occupying soldiers and owe their language to his conquest.

Trajan was also a prodigious builder, some of whose creations like his market in Rome and his famous 100-foot column there can still be admired today. He also implemented Nerva's idea of the *alimenta*, a system of using state funds to support poor children in Italy.

Such was Trajan's popularity that over two centuries after his death the Roman Senate still prayed for each new Emperor to be 'felicior Augusto, melior Traiano' (more fortunate than Augustus, better than Trajan).

Trajan also has a special place in the eyes of the Christian Church, as he was famously lenient with Christians, once instructing his friend Pliny the Younger (then a provincial governor) not to seek them out but to prosecute them only if they disturbed the peace. For this Dante included him in Paradise, unique among pre-Christian emperors, and relates how Pope Gregory the Great prayed for his admission to heaven.

Trajan died of a stroke on 8 August 117, deeply mourned by his people, who saw him as the perfect ruler; indeed, the 2nd-century historian Cassius Dio claims his only vices were wine and young boys.

Pushkin is killed in a duel

1837 On this winter afternoon a duel was fought, pistols at ten paces, in a lonely spot on the outskirts of St Petersburg. The Frenchman fired first, and Alexander Pushkin fell to the ground. Helped to his feet by a second, the poet aimed, then fired off a shot, hitting his adversary in the arm. It would have been a draw if both men had survived their wounds. But Pushkin, Russia's greatest poet, did not survive, dying two days later at the age of 37.

Imperial Russia was never a congenial place for free spirits, especially if the Tsar's government suspected them of harbouring dangerous political views, such as liberalism. Pushkin, however, was no longer the free spirit of his youthful days, his genius increasingly tethered to his desire for social standing in the capital. This desire led not only to ruinous debt but also to a dependence on the Tsar's favour for income and privileges, for which he gave up the right to travel and write as he pleased. The poet turned courtier knew that in court circles he was mocked for his pretensions. He also knew that his correspondence was regularly opened by the police.

Pushkin chose to fight a duel over an anonymous letter alleging that he was a cuckold, owing to his wife's affair with a Frenchman serving in the Russian Horse Guards. He issued the challenge more to protect his position in society than because of the truth of the charge, which, knowing his wife's narcissistic nature, he doubted.

Upon his death, the government ordered his room sealed so police agents could inspect his papers. Troops were posted around the house in case of an outburst from the crowd of mourners gathering in the street. Only the briefest, most formal death notices were allowed in newspapers. Fearing public demonstrations at the scheduled cathedral service, the government secretly transferred the body to a smaller church in a futile attempt to limit attendance.

The public outcry at the loss of Pushkin was widespread among the middle classes and the intelligentsia, who blamed court aristocrats and the Tsar's repressive regime for his death. He became a symbol of liberalism destroyed by autocracy. When a young hussar officer circulated a bitter poem about Pushkin's aristocratic enemies, he was arrested for it and banished to the Caucasus. The officer's name was Mikhail Lermontov, and in time he would be the genius of the next generation, a successor to the great Pushkin.

On 6 February Pushkin's body was buried at Mikhaylovskoe, his country estate, a police spy in attendance to the end. The Tsar forbade the erection of a monument.

In *Eugene Onegin*, composed some years earlier, Pushkin foretold his own fate when he described the poet Lenski's death by duel:

And Lenski, closing his left eye,
Also began to aim – just then
Onegin fired his fatal shot …
The poet's destined hour had struck.
Silent he let his pistol fall.

Also on this day

1756: Austrian composer Wolfgang Amadeus Mozart is born * 1859: Kaiser William II of Germany is born * 1901: Italian composer Giuseppe Verdi dies

28 January

Death comes to Europe's greatest emperor

814 His language was German, his capital in Aachen, and Germans consider him the first German Emperor as well as the greatest.

The French believe him French, point out that he was King of the Franks, and call his capital Aix-la-Chapelle, named in reference to the lovely octagonal chapel that he built there. They, too, consider him their first Emperor and perhaps their greatest.

In English we call him by his French name, Charlemagne, who conquered vast territories to build an empire that included all of modern France, Belgium and Holland, virtually all of Germany and Austria, half of Italy, part of Hungary and a few north-eastern provinces of Spain. He established the Carolingian dynasty that ruled intermittently until 987, and in several Slavic languages (as well as in Turkish) the word 'king' derives from the German version of his name (Karl), for example *král* in Czech and *król* in Polish. He thus shares a distinction with Julius Caesar, whose name was the origin of the words *kaiser* in German and *tzar* in Russian.

Charlemagne died this day almost 1,200 years ago, probably from influenza. He was 71. His tomb lies in his chapel in the cathedral at Aachan. It bears the inscription: 'Sub hoc conditorio situm est corpus Karoli Magni et orthodoxi imperatoris, qui regnum francorum nobiliter apliavit, et per annos XLVII felicites rexit.' (Beneath this tomb lies the body of Charles, Great and orthodox Emperor, who led the Kingdom of the Franks with greatness and ruled it successfully for 47 years.)

Although Charlemagne had been a loyal supporter of the Church and spreader of the faith, he was canonised only in 1165 because, in the words of historian Norman Davies, 'the process was obstructed for 351 years by reports that his sexual conquests were no less extensive than his territorial ones'. Sadly for the Great Charles, he never became a proper saint because he was canonised by Paschal III, an anti-pope set up by Holy Roman Emperor Frederick Barbarossa in competition with the legitimate popes of the Catholic Church in Rome.

Henry VIII dies in St James's Palace

1547 When Henry Tudor had mounted the throne of England in 1509 as King Henry VIII, he had been young, handsome, dashing, athletic, musical – in a word, glorious, all that a king should be. But now, prostrate and close to death, he had become at the age of 57 a megalomaniac, a callous, brutal and self-glorifying tyrant. A giant of a man for his time, he was six feet two inches tall and weighed over twenty stone. Partially crippled by a festering ulcer on his thigh caused by a jousting accident a decade before, his body was so bloated he could not mount the stairs on his own.

At the end, Henry lay dying in St James's Palace in London, surrounded by his counsellors, including the Archbishop of Canterbury Thomas Cranmer.

Legend has it that this great and terrible king died defiant, calling for a bowl of white wine, cursing monks and clerics and abruptly dying with the agonised shout, 'All is lost!'

In truth, however, Henry died as he had lived, refusing to believe that any power, even death, would dare approach him. During the night of 27 January he was asked if he wanted a priest. 'I will first take a little sleep,' he replied, 'and then, as I feel myself, I will advise upon the matter.' So, confident that there was more time – that there would always be more time – Henry slipped off into a coma. At about 2 a.m. on Friday 28 January 1547 bluff King Henry passed from this earth.

Also on this day

1457: Henry Tudor, the future King Henry VII of England and first Tudor king, is born * 1521: The Diet of Worms opens, at which Martin Luther is outlawed by the Church * 1921: American painter Jackson Pollock is born * 1935: Iceland becomes the first European country to legalise abortion

29 January

Napoleon III takes a beautiful Spanish bride

1853 She was 26, Spanish and strikingly beautiful. He was 44 and attractive through his power; 68 days earlier he had become Emperor of France. On this day they were married by civil ceremony, but still she refused to go to bed with him until after the church service the following day. She was Eugénia María De Montijo De Guzmán (Eugénie in French), a Spanish aristocrat of severe Catholic views. He was Louis Napoleon Bonaparte, the nephew of the great Napoleon, and now officially known as Napoleon III.

It seems likely that on her wedding night Eugénie was glad she had rebuffed his advances the day before, for Louis apparently attracted women by his energy, intelligence and great family name, not by his prowess in bed. One of his conquests, the marquise de Taisey-Chatenoy, recalled that the experience was brief and unsatisfying, and his heavy breathing had caused the wax on his moustache to melt.

Although Eugénie bore Louis a son in 1856, she was unenthusiastic about her conjugal obligations, and he was no more monogamous during marriage than he had been before. As is the way in dynastic unions, the couple stayed together despite his philandering. After the disastrous French loss to Bismarck's Prussia at Sedan in 1870, they were exiled to England, where Louis died in 1873. But Eugénie continued in the role of the *grande dame* of Napoleonic politics until her death at the great age of 94 in 1920.

Richelieu discovers Mazarin

1630 France was about to invade Italy, so Cardinal Antonio Barberini was dispatched to seek out France's mighty Cardinal Richelieu to ask for a truce.

The meeting took place on this day in 1630. In itself it achieved nothing, but its real effects would start to be felt on Richelieu's death, twelve years later. For in Cardinal Barberini's train was the son of a Roman steward. His name was Giulio Mazzarini, then just 29 years old.

Richelieu was impressed by Mazzarini's brilliance and invited him to dinner. 'I took to him by instinct', he later wrote.

So the architect of France's greatness met the man who would be his successor, who later shortened his name to Mazarin. On his deathbed in 1642 Richelieu won Louis XIII's promise that Mazarin would take over as First Minister. He kept the post for the next twenty years.

A fatal miscarriage

1536 Anne Boleyn had been married to Henry Tudor, King of England, for three full years yet still had failed to deliver that *sine qua non* of dynastic marriages, a son and heir to the throne. Their daughter Elizabeth, now two, of course didn't count; she was merely a girl. Worse (for Anne), Henry was clearly tiring of his wife, grown shrewish and demanding and no more the only magnet for the King's great lust.

But happily Anne found herself pregnant in January of 1537. At the end of the month, however, calamity struck. Entering a room unexpectedly, she found her obese and rutting husband in the tender embraces of proper, pleasant Jane Seymour, one of Anne's maids in waiting.

Short-tempered and bossy, Anne reacted so violently to the scene she had just witnessed that she lost the child within her, which was in fact a baby boy. The date was 29 January 1536.

Who knows what changes might have occurred had Anne delivered a son to the King. As it was, Henry had her head neatly severed from her body exactly three months and twenty days after the miscarriage. Eleven days after that he married Jane Seymour. Nineteen months later Queen Jane gave birth to the heir Henry so desperately wanted, the future Edward VI.

Also on this day

1737: Political essayist Thomas Paine is born * 1813: Jane Austen publishes *Pride and Prejudice* * 1856: The Victoria Cross is established

30 January

Double suicide at Mayerling

1889 At some quiet hour after midnight at the royal hunting lodge in Mayerling, Archduke Rudolf, only son of the Emperor Franz Joseph and heir to the throne of Austria-Hungary, composed a despairing letter to his mother ('I know that I am unworthy to be your son') and a brief note to his wife with the equivocal phrase, 'I am going calmly to my death which alone can save my good name.' He then placed a pistol to the temple of his seventeen-year-old mistress lying next to him in bed and pulled the trigger. Some hours later he turned the gun on himself. In the morning servants discovered the shocking scene, and word was sent post haste to Vienna.

Rudolf had been strictly raised by his unaffectionate father and, although he was well educated and intelligent, his father denied him any role in government. His arranged marriage to a Belgian princess had produced one daughter but no happiness, and he turned to mistresses for consolation.

In 1887, when Rudolf was 29, he met Baroness Maria von Vetsera at a ball in the German embassy. Although Maria was only sixteen at the time, she and the unhappy prince were soon enmeshed in a passionate affair.

When Franz Joseph heard of his son's liaison he determined to put a stop to it. On 28 January he summoned Rudolf and rebuked him for his conduct, taking the opportunity to tell him that the Pope had refused his plea to have his marriage annulled. The Emperor strongly voiced his own opposition to any divorce.

The next day an anguished Rudolf took Maria to the hunting lodge where he persuaded this seventeen-year-old innocent to join him in suicide, his only solution for their problems.

Wishing to hush up Maria's murder, Franz Joseph immediately dropped a veil of secrecy over the affair and had her body secretly buried. Then the imperial court issued a series of unconvincing lies that served only to inflame public curiosity and generate ever more bizarre rumours about what had actually happened: Rudolf and Maria had committed suicide because she was pregnant; Rudolf had been assassinated by Austrian republicans; Rudolf had committed suicide after killing Maria because she had emasculated him; Rudolf had shot himself after having been caught plotting against his father; Rudolf had killed them both because he had discovered that Maria was his half-sister; Rudolf was murdered in a love triangle duel with another noble. As recently as 1982 the family continued to leave false trails when former Empress Zita told a newspaper that Rudolf had been murdered for unspecified but mysterious 'political reasons'.

Rudolf's death at Mayerling made his cousin, Archduke Franz Ferdinand, the next in line to inherit the throne of Austria-Hungary. Twenty-five years later Franz Ferdinand and his wife also met their deaths by pistol fire, but this time there was an assassin, and the place was Sarajevo.

The scaffold built by a saint

1278 Wandering through Paris in the tenth *arrondissement* near the Gare de l'Est, you will come upon the historic Hôpital St Louis, built for plague victims in 1605. Ironically, it was next to the hospital's site, on the present rue de la Grange-aux-Belles, that St Louis himself had a more sinister edifice constructed during the first half of the 13th century. The saintly king's construction was the infamous gallows of Montfaucon.

Montfaucon was built like a great hall without a roof. It featured sixteen pillars attached to one another by chains of iron, standing on great stone blocks. Here the criminals and traitors of France were hanged – and left hanging until their corpses disintegrated.

On 30 January 1278 an unfortunate victim named Pierre de la Brosse was brought to the scaffold. De la Brosse had started life as a surgeon and valet to King Louis himself and had risen to become Finance Minister under Louis's son Philip III, the Hardy. Sadly, court intrigue eventually brought de la Brosse down, but in his death he started something of a tradition for French Ministers of Finance.

For after de la Brosse, Pierre Rémy (minister to Charles IV), René de Siran (to Philip the Fair), Euguerrand de Marigny (to Louis X), Olivier la Daim (to Louis XI) and Beaune de Samblançay (successively minister to Charles VIII, Louis XII and François I) all met their ends on the gallows of St Louis's Montfaucon. In fact, the dreaded platform endured until 1627 as a place of execution and was finally pulled down only in 1761.

Also on this day

1649: English King Charles I is beheaded, the only English king ever publicly tried and executed as a traitor, tyrant, murderer and public enemy * 1882: American President Franklin Delano Roosevelt is born * 1933: German dictator Adolf Hitler assumes power

31 January

The German Sixth Army surrenders at Stalingrad

1943 Today, the day after the tenth anniversary of his coming to power, Adolf Hitler raised four of his generals to the rank of Field Marshal. At that very moment, one of those newly created marshals was in the process of surrendering his army to the enemy. For Field Marshal Friedrich Paulus and his Sixth Army, and for Hitler and Nazi Germany as well, the tide of Operation Barbarossa, the German army's invasion of Russia, had turned. The high water mark was at the city of Stalingrad.

Not many months earlier, believing that the Red Army was on its last legs and possessed no sizeable reserves with which to mount a counter-attack, the German high command determined to deal its foe a knockout blow before winter set in. Hitler wanted Stalin's city taken, no matter what. In this spirit German ground commanders ignored intelligence reports of large enemy forces building up around the Stalingrad position.

So it was that, beginning on 12 September, when Paulus launched what was supposed to be the final attack, Sixth Army found itself facing the fiercest sort of close-quarter resistance, as it attempted to claw its way through the rubble of the ruined city, block by block, building by building, even floor by floor. When the offensive petered out in late October, the centre of Stalingrad still lay in Soviet hands.

Snow began falling on 12 November. It was followed by heavy Soviet attacks driving through the flanks of the long German salient stretching back west and south of Stalingrad. Suddenly, on 22 November, Sixth Army, 290,000 strong, found itself cut off and surrounded. In the weeks that followed, the Russians hammered in the sides of the German-held pockets. Supplies had to be flown in now, but the Luftwaffe's available air capacity could bring in less than half of what the army needed to keep functioning. From his headquarters in East Prussia, Hitler proclaimed 'Fortress Stalingrad' and forbade any attempt to break out for the safety of the German lines to the west. Men died by the thousands, from wounds, exhaustion, exposure and starvation. Just before Christmas, a rescue mission was fought to a standstill 35 miles short of Sixth Army's lines.

On Christmas Day the temperature was –25° Fahrenheit. On New Year's Day Hitler sent this message to Paulus and his command: 'You and your soldiers ... should enter the New Year with the unshakeable confidence that I and the whole German *Wehrmacht* will do everything in our power to relieve the defenders of Stalingrad ...' It was not to be. Sixth Army had been abandoned.

Surrender discussions began on 31 January. Sick and demoralised, Paulus at one point refused to order the holdout XI Corps to join his surrender, but it made no difference. By 4.00 a.m. on 2 February, the last signs of resistance had flickered out. All that remained of the German Sixth Army – 91,000 soldiers, including 22 generals – was marched away to the Soviet lines. Foreign correspondents witnessing these trophies of the great Soviet victory noted how healthy the German generals appeared compared with their undernourished troops. Of the German soldiers captured at Stalingrad, 95 per cent died in POW camps. Those who survived, around 5,000, were released after the war, the last 2,000 of them in 1955.

Also on this day

1543: Tokugawa Iayasu, founder of the Tokugawa shogunate in Japan, is born * 1606: English terrorist Guy Fawkes and three others are hanged, drawn and quartered * 1797: Austrian composer Franz Schubert is born

1 February

The Bohemian behind La Bohème

1896 Henri Murger was one of the few struggling poets of 19th-century Paris who turned his Left Bank experiences to profitable account.

Born in Paris in 1822, Murger was the son of a tailor and a concierge, and his formal education stopped at the age of thirteen. His early work was undistinguished, and he often lived in poverty with deteriorating health, but the romance and gaiety of 19th-century Paris enthralled him. When he was in his early 20s he started writing serialised stories about Bohemian life in the mid-1840s. Here were the radicals, the rebels and above all the artists who rejected all bourgeois values, choosing instead what they saw as the honesty of artistic creation and the suffering and privation that often went with it, determined to follow a life of independence, work and pleasure. He called the Bohemian life 'la préface de l'Académie, de l'Hôtel-Dieu ou de la Morgue' (the foreword to the [French] Academy, the hospital or the morgue).

If you are an opera fan, one of Murger's stories will sound familiar: 'During that time, the great philosopher Gustave Colline, the great painter Marcel, the great musician Schaunard, and the great poet Rudolphe, as they referred to each other among themselves, regularly frequented the café *Momus*, where they were known as the four musketeers because they were always seen together. In fact, they came together, left together, played together and sometimes didn't pay for their drinks together, always with a harmony worthy of the Conservatory Orchestra.' Rudolphe, of course, was a portrait of Murger himself.

Murger's tales became so popular that he eventually pulled some together into a play called *La Vie de Bohème*, an instant hit of the day. He was celebrated by Victor Hugo, lauded by Louis Napoleon and awarded the Légion d'Honneur. But he enjoyed fame and fortune only briefly. Within a decade he was dead at the age of only 39.

Sadly, Murger did not live to the evening of 1 February 1896 when Giacomo Puccini's opera *La Bohème*, based on Murger's play, was first performed in Turin. More than a century later, *La Bohème* remains the most often produced and most popular opera ever written.

A king's assassination leads to the end of the Portuguese monarchy

1908 Cultured, multi-lingual, sophisticated and an expert in oceanography, King Carlos I of Portugal was better known to his subjects for the less inspiring aspects of his personality, namely his extraordinary extravagance and licentiousness. Perhaps his main distinction is that he is Portugal's only monarch ever to be assassinated.

Carlos had become King in 1889, but his country was beset by severe political and economic problems, including the metastasis of a rabid republican opposition. As problem led towards crisis, in 1906 the King, impatient with politics and popular demands, appointed João Franco as Prime Minister and virtual dictator. Despite Franco's attempts to reform the government's finances, rumours grew that he was illegally siphoning off money from the treasury to help Carlos pay for his profligate lifestyle.

Finally the combined pressure of Franco's stifling dictatorship and a faltering economy brought open revolt, and on 1 February 1908 King Carlos and his son Luís Filipe were gunned down in an open carriage riding through a city square in Lisbon. No one has ever proved whether the killers were anti-monarchical fanatics acting alone or agents of the Carbonária, a republican secret society, but the result was the collapse of the monarchy less than two years later. Carlos's younger son Manuel, only eighteen on his father's assassination, became King, but the Carbonária ignited another uprising in October of 1910, this time successfully chasing him into permanent exile in England, bringing to an end the rule of the House of Bragança, which had first gained the throne of Portugal on 15 December 1640.

Also on this day

1328: King Charles IV of France dies, ending the Capetian dynasty after 341 years, and starting the Valois dynasty with Philip VI * 1650: French philosopher René Descartes dies in Stockholm * 1793: Britain declares war on France, to last for 22 years

2 February

Birth of a 'bold merry slut' destined to become a king's mistress

1650 Born today in an alley off Drury Lane in London was one of history's most beguiling mistresses, Nell Gwyn, the petite, exuberant brunette who was kept for seventeen years by England's King Charles II.

By her own account, Nell had been born in a bawdyhouse run by her mother. Her father died in debtors' prison when she was still an infant. When she was a young girl her mother had enlisted her help 'to fill strong waters [serve brandy] to the guests' at the brothel, and she later sold oranges in Drury Lane. By the time she was fifteen she had switched to a career on the stage – and in the beds of her lovers. The first was an actor named Charles Hart, and a subsequent one was Charles Sackville, prompting her later to refer to Charles II as '*my* Charles III'.

When Nell was nineteen she came to the attention of the King, who was then 39, and soon became his mistress. 'Pretty witty Nell', as Samuel Pepys called her, charmed Charles not only by her pert good looks and exceptional legs but also by her high spirits and even temper. Once installed as the King's favourite (or at least one of them), she neither meddled in public affairs nor demanded money, although Charles treated her generously. Unlike some of his mistresses (and unlike Charles himself), from the time she joined him she remained faithful.

Famous for her quick wit, Nell once had occasion to use it to save herself from a violent mob. England at the time was rabidly anti-Catholic, and when Nell was riding in her carriage she was mistaken for Louise de Kéroualle, another of Charles's mistresses and a Catholic. As some drunken louts approached the carriage hefting iron bars, she poked her head out the window and called out, 'Pray, good people, be civil, for I am the *Protestant* whore.'

Nell had borne the king two sons and was 35 when Charles died in 1685. On his deathbed he entreated his brother James, 'Let not poor Nelly starve.' Honouring Charles's request, James gave her a pension of £1,500 a year. Two years later, on 14 November 1687, that 'bold merry slut' (Pepys again) died in London of a stroke.

Of Candlemas and Groundhog Day

AD 1 Called Candlemas because of the custom of lighting candles during the festival, today commemorates the day in the year 1 when the Virgin Mary went to be purified in the Temple of Jerusalem 40 days after the birth of her son and to present Jesus to God, as described in the second chapter of Luke. Today this religious remembrance bears another name in Britain, and in America it has been transformed into something surprisingly different.

The earliest record of Candlemas comes from 4th-century Jerusalem, when it was celebrated on 14 February, 40 days after Epiphany, which was then celebrated as Jesus' birthday. But there was another, pagan, holiday on 15 February called Lupercalia, the Roman fertility festival honouring the god Pan. To wean good Christians away from heathen rituals, in AD 492 the canny (and saintly) Pope Gelasius I abolished Lupercalia and replaced it with Candlemas. Fifty years later, Byzantine Emperor Justinian moved the date to 2 February, 40 days after Christmas, but the holiday was celebrated only in the Eastern Empire, where Justinian held sway.

In the 7th century Pope Sergius I introduced Candlemas to his Catholic subjects in Rome, and over the centuries it made its way across Europe to the cold and remote outposts of Great Britain. There small children would celebrate the holiday with the song:

If Candlemas be fair and bright,
    Come, Winter, have another flight;
If Candlemas brings clouds and rain,
    Go, Winter, and come not again.

Although the verse is English, it will have a familiar ring to Americans, who need look no further than to America's Groundhog Day, also celebrated on

2 February. American tradition decrees that this is when the hibernating groundhog (really a woodchuck) comes out of his burrow to see if he can see his shadow. All is well if the day is cloudy, for this forecasts an early spring, but if his shadow can be seen, the groundhog returns to his hole for another six weeks' sleep.

Although the basic tradition of predicting the weather originated in Britain, German settlers in Pennsylvania brought with them the tradition of a beaver, transmogrified over time to the groundhog.

Sadly, while Groundhog Day reigns supreme in North America, the evocative name of Candlemas is no longer used in Britain, replaced by the more pious term 'the Presentation of Christ in the Temple'.

Also on this day

1525, 1594: Italian composer Giovanni di Palestrina is born and dies * 1626: Charles I is crowned King of England

3 February

How the butcher of Cesena started the Papal Schism

1377 In 1308 the French Pope Clement V had moved the papacy from Rome to Avignon, principally as a political favour to Europe's most powerful king, Philip the Fair of France. One of the results of this so-called 'Babylonian Captivity' was a revolt of the Papal States in Italy, led by the Guelphs of Florence. But Pope Urban VI was disinclined to let Italy free from his control, and he ordered his legate there, Cardinal Robert of Geneva, to bring the Papal States to heel, if need be by force of arms.

Robert of Geneva was a young man (34) of high cultivation and sophistication. Although both lame and fat, he was also a cousin of the King of France. His manner was highly autocratic and his methods entirely ruthless.

Quickly hiring a band of mercenaries led by a renegade English knight named Sir John Hawkwood, Robert immediately attacked the city-states in revolt. He was at first unsuccessful but then came to the town of Cesena, near the Adriatic coast between Ravenna and Rimini.

To persuade Cesena's citizens to open their city gates, Cardinal Robert promised clemency by holy oath. But once inside the town he summoned his mercenaries and called for 'sangue et sangue' (blood and blood). Beginning on 3 February 1377, the soldiers butchered the town's inhabitants for three days and nights. Women were raped, men slaughtered and hundreds drowned in the moat outside the walls while trying to escape. Almost 5,000 in all were slain, and Cesena was put to the torch.

Cardinal Robert's services to the papacy at Avignon were considered so valuable that in September of the following year he was elected Pope as

Clement VII, although there was already another pope on St Peter's throne in Rome. Thus this noble murderer became the first anti-pope in the papal schism that was to tear Christendom apart for 71 years.

Emperor Charles V lays aside his burdens

1557 On this day began the most celebrated retirement since Diocletian resigned as Roman Emperor 1,252 years before. This time it was a Holy Roman Emperor who was laying aside the burden of office, Emperor Charles V, who today at last reached his chosen sanctuary at the monastery of San Jeronimo at Yuste.

Once the ruler of more land than even Charlemagne, Charles had relinquished his titles one by one, Spain and the Lowlands to his cold-eyed son Philip II, Austria, Italy and the German provinces to his brother Ferdinand. He retained only a small but luxurious villa next to the monastery in the hard country of Spain's Extremadura. There he slept in a room from which, when the door was open, he could see the altar in the chapel from his bed.

For Charles was sick both physically and at heart. Ridden by gout (the disease from which his son Philip was later to die), he arrived at Yuste carried in a litter, too ill to mount a horse. And in his great task of re-uniting the Christian world from the cleavage caused by Martin Luther, he knew he had failed. 'I have done what I could and am sorry that I could not do better. I have always recognised my insufficiency and incapacity', he mourned.

Charles installed himself in comfort with religion to support him and courtiers and his collection of clocks to while away the hours. Humble, saddened and sick, the great emperor died eighteen months later at the age of 58.

Also on this day
1809: German composer Felix Mendelssohn is born * 1913: The 16th Amendment to the US Constitution, authorising the collection of income tax, is ratified

4 February

Yet another disaster for the House of Stuart

1716 Today James Francis Edward, the last Stuart ever born on British soil, kept family tradition alive with yet another Stuart calamity.

For a family that had the good fortune to become kings at all, the Stuarts of Scotland (and later of England) were certainly dogged by bad luck – or at least by their own persistent incompetence. During the four centuries after the first Stuart became King of Scotland, two royal Stuarts were killed in battle, two were murdered, two were executed and three went mad or were too incompetent to rule.

In the 12th century the Stuart family, which had originally been called the Fitzalans, became hereditary High Stewards of Scotland, taking on the name 'Steward' in the process. (Sometime during the 16th century, due to French influence, the name was respelled because there was no 'w' in the French alphabet.)

The first royal Stuart, Robert II, was heir presumptive to the Scottish throne for more than 50 years. He is mostly remembered for his unsuccessful rebellion against his kingly cousin, David II, and the number of his children. He had nine bastards, later legitimised when he married his mistress, and four more by his second wife, and he sired at least eight other illegitimate children on the side for a grand total of 21.

In 1371 Robert was 54 when he finally inherited the throne. By the time he had reached 65 he had become so incompetent that he turned over control of his realm to his son John.

Imprisoned for helping his father in the abortive revolt against King David, John changed his name to Robert when he succeeded but was soon disabled by being kicked by a horse. Hence during his sixteen years as king he never ruled his nation, leaving power in the hands of his brother.

Robert's son, James I, continued the family custom of misfortune when he was murdered in 1437. Then an exploding cannon killed his son James II while he was defending Roxburgh from the English. The next in line, James III, was murdered while running away from a battle at Sauchieburn.

James III's son, predictably named James IV, was yet another war death, unhorsed and killed at the Battle of Flodden in 1513. Then his son James V died insane shortly after another defeat by the English, and James V's daughter Mary (Queen of Scots) died under the axe of England's Queen Elizabeth.

Mary's son James VI – who became James I of England – defied tradition by dying in bed, but his son Charles I was famously beheaded for his dogged insistence on the Divine Right of Kings.

Charles I's son Charles II was the true exception to the Stuart custom of disaster, and he became only the second kingly Stuart to die peacefully and in full control of his faculties. His brother James II also passed away from natural causes, but his life was calamitous nonetheless, for he lost the throne of England through his unremitting pigheadedness.

Through no fault of James II's, the crown stayed in the family, going to his daughter Mary and her husband William of Orange – but poor Mary reigned for only five years, dying of smallpox at just 32. Then Mary's sister Anne inherited the crown after William of Orange's demise. Her particular misfortune was her inability to have children. Pregnant eighteen times, only four of her children were born alive, of whom only one survived infancy, and he predeceased his mother.

On this date it was the turn of James (Francis) Edward, son of the banished James II and brother of Mary and Anne, to find calamity instead of triumph.

James Edward never relinquished his claim to the thrones of England and Scotland even though he had been taken to France at the age of six months.

When his father died in 1701 he gained the support of Louis XIV and styled himself James III of England and James VIII of Scotland.

When he was twenty James Edward made his first attempt to reconquer Scotland but never reached the shore, as British ships forced him to turn tail and return to France.

Seven years later he made one final effort to regain his kingdom by force of arms, landing at Peterhead near Aberdeen on 22 December 1715. Sadly, although a decent and honourable man, the Old Pretender, as James Edward is known in history, was neither warrior nor leader. His troops were too few, his money too little, and just 44 days after his landing, his incursion had become a withdrawal. On this day he hurriedly set sail for the Continent on the *Marie Thérèse*, his invasion a total fiasco. As he abandoned Scotland for ever, he coined the memorable phrase, 'Nous recoulons pour mieux sauter.' (We pull back in order to jump forward better.) Typical of this man who thought he should be King of England, his one famous remark would be made in French.

The Old Pretender spent the remainder of his life in exile in Rome. His son, the romantic Bonnie Prince Charlie, made a final futile attempt to regain the Stuart crowns in 1745 and then died without legitimate offspring, at last putting the House of Stuart out of its misery on 31 January 1788.

Also on this day

1789: George Washington is elected president of the United States * 1861: Seven secessionist southern states form the Confederate States of America, in Montgomery, Alabama * 1945: American, British and Soviet leaders meet in Yalta in the Ukraine to make agreements for post-war Europe

5 February

Birth of the man who gave birth to the Conservative Party

1788 Born today, Robert Peel, the shy, proud man who served as British Prime Minister for over eight years and founded the Conservative Party.

Peel was the grandson of a Lancashire farmer who had set up a calico-printing firm. This eventually provided enough wealth to employ 15,000 people and to buy both a baronetcy and a seat in Parliament for Peel's father, not to mention an education at Harrow and Oxford for Peel himself.

A brilliant student, on graduation Peel followed his father into Parliament and became an under-secretary a year later. Shortly after, he was appointed chief secretary for Ireland, but his involvement failed to lessen his strong anti-Catholicism, and he fought the idea of allowing Catholics to serve in Parliament. Chosen as Home Secretary at only 34, within five years he had resigned his post rather than agree to Catholic emancipation. By the time he was 40, however, he had come to see the necessity (and the justice) of permitting the election of Catholics and their appointment to most public offices, and he incurred the enmity of many of his political allies by his volte-face.

Peel first became Prime Minister in 1834, and it was then that he formed the Conservative Party, a more liberal version of the old Tory Party. But his Conservatives stayed in power for just over two years, eventually defeated by a coalition.

At the age of 53 Peel once again became Prime Minister and over the next six years transformed British law and government. He repealed the restrictive Corn Laws that prevented the import of cheap corn, abolished hanging for most crimes, legalised trade unions and reformed the central bank and the economy. (He also reintroduced a less popular institution that has been with us ever since when he re-established the income tax, originally set up during the Napoleonic Wars as a temporary measure.)

In spite of his achievements, his peers did not love Peel; his title was too new for the true aristocracy and his manner too superior for the rest. His great enemy Disraeli claimed that his bright smile was 'like the fitting on a coffin'.

Robert Peel died on 6 June 1850 after being thrown from his horse. He is still considered by many historians to be Britain's greatest peacetime Prime Minister. For most of us, however, he is remembered for only one of his achievements, the creation in 1829 of the London metropolitan police force, still affectionately called 'bobbies' in his honour.

Also on this day

1881: Scottish historian Thomas Carlyle dies in London * 1897: French novelist Marcel Proust fights a duel with fellow writer Jean Lorrain

6 February

'I have been a most unconscionable time dying; but I hope you will excuse it.'

1685 According to tradition, it was with the words above that England's King Charles II apologised to the courtiers surrounding him shortly before he died on this day, after six days of hovering on the brink.

King for almost a quarter of a century, Charles is one of history's most appealing monarchs, a man of wit, courage and generosity who sincerely cared for his subjects. An all-round sportsman, he loved tennis, hunted, hawked and shot, enjoyed long walks, swimming and rowing, and was an enthusiastic sailor. But the sport that perhaps he enjoyed the most was gallantry; he fathered at least fourteen bastards by various mistresses and was a keen visitor to London's stews. As Pepys observed, 'He is at the command of any woman like a slave, though he be the best man to the Queene in the world, with so much respect and never lies a night from her; but yet cannot command himself in the presence of a woman he likes.' For all of this he was called the Merry Monarch.

Returning from exile to become King after the eleven harsh Puritan years of Cromwell that followed his father's execution, Charles was welcomed by his citizens on his return and mourned by them at his death. As historian Hesketh Pearson has written, 'Lacking [political] passion, he stood for toleration. Having no malignity, he typified charity. Hating retribution, he desired reconciliation.'

Charles first fell sick on Sunday 1 February in Whitehall in London. At 54, he had been in excellent physical condition, troubled only by gout and a running sore on his leg. On that morning he awoke feeling out of sorts, his leg bothering him so much that he forwent his usual walk, taking a carriage ride instead.

The following day he woke 'pale as ashes', his speech slurred and hesitant. Suddenly at breakfast he gave a great shriek and fainted. Later he was attacked by convulsions and fever. It was clear to all that he was seriously ill, and so began the torments to which he was subjected by an array of physicians determined to make him well.

During the next four days the doctors repeatedly bled him, even opening his jugular vein, gave him purgatives, emetics and enemas of rock salt and syrup of buckthorn, branded his shaven head and feet with hot irons, applied blistering agents to his skin and in the end even made him drink spirit of human skull taken from a person who had died a violent death. In all it has been calculated that he was subjected to 58 different treatments by fourteen different doctors.

Charles suffered these tortures stoically, but his condition continued to worsen. On the evening of 5 February, with Charles's permission, his brother James (about to become James II) cleared the room of all but two courtiers and surreptitiously introduced the Catholic priest Father Huddleston, who had once helped Charles in his fugitive days when Cromwell was in power. Now Catholicism was despised and virtually illegal in England, but the fervent James was intent on what he saw as his beloved brother's salvation. The King received the last rites and became a Catholic less than a day before he died.

Charles awoke weak but lucid at six on Friday morning, 6 February. 'Open the curtains that I may once more see day', he whispered, and the curtains were drawn back. Half an hour later he had lost his speech and then fell into a coma. He died at noon.

The debate about exactly what killed Charles raged for many years. In his time it was attributed to 'apoplexy', and of course there were the usual rumours of poison. Later many thought his doctors' administrations had done him in. Still later the most popular theory was a stroke, but today most believe it was some form of kidney failure.

Philip the Fair becomes King of France

1286 When Philip the Fair was crowned in Reims today, it was the start of a 28-year reign that would change French history.

Handsome, silent and cold-blooded, Philip is best remembered for two acts that demonstrated his great and malevolent power. First, he caused the papacy to enter into what is known as its Babylonian Captivity when he pressured it to move its seat from Rome to Avignon. Second, he suppressed the Order of the Templars, eventually causing their innocent leader Jacques de Molay to be burnt at the stake for heresy.

Tradition has it that Molay, as he was being tied to the stake, called down a curse on all those involved. Whatever the reason, Philip, Pope Clement V who acquiesced in this judicial murder, and Philip's Prime Minister Guillaume de Nogaret all died within a year of Molay's immolation. Then Philip's three sons each died in turn without male heirs, bringing to an end the Capetian line of kings after 341 years of power.

Also on this day

1508: Maximilian I becomes Holy Roman Emperor * 1564: English writer Christopher Marlowe is born * 1911: Fortieth US President Ronald Reagan is born

7 February

Charles Dickens – 'the cheerfullest man of his age'

1812 Today in Portsmouth was born the greatest – or at least the most prolific – of the great 19th-century novelists, Charles Dickens. Lionised when alive, still venerated almost two centuries later, he penned a whole pantheon of works so unique in their style and ability to portray character and caricature that we still use a derivation of his name – Dickensian – to describe both squalid living conditions and humorous if sometimes repulsive people.

Although of a middle-class family, Dickens was withdrawn from school and put to work in a shoe blacking warehouse when he was twelve because his father had squandered his money and been imprisoned for debt. He later returned to school but at fifteen abandoned all formal education to become a solicitor's clerk, then a court stenographer and at seventeen a newspaper reporter.

By the time he was 24, however, Dickens had already started to make his mark as a writer, with the publication in instalments of *The Pickwick Papers*, which was a huge success with the public. The same year, he married Catherine Hogarth, who would bear him ten children. From that time onwards, outwardly at least, Dickens was the successful and contented author living the respectable Victorian life (Victoria having assumed the throne in 1837).

Indeed, by all accounts Dickens had both wit and charm. In one house he had a secret door to his study that was disguised to look like a bookcase, with painted shelves and the spines of books bearing fictitious titles. One set bore the title *The Wisdom of Our Ancestors* and included individual volumes on ignorance, superstition, the block, the stake, the rack, dirt and disease. Beside them sat a single slim companion book entitled *The Virtues of Our Ancestors*, so thin that the title on the spine had to be printed vertically.

After the success of *The Pickwick Papers*, Dickens continued to turn out long, successful novels – *Oliver Twist* followed by *Nicholas Nickleby* and *The Old Curiosity Shop*, a book adored by the public particularly for its sentimental handling of the death of Little Nell. (Not everyone has found it so touching, however. Oscar Wilde once remarked, 'One would have to have a heart of stone to read the death of Little Nell … without laughing.')

In 1843 Dickens published his most syrupy work, *A Christmas Carol*, which was an immediate success. His own favourite, the partly autobiographical *David Copperfield*, came out in 1850, followed during the next four years by two novels of social protest, *Bleak House* and *Hard Times*. An enthusiastic public eagerly awaited almost all of these, and Dickens became a national figure.

Suddenly, in May of 1858, when Dickens was 46, his wife Catherine moved out, although nothing was said to the outside world. The reason? Ten months before, Dickens had met and fallen in love with an attractive actress named Ellen (Nelly) Ternan, who was 27 years his junior. Two months prior to the collapse of his marriage Dickens had written to a friend, 'The domestic unhappiness remains so strong upon me that I can't write.'

After his wife's departure, however, Dickens evidently regained his creative flair, turning out such masterful novels as *A Tale of Two Cities*, *Great Expectations* and *Our Mutual Friend*. Meanwhile his sister Georgina came to live with him, caring for his younger children and taking care of the household.

As he grew older, Dickens seems to have become inwardly sad and preoccupied although outwardly as ebullient as ever. His American publisher called him 'the cheerfullest man of his age'. He now increased his workload, contributing to magazines and scheduling public readings of his works around Great Britain and in the United States. He undertook another tour of England in 1869, but abandoned it in April when he collapsed. Even then he continued to work, starting *The Mystery of Edwin Drood* and giving readings in London. Then, suddenly, on 9 June 1870 he died at his country house, Gad's Hill in Kent. So revered was he by the nation that he was buried in Westminster Abbey.

France votes for dictatorship

1800 Along with a new century, France had a new leader, Napoleon Bonaparte, the glamorous 23-year-old general who had triumphed first in Italy and then in Egypt.

Napoleon had staged a virtual *coup d'état* only a couple of months earlier, his celebrated *19 Brumaire* (the date according to France's republican calendar that had been instituted in 1793). But today the French electorate overwhelmingly confirmed him as First Consul, by 3,011,007 votes in favour to 1,562 against.

No doubt the French believed they were electing a strong leader for a democratic republic. Only ten days after the results were in, however, Napoleon moved himself and his wife into the Tuileries, traditional home of the French monarch. It proved a portent for things to come.

1478: English statesman and Catholic martyr Thomas More is born * 1807: Napoleon defeats the Russians and Prussians at the Battle of Eylau * 1950: The United States recognises Emperor Bao Dai of Vietnam rather than Ho Chi Minh, who is recognised by the Soviets

8 February

Mary, Queen of Scots, is beheaded

1587 Mary Stuart, Queen of Scots: once Queen of France, then the reigning Queen of Scotland, but for the past nineteen years a prisoner in gentle confinement in England. She was a fiery and beautiful woman, proud but essentially stupid, brave but vain and astonishingly foolish.

Twenty years earlier she had been driven from Scotland for conspiring in the death of her husband and marrying his murderer. Since fleeing to England she had not ceased from her plotting to regain her freedom and to seize the English throne from the jailer whom she had never met, Queen Elizabeth. (Although two centuries later the German poet Friedrich von Schiller had the two meet once outside Mary's prison in his play *Maria Stuart*, this was for reasons of drama rather than history.)

Now at Fotheringhay Castle a great platform was erected in the main hall. Here Mary was to die, convicted of plotting to kill the Queen.

Proudly she entered, dressed entirely in black, her reddish black hair impeccably coiffed. Crucifix in hand, she signalled for her black cloak to be removed. The 300 nobles in attendance gasped as they saw that underneath she was clad entirely in velvet the colour of blood. Thus she knelt to die.

Shaken, the masked executioner needed three blows of the axe to sever her neck, and then the once beautiful head of the 44-year-old queen rolled across the scaffold. The headsman stooped to pick it up, and suddenly it slipped from his grasp, and he was left holding a dark red wig. The beautiful Mary's real hair was short-clipped and grey, that of an old woman.

According to some sources, the dead queen's lips continued to move for ten minutes.

Peter the Great dies of liver failure

1725 At 5.00 in the morning Peter the Great, Tsar of all the Russias, suffered his last terrible convulsion, and death released him from agony. Modern analysis suggests that he died from acute cirrhosis, a condition doubtless caused by his frequent bouts of brutish drunkenness, bouts that he delighted in forcing his whole court to join in.

Peter's ruthlessness and cruelty are well documented. To his enemies he gave no quarter, and after the Streltsy rebellion in 1698 he beheaded 80 conspirators with his own hand. But he denied that he was cruel, his perverse logic leading him to punish those who claimed that he was by having their tongues cut out. He also had his own son tortured to death.

In spite of it all, Peter was great indeed, as he virtually single-handedly turned Russia from an Asiatic nation into a Western one in just 35 years of dictatorial rule. He introduced scores of European industries to Russia and was responsible for his country's first navy – and first secret police. Most of all, he changed the outlook of his people.

When he died at 52 Peter left his Swedish-born wife Catherine to succeed him as Russia's first woman ruler.

Also on this day

1820: US general William Sherman ('War is hell.') is born

9 February

A queen connives in her husband's murder

1567 Henry Stewart, Lord Darnley had been the worst of husbands – vain, stupid, indolent and drunken, with an insatiable desire to wield the full power of a king through his wife. Darnley's wife of course was 25-year-old Mary, Queen of Scots, who had no intention of sharing her power with anyone, least of all with her detested and quite detestable husband who was still only twenty.

Unfortunately for Darnley, Mary was also passionately in love with a Scottish adventurer named James Hepburn, the Earl of Bothwell, who would execute the murder that Mary so much desired.

On 9 February 1567 Mary rushed to join her husband in his house at Kirk o'Field, outside the gates of Edinburgh. Darnley was there convalescing from either smallpox or venereal disease, and Mary, playing the caring wife, showed her concern. In truth, her purpose was simply to ensure that he would be at home that night.

In the middle of the night the Queen suddenly remembered that she had promised to attend a ball following the wedding of one of her maids-in-waiting that very evening. Giving her husband a last kiss, she departed smiling.

A few hours later a tremendous explosion was heard throughout Edinburgh. Bothwell had moved a barrel of gunpowder to the room directly below Darnley's bedroom and had set it off. Darnley subsequently was found naked and dead in the street outside, apparently strangled, whether caught as he fled or throttled in his room and blown onto the street no one could say. Three months and six days later Mary married Bothwell.

Also on this day

1408: Henry IV defeats and kills Henry Percy, Earl of Northumberland at Bramham Moor * 1881: Russian novelist Fyodor Dostoevsky dies in St Petersburg

10 February

Victoria marries Albert

1840 Today marks the wedding of twenty-year-old Queen Victoria to her German cousin, Prince Albert of Saxe-Coburg-Gotha, in the Chapel Royal of St James's Palace in the heart of London's West End.

In October of the previous year Albert had visited Victoria at Windsor, sweeping her off her feet by his serious demeanour and good looks. After only four days together, the Queen had come to her decision. Albert was the man she wanted to marry, and royal protocol demanded that she do the proposing. As she later recorded in her diary, 'After a few minutes I said to him that I thought he must be aware *why* I wished them [Albert and his brother] to come here – and that it would make me *too happy* if he would consent to what I wished (to marry me).' Then, 'we embraced each other, and he was *so* kind, *so* affectionate.'

Although the Queen was clearly enamoured, Albert married primarily to find a larger, more influential place for himself in the world than would have been possible had he remained at home, the second son in the tiny German principality ruled by his father. In the end, however, the marriage proved to be one of the few true royal love matches. Victoria was besotted from the beginning, and over the years he came to love her deeply – and faithfully, a rarity among aristocrats.

Not that the marriage was without problems. Victoria had strong views about her position and the precedence of a queen over her consort, but Albert wished to participate in royal councils and play the traditional role of the husband. One famous story, perhaps apocryphal, illustrates the dilemma.

Annoyed with Victoria for excluding him yet again from an important state decision, Albert retreated to his room and locked the door. Soon Victoria sought him out, knocking loudly and demanding entrance.

'Who is there?' asked the prince from within.

'The Queen of England', came the reply. But the door remained closed.

Once again Victoria knocked, once again Albert asked who was there, and once again the response was 'The Queen of England'. The door remained resolutely shut.

Victoria knocked a third time and Albert again asked, 'Who is there?'

'Your wife, Victoria', came the answer, after which Albert immediately opened the door and welcomed her in.

Eventually Albert became Victoria's prime advisor and confidant, without whose advice she took no decisions. Hardworking, earnest and somewhat priggish, Albert also set for the British public the example of what we would call the Victorian code of conduct.

Victorian morality may long have vanished, but one of Albert's introductions to British culture is with us still: the Christmas tree, an old German tradition he popularised in Britain in 1841 when he gave one to Victoria as a Christmas present.

The 18th century's greatest general runs from his first battle

1741 When the Prussians met the Austrians in the snows of Mollwitz in Silesia, the battle looked so desperate that the young Prussian King galloped from the field, terrified he would be captured in this, his first battle.

Fortunately for Prussia, the tide of battle was turned by Field Marshal Schwerin, who finally routed the enemy, allowing the King to return.

This was an inauspicious beginning for the King, but it was the last time he would leave the field early. His name was Frederick the Great. During the next 45 years he firmly established himself as the greatest commander of his age.

Also on this day

1258: The Mongols destroy Baghdad * 1482: Italian sculptor Luca della Robbia dies * 1775: English essayist Charles Lamb is born in London

11 February

The long life of America's greatest inventor, Thomas Edison

1847 Today in Milan, Ohio, was born a man who would register 1,093 US patents, the last at the age of 83. He was Thomas Alva Edison, the greatest practical genius America has ever produced, who claimed he 'never waste[d] time inventing things that people would not want to buy'.

Almost deaf since childhood, Edison became a diligent worker who maintained that 'genius is one per cent inspiration and ninety-nine per cent perspiration. Accordingly, a genius is often merely a talented person who has done all of his homework.'

Edison's first invention was an electric vote-recording machine that was immediately rejected by the Massachusetts Legislature, probably because it restricted politicians' ability to rig the vote. Later creations include the first commercially viable mimeograph, the dictaphone and the electric storage battery, as well as the first successful system for generating and distributing electricity.

But Edison's greatest fame came from three inventions that totally changed the world in which he lived. He invented the phonograph in 1877, the incandescent electric light bulb in 1879 and early in the next century the 'kinetiscope', which was used for the first silent film – although the film wasn't projected; the viewer had to see it through a peephole.

Edison claimed that 'My principal business is giving commercial value to the brilliant – but misdirected – ideas of others.' His light bulb is the perfect example; back in 1801 the British scientist Sir Humphry Davy had first used electricity to heat platinum strips to incandescence. Edison's development of a practical bulb for general public use came 78 years later.

Edison died at 9 p.m. on 18 October 1931, on the anniversary of his invention of the light bulb.

The legend of Japan's first emperor

660 BC According to a 14th-century Shinto monk, in the Age of the Gods Japan was known by the snappy name of 'ever-abundant land of reed-covered plains and bountiful rice fields'. Later, at the time of the Sun goddess Amaterasu, another name was used, Yamato, which means 'footprints on the mountains', in remembrance of the time when the soil was still soft and men tracked across the mountains for food.

Amaterasu sent her celestial grandson Ninigi to govern the Earth, giving him the sacred sword and mirror, which became imperial emblems. Ninigi in turn had a great-grandson named Jimmu, who hopped from island to island conquering Japan's early tribes and ending in Yamato, where he became Japan's first Emperor, consecrated at Kashihara on Unebi Mountain this day in 660 BC.

From that day forward the same imperial line has ruled Japan. In 1890 the Japanese government built a Shinto shrine where Jimmu is believed to be buried at Unebi, and even today on every 11 February large crowds gather at the Kashihara Shrine to celebrate that first royal enthronement over two and a half millennia ago.

Also on this day
1732: America's first President George Washington is born * 1879: French caricaturist Honoré Daumier dies

12 February

Lady Jane Grey mounts the scaffold

1554 Today in the Tower of London a beautiful and intelligent sixteen-year-old girl was beheaded for treason. She was Lady Jane Grey, a pawn manipulated and controlled by her weak but ambitious father and her power-hungry and devious father-in-law, the Duke of Northumberland, because they thought she should be – and could be – Queen.

By early 1553 it was clear to all that Jane's cousin, the young and sickly Edward VI, could not long survive. Northumberland and his allies persuaded the dying boy-king to put aside his sisters, Mary and Elizabeth, and designate Jane as his heir. As a devout Protestant and great-granddaughter of King Henry VII, she seemed the perfect replacement, especially for those who feared Mary's morbid Catholicism and her desire to marry Spain's equally Catholic heir to the throne, the future Philip II.

Edward died on 6 July 1553, and four days later Northumberland and his followers proclaimed Jane Queen, while Mary Tudor fled to Norfolk. But it was almost instantly clear that the country would not support this substitution – Mary was, after all, Edward's sister and the legitimate daughter of King Henry VIII. Jane's support soon withered away, and she was easily persuaded to abandon her claim after a 'reign' of a mere nine days. She and her father were incarcerated in the Tower of London, but he was soon pardoned.

It seems likely that Jane, too, would eventually have been spared, but her father seemed incapable of leaving well enough alone. By the end of the year he had joined another plotter, Sir Thomas Wyat, who raised an army to depose Mary by force. On 3 February 1554, Wyat and some 3,000 fellow rebels advanced on London, but soon disbanded in despair when the local populace bolted their doors and refused to join them.

Wyat's revolt – and Jane's father's support of it – was the last straw. Jane was condemned to death.

On 12 February Jane watched from her window in the Tower as first Northumberland was led to the block, and then her young husband Guildford. One hour later the queen-pretender herself was taken to the axeman. Bravely and willingly she went; just five days earlier she had written to her father, 'Yet can I patiently take it, that I yield God more hearty thanks for shortening my woeful days.'

America's greatest president is born

1809 A photograph still exists of the small log cabin – eighteen feet wide by sixteen feet long with only one room and a dirt floor – where America's greatest president, Abraham Lincoln, was born on this day in 1809.

Lincoln's great fame of course rests on his freeing some 4 million black slaves and preserving the United States during the terrible Civil War in the 1860s.

Especially because slavery was such a polarising issue, the war is sometimes seen as a conflict between two radically different parts of the nation, the bucolic and gentlemanly South and the industrious and mercantile North. But in truth the two sides were closely intertwined, and Lincoln's own life contains poignant reminders of the personal nature of a civil conflict.

For example, in the War Between the States, the two leaders were born in the same state. Lincoln's famous log cabin was in Hodgeville, Kentucky – and Jefferson Davis, the President of the Confederate States, was also born in Kentucky. Although married to the President in the North, Lincoln's wife Mary had four brothers and three brothers-in-law who fought for the South, two of whom were killed in action.

Everyone knows Lincoln freed the slaves, won the Civil War, saved the nation and was assassinated. But how many know that he was the first American president to wear a beard?

Also on this day

1804: Prussian philosopher Immanuel Kant dies * 1809: British naturalist Charles Darwin is born

13 February

The bombing of Dresden

1945 Dresden lies in the broad basin of the Elbe just 100 miles south of Berlin. In the late 17th and 18th centuries three electors of Saxony, Augustus I, II and III, turned it into a Baroque bijou whose only rivals in beauty were Vienna and Prague. Exquisite buildings like the Zwinger, the Japanese Palace and the Hofkirche were built, and the electors also assembled outstanding collections of paintings and objets d'art. So brilliant was the city that it earned the nickname of 'Florence on the Elbe'.

That all changed for ever on the night of 13 February 1945 when the first of 773 British Avro Lancaster bombers released its bombs over the city centre. Before the night was over the British had dropped over 2,500 tons of high explosives, of which two-thirds were incendiaries filled with highly combustible chemicals such as magnesium and phosphorus. This firebombing created a self-sustaining firestorm with temperatures over 1,500° centigrade. Almost 90 per cent of the inner city's 28,000 houses were destroyed, including 22 hospitals. Three centuries of architectural magnificence were incinerated in a single night. During the following two days over 500 American bombers joined the attack, although their target area was restricted to the railway yards.

There is still debate on the number of civilians killed. Before the war

Dresden's population was about 650,000, but by 1945 the city was teeming with refugees fleeing from the advancing Russian army, bringing the total closer to 1,000,000. Although Nazi propaganda claimed a quarter of a million had died, modern estimates suggest a lesser figure of some 135,000, still the largest number of casualties ever inflicted in a bombing raid, dwarfing the 70,000 deaths at Hiroshima and almost triple the 51,509 British civilians killed by German bombing during all of the Second World War.

The primary instigator of the attack on Dresden was the head of RAF Bomber Command, Air Marshal Arthur Harris, who derided the type of precision bombing advocated by the US Airforce. Harris insisted that night-time firebombing raids would undermine civilian morale, in spite of the evidence within his own country that indiscriminate German bombing of civilians at Coventry and London simply stiffened British resolve.

The first German cities to suffer from Harris's tactics were Lübeck, Hamburg, Berlin and Cologne, but Dresden remains a special case because it quartered few German troops, had little war-related industry and was virtually undefended by anti-aircraft guns.

Two months after Dresden British Prime Minister Winston Churchill ordered Harris to end the firebombing of German cities 'simply for the sake of increasing the terror' and wrote to the Air Staff, 'The destruction of Dresden remains a serious query against the conduct of Allied bombing.' After the war he conspicuously omitted Harris's name from the list of new peerages, although he awarded them to many less important generals. But perhaps Churchill was a bit disingenuous; there is some evidence that he agreed to Harris's proposed attack in order to intimidate the Russians with the power of Bomber Command.

Although firebombing civilians was Harris's own invention ('The primary objective of your operations should now be focused on the morale of the enemy civil population and in particular of the industrial workers', he briefed his men), he tried to pass the blame upwards, writing in his memoirs, 'Here I will only say that the attack on Dresden was at the time considered a military necessity by much more important people than I.' Nevertheless, post-war criticism was so strong that in 1945 he moved to South Africa. In the end, however, perhaps he was lucky. He was never indicted for war crimes or breaches of the Geneva Convention. Indeed, despite the fervent protestations of the German government, over half a century after Dresden's destruction, Elizabeth, the Queen Mother, led the ceremonies in London at the unveiling of a statue honouring 'Bomber' Harris.

The long, adventurous life of Benvenuto Cellini

1571 Sculptor, author and perhaps history's greatest goldsmith, Benvenuto Cellini was also a notorious adventurer who had been banished from his native Florence for duelling at 15, condemned to death for fighting at 23, and pardoned by the Pope for killing a rival goldsmith at 35.

He was a true Renaissance man. His exquisite jewellery was as famous in his own time as it is today, and his greatest piece of sculpture, the bronze Perseus holding the Gorgon's head, still stands in Florence's Loggia dei Lanzi.

This immensely talented artist was also a fierce soldier. He played a critical role in defending Pope Clement VII in the Castel' Sant'Angelo against the rampaging troops of Emperor Charles V when they sacked Rome in 1527. Cellini claimed to have shot the attacking commander, the Constable of Bourbon.

Later Cellini became court goldsmith to François I of France and, while creating masterpieces, scandalised Paris by using prostitutes for models, whom he would occasionally beat. His own mistress publicly accused him of sodomising her, and he was constantly involved in brawling in the streets.

Yet in the Renaissance talent was all. When asked why he had not had Cellini punished, Pope Paul III replied, 'Men unique in their professions, like Benvenuto, were not subject to the laws.'

Cellini died on this day in his native Florence at the ripe age of 91.

Talleyrand is born

1754 Near the Church of Saint-Sulpice in Paris there still remains a small remnant of the Rue Garancière. On this day at the family 'hôtel' at number 4 a baby boy was born in aristocratic surroundings. His name was Charles-Maurice de Talleyrand, and he was to influence the destiny of France for the next 84 years.

Brilliant, ambitious, greedy and virtually clairvoyant in understanding the great events of his time, Talleyrand would serve four kings, an emperor and a republic before, during and after the French Revolution. In the end he would himself become a prince. The most brilliant diplomat of his time, he summed up his views on human nature with the remark, 'Words have been given to man so that he may disguise his thoughts.'

Also on this day

1542: English Queen Catherine Howard is beheaded at the age of 22 * 1867: Austrian composer Johann Strauss the Younger's waltz the 'Blue Danube' is played publicly for the first time in Vienna * 1883: German composer Richard Wagner dies

14 February

The mysterious death of Richard II

1400 No one really knows how England's King Richard II met his death, and even the exact date is in dispute, but many historians believe that it happened during the night of 14 February at Pontefract Castle in Yorkshire in the year 1400.

Richard had shown a flash of mettle as a fourteen-year-old king when he faced down the Peasants' Revolt, but during most of his time in power he relied on his uncle John of Gaunt to keep England's greedy and ambitious nobles under control. But after Gaunt died in February of 1399, Richard made two grave errors. First he sent Gaunt's son Henry Bolingbroke into exile, and when Gaunt died shortly after, he confiscated Henry's inheritance. Richard's second mistake was to go abroad to Ireland. While he was gone Bolingbroke invaded England and persuaded other powerful barons to join him. Richard returned to find himself outnumbered, isolated and without hope. He surrendered without a fight and was incarcerated in the Tower of London. There, terrified for his life, on the last day of September he abdicated before Parliament, and on 13 October Bolingbroke was crowned King Henry IV.

Richard was now an ex-king at the age of 33, without even his freedom, this ruler who had once declared, 'I am the law.' But even languishing enchained in prison he remained an intolerable threat, a possible centre for conspiracy and revolt by ambitious barons. Parliament now determined that he should be locked away in secret so that he could never be found or rescued. Forced into disguise to leave the Tower, he was moved from castle to castle and eventually imprisoned in Pontefract Castle in Yorkshire. There he was kept in chains.

In January of 1400 the Earl of Salisbury and a group of Richard's former courtiers conspired to free him and restore him to the throne. For Henry IV this was proof enough that Richard was too dangerous to live.

What happened next is debated. Shakespeare tells us that Richard was attacked in his cell by Henry's henchmen, but rose to defend himself, wrenched a sword from one of his executioners' hands and killed two attackers. But creeping up behind him, his jailer, Sir Pierce of Exton, leaped on a chair and felled him with an axe blow to the back of the head. In the 17th century, however, Richard's body was exhumed, and no marks were found on his skull consonant with the blow of an axe. Other sources claim that, depressed by the hopelessness of his situation, Richard starved himself to death, but most contemporaries thought that his jailers, on orders from the new King Henry, simply cut off his food supply.

However he met his end, two weeks after his death Richard's corpse was taken south on a posthumous royal procession for all to see that he was actually dead. After two days of lying in state at St Paul's, he was quietly interred at the Dominican church at King's Langley, but during the reign of Henry IV's son Henry V, the body was transferred to Westminster Abbey.

Richard was the eighth and last of the direct Plantagenet kings of England (although there were six more indirect Plantagenets from the Houses of Lancaster and York), and the third of his house to die by violence.

Also on this day

1776: English economist Thomas Malthus is born * 1779: Captain James Cook is killed by natives on Hawaii * 1929: The St Valentine's Day Massacre: Al Capone's gang machine-guns seven members of Bugsy Moran's gang in a warehouse in Chicago

15 February

The sinking of the battleship Maine triggers the Spanish–American War

1898 Relations between Spain and the United States had been dangerously soured by the continued revolt in Spanish-owned Cuba and the lamentable conditions of the colonised Cubans. Eventually President William McKinley ordered the battleship USS *Maine* to Havana to reassure Americans living there.

At just past nine on the evening of 15 February the *Maine* swung quietly at anchor, most of the crew already gently sleeping in their hammocks while Captain Charles Sigsbee sat quietly in his cabin writing a letter. Then, he later recalled, 'I laid down my pen and listened to the notes of the bugle [playing taps], which were singularly beautiful in the oppressive stillness of the night. ... I was enclosing my letter in its envelope when the explosion came. It was a bursting, rending, and crashing roar of immense volume, largely metallic in character. It was followed by heavy, ominous metallic sounds. There was a trembling and lurching motion of the vessel, a list to port. The electric lights went out. Then there was intense blackness and smoke.'

An enormous explosion had engulfed the front half of the ship, right where most of the men were billeted. The *Maine* settled to the bottom of Havana harbour; of the 350 men on board, 260 died with the ship. The next morning only the ship's charred and twisted stern and bridge could still be seen above the gently lapping waves of the harbour.

Although no one knew who had detonated the blast, the unscrupulous press baron William Randolph Hearst had no scruples about inflaming American public opinion by blaming the Spaniards. His New York *Journal* was in a fierce circulation war with competitive newspapers, and Hearst believed a war against Spain was just what was needed to build readership. The *Journal* even published drawings purporting to show Spanish saboteurs clamping an underwater mine to the *Maine's* hull. Soon most Americans came to believe that the iniquitous Spaniards had blown up the battleship in a gesture of arrogant contempt for America.

Hearst then urgently dispatched writers and the artist Frederick Remington to Cuba to cover a so-called war between the dastardly Spanish and heroic Cuban rebels. Finding no trace of combat, Remington cabled Hearst: 'There is no war. Request to be recalled.' Hearst's answer was to the point: 'Please remain. You furnish the pictures, I'll furnish the war.'

Hearst was true to his word. Driven by the public's great patriotic fervour, the American Congress soon demanded Spanish withdrawal from Cuba, and by April the Spanish–American War had begun. The United States won a pathetically one-sided contest, in only eight months forcing Spain into a peace treaty by which the United States acquired Guam, Puerto Rico and the Philippine Islands.

In the pride of victory, the public began to forget about the *Maine*. Also forgotten was the fact that for many years no one really knew why she had blown up or who was responsible. But in 1976 a study by the US Navy indicated that the most likely cause was an accidental detonation in the ship's coalbunker, entirely the fault of the *Maine* herself and her crew.

Galileo is born in Pisa

1564 Pisa: the home of the Leaning Tower and of course its most famous resident, Galileo Galilei, who today was born there.

Galileo's first great discovery took place in the Pisa cathedral, next to the leaning campanile. There at the age of nineteen he timed the oscillations of a swinging lamp against the pace of his own pulse to find that each swing took exactly the same time no matter what its width. Thus the pendulum was born. Later he used the Leaning Tower itself to demonstrate that two objects of different weights fall at the same speed and acceleration.

At 28 he moved to Padua and later to Florence where, having invented the telescope, he confirmed the heretical theories of Copernicus that the Earth revolves around the Sun. Worse, he wrote in clear, common Italian that any educated man could understand. Horrified, the Jesuits thought Galileo's teachings were more dangerous 'than Luther and Calvin together'. Summoned to Rome by the Inquisition in 1633, Galileo recanted his views, but as he rose from his knees at the end of the trial he muttered the famous, 'E pur si muove.' (But it *does* move.)

The great scientist spent the rest of his days in Sienna and near Florence, never returning to his natal Pisa. He died in his 78th year. Always cautious, the Vatican waited 350 years until finally absolving him of his sins in 1992.

Also on this day
1944: Allied planes destroy the ancient monastery at Monte Cassino in Italy

16 February

The Royal Navy captures the Altmark

1940 Tonight in a remarkable feat of naval derring-do, a British destroyer operating under Admiralty instructions intercepted a German supply ship making her way home along the coast of Norway. With searchlights blazing on her target, HMS *Cossack* pursued the *Altmark* into a narrow fjord where the supply ship ran aground. A boarding party killed seven German defenders, then opened the hatches to get at the cargo in the holds. The *Altmark's* cargo was 300 sailors of the British Merchant Navy, the captured crews of nine merchant vessels sunk the previous autumn by the German raider *Graf Spee*. By midnight *Cossack* was out to sea again, heading with her rescued cargo for the Firth of Forth.

It was, of course, a notable achievement by the Royal Navy and one greatly welcomed by a British public looking for purposeful engagement with the enemy during that trancelike opening period of the Second World War that came to be called the Phoney War or the Sitzkrieg. But the *Altmark* incident had the effect of putting the fat in the fire.

Neutral Norway vehemently protested the British violation of its territorial waters in vain. To Germany the incident demonstrated that Great Britain was willing to violate Norwegian neutrality and that Norway was unable or unwilling to prevent such action. The state of affairs threatened Germany's supply of Swedish iron ore, so vital to the Third Reich's heavy industries and much of it shipped through Norwegian waters. On 21 February Hitler ordered Exercise *Weser* – his planned invasion of Norway and Denmark – moved to the highest operational priority, ahead of Case Yellow, the invasion of France and the Low Countries.

In their reporting of the *Altmark* incident some British newspapers included this description from a *Cossack* sailor's account of the boarding: '... Meanwhile our boys were opening up the hatches. One of them shouted: "Are there any English down there?" There was a yell of "Yes!" You should have heard the cheer when our men shouted back: "Well, the Navy's here."' Some days later in London the First Lord of the Admiralty Winston Churchill appropriated this phrase to good effect addressing a large audience at the Guildhall: 'To Nelson's immortal signal of 135 years ago, "England expects that every man will do his duty," there may now be added last week's not less proud reply, "The Navy's here."'

During the night of 6 April 1940, German naval forces and troop ships left their north-German ports and sailed for Norway. The Phoney War was almost over. The real war was about to begin.

The unscrupulous king who unified Portugal

1279 In spite of having a language distinctively its own, Portugal had great difficulty in becoming a single nation, but its final unification owed much to King Alfonso III, who died on this day.

The country's name stems from Portus Cale, an ancient community established in pre-Roman times on the Douro River. From the 3rd century BC the Romans were in control – Julius Caesar governed the territory for a period before his Gallic conquests. The Romans called it Lusitania, after a local tribe that lived there. Centuries later, as Rome collapsed, the Germanic Suebi took over, only to be conquered by the Visigoths who in turn were brought down by Moors invading from North Africa in the 8th century.

In the centuries that followed, the Portuguese themselves gradually reconquered much of their own country, and the nation finally became independent in 1139, but some of today's Portugal was still under Moorish control. At the beginning of the 13th century Muslims in Portuguese Portugal were theoretically allowed to become citizens, although large numbers were captured and sold into slavery.

Born in about 1225, Alfonso was the son of King Alfonso II. On his father's death the kingdom went to his elder brother Sancho, leaving poor young Alfonso no way forward except to usurp the throne. Aided by a Church enraged by Sancho's confiscation of Church property, he won a two-year civil war, exiled his brother to Toledo and took the title of Alfonso III.

Once in power, however, Alfonso showed little gratitude, first entering a bigamous marriage and then suffering excommunication for commandeering yet more Church property.

In the meantime he was slowly occupying the last remaining Muslim enclaves in the Algarve, completing the reconquest of the country and transferring the capital from Coimbra to Lisbon, where it has remained to this day. When he died, he had ruled his nation for 34 years.

Also on this day

1822: English scientist and founder of eugenics Francis Galton is born * 1862: General Ulysses S. Grant wins the first major Union victory of the American Civil War when Fort Donelson on the Cumberland River in Tennessee surrenders with about 15,000 troops

17 February

Molière's last act

1673 'On ne meure qu'une fois, et c'est pour si longtemps!' (You only die once, and it's for such a long time!) So wrote France's greatest comic dramatist, Molière, who tonight collapsed on the stage at the Palais Royale in Paris to die at home a few hours later at the age of 51.

Molière was born Jean-Baptiste Poquelin but adopted the stage name Molière when he was a 22-year-old actor. By the time he was in his 30s he was not only writing plays but directing them as well, while simultaneously managing a travelling company of actors.

When he was 36 Molière first performed one of his own plays before King Louis XIV, who eventually backed Molière's players and they became the Troupe du roi (the king's troop).

Although Molière was brilliantly original, like Shakespeare he had no compunction about adapting other people's ideas to suit his own purposes. 'Je prends mon bien où je le trouve' (I take whatever belongs to me wherever I find it), he said. He also had little fear of the all-powerful authority of the Church, writing several plays, notably *Tartuffe* and *Don Juan*, that attracted ecclesiastical censure.

By 1673 Molière was at the height of his fame but had become seriously ill. Nonetheless he refused to relinquish his position as star actor in his own works. Today, just before the final curtain of his play *La Malade Imaginaire*, in which he was playing the lead role of the hypochondriac, he collapsed on stage and was rushed to his house, situated in what is now number 40, rue de Richelieu in Paris.

Molière quickly went to bed but soon was haemorrhaging blood. 'Don't be frightened,' he said to a friend at his bedside, 'you've seen me bring up more than that. But you'd better go and tell my wife to come up.' He died an hour later.

Even in death his troubles with the Church were not over. It took the intervention of the King for him to be buried in holy ground, with Church insistence that the burial take place in the dead of night.

Molière's heritage is still with us today. He continues to be one of France's most performed playwrights, and after his death the company he founded went on to become the Comédie Française, of which he is considered the 'father'.

'Peccavi!'

1843 On the morning of this day General Charles Napier entered in his diary, 'It is my first battle as a commander: it may be my last. At sixty, that makes little difference; but my feelings are, it shall be do or die.' He then led his small force of 400 British and 2,200 Sepoys to a crushing victory over 30,000 Baluchis in the battle of Miani in the province of Sindh, now in south-eastern Pakistan. Napier hurled himself into the midst of the conflict, fighting hand-to-hand. At the end of the battle he finished off the enemy by personally leading a devastating cavalry charge.

Five weeks later he scored another major victory at Dabo, near Hyderabad, gaining full control of the province of Sindh. Entering Hyderabad, he ensconced himself in the Emir's palace and reported his triumphs to head-quarters with one of the most remarkable military communications of all time, consisting of a single word: '*Peccavi*!' (Latin for 'I have sinned [Sindh]'.)

Also on this day

1653: Italian composer Arcangelo Corelli is born * 1776: English historian Edward Gibbon publishes *The History of the Decline and Fall of the Roman Empire* * 1909: Apache leader Geronimo dies

18 February

The Duke of Clarence is drowned in a butt of Malmsey

1478 Malmsey is a sweetish wine from Greece that was much favoured by the English nobility in the 15th century. One of its most ardent consumers was George, Duke of Clarence, younger brother of that handsome and calculating monarch, Edward IV.

Unfortunately George had few of his brother's virtues but many vices of his own, of which the worst were blind ambition and disloyalty. Throughout his brother's reign George plotted with one enemy after another to snatch the crown and make himself King.

Finally Edward had had enough. In January of 1478 George was tried before the Lords of Parliament and condemned to death for treason.

Edward hesitated, loath to execute his own brother, but Parliament urged a speedy end. Legend has it that George, terrified of the pain of the axe, requested that he be drowned in his favourite drink. And so it was that, on 18 February 1478, George, Duke of Clarence, was gently lowered into a vast butt of Malmsey, to die with a sweet taste in his mouth.

Martin Luther is happy to die

1546 Perhaps the strain of all the years of defying the Pope and most of the Christian world became unbearable for Martin Luther, because once when the Dowager Electress of Saxony wished him many years of long life, he replied, 'Madame, rather than live another forty years I would give up my chance of Paradise.'

So felt Martin Luther, who was first an Augustinian monk, and then had become, in order, a priest, a university teacher and a celebrity and condemned heretic. Now, at the age of 62 years, three months and eight days, he died in Eisleben, Germany, the town where he was born.

Through his protestations and strength of belief, Luther gave the world Protestantism, as well as several centuries of religious war. But, according to legend, he also gave us a more joyful tradition, the Christmas tree. The story goes that one Christmas Eve he took a walk in a nearby forest where he was profoundly moved by the snowy fir trees shimmering in the starlight. To remind local children of the beauty of God's creation he brought a tree indoors and decorated it with candles to simulate the stars.

Deadly ambush for the duc de Guise

1563 François, second duc de Guise, was the leading member of France's leading Catholic family: proud, reactionary and aristocratic. A general of exceptional talent, he was nicknamed *Le Balafré* (roughly Scarface) for the scars he received in the siege of Boulogne.

Guise had been responsible for the bloody massacre of Protestants at Vassy that had ignited the first French religious war. So extreme was he in his persecution of the Huguenots that he once executed some prisoners, telling them, 'My trade is not to make speeches but to cut off heads.' So the French Huguenot leader Gaspard de Coligny determined to eliminate Guise – for ever. The opportunity came on 18 February 1563.

Riding towards his military headquarters, Guise had unwisely doffed his coat of mail, unaware that one of his own men, a certain Jean Poltrot, was actually a Huguenot spy.

Seeing that Guise was unprotected, Poltrot rode on ahead and then hid behind a hedge. As Guise passed, Poltrot fired. Guise fell senseless to the ground and died a week later, on Ash Wednesday, 24 February, his 44th birthday.

Exactly one month later Poltrot paid the price for his treason. Lying on his back in a field, each arm and each leg was securely tied to a different horse – and then the horses were whipped off in a gallop in four different directions. Nine years later Gaspar de Coligny was murdered by Guise's son.

Also on this day

1455: Florentine painter Fra Angelico dies * 1564: Roman sculptor and painter Michelangelo Buonarroti dies * 1678: John Bunyan's *Pilgrim's Progress* is published * 1861: Victor Emmanuel is proclaimed King of a united Italy at the first meeting of the Italian parliament

19 February

American Marines land on Iwo Jima

1945 Iwo Jima was nobody's idea of prime real estate – five miles end to end, three miles at the widest point, a low hump of island 700 miles south of Tokyo, covered by rock, sand and volcanic ash, its southern tip dominated by an extinct volcano, 556 feet above sea level, named Mount Suribachi. Taking his first look at it, a young US marine pronounced it 'not worth fifty cents at a sheriff's sale'. But considering the price paid in blood to gain possession of it, Iwo Jima had to be one of the most costly places on Earth.

Within its forbidding terrain, the island held three airstrips and a Japanese garrison of 21,000 troops. One observer said it 'bristled with concealed gun emplacements, pillboxes, mine fields, and an elaborate system of underground caves and shelters'. Artillery pieces and mortars were expertly sited to cover not only the beaches but also virtually every square foot of the interior. For the Japanese, Iwo's strategic value was as part of the home islands' defence cordon;

for the Americans it would be as a forward base for B-29s and their fighter escorts taking part in the air offensive against Japan.

Everybody knew Iwo would be tough. Two days before the landings, as US battleships opened up with their pre-invasion bombardment of land targets, rocket-firing minesweepers and gunboats swept close in to scout the beaches where the landings would take place. The tempo of the preliminary operation was so high that the Japanese commander concluded actual landings were underway, and he sent out a communiqué to that effect. That night Radio Tokyo proudly misinformed its audiences that the enemy's first invasion attempt had been repelled.

At 0859 today – one minute ahead of schedule – the first wave of marines hit Red Beach One from landing craft. One battalion came across a small sign erected in the sand reading 'Welcome to Iwo Jima'. It was a thoughtful gesture left by Navy Seals two days earlier as they probed the landing area for shoals, reefs, mines and underwater defences.

Two entire Marine divisions went ashore this day. A third would follow. Eventually, there would be 60,000 marines on the island. Mount Suribachi fell on D+4 (23 February), and the first flag went up at 1035. From the crowded beaches below came cheers. Staring at the tiny figures high up on the summit, one marine said, 'Those guys ought to be getting flight pay.' The immortal photograph of the flag-raising ceremony was taken three hours later.

Suribachi was only the beginning. The Marines' advance up the island was bloodily contested every foot of the way. On the tenth day of combat they held less than half the island. Behind every dune, ridge or gully, defenders lay in deadly wait. Iwo Jima was not secured until D+26, and the final act of resistance – a pre-dawn suicide charge – was not quelled until D+35 (26 March). When the Navy released casualty figures for the first three days of combat, press reaction back home was one of shock. In a front-page editorial for the San Francisco *Examiner*, William Randolph Hearst Jr questioned the heavy price in lives lost.

The price was heavy indeed. Among total casualties of almost 26,000 marines and Navy personnel, there were some 6,000 deaths. Of the Japanese, fewer than 1,000 survived to be taken as prisoners. But even before combat was over, a B-29, low on fuel returning from a bombing mission over Japan, made an emergency landing on one of the landing strips. It was the first of 2,400 B-29s to make use of Iwo during the remaining months of the war. Afterwards, Admiral Nimitz characterised the American effort at Iwo Jima as one in which 'uncommon valor was a common virtue'.

John Wycliffe is tried for heresy

1377 John Wycliffe considered himself a great reformer. He saw the Church and its masters waxing ever fatter and richer and moving ever further from the spiritual needs of mankind. Indeed, he bitterly attacked everyone from the

Pope and his cardinals to monks and friars for their greed and worldliness. He also carried on a somewhat arcane debate about transubstantiation, a subject of interest so typical of the medieval world.

Not surprisingly, the Church struck back. On this day a somewhat frail (he was only 47), white-bearded Wycliffe was brought to trial for heresy in the Lady Chapel of St Paul's Cathedral in London. Surely he would have been condemned and probably put to death if not for the armed intervention of Duke John of Gaunt, son of the King. With the Duke's guard intimidating the prosecuting churchmen, Wycliffe went free, able to return to his greatest work, the first English translation of the entire Bible.

But the mighty Church was not to be denied. At the Council of Constance some 31 years after Wycliffe's death, he was at last condemned of heresy. His corpse was disinterred, burned and thrown into the River Swift.

By then, of course, it was far too late to prevent the spread of his teachings. Church reform became inevitable, and Wycliffe has become known in English history as the Morning Star of the Reformation.

Also on this day

1405: Mongol conqueror Tamerlane the Great dies * 1717: English actor David Garrick is born * 1743: Italian composer Luigi Boccherini is born in Lucca

20 February

Execution of an Austrian patriot

1810 Andreas Hofer looked very much the innkeeper that he was – round-faced, bearded and somewhat roly-poly. But beneath his genial exterior beat the heart of a true Austrian patriot, a man who loved his Emperor but wanted no truck with either Bavarians or Frenchmen, who were intent on claiming his homeland, the Tyrol in western Austria.

In 1809, when Hofer was 46, under pressure from Napoleon, Emperor Franz I ceded the Tyrol to Bavaria, but Hofer led a local insurrection to return the province to Austrian control. After decisively crushing the Bavarians at Berg Isel, he set himself up in Innsbruck as commander in chief of the Tyrol, under the protection of Emperor Franz. In October of that year, however, Franz once again bowed to French pressure and once more relinquished the Tyrol.

Still defiant, Hofer continued to resist the French, causing Napoleon to put a price on his head and dispatch a column of troops to capture him.

Evading his enemies, Hofer fled to the mountains, where he holed up in a deserted herdsman's hut, but his pursuers soon tracked him down, brought him barefoot through the snowy mountain passes and took him to French-controlled Mantua.

There Hofer was subjected to a kangaroo court-martial, convicted of treason and sentenced to death. Even though Franz made no effort to save him, he still might have escaped the ultimate penalty had Napoleon not sent a direct order by heliograph from Milan demanding to know the date of execution.

On this day Hofer was led to the city walls to face the firing squad. Refusing a blindfold, he addressed his executioners with the farewell comment, 'Goodbye, wretched world, this death is easy!' Then he ordered the guns, 'Fire!'

Thirteen years later Hofer's remains were brought back to Austria and interred in Innsbruck. For many years a play celebrating his patriotism was performed each year in Merano, in the Tyrolean part of Italy, and a poem about him was adapted as the Tyrolean anthem.

'Here lies Josef II, who failed in all his undertakings'

1790 Today died one of history's most infuriating and contradictory monarchs, Josef II of Austria.

Josef was a man fired by a mission – to better his people and modernise his country. Unfortunately his lofty aims were matched by his stubborn insistence that only he knew how to achieve these aims and his dogged determination to involve himself in the smallest details.

On the death of his father, at the age of 24 Josef became co-regent with his remarkable mother, the Empress Maria Theresa, but, realising her son's shortcomings, she took all the important decisions herself. But when Maria Theresa died in 1780, Josef was on his own.

A man of boundless energy, Josef formulated innumerable decrees to improve the life of his subjects but never thought to consult those very subjects themselves. He infuriated the richer ones by his own simple lifestyle, putting an end to imperial extravagance, and alarmed those lower down the social scale by his insistence on continual change from traditional ways of doing things.

Josef fought two unnecessary wars with mixed results, but his most contentious acts were domestic. He abolished serfdom, no doubt to the joy of those freed but to the rage of many landowners. Much more controversial, he broke the power of the Church in a highly religious country, dissolving any monasteries he felt were not 'useful' – not involved with teaching or tending the sick. Some 700 were shut down, forcing 36,000 monks to leave their orders. He also established freedom of religion in a highly Catholic country and further infuriated the Church by freeing the Jews from many of their legal constraints, but with this act greatly enriched Austria's cultural life.

All the while Josef's subjects disliked and resisted most of his reforms, largely because they were imposed from above by this arrogant, opinionated monarch. Meanwhile Josef himself became increasingly bitter and self-pitying as he came to realise how little thanks he got for what he saw as vast improvements in the lives of his people. Just before he died he wrote his own epitaph with instruction for it to be carved on his tomb: 'Here lies Josef II, who failed in all his undertakings.'

As the historian Friedrich Schreyvogl has written, 'When Josef died, deserted by all his friends, his efforts to achieve freedom and general welfare for his subjects seemed to have been in vain. Today, however, ... he is considered the benefactor of his subjects, the people's emperor, who by his many voyages and inspections devoted himself to all matters of greater or lesser importance. In his century he had predicted there would be a time when general welfare took precedence over individual prosperity. But he was born one century too soon.'

Also on this day

1437: James I of Scotland is murdered * 1872: The Metropolitan Museum of Art opens in New York

21 February

The Battle of Verdun

1916 At 7.00 a.m. German artillery began a bombardment of the French-held salient north of the historic fortress city of Verdun. It was the deafening prelude to the longest and one of the bloodiest battles of the First World War. Erich von Falkenhayn, the German Chief of Staff and War Minister, chose Verdun for the killing ground because it would compel the enemy into costly counter-attacks from which, he promised an appreciative Kaiser, 'the forces of France will bleed to death'.

The shelling from 1,200 artillery pieces paused at 4.00 p.m., as groups of German infantry edged out of the winter gloom to probe the devastated French forward positions. The battered and deafened defenders just managed to hold on until darkness brought an end to the first day's fighting. Then the bombardment resumed.

And so it went, day after day, savage artillery fire followed by infantry attacks, the French, outgunned and outnumbered, slowly giving way. On the 25th, impregnable Fort Douaumont, the linchpin of the entire French position in the salient, fell to the Germans. Supply routes into Verdun came under fire and were almost severed. Withdrawal to more defensible positions across the Meuse would have been the best military option, but for France, with national honour at stake, withdrawal was unthinkable. Someone would have to organise the defence of Verdun.

The organiser turned out to be Philippe Pétain, an unsung major general who had a talent for defensive warfare and the confidence of the *poilus* that he would not send them out to useless slaughter. He paid special attention to his artillery, co-ordinating its operation into an instrument of punishment for the enemy. He rebuilt and maintained the supply routes, assembling 3,500 trucks that operated day and night bringing in vital supplies and reinforcements for the Verdun garrison. He restored the fighting value of his troops by rotating his divisions in and out of the line. In time, these prudent measures turned the German tide. The 23rd of June saw the farthest extent of the German advance, almost – but not quite – to Verdun itself. Now, reaching the limits of its reserves, German strength began to ebb. Under French counter-attacks, the front line edged back northward. On 24 October Fort Douaumont was retaken. In December the fighting subsided into the ordinary, sporadic rhythm of trench warfare.

Verdun bled both armies white. In ten months of battle, the total casualties numbered over 700,000 dead, wounded and missing. For the French it was an act of stubborn heroism, and they hailed it as a great victory, but in truth, as Alistair Horne wrote, 'Neither side "won" at Verdun.' Among its many consequences were these: General von Falkenhayn was replaced as Germany's Chief of Staff in August after it became painfully clear that his campaign would never prevail; the French Commander-in-Chief General Joffre was sacked in December, in part for having neglected Verdun's defences; General Pétain, beloved by his troops, was replaced in May as army commander by a more offensive-minded general, but the next year, in even grimmer military circumstances, France turned once again to her 'architect of victory' and this time made Pétain Commander-in-Chief of the French Army; and a young company commander in the 33rd Infantry Regiment, Captain Charles de Gaulle, was captured on 1 March 1916, and spent the rest of the war in a German prison camp.

Also on this day

1431: Joan of Arc's trial begins in Rouen * 1613: The Romanov dynasty begins: Michael Romanov, son of the Patriarch of Moscow, is elected Russian Tsar * 1940: The Germans begin construction of a concentration camp at Auschwitz

22 February

Etienne Marcel terrifies the Dauphin

1358 When the English army destroyed the forces of France at the Battle of Poitiers in 1356, one of the trophies they captured was the feckless and pleasure-loving French King, Jean II, called the Good. Deprived of leadership, France fell into anarchy. Of that calamitous time Petrarch wrote: 'On every hand I witnessed a terrible solitude. Fields were abandoned and buildings in ruins. Even near to Paris there were the same signs of fire and desolation. The streets were deserted and grass grew in the high roads. It was as though France had died.'

It was under these tragic conditions that the provost of merchants in Paris, Etienne Marcel, took charge of the city. Walls were repaired, provisions arranged for. Marcel and his followers forced the Dauphin Charles (the future Charles V) to grant reforms, summarised in the Great Ordinance of 1357.

Early in 1358, however, Charles broke his promise by debasing the coinage. Assembling his followers on 22 February, Marcel entered Charles's apartments in the royal palace (today's Palais de Justice). In the Dauphin's presence, without discussion or trial, the mob struck down two of Charles's noble advisors, who fell at the prince's feet, splattering him with blood. Marcel then placed his own cap upon the Dauphin's head, assuring him of protection if he carried out his pledged reforms.

It has been said that this revolt and triumph of the bourgeoisie was the first small step towards liberty and democracy. If so, it was a particularly short-lived one, as Marcel himself was murdered only five months later.

Scandale *at the court of Louis XIV*

1680 It was the greatest scandal of the entire 72-year reign of Louis XIV. First there were ever-increasing rumours circulating at court, and then little by little hard evidence had started to come in: certain members of the French nobility were practising witchcraft. Worse, the evil art extended all the way to murder by poison and blasphemous black masses. Worse yet, there was proof that the leading practitioner was the notorious Mme La Voisin – and that one of her chief clients for love potions was none other than the King's number-one mistress, Mme de Montespan.

Luckily, hearty King Louis survived the love potions with no worse effects than recurring headaches and an upset stomach. But he realised that the only way to end the scandal was to close for ever the mouths of those who knew about it, a sad collection of supposed witches and philtre suppliers.

Some hundreds of poor wretches were locked anonymously in prisons all over France, never to emerge. And on this day the chief culprit, Mme La Voisin, was led to the stake where she died in agony.

But the ripples didn't end there. One of Louis's former mistresses, Olympia Mancini, had been suspected of poisoning her husband and had fled to Brussels. As a consequence her son was rejected for a military career and he in turn fled to Austria. That son was Prince Eugene of Savoy, destined to battle Louis to a standstill as Austria's greatest general.

Also on this day

1788: German philosopher Arthur Schopenhauer is born * 1819: Spain cedes Florida to the USA * 1857: English soldier and founder of the Boy Scout movement Robert Baden-Powell is born

23 February

Emperor Diocletian persecutes the Christians

AD 303 Nicomedia lies east of what is now Istanbul in Turkey, today hardly a memory but at the beginning of the 4th century the de facto capital of the Roman Empire and residence of that fearful oppressor of the Christians, the Emperor Diocletian. It was here on this day that the Christian persecutions began when at dawn soldiers and city magistrates broke into the city's most important church and, finding no idols to destroy, burnt the Holy Scripture and then levelled the building to the ground. The next morning Diocletian issued his famous edict ordering the destruction of churches throughout the Empire.

Diocletian's unwavering objective throughout his 21-year reign was to consolidate his enormous territories under central imperial authority. Although in private hardly a religious man, he had reinstituted the ancient Roman gods as a way to give central focus to his authority as Emperor and had transformed himself into a sort of living god, the son of Jove, whom ordinary mortals could approach only prostrate and supine, to kiss the hem of his robe.

Christianity proved a problem in that its adherents refused to worship the Emperor and thus, Diocletian thought, weakened the state. In addition, squabbles among various Christian sects were a threat to public order, and many considered Christianity to be an attempt to establish a separate state within a state. Finally, Christians were exceedingly unpopular among certain elements of Roman society. As the incomparable Gibbon describes it, 'The Pagans [i.e. ordinary Romans] were incensed at the rashness of a recent and obscure sect, which presumed to accuse their countrymen of error, and to devote their ancestors to eternal misery.'

Within two weeks of Diocletian's first edict, the Emperor's palace was twice set alight, and Christians were the prime suspects. Christian resistance was reported from various places in the Empire. Diocletian vowed that his proscriptions would be effected without bloodshed, but that soon became a promise impossible to fulfil, as many of his governors were even more draconian than he. As the conflict grew, the Emperor issued three more edicts, each harsher than the last. Leading Christians were punished, and the entire clergy was ordered imprisoned, to be released only after sacrificing to the Roman gods. Finally, in April 304, Diocletian commanded all Christians to worship the Roman gods on pain of death, and Christian refusal led to an atrocious slaughter, including feeding believers to the lions.

Only a year later, prematurely aged through ill health, Diocletian stunned the Roman world by announcing his abdication and retirement. After a short stay in Nicomedia he moved to his birthplace in what is now Split in Croatia to live in his magnificent palace until his death in 316. Ironically, the mausoleum in which he was buried is now a Christian church.

Fair Kate is crowned Queen

1421 Catherine de Valois, Queen of England's Henry V, was supposed to have been a beauty, the Fair Kate of legend and Shakespearean renown, so no doubt she looked her handsomest on this February Sunday when she was crowned Queen of England in Westminster Abbey.

Catherine, daughter of the King of France, was only nineteen at the time, having married Henry the previous June. Within eighteen months of her coronation she would bear a child and lose her husband. That child would become anointed King of both England and France, but the more lasting significance of Catherine's queenship was that she would stay in England even after her husband was dead.

Her son Henry VI would reign 40 years but rule for few, a gentle, pious, not quite sane monarch in the midst of the Wars of the Roses. But Catherine would marry a second time, this time a Welsh squire named Owen Tudor. Their grandson would found the Tudor dynasty.

Also on this day

1633: English diarist Samuel Pepys is born * 1792: English painter Joshua Reynolds dies * 1820: The Cato Street conspiracy: Police arrest conspirators who planned to blow up the British Cabinet * 1821: English poet John Keats dies in Rome * 1836: The siege of the Alamo begins under the Mexican general Santa Anna

24 February

Emperor Charles V Day

1500, 1525, 1530 This day belongs to the greatest of all the Habsburg emperors, Charles V. On it he was born at the very dawn of the 16th century in the Flemish town of Ghent. By the time he was nineteen his father and grandfather were dead, his morbidly insane mother was locked up for life in a lonely town in Spain and Charles was the master of more land in Europe than anyone since the Roman emperors, including Charlemagne. As well as wearing an emperor's crown as Charles V, he was also King of Spain as Charles (Carlos) I.

On Charles's 25th birthday, the date 24 February acquired even more significance. Under the command of King François I himself, a French army of almost 30,000 men was besieging the town of Pavia, in northern Italy. To the relief of the city, a slightly smaller Habsburg army arrived to reinforce the 6,000-man garrison within. The French attacked, but just when they seemed to be in the ascendant, 1,500 Spanish harquebusiers devastated the French cavalry and the Habsburg force counter-attacked, annihilating the French. Among the captured was King François himself, who melodramatically wrote to his mother, 'Tout est perdu fors l'honneur!' (All is lost, save honour!). François was taken away to spend over a year in Madrid as a royal prisoner, and from that date forward Spain dominated the Italian peninsula.

The 24th of February was also the date of Charles's coronation, on his 30th birthday (although he had already been Emperor for over ten years). Charles received his crown in the cathedral in Bologna, as Rome was in ruins, sacked by his own troops. Crowning him was Giulio de' Medici, Clement VII, the pope whom Charles had held prisoner during the sack. Charles was the last emperor to be crowned by a pope until Napoleon coerced another one almost 300 years later.

The fall of the last king of France

1848 Louis-Philippe had wanted to be France's Citizen King, and for eighteen years he had apparently succeeded, but finally the French public had tired of his reactionary ways. In February of 1848 the unhappy citizens exploded into revolt.

On the 22nd, protesters demanding political reform were denied permission to march and reacted by burning park benches and overturning buses. The next day Louis-Philippe sacked his Prime Minister, but still the demonstrators mobbed the streets. When they advanced down the rue des Capucines towards the Ministry of Foreign Affairs, the King's troops opened fire, killing 52. The following day the tired and defeated 72-year-old monarch and his Queen fled the country disguised as 'Mr and Mrs Smith', the King wearing a tradesman's hat and goggles.

Thus on 24 February 1848 ended the Bourbon monarchy in France that had commenced 259 years earlier under Louis XIII. So, too, ended the role of kings in France, who, except for the Revolutionary and Napoleonic years of 1793 to 1815, had ruled the country for 1,347 years, since the fifteen-year-old Clovis became the first French king in 481.

Also on this day

1786: Fairytale writer Wilhelm Grimm is born * 1836: American painter Winslow Homer is born

25 February

Renoir is born

1841 For one of France's greatest painters, Pierre Renoir was remarkably unassuming. 'What are paintings for, after all,' he said, 'to decorate walls.' Renoir always underplayed his talent, once denying that he was a great artist on the grounds that he was not syphilitic, homosexual or insane.

Renoir was born today in Limoges, the son of a tailor. During his 78 years he produced over 5,000 oil paintings and, along with Monet, fathered Impressionism. In old age his hands were so crippled with arthritis that the brushes had to be bandaged to them, but still he painted, often the soft voluptuous nudes for which he is famous. But his real attitude towards women was more sentimental than sexual. 'That is what women are so good at,' he once said, 'to make life bearable.'

Renoir died on 3 December 1919 at Cagnes in the south of France.

Essex is executed

1601 At the age of 34 Robert Devereux, Earl of Essex, was a classic Elizabethan adolescent: handsome, courageous, witty, dashing – vain, egotistical, foolhardy, fatuous. He had once been Queen Elizabeth's favourite, but his untempered pride and childish ambition for glory had led him to one foolish adventure after another. To rein him in, the Queen had banished him from court and had at last taken away his monopoly on wines, thus ensuring his financial collapse.

It was then that Essex determined to revolt. On the morning of Sunday 8 February, he rode through the city of London with some 200 supporters shouting 'For the Queen!' with the hope of inciting the populace into rebellion. As the mob rushed down the Strand a royal messenger appeared who informed them that Elizabeth had declared Essex a traitor. Immediately the crowd started to melt away, and Essex, realising that he had failed, desperately returned to his own mansion, only to find the Queen's soldiers there waiting for him. The Essex revolt was over in just a few hours and Elizabeth's one-time favourite was taken to the Tower.

During his last days the once-proud earl wildly confessed to his treasons, trying to implicate as many of his own friends and family as he could. He hoped for Elizabeth's mercy, but had forgotten her warning, 'Those who touch the sceptres of princes deserve no pity.'

Seventeen days after his revolt Essex paid for his treachery. Taken to the scaffold in the Tower yard, he knelt and prayed, then shed his dark coat to expose a scarlet waistcoat and placed his head on the block. It required three blows of the axe to sever his head. He was still only 34.

Start of a disastrous reign

1309 The coronation of Edward II on this day marked the official beginning of one of the most disastrous reigns in English history. Edward may have planted the seed for that disaster at the coronation itself.

The ceremony was at Westminster Abbey. Outside the church the crowd gawked at the arrival of the King's favourite, Piers Gaveston, dressed in royal purple, heavy with pearls. Later at the coronation banquet Edward totally neglected his new Queen Isabella and doted on Gaveston, to whom he had given a large portion of his wife's jewellery. Everyone, including the Queen, knew whom the King was really in love with.

Isabella never forgot the humiliation. Four years later Edward's barons seized and executed Gaveston, probably with her encouragement. And thirteen years after that she deserted Edward for a lover, invaded England from her native France, captured her feckless husband and arranged or at least consented to his appalling execution – he was impaled through the anus with a red-hot spit.

Also on this day

1723: English architect Christopher Wren dies in London

26 February

Napoleon escapes from Elba

1815 'It's better to die by the sword than in this ignoble retirement.' So counselled the Emperor Napoleon's strong-willed mother Letizia, who shared with him his exile on the island of Elba off the Mediterranean coast of Italy.

Less than a year earlier, on 4 May 1814, Napoleon had arrived on Elba, a beguiling island of pastoral hills and scenic bays covering slightly over 75 square miles. His victorious enemies had treated him handsomely (for a man who had kept Europe almost continuously at war for the better part of fifteen years). He was to be considered an independent ruler of the island, he would retain the title of Emperor, and, to the chagrin of the restored Louis XVIII, France would support him with annual payments of some 2 million francs.

But the Emperor was worried. The French government was baulking at paying his yearly stipend, and his agents had learned that many European ministers felt that Elba was too close for comfort, a few mooting the idea of banishing him to some remoter spot. Finally, he missed his wife Marie-Louise, whom he believed his captors were preventing from joining him. (She had in fact no intention of ever seeing him again, as, unbeknownst to the Emperor, she had taken a full-time lover, the fellow Austrian Adam Adalbert, Count von Neipperg.)

So it was that, taking his mother's advice, Napoleon slipped away from his island prison in the dark of the evening of 26 February 1815. The Emperor, 800 loyal soldiers and a few horses boarded a few small sailing boats and a brig with the unfortunate name of *L'Inconstant*. On 1 March they landed in what was then a tiny fishing village called Golfe-Juan, just a few miles from Cannes.

First ashore was General Pierre Cambronne, who handed out tricolour cockades to all who would take them. Up went Napoleon's famous proclamation, 'L'aigle, avec les couleurs nationales, volera de clocher en clocher jusqu'aux tours de Notre-Dame.' (The eagle, with the national colours, will fly from steeple to steeple until it flies from the towers of Notre Dame.) Off to reconquer France, Napoleon marched north towards Paris (you can still drive along his route north from Grasse, proudly labelled the Route Napoléon by the French Ministry of Culture). Hope ran high in the Emperor's camp, but Waterloo was only three months away.

Come the Revolution

1848 Today in London a portly, bearded German gentleman of 29 and his urbane young friend of only 19 published a pamphlet that would lead to three-quarters of a century of global conflict, with the people of half the developed world living in oppressed conditions in totalitarian states. It was entitled *Manifest der kommunistischen Partei*, better known to most of us by its English name, *The Communist Manifesto*. The authors were Karl Marx and Friedrich Engels, two middle-class German revolutionaries who had fled to London on the failure of Germany's workers to seize power during the uprisings of 1848.

The *Manifesto* opens dramatically with the words, 'A spectre is haunting Europe – the spectre of communism.' This was no threat but a promise, as the young authors claimed that 'the history of all hitherto existing society is the history of class struggles', and that united Communists would abolish all private property and 'raise the proletarian to the position of the ruling class'. The pamphlet's closing rhetoric became world-famous: 'The proletarians have nothing to lose but their chains. They have a world to win. Working men of all countries, unite.'

Happily for the authors, Marx died in 1883 and Engels in 1895, far too early to see the revolution they had so hoped for and the appalling consequences it brought for millions of Russians, East Europeans and other states swallowed by Communism. But the monster they had given birth to strangled itself with its own inner contradictions. Had he lived to see the slow implosion of Communism and the peaceful fall of the Berlin Wall on 9 November 1989, Engels might have been bemused by the irony of his accurate prediction that 'Der Staat wird nicht "abgeschafft", er stirbt ab.' (The State is not 'abolished', it withers away.)

Also on this day

1781: British Prime Minister William Pitt the Younger makes his maiden speech in the House of Commons * 1802: French writer Victor Hugo is born * 1871: Prussia and France sign a peace treaty at Versailles, ending the Franco-Prussian War * 1901: Boxer Rebellion leaders Chi-Hsin and Hsu-Cheng-Yu are publicly executed in Peking

27 February

Fire in the Reichstag

1933 In Berlin this evening, shortly after 9.00, Marinus van der Lubbe struck a spectacular blow for the cause of German workers. With a torch he set fire to the Reichstag building and soon had it blazing well out of control.

For van der Lubbe, a 24-year-old Dutch bricklayer, former Communist and loner with no political affiliation, his act of arson was meant to protest against the rampant injustices of capitalism. Still in the building when the police arrested him, he readily confessed to his deed. 'I considered arson a suitable method. I did not wish to harm private people but something belonging to the system itself. I decided on the Reichstag.'

But for the Nazi leader Adolf Hitler, Chancellor of Germany for less than a month, the fire was an undisguised blessing. 'A God-given signal,' he called it, 'the work of the Communists.' Herman Göring, agreeing with his Führer, claimed the fire was the first act of an uprising intended to disrupt the forthcoming Reichstag elections in which the Nazi Party hoped to return a clear majority.

The morning after the fire, the Reich Cabinet passed an emergency decree – 'the charter of the Third Reich', the historian Ian Kershaw called it – disposing of all the rights Germans had enjoyed under the Weimar constitution, including those of free speech, assembly, press freedom and privacy of communications. There followed over the next few days a violent government crackdown against the Left: Communists, Social Democrats, trade union leaders and intellectuals were beaten, tortured, imprisoned and killed – all in the name of saving Germany from imminent bolshevism. It was a sign of things to come.

The emergency decree and the ruthless measures were welcomed by the German electorate. The 5 March elections, although not resulting in an outright majority for the Nazis, were a solid victory with 44 per cent of the vote and 230 seats in the Reichstag, the best they had ever achieved. Better yet, the fire had brought out first-time voters in record numbers, most voting for the Nazi Party.

A German court found van der Lubbe guilty of the crime to which he had confessed. Tried with him were four Communists, including the head of the German Communist party. But with the lack of any evidence contrary to van der Lubbe's explicit declaration that he acted alone, the court acquitted the co-defendants, much to Hitler's outrage.

The arsonist himself was executed on 10 January 1934. Whether he was part of a Communist conspiracy, as the Nazis claimed, has never been clearly established. Many considered it more likely that the Nazis themselves had set the fire as the pretext for their first step towards total power. Whatever the truth, instead of the rope, van der Lubbe surely deserved some sort of medal from the Nazis for providing such a golden opportunity to begin the establishment of the Third Reich.

Americans defeat the Scots

1776 Today, to the sounds of drums and bagpipes, a Highland army of 1,000 soldiers, kilted, wielding muskets and claymores and yelling Gaelic war cries, met disaster at a bridge in North Carolina. A force of patriot militiamen holding a strategic crossing of Moore's Creek met the Scottish charge with musketry, then routed the survivors. The timely American success had the strategic effect of preventing the loyalist force from linking up with redcoats to retake the region for King George.

It is an irony of history that the Highlanders who fought at Moore's Creek Bridge, most of them recent immigrants to North Carolina, chose to fight as loyalists of the British crown rather than remain neutral or join the rebels of their adopted country. But it was not for love of King George that they fought. Many of them had tasted the fruits of rebellion against England before – in the Stuart uprising of 1745 – and found it bitter. Forced then to take oaths of loyalty in the savage aftermath of the Battle of Culloden, they were not prepared, even 30 years later and in another land, to break their word and once more risk defiance of the crown.

So, when their clan leaders seconded the call of the royal governor for His Majesty's subjects to put down the patriot rising, the Highlanders rallied to the King's colours. For despite their new surroundings, they remained what they had always been: clansmen of strong but narrow loyalties, many still speaking only Gaelic, resolute in their historic enmity towards Lowlanders and Ulstermen, so many of whom had joined the rebel camp.

Some 850 Scots were captured at Moore's Creek. The soldiers were disarmed and ordered to their homes. Officers were sent prisoner to Philadelphia and eventually paroled or exchanged, their properties confiscated. Among these last were the husband, son and son-in-law of one Flora MacDonald, who had achieved everlasting renown after Culloden by leading the defeated Bonnie Prince Charlie to the Isle of Skye and safety from his pursuers, a deed that landed her in a British prison ship. Impoverished like so many of her countrymen after the failed uprising, she and her husband, a leader of the MacDonald clan, sailed for the New World. Now once again they were on the losing side.

If Moore's Creek proved a disaster for the Highlanders, it was heady news for Carolina patriots already inspired by the previous year's events at Lexington, Concord and Bunker Hill. Only six weeks after the battle, South Carolina instructed its delegates to the Continental Congress sitting in Philadelphia to declare their support for the complete independence of the American colonies from Britain. It was the first such declaration by a colony and would lead to the Continental Congress's Declaration of Independence on the following 4 July.

Also on this day

AD 274: Roman Emperor Constantine the Great is born * 1807: American poet Henry Wadsworth Longfellow is born in Portland, Maine

28 February

The Republican Party is born

1854 Today a small group of abolitionists, Free Soilers and former Democrats and Whigs met in a church in Ripon, Wisconsin, to join forces in fighting the extension of slavery into American territories. Under the leadership of Alvan Bovay, the participants adopted an anti-slavery resolution and agreed to meet again the following month. From this slight beginning was born the Republican Party of the United States.

Although the American Civil War was still seven years away, slavery was already the great issue of the day, particularly now that the Kansas-Nebraska Act looked certain to be passed by Congress. This act overturned the 1820 Missouri Compromise that had excluded slavery from the Kansas and Nebraska territories, and made it possible that it would be permitted there if supported by popular vote. Abolitionists were outraged at the turnaround and fearful that pro-slavery forces, supported by slave owners from the South, would institute the hateful practice in the territories.

After the first two meetings, the Ripon organisers found their church too small for a major gathering of likeminded people, and scheduled the first official conference of the new party for 6 July in Jackson, Michigan. There the abolitionists formalised the name 'Republican' and positioned themselves as descendants of Thomas Jefferson's Democratic-Republican Party, with its emphasis on equality for all, blithely ignoring the fact that their hero Jefferson had owned 250 slaves.

Two years later the Republicans nominated John C. Fremont for president with the rallying cry 'Free soil, free labor, free speech, free men, Fremont'. Even though they battled against both Democrats and Whigs, they garnered 33 per cent of the vote, considered by Republicans a 'victorious defeat'. In celebration the American poet John Greenleaf Whittier wrote:

Then sound again the bugles.
Call the muster roll anew;
If months have well-nigh won the field,
What may not four years do?

Indeed, four years later Abraham Lincoln was elected the first Republican president.

The Republicans remained in power for all but eight years from 1861 to 1913, including the anomaly of Lincoln's running mate and successor Andrew Johnson, who was a 'war' Democrat who fervently opposed the secession of the Southern states. In total eighteen Republicans have held the nation's highest office since the party's founding, compared with only nine Democrats.

Over the years the Republicans began referring to themselves as the 'grand old party', soon to be short-handed as 'GOP', surely a misnomer in that the Democratic Party (which also took its name from Jefferson's Democratic-Republicans) had been formed in 1832, some 22 years before the Republicans.

Birth of the inventor of the essay

1533 Today was born literature's most famous essayist, Michel Eyquem, seigneur de Montaigne, in his family's château near Bordeaux.

Montaigne's aristocratic father had him brought up entirely in Latin until he was six and subsequently trained him in law. Although he became a judge and later mayor of Bordeaux, Montaigne 'retired' at the tender age of 38 to devote the rest of his life to writing. Living in the family château (which he had by now inherited from his father), Montaigne worked daily in his book-lined library in one of the château's towers. His most famous work is simply entitled *Essays*; Montaigne actually invented the term for short philosophical pieces.

Although Montaigne married and fathered six children, his heart was always in his work. But when he reached his late 50s he was plagued by ill health, perhaps prompting his famous perception: 'Le continuel ouvrage de votre vie, c'est bâtir la mort', he wrote. (The constant work of your life is to build the house of death.)

When he was 59 he was struck by a severe inflammation of the tonsils, leaving him literally speechless. He finally died while hearing Mass on 13 September 1592 in the château where he was born.

Also on this day
1820: John Tenniel, illustrator of *Alice's Adventures in Wonderland*, is born * 1916: American/British writer Henry James dies

29 February

Caesar decrees a new calendar

45 BC Legend has it that the first Roman calendar was instituted by Romulus in 738 BC, but it had only ten months. Then, in the 7th century BC, the Roman King Numa Pompilius added January and February to create a twelve-month year, and the Roman world lived with it for six centuries even though it totalled only 355 days, leading to calendrical chaos.

Finally Julius Caesar stepped in, decreeing a new calendar based on the calculations of Sosigenes of Alexandria, who had worked out that a year should have 365 and a quarter days.

But how to account for that last quarter day? Cleverly, Sosigenes added an additional day at the end of February every fourth year. The new calendar went into effect on 1 January 45 BC and on this day the world celebrated its first Leap Year. Back then, however, they didn't call it Leap Year but *bis-sexto-kalendae*, a term not explainable in fewer than four paragraphs. Luckily, centuries later the Scandinavians coined the term Leap Year, derived from the Old Norse *hlaupa* ('to leap'). This was based on the observation that during a Leap Year any fixed event leaps forward an extra day, falling two days after the day of the week it fell on the previous year rather than only one day later as in normal years.

If the number of days, the number of months and a *bis-sexto-kalendae* weren't change enough, Caesar also changed the name of one of the months, or at least the Roman Senate did, when it renamed Quintilis 'July' in his honour. (Later another obsequious senate renamed Sextilis in honour of Caesar's successor, Augustus, calling it 'August'.)

One thing Caesar forgot was the week – there were none in his calendar. But in the 4th century the first Christian emperor Constantine introduced the seven-day week, based on the Book of Genesis. And while Caesar's calendar looked accurate, in fact it overestimated the length of the year by eleven minutes and fourteen seconds, a problem resolved only in 1582 when Pope Gregory XIII adjusted Caesar's calendar and re-baptised it the Gregorian Calendar.

The pope who started the Counter-Reformation

1468 Today in the small town of Canino in the Papal States was born an Italian aristocrat who would become the first pope to lead the Catholic response to Protestantism, the Counter-Reformation.

Alessandro Farnese came from a family that had already served the papacy for three centuries. Studious and intelligent, as a young man he was educated in Florence, coming under the influence of Lorenzo the Magnificent. During this period he first met Lorenzo's son Giovanni, seven years his junior.

Although the success of Farnese's career in the Church was never in doubt, his prospects took a quantum leap when his sister Giulia became the mistress of the notorious Borgia Pope Alexander VI. Alexander created young Farnese a cardinal deacon when he was just 25. In the corridors of the Vatican young prelates referred to him as the 'petticoat cardinal'.

While serving the Church, Farnese also managed to service his aristocratic mistress, who bore him four children. Even after Alexander died, he continued to progress, as his old friend Giovanni de' Medici kept his career on track when he became Pope as Leo X in 1513.

Finally, on 13 October 1534, when he was already 66, Farnese was elected Pope, taking the name of Paul III. Although sincerely religious, he was always one of Catholicism's more worldly pontiffs, with a strong interest in the arts. He built the magnificent Farnese Palace in Rome, persuaded Michelangelo to finish *The Last Judgement* on the wall of the Sistine Chapel and commissioned him to build St Peter's dome.

Oddly, this sophisticated Italian also had a lasting effect on the Church itself. He is remembered for excommunicating England's Henry VIII and for approving a fledgling monastic order called the Society of Jesus (the Jesuits), naming Ignatius Loyola as its first general. But his greatest achievement came in 1545 when he convened the Council of Trent, Catholicism's first attempt to reform itself in the face of Protestant revolt.

In the autumn of 1549 the 81-year-old Pope Paul was stricken with a raging fever and died in his bed in the Vatican.

Also on this day

1792: Italian composer Gioacchino Rossini is born * 1868: Benjamin Disraeli becomes Prime Minister for the first time * 1880: The St Gotthard railway tunnel through the Alps is completed, linking Italy with Switzerland

1 March

Frédéric Chopin is born

1810 Like his compositions, Frédéric Chopin's life was brilliant in success, wistful in tone and brief in duration. He was born Fryderyk Franciszek Szopen on this day in a village with the unlikely name of Zelazowa Wola, some 29 miles from Warsaw. Despite his name and place of birth, Chopin was Frenchified from the start: his father was a French émigré who sent him to the local French lycée to be educated.

Chopin's genius showed itself at an early age: he gave his first concert at the palace of Polish Prince Radziwill at the age of eight. At twenty the same prince presented him to Paris society at the home of Baron de Rothschild.

Chopin's life was a classic of 19th-century Romanticism: his music, his aristocratic good looks, his final wasting illness and most of all, his doomed affair with George Sand.

By 1836 Chopin, now a celebrated composer and virtuoso, was introduced by his friend Franz Liszt to a Parisian baroness named Aurore Dudevant, who had already become famous under the pseudonym of George Sand for writing about the anguish and exultation of women in love. Six years older than Chopin and still married, she was already the focus of Parisian gossip about her turbulent liaisons with writers such as Alfred de Musset and Prosper Mérimée. Now she fixed upon Chopin and pleaded with him to become her lover. By 1838 he had succumbed to her blandishments, and the two retreated to Majorca, where they lived for two months in an abandoned monastery.

Returning to France, the couple moved first to Sand's country house at Nohant, then to Paris where they lived in the rue Pigalle and later in the square d'Orléans. But by the time Chopin was 37 in 1847, the affair was over, broken by lovers' quarrels and Chopin's deteriorating health.

Free but unhappy, Chopin organised a desultory seven-month tour of Great Britain and then returned to Paris where, four months before his 40th birthday, he died of consumption. He is still considered the greatest composer of piano music in history.

Ethiopians crush the Italian army at Adwa

1896 Colonialism was everyone's favourite national sport in the 19th century, so the Italians, who for the most part had stopped being someone else's colony only 30 years before, felt that honour obliged them to join the game.

By 1887 Italy was at war with Ethiopia, and Italian forces had a taste of the future when the Ethiopians defeated them at Bogali (25 January 1887). But through the next nine years armed conflict alternated with diplomacy, and Italy at least nominally controlled much of the country.

By 1895, however, the Ethiopian King Menelek was rapidly pushing the Italians out. Italian Prime Minister Crispi felt that national honour was at stake and ordered General Baratieri to advance against the King's apparently primitive army at Adwa.

On 1 March 1896, some 25,000 foolhardy Italians attacked over 100,000 Ethiopians – and were annihilated, those not killed being held to ransom. It was one of the worst colonial defeats ever recorded, and it forced Italy to recognise the independence of Ethiopia – until 1934.

A haughty duke sparks religious wars in France

1562 François, second duc de Guise, was arrogant, imperious and impeccably aristocratic. He was France's foremost soldier and the leader of one of the country's three most powerful families. He was also a staunch Catholic, highly conservative and somewhat of a bigot.

On 1 March 1562, Guise happened to be passing through Champagne and stopped in the town of Vassy to hear Mass. Vassy was a largely Huguenot town, and the Duke found the locals defying a royal edict by holding a Protestant service in a barn only a few hundred yards from the Vassy church.

Soon the barn became the scene of a confrontation between Catholics and Calvinists, and Guise and his men attempted to enforce the King's edict by compelling the Protestants to stop their service of worship. In a moment rocks were flying, and the Duke found fresh blood oozing from a face wound.

In an instant Guise's men savagely attacked the Huguenots, killing 30 and wounding over 100 more. To top it off, the enraged Duke ordered a gibbet constructed from the barn's benches and strung up the Protestant minister.

This was the first mass violence between France's Catholics and Protestants – and the spark that lit 35 years of brutal religious conflagration.

Also on this day

1780: Pennsylvania becomes the first US state to abolish slavery * 1815: Napoleon lands at Golfe-Juan on the Côte d'Azur on escaping from Elba * 1845: The USA annexes Texas

2 March

Charles the Bold loses his treasure

1476 In all, Swiss pikemen defeated Charles the Bold, Duke of Burgundy, three times, of which the last cost the Duke his life.

The first victory, however, was in some ways the most profitable for the Swiss. On this day the two armies met at Grandson, near the Lake of Neuchâtel.

Through expert use of terrain and the element of surprise, some 20,000 Swiss defeated three times that many Burgundians.

What's more, they captured Charles the Bold's chief portable treasures. The Swiss seized Charles's gold dinnerware and twelve exquisite enamel apostles, plus an incredible collection of jewels which included:

The 'grand duc de Toscane', a diamond of 139 carats mounted in gold and pearls;
'Le Sansy', a 100-carat diamond;
'Le Federlin', a brooch of five rubies, four diamonds, 70 pearls and three giant pearls, intended for Charles's hat;
'Les Trois Frères', three rubies of 70 carats;
Two huge pearls called 'Non Pareille' and 'La Ramasse des Flandres';
Charles's necklace of the Order of the Golden Fleece;
Charles's hat decorated with sapphires, diamonds, rubies and pearls.

Apart from these incredible jewels, the Swiss also took over an even greater treasure left behind by the fleeing Burgundians: some 2,000 Burgundian *filles de joie*.

Death of the last Holy Roman Emperor

1835 Today died Emperor Franz II, a dry old stick of a man of 64. He had been the 66th Holy Roman Emperor since Charlemagne, and the last one, for under pressure from Napoleon he had resigned the title, demoting himself to Emperor of Austria. Although he reigned for 43 years, Franz was overshadowed by his brilliant minister Klemens Metternich, and is remembered today less than he deserves. He was in fact a tough-minded, sardonic man who managed three events of enduring historical note.

First, he married his daughter Marie-Louise to the upstart Emperor Napoleon, a calculated decision that may have saved his throne. Second, he hosted the Congress of Vienna after Napoleon's final defeat, when the future of Europe was determined for most of the century to come. Third and most memorable, he renounced the title of Holy Roman Emperor and brought an end to the story of the Holy Roman Empire after eight and a half centuries.

Also on this day
1791: British preacher John Wesley dies in London * 1882: Roderick McClean tries to assassinate Queen Victoria

3 March

Ponce de León seeks the fountain of youth

1513 Juan Ponce de León was one of the hardy explorer-adventurers who opened up the New World for the kings of Spain. He had fought against the Moors at Granada and served with Columbus on his second voyage. Eventually he became governor of what today is Puerto Rico and amassed a fortune, largely in the slave trade.

It was in Puerto Rico that Ponce de León first heard of the wondrous Fountain of Youth, the miraculous source of water one drink of which would guarantee a life without old age or death. The Fountain, he was told, could be found on a fabulous island somewhere to the north.

On 3 March 1513 Ponce de León set sail with three ships on his famous quest. At the time of the Easter Feast he sighted land. Thinking he had found an island, he promptly named it after the holiday, in Spanish Pascua Florida or 'Flowery Easter'. And so Florida received its name.

As for poor Ponce de León, instead of a fountain of youth he found quite the opposite. While exploring Florida in 1521 he was killed by an arrow during an Indian attack.

Alexander II frees Russia's serfs

1861 At the beginning of this year there were only two 'civilised' nations that still permitted slavery of a sort: the United States with its black slaves and Russia with its serfs. The serfs were technically better off than the slaves, but in the 18th century Peter the Great had bound them to landowners rather than to the land, so in effect they had little or no control over their own lives.

During the first half of the 19th century, many Russian aristocrats believed serfdom not only a blot on the honour of Mother Russia but also a block to the sort of industrial development they wanted.

So at last, on 3 March 1861, Tsar Alexander II liberated the serfs. In addition to their personal freedom, the serfs received allotments of land for which the serfs-turned-peasants had to repay the government over the next 49 years.

From that time the United States remained the only advanced country with legal slavery – until Abraham Lincoln issued the Emancipation Proclamation 22 months later.

Also on this day

1847: Telephone inventor Alexander Graham Bell is born in Edinburgh * 1875: The first performance of Bizet's *Carmen* is staged at the Opéra Comique in Paris * 1878: The Treaty of San Stefano frees Bulgaria from Turkish rule after almost five centuries * 1931: 'The Star-Spangled Banner' is adopted as the US national anthem

4 March

The great Saladin dies

1193 There is a certain magic to the name Saladin, the legendary Saracen leader who defied Richard the Lion-Heart in his crusade to reconquer Jerusalem (particularly if you know what his name means – 'Righteousness of the Faith, Joseph, Son of Job'). It was Saladin who caused Richard to come on crusade in the first place by destroying Christian power in the Holy Land in the Battle of Hattin in 1187. And although Saladin's armies never bested Richard in open combat, they were in the end too strong for him, and Richard was forced to abandon his crusade without having taken Jerusalem.

Saladin was born in a town called Tikrit in what was then Mesopotamia, today's Iraq. (Eight centuries later, an Arab as despicable as Saladin was admirable was also born in Tikrit – Saddam Hussein.) By all accounts, Saladin was at least as chivalrous as any European knight. Even while battling with Richard he sent him and his captains chilled wine, pears and grapes from Damascus to ease their life in camp. On one famous occasion, when Richard was engaged in combat his horse was killed under him. Saladin saw the English King fall and, instead of ordering his men to finish him off, sent him a fresh horse instead.

Richard gave up his crusade in October 1192. Ironically, Saladin died in Damascus of fever only five months later, on this day in 1193.

Dying, he saw the ephemeral nature of all his triumphs. His last instructions to his followers were: 'Go and take my shroud through the streets and cry loudly, "Behold all that Saladin, who conquered the East, bears away of his conquests".'

Also on this day
1394: Portuguese patron of explorers Prince Henry the Navigator is born * 1461: Edward IV usurps the English throne * 1493: Columbus sails into Lisbon on his return from discovering the New World * 1678: Birth of Italian composer Antonio Vivaldi in Venice * 1861: Abraham Lincoln is sworn in as the 16th president of the USA

5 March

Colonial rebels drive the British out of Boston

1776 Morning light revealed the surprise that the American rebels had prepared for General Sir William Howe, the British Commander-in-Chief in America. During the night they had constructed a fortified artillery position at the top of

Dorchester Heights, across the bay from the city of Boston, and, even more remarkable, they had placed in it a battery of powerful cannon that now commanded not only the harbour, where the British fleet lay, but also the city itself, where 6,500 redcoats had been bottled up by the rebel army since the previous spring.

Unknown to the British, the Americans had acquired the cannon when they captured the British stronghold at Fort Ticonderoga the year before. Then, in an epic of winter logistics planned by Henry Knox, the Boston bookseller turned artillerist, the heavy guns, weighing some 120,000 pounds, were put on sledges and dragged by oxen over 300 miles of frozen terrain to the rebel siege lines around Boston.

Sir William knew the jig was just about up. With artillery in such a position, Boston would be untenable. Because the British guns in the city could not be sufficiently elevated to deliver counter-battery fire on Dorchester Heights, Howe's only hope of dislodging the Americans and capturing their cannon was with a night assault. He ordered an attack for that very evening, but it was first delayed by heavy rains and then cancelled, giving the Americans further time to strengthen their defences.

The next day General Howe consulted his commanders in a council of war, at which the decision was taken to evacuate the city. In an agreement with General Washington, Howe promised not to burn Boston if his command were allowed to leave without hindrance. And so it was that ten days later the British garrison and 1,000 American Loyalists boarded ships and sailed away to Halifax, Nova Scotia.

With the evacuation of Boston by the British, round one of the American Revolution – the New England round of Lexington, Concord and Bunker Hill – went to the rebels. But it would be a long war, over six years of fighting, and round two would begin in just four months with a large British army landing near New York City.

Also on this day

1696: Italian painter Giovanni Battista Tiepolo is born in Venice * 1933: Hitler and Nationalist allies win the Reichstag majority, the last free election in Germany until after the Second World War * 1953: Soviet dictator Joseph Stalin dies

6 March

French cunning captures Richard the Lion-Heart's impregnable castle

1204 Through inheritance, marriage, treaty and conquest, Henry II hammered together the Angevin Empire that included all of England plus roughly half of France, from Normandy in the north through Brittany, Touraine and Poitou, down through Bordeaux to Gascony and the borders of Spain. His son Richard the Lion-Heart inherited this great empire and fought to preserve it from his hereditary enemy, King Philip Augustus of France.

Richard's most significant contribution to the defence was the massive Château Gaillard, of which the ruins still stand atop a cliff at Les Andelys, about 55 miles north-west of Paris. 'Gaillard' in French means strong, large and vigorous, and Richard's fortress was aptly named. With its seventeen massive towers, walls eight feet thick and a moat 45 feet deep, it protected the route the French would have to take to invade Richard's northern possessions. 'I should take it if it were made of steel', Philip is reputed to have boasted. 'I should hold it were it made of butter', was Richard's famous reply.

By the year 1203, however, Richard was dead and his cowardly, incompetent brother John was on the throne. It was then that Philip Augustus moved to conquer Château Gaillard at last.

But the mighty fortress looked just as impregnable now as it had when Richard had built it seven years before. For almost six months the French attackers remained camped outside the walls, suffering the daily jeers from the defenders. But while Philip was failing to take the fortress, John was so unsure of his own barons that he could not raise an army to break the siege. It looked like stalemate.

Then Philip learned that the English had over a year's supply of food on hand, so the garrison could never be starved out. Knowing that the only way to victory was by storming the walls, the French King ordered a direct attack.

First the French troops, protected by screens, built a rough path to the moat and promptly filled it with earth and felled trees. Now they could approach the exterior walls, where they mined one of the corner towers, causing its partial collapse.

But still the attackers were unable to force their way in, so the wily Philip sent in a small team of soldiers who entered the fortress through its latrines and quickly lowered the drawbridge leading to the principal keep. Now able to bring in their massive siege machinery, the French hammered a breach in the last remaining walls, compelling the English garrison to surrender on this day in 1204.

The fall of Château Gaillard marks the start of the destruction of the Angevin Empire. By John's death twelve years later, English-held territory in mainland France had been reduced to a few small holdings in the south-west, and Philip had earned his name of Augustus, father of modern France.

Joan of Arc recognises her king

1429 The castle of Chinon still rises rugged and formidable near the Loire, as it did nearly six centuries ago when France's uncrowned king, Charles VII, held pitiful court there while the English ruled much of his country.

But on 6 March 1429, the young king found the first portent of victory to come, when a seventeen-year-old girl named Joan of Arc arrived at the castle.

When questioned by Charles's courtiers as to why she had come, Joan replied: 'I have been commanded to do two things for the King of Heaven: one, to raise the siege of Orléans, the other, to conduct the King to Reims for his sacrament and coronation.'

Legend says that Charles doubted her purpose and so stood among some courtiers, clad in simple dress, and then had Joan brought into the room. Although she had never seen him before, she instantly picked him out and made reverence to him. 'After leaving her', an eye witness said, 'the King appeared joyful'.

And so he should have been. Within four months Joan had fulfilled both her commissions.

Mary, Queen of Scots' husband murders her counsellor

1566 By eight in the evening the rebellious Scottish barons had surrounded Edinburgh Palace and taken possession of the doors, all in deadly silence. With them was the vain and frivolous King Consort, Lord Darnley, who shared the barons' desire to rid the world of one David Riccio, the advisor to Mary, Queen of Scots. The barons thought that Riccio had too much power to live, and Darnley suspected him of being his wife's lover.

The armed men climbed stealthily to the chamber where Riccio and the Queen were dining. In they rushed, upsetting the table and knocking over all but one candle. In the flickering light Riccio tried desperately to hide behind the Queen, but the violent nobles dragged him away, in spite of Mary's screams of protest. Before the very eyes of the Queen, the little man was repeatedly stabbed and then rushed, still living, from the room. Outside he was set upon again, and this time there was no mistake. Riccio was dead, with 56 stab wounds in his body.

Mary was shattered but soon dried her tears, declaring: 'Enough of grief. I will study revenge.' Less than a year later she conspired to have Darnley blown to bits in his own bedroom.

Also on this day

1475: Italian sculptor and painter Michelangelo Buonarroti is born * 1836: The twelve-day siege of the Alamo ends, with only six survivors out of the original force of 155

7 March

Marcus Aurelius becomes Emperor

AD 161 If ever a man was born to the purple it was the Roman Emperor Marcus Aurelius. His grandfathers had both been consuls, his father's sister was married to the future Emperor Antoninus Pius and one grandmother was heiress to one of Rome's greatest fortunes. His position was further strengthened when at seventeen he was adopted by Antoninus, and seven years later when he married Antoninus' daughter, the beautiful if unfaithful Annia Galeria Faustina.

It was on the evening of this day that Antoninus died of acute indigestion brought on by a surfeit of Alpine cheese two days before. As the 74-year-old emperor lay on his couch, too weak to move, the tribune of the day asked for the nightly password. 'Aequanimitas' (peace), he murmured, his last word.

Indeed, Antoninus' 23 years as Emperor had been among the most peaceful and enlightened in Roman history, and with his customary foresight he had long since designated his adoptive son Marcus Aurelius as the next emperor, who today succeeded to the throne.

Marcus was a few weeks short of his 40th birthday when the reins of power fell into his hands. His first act was to insist that the Senate make his younger adoptive brother Verus co-Emperor, although Marcus was clearly the senior partner. Their co-operation lasted until Verus died of a stroke eight years later.

Early in life Marcus had been fascinated by philosophy, at twelve adopting the rough cloak of the Greek philosophers and sleeping on the ground, until his mother convinced him that he could contemplate the nature of life equally well from a comfortable couch. And, despite nineteen imperial years spent almost constantly and successfully at war against Rome's enemies, it is for his *Meditations* that today he is primarily remembered.

Marcus' *Meditations* were a series of fragmentary musings jotted down over his years as Emperor. It is unclear if he ever intended anyone to read them, as in them he addresses himself and uses them to record his preoccupation with the futility of human life.

Written in Greek, they strongly reflect the Stoic tradition in which Marcus was educated, and once were considered among the greatest of philosophical tracts. Recent historians, however, have been less impressed, noting the Emperor's repeated angst about the transience of man's life and works, especially his own. Furthermore, although expressed in Marcus' own way, the basic ideas put forward are not original but a reiteration of many of the moral precepts of the freed slave and philosopher Epictetus, who taught that the universe is governed by some sort of divine intelligence of which the human soul is a part.

He also held the Stoic belief that men should look on triumph and tragedy with equanimity, and play a constructive role in public affairs. This Marcus did, governing fairly and with moderation (he forbade the execution of any senator and tolerated the troublesome Christians), continually defending the empire from the depredations of Scythians and Germans.

On 17 March 180 Marcus died at 59, possibly of plague, in Vindobona, now Vienna, where today in the historic district you can find a street called Marc Aurelstrasse, named in his honour.

Marcus Aurelius was the last of the 'five good emperors' who ruled Rome for 84 consecutive years, earning the praise of Gibbon who called it 'a period in the history of the world during which the condition of the human race was the most happy and prosperous'. Sadly, this glorious epoch came to a close on Marcus' death when his eighteen-year-old son Commodus (the villain of the film *Gladiator*) inherited the empire.

Also on this day

322 BC: Greek philosopher Aristotle dies * 1274: Christian philosopher St Thomas Aquinas dies * 1875: French composer Maurice Ravel is born * 1876: Alexander Graham Bell patents the telephone

8 March

The first English parliament?

1265 Simon de Montfort is one of the great controversial characters in English history. The bare outline of his achievements is indisputable: de Montfort led a rebellion by English barons against the weak and puerile leadership of Henry III, and after capturing the King at the Battle of Lewes in 1264, Montfort was de facto ruler of the realm. The controversy is whether he was a man ahead of his time, a believer in liberty and some sort of democracy, or whether he was simply another power-hungry noble with an eye to the main chance.

Whatever the verdict on Montfort's character, what is certain is that on 8 March 1265 he gathered together in Westminster Hall some peers of the land, a sprinkling of bishops, two knights from each shire and two to four 'good and loyal men' from each city and borough. This was the first time in history that ordinary citizens had met to discuss the government and to give opinions regarding the laws they were to live under. Historians consider this the first parliament, the start of what is today the House of Commons and, in a broader sense, the start of parliamentary democracy as it now exists.

Death of a self-made duke

1466 Francesco Sforza had been born illegitimate in 1401. His father was a peasant from Romagna named Muzio Attendolo, who had risen to become commander of a band of mercenary soldiers who had once kidnapped him. Such leaders were called *condottieri* because they agreed a contract (*condotta* in Italian) with the city for which they agreed to fight. Always ambitious, often brutal and sometimes capable, *condottieri* preferred armed cavalry for their mercenaries.

Perhaps to enhance his status as a leader and fighter, Muzio Attendolo changed his name to Sforza (*sforzo*: Italian for effort or will) and gave it to his son Francesco, although declining to marry Francesco's mother.

At the age of 22, the younger Sforza took over the band of mercenaries when his father was drowned during a battle, and became one of Italy's most renowned *condottieri*. Tall, strong, direct, honest and shrewdly intelligent, he managed to marry another bastard offspring, Bianca Maria, illegitimate daughter of Filippo Maria Visconti, the last Visconti duke of Milan.

In 1447 Milan was attacked by Venice, and Sforza's father-in-law called on him for help. But before Sforza arrived, Duke Filippo Maria died, unexpectedly leaving his city to the King of Naples. Egged on by Sforza, the disgruntled Milanese proclaimed Milan a republic and appointed him captain general. Shortly thereafter he forced Milan to recognise him as Visconti's heir and the new Duke.

Sforza proved to be an able and energetic ruler as well as a patron of the arts in the blossoming Renaissance. When not fighting wars or commissioning paintings, he sired eight children by Bianca Maria, while producing a further eleven illegitimate ones on the side. When he died today at 65, he left behind the dynasty that bears his name and that ruled Milan until 1535.

Also on this day

1702: Anne becomes Queen of England after William III dies in a riding accident * 1855: Charles XIV of Sweden (the former Napoleonic marshal, Jean-Baptiste Bernadotte) dies

9 March

Napoleon marries Joséphine

1796 Today in a civil ceremony the future Emperor Napoleon married his first wife, née Joséphine Tascher de la Pagerie, better known to us as Joséphine de Beauharnais, the name of her first husband who had been guillotined during the French Revolution. Joséphine herself had been briefly imprisoned during the Terror.

In 1796 Napoleon was just at the start of his giddy ascent, only 26 years old and still spelling his name 'Buonaparte'. Joséphine was 32 and beautiful in a highly erotic way, no doubt impressively polished and worldly for this Corsican *arriviste*.

Both the bride and the groom must have had some doubts about themselves, since Napoleon made himself out to be 28 instead of 26 by using his brother's birth certificate, while Joséphine presented herself as 29.

The marriage must have been a real love match, if we can judge by Napoleon's love letter dated only a month after the marriage. Urging Joséphine to join him in Milan, he wrote: 'But of course you're coming. You'll be here beside me, on my heart, in my arms, on my mouth ... a kiss on your heart, and then one a little lower down, much lower down.'

Later, when her husband was campaigning in Egypt, Joséphine started an affair with another army officer, a scandal that almost brought on divorce. But she finally persuaded Napoleon to forgive her and even talked him into a church wedding that took place on 1 December 1804, the day before he was crowned by the Pope.

By 1810, however, the marriage had finally foundered, battered by mutual infidelity and given the *coup de grace* by reasons of state: it had produced no heir. Joséphine departed to lavish retirement in Malmaison, just outside Paris, where she died a month before her 51st birthday.

The first battle of ironclad ships

1862 The Union ship *Monitor* looked rather like a hatbox on top of a raft, while the Confederate *Merrimac* was shaped like a bar of Toblerone chocolate with a smokestack in the middle. Yet when these two peculiar warships met in combat in Hampton Roads, Virginia, they changed for ever the nature of naval warfare. For on this day took place the first battle ever between ironclad ships.

At first blush the ships seemed very different. The *Merrimac*, at over 100 yards long, was twice the length of the *Monitor*, and her crew of 300 was more than five times as large. Further, she was armed with ten guns to her rival's two. The *Monitor*, on the other hand, sported the first gun turret in history, so her guns could be aimed in any direction without turning the ship.

Prior to the meeting of these metal monsters, the *Merrimac* had destroyed several wooden ships while remaining impervious to cannon fire.

The Battle of Hampton Roads started about eight in the morning. Both ships fired unceasingly at each other, at so close a range that the vessels actually touched five times during the engagement. The *Merrimac* even tried to batter the *Monitor* with its cast-iron ram.

After several hours of fighting the Confederate ship withdrew unharmed. Neither ship had been able to inflict significant damage on the other.

The two ironclads never fought again. The Confederate sailors scuttled the *Merrimac* when the South pulled out of Norfolk, Virginia, while the *Monitor* was lost in a storm off Cape Hatteras on the last day of the year. But naval warfare would never be the same. The wooden warship was relegated to history.

Cardinal Mazarin dies

1661 At 2.30 in the morning the great Cardinal Jules Mazarin passed away at the age of 59. He had dominated France for nineteen years, had been godfather to Europe's most regal king, Louis XIV, and, according to legend, actually became the second husband of Louis' mother, Queen Anne.

All of this would have been an achievement for any man, but for Mazarin it was even more extraordinary. Grandson of a Sicilian fisherman, son of a

Roman steward, Mazarin was born Giulio Mazzarino, neither titled nor rich. Furthermore, he was never ordained and so ruled France without being a Frenchman and became a cardinal without being a priest.

Mazarin owed his rise in power largely to Cardinal Richelieu, to whom he was devoted. Richelieu noted Mazarin's sharp intelligence and was impressed by his physical courage. Once, at the age of 28, Mazarin galloped between opposing French and Spanish armies at Casale in Italy shouting 'Peace, peace!', as if a truce had been signed. The armies fell back, and Mazarin was thereafter remembered as someone who would put his life on the line to stop a war.

When he became a cardinal he accumulated an enormous and priceless art collection, which he probably dipped into government funds to acquire. His mansion in Paris was so grand that today it is the Bibliothèque Nationale.

Also on this day

1074: Pope Gregory VII excommunicates all married priests * 1451: Italian navigator Amerigo Vespucci is born * 1932: Eamon De Valera is elected President of the Irish Free State, promising to abolish all loyalty to the British Crown

10 March

The story of the French Foreign Legion

1831 France's King Louis-Philippe needed some hardened but perhaps expendable troops to pacify Algeria, and he met the need by creating a new military unit. On this date in 1831 his Minister of War Marshal Nicolas Soult formed the French Foreign Legion, specifying that it 'should not be employed in the continental territory of the kingdom'.

The Legion's officers were recruited from veterans of Napoleon's army who had been mouldering on half pay since Waterloo. The enlisted men were drawn from all over Europe, often desperate men who could find no employment or were wanted by the law. Within a year, Legion strength was 5,500 officers, NCOs and Legionnaires.

The Legion first saw combat in April 1832, when two battalions of mainly German and Swiss troops stormed a village called Maison Carrée east of Algiers. Since then, Legionnaires have fought in hundreds of wars and brush fires around the world. They were at the siege of Sebastopol during the Crimean War, and supported the puppet Emperor Maximilian during his ill-fated reign in Mexico. Their African conflicts have included Dahomey, Madagascar, Tunisia, Chad, Lebanon and Algeria. They also served in Vietnam, in Bosnia during the civil war there in 1993 and in the first Gulf War.

Over the years, the Legion has boasted some famous names (although not all of them bore those names when they were Legionnaires). There have been two Napoleons – the Emperor's nephew who was a captain in 1863, and Prince Napoleon, the Bonaparte pretender to the French throne, who served under the name of Blanchard in 1940. Napoleon/Blanchard must have been amused to find a fellow pretender to the throne serving with him – the comte de Paris, who was a direct descendant of King Louis-Philippe, the man who created the Legion. An earlier royal officer was the future Peter I of Serbia, who used the name Kara as his *nomme de guerre* in 1870.

The most illustrious Legion officer undoubtedly was Patrice de Mac-Mahon, who served in 1843–4, went on to lead the French army at the great victory at Magenta in 1859 and rose to be President of the Third Republic in 1873. Two other Legion members have become Prime Ministers of France. Edouard Daladier was Prime Minister for several years in the 1930s (and co-signer with Neville Chamberlain of the Munich Pact with Adolf Hitler's Germany), and Pierre Messmer was Prime Minister under de Gaulle and Pompidou.

The Legion also boasts some cultural lions. The American poet Alan Seeger spent three years in the Legion during the First World War and was killed in action at Belloy en Santerre, and the Hungarian-born English author Arthur Koestler, writer of *Darkness at Noon*, was in service in 1940. Indeed, the Legion's reputation for hard-bitten souls with a chequered past has been seen as so glamorous that even an American *boulevardier* like Cole Porter maintained that he had been a Legionnaire, although historians now universally debunk the claim.

Today the Legion boasts soldiers of fortune from some 99 countries, usually tough, sometimes criminals on the run. There are no Frenchmen in the Foreign Legion except for officers, all of whom are graduates of the French national military academy of St-Cyr. This combination of French leadership and foreign troops has created a formidable fighting force. The British Second World War Field Marshal Viscount Alanbrooke called it 'the grandest assembly of real fighting men that I have ever seen, marching with their heads up as if they owned the world, lean, hard-looking men, carrying their arms admirably and marching with perfect precision'.

The Legion remained stationed abroad for 131 years, until the liberation of Algeria forced it to move, for the first time, to France. Today it boasts between 8,000 and 9,000 men. Each year there are about 500 candidates to join, but less than 10 per cent are accepted.

Should the Foreign Legion's history and glamour tempt you to join, if you're not French you will have to become a Legionnaire, for whom the rules can be daunting:

The minimum term of service is five years
You cannot have a bank account
You are not permitted to live off barracks
You may not own a car or motorcycle
Marriage is forbidden until you attain the rank of sergeant or have served
   for nine years.

Death of 'the most dangerous man in Europe'

1872 Today in Pisa died Giuseppe Mazzini, the man whom the reactionary Prince Metternich once called 'the most dangerous man in Europe'.

To a large degree, the unification of Italy was the work of three very different men: Cavour, the brilliant politician; Garibaldi, the soldier and leader; and Mazzini, the republican and social reformer.

Son of a doctor, Mazzini was born in Genoa. Dark, intelligent, intense, he was committed to Italian independence and unity all his life. He was an outstanding propagandist but also an activist in the cause he loved. So great was his moral influence that he was forced to flee abroad and was condemned to death in absentia. He was felt to be dangerous by every conservative and status-quoer in Europe, most particularly by the Austrians who controlled most of northern Italy. He seemed to be a threat not just because he worked for a united Italy but also because he was seen as a visionary who could elevate his cause. His views had a moral and religious basis, and he passionately believed that justice and individual liberty were the true fruits of the revolution he preached.

When he died at 67 the reunification he had devoted his life to had been completed just two years earlier, with the annexation of Rome completing the task. Could this be the reason his last recorded words were: 'Yes, yes, I believe in God!'

Also on this day

515 BC: The building of the great Jewish temple in Jerusalem is completed

11 March

General MacArthur leaves the Philippines

1942 In the gathering evening darkness, General Douglas MacArthur, commander of United States Forces in the Far East, stepped off Corregidor Island's North Dock onto the deck of PT-41. Minutes later the motor torpedo boat rumbled away on the first stage of a journey that would take him from the Philippines through the Japanese naval blockade to Australia. In Adelaide a week later, he told reporters, 'I came through', then added the phrase that would become famous: 'and I shall return.'

Left behind was a looming defeat whose dimensions were still unknown to the American public. Against a strong Japanese invasion force that landed two weeks after Pearl Harbor, MacArthur had quickly organised his forces in a stubborn, retreating defence. But he knew, as did his superiors in Washington, that without reinforcements buttressed by air and sea power the defence of the Philippines was a lost cause.

No one would have known the cause was lost from the communiqués issued by MacArthur's headquarters on Corregidor, messages one historian described as 'gripping though often imaginary accounts as to how MacArthur's guile, leadership, and military genius had continuously frustrated the intentions of Japan's armed forces'. For the American public, he became the first hero of the war.

From Washington, President Roosevelt promised MacArthur help. In January, Army Chief of Staff George Marshall radioed: 'President has seen all of your messages and directs navy to give you every possible support in your splendid fight.' But in the five-month siege of the Bataan Peninsula and Corregidor, no planes, no ships, no reinforcements reached the Philippines. There were none to spare.

Now the question was whether to risk MacArthur's almost certain death or capture with his troops, or bring him out. John Curtin, the Australian Prime Minister, helped decide. In late February, facing the increasing threat of Japanese invasion, the Australian government demanded of British Prime Minister Winston Churchill either the return of three Australian divisions now with the British Eighth Army in North Africa, or the appointment of an American general as supreme commander of an expanded Allied force for the south-west Pacific theatre. Churchill, who had earlier expressed his admiration in the House of Commons for 'the splendid courage and quality of the small American army under General MacArthur', used his influence with FDR.

Initially, MacArthur refused the President's order to leave his command, but Roosevelt persisted, and the general finally agreed. Boarding PT-41 with him this evening for the dangerous voyage were his wife and four-year-old son.

On 9 April the Philippine defence force – 10,000 American soldiers and some 60,000 Filipino troops, out of food, ammo and medical supplies – surrendered to the Japanese. A month later Corregidor – the Gibraltar of the East – fell, adding the Philippines to the lengthening list of Allied defeats, which by now included Dunkirk, Pearl Harbor, Tobruk, Guam, Wake and Singapore.

By then, however, MacArthur, at Allied headquarters in Melbourne, had taken charge and begun to organise the measures that would in time roll back the Japanese tide. After a brilliant series of air and amphibious operations that leap-frogged across the top of New Guinea, he arrived back in the Philippines on 20 October 1944. Wading ashore on Leyte Island, he reminded the assembled press corps: 'I have returned.'

The end of Cesare Borgia

1507 Today died one of history's most infamous characters, Cesare Borgia, the ambitious, energetic, murderous and totally unscrupulous son of Pope Alexander VI.

During his lifetime – and since – there have been numerous accusations of Cesare's foul crimes, most of them true. Through his father he became Captain General of the papal forces and later was created a duke by Louis XII of France. He was a brilliant general who reduced many an enemy fortress, but he also conquered by guile and treachery. Once he invited four enemy captains to truce talks, disarmed them and then had them publicly garrotted.

Cesare was also not beyond individual assassination to further his ambitions. Historians still debate whether he arranged the murder of his elder brother Juan, although he gained much by his brother's death, inheriting many of his titles and estates.

Regarding the murder of his brother-in-law, however, there is no doubt that Cesare organised it. In 1498 his sister Lucrezia had married Alfonso de Bisceglie, bastard son of the King of Naples and heir to the throne. Two years later, however, it became apparent that instead of a help, Naples was becoming a hindrance to Cesare's plan to make himself ruler of the Romagna in middle Italy.

In July 1500 assassins set upon Alfonso as he left the Vatican. Alfonso escaped, badly wounded, and no one as yet suspected Cesare. But as Alfonso refused to die of his wounds, on 18 August Cesare sent his notorious henchman Michelotto to the room in the Vatican where he lay recovering. After shooing Lucrezia and Alfonso's sister away with threats, Michelotto proceeded to strangle the wounded man, demonstrating Cesare's single-minded determination to succeed at all costs, as suggested by his motto, 'Aut Caesar, aut nihil' (Either Caesar or nothing).

Although Lucrezia grieved at the loss of her husband, Cesare and his father the Pope were well content. Cesare's plans of conquest moved forward. Aided by French troops (his other brother-in-law was the King of Navarre) and the papal army, he captured large swathes of Romagna, including the key cities of Pesaro, Rimini, Faenza and Urbino.

Although Cesare became a duke, he never achieved his ambition to carve out an independent Borgia state and make himself a prince. When Alexander VI died in 1503 he found himself without political support in an area where he was both feared and detested because of his vicious military campaigns. Eventually he escaped to Spain and enlisted in the services of his brother-in-law, Jean d'Albret, King of Navarre. Leading a force of 5,000 troops against the Castilians, today Cesare was ambushed near Viana and hacked to death, his body pierced by 25 wounds. Perhaps reflecting on the evils he had perpetrated, just as he died he lamented: 'I die unprepared.' He was only 31.

It was an unusually bloody career for a man who had been a cathedral canon at seven, a bishop at fifteen, an archbishop at sixteen and a cardinal at eighteen.

Also on this day

537: The Goths lay siege to Rome * 1513: Giovanni de' Medici becomes Pope Leo X * 1905: The Parisian métro is officially opened

12 March

Belisarius' magnificent defence of Rome

537 Today the beleaguered troops of the great Byzantine general Belisarius cheered and jeered from the walls of Rome as the Ostrogoth King Witigis and his downhearted men burned their camps and withdrew towards their capital in Ravenna. In one of the most astonishing defences in history, an army of only 5,000 men had held the city against enemy forces of over 100,000 for a year and nine days.

With its capital in Constantinople, the Byzantine Empire controlled the eastern half of the old Roman world. In the west, the Ostrogoths had ruled Italy since AD 493, when their legendary King Theodoric had completed his conquest. But now the Byzantine Emperor Justinian was determined to wrest back the old western part of the Roman Empire and dispatched his greatest general to do it.

During the previous seven years Belisarius had defeated the Sasanian Persians in Mesopotamia and the Vandals in North Africa. He had also saved Justinian's throne by massacring the rebels during the Nike insurrection in Constantinople. He was about 30 when he advanced on Italy.

His first major operation came in the summer of 536 when he besieged and occupied Naples. Then, on 9 December of the same year, he entered Rome virtually unopposed. The city had been in decline for over a century, ever since the Visigoths had sacked it in 410. Many inhabitants had abandoned it, many buildings and monuments lay in ruins, and cows grazed in the old Roman forum. But Rome was still the largest city in western Europe, and Belisarius knew that the Ostrogoths would soon counter-attack. Less than three months later, King Witigis arrived with a massive army.

Belisarius' exiguous force had to defend circuit walls twelve miles in circumference against an encircling enemy. To strengthen his defences he placed catapults on the city walls and ordered a deep ditch dug beneath the walls. To prevent the Ostrogoths from using boats to row up the Tiber he had a chain drawn across the river, and he garrisoned Hadrian's tomb, the fortress known today as the Castel' Sant'Angelo.

Stymied by Belisarius' defensive tactics, Witigis attempted to force surrender by diverting the city's aqueducts, but his plan backfired when his own camps were turned into malaria-breeding swamps.

Witigis then ordered four siege towers with battering rams to be drawn up by teams of oxen against the Roman walls. As Belisarius watched the enemy's approach, he borrowed a bow from one of his soldiers and killed an Ostrogoth officer at a great distance. He then ordered his bowmen to fire, not at the enemy soldiers but at the oxen. As the oxen fell pierced by arrows, the siege towers were left standing in the open, never having reached the walls.

The Byzantine army's greatest strength was its cavalry of armoured archers. According to the historian Procopius, who was there: 'Their bows are strong and weighty; they shoot in every possible direction, advancing, retreating, to the front, to the rear, or to either flank.' Infantry armed with axes, spears and swords supported the cavalry.

Unable to man all points along the walls, Belisarius mounted a series of surprise sorties. First the horse archers would put the enemy cavalry to flight and then Byzantine infantry would close in to slaughter the unprotected Ostrogoth infantry. In spite of the numerical odds, such attacks were almost invariably successful.

While battling the enemy outside the city, Belisarius also had to guard against treachery from within. At first he feared that the Roman citizens, foreseeing eventual Ostrogoth victory, might throw open the city gates, but with continued Byzantine success, the Romans gained confidence in Belisarius and even volunteered to join the fight. One surprise betrayal, however, was that of Pope Silverius, who wrote to Witigis offering to surrender the city. Belisarius dressed the Pope as a monk and sent him into exile.

Eventually some 4,000 reinforcements reached Rome and entered the city during a truce, bringing with them a large quantity of supplies. Having already lost some 30,000 men, Witigis saw the situation was hopeless and abandoned the siege.

Hitler creates the Anschluss

1938 At 4.00 this Saturday afternoon Adolf Hitler, Chancellor and President of Germany, drove over a bridge across the River Inn and entered Austria at the town of Braunau, where he had been born almost 49 years earlier. The streets were jammed with expectant crowds who cheered his passing motorcade. 'Ein Volk. Ein Reich. Ein Führer' (One people. One state. One leader) they chanted, in celebration of what they hoped the Führer would engineer the next day: the union – *Anschluss* – of their nation with Nazi Germany.

Hitler could scarcely have retained any memory of Braunau itself, for he was not yet three when his father moved the family to Bavaria. Nevertheless, he managed to turn it to good use in 1924 when, in an effort to construct destiny out of chance, he opened *Mein Kampf* with these words: 'Today it seems to me providential that Fate should have chosen Braunau on the Inn as my birthplace. For this little town lies on the boundary between the two German states, which we of the younger generation at least have made it our life work to reunite by every means possible.'

In 1938 Austria was no longer the leading state of a sprawling, polyglot empire but a small German-speaking republic with a repressive government and an active core of pan-German sentiment. But even in reduced circumstances, it offered a resurgent Germany vital advantages: gold and foreign currency reserves, natural resources, heavy industry, labour, and a standing army to swell the ranks of the Wehrmacht.

It took Hitler five years to bring about the Anschluss, during which time he had indeed used against Austria every means at his disposal, including, when other methods failed, subversion, agitation, provocation, intimidation, and assassination. Within Austria itself his efforts enjoyed the active and disruptive support of the illegal Austrian Nazi party.

Even so, it had been a slow process that required the murder of one Austrian chancellor and the intimidation of his successor. Only three weeks previously, in a meeting with Hitler at Berchtesgaden, the latter had agreed under the harshest duress to measures that would lead to an early takeover of his country by Germany. But then, returning to Vienna, the chancellor had reneged and instead announced his intention to call a plebiscite in just four days – on 13 March – allowing Austrian voters to decide the question of their nation's independence.

This unexpected recalcitrance, and the prospect that the plebiscite's results would not support integration with Germany, forced an impatient Hitler to play his last and strongest card, one threatened but never dealt: invasion. This morning at 5.30, with Nazi mobs rioting in the streets of Austrian cities, German troops marched over the frontier to 'restore order', just ten hours before their Führer passed through Braunau on his way to nearby Linz.

And so it was that two days later, on the glorious spring morning of 14 March, the Führer motored from Linz to Vienna, his progress marked by massive demonstrations of public approval (enforced by savage treatment for dissenters). In the Heldenplatz at midday he addressed a quarter of a million delirious listeners, proclaiming 'the entry of my homeland into the German Reich'. The following evening he flew back to Germany, master of a greater Germany, his eyes now on Czechoslovakia.

Also on this day

1881: Turkish leader Kemal Atatürk is born * 1933: President Paul von Hindenburg drops the flag of the German Republic in favour of the swastika and empire banner

13 March

Mata Hari springs full-grown into the world

1905 Before the four-armed statue of Shiva she danced, her arms and calves encircled by bracelets, her breasts covered only by small bejewelled cups. The other dancers snuffed out the candelabra, leaving the stage in the dim light of a flickering oil lamp. Then, with her back to the audience, she threw off her sarong and moved towards the statue, writhing with passion, apparently nude. As she knelt before the statue, another dancer flung a gold lamé cloak over her shoulders. Rising, she turned to face the stunned crowd as the curtain rang down at the Paris cabaret.

Such was the 'birth' of Mata Hari, the notorious dancer and courtesan who made her first stage appearance today under her assumed name, a Malay term for the Sun, literally meaning 'eye of the day'. Twelve years later she would be shot as a spy by a French firing squad.

Mata Hari was born Margaretha Zella, a dark-haired, olive-skinned Dutch girl of middle-class parents. She had been raised in the Netherlands and had later moved to Java with her mean and dissolute husband whose beatings and philandering eventually drove her to divorce.

When M'greet, as she was called, returned from the Far East she was nearly 30. Unable to find either another husband or a suitable job in Amsterdam, she moved to Paris. There she invented a mysterious new identity for herself, claiming that she came from India, daughter of a temple dancer, and had been raised in the service of the god Shiva. Calling herself Mata Hari, she soon landed a role at the Musée Guimet cabaret, where she found instant fame after her début. Shortly she was triumphantly touring Europe, titillating audiences with her risqué routine and taking lovers along the way.

But by the time she was in her late 30s Mata Hari's body was thickening with age, and she progressively earned her keep more as a *demi-mondaine* than as a dancer. Superbly adroit at lovemaking, she found dozens of rich partners, including celebrities such as a Rothschild baron and Giacomo Puccini. At this time, on the eve of the First World War, she also began her career as a spy.

The details and extent of Mata Hari's espionage remain murky. She claimed that she was enlisted by French Intelligence to seduce German officers to learn their secrets, and in at least one case she was successful. But in late 1916 the French intercepted a coded German message referring to her as their 'agent H 21' and were convinced that she had become a double agent.

The French army quickly brought Mata Hari to trial on charges of espionage, and convicted her in a travesty of justice that was held 'in camera' and during which the defence could not cross-examine witnesses. Mata Hari's choice of a 74-year-old corporate lawyer to defend her primarily because he had once been her lover did not help. The jury of six French officers wasted no time in finding her guilty and condemning her to death.

At dawn on 15 October 1917, Mata Hari was led to the internal courtyard of the Parisian prison at Vincennes. There she faced her fate bravely, telling an attendant nun: 'Do not be afraid, sister. I know how to die.' Refusing a blindfold, she faced the twelve riflemen confronting her and blew them a kiss just before the fusillade ended her life.

Such was the finish of the famed Mata Hari, whose body was given to a French medical school so that student doctors could practice their dissecting skills.

Metternich is gone at last

1848 Only three weeks earlier, while Imperial Vienna swirled in the celebration of Fasching before the start of Lent, King Louis-Philippe had been unceremoniously chased from the throne of France, soon to be replaced by Napoleon III. Now the revolution was spreading to Austria, where its focus was on that sardonic old embodiment of frozen conservatism, the arbiter of Europe, Prince Klemens Metternich, now 74 years old and in power since the days of the first Napoleon.

As excitement grew in the streets, exhilarated Viennese students marched towards the Hofburg imperial palace, armed with a copy of the Hungarian patriot Lajos Kossuth's speech demanding the end to Habsburg absolutism and guarantees of liberty for the people. Imperial grenadiers shot a few dead, but the Austrian imperial family came increasingly to realise that the price of salvation was Metternich's ruin, and so he was figuratively tossed to the wolves. On this day he resigned from office and fled into exile in England.

Although detested by the liberal intelligentsia, Metternich had been a genius in his own way, preserving the peace across Europe since Napoleon's defeat at Waterloo. He was hated for his secret police, his arch conservatism and his determination to retain the status quo. But his downfall may also have been hastened by his vanity: only weeks before he was driven from Austria he had pronounced to a French diplomat: 'Error has never approached my mind.'

Also on this day

565: Byzantine General Belisarius dies in Constantinople * 1519: Hernán Cortés lands in what will become Mexico * 1881: Tsar Alexander II is assassinated by a terrorist bomb

14 March

Admiral John Byng faces the firing squad

1757 The start of the French and Indian War three years earlier had pitted England against France as each attempted to gain control of ever larger slices of North America. Once started, hostilities were hard to stop, and both nations continued to spar with each other in Europe on the eve of the Seven Years' War.

In May 1756 the British feared a French attack on their base in Menorca and sent a small fleet under the command of an indolent and indecisive admiral named John Byng to counter French aggression. But by the time he arrived, the base had fallen.

The irresolute Byng launched an attack but in such a desultory manner that he was soon driven off, at which point he decided that he was facing insuperable odds and sailed off to the British base at Gibraltar, leaving Menorca to the mercy of the French.

On hearing the news back in London, British Prime Minister Thomas Pelham-Holles, Duke of Newcastle, bristled with indignation and resolved to punish Byng for his apparent lack of zeal. Charging the Admiral with dereliction of duty, Newcastle guaranteed a biased court-martial by announcing publicly that 'he shall be tried immediately; he shall be hanged directly'.

Brought back to Portsmouth in disgrace, Byng was tried and convicted on his own flagship *Monarch* and on this day taken on deck and shot by a firing squad of marines.

No other British admiral had ever been executed for such a crime, and all of Europe was bemused by the news. Two years later, Voltaire published his masterpiece *Candide* which includes the celebrated observation: 'Dans ce pays-ci il est bon de tuer de temps en temps un amiral pour encourager les autres.' (In this country [England] it's good to kill an admiral from time to time to encourage the others.)

Ferdinand von Habsburg becomes Emperor

1558 Ferdinand von Habsburg had long been loyal vassal to his mighty older brother, Holy Roman Emperor Charles V. But now a worn and weary Charles had retired to his monastery in Spain, leaving half his great possessions – the German half – to Ferdinand.

Along with Austria and the German principalities came the title of Holy Roman Emperor, and on this day Ferdinand assumed the imperial crown in majestic ceremony at St Bartholomew's church in Frankfurt. Ferdinand's Habsburg descendants were to hang on to this title until his great-great-great-great-great-grandson Franz finally dissolved the Holy Roman Empire itself, under orders from Napoleon, some 246 years later.

Also on this day

1492: Queen Isabella of Castile orders the expulsion of 150,000 Jews from Spain * 1804: Johann Strauss the Elder is born in Vienna * 1879: Albert Einstein is born in Ulm * 1883: Karl Marx dies in London

15 March

The Ides of March

44 BC 'Beware the Ides of March!', the augur Spurinna had warned some days earlier, but Julius Caesar had brushed him aside. Was he not, at 55, the most powerful man in the civilised world? For five years he had been dictator, after having decisively defeated the coalition of nobles, including the great Pompey, who had tried to destroy him. Caesar knew there were senators who hated him, who in fact were plotting to kill him, but so sure was he of his position, of the awe (and perhaps, he hoped, the love) in which he was held, that he had even dismissed the troop of Spanish bodyguards that normally escorted him.

So at mid-morning Caesar set off for Pompey's theatre, where the Senate was meeting. En route a friend handed him a note with the details of the assassination plot, but Caesar simply put it with the other letters he was carrying, having no time to read it.

Entering the theatre, he saw Spurinna among the crowd. 'The Ides of March have come', he mocked. 'Yes', replied the augur, 'but they have not yet gone'.

Caesar took his seat, quickly to be surrounded by conspirators who pretended to be paying their respects. One seized him by the shoulder, and Caesar shook him off, but as he turned away one of the Casca brothers central to the conspiracy stabbed him just below the throat. Grabbing Casca's arm, Caesar stabbed it with his stylus and tried to escape the ring of murderers now surrounding him. But suddenly the great man realised it was hopeless. Since Casca's first thrust he had not uttered a word, but when he saw his protégé Marcus Brutus among his assassins, he murmured in Greek, 'You, too, my child?' He then drew the top of his toga over his face while letting the lower part fall so that he would die with both legs covered. The murderers struck out in a frenzied attack, sometimes wounding each other in their eagerness for the slaughter. Twenty-three knife blows struck home as Caesar stood there, defenceless, before he fell dead to the floor.

So died the greatest of all Romans, perhaps, according to Macaulay, the greatest of all men. But he had changed the world. He replaced the corrupt and incompetent rule of the Roman nobility with an autocracy that lasted for half a millennium in the west and 1,500 years in the east, and he gave to France the Latin civilisation that replaced tribal barbarism and that has lasted to this day.

As for the assassins, virtually all were killed within three years of Caesar's murder or, like Marcus Brutus, committed suicide.

History has a special place for Brutus. Caesar had been his mother's lover and had helped him all his life, but nonetheless five years before the assassination Brutus joined Pompey's army against Caesar. Even so, Caesar pardoned him and appointed him governor of Cisalpine Gaul. For his treachery, in his *Inferno* Dante places him in the lowest circle of Hell alongside Judas, hanging from Satan's mouth.

The Bulgar Slayer becomes Emperor

963 On this day more than a millennium ago, five-year-old Basil II titularly became the Byzantine Emperor at the death of his father from dysentery. When he was eighteen, Basil gained full power and went on to become the most successful Byzantine Emperor since the illustrious Constantine 600 years before.

Although born to the purple, Basil was a most unlikely emperor of what at the time was the most powerful and sophisticated empire in the world. He was ugly and coarse with no interest in learning – and apparently never had sexual relations with either sex in all his long life. But he was a dedicated, meticulous

ruler and a great general to boot. He enlarged his empire dramatically, particularly at the expense of the Bulgarians.

Basil's final victory over the Bulgarians took place on 29 July 1014, as he
invaded their country. After ambushing their army in a narrow valley, Basil
captured 15,000 prisoners. In his *Decline and Fall of the Roman Empire* Gibbon
tells us of the Emperor's punishment for those who resisted him: 'His cruelty
inflicted a cool and exquisite vengeance on the fifteen thousand captives who
had been guilty of the defence of their country. They were deprived of sight,
but to one of each hundred a single eye was left, that he might conduct his blind
century to the presence of their king.'

Such was the man whom history has called *Bulgaroctonus*, the Bulgar Slayer.

Basil II died in his Great Palace in Constantinople at nine in the morning on
15 December in the year 1025 at the age of 67. From that day forward the
empire would shrink until its capital fell to the Turks 428 years later.

Catherine de' Medici attends an execution

1560 For an example of pragmatic brutality and logical cruelty, it is hard to beat
today's mass execution of Huguenots sanctioned by one of the Renaissance's
most vicious characters, Catherine de' Medici.

The Protestant Huguenots had made the fatal error of attacking the castle at
Amboise on the Loire, where the French royal family was in residence.
Defeated, the Huguenot leaders were rounded up, and 15 March was set for the
execution of 57 of them in the castle courtyard.

Chief among the spectators was Catherine herself, Queen Mother (and de
facto ruler) of France. In order to demonstrate how the traitorous are
punished, she had placed her fifteen-year-old son beside her with his equally
impressionable wife, young Mary of Guise, better known to us as Mary, Queen
of Scots. Feeling that few were too young to benefit from the occasion,
Catherine also brought along her second son, Charles d'Orléans, age ten.

As the 57 were beheaded or hanged in turn, so the younger generation
learned. Even when the crowd called for mercy for the final condemned man,
Catherine refused. These were the lessons that helped set the tone for the
following 34 years of destruction, barbarism and murder during the French
religious wars.

Also on this day

1792: King Gustav III of Sweden is shot at a ball and dies twelve days later * 1807:
The first performance of Beethoven's Fourth Symphony takes place at the palace of
Prince Lobkowitz in Vienna

16 March

Death of Tiberius the tyrant

AD 37 Like so many Roman emperors after him, Tiberius started his reign in glory and slowly descended into despotism, perversion and paranoia. He died today at the age of 77 after 22 years in power.

Tiberius was the son of Augustus' wife Livia by an earlier marriage and thus automatically a power in the land as stepson to the Emperor. As a young man he was a highly successful general who stayed away from Rome, leaving the politics (and the imperial succession) to Augustus' grandsons. He was austere and distant, some said arrogant. So determined was he to avoid the rivalries of power that by the time he was 36 he had retired to Rhodes. Eight years later he returned to the capital, just days before the death of one of Augustus' two grandsons and less than a year before the demise of the other.

Reluctantly, Augustus then made Tiberius his heir, fearing that his slow deliberation and distant manner would ill prepare him for ultimate power. Reportedly, the old Emperor lamented on his deathbed: 'Poor Roman people, to be ground by those slow-moving jaws.'

On inheriting the throne at Augustus' death, Tiberius at 54 became Rome's second emperor. Initially he was a hard-working and productive ruler. He recognised the difficulty of running the empire, comparing it to 'holding a wolf by the ears'. But after thirteen years he abruptly moved to his magnificent villa on Capri. He never visited Rome again, delegating progressively more power to the commander of his guard and leaving the squabbling Senate to its own devices.

As the years passed, Tiberius became increasingly murderous and vindictive. According to Suetonius, 'Every day brought a new execution', some victims hurled off the cliffs of Capri after unspeakable tortures. One senator was condemned to death for having carried a coin with Tiberius' head on it into a public lavatory. The Emperor also collapsed into paedophilia and pederasty, importing a whole troop of young boys and girls to take part in imperial orgies. Suetonius relates that Tiberius 'would put unweaned babies to his member as though to a woman's breast'. Suetonius also reports that 'since tradition barred the strangling of virgins, when little girls had been sentenced to die this way, the executioner raped them first'.

When he was 71, Tiberius made an error that may have cost him his life when he brought his eighteen-year-old great-nephew Caligula to Capri, eventually naming him as heir to the empire. For six years Caligula remained docile and obsequious, although he already showed signs of the sadism that would mark his years as Emperor.

In early AD 37, Tiberius travelled to Campania to take part in military games. There he injured his shoulder throwing the javelin and then became seriously ill. Returning to his villa on Capri, he lapsed into unconsciousness, and the doctors, shocked by his emaciated condition, declared that death was imminent.

Believing Tiberius to be dead, Caligula slipped his seal ring from the imperial finger to show himself to the waiting crowd as the new Emperor. But suddenly Tiberius woke from what was really a coma and demanded food. Caligula was petrified with terror, but his ally Macro, the quick-thinking commander of the Praetorian Guard, rushed in and stifled the old Emperor with a blanket.

Also on this day

1521: Ferdinand Magellan discovers the Philippines * 1802: The US Military Academy is established at West Point * 1898: English illustrator Aubrey Beardsley dies

17 March

'Neither the sun nor death can be looked at steadily'

1680 The man who wrote this perceptive maxim died early this morning, long a victim of ill health resulting from war wounds. He was François, duc de La Rochefoucauld, who breathed his last in Paris at the age of 66.

Today, La Rochefoucauld is known almost exclusively for his trenchant epigrams, but these were never published until he was in his 50s. In his younger days he had served as a soldier for six years, fighting the Spaniards. It was during this period that he was three times wounded, sustaining severe injuries to his throat and face.

La Rochefoucauld's liking for conflict extended to his civilian life, when he ill-advisedly joined the Fronde, a rebellion by French aristocrats against the constantly increasing power of the throne. Richelieu once imprisoned him in the Bastille, if only for six days, and he came to hate that cardinal's successor, Mazarin, with a virulent loathing. He was also constantly embroiled in a series of lawsuits against other members of the aristocracy on the trivialities of precedence.

At 53, La Rochefoucauld had resigned himself to the unbridled power of Louis XIV's monarchy, and settled in Paris. There he joined the new game in fashion in the city's salons, the invention of epigrams on the manners and mores of the time. And here the mocking La Rochefoucauld came into his own.

'You are never as unhappy as you think, nor as happy as you had hoped', he wrote. Acidly, he pointed out that 'we are all strong enough to bear the misfortunes of others'.

An accomplished courtier of the fair sex, he reserved some of his more pointed thrusts for the field of love. 'If you judge love by the majority of its effects', he wrote, 'it resembles hatred more than friendship'. He observed that 'Jealousy is always born with love but does not always die with it', and 'It is more difficult to be faithful to your mistress when you are happy than when you are treated badly'. He also coined one of the all-time great seduction lines: 'If we resist our passions, it is more because they are weak than because we are strong.'

In 1665, La Rochefoucauld published the first edition of his *Maximes*, perhaps reflecting a cynical view even of himself with the epigram: 'When vanity does not make us talk, there's not much we want to say.' Five more editions appeared before his death fifteen years later.

The start of the greatest career

1787 Today a young man not quite eighteen years of age joined the British Army as an ensign in the 73rd Highland Regiment. He was shy, of indifferent health, and played the violin. Born in Dublin into an old family of the Anglo-Irish nobility now in reduced circumstances, he was a product of Eton and the Royal Academy of Equitation in France, where he had received a year's instruction in riding, swordplay and mathematics.

The young man wasn't looking forward to service in the army – it was a derelict time for that institution after the defeat in North America and before the coming war against republican France – but it was not in his character to protest his fate. To the contrary, he would make the best of it.

The commission came via the head of the family, his older brother Richard, who had importuned the Lord Lieutenant of Ireland, the Duke of Rutland, for it. The ensign signed his name A. Wesley. It was not until 1798, when the older brother was to be made a marquess, that the family name was realigned for heraldic purposes to Wellesley. In that year he was Colonel Arthur Wellesley. One day he would be the Duke of Wellington.

Also on this day
AD 180: Roman Emperor Marcus Aurelius dies of plague * c. AD 389: St Patrick, the patron saint of Ireland, is born * 1861: The Kingdom of Italy is proclaimed and Victor Emmanuel becomes its first king

18 March

Ivan the Terrible dies at last

1584 On this day death finally relieved the world of the burden of Russia's Ivan the Terrible. He had lived for 54 years, over 50 of them as ruler.

Ivan was born near Moscow on 25 August 1530. He became Prince of Moscow when his father died three years later, but he lived in fear of the *boyars* (court nobility) until he began to take an active role in state affairs at thirteen.

One of his initial acts was to have the most hated boyar, Prince Andrei Shuisky, seized and torn apart by a pack of hounds.

In 1547, when he was sixteen, Ivan was proclaimed the first Tsar of all the Russias, a new title derived from the Roman 'caesar' or emperor. He greatly centralised his country and took the first steps in turning it from an Asiatic backwater into a European nation, a task finally accomplished by Peter the Great 100 years later.

Russia was at war during almost the entirety of Ivan's reign. Although he successfully defeated the Tartars and conquered Kazan, his other conflicts, especially against Poland and Sweden, were indecisive. But the losses he endured seemed to embitter him, and he increasingly shrugged off the counsel of his nobles, becoming ever more tyrannical. By the time he was 30 he was enjoying unfettered personal rule and instituted a reign of terror among Russia's nobility, justifying his despotism with the words: 'We have ascended the throne by the bidding of God.'

Prone to fits of insane rage, Ivan saw conspiracy everywhere. His answer was torture and death, and his means of execution included disembowelment, burning at the stake, impalement, drowning and burial alive, punishments that he often supervised personally. It is said that some victims were fed to wild bears.

One of Ivan's worst excesses was his massacre of the citizens of Novgorod, whom he suspected of being on the point of rebellion. Without waiting for confirmation of the charge, he led his army into the city and slaughtered 60,000 men, women and children.

In his paranoia, Ivan established a bodyguard of 6,000 men, known as the *oprichniki*, and authorised them to operate like a gang of malicious cut-throats beyond the law. He considered torture a suitable weapon of state, and once had his personal physician racked and roasted alive on a spit on suspicions of treachery.

Ivan's inhuman contempt for others reached an artistic peak on the completion of St Basil's Cathedral in Moscow. So taken was he by its splendour that he ordered blinded the group of architects who had designed it, to ensure that no other building so beautiful could ever be constructed.

One of the few people Ivan felt he could trust was his son, also named Ivan, who was heir to the throne. But when the younger Ivan was 28, one afternoon he began an argument with his father, who became so incensed that he beat him to death with an iron-tipped rod.

During his last days Ivan's body became swollen and racked with pain. When his doctors could find no cure he turned to clairvoyants and astrologers, but they helped no more than his physicians.

A few days before his death, the Tsar invited the English ambassador to his palace. Showing him some precious stones, Ivan pronounced: 'Look how they lose their colour. They proclaim my end. I have been poisoned.' When death finally came to him, he was playing a game of chess – against himself, for it was unthinkable that anyone could defeat the Tsar of Russia. He was buried in the Cathedral of St Michael in the Kremlin.

Ivan's death has been variously attributed to dysentery, syphilis and other fatal diseases, but over four centuries after his demise his tomb was opened for tests on his desiccated corpse. His body contained toxic levels of arsenic and mercury, suggesting that indeed Russia's first Tsar had died at the hands of a poisoner, proving the old adage that even a paranoid can have real enemies.

Mac-Mahon crushes the Paris Commune

1871 The people of Montmartre were fed up with their new government, the newly formed Third Republic, for they believed that too many concessions were being made to the victorious Prussians who still occupied large parts of France in the aftermath of the Franco-Prussian War.

On 18 March these doughty citizens commandeered 171 cannons to prevent their capture by the Prussians, and when French forces appeared to reclaim them, the crowd seized and shot several French generals. This was the start of the Paris Commune.

In response to the slaughter of the generals, French troops began a siege of Paris that lasted two months. During that time the Commune leaders became more and more extreme, executing enemies and hostages, including the Archbishop of Paris.

Finally, on 28 May, French forces under General Mac-Mahon entered the city. Revenge on the Communards was swift and terrible; some 17,000 were executed, including women and children. So ended the Commune, crushed by the forces of the Third Republic.

Bismarck is forced to resign

1890 For 28 years, Otto von Bismarck had been the virtual dictator of first Prussia and then the united Germany that he had largely created himself.

But for all his achievements, he had enemies aplenty, particularly the liberals of the day who objected to his reactionary domestic policies. 'He is for the Germans', said the historian Brandes, 'what a pair of excellent and extraordinarily strong spectacles are for a short-sighted man: a good thing for the patient that he can get them, but a great misfortune that he should need them'.

In 1888, young Prince Wilhelm had become Kaiser Wilhelm II. He prided himself on his liberal ideas and resented the intransigent dominance of the 75-year-old Iron Chancellor. But perhaps what stuck in his mind was a friend's comment that 'if Bismarck had been his chancellor, Frederick certainly would never have become Frederick the Great'.

Unwilling (or afraid) to fire Bismarck, Wilhelm needed almost two years to manoeuvre him into a forced resignation. But finally on 18 March 1890, the great chancellor resigned. With him went his policies of friendship towards

Russia and benevolent neutrality towards Austria. It was Germany's first long step towards the First World War.

Also on this day

1455: Florentine artist Fra Angelico dies * 1745: Robert Walpole, first Prime Minister of Great Britain, dies * 1913: King George I of Greece is shot and killed

19 March

The last Templar's last curse

1314 Today Jacques de Molay, the last Grand Master of the Templars, was burned at the stake in Paris, his eyes fixed on Notre Dame in the distance.

A French knight from Champagne named Huges de Payns founded the Order of the Temple in 1128, becoming its first Grand Master. The Templars' mission was to guard the passage of pilgrims en route to the Holy Land.

Two centuries later the Templars had grown immensely wealthy, and Jacques de Molay had the misfortune to be in charge when France's King Philip the Fair, greedy for the Templars' riches, decided on the wholesale destruction of the order.

Arrested in 1307 with all the other Templar knights in France, Molay kept a hard silence of seven long years in prison in Paris, strenuously denying any wrongdoing, even after the order was suppressed in 1312. He was determined to take his defence to the only man who could save him, the Pope. Unfortunately for Molay, however, Pope Clement V was virtually a household pet of King Philip's. (It was this same Clement, a Frenchman by birth, who moved the Papal See from Rome to Avignon.) So when the day came for Grand Master Molay to be judged, the Pope dispatched three cardinals to do the job, keeping himself well clear.

Molay was on the point of being condemned to life imprisonment, and he realised that he would have only this one chance to defend himself and the order.

The cardinals were thrown into confusion by Molay's eloquent defence, and decided to take the issue back to Pope Clement. But Philip the Fair would not wait. The same day a royal council was convoked, and the Grand Master was condemned once more, this time to the stake.

As the sun set, guards took Jacques de Molay to the place of execution, dressed only in a cloth shirt. 'God will avenge our death', he said. 'Philip, thy life is condemned. I await thee within a year at the Tribune of God.' He then asked to be turned on the stake to face the towers of Notre Dame, barely visible in the distance.

Just 31 days later Pope Clement suddenly died, and on 29 November of that same year, Philip the Fair too was dead, just as the Grand Master had foretold.

132

La Salle orders one exploration too many

1687 On this day René-Robert Cavelier, sieur de La Salle, one of the great explorers of North America, was murdered at the age of 44. A Frenchman ennobled by Louis XIV for his exploits in North America, this Jesuit-trained adventurer had once wanted to become a priest, but instead became a fur trader and would-be empire builder for France. He was the first white man ever to 'sail' the Mississippi from top to bottom (he did it in a canoe) and in 1682 he claimed the Louisiana Territory for his country, naming it after his sovereign. (For this latter deed, La Salle received scant thanks from King Louis, who wrote to the governor of Canada: 'I am convinced … that the discovery of the sieur de La Salle is useless and that such enterprises ought to be prevented in the future.')

Determined to start a French colony at the mouth of the Mississippi, La Salle returned to France for approval (and money) from King Louis and then in 1684 set sail with four ships and 400 men. His plans extended to conquering part of Mexico, then owned by Spain. But misfortune plagued him. First the Spanish captured one of his ships. Then he missed the mouth of the Mississippi by some 500 miles, and two more ships were wrecked on the coast of what is now Texas.

Desperate, La Salle went ashore at Matagorda Bay. Only 45 of his men remained alive. Unable to locate the Mississippi, he ordered a march north to Canada, then a French colony, the one destination he knew where they would find safety, Frenchmen, and a ship to take them back to France. But Canada was some 2,500 miles away through uncharted wilderness, and his men thought their chances were better if they waited for a rescue vessel. When the headstrong La Salle insisted, his men rebelled, and several ambushed their leader and killed him.

Like many adventurers, La Salle's strong personality was the reason for his success and ultimately the cause for his failure. As one of his subordinates on his last voyage later wrote: 'His firmness, his courage, his great knowledge of the arts and sciences, which made him equal to every undertaking, and his untiring energy, which enabled him to surmount every obstacle, would have won at last a glorious success for his grand enterprise, had not all his fine qualities been counterbalanced by a haughtiness of manner which often made him unsupportable, and by a harshness toward those under his command, which drew upon him an implacable hatred, and was the cause of his death.'

Death of the Dutchman who ruled England

1702 Originally *Stadholder* of the Netherlands, William of Orange married a king's daughter and then chased his poor father-in-law from the kingdom in order to put the crown on his own head. It helped, of course, that the father-in-law was the notoriously unpopular James II of England.

William reigned as King of England for thirteen years, five of them with his wife Mary and then alone after she died from smallpox. Although he was a foreigner, England owes much to him. It was he who forged England's grand alliance with Austria, Holland, Portugal, Denmark, Prussia and Savoy to contain the ambitious and powerful Louis XIV. It was also William who foresaw the greatness of John Churchill, the future Duke of Marlborough, putting him in charge of the Alliance's armies, even though William died before Churchill's illustrious victories.

William was a dour man who cared most about the great international issues of his day. Falsely rumoured to be a homosexual, he let no private feelings sway his judgements in running the nation. As he grew older, poor health plagued him. At the age of 51 he broke his collarbone when he was thrown as his horse tripped over a mole-hill at Hampton Court. Weak as he was, he was unable to recover, dying this day, the first and last King of England of the House of Orange.

Also on this day

1452: Frederick III is crowned in Rome, to reign for 53 years, longer than any other Holy Roman Emperor

20 March

A usurper king meets his maker

1413 His face disfigured by swellings and lesions, his body weakened by a stroke, today England's usurper King Henry IV died repenting his past at the age of 46.

Grandson of Edward III, Henry was born in Bolingbroke Castle in Lincolnshire, and therefore referred to in his time (and by William Shakespeare) as Bolingbroke. As a young man he had been handsome and muscular, a fine athlete who excelled at jousting, loved music and spoke Latin, French and English. When he was eleven his cousin, who was just ten months his junior, inherited the throne as Richard II, and Henry's father, John of Gaunt, became de facto ruler during the young King's minority.

But when Richard started to rule in his own right, Bolingbroke – and most of the country's great nobles – soon lost patience with his spendthrift, feckless ways and joined a group of opposition leaders who forced the King to send his closest favourite, Robert de Vere, Earl of Oxford, into exile. Richard neither forgot nor forgave, and ten years later he exiled Bolingbroke in his turn, confiscating his property. But when Richard made the error of leaving the country for an expedition to Ireland, Bolingbroke returned at the head of an army, seized and imprisoned Richard and claimed the throne for himself as Henry IV. He then had Richard surreptitiously murdered.

Because of this usurpation, Henry faced continuous revolt during his thirteen-year reign. In 1405 he crushed an uprising at the Battle of Shipton Moor, after which he had Richard Scrope, Archbishop of York, hanged, drawn and quartered for siding with the rebels. Contemporaries report that within a few hours of this dreadful execution of a man of God, the King was screaming in pain from rashes that appeared on his face and a tumour that bulged beneath his nose. Many thought he had been stricken by leprosy. It was, his enemies insisted, celestial punishment for usurping the throne and putting the rightful King to death. (Modern science suggests that Henry's loathsome disease was actually syphilis or tubercular gangrene.)

Hoping to escape this curse, Henry made plans to go on crusade to the Holy Land, but continually postponed his departure after he heard a prophecy that he would die in Jerusalem.

On this day in 1413, Henry determined to do penance for his crimes and set out for the shrine of St Edward the Confessor in Westminster Abbey. There, as he knelt to pray, he collapsed unconscious and was carried into an adjoining room. When he came to, the stricken King asked where he was, to be told that he lay in the Jerusalem Chamber of the cathedral (so called because of tapestries depicting the history of Jerusalem hung from its walls). Remembering the terrible prophecy that he would die in Jerusalem, Henry knew his end was at hand.

The dying king blessed his son (about to become Henry V) and whispered to those around him: 'God alone knows by what right I took the crown.' In a few minutes he was dead – in Jerusalem as the prophecy had foretold.

Napoleon's return to Paris

1815 To the consternation of Europeans everywhere but to the joy of Frenchmen, Napoleon entered Paris today in triumph, borne shoulder-high to the Tuileries by a huge crowd crying 'Vive l'Empereur!' Only three weeks earlier he had escaped his exile on Elba to land near Cannes and take the Continent by surprise. As he travelled north through a France war-weary but discontented under the restored Bourbon regime, peasants hailed him as their champion, and his veterans, forgetting the realities of recent campaigns, cheerfully disobeyed orders and flocked to his side.

Napoleon's cause seemed to gather strength with every mile of his progress. In Vienna the Congress pronounced him an outlaw. In Paris King Louis XVIII and the royal court decamped for the safety of Ghent.

A handbill caught the spirit of the day:

The Tiger has broken out of his den.
The Ogre has been three days at sea.
The Wretch has landed at Fréjus.
The Buzzard has reached Antibes.
The Invader has arrived in Grenoble.

The General has entered Lyon.
Napoleon slept at Fontainebleau last night.
The Emperor will proceed to the Tuileries today.
His Imperial Majesty will address his loyal subjects tomorrow.

The Hundred Days had begun.

Ben Franklin vows friendship with France

1778 On orders from the King, the treaty had been signed on 6 February, and Louis XVI of France had invited the American Commissioners to come today to his great palace at Versailles to avow the pact of friendship.

Amid the splendours of mirrored Versailles, among the lace and powdered wigs of Europe's most regal court was the foremost American representative, Benjamin Franklin, who arrived dressed for his role as rustic American philosopher, without wig or sword, clad in brown velvet, hair hanging loose and spectacles on his nose.

'Firmly assure Congress', said Louis to Franklin, 'of my friendship. I hope this will be for the good of the two nations.' Indeed, the treaty was greatly to the good of America, as it brought France into the war against Great Britain, helping to assure American independence.

America's success at throwing off a king, however, brought very little good to poor King Louis, who was the primary victim of his own country's revolt against monarchy only eleven years later. One of democratic France's chief inspirations was democratic America.

Also on this day

43 BC: Roman poet Ovid is born * 1727: English scientist Sir Isaac Newton dies in London * 1815: Switzerland becomes permanently neutral

21 March

Thomas Cranmer perishes by fire

1556 Thomas Cranmer was the diametric opposite of his famous forerunner, Thomas Becket. Both served kings named Henry and achieved Britain's highest ecclesiastical office as Archbishop of Canterbury. Yet while Becket died a martyr defending the Church from the powers of the King, Cranmer martyred himself defending royal authority over the Church.

Cranmer sincerely believed in royal power. To Henry VIII he was the perfect minister, helping him with two divorces, promulgating the Treason Laws and generally increasing the King's authority. Henry died in 1547, but Cranmer retained his influence during the brief reign of Edward VI. When

Edward died at fifteen after only six years as King, Cranmer followed the dying monarch's wish and backed Lady Jane Grey to succeed. But when Bloody Mary Tudor gained the throne instead, Cranmer was tried and convicted of treason for his support of Lady Jane Grey, and of heresy for his anti-papal acts of the past twenty years.

Sentenced to death, Cranmer at first recanted his heresy, but when asked to repeat his recantation in public, he refused, retracting it instead. For this affront to the true Church, today he paid the ultimate price, death by burning.

As the flames leapt up, Cranmer held out his right hand that had signed his recantations, saying: 'This is the hand that wrote it, therefore shall it suffer first punishment.' Then, to the horror of the onlookers, he thrust it into the fire. And so in unspeakable agony died the Archbishop who, more than any other man, built the Church of England.

The most expensive divorce in history

1152 Eleanor of Aquitaine had been married to King Louis VII of France for almost fifteen years and the marriage had produced three daughters. But the lack of a male heir (no woman could inherit the throne of France) drove the King to seek an annulment. Perhaps his judgement was also swayed by his wife's obvious boredom with her solemn husband and her occasional dalliances. But Louis must somehow have forgotten that Eleanor controlled about a quarter of all of France and was in her own right the richest woman in Europe. It was the most costly annulment before or since.

The annulment became official on 21 March 1152, the Pope's consent based on the grounds of consanguinity. Within two months, Eleanor was married once more, this time to young Henry of Anjou, who would shortly become Henry II of England. With her Eleanor brought her immense lands, instantly making Henry one of Europe's most powerful nobles and dramatically lessening the power of France. And only three months after the wedding Eleanor gave birth to Henry's child, explaining her haste to remarry.

The best and worst of Napoleon

1804 History knows few characters as controversial as Napoleon Bonaparte, and today saw him at his best and worst.

The most dramatic event of the day was the execution by firing squad of the duc d'Enghien at the Château de Vincennes east of Paris.

The duc d'Enghien was an attractive and well meaning Bourbon prince who lived in the German castle of Ettenheim in Baden, idly plotting with other aristocratic émigrés the overthrow of the government, of which Napoleon was First Consul. But d'Enghien came from one of France's greatest aristocratic families and thus could be a candidate for the throne should the monarchy be restored. Then Napoleon received intelligence (false, as it turned out) that linked d'Enghien with a serious conspiracy of several generals. Incensed, he sent three brigades of infantry plus 300 dragoons across the Rhine into Germany to seize the poor prince as he lay sleeping peacefully in his undefended house.

Taken back across the border to Vincennes, after a mock trial the 31-year-old d'Enghien was refused a priest, led into the château's moat and summarily shot beside a freshly dug grave. This brutal kidnap and murder horrified most of Europe, and even one of Napoleon's chief advisors, Joseph Fouché, aghast at public reaction, sardonically remarked: 'C'est plus qu'un crime; c'est une faute.' (It's more than a crime; it's a blunder.)

On the very day of the execution Napoleon published a new civil code, the Code Napoleon. This immense body of law was a dramatic improvement over the hodge-podge of existing and sometimes conflicting laws, and its basic fairness was so great that even today it remains the basic law of France, Belgium and Luxembourg.

Also on this day

1685: German composer Johann Sebastian Bach is born * 1806: Mexican President Benito Juárez is born

22 March

'Mehr Licht!'

1832 Johann Wolfgang von Goethe was Germany's and arguably history's greatest poet, but at the age of 83 his end was upon him. Stirring on his bed, his voice steady, Goethe spoke once more. 'Mehr Licht!' he called (More light!), and then he was gone, leaving some of history's most famous dying words behind him.

What did he mean by that final cry? Was he wishing he'd had more clarity and understanding in the past? Or was he seeing ahead into the world to come?

Neither, according to today's iconoclastic historians. What Goethe actually said was: 'Open the second shutter, so that more light can come in.'

Henri IV enters Paris

1594 Even though King Henri IV had abjured the Protestant faith in July 1593, it was almost a year before the strongly Catholic citizens of Paris permitted him in their city. But finally, on 22 March 1594, Paris opened its gates and Henri IV could at last truly call himself the King of France. As Henri himself had famously said: 'Paris vaut bien une messe.' (Paris is worth a Mass.)

1599: Flemish portraitist Anthony van Dyke is born * 1646: The Battle of Stow-on-the-Wold, the last of the English Civil War, is fought * 1820: American Commodore Stephen Decatur dies in a duel

23 March

Another tsar is murdered

1801 In the 302 years that the Romanovs ruled Russia, eighteen members of the family held the throne, four women and fourteen men. Of those fourteen tsars, five were murdered. This day was the turn of Tsar Paul I.

Paul was the son of Peter III and Catherine the Great (or certainly of Catherine, who had taken at least three lovers while Peter was still alive). Paul's natural nervousness and instability were reinforced by the knowledge that his father had been assassinated, almost certainly with Catherine's connivance.

Becoming Tsar on Catherine's death at the end of 1796, Paul already showed signs of insanity, especially the megalomania so common to absolute dictators. 'In Russia, anyone to whom I speak is great', he remarked, 'but only while I speak to him'.

In order to increase his own authority, Paul downgraded the prerogatives of Russia's nobles, constantly changed officials in his government, and reduced the power of local administrations. Fatally, he instituted severe military discipline in the army, occasionally sending high-ranking officers into Siberian exile for errors on the parade ground. Even his foreign policy was disastrous: by 1800 he had broken off diplomatic relations with Austria, was on the verge of war with England and was actually at war with France.

After only four years of Paul's rule, his aristocracy had had enough. A group of high-ranking officers and nobles approached Paul's 22-year-old son Alexander (soon to be Alexander I) and persuaded him of the need for his father's overthrow, assuring him that Paul's life would be spared. Alexander believed the plotters – or wished to believe them – and gave his permission.

On 23 March 1801 the military governor of St Petersburg, Count Peter von Pahlen, and several fellow conspirators entered the Tsar's bedroom in the Mikhaylovsky Palace and cut their ruler down.

Paul was the third Romanov tsar to be murdered in 40 years. The next was his grandson Alexander II 80 years later.

Pope Innocent bests King John

1208 Pope Innocent III was an Italian from Aragni whose primary objective was to increase the temporal power of the papacy. In both Italy and Germany he played one prince off against another to the benefit of Rome, and he liked to show his strength by challenging the marriages of kings. He forced Philip Augustus of France to take back his Danish wife Ingeborg, made Alfonso IX of León give up his wife Berengaria on grounds of consanguinity, and caused Peter of Aragon to break off his intended marriage to Bianca of Navarre.

Innocent's greatest victory came against King John of England. Each had put forward a candidate for Archbishop of Canterbury, and when John refused to yield, the Pope placed all of England under ban of interdict on this day in 1208. Interdict was a potent weapon in the religious 13th century. It meant not only that no church services could be held but also no marriages, baptisms or funerals.

But still John insisted, so Innocent excommunicated him. Even that produced no result, so Innocent used his final weapon: he declared John deposed as King of England and nominated Philip Augustus as his successor, suggesting that Philip might invade with papal blessings.

This last move finally brought John to his knees (or, as Innocent no doubt would have termed it, to his senses). Not only did he accept the Pope's candidate as Archbishop, he declared England a fief of Rome and Innocent his temporal overlord. Innocent had in effect conquered the nation, something that no one had done since William the Conqueror a century and a half before, and that no one would ever do again.

At last Pope Innocent was appeased. He lifted his interdict in May 1213. It had lasted over five years.

Also on this day

1842: French novelist Stendhal (Marie-Henri Beyle) dies * 1887: Spanish painter Juan Gris is born * 1919: Mussolini founds his own party in Italy, the Fasci di Combattimento * 1953: French painter Raoul Dufy dies

24 March

Queen Elizabeth dies

1603 'Nature's common work is done, and he that was born to die hath paid his tribute', once wrote Elizabeth of England in a letter of condolence. Now, as the shadows of age closed in, it was her turn to pay her tribute after 45 years as Queen.

Earlier in her reign Elizabeth had told Parliament: 'As for me, I see no such great cause why I should either be fond to live or fear to die. I have had good experience of this world, and I know what it is to be subject and what to be a sovereign.' But as she grew older, doubts began to enter her mind. She was, according to Sir Walter Raleigh, 'a lady surprised by time'.

Her last years were sombre. Always vain, she wore a tawny wig to hide her grey and thinning hair, and by her decree her palace at Richmond contained not a single mirror. The friends and counsellors of her youth were gone, and she knew her time was near. It was rumoured that her gloomy ghost wandered the palace corridors, anticipating her demise.

During March 1603 for four days she refused to go to bed, remaining seated on her cushions. One day she spent all the daylight hours in silence, her finger in her mouth. Yet she was not senile, but seemingly contemplating her life and past and what was to come. Even at the end she had not lost her authority or her bite; when her closest advisor Sir Robert Cecil presumed to give her instructions, she snapped: 'Must! Is *must* a word to be addressed to princes? Little man, little man!'

On 23 March Elizabeth announced: 'I wish not to live any longer, but desire to die.' At three o'clock the following morning the greatest queen that England (and perhaps any nation) would ever know drifted away, the Archbishop of Canterbury at her side in prayer. Legend asserts that her coronation ring could be removed only by cutting off her finger, symbolising her union with her country. Elizabeth had lived for 69 years, six months and seventeen days.

Also on this day

1401: Mongol leader Tamerlane the Great captures Damascus * 1603: The crowns of England and Scotland are united when King James VI of Scotland succeeds to the English throne

25 March

Trial by Jury *opens in London*

1875 On this date *Trial by Jury* opened at London's Royalty Theatre. It was not the first joint enterprise of William S. Gilbert and Arthur Sullivan – four years earlier they had collaborated on *Thespis*, which ran 64 performances – but it was the first of their operettas that are still performed today. It was also the first to be produced with the theatre impresario Richard D'Oyly Carte. *Trial by Jury* was an immediate success, and in its first two years ran for some 300 performances. Critics and audiences were delighted by the close partnership of Gilbert's words and Sullivan's music, one reviewer noting that they seemed to have 'proceeded simultaneously from one and the same brain'. Only 45 minutes in length, much shorter than any other G&S operetta, *Trial by Jury* was usually performed as part of a double-bill with *HMS Pinafore* or *The Pirates of Penzance*.

Over the next 21 years, Gilbert and Sullivan would collaborate on twelve more of the works that have come to be known as the Savoy Operas, after the Savoy Theatre which D'Oyly Carte opened for his theatre company in 1881 and in which all the operas after *Patience* had their first English performances. Mostly satirical in manner and with 'topsy-turvy' plots, the Savoy Operas poked fun at many prominent features of the late Victorian age.

The object of *Trial by Jury*'s gentle satire is the British legal system. The plot involves a breach of promise of marriage in which the Defendant (Edwin) is being sued for breaking off his engagement to the Plaintiff (Angelina). The trial is complicated when both the Judge and the jury fall in love with Angelina.

'Never, never, never, since I joined the human race', sings the Judge, 'Saw I so exquisitely fair a face'. 'We love you fondly and would make you ours', intone the jurymen. Faced with an unsympathetic courtroom, Edwin makes an offer: 'I'll marry this lady today, and I'll marry the other tomorrow.' Plaintiff's Counsel, however, balks at this solution on the precedent that 'In the reign of James the Second, it was generally reckoned as a rather serious crime to marry two wives at one time.' Exasperated by the parties' inability to reach a settlement, the Judge finally interrupts the proceedings with a notable decision: 'Put your briefs upon the shelf, I shall marry her myself', at which the entire courtroom bursts into a *finale* of song and celebration. Curtain.

Birth of the first Plantagenet king

1133 Today the town of Le Mans in north-western France is better known for its annual motor race, but in the 12th century it belonged to the counts of Anjou, whose domain centred on the fine old town of Angers on the River Loire. It was here on this day that Henry II of England was born, the first king of a dynasty that would reign longer than any other English royal house.

Henry's father was Count Geoffrey of Anjou, a handsome man with a taste for riding, hunting and women. In springtime the Anjou countryside is yellow with a type of gorse called *planta genista*, and as a young man Geoffrey took to wearing a sprig of this cheerful bloom in his hat. He enjoyed this habit so much that he soon came to be known as Geoffrey Plantagenet.

When he reached a precocious sixteen, Geoffrey married 26-year-old Matilda, daughter of Henry I of England, in a grand dynastic marriage. Four years later the future Henry II was born.

Young Henry grew into a thickset, athletic man with red-blond hair, grey eyes and boundless energy. At nineteen he arranged his own dynastic marriage, also to an older woman, the beautiful Eleanor of Aquitaine, eleven years his senior, who was the former Queen of France and the greatest landholder in the kingdom. Two years after that he inherited the throne of England.

Henry II would rule England for 35 years and sire two sons who would become among the most famous and worst kings in British history, Richard the Lion-Heart and John. In all, the Plantagenet dynasty that he founded would hold the English crown for 332 years, until the death of Richard III at Bosworth Field.

The last of Light Horse Harry

1818 On this date Henry Lee, known as Light Horse Harry, died at the age of 62 on Cumberland Island, Georgia, on his way home from a long stay in the West

Indies, where he had gone to restore his health – or, as his enemies insisted, to escape financial and political embarrassments.

Scion of an old Tidewater family, Princetonian, *beau sabreur*, celebrated cavalry commander during the American Revolution, governor of Virginia and member of Congress, Lee was an important leader of the new republic. But he made a series of bad land investments after the war, which eventually led not only to ruin and scandal – it became known that he bounced a cheque on George Washington – but also to time spent in debtors' prison. In 1812, while defending an outspoken Federalist newspaper editor from an angry Republican mob, Lee sustained the injuries that occasioned his retirement to the Caribbean.

Although he left a heavily encumbered estate and a family in penury, Lee also bequeathed to posterity three notable items: his memoirs of the Revolutionary War; the famous phrase from his eulogy to Washington, 'first in war, first in peace, first in the hearts of his countrymen'; and his fourth son by his second marriage, Robert E. Lee, who many years later would lead the Confederacy against the Union that his father had helped found.

Also on this day

1347: St Catherine of Siena is born * 1436: Brunelleschi's Dome in Florence is consecrated * 1804: South American liberator Simón Bolívar leaves Spain for South America * 1821: Greece declares independence from Turkey

26 March

Beethoven bows out

1827 Opinions about Ludwig van Beethoven varied greatly, depending on whether they were about his musical ability or about the man himself. Mozart, under whom he studied, predicted when Beethoven was still only 21 that 'he will give the world something worth listening to'. On the other hand, Goethe, who met him only when he was over 40, cantankerous and almost deaf, thought he was 'an utterly untamed personality, who is not completely wrong in thinking the world detestable, but who certainly does not make it any more enjoyable for himself or for others by his attitude'.

Born in Bonn, Beethoven spent virtually all of his productive years in Vienna. He was a difficult and solitary man totally devoted to his music. Unlike Mozart, who lived and died on the edge of penury for lack of sponsors, Beethoven was recognised and supported throughout his career. Although never rich, he was comfortable. His great affliction was his increasing deafness, which started before he was 30. By the last years of his life he was completely deaf.

In December 1826, Beethoven turned 56 and was showing signs of what was thought to be dropsy but which retrospective diagnosis shows to have been cirrhosis of the liver. His condition continued to worsen until at the end of March he was on the point of death. There is no doubt that he died on the afternoon of 26 March, as a great thunderstorm raged outside, but controversy continues over his last words. One version has him histrionically murmuring the classical ending to Roman plays: 'Plaudite, amici, comoedia finita est.' (Applaud, my friends, the comedy is over.) Elsewhere he is reported to have concluded: 'I shall hear in heaven.' A third story describes him receiving a shipment of special Rhine wine which he had ordered months before. Taking a sip, he mumbled, 'Pity, pity … Too late!'

Three days after his demise Beethoven was buried in Währing churchyard in Vienna, after a funeral attended by 20,000 people.

Beethoven remained a bachelor all his life, in spite of several attempts on his part to marry. When he died, three letters were found locked in his cabinet, all including declarations of love and addressed to his 'Immortal Beloved'. The letters are undated and had never been sent, and the identity of his 'Immortal Beloved' has never been discovered.

Also on this day

1726: Blenheim's architect, Sir John Vanbrugh, dies * 1859: English poet A.E. Housman is born * 1874: American poet Robert Frost is born * 1892: American poet Walt Whitman dies * 1902: British imperialist Cecil Rhodes dies

27 March

The passing of Eleanor of Aquitaine

1204 When she died today she had seen it, done it, lived it all: Eleanor of Aquitaine, the most remarkable woman of her time. She was raised in Poitiers in the traditions of courtly love and the troubadour. In Paris she heard the preaching of Abelard, St Bernard and later St Thomas Becket. A great beauty and sometimes a great scandal, Eleanor was a duchess, descendant of Charlemagne and the richest woman in Europe, her domain covering about a quarter of modern France. (With its own distinct language, Aquitaine was the land of the *langue d'oc*, so named because its inhabitants said 'oc' rather than 'oui'.)

Eleanor had two husbands, both kings. With her first, Louis VII of France, she went on crusade and enlivened the trip by cuckolding him with her own uncle (not an incestuous betrayal, as her uncle was her blood-aunt's husband). With her second, Henry II of England, she founded the Plantagenet dynasty that lasted over three centuries. In all she bore ten children including England's most storied king, Richard the Lion-Heart, and England's worst, King John.

One of Eleanor's granddaughters was Blanche of Castile. When Eleanor was 78 years old she personally brought Blanche from Spain to wed the King of France. At 80 she directed the defence of a town under siege from a marauding army.

144

Finally Eleanor slipped away at 82, an immense age for her time, carried away according to a contemporary chronicle 'as a candle in the sconce goeth out when the wind striketh it'. She lies buried where she died, in the ancient monastery of Fontevrault in the calm of the Valley of the Loire.

Robert the Bruce is King

1306 Today Robert the Bruce was crowned King of Scotland at the age of 30. Scotland had become a fief of England in 1174 but had struggled for independence ever since. Robert was the man who would achieve it.

From the day of his coronation Robert fought against the hated English and finally defeated them resoundingly in the Battle of Bannockburn. In 1328, just a year before his death, England at last recognised Scotland's independence.

Scotland remained independent for another 275 years until James VI of Scotland inherited the English throne as well, as James I.

Also on this day

1625: James I dies in his hunting lodge at Theobalds, Essex * 1770: Italian painter Giovanni Battista Tiepolo dies * 1809: Georges Eugène, Baron Haussman, the man who redesigned Paris, is born

28 March

Constantinople becomes Istanbul

1930 For 1,599 years, ten months and seventeen days the great city had been called Constantinople. On this day the Turkish Post Office officially changed the name to Istanbul, by which it had been identified since some time in the 13th century.

There has been a town on the Istanbul site since at least the 7th century BC, when it was settled by Greeks. They called it Byzantium after the perhaps mythical Greek leader Byzas, who captured the land from wild Thracian tribes in 657 BC.

When Rome displaced Greece as the predominant power in the area, Byzantium became a free city under Roman overlordship, and only in AD 324, almost a millennium after its founding, did it finally become Constantinople.

On 18 September 324 the Western Roman Emperor Constantine defeated his rival Licinius at Chrysopolis to take command of the entire empire. After the battle he retired for the night to nearby Byzantium, where he dreamt that he saw the guardian deity of the city, an old crone, forlorn and failing from age and infirmities. Suddenly she was transformed into a radiant young woman, and in his dream he placed a diadem on her head. When Constantine awoke he interpreted his dream as a sign from heaven, and decided to found a great city on the site.

The Emperor shortly led a group of his assistants on foot around the outskirts of Byzantium (then a smallish town), tracing the boundaries of his new city with his lance. His assistants were astonished by its size, but, according to Christian hagiographers, the Emperor insisted: 'I shall advance till He, the invisible guide who marches before me, thinks proper to stop.'

Constantine immediately undertook a huge building programme, tripling the size of the city, and on 11 May 330 dedicated it as Constantinople (Constantinopolis), replacing Rome as capital of the empire.

Constantinople became the greatest city in the civilised world, but over the centuries it had to weather many storms, including a 6th-century plague that killed most of the inhabitants. It was attacked innumerable times, but thanks to its huge 5th-century walls, it remained unconquerable.

By the 13th century, Anatolian Turks were already referring to Constantinople as Istinpolin, derived from the Greek phrase *eis ten polin* meaning 'in the city'. But even after the Turks finally conquered it in 1453 it remained Constantinople to all but some of its own inhabitants. Over the years the Turks increasingly called it Istanbul, as scarcely a reminder in the city of its Greek or Roman past remained. By the time of the official name change, no trace of Byzantium was left, and the only remnant of the Great Constantine was the eponymous burnt porphyry column that still draws the gazes of tourists in Old Istanbul.

Death of a fat pope

1285 Fat Pope Martin IV, who died today, had only two major objectives during his five-year reign, and he failed at both of them.

Born of noble birth as Simon de Brie in the town now so famous for its cheese, he was short and corpulent, known for his prodigious appetite. Stories abounded of his feats as trencherman, as he spent lavishly for the latest culinary delicacies.

Martin was an advisor to the country's saintly King Louis IX and later his chancellor, but his real patron was Louis's brother, Charles of Anjou, King of Naples and Sicily. It was largely thanks to Charles's influence that he was elected Pope in February 1281.

During the 13th century Christianity was split into two halves, with competing Churches in Rome and Constantinople. Martin's first ambition was to bring all Christians back under the aegis of Rome. In this his powerful ally was King Charles who, according to a contemporary report, 'hoped to become ruler of the world, rejoining east and west to recreate the great empire of Julius Caesar'. The answer for both Pope and King was to conquer the Byzantine Empire.

While Charles would look after the fighting, Martin would use spiritual weapons. In pursuit of his goal he excommunicated the Byzantine Emperor

Michael VIII Palaeologus, while elevating Charles's planned invasion of Byzantium to the level of a 'Holy Crusade'. But Charles made only one serious (and unsuccessful) attack, and the only result of Martin's excommunication was to split the Church irrevocably.

For King Charles, things then went from bad to worse. Having failed to conquer the Byzantine Empire, he then lost his Kingdom of Sicily during the War of the Sicilian Vespers. So Martin decided to help him get it back in the same manner that he had helped against Michael Palaeologus. This time he excommunicated Peter III of Aragon, who had taken control of Sicily.

The result was predictable: another failure, as Peter stayed firmly in control.

Worn out and disheartened, King Charles died in January 1285 at the age of 59. Not three months later, the obese Pope Martin ingested yet another gargantuan meal and died of dyspepsia, an end that was immortalised by Dante when he included the gluttonous pope in his *Inferno*.

Also on this day

1483: Italian painter Raphael is born in Urbino * 1854: France and Britain declare war on Russia to join the Crimean War * 1939: The Spanish Civil War ends as Madrid surrenders to General Franco * 1941: English novelist Virginia Woolf throws herself into the River Ouse * 1946: Juan Perón is elected President of Argentina * 1969: American President Dwight D. Eisenhower dies

29 March

The Rosenbergs are convicted of treason

1951 Today in New York City, a jury of eleven men and one woman unanimously convicted Julius and Ethel Rosenberg of treason under the terms of the 1917 Espionage Act for providing Communist Russia with secret information regarding the construction of the atomic bomb. One week later they were sentenced to death.

The son of a Polish immigrant garment worker from Manhattan's Lower East Side, 33-year-old Julius Rosenberg had long been a member of America's Communist Party, having joined the Young Communists' League at college when he was only sixteen. During the Second World War his wife Ethel's brother David Greenglass had become an army sergeant assigned to Los Alamos, where the development of the bomb was taking place. Soon Julius and Ethel had persuaded Greenglass to ferret out whatever secrets he could find.

Whenever new information was obtained, it was passed on to a podgy, middle-aged courier named Harry Gold, who served as the liaison with the Soviet vice consul in New York City, Anatoly Yakovlev. From there it made its way to Moscow.

Throughout the war years the Rosenbergs must have believed they would go undetected, but in February 1950 Klaus Fuchs, a British scientist and Russian spy working at Los Alamos, was arrested. Fuchs readily admitted supplying atomic data to the Russians, and he, too, had connections with Gold. The trail soon led to David Greenglass and the Rosenbergs, who were taken into custody.

The trial was one of the most contentious in American history, as both Rosenbergs adamantly denied their guilt, and many left-wingers around the world saw the prosecution as an anti-Communist witch hunt, possibly with anti-Semitic overtones. But Julius and Ethel were convicted, mostly by the testimony of Ethel's brother, who had admitted his own guilt and turned state's evidence. The case against Julius Rosenberg was clear-cut, but the key proof against Ethel was Greenglass's wife's testimony that she had seen Ethel typing out Greenglass's handwritten notes. Greenglass was sentenced to fifteen years in prison, while Gold drew a term of 30, but the judge sentenced the Rosenbergs to death, declaring: 'I consider your crime worse than murder.'

The next two years witnessed an explosion of protest around the world, not so much against the verdict as against the sentence of death. Thousands demonstrated in America and Europe, the Pope asked for clemency, letters of protest rained on the White House, and the Rosenbergs' two sons marched carrying signs reading 'Don't Kill my Mommy and Daddy'. But neither the Supreme Court nor President Eisenhower would intervene.

Just after 8 p.m. on 19 June 1953 in Sing Sing Prison in Ossining, New York, first Julius and then Ethel was strapped into the prison's electric chair. Electrodes were applied to the calf of one leg and the shaven scalp, and dampened with a salt solution to make sure of a good contact. Then a current of some 2,000 volts crackled through the system. Unconsciousness was instantaneous, death virtually so for Julius, but Ethel required three long jolts to die. The Rosenbergs were the first American civilians ever executed during peacetime for treason (although their offences had been committed during a war).

For years after the execution, friends, family and assorted left-wingers proclaimed the Rosenbergs' innocence, and David Greenglass later wrote that the prosecution had pressured him into testifying against his sister, threatening to indict his wife if he refused. But in 1997 Alexandr Feklisov, the Rosenbergs' Russian control officer, publicly described his clandestine meetings with Julius in the 1940s, confirming his guilt. He claimed, however, that he had no first-hand knowledge that Ethel had belonged to the conspiracy.

Birth of a man who would inherit the presidency

1790 Today in the Tidewater region of Virginia south-east of Richmond was born John Tyler, who 51 years later would become President of the United States.

The America in which Tyler was born was a small nation of fewer than 4 million people, of whom almost 700,000 were slaves. There were just sixteen states, of which the most populous was Virginia. Only eleven months earlier George Washington had become its first president.

Coming from a powerful Virginia political family, Tyler was elected to the state legislature at 21, the US Congress at 27, the governorship of Virginia at 35 and the US Senate at 37. Finally, in 1840, he made it to the White House, as Vice President to William Henry Harrison, who had been elected on the alliterative campaign slogan of 'Tippecanoe and Tyler too!' (Tippecanoe was a battle against Indians that Harrison had won almost 30 years before.)

Then suddenly, only weeks into office, Harrison died of pneumonia and Tyler became the first American vice president ever to assume the presidency. He was the country's tenth president, the sixth born in Virginia (and the last one born there until Woodrow Wilson).

A devoted believer in states' rights, Tyler was undistinguished at best as leader of the nation, achieving another presidential first when the House of Representatives, led by former president John Quincy Adams, passed a resolution of impeachment because he had vetoed so many bills. The impeachment failed, but at one point his entire Cabinet resigned except for his Secretary of State Daniel Webster, and his own party, the Whigs, repudiated him for his states'-rights views. Not surprisingly, when his term ended he declined to run for re-election.

Settling back in Virginia, Tyler continued to work for states' rights and the prolongation of slavery, although he initially opposed the secession of the Southern states. On the eve of the Civil War the American population had mushroomed to 31 million, almost ten times its total at Tyler's birth, and included some 3.5 million black slaves. When the Confederacy was established, the slave-owning Tyler, now 70, became a member of the Confederate House of Representatives, but he died in less than a year, just seven months before Abraham Lincoln issued his historic Emancipation Proclamation freeing all the slaves.

Also on this day

1461: The Yorkists defeat the Lancastrians under Henry VI at the Battle of Towton in the Wars of the Roses * 1848: American fur and property tycoon John Jacob Astor dies in New York * 1891: French painter Georges-Pierre Seurat dies

30 March

The bloody Sicilian Vespers

1282 Since his brother Louis IX was a crusading French king and certified saint, Charles of Anjou must have inherited the bad half of the family genes.

Master of most of Italy and Sicily, Charles's tyranny and cold-blooded cruelty soon made him detested throughout his territories, particularly in Sicily with its traditions of lawless independence.

On Easter Monday, 30 March 1282, as the citizens of Palermo flocked to vespers in the church of Santo Spirito, a French soldier grossly insulted a pretty young Sicilian woman. The girl's enraged fiancé immediately drew his dagger and stabbed the soldier to his heart. The violence was contagious, and the local populace exploded in fury against the French. Over 200 French soldiers were slain on the spot, and the killing spread to other parts of Sicily the next day. The bloody event is known in history as the Sicilian Vespers.

The overthrow of Charles of Anjou precipitated a long war for the crown of Sicily between the Angevin kings of Naples and King Peter III of Aragon, but the result for Sicily was almost a century of independence.

So inspiring to an Italian is the story of the Sicilian Vespers that Giuseppe Verdi created an opera around it in 1855.

The greatest military engineer in history

1707 Sébastien le Prestre, marquis de Vauban was perhaps the greatest military engineer in history. The fortifications he constructed were practically invulnerable, but even more valuable was his technique of conducting sieges against fortifications. Using his system of parallel trenches, underground mines and ricochet cannon fire, he conducted over 40 successful sieges for his master, Louis XIV.

Vauban was a compassionate man and usually took sympathy on the defeated. He developed the custom by which, when a commander breached his enemy's rampart, he would send for the enemy captain and invite him to surrender, thus sparing the defending garrison and reducing the loss of life.

Vauban also invented the socket bayonet, which was slipped over the muzzle of a musket and so did not have to be removed for firing. King Louis so valued his advice that he made him a marshal, an unprecedented honour for a man who, although thrice wounded, never commanded an army.

When Vauban neglected war, however, he fared less well. In his later years he published a tract attacking Louis's tax policies. The King rejected both Vauban and his views, and he died in disgrace on this day in 1710 at the age of 74.

The disgrace, however, was not permanent. One hundred years later, Napoleon had Vauban's heart disinterred and reburied in the Invalides.

The United States buys land seven times the size of Great Britain

1867 On this date Russia sold Alaska to the United States for $7,200,000. Alaska was formally transferred on 18 October the same year, the result of brilliant negotiations by American Secretary of State William Seward. Although now the intelligence of Seward's purchase is plain to all, at the time so many doubted the sense of buying this enormous area of frigid wilderness that it was colloquially called 'Seward's Folly'.

150

The largest American state, it covers 615,230 square miles (1,593,438 square kilometres), twice as big as Texas and almost seven times the size of Great Britain. But with only 600,000 inhabitants, Alaska has the lowest population of any state.

Seward's purchase was one of the shrewdest in history. Had that $7.2 million been invested at 5 per cent interest for all the years since 1867, it would be worth about $3.6 billion today. But the value of the oil alone beneath Alaska's surface is an estimated $450 billion.

Also on this day

1746: Spanish painter Francisco de Goya is born * 1842: Ether is first used as an anaesthetic during surgery by US doctor Crawford Long * 1853: Dutch painter Vincent van Gogh is born * 1856: The treaty ending the Crimean War is signed

31 March

Commodore Perry opens Japan

1854 After the great Japanese shogun Tokugawa Ieyasu took control of Japan in 1603, successive shoguns attempted to stabilise the country by preventing change. Social classes were frozen, and outsiders – especially Catholic missionaries – came to be seen as a disruptive and threatening influence. By the early 1630s Christianity had been effectively banned, no Japanese was allowed to travel abroad, and the country was closed to foreigners. At times the isolation was so sternly enforced that shipwrecked sailors washed ashore would be summarily executed. For over two centuries Japan lived in near total isolation, although European and North American businessmen yearned for a chance to develop what they were sure would be lucrative commerce.

In early July 1853 a fleet of four American warships anchored in the lower Tokyo Bay. Their commander was Commodore Matthew Perry, haughty, dignified, ponderous and dull, but with determination to fulfil President Millard Fillmore's orders to open Japan to American trade.

On 14 July, Perry landed at Kurihama, a tiny village at the entrance to Tokyo Bay. There he presented American demands to representatives of the shogun. Perry then sailed off to China to await a reply.

In March the following year the Commodore returned, this time with a force of ten ships and some intriguing presents for the Japanese – a telegraph instrument and a miniature locomotive. By now the Japanese had realised that they could no longer fight the inevitable. On the last day of the month the Treaty of Kanagawa was signed, guaranteeing 'a perfect, permanent and universal peace and a sincere and cordial amity' between Japan and the United States.

Perry returned home a hero, to receive $20,000 awarded by Congress. Japan was open at last. As one American observer said at the time: 'We didn't go in; they came out.'

Paris is occupied for the first time in four centuries

1814 Only four years earlier Napoleon Bonaparte had held not just France but almost all of Europe in thrall. His brothers reigned in Spain, Holland and Westphalia. Belgium, most of Italy and a large part of Germany were also under his rule, direct or indirect, and a docile pope was his willing instrument, as was his Austrian father-in-law, Franz II.

But Napoleon's glory had frozen and died on the plains of Russia, and now all of Europe was at his throat.

Retreating, fighting, fighting, retreating – at the end of March 1814 Napoleon fled to Fontainebleau, and the victorious allied powers marched into Paris on the last day of the month. On this day some 230,000 men, headed by the Russian Tsar and the King of Prussia, passed through the Porte Saint Martin and, 30 abreast, marched through Paris's main thoroughfares.

It was the first time Paris had been occupied by a foreign army since the time of Joan of Arc, almost 400 years earlier.

Also on this day

1596: French philosopher René Descartes is born * 1631: The bell tolls for John Donne in London * 1732: Austro-Hungarian composer Joseph Haydn is born * 1837: English novelist Charlotte Brontë dies * 1837: English landscapist John Constable dies * 1881: The Eiffel Tower is inaugurated

1 April

Birth of the Iron Chancellor

1815 Otto von Bismarck was born today in Kniephof, Prussia, a man destined dramatically to change the history of Europe. He was one of the most contradictory leaders in history: he hated political parties, but proved a master politician; a reactionary, he instituted social security for the aged and socialised medicine; a fervent Prussian nationalist, he created a unified German state.

A giant of a man (he was six feet five inches), Bismarck came from a moderately prosperous Junker family. Early in life he showed little promise, but marriage and some sort of religious awakening converted him into the serious and determined man who became aristocratic, autocratic and so self-assured that he was accused of believing in God only because God agreed with him on all subjects. He was also a political genius who would dominate Prussia for nine years and then a united Germany for nineteen more.

An impassioned monarchist, Bismarck became Prussia's Chancellor in 1862. His foremost objective was to wrest control of the German-speaking world from the then dominant Austria and form a unified German state under the leadership of Prussia. To do this, his first task was to build up the army. Called Prussia's Iron Chancellor, his nickname derived from an address to the Chamber of Deputies in which he maintained that 'it is not by means of speeches and majority resolutions that the great issues of the day will be decided ... but by blood and iron'.

In 1864 Bismarck formed an alliance with Austria and used his expanded force to invade Denmark over the Schleswig-Holstein question, a labyrinthine issue that had been simmering since the early 1800s. (Schleswig-Holstein was a Danish province with a substantial German population. The issue was so complex that England's Lord Palmerston once remarked, 'Only three men in Europe have ever understood it, and of those the Prince Consort is dead, a Danish statesman is in an asylum, and I myself have forgotten it.') Bismarck's invasion was immediately successful, and Schleswig-Holstein became a German state.

Two years later, Bismarck launched the Seven Weeks' War against his erstwhile allies the Austrians and some smaller German states. After a major victory at Sadowa, Hanover, Hesse-Kassel, Nassau and Frankfurt, all of which had fought alongside Austria, were annexed, and virtually overnight Prussia, not Austria, had become the Germanic world's major power.

In spite of Bismarck's success (or perhaps because of it), many of Germany's smaller states continued to resist unification, which they quite correctly understood to mean dominance by Prussia. Bismarck's next move was another war – not against the recalcitrant principalities but with France, in the belief that seeing Prussia under attack would awaken pan-German nationalism and lead the way to a consolidated state. Using the ruse of a doctored diplomatic telegram, Bismarck manoeuvred the French into declaring war. Swiftly victorious, Prussia was then able to persuade the other German states to combine into a united empire, of which King Wilhelm became Kaiser Wilhelm I. (Another consequence of this war was Germany's annexation of Alsace and part of Lorraine, two French provinces with large German-speaking populations. Alsace-Lorraine became the ball in a ping-pong match, reverting to France in 1919, recaptured by Germany in the Second World War and finally reunited with France in 1945.)

Thus by 1871 the Continent was dominated by a united Germany, Germany was dominated by Prussia and Prussia was dominated by Bismarck. Confident of the new nation's power, the Iron Chancellor addressed the Reichstag with the words, 'Setzen wir Deutschland, so zu sagen, in den Sattel. Reiten wird es schon können.' (Let's put Germany, so to speak, in the saddle. You'll see that she can ride.)

On 9 March 1888 Kaiser Wilhelm I died just a few days before his 91st birthday, and then on 15 June his son Frederick III succumbed to throat cancer, bringing the intelligent but unstable Wilhelm II to the throne. Kaiser Bill, as the British came to call him, was young (29), arrogant and determined not to be overshadowed by the great chancellor. Within two years he had pressured Bismarck into retirement, an event that sent shock waves across Europe and inspired the great political cartoon in *Punch* (29 March 1890) by John Tenniel called 'Dropping the Pilot'. It showed Bismarck descending a ladder from the German ship of state to be taken off in a pilot boat, while from the deck above the Kaiser as captain calmly surveys his departure.

Bismarck died eight years later, and within three years Kaiser Wilhelm had let Bismarck's keystone treaty with Russia lapse, leading to an alliance between Russia and France, with all its consequences for the future.

In 1914 Kaiser Wilhelm II, to use Bismarck's metaphor, put Germany into the saddle, only to find that without the Iron Chancellor, it could ride only into a brick wall.

Also on this day

1920: Germany's Workers' Party changes its name to the Nationalist Socialist German Workers' Party (Nationalsozialistische Deutsche Arbeiterpartei), or for short, Nazi
* 1924: Adolf Hitler is sentenced to five years in prison for the 'Beer Hall Putsch'

2 April

Charlemagne – the greatest emperor since the Romans

742 Born this day: Charlemagne, who was to become the greatest European ruler since Roman times.

The grandson of the great Frankish leader Charles Martel, Charlemagne became joint King of the Franks along with his father and brother when he was only twelve. After the other two had died he asserted his power over all the Frankish lands, comprising present-day northern France, Belgium and western Germany. Then, over the next 30 years, he subjugated the Saxons, seized Bavaria, fought campaigns in Hungary and Spain and conquered parts of northern Italy. Backed by the Pope (and strongly supporting the Pope in a time of great conflict with the eastern empire in Constantinople), Charlemagne created one vast empire of practically all the Christian lands of western Europe except parts of Spain, southern Italy and the British Isles. He established his capital at Aachen (Aix-la-Chapelle) on the right bank of the Rhine.

One contemporary at Charlemagne's court described him thus: 'He had a broad and strong body of unusual height, but well-proportioned; for his height measured seven times his feet. His skull was round, the eyes were lively and rather large, the nose of more than average length, the hair grey but full, the face friendly and cheerful. Seated or standing, he thus made a dignified and stately impression even though he had a thick, short neck and a belly that protruded somewhat; but this was hidden by the good proportions of the rest of his figure. He strode with firm step and held himself like a man; he spoke with a higher voice than one would have expected of someone of his build. He enjoyed good health except for being repeatedly plagued by fevers four years before his death. Toward the end he dragged one foot.'

This was the man who founded the Carolingian dynasty that ruled an empire for 137 years. So much was he admired that a century after his death the Emperor Otto I emulated the great conqueror by establishing Aachen as his capital, and during the next 600 years more than 30 Holy Roman Emperors and German kings were crowned there.

Charlemagne also appears in several French *chansons de geste* (literally 'songs of deeds') of the Middle Ages, most famously in *Le Chanson de Roland* where he is portrayed leading the Christian fight against the Muslims (or Moors) of Spain.

In 1165 the then Emperor Frederick Barbarossa paid Charlemagne the ultimate compliment in badgering the Pope Paschal III to canonise him. Unfortunately for Charlemagne, Paschal was an anti-pope, claiming to be Pope but unrecognised by the Catholic Church in Rome, so the Church has never accepted his canonisation.

Death of 'a mad dog' in France

1791 Honoré Gabriel Riqueti, comte de Mirabeau, was a lumbering, heavy-set man. His large head was covered by unruly dark hair, his face was scarred by smallpox and his protuberant eyes seemed to glare balefully. Even so, he was inordinately vain, and his vanity was fed by some notable successes with women, including by rumour his own sister. At one stage his amours almost led to disaster when he eloped with the beautiful young wife of an elderly man. Charges were laid and a tribunal condemned him to death for seduction and abduction, a sentence that required all his influence to escape.

Despite his title, Mirabeau was one of France's most prominent revolutionaries. He detested the inequities of the *ancien régime* and dramatically described himself as 'a mad dog from whose bite despotism and privilege will die'. Nonetheless, with the leftward revolution gaining momentum, he found himself on its conservative fringe, as he tried to establish a constitutional monarchy (with himself, of course, as Prime Minister).

By early 1791 Mirabeau was dying but had lost none of his self-assurance. Wishing to sit straighter in bed, he told his valet, 'Support my head, it's the strongest head in France. I wish I could leave it to you.'

Just before he died, that other aristocratic revolutionary, Maurice de Talleyrand, visited him. Sensing the bloody course the revolution would take, which he alone might have prevented, Mirabeau pronounced, 'I take away with me the last shreds of monarchy.'

He proved to be correct. He died on 2 April 1791 at the age of 42. Louis XVI was executed less than two years later.

Did Richard the Lion-Heart really meet Robin Hood?

1194 King Richard hearing of the pranks
Of Robin Hood and his men,
He much admired, and more desired
To see both him and them.

So goes an ancient English ballad, and most of us would like to think that Richard the Lion-Heart did in fact encounter history's most famous outlaw, Robin Hood.

Most historians believe Robin Hood is a sort of composite figure of several different medieval outlaws, while some believe he is complete fiction. But maybe – just maybe – the old ballad is right.

What we know for sure is that on 2 April 1194, King Richard stopped overnight in Clipston Palace, on the edge of Sherwood Forest. This fact and Richard's known love of high and noble drama give some underpinning to the legend that he met Robin here. As every schoolboy knows, Richard went into the forest disguised as an abbot, met Robin and his men and engaged them in sports, outwrestling Little John but yielding to Friar Tuck's superior prowess with the sword. The King then revealed his true identity and, after much swearing of loyalty, king and outlaw dined together in the forest.

Venison and fowls were plenty there,
With fish out of the river;
King Richard swore, on sea and shore,
He ne'er was feasted better.

156

527: Byzantine Emperor Justinian is crowned * 1725: Italian seducer Giovanni Giacomo Casanova is born * 1800: First performance of Beethoven's First Symphony * 1801: The British and Danish fleets met in the Battle of Copenhagen * 1840: Birth of Emile Zola in Paris

3 April

King John commits murder

1203 The four eaglets, as they were called, sons of King Henry II of England, were Henry, Richard, Geoffrey and John. The first died while great Henry was still alive, as did the third, Geoffrey, but not before marrying and producing a son christened Arthur.

In 1189 Henry II died, hounded by his son Richard (the Lion-Heart), who inherited the throne. But Richard's reign was brief, and just ten years later John was crowned after Richard was killed besieging an enemy castle. So John was King, but his nephew Arthur, then a boy of thirteen, was being raised in the courts of France.

By 1203 John was already hated by most of his subjects, and he could no longer ignore his dangerous nephew who had begun to sound his own claims to the throne.

By a fluke of luck, John captured Arthur in a minor battle. First, he imprisoned him at the castle of La Falaise in Normandy, then he moved him to a fortress in Rouen. But no matter where he was kept, Arthur continued to be a threat, one that John had to eliminate.

According to a contemporary source, 'On the day before Good Friday, after dinner, when he was drunk with wine and filled with the devil, he [John] killed him [Arthur] with his own hand and, tying a heavy stone to his body, threw it into the Seine. Later it was dragged up in the nets of fishermen and ... was identified and secretly buried in Notre Dame des Près ... for fear of the tyrant.' The date was 3 April 1203. John the murderer remained King, unpunished and unrepentant, until his death thirteen years later.

Philip the Fair suppresses the Templars

1312 The Order of the Temple had been founded in the early 12th century to guard routes to the Holy Land travelled by devout pilgrims. Its original members were dedicated and selfless knights whose conduct resembled that of warrior monks. Over the years, however, the Templars became secretive and introverted, confused by their own rituals and initiations. With the fall of Acre in 1291, Christianity lost its last toehold in the Holy Land and the Templars their very *raison d'être*. But by then the Order was rich, very rich – a tempting target for Philip the Fair, King of France, who resolved to destroy it.

At first Philip spread harmful rumours about the Order, lies cleverly blended with truth. The Templars were heretics and idolaters who spat on the Cross and practised human sacrifice. They were renegades, sodomites. And then, in a single day on 13 October 1307, Philip arrested every Templar knight throughout France. So began his campaign to convince his pet Pope Clement V to suppress the Order entirely.

The main evidence of the evils of the Temple was admissions of guilt by imprisoned knights. Torture was used to enrich these confessions, the severity of which can be judged by the fact that 36 knights did not survive their inquisition. And when some 500 Templars tried to recant their confessions, five were beheaded and nine burnt at the stake for 'relapsing'. The remainder quickly recanted their recantations.

Philip the Fair finally met in council with the Pope at Vienne on 3 April 1312. Clement and he sat side by side, the pontiff on a slightly higher throne, as befitted his spiritual seniority. The Pope pronounced judgement. The Temple was formally suppressed; after 184 years it no longer existed.

Those knights who confessed and repented were released. The few who continued to proclaim their innocence were imprisoned for life.

Also on this day

1721: Robert Walpole becomes the first Prime Minister of Great Britain * 1882: American outlaw Jesse James is shot in the back by one of his own gang * 1897: Austrian composer Johannes Brahms dies in Vienna

4 April

'A curious, odd, pedantic fellow with some genius'

1774 Ugly to the point of caricature, with a great dome of forehead, a protruding upper lip and very little chin, Oliver Goldsmith yet achieved greatness writing comedy and was a much-loved friend of Samuel Johnson, Joshua Reynolds, David Garrick and Edmund Burke.

Goldsmith was born around 1730 and was a would-be physician before becoming a writer. He studied 'physic' at the University of Leiden in the Netherlands but received no degree, then returned to London as a sometime chemist, and finally lost his job in the medical service of the East India Company. In spite of these setbacks, Goldsmith always insisted he was a doctor. On one occasion he was boasting to his friend Topham Beauclerk of his medical prowess, claiming, 'I do not practise; I make it a rule to prescribe only for my friends.' Nonplussed by Goldsmith's assertion, Beauclerk responded, 'Pray, dear Doctor, alter your rule and prescribe only for your enemies.'

Although Goldsmith clearly failed as a doctor, he did not prosper much as a writer either, for his greatest novel, *The Vicar of Wakefield*, published in 1766, took almost a century to acquire its reputation. His great comic play *She Stoops to Conquer* was first performed on 15 March 1773, only thirteen months before Goldsmith's death of kidney failure on this day in 1774. He died without family (he had never married) and nearly broke. Yet his friends mourned his passing, and none summed him up better than James Boswell, who called him 'a curious, odd, pedantic fellow with some genius'.

A saint dies on Good Friday

AD 397 This was Good Friday and so perhaps a fitting date for the death of a saint.

St Ambrose had been born 57 years earlier of a noble Roman family. Raised as a pagan, he achieved the rank of governor in the empire's civil service and was sent to Milan. There he converted to Christianity, the religion given official status only a few years earlier by Constantine the Great's Edict of Milan in 313. Entering the Church, Ambrose eventually attained the rank of bishop.

Ambrose influenced four separate emperors and had no fear of imperial power. He once personally prevented Theodosius from entering Milan cathedral and kept him out for eight months until he had purged himself for having 7,000 Greeks put to death for murdering their tyrannical governor.

Ambrose was a powerful voice in making pagan worship illegal, but perhaps his most notable achievement was the double baptism of two pagans, a father and his illegitimate son. The father was eventually canonised as St Augustine of Hippo.

Ambrose died of unknown causes. Today, in the Milanese church that bears his name, his bones reside still clothed in bishop's raiment.

The first of the Borgias

1455 When the College of Cardinals met on this day to choose a new pope, the intractable conflicts among Orsinis, Colonnas and the French inevitably demanded a compromise solution. The answer was a 77-year-old Spanish cardinal named Alonso de Borja, who became Pope Calixtus III.

Although Calixtus reigned only three years until his death, he established the Borja (later Italianised to Borgia) dynasty in Rome. Eventually it included another pope, the infamous Alexander VI, Alexander's notorious children, Cesare and Lucrezia, and a saint, St Francis Borgia, who was canonised in 1671.

Also on this day

527: Byzantine Emperor Justinian is crowned * 1648: Dutch-born woodcarver and sculptor Grinling Gibbons is born

5 April

Pocahontas gets married

1614 'Little Wanton' or 'playful, spirited little girl' she was called, better known to us by the Indian word Pocahontas. Today at the age of about nineteen she was married for the second time, bigamously by our standards but not by those of the time, for her first husband, who was still alive, was a heathen Indian.

Pocahontas was an Algonquian, daughter of the mighty chief Powhatan in the Tidewater region of Virginia. As a young girl she had come to know the English settlers in Jamestown, and at fifteen she married an Indian brave named Kokoum.

About two years later an unscrupulous English captain named Samuel Argall lured her onto his ship and then held her for ransom. By the time her father Powhatan had agreed to the terms of payment, Argall had taken her back to Jamestown and then moved to the nearby town of Henrico, where she fell in love with the widower John Rolfe, a leading Virginia planter ten years her senior. In 1613 Pocahontas was briefly reunited with her father, and he agreed with her wish to marry Rolfe.

Rolfe, too, wanted to marry, but he insisted that Pocahontas first become a Christian. After a brief introduction to the faith she was christened with the new name of Rebecca, and on this day the couple married, her first husband Kokoum apparently forgotten. They soon had a baby son.

Two years later John, Pocahontas and their son travelled to England as part of the colony's campaign to raise more funds. There she became an instant celebrity. Still only 21, she was strikingly handsome, dressed in the height of European fashion with her black hair and Indian complexion. She and her husband were presented to the highest members of English society, including King James I.

In March of 1617 the Rolfes set sail for Virginia, but Pocahontas was so ill that the ship returned to harbour at Gravesend. There she died of smallpox, just 22 years old. After her funeral her husband John went back to Jamestown and remarried. In 1622 he perished in an Indian massacre at his farm.

Under normal circumstances the tale of Pocahontas's short life and very minor celebrity would long since have vanished into the lists of historical trivia, but five years after her death the founder of Jamestown, a dashing English adventurer named John Smith, published his *Generall Historie of Virginia* in which he included his now-famous tale of Pocahontas.

According to Smith, in December 1607, when Pocahontas was still only twelve, Algonquian warriors captured him while he was exploring the Chickahominy River. In triumph they brought him before Chief Powhatan. Here, in Smith's own words, is what happened next:

'Having feasted him [i.e. Smith] after their best barbarous manner they could, a long consultation was held, but the conclusion was, two great stones were brought before Powhattan; then as many [braves] as could layd hands on him, dragged him to them, and thereon laid his head, and being ready with their clubs, to beate out his braines, Pochahontas, the Kings dearest daughter, when no intreaty could prevaile, got his head in her armes, and laid her owne upon his to save him from death.'

John Smith's tale immortalised Pocahontas in American folk history. Sadly, today historians conclude that the story was a fabrication, as Smith published it years after the event and it is not mentioned in his diaries. At best this mock execution and salvation was part of a stock Indian ritual of welcome and friendship.

Danton goes to the guillotine

1794 Prior to the French Revolution Jacques Georges Danton had been a successful Parisian lawyer. Despite his bloated and particularly unattractive face he was a powerful speaker who could sway a mob. He became a member of the Legislative Assembly in 1791 when only 32.

From then on his actions became increasingly demagogic – and dangerous, as he practised his own preaching for 'de l'audace, encore de l'audace, toujours de l'audace'. In 1792 he instigated the September Massacres in which suspects already imprisoned were given mock trials and then turned over to the mob for slaughter.

Although Danton at first dominated the Committee for Public Safety, by 1794, led by Robespierre, it had turned on him, jealous of his power and fearful of his ambitions. He was arrested on 30 March.

His trial was a farce, the verdict predictable. On hearing his inevitable sentence, Danton grandly announced, 'My dwelling-place will soon be nothingness. My name is written in the Pantheon of history.'

On 5 April 1794 he was led to the guillotine. As he was carried to the scaffold in a horse-drawn tumbrel, he passed Robespierre's house. Shaking his fist, he called out, 'You will appear in the cart in your turn, Robespierre, and the soul of Danton will howl with joy!'

Stopping to embrace another victim at the bottom of the steps that led to the guillotine, he grandly asked, 'Why should I regret to die? I have enjoyed the Revolution. Let us go to slumber.' He then mounted the scaffold and waded through the sticky blood of previous victims, even then managing to retain his arrogance and courage. 'Show my head to the people', he commanded the executioner seconds before the drop of the blade. 'It's worth seeing.'

Also on this day

1803: Beethoven's Second Symphony is performed for the first time, in the Theater an der Wien, Vienna * 1837: English poet Algernon Charles Swinburne is born in London

6 April

Richard the Lion-Heart's last battle

1199 The tiny village of Châlus lies twenty miles south-west of Limoges. At the end of the 12th century it boasted a minor castle defended by two or three knights and their sons. Nearby a farmer had found a buried treasure of golden coins, probably Roman, and King Richard the Lion-Heart declared he would have it as his right, since he was overlord of the Limousin. Unwisely, the castle's defenders decided to resist.

Accompanied by a strong troop of mercenaries, Richard laid siege to this insignificant fortress. On the evening of 25 March he decided to inspect progress, and he carelessly neared the castle walls protected by a shield but without his armour. Suddenly through the twilight sped a crossbow bolt, striking the King in his unprotected shoulder.

Richard quickly retreated to his quarters, summoning his captain and his surgeon. The bolt had penetrated deep and was at last recovered only by the excruciating torment of laying open the flesh.

Even without Richard, the King's forces soon reduced the fortress and in the process captured the youth who had fired the shot. But by now Richard's wound showed unmistakable signs of gangrene, and the Lion-Heart knew he would soon die. Perhaps because it was the Lenten season, he performed one last chivalrous act.

Summoning the terrified youth, Richard demanded to know why he wished him injury. Emboldened, the young man replied, 'Because you killed my father and brother. Do with me as you want. I have no regrets for the vengeance I have taken.'

'Go forth in peace', said Richard. 'I forgive you my death and will exact no revenge.'

Twelve days later, on 6 April 1199, the great troubadour-knight-crusader-king was dead, at the age of 41. Ignoring Richard's forgiveness, his army captains had the young man flayed alive and hanged.

The Declaration of Arbroath

1320 If 4 July 1776 is remembered for the momentous statement that begins, 'When in the course of human events …' then 6 April should be noted for an equally stirring declaration of independence, written some four and a half centuries earlier, when another nation struggled for freedom from English rule. It read in part:

> For as long as one hundred of us shall remain alive we shall never in any
> wise consent to submit to the rule of the English, for it is not for glory we

fight, for riches, or for honours, but for freedom alone, which no good man loses but with his life.

These brave words were set down in Latin today at the abbey of Arbroath, where Scottish earls, barons, freeholders and clergymen – representing 'the whole community of the realm' – had gathered for the purpose of sending a message to the Pope in Rome. Known thereafter as the Declaration of Arbroath, the document asserted Scotland's independence, militarily confirmed by the great victory at Bannockburn six years earlier, and the assemblage's choice of Robert the Bruce as their King.

In the course of the long and complicated struggle for his nation's independence, Bruce had slain his rival for the Scottish throne, John Comyn, and subsequently had himself crowned King, deeds that won him excommunication by Pope John XXII and an oath by King Edward of England never to rest until Scotland was thoroughly restored to English rule. Against all odds, Bruce and the Scots were victorious in the war that followed. But in the aftermath Edward's son ruling as Edward II would not recognise the independence of Scotland or Bruce as its rightful monarch, a position buttressed by Bruce's excommunication, which while it remained in force cast in doubt the legitimacy of his kingship.

The Declaration of Arbroath, encapsulating as it did the determination of a united people, had effect. The Pope issued a temporary waiver of the excommunication and in 1324 recognised Bruce as the King of the Scots. Border raids and broken truces continued to mark Scotland's relations with England, but in 1328 Edward III signed the Treaty of Southampton recognising Bruce as the king of an independent realm.

Also on this day

1528: German painter Albrecht Dürer dies * 1909: American explorer Robert Peary reaches the North Pole * 1917: The United States declares war on Germany

7 April

'The hope for an easy war and a cheap victory was gone forever'

1862 It was victory snatched from the jaws of defeat. By mid-afternoon today it became clear that the Confederate forces had been shattered by the Union counter-attack and were withdrawing. But 24 hours earlier the shoe had been on the other foot, and General Grant's Army of the Tennessee, reeling backward from the fierce rebel assault, looked on the verge of annihilation.

The Confederates named this Civil War engagement Pittsburg Landing, after a stopping place on the Tennessee River. The Union Army called it Shiloh after a small log meeting-house some four miles from the river. By either designation, it was two days of hell that 'launched the country onto the floodtide of total war'.

As early as 1 April, Confederate cavalry movements and skirmishing near the Union lines indicated an enemy advance was contemplated. Grant's headquarters ignored this evidence. 'The fact is,' Grant wrote later, 'I regarded the campaign we were engaged in as an offensive one and had no idea that the enemy would leave strong entrenchments to take the initiative …' But Albert Sydney Johnston, the Confederate commander, had a different scenario in mind. Just before the attack, he told his senior commanders: 'Tonight we will water our horses in the Tennessee River.' They came very close in an effort that would cost Johnston his life.

At 5.00 a.m. on the 6th, as breakfast fires were being lit in the Union camp, patrols spotted Confederate skirmishers through the woods and underbrush. And suddenly, right behind them, emerged the full Confederate battle line, thousands strong, yelling and firing.

Under the shock of the attack, the Union positions disintegrated. Throughout the long day, the fighting was chaotic and relentless. At dusk, when one more Confederate attack might have destroyed what was left of Grant's army, the rebels halted, exhausted and fought out. During the night it rained and Grant brought up fresh regiments. By daylight today, the Union forces had a sizeable advantage in numbers, and the counter-attack began.

Shiloh was shocking in its carnage: a total of 20,000 men were killed or wounded, about evenly distributed to both sides. Included among the dead was Confederate general Johnston, killed on the first day of battle. That was almost twice the combined losses in all the previous engagements of the war now entering its second year. Bloody Shiloh produced a change in the war, which Bruce Catton summed up this way:

> It had begun with flags and cheers and the glint of brave words on the spring wind, with the drumbeats setting a gay rhythm for the feet of young men who believed that war would beat clerking. That had been a year ago; now the war had come down to uninstructed murderous battle in a smoky woodland where men who had never been shown how to fight stayed in defiance of all logical expectation and fought for two nightmarish days. And because they had done this the hope for an easy war and a cheap victory was gone forever.

A French king's fatal accident

1498 The beautiful château of Amboise on the south bank of the Loire is strongly connected to one of France's least beautiful kings, Charles VIII. Born and raised at Amboise, Charles had a long, drooping nose and mumbled through flabby, wet lips. His oversize head sat atop a small, crippled body. Moreover, he lacked both education and intelligence.

Yet Charles was a well-meaning man with some real sensitivity to beauty. It was he who built much of Amboise, and in many ways he was the man who brought the Renaissance to France, as he had been strongly influenced by Italian art and civilisation during his invasion of Italy.

On 7 April 1498 Charles was back in his beloved Amboise watching a game of tennis being played in the moat of the château. Leaving the court, he hit his head on the low lintel of a doorway. Laughing off the accident, the King returned to the game, but suddenly he collapsed, falling to the ground barely conscious. That evening he died, not yet 28 years old. Amboise, where he had been given life, had taken it back.

Also on this day

1300: The start date of Dante's *Divine Comedy* ∗ 1614: Greek/Spanish painter El Greco (Domenikos Theotokopoulos) dies ∗ 1770: English poet William Wordsworth is born

8 April

The Prince Regent makes a calamitous marriage

1795 'Her figure was very bad, short, very full-chested and jutting hips. She was stockily built, dressed dowdily, lacked moral reticence and good sense, and washed so seldom she was malodorous.' Such was the potential bride of England's future King George IV, Caroline of Brunswick, as described in the private diaries of the Earl of Malmesbury who had been sent to Braunschweig in Germany to vet the prospect.

Unfortunately for Prince George, Malmesbury equivocated in his official report, and the Prince's dynastic need for a wife was so strong that he agreed on the match, sight unseen.

Caroline of Brunswick turned out to be just as unattractive as Malmesbury's description. When George first met her he famously turned to his valet with the appeal, 'I am not very well, Harris; pray get me a glass of brandy.'

The couple were married on this day in 1795. After the official ceremony the groom resorted to the bottle to give him fortitude for the night ahead. Blind drunk, he managed to make love to his new wife that night, implanting a daughter in her womb. They never slept together again.

By 1811 when George had become regent for his mad father, George III, he banished Caroline from court, and she decamped to Montague House in Greenwich Park. Three years later she left for Italy, where she took up with an Italian named Bartolomeo Pergami, who apparently had a stronger stomach and emptier purse than Prince George. As one might throw out a mattress infested with fleas, George had Montague House demolished the moment she was gone.

When George inherited the throne in 1820 he tried to persuade Parliament to dissolve the marriage and take away Caroline's royal title on the grounds of her adultery. During a hearing, a servant testified that 'Her Royal Highness had heard of the enormous size of [Pergami's] machine and sent for him by courier.' But the House of Lords, only too aware of George's own feckless and selfish character, let the bill drop.

George's final rejection of his wife came at his coronation on 19 July 1821 when he banned her from the ceremony in Westminster Abbey, although she caused a scandal by pounding on the church door demanding to be let in.

This last denial may have finally done Caroline in, as she immediately fell ill and died nineteen days later at the age of 53.

Death of King Jean the Good

1364 Jean II was one of France's weakest kings. Captured by the English during the Battle of Poitiers, he spent four years in opulent captivity in London while his own nation was suffering one disaster after another. An epidemic of plague referred to as the Black Death devastated the population, organised bands of marauding soldiers known as the Great Companies pillaged the country at will, and the violent peasant uprising called the Jacquerie cost the lives of thousands. Perhaps half of the people of France died.

Released from England in 1360, Jean was unable to raise the enormous ransom of 3 million crowns he had agreed to pay and so in 1364 he returned voluntarily to London where once again he was lodged in the Savoy Palace (where the Savoy Hotel stands today). But only three months afterwards he fell sick and died on this day at the age of 44.

Jean was enamoured of display, luxury and pleasure and was a strong believer in knightly chivalry, the code of conduct so totally unsuited for the calamitous times in which he lived. For reasons obscure, he is known to history as Jean the Good.

Also on this day
563 BC: The founder of Buddhism, Gautama Buddha, is born

9 April

Lorenzo de' Medici, the Renaissance's Renaissance Man

1492 Lorenzo de' Medici was the Renaissance's Renaissance Man. Italy's shrewdest balancer of power, he spent 23 years as virtual ruler of Florence, juggling the interests of Milan, Venice, Naples, the Papal States and various other powers, notably France, to the benefit of Florence. Indeed, he held the unfashionable view that war was undesirable, and while no coward, he showed little inclination for combat on the few occasions when war was thrust upon him.

But Lorenzo's greatness was not as a ruler or even a banker (the Medici bank that he controlled was Europe's most powerful), but as a man of the arts. He was an outstanding vernacular poet with a broad range from bawdy songs to celebrations of nature to laments on love and mortality:

Quant'è bella giovinezza	How beautiful is youth
Che si fugge tuttavia.	Which flies away soon.
Chi vuol esser lieto, sia;	Let him who would be happy, be it;
Di domani non c' è certezza.	For tomorrow is never certain.

Finally, Lorenzo was the greatest patron of Renaissance art. Andrea del Sarto painted the walls of his villa at Poggio a Caiano, while Ghirlandajo, Filipino Lippi and Botticelli decorated the one at Spedaletto. Sandro Botticelli was virtually Lorenzo's 'court painter' as well as frequent dinner companion. Other artists Lorenzo patronised included Perugino, Verrocchio and Antonio Pollaiuolo. He met and helped Leonardo da Vinci when Leonardo was only twelve, and he 'discovered' Michelangelo at the age of thirteen. Michelangelo in fact lived in the Medici palace for four years, and, according to the contemporary painter-historian Giorgio Vasari, he 'always ate at Lorenzo's table with the sons of the family'.

Ruler, diplomat, banker, lover of women and loving husband, philosopher, patron, poet: no wonder he is known as Lorenzo the Magnificent. The world had become a richer place because of him when he died at his villa in Careggi near Florence on this day at the age of 43.

The American Civil War comes to an end

1865 Palm Sunday at Appomattox Courthouse, a small village in Virginia, the final scene of the American Civil War. In the morning the Southern rebels had launched one last attack – and failed. Outnumbered, outgunned, worn out, the rebel army was near collapse. The great Southern general Robert E. Lee was making a last desperate attempt to reach Lynchburg where he could head for the mountains and take up guerrilla warfare, but the huge Union army under the command of General Ulysses Grant dogged their every step.

Suddenly the Southern vanguard ran into a concentrated troop of Union cavalry. Refusing to attack, the cavalry simply opened their lines so that the Confederates could see a solid wall of Union infantry backed by cannon blocking the Confederate path. There was nowhere left to go.

Now Lee knew the end had come. 'There is nothing left for me to do but go and see General Grant, and I would rather die a thousand deaths', he said.

The two generals met in the parlour of a local farmer, Lee immaculate in his best uniform and gold-mounted sword, Grant rumpled and scruffy in a second-hand private's jacket on which he had pinned his general's stars. Grant offered the terms of surrender under which Lee's men were allowed to keep their horses and Southern officers their sidearms. Lee signed his acceptance, shook the hand offered by Grant and stepped out the door. The war was over.

In all, some 620,000 American soldiers died during the Civil War, almost 60 per cent of whom were from the victorious North. The total is more than the American dead from all other wars combined, from the Revolution through the two World Wars to Korea, Vietnam and the two Gulf Wars.

Henry V is crowned King

1413 Henry V's father Henry IV had died the previous month after spending much of his last years with his face swathed in bandages to hide a loathsome skin disease. The elder Henry's critics were quick to attribute the affliction to leprosy or venereal infection, and claimed that either or both were God's chastisement for having murdered his King, his cousin Richard II.

But now it was time for the younger Henry to assume the throne, a man who to date had been a notoriously irresponsible carouser and womaniser. The coronation was set for Sunday 9 April 1413. Curious for so late in the season, the day dawned to a frightful blizzard of sleet and freezing snow. Once again observers were busy interpreting the omens. Somewhat hopefully they claimed that the raging wind signified the new King's rage in battle while the cold, hard snow symbolised Henry's cold, hard justice.

During the nine years that Henry V reigned, the prophets were shown to be right. He invaded France and crushed the French at Agincourt, and from the moment he wore the crown of England he abandoned the women, wine and revelling of his youth to become the harsh and unyielding ruler who controlled two countries.

Also on this day

1553: French writer and priest François Rabelais (a pseudonym for Alcofribas Nasier) dies in Paris * 1940: Germany invades Denmark and Norway * 1942: The Americans surrender to the Japanese at Bataan * 1945: German Admiral Wilhelm Canaris is executed in the dying days of Nazi Germany

10 April

The pope who gave us our calendar

1585 Today in Rome, just two months short of his 83rd birthday, died one of the most contradictory characters of the 16th century, Pope Gregory XIII.

Gregory had been born Ugo Buoncompagni in Bologna in 1502. He had attended the city's famous university, the oldest in Europe, and then taught jurisprudence there. It was Buoncompagni's legal expertise that brought him to the attention of Pius IV, who sent him to the Council of Trent, the ecumenical assembly that brought wide reform to the Roman Church under Protestant attack. Buoncompagni continued slowly to rise in the Church hierarchy until in May 1572 he was finally elected Pope, just 37 days before he turned 70.

Despite a somewhat intemperate youth (he had fathered a child while living in Bologna), Buoncompagni devoted himself to the spiritual and particularly the temporal wellbeing of the Church. He took the name of Gregory, probably in honour of his saintly predecessor Gregory I, who had reigned a millennium before.

Gregory XIII's irresponsible spending brought the Church to financial chaos, and his reputation suffered from his complacent nepotism (he created two of his own nephews cardinals). But he is remembered most for his militant efforts to suppress emerging Protestantism. Twice he sent small armies to Ireland to bolster Irish Catholics in their revolt against England's Protestant Queen Elizabeth, and he famously celebrated the slaughter of French Huguenots during the St Bartholomew's Day Massacre by ordering a *Te Deum* sung in Rome. He then commemorated the event with a medal showing an angel holding a cross while striking down Huguenots with a sword. Gregory's own effigy decorates the back.

But Gregory also had a more productive side. In 1574 he built the monumental Quirinal Palace as a summer retreat to escape Rome's stifling heat and endemic malaria but soon turned it into the official papal residence, which it remained until 1870. Today it is the presidential palace of Italy. He also ordered the construction of beautiful fountains in the Piazza del Pantheon and the Piazza del Popolo.

But Gregory's most notable achievement is one that still affects all of us every day. In the 6th century his namesake had given the world the Gregorian chant, and in 1582 Gregory XIII gave us the Gregorian calendar and decreed that the year would always begin on 1 January.

The greatest explosion in the recorded history of man

1815 At dawn today on the coast of the Indonesian island of Sumbawa a huge volcano named Mount Tambora stood facing the sea, rising to a height of 13,500 feet, just shorter than Mont Blanc. But in a few hours three gigantic columns of fire would rise from its crater and an apocalyptic explosion would decapitate the mountain, blasting almost 4,500 feet from its summit. This gigantic eruption, which lasted two days, would kill 12,000 people outright and leave another 50,000 to starve to death as volcanic ash stifled their crops. It was the greatest explosion in the recorded history of man, equivalent to about 60,000 Hiroshima-type atom bombs.

For about three years prior to this cataclysmic blast, natives could observe steam and minor eruptions coming from Tambora, and these intensified during the seven months immediately prior to 10 April. When the full eruption came, the volcano spewed out some 12 cubic miles of ash, more than twice the amount from the more famous eruption of Krakatoa 68 years later. Near the volcano, ash deposits accumulated to a depth of 90 feet, and about 200,000 square miles of sea and land (about the size of France) were covered to a depth of half an inch.

The outside world first heard of the Tambora explosion literally. The sound could be detected as far as 1,000 miles away. Gradually the colossal cloud of dust and ash made its way around the world, and by late June Londoners began to observe prolonged and brilliantly coloured sunsets, orange or red on the horizon, purple or pink above it. Today you can still see what the English saw two centuries ago, as these spectacular sunsets were captured in the works of the great English painter J.M.W. Turner. Lord Byron, on the other hand, ignored the beauty and wrote a poem called 'Darkness' about the ash cloud's effect in dimming the sun.

A year after the eruption both North America and Europe experienced what was called 'the year without a summer', as cold and rain gripped the land, leading to disastrous harvests. In Paris the rainfall was three times normal.

Today a vast and tranquil lake occupies Tambora's crater, and the volcano seems to sleep. But those unwary enough to live too close should remember that Tambora erupted again in 1819, 1880 and 1967.

Also on this day

1829: Founder of the Salvation Army William Booth is born * 1864: Austrian Archduke Maximilian is made Emperor of Mexico * 1919: Mexican revolutionary leader Emiliano Zapata is shot by Mexican government troops * 1925: F. Scott Fitzgerald publishes *The Great Gatsby*

11 April

A king's mistress dies for her sins

1599 Henri IV's women were many and varied, for which he earned himself the nickname 'Le Vert Galant' (the Old Playboy). But the one for whom he cared the most was the beautiful and witty Gabrielle d'Estrées, with whom he had two sons and a daughter during their nine-year relationship. Since Henri's wife, the famously promiscuous Queen Margot, had borne the King no children during 26 years of marriage, the King announced his intention to annul his marriage to Margot, wed Gabrielle (who was pregnant once again) and legitimise her sons as heirs to the French throne.

Now, as long as Henri was married to Margot, no one (least of all Margot herself) seemed to mind his love for Gabrielle. But keeping a mistress was one thing, marrying her was something else altogether. Henri tried to win the Queen's agreement to the annulment, but she was resolutely opposed. Nonetheless he petitioned Pope Clement VIII to dissolve the marriage.

All of Henri's courtiers were aghast at the King's proposed *mésalliance* with Gabrielle, and the Pope agonised over his decision regarding the annulment. (The fact that Clement was Margot's first cousin thrice removed through their mutual Medici blood may have played a role in his vacillation.)

In fact, Clement was so distraught that he prayed daily for divine guidance. On 3 April, at the end of prayer, he looked up towards heaven, apparently having seen a vision. Turning to one of his household, the Pope murmured with evident relief and apparent prescience, 'God has provided the answer.'

Six days later Gabrielle gave birth to a son – but he was stillborn. She then quickly lost first her speech, then her hearing, and finally her sight. On 11 April she died in agony, her beautiful face a tormented and hideous mask.

Gabrielle's friends said it was God's will, while her enemies credited the Devil, to whom they said she had sold herself to become mistress to a King.

Now that the scandal of Henri's marriage to Gabrielle had been avoided, Margot at last agreed to the dissolution of her own, and in December Pope Clement granted the annulment. The following October the King wed a distant cousin of both Margot and Pope Clement, the Florentine princess Marie de' Medici, a scheming but slow-witted shrew who, unlike his first wife, took strong (and fruitless) objection to his philandering. But Marie did produce the desired son and heir, and the descendants of this unhappy union ruled France without interruption for another 182 years.

Napoleon abdicates (the first time)

1814 Napoleon had been the master of some 70 million people, including 25 million French, and his empire extended to Belgium, Holland, Spain, Portugal, most of Italy and Germany and parts of Poland and Yugoslavia. But today his territories were reduced to a single grand building, the château of Fontainebleau. Most of his Grande Armée lay dead on the Russian steppes and his victorious enemies occupied Paris. And so today his ten-year reign came to a close, as he abdicated as Emperor, declaring grandly in the third person that 'There is no personal sacrifice, even life itself, which he is not ready to make for the good of France.'

As if to prove his point, the next day Napoleon attempted to poison himself, but after some painful vomiting he recovered. In seventeen days he was en route to exile in Elba, there to wait and plot his brief return.

Also on this day

1713: The War of the Spanish Succession ends by the Treaty of Utrecht * 1945: The Buchenwald concentration camp near Weimar in Germany is liberated

12 April

The South fires the first shot of the American Civil War

1861 Four months earlier, in December 1860, South Carolina had seceded from the United States, quickly followed by six other southern states. Jefferson Davis had been elected President of the Confederacy, but still no battle had been fought in the American Civil War.

Fort Sumter sits on a small island of rock opposite Charleston, the capital of South Carolina. Occupied by Union troops, it was a thorn in the flesh (and pride) of the South.

Fearing Union reinforcements to the fort, Davis ordered the Southerners to attack. At 4.30 in the early dawn of 12 April 1861 a huge mortar shell rose from the shore and exploded on Fort Sumter, followed by an intense artillery barrage from four directions. Although the fort was solid enough – walls 40 feet high and eight to twelve feet thick – the small garrison there, with supplies exhausted, was forced to surrender after 33 hours and 4,000 rounds of artillery fire.

This was the first battle of the American Civil War, which was to continue for exactly four more years, less three days. During that time over 600,000 soldiers on both sides would die and 4 million black slaves would be freed.

Was he the highest-paid lover in history?

1783 Today died Grigory Orlov, once the lover of Catherine the Great, probably the father of one of her three children and the man who had conspired with her to put her on the throne of all the Russias.

Orlov had been only 28 – five years Catherine's junior – at the time of her celebrated coup. Their affair faded a few years later, but, as was customary with Catherine and her lovers, they remained good friends and he kept his power at the Russian court.

When Catherine finally dismissed Orlov from government service he did not go unrewarded. Apart from a year's leave he received an annual pension of 150,000 roubles, another 100,000 roubles to set up his household, two silver dinner services, the title of Prince of the Holy Roman Empire, 10,000 serfs and use of all imperial palaces outside St Petersburg until his own palace was finished.

Also on this day

1204: Soldiers from the Fourth Crusade sack the Christian city of Constantinople * 1945: Thirty-second President of the USA Franklin Delano Roosevelt dies of a stroke

172

13 April

The man who wrote the American Declaration of Independence

1743 'We hold these truths to be self-evident, that all men are created equal, that they are endowed by their creator with certain unalienable rights, that among these are life, liberty, and the pursuit of happiness.' Today was born the man who wrote these famous words from the American Declaration of Independence. He was of course Thomas Jefferson.

Jefferson was born in Shadwell, Virginia, on the banks of the Rivanna River. He represented Virginia during the forming of the United States, served as the first Secretary of State, the second Vice President and the third President.

Jefferson was America's greatest political thinker, with a passion for liberty, freedom of religion, public education and the welfare of the common man. But not all of his writings were as high-minded as the Declaration of Independence. 'The tree of liberty', he wrote in 1787, 'must be refreshed from time to time with the blood of patriots and tyrants. It is the natural manure.'

Apart from being a politician/philosopher, Jefferson was also an inventor (of, among other things, the dumb waiter), architect, musician, scientist and founder of the University of Virginia. More than two centuries after his birth another American president paid tribute to his intellect. In 1962 Jack Kennedy welcomed 49 Nobel Prize winners as 'the most extraordinary collection of talent, of human knowledge, that has ever been gathered in the White House, with the possible exception of when Thomas Jefferson dined alone'.

In spite of his passionately liberal views about democracy, Jefferson had less conviction about certain subgroups. The business of women, he said, is 'to soothe and calm the mind of their husbands', and when he died at the age of 83 he still owned 250 slaves including one, Sally Hemings, who modern science has proved bore him a child.

The story of Queen Crazy Joan

1555 Her parents were the great Catholic Monarchs of Spain, Ferdinand and Isabella, and she married Philip the Handsome of Burgundy. Her name was Juana (in English, Joan).

Juana's husband apparently was handsome indeed, and his affairs were numerous and unconcealed. But Juana loved him passionately and frantically. She was only 25 when he suddenly died in Burgos on 25 September 1506, and her passion turned to mania.

At first she brooded in her darkened room for almost two months, exclaiming, 'A widow who has lost the sun of her own soul should never expose herself to the light of day.' Juana then set out around Spain with her husband's body. For almost two years she took Philip's coffin with her wherever she went and periodically prised off the lid for a loving look at his corpse. She ordered an armed guard around the coffin at all times to prevent the approach of any other woman. Eventually the entourage arrived in Granada, where Philip was at last laid to rest.

Finally her son, the Emperor Charles V, had Juana restricted to a castle in Tordesillas, and here she remained year after year, often lucid, sometimes not, until death came to her on 13 April 1555.

When Juana died she was 76, already known as Juana la Loca, Crazy Joan. But the family that had sprung from her womb was in power everywhere. In the Holy Roman Empire, Italy, Spain, Portugal, France, Hungary, England and Poland, the reigning monarchs were her children or grandchildren or their husbands.

Louis XIV declares he is the State

1655 Nothing illustrates the saying that arrogance is born early and dies late better than today's quotation from seventeen-year-old Louis XIV of France. 'L'Etat, c'est moi', he said in addressing the Parlement of Paris.

Louis had been hunting in the woods around Vincennes when he heard that some members of the Parlement were challenging some of his financial policies. Galloping to Paris, he charged into the assembly chamber whip in hand and ordered the speechless officials to stop questioning his decisions, haughtily informing them that he was the State.

Six years later the great Cardinal Mazarin, who had been acting as the King's Prime Minister, died. Several of the cardinal's subordinates asked Louis from whom they should now take their orders. 'From me', he told them curtly. For the next 30 years he was his own Prime Minister.

Also on this day

1598: Henri IV of France issues the Edict of Nantes, giving religious freedom to the Protestants * 1605: Russian Tsar Boris Godunov dies * 1742: Handel's *Messiah* is first performed in Dublin * 1829: The British Parliament passes the Catholic Emancipation Act, lifting restrictions on Catholics

14 April

Abraham Lincoln is assassinated

1865 On 11 April, just two days after the South had finally surrendered in the American Civil War, President Abraham Lincoln addressed a crowd from the balcony of the White House. After promising that there would be no revenge against the defeated Confederates, he expressed hope that some blacks – 'very intelligent' men and those who had served in the Union army – would be permitted to vote.

Listening from the lawn below was a sometime actor and Southern fanatic, John Wilkes Booth. A 23 year old with dark curly hair and a droopy moustache, he had been a militia volunteer in the troop that had hanged the Abolitionist John Brown in 1859. His hatred of Lincoln and of blacks was visceral. On hearing the President, he exclaimed to a friend, 'That means nigger citizenship! Now, by God, I'll put him through!'

Three days later, on Good Friday, Lincoln and his wife Mary went to Ford's Theater in Washington to enjoy a new play called *Our American Cousin*. There the President's bodyguard, a bored Washington policeman, went into the alley behind the theatre for a drink.

During the third act Booth stepped into the President's unguarded box. Drawing a small Derringer pistol, he shot Lincoln in the back of the head, theatrically crying 'Sic semper tyrannus!' (As always to tyrants! – Brutus's words to Caesar). He then leaped to the stage, but the spur in his boot caught in a decorative flag so that as he landed he fractured his left leg. Despite his injury, he fled from the theatre.

Mortally wounded, America's greatest president was carried to a house across the street, where he died without regaining consciousness at 7.22 the following morning. He was 56 years old.

Although Booth had escaped from the theatre, two weeks later Secret Service agents and Federal troops tracked him to a barn in Virginia. They set the barn alight, and as Booth moved from corner to corner in the burning building, one of the soldiers, Boston Corbett, saw him through a crack and opened fire with his Colt revolver, hitting him in the neck. Corbett was later to claim that 'God Almighty directed me.'

Dragged from the barn, Booth lay all night on a nearby farmhouse porch, slowly bleeding to death and sucking a brandy-soaked rag given him by a charitable soldier. At dawn the next day he realised he could no longer move his hands. 'I thought I did it for the best. Useless, useless', he muttered to one of his guards just before he died. His body was whisked to a nearby federal arsenal and secretly buried under the floor.

Also on this day

978: Ethelred the Unready is crowned at Kingston upon Thames * 1471: Warwick the Kingmaker is killed at the Battle of Barnet * 1759: German composer George Handel dies in London

15 April

Mass suicide at Masada

AD 73 Masada – an unassailable fortress of rock on eighteen acres of flat, treeless mesa, baking in the Palestinian sunlight at a height of 1,400 feet. Here, near the Red Sea's south-west coast, a garrison of Jewish Zealots defied a Roman army of 15,000 men for two years before finally committing mass suicide on this day rather than surrender.

The Zealots were a fanatical group of fundamentalist Jews who were determined to establish a theocracy and destroy the hated regime of the pagan Romans in Palestine. Founded by an extremist with the historically unfortunate name of Judas, the Zealots instigated their first rebellion in the year 6, and in 66 struck again, leading a revolt in Judea during which the Roman governor was murdered and a militant regime was established in Jerusalem.

Within a year a Roman army under the command of future Emperor Vespasian had arrived in Palestine, crushing all rebel resistance. Before completion of the task, however, the then Emperor Vitellius was toppled and killed, and Vespasian left Palestine to take over the Empire, leaving his son Titus in command.

By AD 70 the Romans had recaptured Jerusalem, destroying the Second Temple in the process. But the Zealot garrison at Masada, although only 1,000 strong, thought their position could never be stormed and steadfastly refused to submit. They had not counted on the Romans' resolve and formidable siege techniques. The Roman commander Flavius Silva saw that frontal attack was impossible, and Masada's huge aqueduct-fed cisterns could keep the fortress in water almost indefinitely. His answer was to build a monumental siege ramp against the fortress's western face, which finally permitted the attackers to breach the massive defensive walls.

When the Romans at last entered the fortress, however, all they found was corpses, as the defenders, led by one Eleazar ben Jair (a descendant of the Judas who founded the Zealots), had killed themselves to a man, slaughtering even their own women and children. Only after the Romans had occupied the stronghold did two women and five children emerge from a water conduit, where they had hidden to avoid the massacre. They were the only Jewish survivors.

Suleiman the Magnificent's disastrous Russian bride

1558 Throughout history Russia and Turkey have been at each other's throats, but Russia's greatest success came by accident, through a woman who died today.

For almost 40 years Suleiman the Magnificent had been Sultan of Turkey, undoubtedly the greatest leader in the history of the Ottoman Turks. During most of that time his favourite concubine had been a woman known as Roxelana. Roxelana was not a Turk but a Russian, the daughter of an Orthodox priest. She had been captured during a Turkish raid and was promptly sent to Suleiman's harem.

Over the years Roxelana gained increasing influence over her master while bearing him three sons. Sadly for Turkey, her favourite was Selim, a man of little ability but a great thirst for alcohol.

But Roxelana was blind to Selim's faults while contriving to make Suleiman blind to the virtues of his brothers. First the older brother was framed for treason and ordered strangled by his own father. In 1558 Roxelana died, but by then the animus against Selim's younger brother was deep in Suleiman's system. Eventually this brother too was executed, leaving the path to the throne free and clear for Selim, who became Sultan on Suleiman's death in 1566.

Selim, called Sari (the Blond) for the colouring he inherited from his mother, was a weak and indolent ruler, dominated by the women of his harem and his Janissary guards. Although Turkey under Selim managed to regain Cyprus, the act prompted the formation of an anti-Ottoman alliance of Spain, the Pope and the Italian states that eventually routed the Turkish fleet at the Battle of Lepanto.

Turkey never recovered its former power all because of the myopia of a Russian mother.

Titanic

1912 She was the greatest ship afloat, the mighty *Titanic*, the most luxurious ocean liner in history. But for all her bars and dance floors, restaurants and fine cabins, she had one grievous shortage. For the 2,200 people aboard her maiden voyage, there were only 1,084 lifeboat places.

Speeding through an ice field near Newfoundland at 22 knots, the *Titanic* slammed into a submerged iceberg. At ten past two in the morning of 15 April 1912 the great liner plunged to her watery grave, carrying with her over 1,500 of her passengers and crew. It was the greatest maritime disaster of all time.

Also on this day

1452: Leonardo da Vinci is born * 1764: Mme de Pompadour, mistress of Louis XV, dies of lung cancer * 1891: US inventor Thomas Edison gives a public demonstration of his kinetoscope, a moving-picture machine

16 April

Bonnie Prince Charlie is defeated at Culloden Moor

1746 Today Bonnie Prince Charlie and his Highland troops were crushed at Culloden Moor and all hopes of a Stuart restoration to England's throne were crushed for ever with them.

Fifty-eight years earlier Charlie's grandfather, the inept and arrogant James II, had fled into exile in France, and ever since the Stuarts had been trying to regain their kingdom. In 1745, young Charlie (then only 25) determined to win back the throne for his father, the Old Pretender, who lived in exile as *de jure* James III.

Bonnie Prince Charlie's first efforts were triumphant. Having landed successfully in Scotland, he occupied Edinburgh and led his troops south as far as Derby, well into England.

Then the English army pushed him back into Scotland until this fatal day when they met a far larger English army of 9,000 men under the Duke of Cumberland at Culloden Moor.

The English opened the battle with intense and accurate cannon fire and then attacked Charlie's band of about 5,000 Scots. As the armies closed, each English soldier ignored the man directly in front of him to bayonet the vulnerable side of the man to the right. A thousand Scots were killed outright, and another thousand were hunted down and slaughtered in the following weeks. Only 50 English perished in the battle. The combat itself lasted just over half an hour.

The charismatic, charming Prince Charlie finally managed to re-cross the Channel after five and a half legendary months on the run. During the next 42 years he maintained the Stuart claim without ever being able to raise another army, and he died in France a haughty, disagreeable, dropsical old man at the age of 68.

St Francis renounces his worldly goods

1207 Born to a rich merchant father from Assisi, he had been baptised Giovanni, but his father called him Francesco (meaning French one) in honour of his French mother, and the name stuck. Francesco spent most of his youth squandering his father's money in a conspicuous and lordly fashion. By the age of 21 or 22, however, he began to change the nature of his extravagance. He sold some of his magnificent clothing as well as his house to pay for repairs to a chapel and to support an indigent priest.

Francesco's father was so alarmed by this transformation in his son that he had him brought up before an ecclesiastical court in order to disinherit him.

The hearing took place on 16 April 1207. The presiding bishop ruled that Francesco must give up all his property, since it all came from his father, and the young man, now 24, promptly stripped to the skin in the courtroom, declaring that from now on the only father he would recognise would be God. So touching was the scene that the bishop was brought to tears. Rising, he wrapped Francesco in his own cloak.

From that time on Francesco forswore property altogether, entirely devoting himself to God. During the next twenty years he founded one of the great religious orders, the Friars Minor, commonly called Franciscans. Two years after he died he was declared a saint, whom we know as St Francis of Assisi.

Also on this day

1828: Spanish painter Francisco de Goya dies * 1867: American aeroplane inventor Wilbur Wright is born

17 April

Benjamin Franklin 'lies here, food for worms'

1790 'In this world, nothing can be said to be certain except death and taxes.' So had Benjamin Franklin written to a friend, just a year before his death on this day in 1790. An emphysema had burst in his left lung and Franklin passed into a coma. At about eleven o'clock that night he quietly passed away at the advanced age of 84 years and 3 months.

During his long and eventful lifetime Franklin had been many things: diplomat, writer, postmaster, militia colonel, printer, politician, inventor, philosopher. He was the most famous American of his time, and the breadth of his fame – and of his activities – can be seen in a roster of the people he had known personally.

Naturally he knew Washington, Hamilton, John Adams and Jefferson. The last of these had taken over from Franklin as ambassador to France. When asked if he 'replaced' Franklin, Jefferson replied, 'No one can replace him, sir. I am only his successor.'

Franklin's acquaintance also included: the American naval hero John Paul Jones and the British sea captain and explorer James Cook, Louis XVI and Marie Antoinette, Christian VII of Denmark, James Boswell, Edward Gibbon and Horace Walpole, Pitt the Elder, Voltaire, Edmund Burke, Joseph Priestley, Mirabeau, Danton and the French aristocrat who fought in the American Revolution, the marquis de Lafayette (before Lafayette went to America).

Many years earlier, when he was only 28, Franklin had written his own epitaph: 'The body of Benjamin Franklin, Printer (Like the cover of an old book, its contents torn out and stript of its lettering and gilding), Lies here, food for worms; But the work shall not be lost, for it will (as he believed) appear once more in a new and more elegant edition, revised and corrected by the author.'

The San Francisco earthquake

1906 San Francisco was a smaller city then, with only about 400,000 residents. Most of them were asleep at 5.12 a.m. when the immense quake hit. Today's scientists have calculated that it reached an awesome 8.3 on the Richter scale.

The great San Francisco earthquake destroyed many of the city's buildings, but the ensuing fire that leaped from house to house in a city mostly built of wood caused even more damage.

When it was over, 514 city blocks – or over four square miles – had been devastated. Some 28,188 buildings were in ruins and under them lay over two and a half thousand bodies. It was the most destructive event, natural or man-made, ever to take place on American soil.

Despite the enormous damage, San Francisco was quick to recover. Within three years over 20,000 new buildings had been constructed.

Also on this day

1895: The Sino-Japanese War ends with the Treaty of Shimonoseki

18 April

Martin Luther defies an emperor

1521 The Diet of Worms is remembered for the clash of wills of two of history's most strong-willed men. Sitting in judgement was the young Holy Roman Emperor Charles V, only 21 but already the most powerful monarch in the long millennium between Charlemagne and Napoleon. Testifying to his faith was a German monk who defied the True Church, Martin Luther.

Luther came to Worms eager to defend himself from accusations of heresy, in spite of warnings from his friends that Worms was a town 'where his death had already been decided upon'. Begged by a supporter not to enter the city, the monk replied, 'Wenn so viel Teufel su Worms waren Siegel auf Dachern, so wollt' ich hinein.' (I am resolved to enter Worms although as many devils should set at me as there are tiles on the housetops.)

Appalled by the corruption in Rome and certain of his own principles, Luther refused to accept the absolute authority of the Church, bowing only to 'scripture and plain reason'. But Charles could not tolerate that 'a single monk, deluded by his own judgement' could presumptuously conclude 'that all Christians up till now are wrong'.

The prosecution put its case, to which the 38-year-old monk refused to agree. Finally, on this day, Luther concluded his defence with the famous words, 'Hier stehe ich. Ich kann nicht anders.' (Here I stand. I cannot do otherwise.)

Luther was condemned, but the Emperor, who had previously promised him safe conduct, refused to have him seized. Charles spent the remaining 37 years of his life unsuccessfully trying to undo what Luther had started. Luther spent the remaining 25 years of his life preaching the same 'heresy' in Protestant Germany.

Paul Revere's ride

1775 It was at ten o'clock on a Tuesday evening filled with bright moonlight that Paul Revere set out on the most celebrated ride in American history to alert his countrymen that British troops were marching.

The British were to leave Boston for nearby Lexington, where two dangerous radicals, Sam Adams and John Hancock, were in hiding. Then the soldiers would fall on Concord, only a few miles further, to seize rebel arms and supplies.

'One if by land, two if by sea', Revere is traditionally supposed to have said, referring to the lanterns he instructed two friends to place in Boston's North Church as a signal to patriots across the bay in Charlestown that the British troops were leaving Boston by boat across the Back Bay to Cambridge. Then he set off for Lexington on a borrowed horse called Brown Beauty to warn Adams and Hancock. Revere then galloped off on his historic twelve-mile run to Concord, waking every household and warning every Minuteman (members of the local militia who promised 'to be ready in a minute') on the way.

Revere's ride was more than effective. Adams and Hancock both escaped, and about 350 American patriots came to defend against the British.

The next day the undisciplined Americans, many hunters and Indian fighters, used every trick of concealment and stealth to rout a British force at Lexington and Concord during the first battle of the American Revolution. At day's end some 73 British lay dead with a further 200 missing or wounded. Forty-nine Americans were killed plus 46 more wounded.

Although Paul Revere is remembered most because of his famous ride, his real talent was as an artisan. He was the greatest silversmith America has yet produced.

Napoleon restores the Church

1802 Ever since becoming First Consul, Napoleon had tried to reconcile France to the Church of Rome. Not only was there much confusion regarding whether pre- or post-revolutionary priests should control certain dioceses but, more important, as Napoleon himself had commented, 'Only religion can make men support inequalities in rank, because it consoles for everything.' Finally, on 18 April 1802, the famous Concordat was signed in fine ceremony at Notre Dame, and Catholicism was restored to its place as France's premier religion. Napoleon himself attended the ceremony, decked out in his First Consul's uniform of bright red.

The following day Napoleon asked General Augerau what he thought of the ceremony. 'Very beautiful', responded the general. 'The only thing missing were the millions of men who killed themselves to destroy that which we've re-established.'

Also on this day

1480: Lucrezia Borgia, illegitimate daughter of the future Pope Alexander VI, is born * 1506: The first cornerstone of a new St Peter's Cathedral in Rome is laid * 1593: Shakespeare's poem *Venus and Adonis* is entered for publication

19 April

Sir Francis Drake singes the King of Spain's beard

1587 Today the man Queen Elizabeth called 'my deare pyrat' sailed his fleet into the Spanish port of Cadiz and launched a pre-emptive strike against England's great enemy, King Philip II of Spain.

Flying no flags to indicate his force was anything but a friendly fleet, Sir Francis Drake, aboard his flagship the *Elizabeth Bonaventure*, led sixteen warships into an unsuspecting harbour packed with merchant shipping. Spanish galleys defending the port proved no match against English broadsides. By the next day, 24 Spanish ships laden with supplies for the Spanish armada had been looted and burned or sunk. His work done, Drake sailed out of Cadiz to continue his depredations elsewhere.

In his long career in the twin roles of bold pirate and naval commander, Drake literally covered the world. He was the first Englishman ever to sight the Pacific Ocean. He was also the first man after Magellan to sail around the world, a feat for which Elizabeth knighted him in 1580. For his repeated incursions against their treasure fleets in the Caribbean and on the Spanish Main, the Spanish called him 'El Draque' (the Dragon). They also called him 'the devil', which, not surprisingly, was the very same term the English used for King Philip

Drake's raids against Cadiz and other enemy supply bases during the year 1587 – 'singeing the King of Spain's beard', he termed these actions – had the valuable strategic effect of disrupting Spain's preparations for the armada and delaying for a year its sailing, so gaining precious time for England to prepare for invasion. They were also a foretaste of what the armada would encounter in the way of naval combat when it ventured up the English Channel the next year.

The first battle of the American Revolution

1775 Determined to crush a nascent rebellion, British General Thomas Gage today ordered some 700 soldiers on a pre-dawn raid towards the small Massachusetts town of Concord, where the American colonists' military supplies were stored. En route he captured Paul Revere, one of America's staunchest patriots, who only the previous day had ridden to warn his compatriots that the British were coming. Here is his eyewitness account of the start of the first battle of the American Revolution:

> '... I [took] to the right, towards a Wood, at the bottom of the Pasture, intending when I gained that, to jump my Horse & run afoot; just as I reached it, out started six [British] officers, siesed my bridle, put their pistols to my Breast, ordered me to dismount, which I did. One of them,

who appeared to have the command there, and much of a Gentleman, asked me where I came from; I told him, he asked me what time I left it; I told him. He seemed surprised, said Sr., may I crave your name. I answered my name is Revere, what said he, Paul Revere; I answered yes; the others abused me much; but he told me not to be afraid, no one should hurt me. I told him they would miss their aim. He said they should not, they were only waiting for some Deserters they expected down the Road. I told him I knew better, I knew what they were after; that I had alarmed the country all the way up, ... and I should have 500 men there soon; ... one of them ... clapd his Pistol to my head, and said he was going to ask me some questions, if I did not tell the truth, he would blow my brains out. ... he then ordered me to mount my horse, ... He said to me "We are now going towards your friends, and if you attempt to run, or we are insulted, we will blow your Brains. ..."

'We rid towards Lexington, a quick pace; they very often insulted me calling me Rebel, &c &c. after we had got about a mile, I was given to the Serjant to lead, he was Ordered to take out his pistol ... and if I run, to execute the Major's sentence. When we got within about half a Mile of the Meeting house, we heard a gun fired; the Major asked me what it was for, I told him to alarm the country; ... when we got within sight of the Meeting House, we heard a Volley of guns fired, as I supposed at the tavern, as an Alarm; the major ordered us to halt ... he then asked the Serjant if his horse was tired, he said yes; he Ordered him to take my horse; I dismounted, the Sarjant mounted my horse ... & rode off down the road. I then went to the house where I left [Sam] Adams & [John] Hancock, and told them what had happened; their friends advised them to go out of the way; I went with them, about two miles a cross road; after resting myself, I sett off with another man to go back to the Tavern [at Lexington], to enquire the news; when we got there, we were told the troops were within two miles. We went to the Tavern to git a Trunk of papers belonging to Col. Hancock, before we left the house, I saw the [British] troops from the Chamber window. We made haste & had to pass thro' our Militia, who were on the green behind the Meeting house, to the number as I supposed, about 50 or 60. I went thro' them; as I passed I heard the commanding officer speake to his men to this purpose. "Lett the troops passby, & don't molest them, without they begin first." I had to go a cross Road, but had not got half Gun shot off when the [British] Troops appeared in sight behinde the Meeting House; they made a short halt, when a gun was fired. I heard the report, turned my head, and saw the smoake in front of the Troops, they imeaditly gave a great shout, ran a few paces, and then the whole fired ...'

Of the Lexington militiamen who had assembled on the green at daylight, seven lay dead; nine more were wounded. Now the British column marched west towards Concord.

But when the British finally reached Concord, a force of about 350 armed Americans compelled them to withdraw to Boston some fifteen miles away. This ignominious retreat was a disaster for the British as Americans sniped at them from behind trees and stone walls along the roadside. By the time the British reached safety they had suffered 273 casualties against only 95 for the rebels and the American Revolution was well under way.

Also on this day

1824: George Gordon, Lord Byron, dies of malaria in Missolonghi on his way to fight for Greek independence * 1881: British Prime Minister Benjamin Disraeli (Lord Beaconsfield) dies * 1882: British naturalist Charles Darwin dies

20 April

Adolf Hitler is born

1889 At 6.30 in the evening of this chilly, overcast Easter Saturday, in the Austrian border town of Braunau am Inn, near Linz, Adolf Hitler was born to a middle-class Catholic family living in modest but comfortable circumstances. He was the fourth child of the union but the first to survive infancy. The household, which included two older children from the father's previous marriage, would in time be enlarged by the addition of two more children (one of whom died at six), an aunt (the wife's younger sister), a maid and a cook.

The parents were second cousins, a relationship that had required dispensation from Rome before they could be married in 1885. The father, Alois, was a customs collector in the Austrian service whose hobby was bee keeping. He had been born out of wedlock with his mother's family name Shickelgruber. At the age of 39 he attempted to legitimise himself by adopting his father's name, but changing Heidler to Hitler. He was a bastard in more ways than one, being also a strict, domineering personality and, when drunk, a harsh disciplinarian inclined towards violence with family members, especially his sons.

Klara (née Polzl), Adolf's mother, was Alois Hitler's third wife. She had worked in the household as a servant during both of her husband's previous marriages. She was submissive, churchgoing, and desperately protective of her children and stepchildren, especially Adolf, who, his younger sister Paula remembered, 'challenged my father to extreme harshness and who got his sound thrashing every day'.

These events, which provide no sign of what was to come, are among the few verifiable facts of Adolf Hitler's first years. The rest is speculation or myth. Ron Rosenbaum described the record of Hitler's early life as 'a realm disguised by his own deceitfulness, camouflaged by thickets of conflicting evidence, a tangled undergrowth of unreliable memory and testimony, of misleading rumor, myth, and biographical apocrypha'.

Napoleon III is born

1808 Born this date was one of history's few dreamers who actually accomplished most of his dreams, Louis Napoleon Bonaparte. Forty-five years later he was to become Emperor Napoleon III of France, having staged a *coup d'état* the previous year because the French constitution prohibited him from seeking a second term as President. He managed to retain that glorious position for eighteen years, some eight years longer than his famous uncle Napoleon I had done.

Napoleon III was a curious mixture of tyrant and liberal. Fearing a challenge from French republicans, he strongly curtailed individual liberty, resorting to the methods of the police state. Until late in his reign he dictated to all government departments, ensuring that his will and his alone would prevail. In many ways he resembled a rather more benign Hitler. He capitalised on false crises (like a non-existent revolution in 1851) and was a master of propaganda.

On the other hand, Napoleon restored universal suffrage and promoted public works, industry and agriculture. He backed the building of the Suez Canal and the construction of railways in France. He was deeply involved in the rebuilding of Paris and empowered his prefect of the Seine, Baron Haussmann, to rebuild great swathes of the city.

Louis was the son of the first Napoleon's brother Louis (erstwhile King of Holland) and Hortense de Beauharnais, the daughter of Napoleon's first wife Joséphine. Therefore Napoleon I was both Louis's uncle and his step-grandfather.

Also on this day

1768: Italian landscape painter Canaletto (Giovanni Antonio Canal) dies in Venice * 1770: Captain James Cook discovers Australia

21 April

The tragic romance of Abelard and Héloïse

1142 'Sweet as cinnamon' were her embraces, wrote Pierre Abelard of his beloved mistress Héloïse, and the romance of Abelard and Héloïse still speaks to us today across almost nine centuries.

Abelard was born in Brittany near Nantes but went to study in Paris at the age of twenty. A master dialectician, his brilliant mind and impassioned oratory soon won him the mastership of Notre Dame. When he was in his early 30s he established his own school just outside the gates of Paris, drawing a large number of admiring students. For this Abelard is considered to be the founder of the University of Paris.

Shortly, however, his career was to be cut short by the most famous love affair of the Middle Ages. When Abelard was about 40, Fulbert, the canon of Notre Dame, entrusted him with the education of his beautiful niece Héloïse, then nineteen or twenty. They fell deeply in love, and she bore him a son to whom they gave the peculiar name of Astralabe. Subsequently the couple were secretly married. But Uncle Fulbert was convinced that her lover intended to abandon her. Thirsting for revenge, he had Abelard seized by hired hooligans and castrated.

Despairing for a love now irretrievably lost, Abelard then became a monk at the royal abbey of Saint-Denis and browbeat Héloïse into becoming a nun at Argenteuil. The couple exchanged some beautifully poignant love letters, most now lost. Later, when Argenteuil was dissolved, Héloïse moved into a religious community called the Paraclete, which Abelard had founded. There she became the abbess.

Abelard continued to teach but eventually found himself in opposition to Rome and so retired to the famous Benedictine abbey at Cluny in Burgundy. On this day in 1142 he died there at the age of 63. Perhaps in extremis he was not as certain of his religious principles as he had always been in the midst of life, for his final words were a plaintive 'I don't know! I don't know!'

Abelard was buried in the Paraclete church, as he had requested. Héloïse outlived him by 22 years and according to legend died with the words: 'In death, at last, let me rest with Abelard.' Initially she was buried beside her lover at the Paraclete. In the 19th century they were moved to the Père-Lachaise cemetery in Paris.

Rome — the beginning

753 BC On this day, according to Plutarch, the city of Rome was founded.

The tale starts at Alba Longa, a town about twelve miles south-west of Rome. Virgil tells us that Aeneas, a Trojan who escaped from Troy after its fall, established the tribe that lived there.

Years later Alba Longa's King Numitor was betrayed by his brother Amulius, who seized the throne and forced Numitor's daughter Rhea Silvia to become a Vestal Virgin to preclude her producing a child to threaten his rule.

But Rhea Silvia was less virginal than her order. Seduced by the god Mars, she produced twin sons, Romulus and Remus.

When Amulius learned of the birth he imprisoned poor Rhea Silvia and ordered her twins to be drowned in the Tiber. But the man who should have drowned them took pity instead and left them in a shallow trough that floated down the river until they reached the spot where Rome now stands.

Here Romulus and Remus were suckled by a she-wolf until they were found by a farmer, who raised them. In time they returned to Alba Longa thirsting for revenge. They succeeded in killing their uncle Amulius and restored their grandfather to the throne.

Having satisfied family honour, they returned to the exact place on the Tiber where the she-wolf had found them and founded Rome on 21 April 753 BC.

Romulus's career did not end there, although Remus's shortly did, as his brother killed him in a dispute over a city wall. Romulus became King of Rome and later organised the rape of the Sabine women. But he never died. One day he mysteriously disappeared in a storm, and Romans believed he had been turned into a god.

The last of the first Tudor

1509 After crushing the murderous Richard III on Bosworth Field, Henry VII provided England with 24 years of uninterrupted peace from foreign wars and laid the foundations for the great Tudor flowering that was to come under his son and particularly under his granddaughter, Elizabeth I.

Henry was a contradiction to the age in which he lived. He preferred peace to war, fidelity to licentiousness, frugality to the building of palaces. His narrow face, with thin, pursed lips and suspicious eyes, shows a rather cold-blooded and calculating man, wary of his fellows.

Yet the England of only 3 million souls over which he ruled owed him much for the tranquillity he gave them after the calamitous Wars of the Roses. But although Henry fought no foreign wars, he had trouble enough at home.

Henry had no difficulty in defeating the first uprising led by Richard III's chamberlain, Lord Lovell, but fought a full-scale battle against rebellious forces led by Lambert Simnel, a simple country boy who was duped into claiming he was the Earl of Warwick. Simnel was defeated and captured, and Henry put him to work as a scullery boy in his own kitchens.

Later another impostor led a more dangerous revolt. A handsome Flemish lad named Perkin Warbeck claimed to be Richard, one of the princes that Richard III had locked up in the Tower of London. He invaded England three times with backing from half a dozen Continental powers, but Henry finally captured him in 1497 and executed him two years later.

When Henry breathed his last at Richmond Palace on 21 April 1509 he was a worn-out 52. After giving his country 24 years of peace his last gift was 38 years of tyranny – the reign of his son, Henry VIII.

Also on this day

1574: The first Medici duke, Cosimo de' Medici dies of an apoplectic fit in the Medici Palace, Florence * 1699: French playwright Jean-Baptiste Racine dies in Paris * 1836: American political leader Sam Houston defeats Mexican general Santa Anna at the Battle of San Jacinto * 1910: American writer Mark Twain (Samuel Clemens) dies

22 April

The tale of the Potemkin villages

1787 On this day the fat and ageing Empress Catherine the Great of Russia sailed down the Dnieper from Kiev with a fleet of seven imperial galleys and over 80 other boats on one of the most astonishing royal outings in history. The Master of Ceremonies was her former lover and current Chief Minister Grigory Potemkin. Other passengers included a full entourage of courtiers and foreign envoys and her current lover, Alexander Yermolov, 24 years her junior.

The purpose of the voyage was to inspect the towns and military installations that Potemkin had established along the river and in the Crimea, recently annexed from Turkey. A secondary motive was to meet with Holy Roman Emperor Josef II to plot the destruction of Turkey and the dismemberment of Poland.

Grigory Potemkin was one of the most profligate and effective showmen the world has known. Determined to show Catherine his achievements in the best possible light, he spent millions of roubles refurbishing the towns and palaces along the route and organising fantastic military displays to impress his sovereign. It was he who had arranged the fleet with its 3,000 oarsmen and crew, including an orchestra of 120 musicians. Local peasants were rounded up to line the riverside to watch the royal procession – not difficult to arrange for serfs who had never before seen the Empress and were curious. Firework displays were frequent and stops along the way featured huge military demonstrations such as a mock attack by some 3,000 Cossack horsemen.

Eventually the procession continued by carriage into the Crimea to inspect the formidable war fleet that Potemkin had built in only two years (and that the following year the American captain John Paul Jones would command in victory over the Turkish navy). At the end of the three-month journey he brought the Empress back through Poltava, scene of Peter the Great's historic victory over the Swedes 78 years before. There he staged yet another military spectacle using 50,000 troops playing Swedes and Russians.

One reason Potemkin so desired to impress Catherine was to counter the incessant and dangerous criticism aimed at him by jealous nobles whom he had supplanted in the corridors of power. His stage management of the Empress's journey down the Dnieper was brilliant and momentarily successful, but he had reckoned without the wiles of a disgruntled Saxon diplomat named Georg von Helbig, who had not been invited on the trip. Miffed, Helbig started rumours that the towns past which the imperial fleet had sailed were in fact only pasteboard façades. He also maintained that the crowds of peasants thronging the riverbank were in fact only one group, transported each night down the river with a change of costume to deceive the onlookers. In dispatches to his masters in Germany, he coined the phrase 'Potemkinsche Dörfer' – Potemkin Villages.

Potemkin's rivals quickly took up these stories, spreading them throughout first Russia and then Europe. They were given additional substance by the testimony of Catherine's son Paul, who hated Potemkin both as his mother's lover and because of his unlimited power. Sadly for Potemkin – one of Russia's greatest ministers – today it is for the mythical Potemkin villages that he is best remembered.

Birth of a great salonière

1766 Although born today in Paris, Germaine de Staël was actually a Swiss née Necker who later married a Swede. She was a rabid republican whose theatrical antics amused many but infuriated a few, including Napoleon, who eventually banned her from France. She was also, by any standards, an accomplished intellectual, and invitations to her Parisian salon were prized.

Most of Madame de Staël's life was spent intriguing, writing now forgotten books, changing men and overdramatising herself. 'Jamais, jamais, je ne serai jamais aimée comme j'aime!' (Never, never, never shall I be loved as I love!) she once famously lamented.

She took many lovers but typically considered her relationships as noble womanly sentiments, writing 'L'amour est l'histoire de la vie des femmes; c'est un épisode dans celle des hommes.' (Love is the story of a woman's life; it is an episode in a man's.)

The lover with whom she was most associated was another Swiss, the novelist Benjamin Constant, with whom she spent a see-saw fourteen years, but an earlier one, Talleyrand, by whom she had a child, probably knew her best. 'She is such a true friend', he said, 'that she would throw all her friends into the water for the pleasure of pulling them out again.'

Germaine de Staël had a romantic fear of death as well as her share of sexual conceit. 'When I look on these arms, these breasts at the sight of which every eye is filled with lust,' she confided to a friend, 'and when I think that this splendour must one day be food for repulsive reptiles, a cold shudder passes through me, a combination of horror and pity.'

She died in 1817 at the age of 51.

Birth of the man who fathered Tom Jones

1707 If you have read *Tom Jones* you already know a good deal about its author Henry Fielding, who was born this day in 1707. Not that *Tom Jones* is auto-biographical, only that the character of its hero so closely reflects that of its author.

Fielding was born into a family of some social pretence – descended from the Earls of Denbigh. But his father had gambled away whatever fortune he had inherited during the course of four marriages. Henry attended Eton but then had to earn the money on which he lived. Like his father, and like Tom Jones, he was both improvident and intemperate. He loved his food, his drink and his snuff. In spite of this, he was an avid scholar and amassed a huge library, investing in books whatever money he failed to lose at gambling.

Fielding's other passion was women. He felt strongly 'the Desire of satisfying a voracious Appetite with a certain Quantity of delicate white human Flesh'. Although happily married, he was not above temptation, and after the death of his wife he impregnated and married his cook, in that order.

At heart Fielding was a truly decent man who, apart from writing for a living, also served as a fair and compassionate magistrate.

Henry Fielding died on 8 October 1754 in Lisbon at the age of only 47, perhaps exhausted by a life of hard work and high living.

Also on this day

1500: Portuguese explorer Pedro Cabral lands on the coast of Brazil, claiming it for Portugal * 1724: Prussian philosopher Immanuel Kant is born * 1827: English caricaturist Thomas Rowlandson dies

23 April

The coronation of Charles II

1661 It was a brilliantly sunny St George's Day when King Charles II was ferried from Whitehall Palace down the Thames to the Tower of London to start the magnificent procession to Westminster Abbey where he was to be crowned. For monarchists it was a day of rejoicing, but also one with small reminders of the Civil War and the execution of Charles's father Charles I a dozen years before.

Flanked by wildly cheering crowds, the royal cavalcade proceeded from the Tower along unpaved streets strewn with gravel towards Whitehall, where the elder Charles had been beheaded. According to the eyewitness Samuel Pepys, the procession of carriages and horses was 'so glorious ... with gold and silver that we were not able to look at it.' Reaching Whitehall at three in the afternoon, the King and his retinue dismounted to walk on a blue carpet to the Abbey, where the same Archbishop of Canterbury who had attended Charles I on the scaffold placed the crown upon the new King's head.

To mark the joyous restoration, Charles's coronation was ostentatiously splendid – it cost over £30,000, a stupendous sum in the 17th century. The ceremony at the Abbey was followed by a magnificent banquet in Westminster Hall, the same great chamber where the first Charles had been tried and condemned. But this time there was only jubilation, as the great and good of the land drank the King's health and the King's Champion rode through the hall in full armour challenging, 'If any dare deny Charles Stuart to be lawful King of

England, here is a champion that calls him a liar and a false traitor and would fight with him.' Outside in the streets drunken crowds celebrated to the light of bonfires.

Charles reigned until his death almost 24 years later. His greatest achievement was the tranquillity he gave his nation after years of civil war and Cromwell's dour protectorate. He was a popular king who became known as the Merry Monarch for his carousing and whoring, supposedly fathering over twenty bastards. As one of his contemporaries recorded, 'A king is supposed to be the father of his people, and Charles certainly was father to a good many of them.'

Also on this day

1564: William Shakespeare is born * 1616: William Shakespeare and Miguel Cervantes die on the same day * 1775: British painter J.M.W. Turner is born * 1850: British poet William Wordsworth dies at Grasmere

24 April

The ill-starred marriage of Sisi and Emperor Franz Joseph

1854 Today, in Vienna's Augustinerkirche just outside the Hofburg, Austria's tall, blond 23-year-old Emperor Franz Joseph married Elisabeth Wittelsbach, his strikingly beautiful sixteen-year-old cousin known to friends and to history as Sisi. It looked to be a fairytale marriage, but the demands of empire, a domineering mother-in-law and Sisi's neurotic restlessness transformed it into a tragedy.

Franz Joseph had been meant to marry Sisi's older sister the year before but at the very first encounter – a family luncheon at Bad Ischl – his eye fell on the stunning Sisi. Two days later they became engaged. The following year she was brought down the Danube to Vienna in a great bridal ship decorated with flowers. Church bells rang and crowds cheered as her procession made its way across the city. Nearly a thousand people crammed into the church to witness the marriage ceremony, conducted by a cardinal with the assistance of 70 archbishops and bishops. At the great Coronation Ball two nights later, Johann Strauss the Younger conducted the orchestra.

So, in a setting from a Lehar operetta began a long and unhappy marriage that lasted 44 years and produced four children, among them Rudolph, the long-hoped-for male heir to the Austrian throne. But right from the beginning troubles multiplied. Franz Joseph's mother Sophie, a powerful and domineering woman, constantly interfered, virtually bringing up the first two children herself rather than letting Sisi do it. Meanwhile Franz Joseph was above all a slave to Habsburg duty and the obligations of empire, and the marriage was further weakened by his infidelities.

Sisi, an undisciplined free spirit, was unable or unwilling to adapt herself to the role of Empress, a failing suggested even before the marriage, when she told her nanny two days after Franz Joseph's proposal, 'Yes, I do love the Emperor – if only he weren't the Emperor!' She claimed she would rather marry a butcher.

Although she could be gay and vivacious, Sisi remained at heart a child, incessantly complaining and moping and bearing grudges for life. Not unlike Diana, Princess of Wales, in the next century, this dazzling woman was fixated with being thin and beautiful. Her riding became her obsession, and she became the finest horsewoman in Europe. She found court life oppressive and her husband unresponsive, and after six years of marriage she repeatedly left her family to live in seclusion on Madeira, on Corfu and in Venice. Franz Joseph's infidelities soon made her seek her own, and she entered an affair with her handsome Magyar secretary, Count Imri Hunyadi. She kept a diary in verse that reveals both her isolation and her rather jejune self-dramatisation:

Ich wandle einsam hin auf dieser Erde,	I wander lonely on this earth,
Der Lust, dem Leben längst schon	Enjoyment and life rejected
abgewandt;	long ago;
Es teilt mein Seelenleben kein Gefährte,	My inner soul has no companion,
Die Seele gab es nie, die mich verstand.	There was never another soul that
	understood me.

But neither Sisi by her travels nor Franz Joseph by his work could escape the tragedies that dogged the Habsburg family. In 1867 Franz Joseph's younger brother Maximilian, briefly Emperor of Mexico in a disastrous colonial venture, was shot to death by a Mexican firing squad. In 1889, in one of the great scandals of the century, Crown Prince Rudolph killed his mistress and himself in the royal hunting lodge at Mayerling.

In her diary Sisi once wrote, 'Nonetheless I always go in search of my fate. I know that nothing can stop me from meeting it on the day when I must. All men must meet their fate at a given hour. Fate closes its eyes for a long time, but one day it finds us anyway.' In 1898 fate found Sisi on a trip to Switzerland.

While she was waiting on the quayside in Geneva for a steamer to take her up the lake to Montreux, a 24-year-old anarchist named Luigi Lucheni stabbed her in the side with a sharpened file. Because she was so tightly corseted she was unaware of how badly she had been hurt and walked aboard the ship. There she collapsed and died, her last words a plaintive 'What happened to me?'

Even then tragedy continued to stalk the Habsburgs. Franz Joseph's nephew Franz Ferdinand, who became Austria's heir apparent on his cousin Rudolph's suicide, was shot to death, along with his wife, at Sarajevo in 1914. With most of his family dead and the empire he was meant to preserve crumbling around him, Franz Joseph, duty-bound to the last, died at the age of 86 on 19 November 1916, having spent most of the previous night at his desk signing wartime orders.

Halley's Comet heralds an invasion

1066 Comets blazing across the sky were regarded as sure signs of great events, and in England men wondered what the heavens had ordained as the sky was lit 'with a mighty mass of flame' on this Monday just after Easter.

This comet did indeed portend the extraordinary; only five months later England was to be successfully invaded – for the last time in history.

The invader of course was the Norman William the Conqueror. The comet's significance to the medieval mind is shown by its prominent inclusion in the historic Bayeux Tapestry.

In 1682, after it had appeared eight more times, the comet that foretold William's coming was christened Halley's Comet after the astronomer who calculated that it would appear every 77 years. We now know that Halley's Comet measures about nine miles by five, with a tail that stretches thousands of miles. It is made of ice and tiny rock particles and travels at over 80,000 miles per hour.

Emperor Charles V wins the Battle of Mühlberg

1547 The 47-year-old Holy Roman Emperor Charles V was in his strength. Over two decades earlier he had seen the heretic Martin Luther outlawed; later he had held the King of France in captivity in Madrid for a year; still later he had chased Suleiman the Magnificent and his vast army from the gates of Vienna. And now he was on the verge of crushing the rebellious Protestant princes of Germany who dared challenge the authority of their Emperor.

Charles's army was like its master, of no fixed nationality. There were Netherlanders and Italians, good German Catholics and those prime shock troops, the Spanish *tercios*. Reaching the Elbe early on a misty morning, some valiant Spaniards under the command of the Duke of Alba took their swords between their teeth and swam the frigid river. Soon the rest of the army was across, and the enemy, caught completely by surprise, was shortly scattered in defeat.

This was the famous Battle of Mühlberg, which gave Charles control of all of Germany. He was then at the pinnacle of his power, master of much of Europe, without challenger. Today Titian's great equestrian portrait of Charles celebrating the victory hangs in the Prado in Madrid. The armoured Emperor rides a prancing horse of unnerving black; the skies overhead are somehow full of menace, and Charles's sad eyes seem to reflect the disillusions of a lifetime rather than triumph. Indeed, within eight years, the great Emperor would take his retreat, defeated by the knowledge that his aim to unite his Empire in the religion of Rome could never be accomplished.

Also on this day
1731: English novelist Daniel Defoe dies * 1770: English writer Thomas Chatterton commits suicide * 1898: Spain declares war on the US to start the Spanish–American War

25 April

Birth of a king who built a chapel and became a saint

1214 Today a baby boy was born in the town of Poissy, about 15 miles west of Paris. His father was a prince, one day to be Louis VIII of France; his mother was a redoubtable Spanish princess named Blanche of Castile. The baby, too, would be christened Louis and he also would become King of France.

Louis IX would be one of the few monarchs in history whose greatness – universally recognised by his contemporaries – would be in his character alone. He would become the great ideal of the Middle Ages, devout, charitable and just, with greater moral force than the Pope. So great was his reputation for fairness that he was often asked to adjudicate in major disputes in foreign countries.

Louis's most lasting contribution to civilisation is the magnificent Sainte-Chapelle in Paris, which he had constructed between 1243 and 1248. Sainte-Chapelle's superlative stained glass covers most of three sides of the chapel, with over 1,100 scenes in the fifteen windows.

Young Louis would reign for 44 years as Louis IX, and after his death from plague while on crusade he would be canonised a saint.

The first Prince of Wales

1284 The Welsh have always been an independent lot, and even when conquered by England's Edward I they placed great restrictions on the sort of prince they would accept to rule them. Whoever the King would choose, said the Welsh barons, he must speak neither English nor French and must have been born in Wales.

Fortunately for Edward, just a few months earlier, on 25 April 1284, his wife Eleanor had given birth to a son in the King's new castle at Caernarvon in Wales. Thus Edward met the barons' demands in full by presenting to them his infant son, who at the time spoke neither English nor French and who was born in their native country.

The son in question was also called Edward, eventually to rule England as Edward II. Because he was born there he became the first Prince of Wales, the title by which the male heir to the English throne is still known more than seven centuries later.

Joseph Conrad publishes his first book

1895 In London this day the firm of T. Fisher Unwin published a first novel by an unknown author. It was a romance set in an exotic locale, East Borneo, with a plot that involved an obscure Dutch trader who presided over a derelict trading post, his very large but unfinished house, his Malay wife, his beautiful half-caste daughter, and his dreams of wealth, now all but crumbled.

The title of the novel was *Almayer's Folly* and the author, a 37-year-old Polish-born ship's officer in the British maritime service, was named Joseph Conrad. He had begun writing the novel in 1889, and it took him five years to complete, during which he had been at sea for considerable periods. He had nearly lost the manuscript twice, once in a Berlin railway station, later in the rapids of the Congo River.

Before a typescript was delivered by messenger to the publisher, only one other person had read the novel. In 1893 Mr W.H. Jacques, a young Cambridge graduate suffering from tuberculosis, was travelling for his health aboard the full-rigged clipper *Torrens* on its Adelaide–London run (126 days). In the course of the voyage he had struck up an acquaintance with the ship's first mate, who on an impulse asked if the passenger would care to read nine hand-written chapters of an unfinished novel. Jacques took the manuscript to his cabin. The next day Conrad asked him whether the book was worth finishing. Jacques said, 'Distinctly.' Had he been interested, asked the mate. 'Very much', replied Jacques.

The two house readers for T. Fisher Unwin must have agreed with Jacques's opinion, for the novel was quickly accepted for publication. When it came out, reviews were generally favourable, romances set in exotic places then being very much in fashion, thanks to the works of Rudyard Kipling, Robert Louis Stevenson and others. One reviewer wrote that Conrad might well become the 'Kipling of the Malay Archipelago'.

A better indication of Conrad's future was the fact that by the time *Almayer's Folly* was published he was at work on a second novel which would appear in print the following year as *An Outcast of the Islands*.

Also on this day

1599: English dictator Oliver Cromwell is born in Huntingdon * 1945: American and Russian troops meet on the Elbe River during the Second World War

26 April

The Pazzi Conspiracy: murder in the cathedral, Italian style

1478 Lorenzo the Magnificent was only 28 years old, but he was already senior among the Medici and as such de facto ruler of republican Florence. Athletic, fun loving, both shrewd and intelligent, he had a dark, masculine face of no beauty but strong appeal. But as the greatest man in Italy's grandest family he also had his enemies, and in early 1478 Florence's other leading family, the Pazzi, were conspiring to take over the state.

The chief conspirator was young Francesco de' Pazzi, who schemed with Francesco Salviati, Archbishop-designate of Pisa, whom Lorenzo had prevented from taking over his bishopric. The two plotters worked with tacit approval of conniving Pope Innocent VIII.

The plot was simple. Lorenzo and his brother Giuliano had to die, and the most convenient time and place would be in church, when they would be together, unsuspecting, and, with luck, unarmed. So the murder was planned for Sunday 26 April, in the red-domed cathedral of Florence. The signal for attack was to be the ringing of the sanctuary bell for the Elevation of the Host. In such a setting, it seemed appropriate that those enlisted to stab Lorenzo in the back were two disguised priests.

As the bell sounded the priests struck, but so ham-handedly that only one even wounded Lorenzo, slashing him across the back of his neck. Pouring blood, Lorenzo spun to avoid his attackers and escaped through a side door of the cathedral. His brother Giuliano was not so lucky; in a frenzy of blood lust, Francesco de' Pazzi and an accomplice stabbed him nineteen times and left him dead on the cathedral floor.

Still trying to carry out the coup, the conspirators rushed to the Palazzo della Signoria, Florence's town hall, to seize control of the city, but there Medici supporters surrounded and cornered them. Seizing Archbishop Salviati, Lorenzo's allies tied a rope to his neck and lowered him out of the window.

Francesco de' Pazzi was stripped naked and then hanged from another window to dangle alongside the archbishop. Rioting citizens in the piazza below saw the archbishop fix his teeth into Pazzi's naked body as they swung choking and goggle-eyed at the end of their ropes.

Some 80 conspirators were hunted down and executed, including the two priests, who were first castrated, then hanged. When all was over the Medici were more powerful than ever, thanks to the crushing of what has become known as the Pazzi conspiracy. To this day *pazzo* in Italian means 'crazy'.

Guernica

1937 At 4.30 this Monday afternoon – market day – Adolf Hitler's Condor Legion, using the Spanish Civil War as a testing ground, tried out some new techniques of blitzkrieg on the residents of the historic Basque town of Guernica.

It was a success. Heinkel 111s, flying over in waves, worked for four hours dropping high-explosive and incendiary bombs on Guernica, whose normal population of 7,000 had been greatly increased by the presence of Loyalist troops and of civilians getting out of the way of the Nationalist advance. When the bombers finished, most of the town had been destroyed or was on fire. At that point Junkers took over the action and strafed civilians in the streets.

Two days later Nationalist ground forces captured Guernica. Franco's propagandists reported that Basques had set fire to Guernica as a device to whip up Loyalist resistance. But the German pilots of the Condor Legion were soon boasting of their success, and the newspapers quickly got hold of the story. There was a great deal of international outrage, but not much in the way of action. When two Basque priests, both eyewitnesses to the bombing, went to Rome hoping to inform the Pope of the atrocity, they were shunted off to Cardinal Pacelli (soon to become Pope Pius XII), whose only response was, 'The Church is persecuted in Barcelona.'

The Spanish Civil War moved on to produce more bloody events that might have obscured what happened at Guernica, except that Pablo Picasso reminded the world with his most famous painting. Guernica was a preview of what would happen in places like Warsaw, Coventry, London, Berlin, Dresden and Tokyo.

Delacroix, the son of Talleyrand?

1798 On this day a great painter was born: Eugène Delacroix, who one day would lead the Romantic Movement in French painting with great works such as *The Death of Sardanapalus*, *Women of Algiers in Their Apartment* and his most famous painting, *Liberty Leading the People*.

Officially, Delacroix's father was the one-time French Foreign Secretary, Charles Delacroix. But after his birth, rumours in the best salons insisted that his real father was none other than Charles Delacroix's successor as Foreign Secretary, that worldly cleric and womanising prince, Charles-Maurice de Talleyrand. Indeed, the greatest contemporary *salonière* of them all, Germaine de Staël, acidly remarked about Delacroix senior, 'M. Delacroix isn't a minister, he's an old pregnant woman', apparently endorsing the rumour. And who should know better than Mme de Staël, who once herself bore an illegitimate child to Talleyrand?

A tale of two dishes

1707, 1859 Countries, loyalties, nationalities, even empires have changed so often in Europe that most of what's left is confusion. Take two events that happened on this day to illustrate the point.

In 1707 the War of the Spanish Succession was in full swing, with Louis XIV's France embattled by the forces of England, Holland and Austria. On this day Prince Eugene of Savoy (himself a French subject) led his Austrian army through the open gates of Milan, having roundly defeated the French at Turin a few days before. Milan would remain subject to Austria for a century and a half.

Exactly 152 years later to the day, Count Camillo di Cavour rejected an Austrian ultimatum that Piedmont (of which Cavour was Prime Minister) disarm, thus drawing Austria and France into another war. By July Austria had been defeated, Austrian control of Milan (the capital of Piedmont) was ended for ever and the unification of Italy had begun.

It may appear that Austria's 152-year domination of Milan, which started and in a sense ended on the same day, was an inconsequential political interlude, without lasting results. But it is not so.

A favourite and famous dish in Milan today is a piece of veal beaten paper-thin, breaded and fried, called *cotelleta Milanese*. In Vienna, however, the self-same dish, claimed to be Vienna's greatest speciality, is called *Wienerschnitzel*, and no one knows if the Austrians stole it from the Italians or the other way around, but it certainly happened during those 152 years. Better call it breaded veal cutlet.

Also on this day

AD 121: Sixteenth Roman Emperor and sometime philosopher Marcus Aurelius is born * 1765: Nelson's mistress, Emma Hamilton, is born

27 April

Magellan the great explorer is killed in the Philippines

1521 Fernão de Magalhães, better known to us as Ferdinand Magellan, was born of a noble Portuguese family in 1480 and raised in the royal household. In his late 30s, Magellan approached the Portuguese King Manuel I to finance a voyage to the Moluccas (today part of Indonesia) by a western route. Manuel had no confidence in his countryman, so Magellan turned to Spain. Luckily for him, and for us, the Spanish King was the future Holy Roman Emperor Charles V, grandson of the Catholic Monarchs Ferdinand and Isabella who had financed Columbus. A man of imagination and intelligence, Charles agreed to underwrite the voyage, and Magellan set sail across the Atlantic on 20 September 1519.

A little over a year later Magellan had crossed the Atlantic and then bore ever southward along the coast of South America to find a way through to the 'Spice Islands' for which he was searching. On 28 November 1520, having discovered the straits at the tip of South America that now bear his name, he reached the Pacific Ocean, which he then set out to cross.

As provisions dwindled, conditions aboard Magellan's ships became appalling. His men were reduced to eating putrid and worm-infested biscuit, sawdust and grilled rat. Their only good luck was the weather, which remained miraculously calm for almost four months, without a single storm. Because of this one bounty they named this new ocean the Pacific.

Continuing westward, Magellan landed on the Philippines in March and set out to explore these largely unknown islands. But on 27 April 1521 on the beach of the tiny island of Mactan, Magellan and his crew were caught up in a minor skirmish with a local tribe. Overwhelmed, Magellan tried to cover the retreat of his men and was cut down by the spears and poison arrows of the natives. He was still only 41.

Magellan's crew continued the voyage, finally returning to Spain in September of 1522, completing the first circumnavigation of the globe. This was one of the pivotal moments in history, as the voyage not only proved the world was round but also revealed that the Americas were indeed a New World, separate from Asia.

Also on this day

1737: English historian Edward Gibbon is born at Putney * 1791: Telegraph inventor Samuel Morse is born * 1822: American President and general Ulysses S. Grant is born * 1840: American writer Ralph Waldo Emerson dies

28 April

Mussolini is lynched with his mistress

1945 Caught like a rat and dispatched like one. This is the fate that befell Benito Mussolini this afternoon not far from Lake Como. He was pushed out of an automobile by Communist partisans and shot to death at the side of the road. It is ironic that the man who brought on the downfall of Italy by joining it to the Axis cause in the Second World War should die on a road named Via XXIV Maggio to honour the date in 1915 (24 May) when Italy joined the Allies in the First World War.

Gunned down by his side was his mistress Claretta Petacci. Executed nearby were fifteen members of his fascist government fleeing with their Duce to Switzerland ahead of the Allied advance and anti-fascist resistance. When the partisans stopped the column the day before, they had discovered Mussolini disguised in a Luftwaffe overcoat and helmet. After the shootings, the corpses were trucked to Milan. There in the Piazzale Loreto, the site of a fascist massacre of resistance fighters the year before, the bodies were strung up by their heels at a gas station and displayed the next day to a jeering mob. Someone tied Claretta's skirt around her legs to preserve modesty. It was a fittingly shabby end for the man whom A.J.P. Taylor described as 'a vain, blundering boaster without either ideas or aims'.

Mussolini's father named him Benito after the Mexican revolutionary Benito Juárez with whom the elder Mussolini shared an antipathy for Habsburg rule. Benito Mussolini electrified Italy and the world in 1922 with the march on Rome, a propaganda event that bluffed a timid King Victor Emmanuel III into making him Prime Minister. Mussolini was fascist dictator of Italy for the next 21 years, at one point simultaneously holding the offices of Prime Minister, Minister of Foreign Affairs, Minister of War, Minister of the Navy, Minister of Aviation and Minister of the Interior. He dazzled his countrymen with dreams of empire in Ethiopia and Albania. In foreign policy there were other courses available, but he chose the fatal alliance with Hitler. The realities of war proved his, and Italy's, undoing.

On 25 July 1943, as Sicily fell to the Allies, a majority of the Fascist Grand Council, one that included his son-in-law Galeazza Ciano the Foreign Minister, voted to deprive Mussolini of supreme military command. The King, now determined to save his country by suing for peace with the Allies, dismissed Mussolini as Prime Minister and ordered him from Rome to confinement on the island of Ponza. There he was the object of a daring rescue by SS paratroopers acting on Hitler's orders. He was flown first to safety in Germany, where news of his survival was broadcast to the world. Then Hitler returned him to Italy, to the town of Salvo on Lake Garda, where he was installed as leader of a puppet regime under German protection, intended to maintain fascist control of northern Italy. But in the spring of 1945, with defeat now inevitable, Mussolini and his followers began to pack.

Whatever else he may have been, the Duce was a family man: an Italian historian calculated that by the year 1943 over 300 relatives of Mussolini or his wife Rachele were receiving government handouts. But even family feeling could not save his son-in-law whom he sent, with others similarly guilty, before a firing squad in January 1944 for the 'treachery' of his vote the previous year.

The Duce died just two days ahead of his partner in crime Adolf Hitler, who, similarly accompanied in death by a mistress (whom he had actually married a couple of days before), committed suicide in Berlin on 30 April.

Mutiny on the Bounty

1789 Humiliated and harassed beyond endurance, Lieutenant Fletcher Christian of HMS *Bounty* on this day forced tyrannical Captain William Bligh into an open boat at sword-point and took command of the ship.

Bligh and eighteen men loyal to him sailed 3,600 miles in 41 days before reaching Timor and safety, a remarkable feat of seamanship and leadership.

Only 26 at the time, Christian fled in the *Bounty* with 24 other crewmen, but eventually all but nine returned to Tahiti, where three were taken to England and hanged. Christian and eight other mutineers sailed on to the isolated, volcanic Pitcairn Island, 1,350 miles south-east of Tahiti, where they scuttled the ship and settled down with some Tahitian women who had accompanied them.

The whereabouts and fate of Christian and his fellows remained a mystery until 1808 when a single survivor and the crew's descendants were found on the remote island. According to their story, a year or two after settling on the island Christian's comrades had killed him in an argument over the shortage of wives.

Also on this day
1758: Fifth US President James Monroe is born, whose doctrine warned European countries against interfering in the Western hemisphere

29 April

Catherine of Siena, a saint who changed history

1380 Today died one of the few saints who truly helped change the course of history, St Catherine of Siena.

Daughter of a Siennese dyer, the mystical Catherine joined the Dominican Order at the age of sixteen at a time when the papacy was located in Avignon during the so-called 'Babylonian Captivity'. Noted for her piety and self-abnegation, she prayed that Christ would be her Heavenly Bridegroom and eventually developed stigmata on her hands and feet (although they were visible only to herself until after her death).

In 1376 the city-state of Florence rebelled against the Pope, and Catherine travelled as a sort of holy ambassador to Avignon, then the seat of the papacy. All popes had lived there since 1309 when the French King Philip the Fair, after years of conflict regarding papal versus royal authority, had persuaded the Gascon-born Pope Clement V to move there from Rome.

Now Catherine determined not only to intervene on behalf of her native Florence but also to end the papacy's stay in Avignon and bring about its return to Rome. Having no doubt that God should be on her side, she impatiently commanded the Lord, 'It is my will that you do not delay any longer.'

At least Pope Gregory XI heard her. He was so impressed with her religious fervour as well as her common sense that he not only forgave the Florentines but also agreed to come back to Rome. In January of 1377 he entered the Holy City with Catherine at his side.

Catherine died in Rome only three years later at the age of 33. Earlier she had deliberately scalded herself in the hot springs at Vigone to prepare herself for Purgatory. Evidently, however, it was wasted preparation, for she was declared a saint in 1461.

Hirohito – the longest-reigning Japanese emperor

1901 According to tradition (and official Japanese history until 1945) the Japanese Empire was founded in 660 BC by the Emperor Jimmu, descendant of the Sun goddess Amaterasu and direct forebear of every emperor since. And in all these two and a half millennia, no emperor reigned as long as Hirohito, born this day in Tokyo.

Emperor Hirohito inherited the throne in 1926. He played a questionable role in the start of the Second World War and an honourable one in ending it. A mild, bespectacled man, his real interest was marine biology.

When Hirohito died on 7 January 1989, just two months before his 88th birthday, his reign had lasted 62 years. His funeral was attended by the largest collection of world dignitaries ever assembled, with representation from 163 countries, including 54 heads of state.

Also on this day

1429: Joan of Arc enters Orléans after relieving the English siege * 1945: US soldiers liberate Dachau concentration camp in Germany

30 April

Hitler commits suicide

1945 The huge 30-room bunker beneath the Reich Chancellery was dim and dank, the electricity faltering under the unceasing bombardment of Russian guns. The twenty or so people inside included two of the most sinister still alive in the crumbling Third Reich: the second most powerful man in Germany, the shadowy Martin Bormann, and the Nazi Minister of Propaganda, Joseph Goebbels. All waited solemnly, some with dread, others with impatience, for the death of their master Adolf Hitler. They knew that he had sworn to commit suicide with Eva Braun, the 33-year-old mistress he had married only two days before.

Outside the bunker some 100,000 Russian troops were taking Berlin street by street, vastly outnumbering the German defenders, composed of only a few seasoned soldiers leading a ragtag collection of old men and Hitler youths, boys of less than sixteen, armed for this final apocalypse. The Russian tyrant Joseph Stalin had ordered his generals to take the city no later than 1 May at all costs so that its fall could be announced in the May Day parade in Moscow.

Hitler seemed in shock, his face ashen, his left arm trembling uncontrollably as if with Parkinson's disease, his green jacket stained with spilled food. Two days earlier his friend and ally Benito Mussolini had been executed by Italian partisans and hung by his heels in a square in Milan, and Italy had capitulated yesterday. Now Hitler had learned that his most faithful lieutenant Heinrich Himmler had betrayed him by trying to negotiate surrender through neutral Sweden. The last message ever sent from the Führerbunker was an order for the arrest and execution of this traitor.

The first to die was Hitler's German Shepherd bitch Blondi, who was fed a capsule of cyanide to test the poison's efficacy. Now in the early afternoon Hitler summoned his last remaining supporters, distractedly shook their hands and bid them a listless goodbye. Just after three he led Eva to his sitting room in the lower bunker and closed the door. Two loaded pistols and two cyanide capsules were waiting for him there.

Finally at four o'clock Hitler's valet, accompanied by Goebbels, Bormann and two generals, opened the closed door to the room. Eva lay dead from the poison while Hitler slumped in his armchair, a bullet hole in his right temple.

Obedient to the last, his supporters carried the bodies to the bunker courtyard, doused them with petrol and set them alight. They then honoured the burning corpses with a final Nazi salute. Shortly afterwards Goebbels and his wife Magda poisoned their six small children and committed suicide, a deluded Magda boasting, 'You see, we die an honourable death.' Bormann made his way out of the bunker but was killed not in the fighting but from having taken poison to avoid falling into Russian hands. His body was buried in the rubble.

At 10.50 that evening Russian soldiers finally seized the Reichstag, but the victorious troops were quickly shouldered aside by agents from SMERSH, a directorate of the Russian state security apparatus. Hitler's burnt skull was secreted back to Stalin in Moscow, and only years later did the Russians reveal that Hitler's body had been found.

One week later what was left of the Nazi government signed an unconditional surrender. Hitler's Thousand Year Reich was dead after thirteen years.

Thomas Jefferson doubles the country for $13.50 a square mile

1803 Thomas Jefferson's greatest contribution to the United States was his understanding of and commitment to liberty. But he also doubled the size of the country.

From the start of his presidency in 1801 Jefferson had been looking for ways for the United States to expand to the west beyond the land of the original thirteen states. During this time Napoleon had been looking for cash and an ally against Great Britain. As a result, when Jefferson offered to buy New Orleans, Napoleon offered the entire Louisiana Territory.

On this day in 1803 the deal was finally struck. The United States paid a mere $11,250,000 and at a stroke gained some 833,000 square miles of territory. Called the Louisiana Purchase, the land included eleven states: Montana, Wyoming, North Dakota, South Dakota, Minnesota, Nebraska, Iowa, Arkansas, Kansas, Missouri and Louisiana.

The US at this time had a population of only a little more than 4 million. But the Louisiana Purchase hardly added to that. Apart from several thousand indigenous Indians, the only people to come with the deal were some 40,000 Creoles.

St Petersburg is born

1703 By the spring of 1703 Peter the Great's war with Sweden to determine what country would dominate the north of Europe had already lasted for almost three years, and it still had another eighteen to run. On the last day of April Russian troops under the command of General Sheremetev started the first bombardment of a small Swedish fortress at Nyenskans, which was located on an island at the mouth of the Neva River.

The Swedes soon surrendered to the superior Russian force, and Peter became the owner of a grim, swampy, clammy and cold piece of real estate. But to Russia this conquest was of great importance; it at last gave the country true access to the Baltic Sea.

So enamoured was Peter with his new island that he resolved to build a city there – and to name it after his own patron saint and therefore in a way after himself. So Swedish Nyenskans became St Petersburg – and later Leningrad and then St Petersburg again – serving as Russia's capital from the time of Peter the Great until the Russian Revolution.

Mary Tudor's child

1555 Church bells pealed out over London, the *Te Deum* was sung in St Paul's, tables were readied for feasts in the streets and wood was stacked for celebratory bonfires. The Queen had been in seclusion at Hampton Court for ten days, waiting for the birth of her child, and now at last the birth pangs had begun. Queen Mary was to give to the world the baby she so hungrily desired, the infant that would save her England and lead it back to Catholicism.

But where was the baby? As the hours passed the incredible truth became more and more apparent. There was no baby, the Queen wasn't pregnant in her body, only in her mind. Slowly the word spread. The bells ceased their pealing, the tables were returned to storage, the wood carted away.

At this time Mary had been Queen for only two years, and she had been a moderate and benign sovereign. But now she understood. God was punishing her for two terrible, unexpiated sins, the signing of a document denying the supremacy of the Pope (signed under duress from her father Henry VIII) and her leniency towards Protestant heretics.

From this moment on Mary earned her name of Bloody Mary. During the three and a half years that remained to her the frenzied Queen sent over 300 people to the stake as she tried to burn Protestantism from the land. She died a morbid fanatic at the age of 42.

Also on this day
1396: The last crusade leaves from Dijon under the command of Burgundian Jean de Nevers (Jean Sans Peur) * 1883: French painter Edouard Manet dies in Paris

1 May

Dante meets Beatrice

1274, 1283 From across a crowded room, love, total and imperishable, came to young Dante Alighieri today as he set eyes for the first time on the divine figure of Beatrice Portinari. 'From that time forward', he later wrote, 'love fully ruled my soul'.

Dante was not quite nine years old when he first saw Beatrice at a party given by her father Folco Portinari in his palazzo on the Corso in Florence, already a considerable walled city of about 80,000. Dressed in crimson, she was a few months younger than he. For the next nine years he worshipped her from afar, and only in 1283, also on 1 May, did she speak to him for the first time as they passed each other in the street. During the following years, Dante's love for Beatrice continued unabated, although there is no reason to think it was returned.

In 13th-century Florence, marriages among the upper classes (to which both Dante and Beatrice belonged) were invariably arranged by the families involved. In 1286 Dante married Gemma Donati, to whom he had been betrothed since the age of twelve. A year later Beatrice also married, only to die three years later, still only 24.

Despite his adventurous life and years in exile, Dante remained devoted to Beatrice (or her memory) throughout his life, writing of her in his *La Vita Nuova*, published when he was 28, and recreating her as his guide to Paradise in his *Divine Comedy*, completed when he was about 55. Spare a thought for his poor wife Gemma, who is never mentioned in any of Dante's writing.

La Serenissima *comes to an end after 1,071 years*

1797 Lodovico Manin had been elected Doge of the Republic of Venice eight years earlier. He was the 118th noble to carry that grand title since the Republic had installed its first doge, Orso Ipato, in the year 726.

But now a ruthlessly ambitious French general named Bonaparte had given Doge Manin an ultimatum, backed up by an army of over 4,000 troops. The Doge was to abdicate and the Republic to cease to exist. Bonaparte had offered Venice to the Austrians if they would give up their claims to Bologna, Ferrara and Romagna.

Outmanoeuvred and outgunned, Manin agreed to Bonaparte's demands, and on this day the Republic of Venice, *La Serenissima*, came to an end after a glorious history of 1,071 years.

Along with the Republic, the office of doge of course also vanished, although a strange echo of the name would resonate in the 20th century. 'Doge' is the Venetian for the Latin *dux*, or leader, a title to be revived by Benito Mussolini as 'Il Duce'.

The King gets flowers from the court's filles de joie

1515–47 'The King's life is like this. He gets up at eleven o'clock, hears Mass, has dinner, passes two or three hours with his mother, then goes whoring or hunting and finally wanders here and there throughout the night.' So wrote a Venetian envoy at the court of France's licentious monarch, François I.

Later one of François's own ministers wrote: 'Alexander the Great saw women when he had no business; François took care of business when he had no more women.'

Thus on 1 May during François's reign took place a bizarre ceremony fit for a king, or for this king at least. Each year on that day the court prostitutes presented François with a bouquet of flowers, a token of their gratitude for the year just past and a promise for the year to come.

England and Scotland become Great Britain

1707 Today Great Britain became a historic reality as the English and Scottish parliaments were combined for the first time.

England had invaded and attempted to rule Scotland countless times over the centuries, but the two countries had first truly been brought together only on the ascension of England's first Stuart king, James I, in 1603. James was already King James VI of Scotland, and it was he who added Scotland's unicorn to England's lion in the royal coat of arms.

But it was another 104 years, during the reign of James's great-granddaughter Anne, before the parliaments were finally combined and the two countries became subject to a single government.

David Livingstone dies

1873 David Livingstone had spent 33 years in Africa and was widely recognised as its greatest explorer. Yet few remember that he had failed in the three tasks he had set himself: to find the source of the Nile, to stop the slave trade and to convert to Christianity black Africans whom he called 'these sad captives of Sin and Satan'.

In April 1873 Livingstone was wandering through the heart of Africa, penniless and virtually deserted by his guides and bearers, sick and feeble from dysentery, malaria and skin ulcers. He had seen only one white man in the past seven years at his celebrated meeting with the journalist Henry Stanley. Finally Livingstone's illnesses overwhelmed him. Unable to walk, in too much pain to be carried, he camped at a place called Chitambo, on Lake Bangweulu. There he died on 1 May.

Even then Livingstone's travels were not over. Two of his native followers buried his heart and viscera beneath a tree on which they carved his name. They then carried his corpse out to civilisation. Eventually it was shipped back to England where it was interred with great ceremony beneath the floor of Westminster Abbey.

Also on this day
1769: Arthur Wellesley, later Duke of Wellington, is born in Dublin * 1851: The Great Exhibition opens at the Crystal Palace in London

2 May

Leonardo da Vinci dies in a king's arms

1519 In his determination to have the most splendid court in Europe, France's François I entreated Leonardo da Vinci to become his court painter, and in 1516 the ageing Leonardo at last consented. The King gave him a charming manor house in Cloux, only a few hundred yards from the royal château of Amboise on the Loire River.

Here the great painter-sculptor-architect-inventor-engineer passed his last three years until he succumbed to a stroke on 2 May 1519 at the age of 67. Tradition has it that he died in the arms of a grieving François, certain that his death was just punishment for his artistic failures. 'I have offended God and man', he said, 'because my work did not achieve the quality it should have'.

Since he was already infirm when he arrived in France, Leonardo created little of note for François, but he did bring several of his own paintings with him when he came. One of these has remained in France ever since, probably the most famous work of art on Earth, the Mona Lisa.

Sophia von Anhalt-Zerbst (aka Catherine the Great) is born

1729 Today is the birthday of Catherine the Great of Russia. Her name was not Catherine, she was not Russian and, at least by modern standards, her only form of greatness was her girth.

She was born in Stettin, Germany, daughter of a minor prince. Her name was Sophia von Anhalt-Zerbst.

Sophia became Catherine (or, more properly, Ekaterina) and Russian when she married the heir to the Russian throne, the future Tsar Peter III, at the age of sixteen. Seventeen years later she and her lover Grigory Orlov staged a *coup d'état* against Peter, who was quickly captured, imprisoned and murdered.

Catherine ruled Russia for 34 years and gained an unjustified reputation for liberal thinking thanks to her correspondence with some of France's greatest intellects such as Voltaire and Diderot.

In fact, Catherine's regime was progressively reactionary. She freed all nobles from both taxes and service to the state while making their positions – like those of the serfs – hereditary and permanent.

Also on this day

1611: The Authorised Version of the Bible (King James Version) is first published * 1660: Composer Alessandro Scarlatti is born in Palermo, Sicily * 1808: The population of Madrid rises against Napoleon, inspiring Goya's painting *Dos de Mayo*

3 May

Death comes to the Turkish sultan who brought an end to the Byzantine Empire

1481 Today died the Ottoman Sultan Mehmed the Conqueror, so named for conquering Constantinople and bringing an end to the Byzantine Empire after 1,058 years.

At the beginning of May Mehmed had complained to his chief physician of abdominal pains, but the doctor's prescription had failed to cure, and two days later the Sultan died – probably not from natural causes, but poisoned on orders from his ambitious son Bayezid. It was perhaps a fitting ending for a man who had welcomed the news of his own father's death with public joy and whose first act afterwards was to have his infant brother drowned in his bath.

Mehmed (II) was the son of Murad II by a slave girl, but his father seemed to favour him, and when Murad abdicated after fearful losses to crusader forces, he placed Mehmed on the throne at the age of twelve. Two years later Murad returned to command the empire's armies, this time victorious, but he died in 1451 when Mehmed was nineteen, and thenceforth until his death Mehmed ruled with a hand of iron.

Mehmed's abiding obsession was the capture of Constantinople, the last stronghold of the Christian Byzantine Empire that had been born in 395, when Emperor Theodosius I had split the Roman Empire between his two sons, never to be reunited.

First Mehmed neutralised Constantinople's Christian allies, Hungary and Venice, by offering them peace treaties on very favourable terms. Then he added a fleet of 31 galleys to his army, hired a Hungarian gunsmith to cast a cannon larger than any then in existence, and, to control the Bosphorus, built the Rumeli Hisari fortress (which still stands in intimidating glory) only a few miles from Constantinople.

Not all agreed with Mehmed's determination to conquer the great city, especially the grand vizier Candarli, but Mehmed would brook no argument and besieged the city on 6 April 1453, himself as commander in the field. After a siege of 54 days Constantinople fell; one of Mehmed's first acts was to order the arrest and execution of the reluctant Candarli.

But there was more to Mehmed than pure military prowess. Immediately on capturing Constantinople he headed straight for the magnificent Hagia Sophia church and converted it into a mosque. He not only fostered the Muslim faith but also brought in an Armenian patriarch and a Jewish head rabbi and re-established the Greek Orthodox Patriarchate. Transferring his capital to the city, he imported Christian merchants and offered guarantees of safety to Greek and Italian traders. Within 75 years Constantinople (by then increasingly called Istanbul) had become the largest city in Europe.

Nor were these all of Mehmed's accomplishments. He gave the Ottoman Empire a new constitution and brought philosophers and scholars to his court while accumulating a huge library of Latin and Greek works. He summoned the Venetian painter Gentile Bellini to paint his portrait (now in London's National Gallery) and to embellish the walls of his palace. Mehmed even penned a collection of his own poems.

Throughout this cultural renaissance, Mehmed remained a merciless tyrant, meting out the harshest punishment to any who opposed his wishes, becoming the prototype for the despotic Ottoman sultans who would rule in the centuries to come. He put in place the basic structures that would sustain the empire for half a millennium, largely the same structures that would bring about its final collapse in 1922.

The sad story of Europe's first modern constitution

1791 Inspired by the creation of the United States and frightened by the chaos in France, today Poland's King Stanislaw Augustus and the Polish Sejm (parliament) agreed the first modern written constitution in Europe, creating a constitutional monarchy.

Although the new constitution retained many Polish traditions, it established fundamental democratic reforms. Henceforward the King's decrees had to be countersigned by his ministers, who in turn were responsible to the Sejm. The Sejm itself was elected by Polish citizens, although there were some property qualifications. There were even some new civic freedoms, as religious discrimination was abolished.

Sadly, there was still a strong reactionary force among the Polish aristocracy, and Poland's watchful neighbours, Russia and Prussia, looked with alarm on both a more democratic state and the possibility of a strengthened Poland.

The following year, Russia's Catherine the Great came to the aid of the reactionaries and sent in her army to crush both the small Polish army and the democratic reforms. After a series of defeats, the King and government realised their cause was hopeless and agreed to abolish the new constitution.

Even a return to the past was not enough for Catherine and her Prussian allies. In 1795 they partitioned Poland for the third time since 1768, including Austria in the spoils. Russia took 62 per cent of Poland's territory, Prussia 20 per cent and Austria 18 per cent. King Stanislaw abdicated, the last king of Poland. And Poland as a nation ceased to exist.

Wellington becomes a duke

1814 He had been made a viscount in 1809 for his victory at Talavera; elevated to an earl in 1812 for his successful siege of Ciudad Rodrigo; and raised to a marquess the same year for Salamanca. He even had his portrait painted by Francisco Goya for chasing Joseph Bonaparte out of Madrid.

Today, with the Peninsular War won, Napoleon gone to Elba, and King Louis XVIII on the throne of France, Lieutenant-General Arthur Wellesley, hailed affectionately as 'Nosey' by his veterans and 'El Liberador' by a grateful Spain, received the title by which the world would know him for all time: duke – the Duke of Wellington. To a letter that he wrote to his brother Henry the next month he added: 'I believe I forget to tell you that I was made a Duke.' No one else forgot. To his countrymen, as one biographer noted, 'he was henceforth *the* Duke'.

Also on this day

1410: Anti-pope Alexander V dies, reportedly poisoned by anti-pope John XXIII * 1469: Niccolò Machiavelli is born in Florence * 1493: Pope Alexander VI publishes the first Bull Inter Caetera dividing the New World between Spain and Portugal

4 May

Sherlock Holmes goes over the falls

1891 Mr Sherlock Holmes vanished today in Switzerland and was presumed dead, most probably at the hands of his arch-antagonist Professor James Moriarty, the 'Napoleon of crime'. The celebrated London consulting detective was on a walking trip of several miles from the village of Meiringen to the hamlet of Rosenlaui, and had taken a recommended detour to see the falls of Reichenbach. Shortly before the detour, his travelling companion on the journey, a Dr Watson, also of London, had been called back to Meiringen on a medical emergency (which proved a ruse), so that Holmes was alone when he approached the falls.

Evidence gathered at the scene – two sets of footprints going towards the gorge but none returning – suggested that Holmes and his assailant met and struggled on the narrow path, then fell, locked together, into the abyss, their bodies unrecoverable in the 'dreadful cauldron of swirling water and seething foam'. The crime-scene investigation, which was conducted by local police and Dr Watson, also found an alpenstock belonging to Holmes, his silver cigarette case, and his note to Dr Watson, evidently scribbled some minutes before the end, stating that he and Moriarty were about to have a 'final discussion of those questions that lie between us'.

Holmes's death was a serious blow – not only to crime prevention but also to literature. True to his mysterious form, however, Holmes reappeared in London almost three years later, in April 1894, to resume his career as the world's first consulting detective. It turned out that it was Moriarty, and not Holmes, who had died in the falls of Reichenbach. Holmes was brought back – from the very brink – at the insistence of millions of his devoted fans around the world left shocked and grieving over his unexpected demise. For them the three years of his absence seemed more like ten – which in fact they were. 'The Final Problem', Arthur Conan Doyle's story in which Holmes met his terrible fate, was published in the December 1893 issue of the *Strand Magazine*. But Conan Doyle did not effect his detective's remarkable reappearance until October 1903, with the publication of 'The Empty House'.

The Battle of the Coral Sea begins

1942 At 6.00 a.m. today, carrier-launched American aircraft made a surprise bombing raid on Japanese shipping at Tulagi in the Solomon Islands, doing only minor damage but beginning a five-day naval battle that would be the first check to Japan's bid for supremacy in the Pacific.

In the spring of 1942, flushed with their recent successes against the British, the Dutch, and the Americans in South-east Asia and the Pacific, the Japanese decided to extend their reach by capturing bases from which they could sever the vital supply line from the United States to isolated Australia. In April they gathered strong naval and invasion forces at their great base at Rabaul, then sent them south-eastward, supported by a striking force of two big aircraft carriers, towards the Coral Sea.

By this time, however, Allied cryptographers had broken the Japanese naval code. Learning that the enemy's first moves would be to take Port Moresby in New Guinea and Tulagi in the Solomons, Admiral Nimitz, the US Pacific commander-in-chief, dispatched a task force with the carriers *Yorktown* and *Lexington* to spoil the game. The United States drew first blood when the *Yorktown* launched its surprise attack this morning on Tulagi, seized by the Japanese only the day before.

What followed over the next four days in the Coral Sea was the first naval battle in history in which no ship on either side ever sighted the enemy. It was also an engagement of air attacks and counter-attacks that Samuel Eliot Morison described as 'full of mistakes, both humorous and tragic, wrong estimates and assumptions, bombing the wrong ships, missing great opportunities, and cashing in accidentally on minor ones'. Battle ended on 8 May and both forces withdrew, the US having lost more tonnage sunk, including the *Lexington*, the Japanese more aircraft.

In other circumstances the Battle of the Coral Sea might have been judged a tactical draw. The outcome, however, was a strategic American victory because it forced the Japanese to halt their expansion around the perimeter of Australia. Moreover, ship damage and aeroplane losses sustained in the battle prevented both of the big Japanese carriers from joining their fleet the next month at Midway, where the US Navy achieved an even greater and more decisive victory.

Also on this day

1814: Napoleon arrives on the Island of Elba

5 May

Napoleon is murdered?

1821 Today at 5.49 in the late afternoon Napoleon Bonaparte, once emperor of half of Europe and lord to 70 million people, died on the remote island of St Helena a few months before his 52nd birthday, of what was thought to be stomach cancer. His last word was a faintly whispered 'Joséphine', a wistful final thought for his first wife who had died seven years before.

Napoleon spent the last five and a half years of his life on St Helena, an island with a population of only 2,000 but with 1,400 British troops to guard against his escape. Bored to distraction and bitter at both the enemies who had defeated him and the supporters who had betrayed him, he kept a minor court of a few French officers and their wives who had followed him into exile. His last eighteen months were passed in pain and growing weakness, characterised by extreme nausea, headaches, weakened sight, insomnia, deafness and bleeding gums. Although he faced death without flinching, on the evening of 3 May 1821 he lapsed into unconsciousness, apparently paralysed, after taking a huge dose of calomel laxative that his doctors hoped would help him. Two days later he was dead.

Napoleon was buried on the island where he died in a grave twelve feet deep, lined with stone. There he remained for nineteen years until his body was returned to Paris for entombment in Les Invalides.

In the late 20th century, scientific analysis of Napoleon's hair showed residual traces of arsenic, prompting some historians to conclude that he had not died of cancer but had been murdered, probably by one of his courtiers, Count Charles Tristan de Montholon, who had poisoned his wine. Montholon's putative motive was revenge for Napoleon's affair with his wife. Equally likely is the suggestion that the British and the restored French monarchy together persuaded Montholon to administer the fatal dosage, fearing that Napoleon might once again escape and overturn the autocratic monarchies of Europe.

Garibaldi launches the Risorgimento

1860 Today began the greatest military adventure of the Italian Risorgimento (literally 'rising again', the resurgence of nationalism which resulted in the reunification of Italy), the conquest of Sicily by Giuseppe Garibaldi and his Thousand.

In 1860 Sicily and southern Italy still formed the Kingdom of the Two Sicilies, an economic backwater ruled by a reactionary and repressive king.

On this day Garibaldi and his Thousand irregulars set sail from Genoa to free Sicily from its king and his 30,000-man army. The irregulars had no proper uniforms but to identify themselves all wore red shirts, and it was as Red Shirts that subsequently they were known. The actual count was 1,089, consisting of lawyers, brigands, middle-aged clerks, teenage boys, doctors, vagrants and one woman.

Astonishingly, the Thousand outmanoeuvred and outfought Sicily's demoralised troops, gathering local peasant reinforcements as they went. The bearded Garibaldi, who brilliantly planned the campaign, led continually from the front, risking himself for his cause. By June the island had been liberated and Garibaldi proclaimed dictator. It was the first truly significant step towards the reunification of Italy that would finally be completed with the taking of Rome some ten years later.

Also on this day

1818: Karl Marx is born in Trier, Prussia * 1835: The first passenger railway line in continental Europe opens at Allée Verte in France, eleven years after the first British line

6 May

The duc de Bourbon is killed sacking Rome

1527 Charles II, duc de Bourbon, was the last of France's great feudal lords. Although Constable of France, he had long been at odds with his sovereign François I and even more so with François's mother Louise, whom he had rejected with disgust when she suggested he marry her.

In 1523, Bourbon became an outlaw in France by signing an illegal alliance with Holy Roman Emperor Charles V which, if effected, would have reduced France to a state of feudal anarchy.

Abandoning his own country, Bourbon was awarded command of Charles's army in Italy. By the spring of 1527, however, the army was near mutiny, having been unpaid for months. Ever the opportunist, Bourbon joined the mutineers and on 6 May led the army to Rome to perpetrate one of the bloodiest and most violent sacks of a major Western city since crusaders had sacked Constantinople half a millennium before.

As terrified Pope Clement VII took refuge in the Castel' Sant'Angelo, the city was assaulted with brutality and thoroughness. Nuns were raped, priests murdered, and horses were stabled in St Peter's. Some 4,000 people were slain.

Despite the army's best efforts, the Castel' Sant'Angelo resisted all attempts to storm it as the Pope cowered in one of the inside rooms. The duc de Bourbon, however, was not so lucky. While directing the assault on this day he was cut down by a harquebus bullet fired by one of the Pope's defenders, the Florentine sculptor Benvenuto Cellini.

'The Incorruptible' is born in Arras

1758 On this day Maximilien de Robespierre was born to middle-class parents in the town of Arras. Later he would move to Paris to become, for a while, one of the bloodiest and most fanatical of France's revolutionaries, chief author of the Reign of Terror.

Robespierre had trained as a lawyer and was appointed a judge in his home town. Later he became president of the Arras Academy for the advancement of the arts and sciences, and when he was 30 the citizens of Arras elected him as one of their representatives in the National Assembly. A fervent and frequent speaker there, he did not go unnoticed. Mirabeau astutely observed: 'Cet homme ira loin, car il croit tout ce qu'il dit.' (This man will go far, for he believes everything he says.)

Although reputed honest (he was called 'The Incorruptible'), Robespierre was a mean and vengeful man, implacable to his enemies. According to a contemporary, he 'never forgave men for injustices he had done them, nor for the kindnesses he had received from them, nor for the ability that some of them possessed and that he did not have'.

In one of history's most perfect cases of poetic justice, Robespierre himself died by the guillotine less than a year after the beginning of the Terror he had started.

The French government moves to Versailles

1682 After two decades of labour, today Versailles became the seat of the French monarchy and government, even though the great château would not be completed until well into the next century.

This draughty, uncomfortable palace housed not only Louis XIV and his family and mistresses but also a court of over 1,000 nobles with their 4,000 servants.

Even at the time, Versailles was attacked for its vainglorious ostentation. One contemporary bishop wrote: 'This city of riches would have great splendour and pomp but it would be without strength or solid foundation ... and this pompous city, without needing other enemies, will finally collapse by itself, ruined by its own opulence.'

The bishop's direful prediction proved correct. Versailles removed the French king from daily contact with his people, and its very richness and arrogance helped set the stage for the destruction of the monarchy a century later.

Also on this day

1856: Sigmund Freud is born in Freiberg, Austria (now Pribor, Czech Republic) * 1910: King Edward VII dies in London * 1937: The German zeppelin *Hindenburg* catches fire in New Jersey, USA, killing 36 passengers * 1954: Roger Bannister runs a mile in three minutes, 59.4 seconds, the first to break the four-minute barrier

7 May

German U-boat sinks the Lusitania

1915 The great Cunard steamship *Lusitania* was 790 feet long with four tall stacks billowing black smoke. She was carrying a crew of 702 plus 1,201 predominantly British passengers, but including 188 Americans, as she headed for Southampton from New York. Although Britain was at war, no one thought the deadly German U-boats would attack a vessel carrying only passengers, especially since so many were citizens of a neutral – and powerful – United States.

In the early afternoon of 7 May the liner was nearing the west of Ireland. Lurking unseen was the German submarine U-20.

Suddenly a torpedo rocked the ship, quickly followed by a huge second explosion. In eighteen minutes the *Lusitania* was gone – with 1,198 of its passengers and crew, including 128 Americans and 63 children.

As the German submarine commander recorded in his log: 'Clean bow-shot from 700-metre range. Shot hits starboard side behind bridge. Unusually heavy explosion follows ... Many [life] boats crowded, come down bow or stern first and immediately fill and sink ... I submerge to 24 metres and go to sea.'

The German government insisted to an appalled American public that the ship had been carrying a huge quantity of explosives intended for Britain's war effort. Not so, cried the British Admiralty. High explosives on an ocean liner, endangering hundreds of innocent civilians? An evil German fabrication. By and large the Admiralty was believed, and although the US stayed out of the war for two more years, the sinking of the *Lusitania* was a critical turning point in American opinion.

Some 67 years later a British salvage team examined the wreck – only to find that someone had beaten them to it. A large square hole had been cut in the ship's deck, and the forward hold – officially carrying only foodstuffs – had been stripped clean. Further examination revealed a gaping hole in the portside bow, which could have been caused only by a huge internal explosion. But to this day the British Admiralty sticks desperately to its story.

The fall of Dien Bien Phu

1954 Gabrielle, Huguette, Claudine, Isabelle, Dominique, Béatrice, Eliane, Marcelle. What charming names. So Gallic, so feminine. You can almost smell their perfumes, hear the soft tones of their voices. But today Gabrielle and all her sisters had fallen. And so, most tragically, had the very centre of their existence, what they were meant to surround and protect: the French base at Dien Bien Phu, in Vietnam, overrun this afternoon by Communist troops after a siege of four and a half months.

And Gabrielle, Claudine, *et les autres*? They were the outlying strongpoints and artillery bases protecting the main position, all named, so it was believed, for the current and former mistresses of the garrison commander, a dashing cavalryman with a fine record in the Second World War, and – it hardly needs saying – irresistible to women.

Dien Bien Phu, scarcely more than a place name on a map, lies in a remote valley some 220 miles west of Hanoi, near the Laotian border. Its strategic value for the French army was as a launching point for operations against the Communist Viet Minh forces, led by General Giap, fighting for the independence of Vietnam from French control. In November 1953, the French sent in paratroopers to occupy the place, built a fortified position, constructed an airstrip, and airlifted in the first of what would eventually be 16,000 men. But the strategy was faulty in several key respects: the French were outnumbered and outgunned, the position could be resupplied only by air, and the French lacked the air power that might change an adverse outcome on the ground.

So General Giap brought up his men, 40,000 of them, and his guns, and Dien Bien Phu turned into a trap for the French. As the weeks went by, the perimeter, entrenched and protected by barbed wire, shrank under heavy Communist artillery fire, tunnelling tactics, and savage infantry assaults. It was Vicksburg, or Stalingrad. The airfield fell to the attackers on 27 March. Now the defenders were forced to rely on air-drops from low-flying planes that proved all too vulnerable to anti-aircraft fire. The strongpoints fell one by one, faithful Isabelle holding out to the very last. Dien Bien Phu now became, in Bernard Fall's phrase, 'Hell in a very small place'.

And so today, 7 May, with the Communist lines only yards away, the French prepared for the end by destroying everything of military value: artillery pieces, engines, rifles, optical equipment, radios. At 17.50 hours the last radio message went out to French headquarters in Hanoi: 'We're blowing up everything. Adieu.' The firing slackened, then ceased. There was no white flag of surrender. Instead, three Viet Minh soldiers hoisted a red flag with a gold star over the command bunker.

Of the 16,000 French soldiers who fought at Dien Bien Phu, only 73 were able to escape. Some 10,000 were captured, many of them wounded, and marched away to prison camps. The rest were dead. Communist losses were estimated at 25,000. The debacle of Dien Bien Phu marked the effective end of French control in South-east Asia, and the beginning of an increasing role in the region for the United States, which within a decade would be drawn into a much expanded conflict, the Vietnam War.

Beethoven conducts his Ninth Symphony

1824 By 1818 Ludwig van Beethoven was severely afflicted by the most terrible curse for a composer – deafness. By this time even his ear trumpet no longer helped, and he was reduced to communicating with conversation notebooks. Nonetheless it was in 1818 that Beethoven once again started to work on an idea that had tempted him for over twenty years, making Schiller's 'Ode to Joy' thematic to a great work of music. Even this objective, however, was not ambitious enough for Beethoven, so he combined it with another long held goal, the integration of the human voice into a symphony, something he had never done before.

By early 1824 the masterpiece was ready: Beethoven's Ninth Symphony. And on this day, 7 May 1824, it was performed for the first time, in the Kärntnertortheater in Vienna, with Beethoven himself conducting. At the symphony's conclusion the audience shook the concert house with their wild applause – but the stone-deaf Beethoven, facing the orchestra, was completely unaware of the ovation until one of the soloists made him turn to face the cheering crowd. Beethoven's Ninth Symphony was the longest, perhaps the greatest, and the last symphony that he ever composed.

A Swedish maid becomes Empress of Russia

1724 Martha Skovronskaya was a simple, unpretentious girl who, orphaned at an early age, found work as a domestic in the house of a pastor in the Swedish town of Marienburg. Soon, however, her rather moon-faced dark good looks brought the men around, and in 1702 she married a Swedish dragoon at the age of seventeen.

Only a few days after her marriage a Russian army conquered the town, and Martha soon transferred her allegiance to the victorious general, Boris Sheremetev. Such was Martha's appeal, however, that one of the Russian Tsar's chief advisors, Alexander Menshikov, soon snatched her from the general for himself. But Menshikov had the soul of a pimp, for within the year he had introduced his mistress to his master, Tsar Peter the Great, and Martha became the lover of the most powerful man in the land.

Jolly, coarse, straightforward and physically appealing, Martha struck a special chord with Peter, and after the birth of two children, to the hidden astonishment of his court, he married her in 1706.

After eighteen years of marriage Peter decided to elevate Martha from wife to Empress, which he did on 7 May 1724 after she converted from Protestantism to the Russian Orthodox Church and changed her name to Catherine.

Less than a year later, Peter was dead of cirrhosis and Martha became Empress in her own right as Catherine I. Thus a simple Swedish peasant became the first woman ever to rule mighty Russia.

Also on this day

1812: English poet Robert Browning is born * 1833: German composer Johannes Brahms is born in Hamburg * 1840: Russian composer Pyotr Tchaikovsky is born in Kamsko-Votkinsk * 1892: Yugoslav dictator Josip Broz Tito is born in Zagreb

8 May

The American president who was the 'reductio ad absurdum of the common man'

1884 Harry S. Truman, 31st president of the United States, was born today in a small bedroom in his parents' house in the dusty market town of Lamar, Missouri. He was another in the line of American presidents – including Lincoln and Grant – to spring from an unremarkable background.

Truman was poorly educated and never attended college. Early in life he failed as a haberdasher and spent almost a decade barely surviving as a farmer before he entered politics as a classic 'machine politician', a creature of the corrupt Kansas City party boss, Thomas Pendergast, who controlled the city's Democratic organisation. Even his election to the US Senate was largely engineered by the Pendergast machine, and his nomination to run as Franklin Roosevelt's vice-president in 1944 was the result of more back-room politics.

But with Roosevelt's sudden death in 1945, Truman found himself President of the United States, the most powerful man in the world, in the midst of a world war.

Because of his previous association with Pendergast (who was jailed for a year in 1939 for income tax evasion), small-town lack of sophistication and innate distrust of the rich and powerful, Republicans characterised the Democrat Truman as the '*reductio ad absurdum* of the common man'. And in certain ways they were right: privately Truman was strongly prejudiced against blacks and Jews. But despite these prejudices, he was a character of uncommon sense and granite integrity who famously kept a sign on his desk with the words: 'The buck stops here.'

Truman served almost eight years as President, achieving the greatest election upset in American history in 1948. His accomplishments were decisive in the 20th century: he authorised the first use of the atomic bomb to end the war with Japan, helped create the United Nations and NATO, initiated the Marshall Plan to rebuild Europe after the Second World War, and led the free world's confrontation with Communist aggression by authorising the Berlin Air Lift and intervening in Korea.

Harry Truman died on 26 December 1972, a few months short of his 89th birthday.

Gauguin expires in Polynesia

1903 Today, in the sultry heat of the Marquesas Islands just north-east of Tahiti, Paul Gauguin finally passed away a month before his 55th birthday. His death was no surprise, as he had suffered a series of heart attacks and was frequently afflicted by fever, faintness and vertigo, his body severely marked by syphilitic lesions.

Gauguin spent twelve years living in grass-roofed huts in the South Pacific, and during that time he helped transform the world's idea of painting. Traditionally a painting had been an attempt to represent a three-dimensional world on a two-dimensional canvas, but Gauguin helped to redefine it as a flat surface covered with colours – important not for what it represented but for what it was. He wanted his pictures to provoke a feeling in the viewer, not just represent a scene.

Gauguin has long enjoyed the reputation of being the man of commerce who gave up his family and his business for his art and a life of adventure. The truth is more pedestrian. He had been painting since his early teens but earned his living as a stockbroker. In his spare time he developed his artistic talent and was good enough to be invited to display a landscape at the Paris Salon in 1876, about the same time that he came under the influence of the Impressionist Camille Pissarro. In 1880 Gauguin was asked to show his works at the fifth Impressionist exhibition, an invitation repeated in 1881 and 1882.

In 1882, however, a financial crash cost him his broker's job, and he fled to Copenhagen with his Danish wife and four children. There his marriage collapsed, and he returned to Paris to devote himself to painting while living in penury, despite the admiration of fellow artists like Cézanne and van Gogh.

In 1887 Gauguin travelled to Martinique, where he developed his taste for exotic backgrounds and flamboyant colours. Fed up with city life, he first moved to Brittany and then in 1891 decamped to Tahiti to paint 'primitive' men and women living as he thought nature intended. In exchange for a small gift to her parents, he set up house with a thirteen-year-old girl named Teha'amana.

It was in Tahiti that Gauguin painted the first of his many boldly coloured visions of bare-breasted Polynesian women and developed the art that would lead the way to post-Impressionism. It was here, too, that he contracted the syphilis that would eventually kill him.

In 1901 Gauguin moved to the Marquesas Islands, in part because his syphilitic sores repelled the girls from Tahiti. Setting up house in Hiva Oa, he found a fourteen-year-old girlfriend who agreed to move in with him. There he continued to paint until his death two years later.

It seems fitting that the South Pacific should be the place of Gauguin's demise, as it was there that he created his greatest works. Perhaps this day

Gauguin found the answers to the three stark questions that he had written on the face of his greatest painting: 'D'où venons nous? Que sommes nous? Où allons nous?' (Where do we come from? What are we? Where are we going?)

Joan of Arc relieves Orléans

1429 The English had laid siege to Orléans for a year and a half, but finally French reinforcements had arrived. But what reinforcements! They were commanded by a seventeen-year-old girl.

As every French (and even every English) schoolchild knows, the girl was Joan of Arc. Through her inspired leadership the French troops broke through the encircling English, although Joan was wounded in the shoulder during the mêlée. No doubt the terrible power of this armour-clad 'witch' (as the English considered her) demoralised the besiegers, for they packed up camp and left the following day.

That day was Sunday, 8 May 1429. The English army crept away as Joan was hearing Mass.

Also on this day

44 BC: Julius Caesar adopts Octavian, the future Emperor Augustus * 1660: Charles II of England is proclaimed King by Parliament * 1794: Antoine Laurent Lavoisier, the French chemist, is guillotined * 1873: English philosopher John Stuart Mill dies * 1880: French novelist Gustave Flaubert dies

9 May

Birth of the last Habsburg empress

1892 She was called Zita Maria Grazia Adelgonda Michela Raffaella Gabriella Giuseppina Antonia Luisa Agnese, born this day near Viareggio in Italy. Her father was the Duke of Parma, but the family was poor, even if it did claim descent from Louis XI of France.

At nineteen Zita married Archduke Charles, the great nephew of Emperor Franz Joseph of Austria. The world was at peace and the Austro-Hungarian Empire looked as if it could survive for ever, with its tireless leader Franz Joseph on the throne.

But fate would change all that. First, the heir to the throne Franz-Ferdinand was gunned down at Sarajevo. Then the Emperor died in 1916. Suddenly Zita's husband was Emperor and she the Empress in the middle of a world war.

But not for long. Just two years later Austria-Hungary had lost the war and Charles was forced to abdicate. Twenty-nine months later he was dead.

Empress Zita lived on, mostly in exile, spending 63 years in Switzerland and the United States, never relinquishing her claim to a throne that no longer existed.

Finally, at the grand age of 96, Zita died on 14 March 1989. She was buried with a massive state funeral in Vienna's St Stephen's Cathedral, her horse-drawn hearse carrying her casket past thousands of spectators through the heart of the city to the Capucin Church, where she was to be buried in the crypt with 142 other members of the Habsburg dynasty. There the traditional ritual for Habsburg dead was performed once more.

At the door to the crypt the Master of Ceremonies knocks three times with his staff.

'Who desires entrance?', asks a simple monk from within.

'Zita, the Empress of Austria', responds the Master of Ceremonies, 'crowned Queen of Hungary, Queen of Bohemia, of Dalmatia, Croatia, Slavonia, Galicia …', and so on and on with Zita's dozens of titles.

'I know her not', says the monk.

Once more the Master knocks; once more the monk demands, 'Who desires entrance?'

'Zita, her majesty, Empress and Queen.'

'I know her not.'

A third time the Master knocks. 'Who desires entrance?'

'Zita', he replies, 'a mortal, sinful human.' (*Ein sterblicher, sündiger Mensch.*)

'So let her come in', at last answers the monk as he opens the door.

So was buried an impoverished Italian noblewoman who was the last Habsburg to wear a crown, in a line that had worn its first in the year 1282.

The oldest peace treaty in Europe

1386 The ancient sheepskin document lies at Windsor Castle, yellowed and wrinkled with age. Written in Latin, it affirms an alliance 'for ever' between England and Portugal, as young King Richard II and João I pledged 'an inviolable, eternal, solid, perpetual and true league of friendship'. Dated this day over six centuries ago, the Treaty of Windsor is the oldest unbroken alliance in European history – and it is still actively in force. England has invoked it as recently as 1982 in asking Portugal for air bases during the Falkland Islands War with Argentina.

Also on this day

1805: German poet Friedrich von Schiller dies in Weimar * 1936: Italian troops capture Addis Ababa in Ethiopia and annexe the country * 1941: British ships capture the German submarine U-110 along with its Enigma encoding machine

10 May

Michelangelo starts work on the Sistine Chapel

1508 Today Michelangelo Buonarroti started work on what is often considered the greatest masterpiece – or collection of masterpieces – the world has yet known, on the ceiling of the Sistine Chapel.

This breathtaking fresco was painted on the orders of that irascible pope, Julius II, who was the greatest patron of the arts who ever presided over the Vatican. At first Michelangelo was furious at the commission because he considered himself a sculptor, not a painter, and had done little painting since he was an apprentice in Ghirlandajo's studio in his teens. He suspected that the Pope had chosen him on the cunning recommendation of the architect Donato Bramante, who, jealous of Michelangelo's talents, had proposed him only because his lack of experience painting frescoes would doom him to failure. But Michelangelo knew that, if he declined the commission, he might never get another from Julius, and he undoubtedly thought his own genius would carry him through.

Julius wanted the ceiling to feature scenes from the New Testament, but the obdurate Michelangelo doggedly insisted on the Old Testament, believing it more dramatic, and proved his point with the work's centrepiece, 'The Creation of Adam'.

It took almost four and a half years to complete this great work (although Michelangelo downed brushes for almost a year in 1510–11 when no payments were forthcoming), and in all the painting covers some 10,000 square feet where more than 300 individuals are depicted. Mixed with the profound religious symbolism of the work are innumerable oak trees and oak leaves. These were the homage that Michelangelo paid to his papal patron, whose family name, della Rovere, means 'of the oaks'. Some critics have noted that Michelangelo's women are as sturdy and muscled as his men, possibly because his models for all the figures were men.

The painting of the Sistine Chapel was not only time consuming, it was also back-breaking, as Michelangelo spent hours at a time lying on his back on a scaffold as he painted. All of his work required tremendous effort. As the great painter once earthily remarked: 'Nelle mie opere caco sangue.' (In my works I shit blood.)

The chapel was officially opened on 31 October 1512 when Pope Julius II first celebrated Mass there, but even then Michelangelo's work in the chapel was not done. Julius died early in 1513, and the great painter took a twenty-year rest. But in 1534 he returned to create 'The Last Judgement' under the patronage of Pope Paul III.

Stonewall Jackson passes over the river to rest under the shade of the trees

1863 Chancellorsville, Virginia: scene of one of the American Civil War's bloodiest battles. The North suffered 17,000 casualties to the South's 13,000, but the greatest loss to the Confederates was the legendary general, Thomas Jonathan Jackson, known then and now as 'Stonewall'.

A stern and righteous man, Jackson was not liked by his men, but his courage under fire, his cool head and his brilliant tactical abilities made him the kind of general that soldiers willingly follow. As one observer commented: 'He lived by the New Testament and fought by the Old.' He had earned his nickname at the First Battle of Bull Run when, greatly outnumbered, he resisted a strong Union attack, helping the South to a major victory.

The Battle of Chancellorsville started in earnest on 2 May with Jackson leading the 26,000 men of his II Corps on a bold fourteen-mile march to strike the exposed Union right flank and drive it back in confusion with heavy losses. At dusk Jackson rode out on a moonlight reconnaissance. Some of his own nervous soldiers mistook the general and his aides for Yankees and opened fire, hitting Jackson twice in the left arm, which had to be amputated. The wound looked serious but not mortal. When the Southern commander Robert E. Lee heard about Jackson's injury he sent him the complimentary message: 'You are better off than I am, for while you have lost your left, I have lost my right arm.'

But the wound and the amputation gravely weakened Jackson, who contracted pneumonia. Soon he was half-delirious. On 10 May he seemed to wake from his restless sleep and clearly pronounced his last words: 'Let us pass over the river, and rest under the shade of the trees.' When he died the great general was only 39.

Almost a century later Jackson's enigmatic farewell found an echo in Ernest Hemingway's novel about the death of an officer entitled *Across the River and into the Trees*.

Hitler invades the West as the seeds of his own destruction are sown

1940 Smug with his achievements and supremely confident of future success, Adolf Hitler stood poised to obliterate all opposition to his plans to dominate Europe. With 122 infantry and twelve panzer divisions, 3,500 tanks and 5,200 warplanes on the Western front, he was ready to invade the preposterous French and any other nation that opposed his plans for expansion.

And why not? Four years earlier Hitler had called Europe's bluff in remilitarising the Rhineland. Two years after that he had absorbed Austria without firing a shot. Then he had seized the Sudetenland in Czechoslovakia while Continental and British leaders had only wrung their hands in alarm.

Then came the non-aggression pact with Russia, effectively ending any Soviet threat, and finally, after manufacturing a spurious border incident, the German army swept into Poland on the morning of 1 September 1939. The German blitzkrieg destroyed the Polish air force in 48 hours, and the last resistance in Warsaw surrendered in only 27 days.

Since the invasion of Poland, Germany had in theory been at war with France and England, but typically the European powers' words were louder than their actions, as no battles were fought during a period sardonically known as the 'Phoney War' or 'Sitzkrieg'. But while the Allies were dawdling, on 9 April 1940 Hitler sent his armies to occupy Denmark and Norway.

Now the time had come to put Western Europe in its place. Following the brilliant plan of German General Erich von Manstein for a panzer attack through the Ardennes Forest, at dawn today the Wehrmacht began its invasion of Luxembourg, Belgium, Holland and France. By afternoon, German forces had penetrated as far west as Maastricht and Liège.

Now an icily self-assured Hitler knew that Europe soon would be his. Who could resist the mighty German onslaught? He was probably only vaguely aware of a change across the English Channel and discounted its importance, but it would be the first nail in his coffin.

In Great Britain the frail and ageing Prime Minister Neville Chamberlain, following the advice of his friends in the Conservative Party and the Opposition of the Labour Party, resigned. His successor was a dark horse candidate, Winston Churchill, First Lord of the Admiralty, whose 40 years in politics had convinced many in his party that he was unreliable, mercurial, and a lone wolf not to be trusted with supreme political power. Moreover, he had been in charge of the Royal Navy during its recent failure to prevent the German invasion of Norway. But the younger Conservatives, like the nation at large, were behind Churchill, for they saw that he, virtually alone among the senior leadership of the nation, had been outspokenly right on the great issues of the decade – Hitler, rearmament, and appeasement.

And so it was that at 6.00 p.m. on the same day that Hitler charged into Western Europe, Winston Churchill, the man who would do most to destroy him and his Third Reich, took over the leadership of Great Britain. 'We cannot yet see how deliverance will come, or when it will come', declared the new Prime Minister, 'but nothing is more certain than that every stain of his infected and corroding fingers will be sponged and purged and, if need be, blasted from the surface of the earth'.

It was not a moment too soon. The preliminaries were over and the main bout had begun.

Also on this day

1774: Louis XV dies of smallpox at Versailles * 1818: American revolutionary Paul Revere dies * 1857: Sepoy revolt at Meerut triggers the Indian Mutiny

11 May

An English PM is assassinated

1812 Had he not been assassinated, Spenser Perceval would have remained one of England's most obscure Prime Ministers, even in his own time noted primarily for his icy demeanour and religious bigotry.

At 49, Perceval had been a totally undistinguished Prime Minister for three years when, on 11 May 1812, he walked into the lobby of the Houses of Parliament just after five in the evening. As he entered, a failed English businessman named John Bellingham stepped in front of him and shot him in the chest. Bellingham had no personal grudge against Perceval, but believed that somehow the government should recompense him for a lifetime of failures in business.

Hands flying to his chest, Perceval fell to the floor crying, 'I am murdered, murdered', just before he died.

The government wasted no time with Bellingham, who had made no attempt to escape. In less than a week he had been tried and hanged.

Perceval remains the only British Prime Minister ever to have been assassinated, not a bad record compared with four American presidents and five Russian Romanov tsars.

Birth of a balladeer

1888 Today in Temur, Siberia a Jewish boy was born named Israel Baline. Four years later his family moved to New York, where young Israel grew up with a talent for song writing. Eventually he would become America's greatest composer of popular ballads, writing both music and lyrics for songs that in themselves would form an all-time hit parade.

His list includes 'Alexander's Rag Time Band', 'A Pretty Girl is Like a Melody', 'Easter Parade', 'Let's Face the Music and Dance', 'Always', 'There's No Business Like Show Business', 'Blue Skies', 'Puttin' on the Ritz', 'What'll I Do?', 'God Bless America', 'Cheek to Cheek' and a song that has sold more than 50 million records, still going strong, 'White Christmas'.

Israel Baline of course was Irving Berlin – a name adopted after a printer's error on an early piece of sheet music.

Berlin defined four themes for popular songs: home, love, happiness, and self-pity. As fellow composer Jerome Kern said of him: 'Irving Berlin has no *place* in American music. He *is* American music.'

Berlin wrote until he was in his 90s, composing thousands of songs in all. He died in September 1989 at 101 years old.

General Jeb Stuart meets his match

1864 Nowhere is the legend of Southern valour, dash and taste for adventure better embodied than in James E.B. 'Jeb' Stuart, the flamboyant Confederate cavalry general during the American Civil War.

Tall and handsome with a full flowing beard, Stuart wore leather hip boots and sported a plume in his hat. His first notable appearance in history comes in the capture of abolitionist John Brown at Harper's Ferry. Later he led his cavalry in many of the Civil War's most famous engagements, including Gettysburg, Chancellorsville, Antietam and both battles of Bull Run.

Towards the end of the war, Northern cavalry had at last matched the South in verve and ability – and were far better armed, with rapid-fire carbines. They also had a leader equal to Stuart in Philip Sheridan.

In May 1864 Sheridan led his men on a long foray through Virginia, hoping to entice Stuart into a head-on clash. Finally, on 11 May, the Southern cavalier met the Yankee at Yellow Tavern, a few miles outside Richmond. Out-numbered two to one, the Rebels were routed and dashing Jeb Stuart was mortally wounded, dying at the age of 31.

Also on this day

AD 330: Emperor Constantine dedicates Constantinople as the capital of the Roman Empire * 1778: William Pitt the Elder (First Earl of Chatham) dies at Hayes, Kent * 1857: Indian mutineers seize Delhi

12 May

Florence Nightingale, the Lady with the Lamp

1820 'Flit on, cheering angel!' With this whimsically appropriate anagram did Lewis Carroll of *Alice in Wonderland* fame celebrate Florence Nightingale, the dedicated, heroic, neurotic nurse who transformed the idea of military hospitals during the Crimean War.

Florence Nightingale was born today in Florence, where her wealthy parents were living. They named her after the city they loved. When her family moved back to Derbyshire, she was educated at home by her father, who taught her history and philosophy as well as Latin, Greek, French, German and Italian.

Earnest and somewhat of a mystic, at sixteen Nightingale thought she had heard God's voice telling her she had a serious mission in life, but it was only ten years later that she came to realise that the mission was to help mankind by becoming a nurse, no fit occupation at the time for a woman of her station and means.

Despite her father's strong reservations, in 1850 Nightingale went to Alexandria to study nursing, then moved on to Germany and finally, in 1853, returned to England where she became the superintendent for the Hospital for Invalid Gentlewomen in London. Then came the Crimean War. Soon grisly descriptions of the ghastly conditions of the British wounded flooded into England.

Determined to help, Nightingale offered her services to the War Office and was given authority over all nursing in British military hospitals in Turkey. In November 1854 she arrived with 38 other nurses in Scutari near Istanbul, the place to which thousands of wounded and sick British soldiers were shipped across the Black Sea from Crimean battlefields. After she saw the filthy, rat-infested conditions of the main hospital, she wrote: 'I have been well acquainted with the dwellings of the worst parts of most of the great cities in Europe but have never been in any atmosphere which I could compare with that of the Barrack Hospital at night.' At first both resented and ignored by male doctors, who thought a theatre of war no place for a woman, she quickly set about tending the sick and wounded and improving the appalling level of hygiene.

Reflecting the stern morality of the day, no nurses were allowed in the wards after eight in the evening, the only exception being Nightingale herself. Every night she made her rounds carrying a lantern, chatting with the wounded and giving encouragement. From this she earned the nickname of 'The Lady with the Lamp'. But most important, thanks to her tireless efforts and understanding of the need for cleanliness, the mortality rate among the wounded was significantly reduced.

When the war finally dragged to a close in 1856, Nightingale returned to London, a very famous, widely beloved, and almost mythic person for her heroic deeds. But she refused all honours while continuing to be involved in what she saw as her mission, advising on hospital administration and founding schools for nurses. In pressing her reforms she was dealing – as probably only a wealthy, well-connected woman could in those days – with the very highest people in the British government and society, including Queen Victoria, who gave her a diamond brooch designed by Prince Albert bearing the inscription 'Blessed are the merciful'. Among her innovations were bells for patients to summon nurses, dumb-waiters to move food up from the kitchens, and hot water piped to all floors.

But, unwilling to accept awards or be lionised, publicly Nightingale had virtually vanished, and she became a bed-ridden invalid, apparently suffering from some kind of post-traumatic stress disorder. Even then she continued to receive official visitors and to write.

In 1861 she wrote *Notes on Nursing*, in which with tart good humour she revealed: 'No man, not even a doctor, ever gives any other definition of what a nurse should be than this – "devoted and obedient". This definition might do just as well for a porter. It might even do for a horse.'

Growing older, confined to her bed, Nightingale started to lose her sight, and when she passed 80 she became completely blind. At 87 she achieved another first for a woman when Edward VII awarded her the Order of Merit.

Florence Nightingale finally died on 13 August 1910 at the age of 90. Just prior to her death she had declined the offer of burial in Westminster Abbey.

The amazing recuperative powers of Cesare Borgia

1499 Cesare Borgia, illegitimate son of Pope Alexander VI, was both an out-standing athlete and exceptionally strong. Renowned for his swordsmanship and equestrian skills, he occasionally staged bull fights in which he alone killed all the bulls. He reputedly could bend an iron bar with his bare hands, and he is supposed to have been Machiavelli's model for his book *The Prince*.

In addition to all that, this black-haired nobleman with piercing eyes was said to be the handsomest man in Italy, so it is no surprise that his conquests of the fairer sex were legion.

When he was 23, on 12 May 1499, Cesare married the beautiful Charlotte d'Albret, sister of the King of Navarre, in King Louis XI's imposing château at Blois on the Loire River. Apparently, Cesare then brought his athletic ability and manly charm into perfect harmony. According to an Italian envoy present, Cesare consummated the marriage twice before supper 'since it is the custom there to consummate the marriage by day', and then six more times at night.

Despite this glorious beginning, Cesare stayed with Charlotte only two months before leaving her for the adventures of the battlefield. He was killed in battle eight years later, having never again seen his wife.

Also on this day

1812: English painter and author of the *Book of Nonsense* Edward Lear is born in London * 1949: The Russians call an end to the Berlin Blockade

13 May

The Terror begins

1793 Today began the Terror, that frenzy of republican butchery with which the rabid revolutionaries of the French Revolution cleansed the state of aristocratic blood. Later the ferocious Joseph Fouché offered this heartless justification: 'The blood of criminals fertilises the soil of liberty and establishes power on sure foundations.'

The very epicentre of the Terror was the great open square on the Seine that today we know as the place de la Concorde, now one of Paris's most spectacularly beautiful. But in 1793 its beauty was overshadowed by the sight of the guillotine, raised on a platform to give the spectators a better view, where 1,343 victims were beheaded.

The place de la Concorde was built between 1755 and 1775 and originally named for the man who ordered its construction, King Louis XV. Initially a large equestrian statue of the King dominated it, but that was demolished during the early days of the Revolution, and the place Louis XV fittingly changed its name to the place de la Révolution.

During the Terror, thousands of people congregated here daily to see the tumbrels of the condemned arrive. Seated around the scaffold with wine and bread bought from enterprising grocers, the spectators enjoyed the sight and smell of running blood. The notorious *tricoteuses* sat knitting to the swish of the blade and the cries of terror from those waiting their turn on the scaffold.

Here the Revolution devoured its first victims and eventually itself. Not only Louis XVI, Marie Antoinette, Philippe Égalité and Charlotte Corday but also Danton, Saint-Just and Robespierre were all beheaded here.

One of the most pathetic must have been poor Madame du Barry, who on 8 December 1793 was carried to the guillotine screaming in terror, 'You are going to hurt me! Please don't hurt me!' Now a haggard 50, she had once been the ravishing, silly and frivolous mistress of Louis XV. Since Louis's death nineteen years before, she had been living in luxury outside Paris, but the mob had not forgotten her. Dragged from her château, she rent the air with pleas for her life, offering her riches to any who would spare her, as the tumbrel carried her through the city. As the poet Lamartine later remarked: 'She died a coward because she died neither for her views, her virtue nor her love, but for her vice. She dishonoured the scaffold as she had dishonoured the throne.' So, paralysed by fear, the courtesan who had once accompanied a king lost her head in the square that he had built.

Churchill offers blood, toil, tears, and sweat

1940 Today, with German armour advancing invincibly across the Continent towards the English Channel, Winston Churchill entered the House of Commons for the first time since becoming Prime Minister of Great Britain three days earlier. In this moment of military crisis, he had come to present his administration's policies and ask for a vote of confidence. We remember the great words he spoke on this occasion and through them we imagine his voice already to be that of a nation united behind him. It was not so. Instead, the new Prime Minister faced an uncertain, almost hostile political atmosphere in the Commons. As he strode into the chamber, the Opposition Labour benches greeted him with loud cheers, but across the aisle the Conservatives – his party – remained silent. Their hearts were still with his predecessor, Neville Chamberlain, brought down by the fiasco in Norway that many thought should have been laid at Churchill's door.

This first speech was a test. Here are the words he gave them: 'I have nothing to offer but blood, toil, tears, and sweat. … You ask, what is our policy? I will say: it is to wage war, by sea, land, and air, with all our might and with all the strength that God can give us; to wage war against a monstrous tyranny, never surpassed in the dark, lamentable catalogue of human crime. That is our policy.

'You ask, what is our aim? I can answer in one word: Victory – victory at all costs, victory in spite of all terror; victory, however long and hard the road may be; for without victory there is no survival. Let that be realised: no survival for the British Empire; no survival for all that the British Empire has stood for; no survival for the urge and impulse of the ages, that mankind will move forward towards its goal.

'But I take up my task with buoyancy and hope. I feel sure that our cause will not be suffered to fail among men. At this time I feel entitled to claim the aid of all, and I say "Come, then, let us go forward together with our united strength."'

It was a good beginning. Churchill got a unanimous vote from the House that afternoon, and if some members grumbled that showy rhetoric might be all he had to offer, and others predicted a short life for his administration, he soon proved the doubters wrong on both counts.

Also on this day

1717: Austrian Empress Maria Theresa is born * 1787: British ships with 778 prisoners leave Portsmouth to found Sydney * 1846: The United States declares war against Mexico * 1882: French painter Georges Braque is born at Argenteuil

14 May

Henri IV is murdered

1610 On one of the blackest days in French history, today King Henri IV, France's greatest king, was stabbed to death as he rode in his carriage.

Henri was France's first Bourbon king. Inheriting the throne when the country was being torn asunder by the Religious Wars, he ended nearly 40 years of religious conflict and reunified the country. His most significant single achievement was the Edict of Nantes that gave freedom to France's Protestants, including the right to hold public office. 'Those who follow their consciences are of my religion', he declared, 'and I am of the religion of those who are brave and good'.

Once peace was restored, Henri gave the nation the kind of economic impetus it needed, with innovative programmes such as the introduction of the silk industry. He was famous for his wish to give every Frenchman *une poule au pot*, a chicken in the pot, every Sunday. He also added greatly to the beauty of Paris by building the place Royale, now the place des Vosges. On top of his many achievements for the nation, Henri also had time to indulge himself in numerous scandalous love affairs and came to be known as *le vert galant* (the old playboy).

By 1610 Henri was 56 years old and, perhaps fearing death, had premonitions of a violent end. His wife Marie de' Medici had foretold the specific method, having dreamed that Henri would be stabbed, and an astrologer even predicted the correct date. But when 14 May arrived, Henri shrugged off the warnings, determined to visit a sick friend.

When Henri's carriage stopped momentarily at the corner of the rue de la Ferronerie and the rue Saint-Honoré, a fanatical Catholic named François Ravaillac reached through the carriage window and stabbed the King. Henri tried to defend himself, only to be stabbed a second time, this time mortally, as the knife pierced his lungs.

Henri's murderer claimed he was executing a divine mission for the Church. In truth he was probably the tool of some of Henri's enemies, notably the duc d'Eperon (who was with Henri in the carriage and had singularly failed to prevent the assassination) and one of Henri's ex-mistresses, Henriette d'Entrangues. Fittingly for such a crime, Ravaillac was drawn and quartered thirteen days later in the beautiful square that Henri had created, the place des Vosges.

Also on this day

1607: John Smith and other colonists disembark at what was to become Jamestown on the Chesapeake Bay in North America * 1727: English landscape painter Thomas Gainsborough is born * 1796: English doctor Edward Jenner administers the first smallpox vaccination

15 May

The first Streltsy revolt in Russia

1682 The Streltsy (or musketeers) were Russia's only permanent armed force, acting as guardsmen, policemen and firemen, all in one. In May 1682 there was a power vacuum at the heart of Russia. Tsar Fedor had died the previous month and his only male heirs – a son and his half-brother – were both under age. This left two formidable women to struggle for power. One was Sophia, elder sister to one brother and half-sister to the other. The other was Natalya, second and surviving wife of Fedor and mother of the younger son named Peter.

Fearing her stepmother but desperate for power, Sophia secretly began to encourage the Streltsy to assert themselves and take charge of the land. On 15 May violence broke out. Thousands of Streltsy surrounded the Kremlin and then, before the eyes of ten-year-old Peter and his brother, literally tore to pieces two chief government ministers. And this was only the beginning. For the next six months the Streltsy looted and murdered, out of control, until Sophia's power was finally consolidated. By November the Streltsy revolt was over, but young Peter was never to forget it.

Peter waited sixteen long years, but by 1698 he had become Russia's sole and undisputed Tsar. Then, once again, the Streltsy staged a rebellion. But this time Peter had an army, and the revolt was quickly broken.

Not content simply at reaffirming his power, Peter wanted revenge. He ordered all 1,750 prisoners to the torture: they were flogged, roasted, burned with timbers and subject to the strappado (a torture by which the victim is tied to a rope, made to fall from a height almost to the ground and then stopped with a sudden jerk). Only to younger Streltsy did he show 'mercy'. They were branded, flogged, had their noses slit and their ears sliced off and were sent into exile. All the others were executed, some 80 by Peter himself, who had also personally conducted much of the torture.

Not surprisingly, there were no more revolts against Tsar Peter, known to history as Peter the Great.

Mary, Queen of Scots, marries Bothwell

1567 Mary Stuart had become Queen of Scots at the age of six days on the death of her father, but she had been sent to live at the royal court in France when she was only five. At seventeen she married François II, thereby becoming Queen Consort of France. But the weak and sickly François shortly died, so this two-time queen returned to her native Scotland still just nineteen years old.

The next five years were among the most calamitous in the history of queens, as Mary married husband number two, Henry Stewart, Lord Darnley, a drunken groper with a yen for power and money. In addition to her ill judgement in wedding Darnley, she brought more trouble on herself by alienating her rather uncivilised subjects by trying to tell them what to do, and infuriating her mainly Protestant population by her devout Catholicism. To top it off, Mary then cuckolded her husband and probably colluded in his murder. There was more to come.

On this day Mary took James Hepburn, Earl of Bothwell as husband number three, a man who three months earlier had slaughtered husband number two. He had ignited a keg of gunpowder in the room beneath him as he slept, and Darnley subsequently was found naked and strangled in the street outside, whether caught as he fled or strangled in his room and blown onto the street no one could say.

Even among Scottish aristocracy this was considered *de trop*, so none of Mary's nobles would attend the wedding. The only willing priest to be found was the Bishop of Orkney, one of Bothwell's relations. Nonetheless, Mary observed the proper forms by dressing in deepest mourning in remembrance of the husband she had just lost.

Of all of Mary's passionate and stupid mistakes, the marriage to her accomplice in her husband's murder was the worst. Her nobles, including even her own half-brother, rose against her. Within a month Bothwell had fled the country and vanished for ever from her life. (Nine years later he died insane in prison in Norway.) Within two months of her unseemly wedding Mary had been forced to abdicate the Scottish throne in favour of her infant son, and exactly one year and one day after her marriage she fled from Scotland, never to return.

Semmelweiss introduces hygiene in the hospital

1847 This morning made medical history, but no one knew it, when the following notice appeared on the door of the obstetrical clinic of the Vienna General Hospital: '... every doctor or student who comes from the dissecting room is required, before entering the maternity ward, to wash his hands thoroughly in a basin of chlorine water which is being placed at the entrance. This order applies to all without exception.'

The hospital staff was outraged. Surgeons and obstetricians resented the washing up and sterilisation order as scientifically senseless and an affront to Viennese medical tradition; medical students and nurses took their cue from the senior staff. But the notice was the result of a truly great scientific discovery – and of one young doctor's zeal.

Ignaz Semmelweiss, a 28-year-old Hungarian doctor and the author of the new regulation, had concluded on the basis of his own observation that infection – in this case, puerperal fever – could be transmitted to the mothers in the obstetrical clinic by the hands and instruments of doctors who had just come from conducting autopsies on corpses. Semmelweiss also found that in the same manner diseases could be passed from a sick patient to a healthy one. And he was soon to discover that unclean bed linens were yet another source of infection in patients.

The facts were incontrovertible: in the spring of 1847, before Semmelweiss put his regulations into effect, the mortality rate in the obstetrical unit was 11.4 per cent of mothers admitted; in 1848 the rate dropped to 1.33 per cent.

For his troubles, the Vienna General Hospital refused to renew his two-year medical contract and his successor promptly cancelled his orders. Semmelweiss then went to Budapest where in 1851 at St Roch's Hospital he initiated the same regulations, encountered the same institutional opposition and resentment, and duplicated his Viennese success. His ideas became accepted in Hungary, but Vienna remained hostile to them.

Through lectures and writing, Semmelweiss tried to persuade doctors and medical professors of the efficacy of his discoveries, but he found his doctrine ignored and himself ostracised. The effect on him was tragic: as time went on he became increasingly erratic in his behaviour, and in 1865 he was confined to an insane asylum in Vienna. He died there on 14 August – of septicaemia, the very disease he had been fighting for twenty years, contracted in one of his last operations in Budapest.

Semmelweiss died forgotten, but the principle he discovered would soon be rediscovered – and eventually introduced as scientific truth in the practice of medicine – by medical scientists like Joseph Lister in England and Robert Koch in Germany.

Corsica becomes French

1768 Even today most Corsican towns bear Italian names, and some of the inhabitants are noted for their clannish brigandry so like that of Sicily and Sardinia. Yet Corsica has been French for over two centuries, as it was on this day in 1768 that King Louis XV of France signed the deed of purchase from the Genoese.

Louis's buy had incalculable consequences, as only fifteen months later one of the world's most dramatic characters was born in Corsica – Napoleon Bonaparte, who originally bore the Italian name of Napoleone Buonaparte. It seems likely that the entire history of Europe might have been radically different had Napoleon been born Italian rather than French.

Also on this day

1702: The War of the Spanish Succession begins * 1773: Future Austrian chancellor Klemens Metternich is born in Coblenz, Germany

16 May

End of a fairytale

1703 Charles Perrault thought of himself as an accomplished poet, and when he died today in Paris at the age of 75, no doubt he hoped it would be for his classic French verse that he would be remembered.

Sadly for Perrault, his poetry is now long forgotten, but happily his greatest work lives on. For Perrault was the first to write down classic fairy tales such as 'Sleeping Beauty', 'Cinderella', 'Puss in Boots' and 'Little Red Riding Hood'. (He beat the Grimm brothers to publication by 115 years.)

Perrault entitled his collection *Histoires ou contes du temps passé*. In the book's frontispiece is inscribed: 'Contes de ma mère Loye.' ('Loye' being a play on *l'oie*, goose.) Virtually every European and British child has loved Mother Goose ever since.

Prince Louis's troubles with Marie Antoinette

1770 Young Louis the groom was only fifteen, slim, shy, ignorant and, unknown to himself, just four years from becoming King of France, as he would when his grandfather Louis XV would die of smallpox.

The bride was Marie Antoinette, christened Maria Antonia, ninth child of Austrian Empress Maria Theresa. She was only fourteen when she married young Louis at Versailles on this day in 1770.

Although the wedding ceremony was a lavish success, the wedding night was less so, as Louis found himself unable to perform. In fact, the marriage was not consummated for another three years, when Louis reportedly underwent an operation on his foreskin.

Marie Antoinette's continuing failure to produce a child alarmed the courts of both France and Austria. Her brother Joseph, now the Holy Roman Emperor, even visited Paris to investigate the problem. He sent his brother a detailed report of his astounding findings: 'Louis has fine erections, introduces his member, and then stays there without moving for a minute or two and then pulls out without climaxing.' Joseph's solution was direct: 'He should be beaten to make him ejaculate as you beat a donkey.'

Eventually Louis somehow learned to perform, and the marriage produced two children.

Also on this day

1763: James Boswell meets Dr Samuel Johnson for the first time * 1804: Napoleon is declared Emperor * 1928: The first Academy Awards ceremonies take place in Hollywood

17 May

British troops relieve Mafeking

1900 When the war in South Africa broke out in the autumn of 1899, the Boers immediately laid siege to several British-held towns. The longest and bloodiest of these sieges – and the only one to introduce a new word to the English language – took place at Mafeking, finally relieved by a British column at 7.00 this evening after 217 days of constant blockade, intermittent shelling, and occasional raids.

At first, the Boers outnumbered the Mafeking defenders by six to one, but they reckoned without the commander of the British garrison. He was a cool customer, a veteran African campaigner named Colonel Robert Baden-Powell (B-P, he was called) who offered a skilful and imaginative defence throughout the ordeal. For the British, the strategic value of holding Mafeking was simply to draw Boer forces away from the lightly defended Cape Colony until reinforcements arrived from Great Britain. B-P was the right man for the job.

With the garrison in Mafeking were several newspaper correspondents who filed their stories by telegraph, filling in their readers around the world with the events and atmosphere of the siege: tales of heroism, cowardice, raids, escapes, near misses, and the like. The public was enthralled. On 30 April, the 200th day of the siege, a cocky Boer commander sent a message into Mafeking proposing a cricket match between the two sides, to which B-P responded: 'I should like nothing better – after the match in which we are at present engaged is over. But just now we are having our innings and have so far scored 200 days, not out ...

and we are having a very enjoyable game.' As it turned out, the game was just about over.

News of the relief of Mafeking produced riotous, hysterical street demonstrations around the British world, especially in London. It also produced this entry in the *Oxford English Dictionary*: 'Maffick. v.i. Celebrate uproariously, rejoice extravagantly, esp. on an occasion of national celebration (orig. the relief of the British garrison in Mafeking, South Africa, in May 1900).'

After the mafficking was over, the Boer War continued for another two years, extracting from all concerned inordinate amounts of human suffering, devastation, and money. In time, B-P went home to England, eventually retired from the Army a general, and in 1907, employing the fieldcraft he had learned and taught his troops during his days in the veldt, he founded the Boy Scouts and, a few years later, the Girl Guides.

Birth of an anarchist

1814 'All exercise of authority perverts and all submission to authority humiliates.' So wrote Mikhail Bakunin, born today in Premukhine, Russia, and destined to create the cult of anarchism with his friend Pierre Joseph Proudhon.

Son of a Russian landowner, Bakunin was a giant of a man. He weighed in at twenty stone, his gargantuan body topped by a large, bearded, balding head. Sexually impotent, he poured his energy into endless if often adolescent plotting. (He occasionally sent coded letters mailed in the same envelope as the code itself.) Personally gentle and kind, Bakunin also favoured terror, maintaining that 'the passion for destruction is also a creative passion'.

Bakunin fought in Paris during the Revolution of 1848, and a year later manned the barricades in Dresden in the company of his lasting friend, Richard Wagner. Twice arrested and condemned to death, he escaped execution by having his sentence commuted to imprisonment in Russia and exile in Siberia. He later escaped and worked with Karl Marx, but in 1872 he attempted to hijack control of the First International, forcing Marx to move the general council from London to New York.

As much as any man, Bakunin created the connection between simple anarchism (i.e. a world without laws or restraints) and terrorism. His heritage lives with us to this day.

History's greatest diplomat dies

1838 He had been a Catholic bishop and had married a woman of easy virtue. He had brilliantly advised four kings, an emperor and a republican government while amassing a huge fortune by soliciting bribes. His many mistresses included his own nephew's wife – and her mother. His private *hôtel* was in the rue de Rivoli in Paris, where for twelve years his personal chef was the fabled Antoine Carême.

Such a man was Charles-Maurice, Prince de Talleyrand, a small French aristocrat (he was just five foot five) who walked with a limp due to a foot crushed by a nurse when he was an infant.

This extraordinary man served as Foreign Minister to the Directory, the Consulat, the Empire and the Restoration. In 1814 he was President of the provisional government, and he was twice made a prince, once by Napoleon and once by Louis XVIII. His final post was Ambassador to England, where he served until he was 80.

Talleyrand's immense abilities were surpassed only by the cynicism by which he lived. 'You must guard yourself against your first impulse', he said. 'It is almost always honest.'

Talleyrand died today at the ripe old age of 84, surrounded by mourning nobles, including King Louis-Philippe. Told that the Archbishop of Paris had said he would sacrifice his own life if it would save Talleyrand's, the statesman laconically commented: 'He can find a better use for it.'

The same morning Talleyrand signed his last treaty – an agreement between himself and the Church that in essence renounced much of his life (including a wife of 35 years) and that presumably gained for him an influential post in heaven.

Also on this day

1510: Italian painter Sandro Botticelli dies in Florence * 1792: The New York Stock Exchange is established at 70 Wall Street in New York

18 May

Eleanor of Aquitaine marries her second king

1152 Little in documented history sings with such romance as the passionate, glorious and ultimately tragic saga of King Henry II of England and his beautiful wife, Eleanor of Aquitaine.

Eleanor was unquestionably the most fascinating woman of the Middle Ages. Duchess of Aquitaine in south-west France, she was Europe's richest woman in her own right, and her capital was Bordeaux, city of troubadours. Dark haired and dark eyed, she is reputed to have been both witty and physically alluring.

First married to dull Louis VII of France, Eleanor drove him to annulment after fifteen years of marriage and not a little dalliance on her part, once complaining that she 'had married a monk, not a king'. But within two months of shedding one king she married a man shortly to be another, for on this day in 1152 she wed young Henry Plantagenet, duc d'Anjou, in her capital city. Henry was only nineteen while Eleanor was 30, but it didn't seem to matter. They may have married to combine their vast inheritances, but the attraction between the two was certainly strong; Eleanor was nearly six months pregnant.

Henry and Eleanor had eight children together, and only a year and a half after their marriage he became King of England. He would be a great king, too, and found a dynasty that would last over 300 years.

Even Henry's and Eleanor's children were from storybooks: Richard the Lion-Heart, the great warrior, and King John, England's most despicable king.

Ultimately there would be tragedy. Henry would tire of his wife and above all of her political scheming, and he would imprison her in gentle confinement for sixteen years. Eventually Henry himself would be hounded to death by his own rebellious sons.

Also on this day

1525: Flemish painter Pieter Bruegel the Elder is born * 1803: England declares war on Napoleon's France * 1846: Russian jeweller Peter Carl Fabergé is born * 1868: The last Russian tsar, Nicholas II, is born

19 May

The mysterious life of Lawrence of Arabia

1935 Today T.E. Lawrence died in self-imposed obscurity, at the age of 46, from injuries sustained in a motorcycle accident. The obscurity he maintained for thirteen years was shelter from the intense public enthusiasm and media scrutiny that greeted his exploits in the First World War as 'Lawrence of Arabia'. He had suddenly become world famous after the American journalist Lowell Thomas visited Palestine in 1917 and made films of the Arab Revolt, in which Colonel Lawrence, a British intelligence officer, had been instrumental as an advisor and leader.

As the war ended, Thomas's film and lecture presentations, seen by millions in Britain and America, showed Lawrence in Arab dress against desert land-scapes, surrounded by fierce tribesmen mounted on camels and waving rifles. For audiences weary of four years' stalemate and carnage on the Western front, the scenes were irresistible: a diminutive Englishman leading Britain's Arab allies in a series of daring – and successful – guerrilla raids against the Turks, all in the promise of an independent Arab homeland in Syria when the war was over.

At war's end, however, it became known that Britain had signed a secret wartime treaty with France in which the two nations agreed to carve up between them Turkish possessions in the Middle East. Under the treaty, France was to receive Syria, which the Arabs had helped conquer during the war and fully expected to be within their homeland. Lawrence was dismayed at

Britain's betrayal of its original promise to the Arabs. At a private ceremony with King George V at Buckingham Palace, where he was about to receive a DSO and the Order of the Bath, Lawrence unexpectedly refused the decorations. Surprised, the King was left, in his own words, 'holding the box in my hand'. Later, Lawrence told Winston Churchill that the refusal was the only way he knew to make the King aware of what had been done in his name.

In 1919 Lawrence, dressed once again in Arab attire, attended the Versailles Peace Conference to argue the Arab case, but the post-war settlement endorsed the Syrian mandate in France. For a while, Lawrence worked as an advisor on Middle Eastern matters to Churchill at the Colonial Office, but with the cause betrayed in which he had invested so much of himself and for which he had become a legend, he found the hero's role impossible to sustain.

Seeking anonymity and perhaps the comradeship of his war years – and no doubt as atonement for what he considered his failure – Lawrence abruptly gave up public life in 1922 and under a pseudonym enlisted as a recruit in the Royal Air Force. His cover soon blown by an attentive press, he joined the Tank Corps as a private. He returned to the Air Force as T.E. Shaw, serving for a time in Karachi where he translated *The Odyssey*. In 1926 *The Seven Pillars of Wisdom*, his account of the Arab Revolt, was published in a limited edition. In time it would be acknowledged a great classic of war writing. Lawrence left military service in 1935 to live in Dorset.

Among those who attended his funeral were Winston Churchill and the poet Siegfried Sassoon. King George V wrote to Lawrence's brother: 'Your brother's name will live in history and the King gratefully recognises his distinguished services to his country and feels that it is tragic that the end should have come in this manner to a life so full of promise.'

Anne Boleyn is beheaded

1536 'Madame Anne is not one of the handsomest women in the world', reported a Venetian ambassador about Henry VIII's second wife, Anne Boleyn. 'She in fact has nothing but the English king's great appetite and her eyes, which are black and beautiful.' After three years of marriage, however, Henry's appetite for Anne had dulled, while his taste for Jane Seymour had sharpened.

When Henry's interest in Anne had entirely vanished, she soon found herself charged with adultery, an indictment that most historians consider a convenient fiction to release Henry from his marriage. No sooner had the charge been laid than Henry's chief minister Thomas Cromwell assured the King that it was equivalent to treason, for which the only penalty was death.

To commit adultery one requires a partner, but in a divorce case four would be even better than one. Francis Weston and William Brere were members of Anne's Privy chamber. Henry Norris was a courtier, and Mark Smeaton a court musician. All were friends of Anne.

Henry had the four men tried for adulterous relations with his wife. Although only Smeaton admitted the crime (under torture), all four were condemned and, on 17 May, went to the block, perhaps a merciful punishment for treason, which usually was rewarded with hanging, drawing and quartering. Possibly Henry had taken into account the fact that they were innocent.

Two days later it was Anne's turn. Not that Henry was callous towards his wife; instead of turning her over to the public axeman, as a special favour he imported an expert executioner from France who employed a sharp French sword instead of a common axe, which often required several chops to decapitate the victim. Anne knelt before her executioner, not required to place her neck on the block. He deftly decapitated her with one sideways blow from his sword.

Henry married Jane Seymour eleven days later.

Also on this day

1890: Vietnamese leader Ho Chi Minh is born * 1898: British politician William Gladstone dies in Hawarden

20 May

Napoleon creates the Légion d'Honneur

1802 When we see a Frenchman with a red rosette or thin red ribbon in his buttonhole we know he has been recognised by his government for some significant achievement. We know he has been awarded the Légion d'Honneur or Legion of Honour.

During the French Revolution all the orders and decorations of the monarchist regime were abolished, so on 19 May 1802 (28 Floréal, Year X, according to the Revolutionary calendar) First Consul Napoleon Bonaparte proposed the Legion of Honour, insisting that, unlike most medals, it be open to all, soldiers and civilians alike, without regard to birth or religion. The following day the law setting up the new Order was passed.

In Napoleon's time about 48,000 men became part of the Legion, only 1,200 of them civilians. Even after Napoleon's fall the Legion of Honour was retained by kings and republics alike, but with ever increasing inflation of those elected. Just before the Second World War there were almost 320,000 members. Finally in 1962 the French government set the limit at 125,000. As evidence of the high regard in which this award is still held, the Legion's highest-ranking member is the President of France.

About two-thirds of those awarded with the Legion of Honour have been from the military services, the remainder being civilians. To earn it, civilians must have at least twenty years of significant achievement, while soldiers must have displayed extraordinary bravery.

For its first hundred years there were virtually no women recipients of the

Legion of Honour (less than 1 per cent in 1912), but now women represent about one fifth of the new appointments.

Today, some two centuries since Napoleon first conceived the idea, the Legion of Honour remains France's highest award, civilian or military.

Death of a revolutionary aristocrat

1834 Guess who died today. He:

- Was an American major general at the age of nineteen.
- Once wrote to George Washington that 'I always consider myself, my dear General, as one of your lieutenants on a detached command'.
- Was present at the British defeat at Yorktown.
- Was spirited, energetic and enthusiastic, but, according to James Madison, had 'a strong thirst of praise and popularity'.
- Arrived in America for the Revolution in his own private brig.

If you haven't guessed yet, he also:

- Had Louis XVI brought back from his flight to Varennes.
- Ordered the final demolition of the Bastille after 14 July.
- Created the modern French flag by combining the blue and red of Paris with the Bourbon royal white.

The answer is Marie-Joseph-Paul-Yves-Roch-Gilbert du Motier, the marquis de Lafayette, revolutionary aristocrat in both France and America, who died today at the age of 76.

Although he died in France, Lafayette was, literally, buried in American soil. When he left the United States after the American Revolution, he had become such a fervent Americanophile that he carried with him enough earth to fill a grave. As he had wished, he was buried in it.

Christopher Columbus dies in Valladolid

1506 Today at the age of 54 the greatest navigator the world has known died in Valladolid in northern Spain.

Christopher Columbus (or, more properly, Cristoforo Colombo), the son of a Genoese weaver, crossed the Atlantic four times, discovering the Bahamas, Santo Domingo and Cuba (which he thought was Japan) in 1492, Puerto Rico and Jamaica in 1496, Trinidad and South America in 1498 and Honduras and Panama in 1503–4. He also brought the pineapple and tobacco back to Europe, although he did not know what tobacco was for.

Even after he died, Columbus's travels were far from over. Initially he was buried in Valladolid, but three years later he was transferred to Seville, then later to Santo Domingo. Almost three centuries after his death he was dug up once again and moved to Havana, and in 1898 he made a return voyage across the Atlantic to his final resting place (until now) in Seville Cathedral.

Also on this day

1444: Italian painter Sandro Botticelli is born * 1688: English writer Alexander Pope is born * 1799: French novelist Honoré de Balzac is born in Tours * 1902: The US ends the occupation of Cuba and it becomes a sovereign, independent nation

21 May

Lindbergh solos the Atlantic (followed by a woman)

1927, 1932 'I first saw the lights of Paris a little before 10 p.m., or 5 p.m., New York time, and a few minutes later I was circling the Eiffel Tower at an altitude of about four thousand feet.' Minutes later he touched down at Le Bourget Airport, where 10,000 delirious onlookers brushed aside the police cordon and rushed onto the runway to cheer his arrival. As he stepped down from his plane the police lifted him to their shoulders and carried him through the frantic crowd. Charles Lindbergh had just become the first person ever to fly non-stop from New York to Paris, covering 3,610 miles in 33½ hours.

At 7.52 the previous morning Lindbergh had trundled down the dirt runway at Roosevelt Field in Long Island in *The Spirit of St Louis*, his single-engine, high-wing monoplane only 28 feet long with a wingspan of just 46 feet. Heavily laden with fuel, he barely cleared some obstructions at the runway's end: 'I passed over a tractor by about fifteen feet and a telephone line by about twenty', he later recalled.

Lindbergh's route took him over Long Island Sound and north to Cape Cod and Nova Scotia, and then across the Atlantic as night fell. Flying through a heavy fog with no moon, he manoeuvred around threatening cloudbanks, sometimes only a few feet above the wave tops.

The following day he first knew he was approaching Europe when he sighted a small fishing boat. Soon he was flying over Ireland, then England and across the English Channel. Then 'the sun went down shortly after passing Cherbourg and soon the beacons along the Paris–London airway became visible'. Before long he was landing at Le Bourget.

The day following his flight more huge crowds cheered Lindbergh in front of the American Embassy in Paris, and President Gaston Doumerque awarded him the Legion of Honour. When Lindbergh returned to the United States (by ship this time), a convoy of warships and fighter craft accompanied him as he approached Washington, where President Coolidge presented him with the Distinguished Flying Cross.

On Lindbergh's arrival in New York the financial markets were closed for 'Lindbergh Day'. Ten thousand soldiers and sailors led the parade up Broadway through cheering throngs and ticker tape. Over 4 million people lined the route, the biggest welcome the city had ever given.

On 21 May 1932, exactly five years after Lindbergh had landed in Paris, a slender, dark-haired American named Amelia Earhart touched down in a field near Londonderry in Northern Ireland after only fourteen hours and 56 minutes in the air. 'After scaring most of the cows in the neighborhood', she later wrote, 'I pulled up in a farmer's back yard'. As she had somewhat lost her way, she asked the farmer where she was. 'In Gallagher's pasture', he replied. She had just become the first woman ever to solo across the Atlantic.

Earhart had started her historic flight from Harbor Grace, Newfoundland in a Lockheed Vega. Carrying only soup and tomato juice to sustain her, she used smelling salts to keep her awake, as she drank neither coffee nor tea. In spite of the strong winds and mechanical problems that slowed her down, her flight was faster than Lindbergh's (although the distance was also shorter).

Earhart's transatlantic solo catapulted her into enduring fame, especially with American women, for whom she became an early feminist icon. Like Lindbergh, she was feted and celebrated, receiving the National Geographic Society gold medal from President Herbert Hoover and the Distinguished Flying Cross from Congress – the first woman so honoured.

About the sad life of dismal Henry VI

1420, 1471 At the beginning of the 15th century, King Charles VI of France had become incapable of ruling his country due to frequent fits of madness. Into this power vacuum stepped two competing dukes, Bernard VII of Armagnac and Jean Sans Peur of Burgundy, who enlisted the English to his cause.

Thinking it would help her retain her own position, Charles's wife Queen Isabeau sided with Burgundy and his English allies. Abandoning Paris to the Armagnacs, the Queen chose Troyes for her capital.

On 21 May 1420 Isabeau signed a treaty with the English called the Treaty of Troyes. This dishonourable pact disinherited Isabeau's own son and delivered France to the invaders. The treaty was sealed by the marriage of the English king, Henry V, and the Queen's daughter, Catherine de Valois. Henry was named Regent of France, with the solemn pledge that the French throne would descend to Henry's and Catherine's male heir, should they have one. On 6 December of the following year the couple celebrated the birth of a healthy boy and christened him after his father.

Then, in August 1422 the English king died, only to be followed within two months by mad King Charles, leaving the thrones of both France and England to a baby boy of less than a year. Thus an infant became Henry VI of England and Henri I of France, the only monarch ever to be crowned king of both countries, although he never ruled France for a day.

243

Unfortunately, young Henry succeeded to more than two thrones. He also inherited a streak of insanity from his grandfather that progressively incapacitated him as he grew older. To make matters worse, he was caught up in that great baronial struggle, the Wars of the Roses, and after 40 years on the English throne he was abruptly deposed by Edward of York and his mentor, the Earl of Warwick. York then proclaimed himself Edward IV.

Poor Henry spent the next ten years alternately imprisoned or in hiding in various monasteries, of which the latter may at least have been pleasing to this pious and simple-minded man.

In 1470, however, the innocent Henry was dramatically returned to the throne (if not to power), as Warwick changed sides and unhorsed his former protégé, an act for which he earned the title of 'Kingmaker'. But this momentary return to glory in fact spelled the end for Henry. Edward IV defeated and killed the Kingmaker at the Battle of Barnet on Easter Sunday 1471, and quickly had old Henry clapped back into the Wakefield Tower of the Tower of London.

On the morning of 22 May 1471, word was given out that the ageing Henry had died the previous night of 'pure displeasure and melancholy', and his body was laid out in St Paul's for all the citizens to view. But in all likelihood Edward had simply realised that England could not hold two living kings and had put Henry to death during the night of 21 May. Proof of this royal murder surfaced over 400 years later when Henry's remains were analysed in 1910. A blunt instrument had caved in the back of his skull, and his tangled hair still bore traces of blood.

The old king died exactly 51 years to the day since he had become heir to the throne of France.

Today Henry VI is largely forgotten, considered a pious pawn among the unscrupulous barons. But he has one lasting memorial: he founded the world's most famous boys' school at Eton.

Also on this day

427 BC: Plato is born * 1471: German painter Albrecht Dürer is born in Nuremberg * 1881: Clara Barton founds the American Red Cross

22 May

Constantine the Great, the emperor who legalised Christianity

AD 337 Today on Whit Sunday at Ankyrona, on the outskirts of Nicomedia in Bythnia (now Izmit in Turkey), the Roman Emperor Constantine the Great died after a reign of 31 years, the longest since Augustus three centuries before.

During his time in power Constantine transformed for ever the world he lived in. He reunited the Roman Empire for the first time since Diocletian had divided it in AD 284, he created the great city of Constantinople and moved the empire's capital there from Rome, and he made Christianity the favoured religion of Western civilisation.

Nonetheless, through the long telescope of history, Constantine remains somehow opaque, lacking human dimension. We know he was imposing in stature and strength, and in 4th-century statuary he looks like an amiable but somewhat slow-witted rugby fullback, with his cap of curly hair, his large trusting eyes, his slightly jutting ears and his thrusting full jaw. His personality is more difficult to understand.

Even the historians of his time were split about Constantine's nature. Christians portray him (as he seemed to see himself) as the thirteenth Apostle for his conversion of his Empire to Christianity, while contemporary pagans describe him as an evil tyrant who savagely crushed all opposition and squandered the empire's money for his own pleasure.

By all accounts, the laws that Constantine promulgated were repressive. Apparently a faithful husband, he seems to have been particularly disturbed by what he saw as sexual misconduct. Rapists, including men who simply ran off with their girlfriends, were burned alive, as were girls who eloped from their family's home. Any servant who aided an elopement was executed by having molten lead poured down his throat. Constantine even had his own son Crispus executed, believing him guilty of adultery. When he later discovered that his son was innocent and his second wife Fausta had falsely implicated him (or, another story goes, when she was caught in bed with a slave), she too was killed, held in a bath where the temperature was raised until she suffocated in the steam.

Constantine was 63 when he died. He had been campaigning against Persia when he fell ill and, en route back to his capital at Constantinople, he was forced to stop near Nicomedia, too sick to travel further. With the approach of death, he discarded his robes of imperial purple for the white of a Christian Neophyte and at last agreed to be baptised, this emperor who had been attempting for the past 25 years to convert an entire empire.

No sooner was Constantine dead, however, than on his instructions his corpse was brought to Constantinople where his attendants stretched him out on his golden bed in the imperial apartments. The body was reclothed in royal purple, with the imperial diadem on its head. Then, as Gibbon describes: 'The forms of the court were strictly maintained. Every day, at the appointed hours, the principal officers of the state, the army and the household, approaching the person of their sovereign with bended knees and a composed countenance, offered their respectful homage as seriously as if he had been still alive ... Constantine alone, by the peculiar indulgence of Heaven, had reigned after his death.'

Shortly, however, he was buried in the Church of the Apostles that he had built. Meanwhile, back in Rome, the capital he had visited only once in the last twenty years of his life, the Senate deified him like the pagan emperors of old.

King Henry VI is captured at the first battle of the Wars of the Roses

1455 Today the English royal army met that of the rebellious Richard, Duke of York, at St Albans, just north of London, in the first battle of that bloody internecine slaughter picturesquely called the Wars of the Roses.

Leading the royal army of perhaps 2,000 men was King Henry VI, son of the great warrior Henry V, who had died without ever seeing his infant son. But Henry VI was the very opposite of his cold and belligerent father. A studious and pious loner who just five months earlier had suffered a nervous breakdown, he was dominated by his wife, the ambitious Margaret of Anjou.

At the head of an enemy force some 6,000 strong was Richard, Duke of York, supported by the Earls of Salisbury and Warwick, the latter known to history as Warwick the Kingmaker.

There was a legitimate question whether Henry or Richard had the better right to the throne, for both men claimed it through descent from Edward III. The House of Lancaster now held it only because Henry's grandfather Henry IV had usurped it from the hapless Richard II.

But Richard of York had no real desire to make himself King. The conflict stemmed from the anarchy caused during Henry VI's long minority, when every baron maintained a private army in a lawless country. During one of Henry's fits of insanity Richard had become protector of the realm, but had been forced out by Henry's wife Margaret when Henry regained his senses. Hated by Margaret, Richard feared for his position, his wealth and his head, and took up arms in self defence.

As the armies jockeyed for position around St Albans, Richard sent word offering to negotiate, swearing fealty to the King. Perhaps enraged by his subject's refusal to submit instantly, Henry sent back a message vowing to hang, draw and quarter any who questioned his authority. Now battle became inevitable.

The first Battle of St Albans lasted less than an hour, as Henry's troops wilted before the rebel charge, especially when Warwick got round behind them. Many were killed and King Henry, wounded in the neck, was captured. Now in full command, Richard allowed Henry to remain King, subject to his control, but the uncertain peace lasted only until 1458. The terrible dynastic brawl continued to drench England in blood for 30 years, until the pivotal Battle of Bosworth Field ended the struggle of rival Plantagenets and Henry VII, the last representative of the House of Lancaster, founded the Tudor dynasty.

According to Shakespeare, the Wars of the Roses gained its name one day when Richard of York was walking in the garden of the Inns of Temple in London, where he encountered one of King Henry's advisors, the Duke of Somerset. During an argument, Somerset picked a red rose from a bush, saying: 'Let all of my party wear this flower!' In retort, Richard simply plucked a white rose to represent the House of York.

Although Shakespeare's version is apocryphal, the white rose was certainly one of the symbols of the House of York. Historians disagree, however, on the red rose. Some say it was originally a symbol of Henry's great-grandfather John of Gaunt, while others insist that it was assumed by the House of Lancaster by Henry VII only after the wars were over. In any case, the actual nomenclature – the 'Wars of the Roses' – was coined only in 1829 when Sir Walter Scott used it in his novel *Anne of Geierstein*.

Also on this day

1813: German composer Richard Wagner is born in Leipzig * 1859: British writer Sir Arthur Conan Doyle is born in Edinburgh * 1885: French novelist Victor Hugo dies in Paris * 1939: Adolf Hitler and Benito Mussolini create the Axis by signing a 'Pact of Steel'

23 May

Savonarola is burned at the stake in the Piazza della Signoria

1498 Girolamo Savonarola had the death's head of a fanatic: ascetic, hollow cheeks beneath his great beak of a nose, full, rubbery lips and piercing green eyes that were said to glow with inner zeal. Born in Ferrara in 1452, he became a Dominican friar whose principal concern was to attack pleasures of the flesh and independence of the spirit for the glory of a cleansed and purified Church.

Savonarola moved to Florence in 1489 and within two years was the most controversial figure in the city, castigating the gentry for corruption, pleasure-seeking and vanity. His aim was nothing less than the subjugation of all Florence, including the government, to his version of God's law.

Savonarola's influence grew; he had accurately predicted the deaths of Lorenzo the Magnificent and King Ferrante of Naples, and he interpreted Charles VIII of France's invasion of Tuscany in 1494 as the scourge of God he had so long foreseen.

The power vacuum left when Charles VIII left Tuscany thrust Savonarola into de facto control of Florence, and the next four years were filled with grim religiosity that often included the ritual burning of 'vanities' ranging from make-up to sumptuous clothing and jewellery. The bonfires sometimes incinerated sensual paintings even by such masters as Botticelli.

As Savonarola's power grew, so did his list of enemies. The most dangerous of these was Alexander VI, the dissolute and calculating Borgia Pope who was determined to bring the friar to heel. Alexander particularly objected to Savonarola's claim to direct communication with God, thereby putting himself above the Church and, by implication, above even the Pope himself.

After Savonarola refused to come to Rome to explain himself, Alexander tried to bribe him into silence with the offer of a cardinal's hat. 'A red hat?', Savonarola replied with scorn, 'No hat will I have but that of a martyr, reddened with my own blood.' Finally Alexander excommunicated him, but Savonarola merely advised the Pope to take immediate care of his own salvation and continued to harangue the crowds of Florence.

Savonarola's intransigence led to Alexander's final threat: unless the friar was sent to Rome, all of Florence would be placed under interdict, meaning that there could be no Mass, no taking of Communion, and no weddings, baptisms or funerals. This was the moment his enemies were waiting for. The Franciscan monks of the town, long jealous of the Dominicans' predominance, challenged his religious supremacy, and the rich and powerful families, longing for a return to more civilised days, stirred up the Florentine mob. Finally, on Palm Sunday in 1498, Savonarola was chased from his pulpit and arrested by the civil government. Torture soon led to confession and confession to conviction for heresy and promoting a schism in the True Church.

On 23 May a great scaffold was erected in Florence's Piazza della Signoria, and on it Savonarola and two of his most faithful followers were executed by fire. 'The culprits were burned in a few hours', wrote one eyewitness, 'and their arms and legs gradually dropped off. Then stones were thrown at the parts of the bodies still hanging, in order to make them fall, as there was a fear that the mob would get hold of them. Then the executioner and his helpers cut down the post and burned it to the ground, bringing up more wood and stirring the fire over the dead bodies so that every piece was consumed. They then brought wagons and ... took the last of the ashes to the Arno near the Ponte Vecchio so that no remains should ever be found.'

The Second Defenestration of Prague

1618 At the time it must have seemed like a comic opera. The previous year, Catholic representatives of Holy Roman Emperor Matthias had ordered the closing of new Protestant chapels in the Bohemian towns of Hrob and Broumov. Then in May 1618 the Emperor sent three imperial regents to Prague, the capital of Bohemia, further to enforce his stand against Protestantism. When these august representatives came on this day to the Hradcany Palace with Matthias's demands, they were seized by a group of local deputies and flung from the first floor windows.

'Now let your Virgin Mary save you', cried one of the attackers as the envoys went over the sill.

The fall was only a few feet, and the shaken deputies scuttled away unharmed. This was the famous Second Defenestration of Prague (the first took place on 30 July 1419).

Ridiculous perhaps, but with dire consequences. This marked the first violence between Protestants and Catholics, the first open opposition to Vienna. By August, Imperial troops were on the march in Bohemia and Europe's worst religious war, the Thirty Years' War, had begun.

Also on this day
1335: Mongol leader Tamerlane the Great is born * 1533: Henry VIII divorces Catherine of Aragon * 1701: Scottish-born buccaneer Captain Kidd is hanged for piracy * 1706: The Duke of Marlborough defeats the French at the Battle of Ramillies * 1945: Hitler's second-in-command Heinrich Himmler commits suicide

24 May

The sun sets on Nicholas Copernicus

1543 No less an authority than Martin Luther said of him: 'The fool will overturn the whole art of astronomy.' Luther was referring to Nicholas Copernicus, the Polish astronomer who would change for ever our way of seeing the universe, and whose work would eventually destroy much of the underpinning of the medieval world.

Copernicus (Mikolaj Kopérnik in the original Polish) was born in the small town of Torun in 1473. He was a canon who practised medicine, but his great contribution of course was in astronomy. He was the first to postulate a heliocentric view of the universe in which the Sun, not the Earth, is at the centre.

Copernicus spent much of his life in East Prussia, and it was there that he wrote his immortal work, *De revolutionibus orbium coelestium* (On the Revolutions of the Celestial Spheres), which laid out his theory. Earlier he had summarised his main points, among which were: 'The centre of the Earth is not the centre of the world. All the planetary orbits circle around the Sun at the centre of them all.' In the 16th century such a theory was not only psychologically threatening, but heretical. If it was true, the Earth was no longer the constant, unmoving centre of the universe but just a planet like any other. Copernicus was challenging head-on Ptolemy's geocentric theory that had been accepted for 1,400 years. His theory was also directly counter to the teachings of the Church.

The great astronomer finished *De revolutionibus* when he was 57 but, due to its contentious subject matter, he was unable to publish. Finally, in 1543, a Lutheran printer in Nuremberg, free from the pressures of the Church in Rome, brought out the great work. This same year, when he was 70, Copernicus was living in Frauenberg, Poland. Before even seeing his book in print, he suffered a stroke and soon lapsed into unconsciousness. Then one of his colleagues placed a copy of the work, printed at last, in his unfeeling hands. Immediately before he died he regained consciousness just long enough to realise that his theories had at last been published.

Peter Minuit buys Manhattan for 60 guilders' worth of trinkets

1626 On this day Peter Minuit, a director of the Dutch West India Company's North American colony, made a historic barter with a local Indian tribe: in exchange for some 60 guilders' worth of pots, pans, fish hooks, tools and cloth, the Company received possession of a large island at the mouth of the Hudson River.

Peter Minuit, a ruddy, round-faced man with a goatee and large upward-sweeping moustache, was a Dutch-speaking German, born in Wesel in Germany. Two years before his appointment as director, the Dutch West India Company had established the colony of New Netherland in the lower Hudson valley and had landed its first settlers there, setting up shop in small communities on the shores of the great bay. But just as the new settlements were finding their feet, war broke out between local Indian tribes over the fur trade with the colonists. In an attempt to provide protection for the fledgling settlements, Director Minuit bought Manhattan Island – a name derived from an Algonquin Indian word meaning 'island of hills' – and moved the settlers to its southern tip. He called the new town New Amsterdam and ordered a wooden fort built at its centre. (The traditional tale that Minuit bought Manhattan for $24 is of course apocryphal, since at the time the dollar did not exist.)

In 1631 the Dutch West India Company called Minuit back to Holland and after more New World adventures, some for the Swedes, he was drowned in a hurricane in the West Indies in 1638.

Even without Minuit's leadership, however, New Amsterdam continued to prosper, but in 1664 the despotic and controversial governor Peter Stuyvesant was forced to cede it to the British during the Second Anglo-Dutch War when a powerful fleet of British warships sailed into the harbour. The British renamed the city New York in honour of the King's brother, the Duke of York (later James II).

Also on this day

1685: Physicist Gabriel Fahrenheit is born in Danzig, Poland * 1743: French revolutionary Jean-Paul Marat is born * 1819: Queen Victoria is born in Kensington Palace * 1844: Samuel Morse sends the first telegraph message, from Washington to Baltimore

25 May

Oscar Wilde is convicted of the love that dare not speak its name

1895 On this date a London jury found Oscar Wilde, the internationally famous author of *Dorian Gray*, *The Importance of Being Earnest* and *Lady Windermere's Fan*, guilty of committing indecent acts, and the trial judge immediately sentenced him to two years' hard labour. Three months earlier, Wilde had brought a charge of libel against the Marquess of Queensbury for calling him a 'sodomite', but the charge backfired disastrously when abundant evidence offered by the defence showed Wilde to have indulged with numerous young men in homosexual acts illegal under the English law of the time. The libel action ended in acquittal for Queensbury and arrest for Wilde.

Wilde's troubles had really started in 1892, when he had met Lord Alfred Douglas and the two had entered into a notorious love affair. Douglas's father, the Marquess of Queensbury, was already enraged at his son's behaviour on several fronts. Now seeing him bent on pursuing 'intimacy with that man Wilde', the Marquess determined to bring his son to heel by bringing the author to ruin. He succeeded only in the second goal. As Wilde wrote to Douglas: 'In your war of hate with your father I was at once shield and weapon to each of you.'

Wilde was at the top of his form at the beginning of 1895, celebrated, hated, mocked, and cheered as an outrageous wit, a flamboyant personality, a genius with language, an outrager of Victorian sensibilities, and the leading spokesman for the cult of aestheticism. Married with two sons, he had also begun to lead a dangerous and not-so-secret double life as a homosexual, meeting in hotel rooms with young men, often lower-class and paid for their services. 'Feasting with panthers' was his phrase for these encounters.

After the sensational trial and conviction, Wilde's life was completely ruined. Upon his release from prison in 1897, he fled England and his family for Europe, where he stayed for the rest of his brief life, broken if not reformed, and dependent on his remaining friends for handouts. The man who had written so many poems, novels and plays in the years before prison, and left the world so many quotable gems, wrote only one more work, *The Ballad of Reading Gaol*. He died at the age of 46 in a Paris hotel room on 30 November 1900. As he quipped in better days: 'The public is wonderfully tolerant. It forgives everything but genius.'

Louis Napoleon escapes from prison

1846 In September 1840, Prince Louis Napoleon Bonaparte had been sentenced to life imprisonment for having the temerity to invade France with a force of 56 men. He had been imprisoned at Ham, in the north of France near Amiens.

Although the prison was grim and dark (it was a castle constructed in the 10th century), conditions were not insupportable, as witnessed by the fact that Louis kept a mistress while he was there, and she bore him two sons.

By 1846, Louis had decided that he had had enough. Early on the morning of 25 May he disguised himself as a prison workman, having shaved off his moustache and dyed his hair. Throwing a plank over his shoulder, he simply walked out of the guarded but open door and then through the main prison gate to freedom.

Within 24 hours Louis was in London, where he was to wait for only four more years before returning to France to win an overwhelming victory for the presidency.

Also on this day
735: The Venerable Bede dies * 1521: The Edict of Worms declares Martin Luther an outlaw * 1681: Spanish playwright Pedro Calderón de la Barca dies in Madrid * 1703: English diarist Samuel Pepys dies * 1803: American philosopher Ralph Waldo Emerson is born in Boston

26 May

A saint meets his bride

1234 When Marguerite of Provence met her future husband on this day in 1234, perhaps she should have paid more attention to her future mother-in-law. Her fiancé, whom she married a few days later, was Louis IX of France, whose domineering mother was the redoubtable and possessive Blanche of Castile.

During the years ahead Blanche would continually nag her son for spending too much time with his wife, once even commanding him away from her sickbed when her death seemed imminent.

Nothing illustrates the theme of the mother-in-law from hell better than the famous tale of Marguerite and Louis at the castle of Pontoise.

The castle contained a spiral staircase, with Marguerite's bedroom at the bottom and Louis's at the top. According to a contemporary source, the royal couple were so afraid of battle-axe Blanche that 'they were wont to hold their converse on a winding stair that went from one chamber to the other, and their affair was so well planned that when ushers spied Queen Blanche coming toward her son's chamber they would knock at the door thereof with their staffs and the King, hearing it from the stair, would hastily run up into his room so that his mother might find him there'.

In spite of her possessiveness, Louis was devoted to his mother. But perhaps patience came naturally to him; eventually he was declared a saint.

Birth of the first great Churchill

1650 Ruined by having fought for the wrong side in the English Civil War, his father had at last moved in with his widowed mother-in-law, a certain Lady Drake, in her house near Axminster in Devon. Here on this day in 1650 the father celebrated the birth of a son, an aristocratic baby with few prospects and less money, one John Churchill.

Churchill was to become the greatest general-statesman of his time, rivalled in military skills only by the great Prince Eugene of Savoy. He was eventually awarded the title of Duke, and assumed the name of Marlborough.

The Duke of Marlborough established the great family that still ranks among

252

England's highest nobility, and his most famous descendant bore the same name as the original duke's father, Winston Churchill.

Also on this day

604: St Augustine dies in Canterbury * 1799: Writer Alexander Pushkin is born in Moscow * 1859: English poet A.E. Housman is born * 1868: Michael Barrett is hanged at Clerkenwell for trying to free two Irish revolutionaries, the last public hanging at Newgate

27 May

Stern John Calvin goes to his rest

1564 As the author of *The Institutes of the Christian Religion*, John Calvin earned himself a place in history as the great simplifier and systematiser of Protestant thought. He also founded the merciless creed that bears his name, Calvinism, with its theories of predestination.

Born in France (and in reality named Jean Cauvin) and educated at the University of Paris, Calvin fled Catholic France for Switzerland at the age of 26 and a year later started the transformation of Geneva into a grim Protestant theocracy. The clergy were authorised to spy on men's private lives to ensure straightforward rectitude, gambling was prohibited, restaurant diners were compelled by law to say grace before eating, and Christmas celebrations were barred. Calvin himself, with his ascetic face and long, straggling beard, ruled the community like an Old Testament prophet, strict, priggish and unforgiving.

Calvin also organised militant Protestantism throughout France, thus preparing the ground for the ferocious religious wars of half a century later.

As he grew older, Calvin suffered from a series of debilitating diseases, but still he worked on, a remote, austere figure totally devoted to his cause. In spite of his deteriorating condition, he slept little and ate only bread and water once every 36 hours. When friends saw that he was dying, they begged him to reduce his workload, but his response was typical: 'Would you that the Lord should find me idle when He comes?'

John Calvin died on this day at the age of 54, but his religion lives with us still in a much more tolerant form. No doubt it was the character of Calvin himself that inspired H.L. Mencken's famous description of Calvinism as 'the haunting fear that someone, somewhere, may be happy'.

The coronation of England's worst king

1199 When his elder brother Richard the Lion-Heart died in battle in April 1199, John Plantagenet put as his first priority his most valuable inheritance: he had himself crowned Duke of Normandy and confirmed as overlord to his territories in Touraine, Anjou and Aquitaine. Only then did he cross the Channel to England. After all, England boasted fewer than 3 million inhabitants in those days, against perhaps twice that number in John's French possessions.

John's coronation took place in London on Ascension Day, 27 May 1199. His seventeen-year reign was one of the worst in English history, as John sparred with the French, the Pope and his own barons. Treacherous and vengeful, he personally murdered his own cousin and once left the wife and son of a rebel baron to starve to death in a royal prison. By the end of his reign, virtually all of those proudly possessed French territories had been lost to the King of France.

Possibly John's ruinous rule was signalled from the start. He was the only king in English history not to receive the sacraments at his coronation.

Also on this day

1332: Italian poet Dante Alighieri is born * 1837: American cowboy legend Wild Bill Hickok is born in Troy, Illinois * 1840: Genoese violin virtuoso and composer Niccolò Paganini dies in Nice * 1941: The British navy sinks the German battleship *Bismarck*

28 May

Jacques Bonhomme revolts against his masters

1358 France was triply devastated: the Black Death had killed a third of the population, bands of marauding mercenaries called the Great Companies ravaged the countryside, and the English had beaten and humiliated the French nobility at war. Less than two years earlier England's Black Prince had destroyed the French at Poitiers, and the French King Jean II had been captured and hauled away to England.

Those who suffered most, of course, were the peasants, many of whom lived at a subsistence level, eating little but bread and onions, living in huts without furniture, water or heat, sleeping on straw. The peasant – or Jacques Bonhomme as the nobles contemptuously called him – lived in misery, filled with hate for the lords who repressed him.

On this day in the village of St Leu some 25 miles north of Paris, about 100 hate-filled peasants armed themselves with pitchforks, knives and clubs and attacked the nearest noble manor, burning it to the ground and killing the owner and his family. This was the first violence in what became known as the Jacquerie, the terrible peasant revolt that lasted only a month but which destroyed some 150 castles and manors. Led by Guillaume Callet, the rampaging peasants killed or tortured many nobles, and in one case a wife and her children were forced to watch a knight roasted on a spit and then to eat his flesh. As the revolt spread, peasants from the countryside teamed up with insurgents from Paris following the banner of Etienne Marcel. Perhaps as many as 100,000 peasants were on the rampage.

Even royalty was threatened. On 9 June a mob surrounded the royal family in the market-place at Meaux, but were then attacked and slaughtered by a loyalist force led by Gaston Phoebus de Foix. The following day, an army led by Charles the Bad of Navarre crushed Guillaume Callet's peasant force at Clermont-en-Beauvaisis.

By the end of June the Jacquerie was over, and an enraged and fearful nobility savaged the bands of peasants, drenching the country in blood. According to a proverb of the time: 'Oignez vilain, il vous poindra, poignez vilain, il vous oindra.' (Spare a villain, he'll cut your throat, show a villain your steel and he'll kneel.) Up to 20,000 peasants were slaughtered, and Guillaume Callet, who had styled himself their king, was crowned with a red hot iron brand and then decapitated. Etienne Marcel was killed by one of his own men, who thought he was selling out to the enemy. Jacques Bonhomme would have to wait over 400 years for his revenge to begin in Paris.

Also on this day

1738: French doctor and inventor Joseph Guillotin is born * 1759: British statesman William Pitt the Younger is born * 1779: English furniture-maker Thomas Chippendale dies

29 May

Joan of Arc is condemned to death

1431 One of the most famous – and iniquitous – trials in history ended today with the accused found guilty and condemned to a heretic's death by fire. Five centuries later she would be declared a saint. Her name was Joan of Arc.

After leading the French army to a string of victories, on 24 May 1430 Joan was captured by the Burgundians at Compiègne. Sold to the English for 16,000 francs in one of the most sordid bargains in history, she was transferred to the English headquarters at Rouen. There, facing her English jailers with courage, she defied them while showing her knowledge of English swear words: 'You think when you have killed me you will conquer France, but that you will never do. Even if there were a hundred thousand Goddammees more in France than there are, they will never conquer that kingdom.'

Joan of Arc's trial in Rouen took far longer than most in a day when justice rarely needed more than a few hours to reach its conclusion. The judges had first been assembled in February 1431, but under the leadership of the infamous Bishop of Beauvais, Pierre Cauchon, these ecclesiastical worthies required three months to find adequate proof against this nineteen-year-old religious innocent.

Found guilty, Joan was turned over to civil justice for her punishment, as the Church itself could not or would not carry out the sentence.

Twenty-four hours later, on a Wednesday, Joan was brought to the old market-place of Rouen and burned at the stake for witchcraft, heresy and, principally, for having defeated the English army.

She remained the religious mystic until she died, claiming to the last her faith in the saintly voices that had directed her most of her life. Chained to the stake, she asked for a cross, which an English soldier made for her out of two small sticks. As she died, her last words were 'Jesus, Jesus'.

After all was over, Joan's executioner threw her ashes into the Seine so that no relic might remain. And so ended the incredible story of an illiterate peasant girl from Domrémy who led an army, restored a king and changed the course of history.

Hillary and Tenzing conquer Everest

1953 The two men had spent the night before in a tent at an elevation of 27,900 feet above sea level, surely the highest camp ever made by humans since the world began. At 3.30 this morning they roused themselves, thawed their boots over a Primus stove, and ate a little breakfast. At 6.30 they started climbing, Tenzing in the lead, Hillary behind, their positions changing from time to time to spell each other in the hard work of chopping and kicking steps in the unstable snow. The weather was perfect for the attempt: clear and almost windless.

Reaching the south summit by 9.00, they jettisoned empty oxygen bottles to lighten their loads. Hillary took the lead as they started up the final ridge, where the snow was firmer. A vertical rock step blocked their way, but with Tenzing belaying him, Hillary found a route by jamming himself between a cornice and the rock face. Now, as they proceeded, the ridge became less steep. Suddenly, at 11.30, there was no place to go but down. They had reached the very top. They were the first human beings ever to stand at the summit of Mount Everest.

Breathless and exhilarated, they thumped each other on the back, shook hands, and looked around at the Himalayas ranged below. They turned off their oxygen, and Hillary took a photograph of Tenzing holding the flags of Great Britain, Nepal, India and the United Nations. Fifteen minutes later, they started down. When they reached the camp at the South Col, Hillary told George Lowe: 'Well, we knocked the bastard off!'

News of the ascent reached London the next day, a fitting present for Queen Elizabeth II's coronation. The feat was acclaimed worldwide. Edmund Hillary, the New Zealand beekeeper, was knighted. Tenzing Norgay, the veteran Sherpa climber for whom this expedition was his seventh on Everest, was suddenly the hero of all Asia.

Enthusiastic crowds greeted the expedition in Kathmandu, Calcutta and New Delhi, where Prime Minister Nehru gave the climbers a reception attended by thousands. But amid the celebration, and while the official account of the climb was being prepared for publication, the human triumph was marred by those who wished to turn it into one of politics or race. Who had set foot on the summit first, the Sahib or the Sherpa? Misinformation and speculation abounded, with some Asian papers reporting that Tenzing had led the way.

The truth was issued in a statement written by Hillary and signed by both men in late June: 'On May 29th Tenzing Sherpa and I left our high camp on Mount Everest for our attempt on the summit. As we climbed upwards to the south summit first one and then the other would take a turn at leading. We crossed over the south summit and moved along the summit ridge. We reached the summit almost together.' Later, in his autobiography, Tenzing described the moment this way: 'The rope that joined us was thirty feet long, but I held most of it in loops in my hand, so there was only about six feet between us. … Hillary stepped on top first. And I stepped up after him.'

Constantinople falls to the Turk – the end of the Middle Ages

1453 Tradition says that today marked the end of the Middle Ages, as Constantinople finally fell to the Turkish forces of Sultan Mehmed II, the Conqueror.

The siege had started in February, when the Byzantine Emperor Constantine XI Palaeologus tried to defend the city with only 10,000 troops against a Turkish army of 150,000 men.

In spite of their numbers, the Turks made little headway during the first months of the siege. Constantinople's massive stone walls seemed unbreachable and a great iron chain shut the Turkish fleet out of the Golden Horn, the narrow body of water forming the north boundary of the old city. Finally, however, Mehmed had 70 of his ships dragged overland from the Bosphorus to the Golden Horn, forcing Constantine to fight on two fronts. Even then the defenders held firm.

But then nature came to the aid of the attackers. Back in the 15th century, all believed in signs and portents, and during the preceding months exceptionally explosive thunderstorms had pummelled the city. By their abstruse calculations Byzantine astrologers took this to signify that Constantinople would hold out against attack. But on 22 May came a very different omen: the Moon entered an eclipse so that all that was visible was a thin crimson sickle – the very image of the Turkish crescent moon emblazoned on Mehmed's banners.

Four days later another ominous sign appeared. A dense fog enveloped the city, and when it started to lift, the refracted evening sunlight was reflected in the city's windows and on the great copper dome of the Hagia Sophia church, making it appear to be wreathed in flame. As the Byzantines began to lose heart,

Mehmed's soldiers' confidence grew. The Turkish sultan ordered three days of massive cannon bombardment, and on 29 May his inspired troops stormed the Romanos Gate to enter the city.

In despair at his plight, Emperor Constantine cried out: 'Is there no Christian to cut off my head?' His own men refused, but shortly Turkish soldiers dispatched him. Mehmed ordered his head to be severed from his corpse and displayed to those few Greeks who had survived the slaughter. He subsequently gave Constantine an honourable burial. Constantinople was lost for ever to Christendom just 1,123 years after the first Emperor Constantine – the man who legalised Christianity across the Roman Empire – had made it his capital.

Also on this day

1415: Anti-pope John XXIII is stripped of his title * 1814: Napoleon's first wife, Joséphine de Beauharnais, dies of pneumonia at Malmaison

30 May

The bons mots *of a great French writer*

1778 He corresponded with Catherine the Great, was friend and councillor to Frederick the Great and was for a while the official historian to the court of Louis XV. He was a Frenchman who lived in England, Germany and Switzerland as well as France and who amassed a great fortune through speculation.

He was also one of the greatest writers that France has produced, writing poetry, novels, philosophy and satire. Among his most famous *bons mots* are:

'Men use thought only to justify their injustices and speech only to conceal their thoughts.'
'If God did not exist, it would be necessary to invent him.'
'This body which was called and still is called the Holy Roman Empire was neither holy, nor Roman, nor an empire.'
'I disapprove of what you say, but I will defend to the death your right to say it.'
'All is for the best in the best of possible worlds.'

He was, of course, Voltaire, that Parisian son of a notary who was born plain François Marie Arouet. He died today in Paris.

Typically, Voltaire even had *bons mots* on his deathbed. When asked to renounce Satan, he declined, ruefully answering: 'This is no time to make any more enemies.' Later, on seeing the lamp next to his bed flare up, he quipped, 'What? The flames already?' Those were his last words.

A French king dies in terror

1574 King Charles IX of France lay dying from tuberculosis at the tender age of 24, and his mother, the notorious Catherine de' Medici, would do anything to save her precious son, the king who had ordered the St Bartholomew's Day massacre against the Huguenots less than two years earlier.

Summoning her astrologers, the Queen Mother determined to have performed the appalling black magic rite, the Oracle of the Bleeding Head.

As the clock struck midnight on 29 May, Catherine and her apostate chaplain began the celebration of the Black Mass in the room of the dying king. A young child was brought in, given communion and then beheaded at the altar. The chaplain then beseeched the Devil to speak through the dead child's mouth.

The severed head was heard to murmur, 'Vim Patior'. (I suffer violence.) Seized with terror, the King cried out, 'Take the head away! Take the head away!' Shivering in fear and loathing, and apparently repenting of the St Bartholomew's Day massacre, he then cried out: 'What streams of blood, how many murders! What wicked counsel I have had!' He continued to scream until a few hours later he gave a terrible groan and died.

The horrible circumstances of Charles's death did not, however, break his mother's grip on the throne of France. The new king was Charles's brother Henri III, through whom Catherine continued to rule.

Also on this day

1431: Joan of Arc is burned at the stake * 1593: Playwright Christopher Marlowe dies in London * 1640: Flemish painter Peter Paul Rubens dies

31 May

The cardinal, the queen and the diamonds

1785 Louis René Edouard, Cardinal de Rohan was perceptibly slow of wit, but he happened to head one of France's wealthiest families. Also living in Paris was a countess named Jeanne de La Motte, who carried royal blood in her veins (she descended from Henri II) but no cash in her pockets. Jeanne decided that Rohan could be bilked to her advantage.

A few years earlier, a Parisian jeweller named Böhmer had crafted a diamond necklace of extraordinary value and vulgarity. It contained 4,647 stones weighing 2,800 carats and lay on the breast fifteen inches from top to bottom. Unhappily for Böhmer, even the extravagant Queen Marie Antoinette found the asking price of 1,600,000 livres too steep.

Here Jeanne de La Motte saw her opportunity. Pretending she was acting as go-between for the Queen, she presented to Cardinal de Rohan a series of letters purportedly from Marie Antoinette. In fact, they were forgeries prepared by Jeanne's lover. The letters asked Rohan to purchase the diamond necklace for the Queen, who, being short of ready cash, wanted to repay in three instalments. The Queen needed the Cardinal (said the letters) to act as guarantor to the jeweller for so large a sum. Jeanne de La Motte clinched the deception by having a veiled prostitute disguised as the Queen meet Rohan one evening in the gardens at Versailles.

Completely duped, the Cardinal arranged for the purchase of the diamonds and handed them over to Jeanne, ostensibly for delivery to Marie Antoinette. Jeanne immediately broke up the necklace and sold the stones.

A few months later the first instalment to the jeweller fell due. Jeanne knew the truth would have to come out, but calculated that the vain and rich Rohan would pay for the necklace himself rather than publicly admit to being so humiliatingly gulled. But she had not counted on the reaction of the jeweller. On learning of the sting, he went straight to the Queen, who promptly informed her husband, Louis XVI.

In the resulting confusion Louis and Marie Antoinette concluded that Cardinal de Rohan had used the Queen's name in order to purchase the diamonds for himself. Rohan was immediately arrested, to stand trial before the French *parlement*.

The trial was brief, Rohan admitting to his credulity rather than criminality. 'I used the full scope of my intelligence to prove that I am a fool', he said. *Parlement* believed him and, on the evening of 31 May 1785, acquitted him of all charges.

Jeanne de La Motte was not so lucky. Sentenced to prison for life, she was whipped and branded with a 'V' for *voleuse* (thief). Two years later she escaped to England, to live out her life writing scurrilous pamphlets accusing the Queen of fictitious crimes, including a passionate liaison with Rohan.

For Marie Antoinette, the whole affair was a disaster. In spite of the evidence, the French public tended to believe that somehow she had contrived to spend a fortune on diamonds, and hatred for her continued to grow.

Of Prussian kings

1740 Frederick William of Prussia was one of history's oddball kings. Ruler of a smallish nation of 5 million people, he restored economic stability and laid the foundations for the powerful and professional Prussian armies of the future.

Yet Frederick William also had a peculiar side. He established a corps of guards of the tallest men in Europe – most were over six feet six inches tall. To get new recruits he sent agents across the continent who didn't hesitate to kidnap unwilling candidates. It was also Frederick William who instilled the most ferocious discipline among his troops, believing that his soldiers should fear their officers more than the enemy.

Although intelligent, Frederick William was also violent and totally insensitive to others, even his own son. He suffered from a metabolic derangement called porphyria (the same illness that plagued England's George III) that afflicted him with gout, piles, boils and unendurable pains in the stomach. Such suffering triggered off insane rages, when the maddened king would assault his courtiers with his cane.

None suffered more than the King's son, the future Frederick II, the Great. His father beat him, spit in his food to keep him from eating too much, and once imprisoned him. He had his son's best friend beheaded before his very eyes for plotting to 'escape' with young Frederick (and possibly for suspected homosexual behaviour). Voltaire called Frederick William 'a crowned ogre'.

Frederick William died today at the age of 51. His son Frederick the Great inherited his kingdom and his disciplined army. He ruled from this day for over 46 years, making Prussia one of the great powers in Europe.

Alfonso XIII survives an assassination attempt on his wedding day

1906 The royal wedding had taken place at the Church of San Jeronimo in Madrid. The bride was Princess Victoria Eugenia, granddaughter of Queen Victoria, the bridegroom was twenty-year-old Alfonso XIII of Spain, who had been born a king, his father having died while his mother was still expecting him.

The royal couple's procession was heading back towards the Palacio Real, but on a balcony along the route lurked Matteo Morral, a revolutionary assassin.

As the wedding procession passed beneath him, Morral dropped a bomb disguised as a wreath of flowers. The explosion was horrendous, the carnage extreme. Over twenty people lay dead – but miraculously both bride and bridegroom escaped untouched.

Later, when asked how he reacted to the constant threat of assassination, Alfonso is reputed coolly to have answered: 'C'est le risque du métier.' (It's the risk of the trade.)

Alfonso's equanimity in the face of danger was his strongest if not sole virtue. After trying to increase his own authority at the expense of the Spanish parliament, he was at last forced into permanent exile in 1931 when Republican parties scored an overwhelming victory in national elections. He died ten years later, unaware that in 1975 his grandson Juan Carlos would return to Spain as King.

Also on this day

1594: Italian painter Jacobo Tintoretto dies in Venice * 1672: Peter the Great of Russia is born * 1809: Austro-Hungarian composer Joseph Haydn dies * 1819: American poet Walt Whitman is born on Long Island * 1902: The Peace of Vereeniging ends the Boer War in South Africa

1 June

The brave, futile end of Napoleon IV

1879 Louis was an imperial prince, only son of France's ex-Emperor Napoleon III. At the age of 23 he found himself in England, having fled with his father into exile after the disastrous French defeat in the Franco-Prussian War. When his father died in January 1873, Louis became the head of the family, with only one goal in life: to regain power for himself and his family, in that order. In this he was ardently supported by Bonapartists everywhere, who proclaimed him Napoleon IV.

The first step in Louis's quest was to gain military glory, and Britain's war of conquest against the Zulus seemed to provide the perfect opportunity.

Britain already ruled neighbouring Natal, and in January 1879 demanded that the Zulu King disband his army and pay reparations, under the pretext that he had insulted the British. When he refused, the British invaded. Although calamitously defeated at the first battle at Isandhlwana, they soon had the Zulus on the run. It was then that young Louis used his extensive political connections to have himself attached to the British.

On 1 June Louis was on a reconnaissance patrol near Ulundi when the Zulus suddenly launched a surprise attack. Thrown from his horse during the action, while his comrades cautiously pulled back, Louis bravely but rashly moved directly towards the attackers, firing his pistol. As he made this hopeless assault he tripped and fell, and the surrounding Zulus instantly hacked him to pieces.

Louis's body was recovered and brought back to Chislehurst for burial. The Napoleonic dream of resurrection was buried with him.

'Don't give up the ship!'

1813 Today a mortally wounded American naval captain earned immortality for himself by commanding his crew, 'Don't give up the ship!'

James Lawrence had been an unruly youth brought up in Burlington, New Jersey. At seventeen he joined the American navy and soon saw action against Barbary pirates. But it was in the War of 1812 against Great Britain that he gave his life and gained his fame.

When the war started the 31-year-old Lawrence was given command of the USS *Hornet* and sank the British ship HMS *Peacock*. Promoted to captain, he then took over the 49-gun frigate USS *Chesapeake* with a new and untrained crew.

On this day Lawrence was refitting the *Chesapeake* in Boston harbour when the British 38-gun HMS *Shannon*, commanded by the experienced Captain Philip Bowes Vere Broke, hove into view. Broke, whose crew was one of the best trained in the Royal Navy, issued a challenge to the American, to meet 'ship to ship, to try the fortune of our respective flags'. Unwisely, Lawrence sailed out to fight.

The battle was over almost before it began, as the *Shannon* battered the *Chesapeake* into a helpless hulk in less than fifteen minutes and fatally wounded her captain. 'Tell the men to fire faster and not to give up the ship,' Lawrence cried, 'fight her till she sinks!' Inspired by their captain's bravery, every officer aboard the *Chesapeake* fought until killed or wounded. Nonetheless the American ship was captured in less than an hour, and taken to Halifax in Nova Scotia under a prize crew. Lawrence died en route four days later.

To pay tribute to the gallant captain a group of women stitched 'Don't Give Up The Ship' into a flag which was given to the American commander Oliver Hazard Perry, whose flagship was a ship renamed the USS *Lawrence* in honour of Captain Lawrence. Only three months after the capture of the *Chesapeake* Perry avenged Lawrence's death by defeating an entire British squadron in the Battle of Lake Erie, although the *Lawrence* was so badly damaged that Perry had to transfer his flag to another ship.

After the war Lawrence's famous exhortation became the motto of the US Navy, and Perry's flag emblazoned 'Don't Give Up The Ship!' is now proudly displayed in the United States Naval Academy. Little mention is usually made of Captain Lawrence's final order on the *Chesapeake*. Seeing the situation was hopeless, he commanded, 'Burn her!'

Also on this day

836: Viking raiders sack London * 1794: The Battle of the First of June, or the Battle of Ushant, the first great naval engagement of the French Revolutionary Wars, takes place

2 June

Death comes to Giuseppe Garibaldi

1882 South of Corsica, north-east of Sardinia lies the tiny island of Caprera, stony and dry like its neighbours, where the weather is mild but the farmer's life is hard.

Caprera's most eminent resident was the gnarled but still hardy Giuseppe Garibaldi, the great Italian patriot, revolutionary and general. Even in old age he carried a sizeable beard, and his high, noble brow gave him a rather messianic appearance. The most famous man in Europe in the second half of the 19th century, Garibaldi had captured Europe's imagination (and indeed the fear and hatred of many European governments) with his flamboyant leadership.

'Non posso offrirgli né onori né stipendi; gli offro fame, sete, marcie forzate, battaglie e morte', he dramatically told his followers. (I can offer you neither honour nor wages; I offer you hunger, thirst, forced marches, battles and death.) And they came in their thousands, donning the famous red shirts that became their emblem (although tradition has it that Garibaldi chose the colour so that his followers would know they would be visible if they ran away in the heat of battle). Together they outfought and outfoxed the decaying monarchy of Sicily and forced the papacy to relinquish most of its territorial claims.

Garibaldi had been born on 4 July 1807. His first battles for freedom were not for Italy but for South America, where he spent twelve years fighting in one country or another, striving to throw off Spanish rule. There he learned the business of soldiering and of fighting guerrilla style. At various times he was shot, imprisoned, starved and tortured. He returned to Italy a formidable fighting man.

More than any other man, Garibaldi created the united Italy of today. He spent his last days in Caprera and here, at the age of 74, he died on this day. Here also he is buried.

The man who gave pornography a bad name

1740 Today in Paris was born the most infamous writer in history, Donatien Alphonse François, marquis de Sade. Son of a nobleman, he was partially raised by his dissolute uncle, the Abbé de Sade, and early showed signs of the fascination with sexual perversion for which he became famous.

At the age of fifteen, however, de Sade seemed to be headed for the normal life of any French aristocrat when he joined the King's light cavalry regiment as a sub lieutenant. A year later he was in combat in the Seven Years' War, in which he showed himself to be a courageous soldier, personally leading a successful attack against the British at Port Mahon. He stayed in the army for twelve years.

But in 1768 de Sade both left the army and suffered the first of many arrests when he incarcerated a young prostitute named Rose Keller in his house in Arcueil. She managed to escape and went straight to the police, claiming that de Sade had cut her with a knife, whipped her with a knotted rope and poured molten wax into her lacerations. De Sade was sent to prison.

The next half-century of de Sade's life was a sordid story of repeated sexual perversion and imprisonment. Once the Parlement at Aix even sentenced him to death in absentia and executed him in effigy. His marriage had mixed results; for a while his wife helped de Sade arrange his orgies, but eventually she divorced him.

On 13 February 1777 de Sade was jailed once again, this time in the gloomy Château de Vincennes. It was here that he started to write, as a defence against the intolerable boredom of prison. In 1784 he was transferred to the infamous Bastille, where on a continuous 13-yard roll of paper he wrote the explicit and perverted novel *Les 120 Journées de Sodome* (One Hundred and Twenty Days of Sodom).

Apprehensive that the discovery of such a corrupt work would only ensure he stayed in prison, he concealed the scroll in a hollow bed frame.

Suddenly, on 14 July 1789 the Paris mob stormed the Bastille, but de Sade, instead of being freed, was transferred to the insane asylum at Charenton for another nine months. Believing that his scroll of *Les 120 Journées* had gone down with the Bastille, he started work on his most notorious work, *Justine*. (By a quirk of fate, in 1904 the original *Les 120 Journées* manuscript was discovered still in the bed frame.) *Justine* was published anonymously in 1791, when de Sade was 51.

Now de Sade was once more at liberty while all around him France fell into revolutionary chaos. He had the wit to pretend to be a republican, even advocating the abolition of all personal property, but with exquisite irony he was charged with *modérantisme* – being too moderate – and only escaped the guillotine by the fortunate fall of Robespierre.

Then, in 1801, came his final prison spell when he was seized at his publisher's, along with several copies of *Justine*. Once again he was consigned to the lunatic asylum at Charenton, where Napoleon personally intervened to make sure he remained confined. There de Sade died on 2 December 1814. His elder son burned all copies of any work in progress.

So notorious was de Sade that by 1834 the word 'sadisme' was already included in French dictionaries. At the beginning of the 20th century the French bohemian poet Guillaume Apollinaire attempted to rehabilitate his reputation, claiming that, although a pornographer, he was also a philosopher and artist, the human embodiment of *plaisir à tout prix* (pleasure at any price). Now the subject of serious intellectual discussion, de Sade would have been delighted when in his last film the Italian director Pier Paolo Pasolini produced *Salo o le 120 giornate di Sodoma* (*Salo, or the 120 Days of Sodom*) which linked de Sade with Mussolini.

Also on this day

1420: Henry V marries Catherine de Valois * 1840: English writer Thomas Hardy is born

3 June

Franz Kafka dies unpublished

1924 'Someone must have been telling lies about Joseph K., for without having done anything wrong he was arrested one fine morning.' The man who wrote this famous opening line died today in a sanatorium in Kierling just outside Vienna. He was Franz Kafka, a writer now considered one of the 20th century's greatest, even though almost all of his enigmatic works were published posthumously.

Kafka was born in Prague, then part of the Austro-Hungarian Empire. He came from a German-speaking assimilated Jewish family dominated by his insensitive merchant father. His early life was unremarkable. After receiving his doctorate in law at the University of Prague, he settled down into undemanding jobs at various insurance companies until, when he was 34, he was diagnosed with tuberculosis, the disease that was to kill him, and was forced to take intermittent leaves of absence. In contrast to his works of fiction, Kafka was a charming and amusing companion. Although strongly attracted to women (he never married but had several serious affairs), he seems to have suffered some anxieties about sex. At 30 he noted in his diary, 'Der Coitus als Bestrafung des Glückes des Beisammenseins.' (The sexual act is the punishment for the happiness of being together.)

But nothing about Kafka's life explains his unfathomable stories and novels or his dark vision of life. He created what one critic calls 'a baffling mixture of the normal and the fantastic'. *The Metamorphosis* opens, 'When Gregor Samsa awoke one morning from uneasy dreams he found himself transformed in his bed into a gigantic insect.' In *The Judgement* a son commits suicide at the request of his father. In Kafka's most famous work, *The Trial*, the protagonist, named simply Joseph K., endlessly queries a faceless bureaucracy but fails to discover the nature of the charges against him even though he is found guilty and eventually killed in the street 'like a dog'.

When Kafka died he left instructions for his executor Max Brod to burn all his works, but fortunately for readers everywhere, Brod disregarded his orders and prepared many of them for publication. Ever since, critics have offered endless interpretations regarding the true meaning of Kafka's works. Brod considered his novels allegories of divine grace, while others have believed the essence of his work to stem from his neurotic involvement with his father. Some credit him with anticipating the impassive and implacable totalitarianism of Nazism and Communism in novels like *The Trial* and *The Castle*. Others see his work as a metaphor for modern man's angst and alienation in an incomprehensible and indifferent world. One critic has even interpreted the men who murder the central character in *The Castle* as symbols for his testicles.

Like Dickens, Orwell, Rabelais and de Sade, Kafka is one of the very few novelists whose name has become an adjective in our everyday speech. 'Kafkaesque: impenetrably oppressive, nightmarish.' But even he would not have imagined that the nightmares he fashioned in prose would attain an even more terrible reality among those he left behind when he died; his three sisters and one of his lovers perished in Nazi concentration camps.

ULTRA *wins the Battle of Midway*

1942 On this day, in the middle of the vast Pacific Ocean, David met Goliath. Goliath was, of course, by far the stronger of the two and very confident of his ability to prevail. David, however, came to the contest armed, not with a sling and five smooth stones, but with ULTRA.

In the spring of 1942 Allied cryptographers managed to break the Japanese

Navy's operational code. The ability to read the enemy's coded messages, one of the war's most closely guarded secrets, was known as ULTRA. From decrypts of the radio traffic, US naval intelligence pieced together what appeared to be the Japanese strategy for achieving total victory in the Pacific. Under the cover of a diversionary attack in the Aleutians, the first step was to be the capture of Midway Island, scheduled for 4 June. Forewarned by ULTRA, Admiral Chester B. Nimitz, commander of the US Pacific Fleet, gathered his carriers under Admiral Jack Fletcher to counter the enemy's main thrust.

Seizing Midway Island, now the westernmost American base in the Pacific, looked to be a pushover for the huge Japanese Combined Fleet, 163 vessels strong and steaming eastward in several groups spread across the ocean. Shortly before sunrise this day, Japanese bombers left their carriers for the initial strike on Midway. Admiral Nagumo, who had led the great raid on Pearl Harbor six months before, had no suspicion that just over the horizon three US carriers, *Yorktown*, *Enterprise* and *Hornet*, carrying 233 planes, were closing in. When he found out, it was too late.

Shortly before 10.00 a.m., while the flight decks of Nagumo's four carriers were jammed with returning aircraft refuelling and rearming for a second strike against the island, the first American attack came in. Three waves of low-flying torpedo bombers were almost entirely destroyed by Japanese anti-aircraft fire and fighter planes. 'For about one hundred seconds,' wrote Samuel Eliot Morison, 'the Japanese were certain they had won the Battle of Midway, and the war.' But on the heels of the first attack, swarming down from 14,000 feet, came 36 Dauntless dive-bombers. Within six minutes three of the Japanese carriers lay in flames, sinking. Later in the day the fourth carrier was so badly bombed that it had to be scuttled. During the evening Nagumo withdrew his invasion force from around Midway to avoid further losses, but hoping the American carriers would follow in the night and encounter the destructive power of Japanese battleships and cruisers converging on the scene. Admiral Fletcher, with his flagship the *Yorktown* fatally damaged and heavy losses in aircraft, declined pursuit.

Thus David, armed with ULTRA, prevailed over Goliath: Midway remained in American hands and the Japanese Combined Fleet withdrew westward, its vital carrier strength crippled. The defeat was so momentous for Japan, which until now had enjoyed almost unbroken success against the Allies in the Pacific, that the Imperial Navy did not inform Prime Minister Tojo of the outcome for over a month. Later, Admiral Nimitz acknowledged ULTRA's crucial role in the victory, concluding: 'Had we lacked early information of the Japanese movements, and had we been caught with carrier forces dispersed … the Battle of Midway would have ended differently.'

Also on this day

1162: Thomas Becket is consecrated as Archbishop of Canterbury * 1811: American/ English writer Henry James is born * 1875: French composer Georges Bizet dies * 1877: French Fauvist painter Raoul Dufy is born

4 June

Dunkirk: 'Wars are not won by evacuations'

1940 Early this morning, as German armour pressed to within three miles of the harbour, Operation Dynamo – the evacuation of Allied forces trapped at Dunkirk – was abandoned. Left behind in the shrinking bridgehead were the remains of the rear guard, several thousand soldiers of the First French Army still defending the perimeter. But brought across the Channel to safety in Britain over the course of nine perilous days were almost 340,000 British and French troops.

On 28 May, when Operation Dynamo began, the situation of the British Expeditionary Force had seemed hopeless, its left flank suddenly exposed by the surrender of the Belgian Army. Winston Churchill, Prime Minister of Great Britain for less than three weeks, doubted whether more than 50,000 troops could be extracted. At the end, however, the rescue effort succeeded beyond all expectation – owing to good luck, German errors, and the magnificent performances of the Royal Navy and the RAF, who conducted and protected the operation.

To a British public understandably relieved at the salvation of its army, the narrow escape became 'the miracle of Dunkirk', almost a triumph in its own right, a way of disguising the magnitude of the Allies' defeat at the hands of the all-conquering Wehrmacht. But later that day, speaking to the House of Commons, Churchill chose these words to describe what had happened across the Channel: 'We must be very careful', he told the MPs, 'not to assign this deliverance the attributes of a victory. Wars are not won by evacuations.'

In spite of his caution, however, Churchill roared defiance with one of history's most stirring speeches, including the famous lines, 'We shall not flag or fail. We shall go on to the end. We shall fight in France, we shall fight on the seas and oceans, we shall fight with growing confidence and growing strength in the air, we shall defend our island, whatever the cost may be. We shall fight on the beaches, we shall fight on the landing grounds, we shall fight in the fields and in the streets, we shall fight in the hills; we shall never surrender.'

The first hot air balloon

1783 America may be the mother of the aeroplane, but France is the mother of flight.

In the first half of the 18th century one Pierre Montgolfier and his wife were busy producing children, sixteen in all. Two of the boys were named Joseph-Michel and Jacques-Etienne; together they would make man's first step towards the stars.

On 4 June 1783 the brothers conducted an earth-shaking public experiment in their home town of Annonay, a few miles from Lyon. Before an intrigued crowd in the town's market-place, they lit a fire of wool and straw under the opening of their large paper balloon. As the balloon filled with hot air it gently rose from the ground, eventually attaining an altitude of about 3,000 feet. After staying aloft for more than ten minutes, it drifted to earth more than a mile away.

The age of flight had been born. Before the end of the year man's first ascent had been accomplished. That, too, was in a Montgolfier-designed balloon.

Also on this day

1798: Italian seducer Giovanni Casanova dies * 1831: The Belgians elect Queen Victoria's uncle Leopold of Saxe-Coburg as King * 1941: Ex-Kaiser Wilhelm II dies in exile in the Netherlands

5 June

Kitchener goes down with the ship

1916 A great hero and symbol of his nation died this evening in the North Sea.

We remember him from the famous recruiting poster reproduced in history books: his glowering, square-jawed countenance with its bristling moustache and piercing eyes, his forefinger pointing directly at the viewer, and below it the caption, 'Your Country Needs YOU'. He was, of course, Field Marshal Herbert Horatio Kitchener, avenger of Gordon, reconqueror of the Sudan, hero of Fashoda, protector of the Northwest frontier, Commander-in-Chief in South Africa, Earl Kitchener of Khartoum, and now Secretary of State for War in the Asquith government.

When Great Britain declared war in 1914, the day after Germany's invasion of Belgium, Kitchener's name was on every lip. The Conservatives in Parliament called for him, the big newspapers demanded him, and Winston Churchill, already in the Cabinet, urged his appointment on Asquith.

'What he symbolised, I think,' wrote the Prime Minister's daughter many years later, 'was strength, decision and above all success. South Africa, Khartoum – everything that he touched "came off." There was a feeling that Kitchener could not fail. The psychological effect of his appointment, the tonic to public confidence were instantaneous and overwhelming.'

For all his immense reputation and military successes, however, he was a warrior of the 19th century facing warfare on an unprecedented industrial scale. He did foresee from the outset, when few others did, what a long war would demand in the way of manpower, and he prepared to meet the enormous expansion of Great Britain's military strength through the formation of new 'Kitchener divisions'. But he could not find a strategy to break the stalemate on the Western Front. Nor was he in favour of flanking side-shows in other theatres. He flip-flopped badly on the Dardanelles/Gallipoli campaign and ended up by opposing the only part of the operation that was a success: the final evacuation. As the war dragged on with no conclusion in sight, his influence in the Cabinet waned, and his colleagues began to challenge his decisions.

A Chief of the Imperial General Staff was appointed to handle much of the management of the war that had been Kitchener's alone. Asquith, wishing to avoid the political embarrassment of a Cabinet resignation, sent Lord Kitchener off to Russia to assess the situation on the Eastern Front. He was on the armoured cruiser *Hampshire*, sailing from Scapa Flow for Archangel, when on the evening of 5 June 1916 she hit a mine in the North Sea and quickly sank, taking with her virtually everybody on board.

David Fromkin offered this assessment of Kitchener: 'If he had died in 1914 he would have been remembered as the greatest British general since Wellington. Had he died in 1915 he would have been remembered as the prophet who foretold the nature and duration of the First World War and as the organiser of Britain's mass army. But in 1916 he had become the ageing veteran of a bygone era who could not cope with the demands placed on him in changing times.'

'A lawless shepherd, of ugly deeds' becomes Pope

1305 Bertrand de Got was born in Gascony and practically from birth was destined for a high career in the Church. Since the lord of Gascony at the time happened also to be the King of England, Bertrand grew up adept at balancing three masters, the King of England, the Pope and the King of France, who was the English King's suzerain for his Gascon territories.

Bertrand's talent for fair compromise led him ever higher in the Church until, on 5 June 1305, he was chosen as Pope in an election manipulated by King Philip the Fair of France. Bertrand took the name of Clement V.

Although the papacy was situated in Rome, Clement was a true Frenchman. Even after becoming Pope he remained in France, never once setting foot in the Eternal City. His motives were mixed. He feared that the frightful political conflict convulsing Italy between Guelphs, who supported the papacy, and Ghibellines, who backed the Holy Roman Emperor, might endanger the Church government, and he desperately wanted to please King Philip, who had engineered his election. In March of 1309 he formally settled in Avignon, bringing the whole papal court with him. There he led the Church and did Philip's bidding, most notoriously in helping the French King to outlaw and condemn the Templars. He also followed common lay practice of offering high office to his relatives, and those places not filled by family were often sold to the highest bidder.

Today Bertrand/Clement is largely forgotten even though his move to Avignon started the 70-year Babylonian Captivity before the papacy returned to Rome. Perhaps scholars of classical literature remember him best, for he earned a place in Dante's *Inferno*, where the great poet called him 'a lawless shepherd, of ugly deeds'.

Also on this day
1594: French painter Nicolas Poussin is born * 1947: US Secretary of State George Marshall calls for a European Recovery Programme (the Marshall Plan)

6 June

Of two men who created Italy

1861 The two greatest builders of Italian unification were both born French. Giuseppe Garibaldi was born in Nice only ten years after Napoleon had grabbed it from Italy, and Camillo di Cavour was born in Turin, which, for a while, Napoleon had annexed to France.

The two men could not have been more different. Son of a sailor, Garibaldi proved to be a great guerrilla fighter and leader, a simple, uncomplicated man more at home on a farm than in a palace. He was tall, dark and heavily bearded, with an air of noble sincerity about him.

Cavour was the second son of a marquis, small and podgy with a fringe of beard and pig-like eyes behind rimless spectacles. He was also one of the most intelligent, resourceful and calculating politicians of the 19th century. Disraeli called him 'utterly unscrupulous'.

Cavour's life's ambition was the creation of an Italian state under the authority of the King of Sardinia, Victor Emmanuel II. Playing off the French against the Austrians, charming the British and using Garibaldi when he had to, Cavour was the great architect of the Risorgimento, the 'rising again' that eventually led to a united Italy. When the Kingdom of Italy was finally created in 1860, he was Victor Emmanuel's first Prime Minister.

Starting from about 1850, Cavour had suffered from what today we recognise as malaria, then endemic in parts of Italy. By the spring of 1861 he was almost overwhelmed by the titanic task of reunification (Tuscany, Parma and Sicily had all recognised Victor Emmanuel the year before, and the Kingdom of Italy had been proclaimed in March). Struck down by fever and weakened by repeatedly being bled, Cavour died on 6 June. According to contemporary records (and hagiographies) his last words were, 'Italy is made – all is safe.'

Sergeant Dan Daly creates a Marine Corps legend

1918 German armies were stretched out along an endless front anchored in the English Channel east of Calais and extending east and south across northern

France. Nowhere was the pressure greater than in Belleau Wood, a small wooded tract just 40 miles from Paris. Should the Boche break through the crumbling French defence there, the capital was theirs for the taking – and perhaps the war.

In early June the French received long-awaited reinforcements, two battalions of United States Marines. Today a legend was born, based on the heroism of one man, a 49-year-old Marine gunnery sergeant named Dan Daly.

The Marines attacked early in the morning, but the attack faltered when it was met by murderous machine gun fire from the entrenched Germans. Daly and his men were pinned down in a wheat field as casualties mounted. A newspaperman present at the battle reported what happened next:

'[Daly] stood up and made a forward motion to his men. There was slight hesitation. Who in the hell could blame them? Machine gun and rifle bullets were kicking up dirt, closer and closer. The sergeant ran out to the centre of his platoon – he swung his bayoneted rifle over his head with a forward sweep. He yelled at his men: "Come on, you sons of bitches! Do you want to live forever?"'

Daly's men charged, and the Germans fell back, their momentum towards Paris broken, never to be regained. Although the Marines did not capture the Wood, it fell nineteen days later to American army reinforcements. But the Marines had made the difference. One hyperbolic US Army general even claimed, 'They saved the Allies from defeat ... France could not have stood the loss of Paris.' Later the grateful French renamed Belleau Wood the *Bois de la Brigade Marine*. And to this day every new Marine recruit hears the tale of Sergeant Dan Daly.

Also on this day

1599: Spanish painter Diego Rodríguez da Silva y Velázquez is born * 1807: Napoleon's brother Joseph becomes King of Spain * 1944: The Allies land in Normandy during the Second World War

7 June

The first ship through the Panama Canal

1914 Today, after four centuries of deliberation and 32 years of intermittent construction, the Panama Canal opened for its first ship, as the concrete carrier *Cristobal* passed through the 51-mile zigzag course of dams and locks that links the Atlantic and Pacific Oceans through the Isthmus of Panama. Now, at last, ships could reach one ocean from the other without having to sail thousands of extra miles around the tip of South America.

In the 16th century Holy Roman Emperor Charles V had ordered a route surveyed for such a canal to shorten the time and reduce the risks of shipping gold from Ecuador and Peru back to Spain, but work was never started. Three hundred years later the Spanish government again studied the idea but abandoned the task after contemplating 50 inhospitable miles of jungle and mountain.

In 1882 a French company headed by the renowned Ferdinand de Lesseps, builder of the Suez Canal, began work in the isthmus, then part of Colombia. Within eight years the venture was foundering, with almost 20,000 workers dead of malaria or yellow fever, the costs of construction escalating in the difficult terrain, and the company itself engulfed in a scandal of bribery and corruption that threatened to bring down the Third Republic in France.

By the end of the century the United States government had come to realise the strategic value of a canal. In the recently concluded Spanish–American War it had taken the battleship *Oregon* two full months to sail from its home port of Seattle to reach its battle station in the Caribbean Sea. Congress therefore voted to buy out de Lesseps' moribund enterprise for $40 million and to pay Colombia another $10 million for construction rights. When Colombia dithered and then refused the offer, President Teddy Roosevelt wielded his big stick. In 1903 he sent a battleship to the isthmus to 'protect American lives', encouraged the Panamanians to declare their independence, and quickly recognised the new regime. Clearly unrepentant for fomenting an uprising, Roosevelt fumed, 'We were dealing with a government of irresponsible bandits. I was prepared to … occupy the Isthmus.' He then added disingenuously, 'But I deemed it likely that there would be a revolution in Panama soon.'

Work on the canal began in 1904, with the President very much in charge. The first major problem was to protect the canal workers from the mosquito-borne diseases that had crippled the French effort. When the doctor in charge needed special equipment to drain the swamps, Roosevelt made sure he got it. Within two years the canal route was relatively mosquito-free. Then, when the pace of construction remained slower than hoped for, the President replaced the two civilians in charge with an Army engineer named George Goethals, who proved to be the master of all the complex challenges of the immense project.

The canal's final design followed ideas developed earlier by the French. The Chagres River was dammed to create an artificial lake (the largest in the world at the time), and electricity produced by the dam fuelled five enormous locks to raise or lower a ship 85 feet. But the biggest challenge was digging a ten-mile trench through Culebra Mountain. Almost 40,000 workers were put to the task, using 19 million pounds of dynamite to break through the rock. Four thousand wagons were needed to cart away the excavated material.

When the canal was finally opened for business in 1914, it had cost $350 million – but that was $27 million under budget. Today over 15,000 ships a year pass through it, each needing 15 to 20 hours, including waiting time. Each pays a toll dependent on her size, the most expensive ever levied coming to $141,345. The cheapest was 36 US cents, paid in 1928 by one Richard Halliburton when he swam the canal.

Two vain monarchs meet at the Field of the Cloth of Gold

1520 Henry VIII of England and François I of France were two of the vainest of history's monarchs, and nothing vainer can be imagined than their behaviour at their first meeting, which took place today in the Val d'Or near Calais in France. It has come to be known as the Field of the Cloth of Gold.

To symbolise their immortal friendship, the two kings erected virtually an entire town of luxurious tents, nearly 400 of them. Henry also had a prefabricated castle of wood and canvas that covered two and a half acres. Gold and silver cloths were used extensively, and some 10,000 French and English courtiers joined this eighteen-day festival of jousting, dancing, drinking and singing. The total cost nearly bankrupted both monarchies, especially the English, with a population of only 3 million at the time, compared with some 15 million in France.

In the end, of course, the Field of the Cloth of Gold changed nothing. François went back to seducing women, Henry to beheading them. Shortly they were at war.

Also on this day

1494: By the Treaty of Tordesillas, Spain and Portugal agree to divide the New World between themselves * 1654: Louis XIV is crowned King of France * 1778: English dandy Beau Brummel is born * 1848: French painter Paul Gauguin is born

8 June

Death of the Black Prince

1376 On this mild Sunday in June died Edward, the Black Prince, in his palace south of the Thames in London.

Son of Edward III (who was still alive when the younger Edward died), the Black Prince was the most notable fighting man of his age. He distinguished himself at the famous English victory at Crécy. (As his father said, 'Also say to them, that they suffre hym this day to wynne his spurres, for if God be pleased, I woll this journey be his, and the honoure therof.' – commonly quoted as 'Let the boy win his spurs.')

It was at Crécy that Edward won his famous nickname, which came not from his colouring (he was blond and blue-eyed) but from the black armour he wore. It was also after Crécy that he adopted the motto *homout; ich dene* (courage, I serve), later shortened to *ich dien*. It seems this was previously the motto of blind King John of Bohemia, who perished during the battle fighting against the English. All subsequent Princes of Wales have used *ich dien* as their motto.

Later Edward commanded at the victory of Poitiers, where the French King

Jean II was captured. Because of his conspicuous gallantry, he was the first member of the Order of the Garter, created by his father.

When the Black Prince died just seven days short of his 46th birthday, he succumbed to a lingering and painful disease, probably dropsy. He left behind a blond-haired son of nine, who would one day gain the throne as the tragic Richard II.

The miserable end of the Dauphin

1795 On this day died poor Louis XVII of France at the age of ten. Son of Louis XVI and Marie Antoinette, in August 1792 the young dauphin, as he was then, was imprisoned with his parents in the Temple, a 12th-century fortified monastery so named because it once housed the Templar order. In theory he became the King of France the following January when his father was executed.

Six months later Louis-Charles, as he was called, was put in the charge of a rabidly republican cobbler named Antoine Simon, who treated him with the brutality and contempt that revolutionaries reserve for royalty. Three months later it was Louis-Charles's mother's turn with the guillotine, and shortly afterwards Louis-Charles was once again imprisoned in the Temple. (The only poetic justice in the story is that Simon perished on the guillotine shortly thereafter, executed in the same group of victims as the Terror's main terrorist, Maximilien Robespierre.)

Louis-Charles was held in solitary confinement in the Temple for a year and a half, in conditions of indescribable squalor. The damp and cold and the filth of a never-cleaned cell that doubled as a toilet destroyed his health, and his mental state can only be imagined, after the loss of both parents to the guillotine. Modern scholars believe he died of tuberculosis.

As no one had access to Louis-Charles during his last months, rumours soon started to spread. Some said that he had been deliberately poisoned by his jailers, others that he was not dead at all but had somehow been rescued from the Temple. During the following years there were almost 40 pretenders who claimed to be 'the Dauphin', most famously and fictitiously in Mark Twain's great novel *Huckleberry Finn*.

Over two centuries after Louis-Charles's death, forensic scientists used DNA extracted from his preserved heart to prove conclusively that the boy who died in the Temple was indeed Louis XVII of France.

Also on this day

1290: Dante's heroine Beatrice Polinari dies at the age of 24 * 1784: Fabled French chef Antoine Carême is born in Paris * 1804: Revolutionary pamphleteer Thomas Paine dies * 1870: Charles Dickens dies of a stroke

9 June

Nero takes his own life

AD 68 Today the notorious Roman Emperor Nero committed suicide as soldiers from his rebellious army closed in for the kill.

Only sixteen when he came to power in 54, Nero had for a time been a hard-working and generous ruler, but within five years he had become the ogre of legend, murdering at will (including his mother and two wives) and engaging in sickening sexual conduct with both sexes. (At one point he had a young slave named Sporus castrated and then married him, taking him to bed like a wife. This prompted a Roman joke that the world would have been a better place had Nero's father chosen such a wife.)

By the time Nero was in his late 20s, conspiracies were rising against him everywhere for his cruelty, extravagance and greed. The early ones were snuffed out, but in March 68 Julius Vindex, the Roman governor of Lugdunum (today's Lyon), revolted. At first Nero simply scoffed, 'I have only to appear and sing to have peace once more in Gaul.' Indeed, the Roman army easily crushed the rebels, but not before Julius Vindex had been joined by Servius Galba, the governor of Spain.

Soon other provinces joined Galba, and the Senate proclaimed him as Emperor while condemning Nero to death by flogging with rods. Then, on 8 June 68, Nero's own Praetorian commander Nymphidius Sabinus abandoned him. Knowing he could no longer cling to power, the Emperor tried to flee Rome for his eastern provinces, but his guards refused to help him, one asking derisively, 'Is it so terrible a thing to die?'

Nero then retreated to the imperial palace, only to awake at midnight to find himself alone, deserted even by his slaves. Leaving in panic, by chance he encountered one of his freedmen, Phaon, in the street. Phaon smuggled the disguised Emperor to his villa outside the city where the terrified fugitive hid in a dingy room. But soon soldiers were at the door, probably tipped off by Phaon, desperately trying to save his own skin.

Seeing no way out, Nero exclaimed at the last, 'Qualis artifex pereo!' (What a great artist the world is losing!) He then stabbed himself in the throat, but, botching the job, he had to call on his private secretary Epaphroditus to finish him off. According to Suetonius, he died 'with glazed eyes bulging from their sockets'. (Epaphroditus later became the Emperor Domitian's secretary but was executed by him on the grounds that a freedman should never help in his master's suicide.) When Nero died he was still only 30.

With Nero ended the so-called Julio-Claudian dynasty of Roman rulers that had started 116 years before, when Julius Caesar defeated Pompey and assumed dictatorial powers. They all died miserably:

- Caesar was assassinated in the Senate, bequeathing money and troops to his great-nephew
- Augustus, who (some say) was poisoned by his wife Livia so that her son
- Tiberius would rule. Tiberius was smothered on orders from his nephew and successor
- Caligula, who was murdered by officers of his own guard, to be succeeded by his uncle
- Claudius, who was poisoned by his wife Agrippina to gain the title for her son
- Nero, who was driven to suicide.

On Nero's death Galba became Emperor, but he too came to a bloody end, hacked to death by his successor Otho's soldiers after only seven months of power.

Also on this day

1672: Russian Tsar Peter the Great is born * 1815: The final act of the Congress of Vienna settles Europe's boundaries until 1870 * 1866: Bismarck's Prussian troops invade Holstein

10 June

Barbarossa drowns crossing a river

1190 On this day died one of the great rulers in German history, Holy Roman Emperor Frederick I, of the Hohenstaufen dynasty, popularly known as Frederick Barbarossa because of his full red beard.

Frederick Barbarossa was Emperor for 35 years, during which he spent much of his time trying to subject Italy to his control. He invaded the country five times and had the distinction of being on the losing side at the Battle of Legnano, one of military history's watershed battles, where, for the first time, infantry defeated a mounted army of feudal knights.

Another reason Italy was a problem for Frederick was that the temporal power of the Church was greatest there. In 1159 the conclave of cardinals chose as the new pope Alexander III, who was committed to reducing Frederick's authority, but the Emperor used his influence to persuade a minority of cardinals to elect Victor IV, who was declared anti-pope by the Church. Alexander quickly excommunicated Frederick.

Emperor and Pope remained at loggerheads for eighteen years, but eventually were reconciled two years before Alexander died.

Now back in the good graces of the Church, Frederick determined to go on crusade to the Holy Land even though he had reached the advanced age (for the time) of 66. He departed in 1189, but a year later drowned while crossing the Calycadnus (now the Göksu) River in Anatolia.

But did he die? German legend has it that an enchanted Frederick Barbarossa still sleeps in a limestone cave in the Kyffhäuser mountains in Germany. He is said to sit at a stone table around which his great red beard has grown, waiting for the time to come when he will return to restore Germany to greatness.

Perhaps Frederick Barbarossa did die, but the legend did not. During the Second World War Adolf Hitler evoked the myth when he named the invasion of Russia 'Operation Barbarossa'.

Marlborough meets Eugene of Savoy

1704 Today began one of the most productive partnerships in military history when England's greatest general, John Churchill, the Duke of Marlborough, first met Prince Eugene of Savoy, the greatest general ever to serve the Holy Roman Empire.

At the time England and the Empire were allied to halt the expansion of Europe's largest and most powerful nation, the France of Louis XIV. At about five in the evening Prince Eugene rode into Marlborough's camp at Mundelsheim, south-east of Stuttgart. At 40 the Prince was thirteen years younger than the Duke but at the time a more celebrated general. The two men took to each other instantly, and their partnership was to last for almost ten years.

The first fruits of their friendship came just two months later when their combined forces destroyed the French at the Battle of Blenheim. Subsequent triumphs included French defeats at Oudenard and Malplaquet. Between the two of them, Eugene and Marlborough demolished Louis XIV's hope of hegemony over Europe.

Also on this day

1688: James Francis Stuart, the Old Pretender, is born * 1819: French painter Gustave Courbet is born * 1926: Spanish architect Antonio Gaudí dies in Barcelona

11 June

'Doctor Mirabilis'

1292 They called him 'Doctor Mirabilis' (Wonderful Teacher), Roger Bacon, perhaps the greatest intellect of the Middle Ages, who was laid to rest today in the university city of Oxford.

Bacon was born in Ilchester in Somerset 78 years before. He studied first in Oxford, then in Paris, where he joined the Franciscan order.

Bacon was a medieval polymath, excelling in mathematics, optics, languages and astronomy, with a particular interest in alchemy, the transformation of base metal into gold. He conceived the telescope and found that he could cause explosions by combining charcoal, sulphur and saltpetre, a mixture we call gunpowder, hundreds of years before its introduction into Europe. His greatest contribution, however, was the 'invention' of the scientific method – that is, the repetition of carefully controlled experiments until the certainties of cause and effect can be demonstrated and proved.

Because Bacon was so far ahead of his own time – and ahead of his own Church – he spent ten years imprisoned in a dark cell in his monastery, without communication with the outside world. His own Franciscan order condemned him to solitary confinement because of his heretical views about science and his virulent criticism of other scholars and theologians, while the Pope banned the reading of his works.

When Roger Bacon died two years after his release from prison, he believed his life and work to have been failures; today he is considered one of the fundamental founders of modern science.

The start of the Second Crusade

1147 The First Crusade had ended triumphantly in 1099 with Antioch and Jerusalem conquered and a Frenchman proclaimed King of Jerusalem. Half a century later, however, the Christians of Jerusalem were living precariously, as the Saracens continually threatened to overrun them. Mindful of both the heavenly glories and the earthly riches to be gained, Louis VII of France and Holy Roman Emperor Conrad III determined to lead a second crusade.

The French set out on 11 June 1147, the feast of their patron saint, St Denis, and were joined in the Holy Land in November by Conrad's Germans, or what was left of them – they had been virtually annihilated en route by the Turks in Anatolia.

The Second Crusade lasted two years and was as much a failure as the First Crusade had been a success. No great cities were taken, and nothing remained of the huge treasure collected to finance the adventure. Of the host that left Europe in 1147, few returned in 1149.

Nonetheless, the Second Crusade may have helped change history, as one of its saltier features was an illicit romance between the French Queen Eleanor of Aquitaine and her own uncle, Robert of Antioch, both of whom had joined the crusade. It is likely that Eleanor's adventure was a prime reason why her husband Louis sought an annulment of their marriage on his return to France.

Eventually, their marriage was dissolved (1152) and the spirited Eleanor went on to marry the future Henry II of England and to be mother of the Plantagenet dynasty.

Also on this day

1572: English dramatist Ben Jonson is born in London * 1776: English painter John Constable is born

12 June

Stalin purges his army

1937 Today in Moscow, after the briefest of trials, Marshal Mikhail N. Tukhachevsky, one of the highest-ranking officers in the Red Army and its former Chief of Staff, was shot to death for treason, espionage and conspiracy. His execution took place in the headquarters of the NKVD, Soviet Russia's secret police. Shot along with him on similar charges were seven other top commanders who, with the marshal, were among Soviet Russia's best and most experienced military officers.

In the 1930s Stalin began a series of purges to 'purify' Soviet Russia of all potential opposition to his regime. By 1937 it was the Army's turn. Among the targets of scrutiny were former aristocrats, tsarist officers and anyone associated with Trotsky's command of the Red Army during the Civil War. Despite his elevation to the rank of marshal by Stalin only two years earlier, Tukhachevsky was vulnerable on all counts.

It made no difference that he was also a brilliant military reformer who had led the Soviet armed forces into much-needed innovations in combined arms, armoured formations, airborne units, tactical air support and an independent bomber force. These contributions were evidence of a capacity for 'independent thought', now the deadliest of Soviet sins.

Naturally, there was 'proof' of Tukhachevsky's involvement in a plot to seize the Kremlin and overthrow the Soviet leadership: a faked dossier of correspondence between the marshal and two German generals. Under torture the marshal confessed to all charges against him.

The purge did not stop with Tukhachevsky and his colleagues. Over the next year the 'show' trials resulted in the following losses to the Red Army through death or imprisonment: three of five marshals; fourteen of sixteen army commanders; 60 of 67 corps commanders; 136 of 199 division commanders; 221 of 397 brigade commanders; and some 35,000 lower-ranking officers – in all amounting to about half the officer corps. Their replacements were for the most part unfit or untrained as commanders.

One result of these leadership losses was the Red Army's poor showing in its 1939–40 campaign against Finland, a performance carefully noted by the German military. What followed in 1941 was worse yet: full-scale disaster at the hands of the Wehrmacht in the opening phase of Operation Barbarossa. If there was a silver lining to this defeat, it was the speedy elimination through death or capture of thousands of incompetent Soviet officers to be replaced by better material. And in the nick of time, as the German army neared Moscow late in the year, the Soviet high command reinstated many of Tukhachevsky's doctrinal innovations. It was almost too late.

Also on this day
1931: Gangster Al Capone and 68 of his henchmen are indicted for violating Prohibition laws

13 June

Alexander the Great dies in Babylon

323 BC Towards evening today in the fabled city of Babylon he died, still only 32. In his twelve years and eight months as King of Macedonia he changed for ever the Western world. He was Alexander the Great.

As always in antiquity, when a great man died young, there were stories of plots and murders. Plutarch tells us of the bad omens that foretold a coming calamity. Alexander's pet lion was kicked to death by a donkey, and ravens attacked each other over the walls of Babylon, one falling dead at the King's feet. After Alexander's death a story grew that conspirators had given him poisoned wine. Feeling as if 'an arrow had struck him in the liver', he tried to throw up the poison by forcing a feather down his throat, but the feather, too, had been poisoned, compounding the original dose.

Modern historians are sceptical, most believing that, already weakened by alcohol, the great conqueror was finally consumed by malaria.

Alexander had inherited the throne of Macedon from his assassinated father, Philip II, along with an even more valuable legacy, the finest army in the world. In addition, his mind had been trained by one of the greatest of all thinkers, Aristotle.

In late 335 BC or early 334 BC Alexander set out on his fabled conquests – first all of Greece, then Turkey, the Levant, Egypt, Syria and back through modern-day Iraq and Iran, conquering the Persian Empire. And still onwards he went, into Parthia, skirting the southern edge of the Caspian Sea into today's Afghanistan and across the Hindu Kush into Pakistan and India, where his troops finally said 'enough' and refused to go further.

Such were the conquests of the great Alexander, the man who founded at least seven Alexandrias, including the one that remains, in Egypt, where he was buried. Although Alexander's only son was born posthumously and therefore had no real chance to inherit his father's empire, Alexander did leave behind two dynasties, not in Greece but in the Middle East, and not of his own blood but through two of his generals who had been his boyhood companions. The first was Seleucus, who was about 32 at Alexander's death. After several years of in-fighting with Alexander's other generals he took control of what today is mostly Syria and Iran to form the Seleucid Empire, which lasted for 240 years.

The other was Ptolemy, who became King of Egypt. His family ruled for 293 years until his descendant Cleopatra clasped an asp to her bosom in 30 BC.

Shortly before he died Alexander ordered all Greeks to worship him as a god, which he sincerely believed he was. He had been well prepared for this role; his mother had told him that Zeus rather than King Philip was his real father, and when he conquered Egypt he became Pharaoh and thus officially the son of the greatest Egyptian deity, Amon-ra. He thus established the idea of a god-king in Europe, a concept that reached full bloom in Rome three centuries later with the Emperor Augustus and eventually transformed itself into the divine right of kings.

Nazi Germany fires the first guided missile

1944 Today the world moved into a new and more terrifying age of offensive weaponry as Hitler's Germany fired the first V-1 jet-powered guided missile against London, killing six civilians.

In all some 8,000 of these 'doodlebugs' were launched from the Pas-de-Calais on the northern coast of France, and about a third successfully reached their targets, killing or wounding an estimated 24,000 people. Flying at only 360 miles per hour, the buzz bombs became increasingly vulnerable targets for British anti-aircraft and fighter pilots.

Less than four months after the launch of the first V-1, on 6 September Germany launched the more formidable V-2, a 47-foot ballistic missile with a 1,500-pound explosive payload that flew at 3,000 miles per hour and was thus invulnerable to both anti-aircraft and fighter plane attack. The first V-2 was aimed at Paris, but two days later the first of 1,100 of these sophisticated rockets started to rain down on Great Britain. Belgium was attacked almost as vigorously.

V-2s were developed and launched from Peenemünde, a village on the Baltic coast of north-east Germany. The name V-2 stood for Vergeltungswaffen 2 (Vengeance Weapon 2), a designation created by the German Ministry of Propaganda.

The V-2 was largely the brainchild of the brilliant German scientist Wernher von Braun, who was Peenemünde's technical director. Captured by American troops in the closing days of the war, von Braun and his colleagues were quickly moved to White Sands, New Mexico, to continue their work on rockets, under different masters. Later von Braun became chief of the American ballistic weapons programme at Huntsville, Alabama, that developed the Redstone, Jupiter-C, Juno and Pershing missiles.

Von Braun always maintained that scientific research is inherently impartial and that governments, not scientists, must bear the responsibility for the use that scientific developments are put to. Or, as satirised by the American composer and lyricist Tom Lehrer,

'Once the rockets are up, who cares where they come down?
That's not my department', says Wernher von Braun.

14 June

Death of a traitor

1801 At 6.30 this Sunday morning at Gloucester Place, London, a British general died of dropsy and gout at the age of 60. In debt and out of favour, he was buried without military honours in a church crypt in unfashionable Battersea.

He had once been one of the best combat commanders on either side in the American Revolution, his name linked with such celebrated exploits as Quebec, Valcour Island and Saratoga. In those days, however, he had been an American general, not a British one. His name was Benedict Arnold.

In 1780 Arnold turned traitor and began a secret correspondence with the enemy Commander-in-Chief in New York City, Sir Henry Clinton. He proposed to give Clinton the strategic American position at West Point in return for £20,000 and a commission in the British Army. But the plot was discovered when Major John André, Sir Henry's intermediary with Arnold, was caught in disguise behind American lines, bearing papers that revealed the betrayal. André was hanged as a spy, and Arnold himself narrowly escaped to British-held New York City.

The British paid Arnold only about one third of the promised money, but they did make him a brigadier general. As the war carried on, he led British troops in operations against his former countrymen in Virginia and Connecticut. Then came the notable American victory at Yorktown.

Arnold had counted on the British continuing military operations in North America, thus providing him with a career in the Army, perhaps as commander of Loyalist forces in America. To argue that case, he took himself and his family to England in 1782, but not long after his arrival an anti-war Whig government gained office in London. He would find a home neither in English society, where he came to symbolise the now-unpopular conflict, nor in the British Army, where fellow officers considered his motives mercenary and dishonourable. Moreover, the loss to the service of the highly popular André was still mourned.

Arnold was forced to spend much of his last twenty years abroad in search of fortune in Canada and the West Indies. During his final days he was wracked with remorse, and shortly before his death he once more donned his American uniform, exclaiming, 'Let me die in this old uniform in which I fought my battles for freedom. May God forgive me for putting on any other.'

In contrast to Arnold's humble interment in Battersea, Major André received a monument in Westminster Abbey on which the inscription proclaimed him 'universally beloved and esteemed by the Army in which he served'.

France's most victorious day

1658, 1800, 1807 The 14th of June was perhaps the most victorious day for French arms in the nation's history.

In 1658 the pre-eminent French general of the 17th century, Viscount Henri de Turenne, defeated a Spanish force reinforced by a contingent of English royalists commanded by the Duke of York, the future James II. (It was after this victory that Turenne summed up the results in his famously terse report to King Louis XIV: 'The enemy came, was beaten, I am tired, good night.') Fought near Dunkirk, the conflict is called the Battle of the Dunes.

In 1800 the greatest French general of the 19th century (and probably of all centuries), Napoleon Bonaparte, grasped victory from the jaws of defeat in counter-attacking and routing an Austrian force in the Battle of Marengo in northern Italy. (He simultaneously provided the historical background for Victorien Sardou's play *La Tosca*, which Puccini later transformed into his glorious opera.)

In 1807 it was Napoleon's turn again, when he annihilated a Russian army at Friedland (then in Prussia, now in Russia) in a battle of about 60,000 troops on each side which resulted in 19,000 Russian casualties.

Except for Turenne's brusque summary, even the French have now largely forgotten the Battle of the Dunes, but Marengo and Friedland are avenues in Paris, named in honour of the great Napoleonic victories. Apart from the street names, however, all three battles today conjure up little for most of us – just battles in which men died for questionable ends and the ego of nations. Marengo, however, leaves a somewhat better taste.

On the evening after the battle Napoleon's chef Dunan sent out some soldiers to scavenge for food for his general. They returned with some tomatoes, onions, garlic, olives, a few crayfish and a chicken. Braising them skilfully with some white wine, Dunan then added some scrambled eggs on the side, creating Chicken Marengo, a dish still found today in good French restaurants.

Also on this day

827: Arabs first invade Sicily * 1645: Oliver Cromwell assumes power by his victory at the Battle of Naseby

15 June

Wat Tyler and the Peasants' Revolt

1381 In 14th-century England the villein or ordinary farmer was close to a serf, taxed by the King, used by the nobles and bound to the land. But as the peasants toiled in their misery, two extraordinary leaders urged them to demonstration and violence, starting the Peasants' Revolt.

One was John Ball, an itinerant and slightly crazed preacher who included in his anti-aristocracy sermons his revised text of a popular ballad: 'When Adam delved and Eve span, who was then the gentleman?' The other was an ex-soldier named Wat Tyler, the Revolt's chief instigator.

In early June 1381 these two men led a motley army of some 20,000 villeins to London, which they shortly occupied, terrifying the richer inhabitants, murdering many, and burning the great Savoy palace belonging to the King's uncle, John of Gaunt. As the flames licked higher it seemed as if the royal government could be on the verge of being swept away.

On 15 June the beautiful blond young King, Richard II, then only fourteen, was forced to parley with Wat Tyler outside the city walls at Smithfield. Several nobles, including the Mayor of London, William Walworth, accompanied him.

Separating himself from his peasant followers, Tyler approached the King and harangued him on his demands. Suddenly there was a scuffle, and Tyler pulled out his knife but was felled by a blow from Walworth's sword.

The peasant army reached for their weapons, but Richard rode out to them alone, ordering them to obey him, their true King. Miraculously, the mob obeyed, and the crowd dispersed. The Peasants' Revolt was over, Wat Tyler lying dead on the ground.

The nobles' vengeance was swift. John Ball was caught and hanged, as were other leaders. The poor peasants gained nothing. 'Villeins you are,' said the King, 'and villeins ye shall remain.'

King John signs the Magna Carta

1215 Runnymede (or Running Mead, as it was called then) was a meadow lying on the south bank of the River Thames a few miles from London, just a little south-east of Windsor Castle. It was here on this day eight centuries ago that England's feudal barons forced the shifty, feckless and untrustworthy King John to sign the Magna Carta, the formal foundation of British liberty.

During his sixteen years as King, John had alienated his barons by excessive taxation without their consent, and exacerbated the situation by his failure to hold on to his possessions in Normandy. He had also infuriated the Church by initially refusing the Pope's nominee for Archbishop of Canterbury, leading to the Church's placing all of England under interdict, which halted all marriages, baptisms and funerals.

Finally the barons, led by the Archbishop of Canterbury, threatened to rise in revolt if John would not guarantee what they saw as their rights.

The Magna Carta both strengthened the rights of the common man (especially those of the barons) and restricted the use of capricious power by the King, establishing in principle the ruler's responsibility towards his subjects.

The most famous principle of the Magna Carta is Clause 39, which reads, 'No free man shall be taken, or imprisoned, or dispossessed, or outlawed, or banished, or in any way injured, nor will we go upon him, nor send upon him, except by the legal judgement of his peers, or by the law of the land.' It thus forces the King to follow legal procedures and guarantees all citizens equal access to the courts.

The Magna Carta was modified over the centuries, as many of its original provisions became outdated or irrelevant. But it remains today a symbol against oppression and a guarantee of individual liberty.

The Duchess of Richmond's ball

1815 There was danger afoot on the Continent of Europe. Napoleon had recently escaped his exile on Elba, had returned to Paris, and this very day was at the head of an enormous army advancing on Belgium. In Vienna, news of these disturbing developments caused the Congress to give up its waltzing, but in Brussels this evening the Duchess of Richmond gave a ball, maybe the most famous ball in history, where the assembled company feasted and danced the night away, 'up to the very brink of battle'.

'There never was, since the days of Darius,' wrote Thackeray, 'such a brilliant train of camp followers as hung around the train of the Duke of Wellington's army in the Low Countries in 1815.' Chief among the attendees at this evening's ball was the cream of British and European military leadership, headed by the Prince of Orange, the Duke of Brunswick and the Duke of Wellington, now Commander-in-Chief of the Allied armies in Flanders. Ambassadors, military officers and aristocrats thronged the spacious rooms. Beautiful ladies abounded in a dazzling array of wives and daughters that included, in addition to the hostess herself, her daughter Lady Georgiana Lennox, Lady Charlotte Greville – a favourite of the Commander-in-Chief – and, if we wish to believe Thackeray's account in *Vanity Fair*, that arch-schemer Mrs Rawdon Crawley, better known as Becky Sharp.

The Duke of Wellington came late and left early. At midnight a rider arrived with a dispatch, and when he had finished reading it, the Duke began issuing orders to aides and conferring with senior officers. Later at supper, where he sat next to Lady Charlotte, he was composed and attentive as always, but afterwards he asked the Duke of Richmond for a map, which he consulted in the privacy of the study.

Sometime after 2.00 a.m., with the festivities in full swing, Wellington left for his quarters. The French army was drawing very near now – had crossed the Sambre, in fact – and there was much to be done to prepare his own army for events. It was no longer the eve of battle, and the approaching dawn would see the commencement of a great military campaign that would culminate in three days' time at Waterloo.

Also on this day

1330: Edward, the Black Prince, is born * 1520: Pope Leo X excommunicates Martin Luther * 1775: The Continental Congress makes George Washington Commander-in-Chief of the Continental Army

16 June

Henry VII captures Lambert Simnel

1487 Henry VII was the rarest of kings in that he sometimes exhibited both a sense of humour and a sense of mercy. An example is the tale of Lambert Simnel.

Simnel was the eleven-year-old son of an Oxford organ maker. He had been chosen by a local priest to impersonate the Earl of Warwick (who was in fact imprisoned in the Tower of London) and thus claim the throne as the rightful heir. (Warwick was the son of the dead Duke of Clarence, brother of Richard III, whom Henry had deposed.) Tutored and bedecked in fine clothes, Simnel and his mentor succeeded in this deception, and an army of dissidents and opportunists grew up around him.

Eventually King Henry took the field against Simnel and, on 16 June 1487, utterly crushed the insurgents at Stoke. Young Simnel was captured and must have expected to be executed. But the King's humour and compassion came into play, and Henry put him to work in the royal kitchens with the lowest of jobs, turning the spit. Simnel eventually rose to the job of falconer and many years later died quietly in bed.

The longest pontificate in history

1846 When wisps of white smoke drifted from the Vatican chimney on this sultry day in June, the waiting crowds knew that, through his cardinals, God had chosen another pope. The new pontiff was Giovanni Mastai-Ferretti, formerly Bishop of Imola and now enthroned with the name of Pius IX.

Pius was a sincere man of some sophistication, with a deep sense of humanity, a sharp intelligence and a disarming appearance of humility. Legend has it that he had the 'evil eye', the power to injure people just by looking at them. In consequence villagers would hide their children when he rode through Italy.

Initially somewhat of an ecclesiastical liberal, Pius became Pope at a time when the papacy was under sharp attack on both spiritual and temporal grounds.

The revolutions of 1848 across Europe terrified him, turning him ever more conservative in his views. Then came a direct threat to the temporal power of the papacy as Italy struggled to unify itself. The papal territories at its centre blocked the creation of a single Italian state.

Pius could not imagine the papacy depending on spiritual power alone and was aghast at the idea of the Church losing its lands and secular authority. Reacting against this threat, he turned his back on all progress and, in 1864, published his famous *Syllabus* listing 80 'principal errors of our times'. Of these, the 80th was the most doggedly reactionary, refuting entirely the view that 'the Roman Pontiff can and should reconcile himself to and agree with progress, liberalism, and modern civilisation'.

Pius is also associated with two of Catholicism's most contentious doctrines, those of the Immaculate Conception and of papal infallibility, both of which were defined and accepted as Church doctrine during his pontificate.

In spite of his refusal to compromise (or perhaps because of it), in the end Pius lost everything he valued most when King Victor Emmanuel's troops marched into Rome in 1870. Church and state were finally separated.

Pius IX soldiered on until he died in 1878. His pontificate of 32 years is the longest in all the twenty centuries of Church history.

Also on this day

1722: John Churchill, Duke of Marlborough, dies * 1866: Bismarck launches a Prussian attack against Austria as the first step in the unification of Germany

17 June

Americans lose a battle but gain heart at Bunker Hill

1775 The first battle of the American Revolution had been fought only two months earlier and twelve miles away, and now rebel soldiers occupied three hills looking down on Boston Harbor, threatening British ships. The highest of the hills rose to some 110 feet. It was called Bunker Hill.

When cannon fire from the ships failed to dislodge the Americans, the British commander General Sir William Howe led his force of 2,300 men to remove the Yankees. Most of the action actually took place on neighbouring Breed's Hill. As the British advanced, American General Israel Putnam gave his famous order, 'Don't shoot until you see the whites of their eyes.' (Putnam's command was not altogether original. In destroying the Austrian army at

Jagerndorf in 1745 Prince Charles of Prussia gave an almost identical order, as did Frederick the Great in 1757 at the Battle of Prague.)

The American soldiers were barricaded behind makeshift barriers of old fences packed with hay and brush. Initially the accurate colonial gunfire stopped the British attack, but eventually the Americans were forced to retreat when they began to run out of ammunition and weapons.

By nightfall the Battle of Bunker Hill was over. Some 226 British lay dead on the field, with another 826 wounded. The Americans suffered 140 killed in action with 301 more wounded. Even though they lost the battle, the Americans were jubilant. They had demonstrated that untrained militia, hastily assembled, could trade blow for blow with professional British soldiers, and American determination was strongly boosted. But the Revolution still had another six years and four months to run.

The king who stole the Stone of Scone

1239 His grandfather, King John, had been treacherous and cruel, while his father Henry III was weak and vacillating. But Edward I, born this day at Westminster, was one of England's greatest kings.

Edward was a splendid athlete and horseman, blond, handsome, regal and so tall (six feet two inches) that he was known as Edward Longshanks. He was also highly intelligent and fluent in English, French and Latin. His main problem was his temper, which matched that of his legendary Plantagenet great-grandfather, Henry II. In his younger days he showed all the worst characteristics of a spoiled prince: cruelty, violence, intolerance and arrogance. But fortunately he did not inherit the throne until he was 33, by which time he had curbed his unpleasant excesses except for the occasional terrifying rage.

Edward married twice and was a virile and faithful husband, a rarity for kings, especially in the Middle Ages. His two wives bore him at least twenty children, the last arriving when he was 67 years old.

Edward reformed the body of English law, moving the nation away from feudalism in the long, slow march towards democratic freedom. He was also a warrior of note and a superb general. His most famous victories were over the Welsh, whom he subdued to such a degree that they remained cowed for the best part of a century. He had less success with the Scottish, although he did manage to capture William Wallace, whom he had hanged, drawn and quartered, a punishment for treason that Edward was the first English king to use.

Edward's more lasting Scottish triumph concerned the Stone of Scone.

The Stone of Scone is a 350-pound block of pale yellow sandstone decorated with a Latin cross measuring 26 by 16 by 11 inches. The Scots believed the patriarch Jacob had once used it as a pillow when he experienced visions of angels. The stone had somehow been taken from the Holy Land through North Africa and on through Sicily, Spain and Ireland before reaching Scotland, where it was taken to the village of Scone in the 9th century. There it was built into a throne on which Scottish kings sat during their coronation ceremonies for 400 years.

In 1296 Edward moved the stone to London and had a new coronation chair built with the stone fitted under it. It was to symbolise that kings of England were also kings of Scotland. The Stone of Scone remained in Westminster until the end of the 20th century when, in a gesture of political rapprochement, it was returned to Scotland.

Also on this day

1600: Spanish playwright Pedro Calderón de la Barca is born * 1719: English writer Joseph Addison dies

18 June

The sayings of Waterloo

1815 Waterloo, a Flemish farming village nine miles south of Brussels. Today the 72,000-strong army of Napoleon Bonaparte lost the Emperor's last great gamble there to a mixed force of 68,000 British, Dutch, Belgian and German troops, strongly reinforced by some 45,000 Prussians led by the 72-year-old Field Marshal Prince Gebhard Leberecht von Blücher. In command of the entire Allied army was Britain's finest general since Marlborough, Arthur Wellesley, the Duke of Wellington. As subsequently pronounced by Victor Hugo, 'Wellington was the technician of war, Napoleon its Michelangelo.'

The battle started at midday with Napoleon's first attack and continued until the battered and defeated French forces started to retreat from the field at eight o'clock in the evening. In all, the French suffered over 25,000 men killed or wounded, with another 9,000 captured.

After the battle the self-assured Duke reflected on the result. 'It has been a damned serious business,' he said, 'Blücher and I have lost thirty thousand men. It has been a damned nice thing – the nearest run thing you ever saw in your life … By God, I don't think it would have done if I had not been there.' Later he is reputed to have remarked on the steadfastness of his officers with the famous observation, 'The battle of Waterloo was won on the playing fields of Eton.'

Wellington was not the only general at Waterloo to coin a phrase. Tradition has it that the French Guard Commander Pierre de Cambronne answered a call to yield with 'La Garde meurt, mais ne se rend pas.' (The Guard dies but never surrenders.) After the battle, however, Cambronne denied the comment, claiming he made only the one-word reply 'Merde!' – the word since known to the French as 'le mot de Cambronne'.

Waterloo ended the career of the great Napoleon – he abdicated four days later. It must have galled him that his defeat came at the hands of the British, whom he had once derided as 'a nation of shopkeepers'.

America declares war on Great Britain

1812 Caught in a trade vice between Great Britain's blockade of Napoleon's Europe and Napoleon's Continental System isolating Great Britain, today the United States Congress declared war on Great Britain to start the War of 1812.

'As for France and England,' wrote former president Thomas Jefferson, 'the one is a den of robbers, the other pirates.' The British, however, were considered worse, as they impressed American sailors to serve in their navy as well as seizing American ships.

To the British, on the other hand, America's belligerency was merely an annoying gnat to be batted aside compared with the true enemy, the eagle of Napoleon. Later generations of Americans also failed to understand why the US had gone to war. It was, according to another president, Harry S. Truman, 'the silliest damn war we ever had, made no sense at all'.

The War of 1812 is today principally remembered for the humiliation of British troops capturing Washington and putting the White House to the torch. But it also provided the inspiration for an American lawyer named Francis Scott Key to write 'The Star-Spangled Banner' and provided one further interesting historical footnote. During the conflict 63-year-old James Madison became the only US president to face enemy gunfire while in office, as he led an artillery battery during the attack on the capital.

Also on this day

1155: Holy Roman Emperor Fredrick Barbarossa is crowned in Rome * 1429: The French, led by Joan of Arc, defeat the English at the Battle of Patay

19 June

Mexican Emperor Maximilian faces the firing squad

1867 At dawn this morning in Querétaro in central Mexico a tall, blue-eyed Austrian with a foot-long golden beard carefully donned his black frock coat in his prison cell and mounted a carriage accompanied by a priest, en route to his execution. By 6.40 a.m. he was dead, cut down by the bullets of a seven-man firing squad of Mexican soldiers. Just 34, he had been Emperor of Mexico for three years and nine days. His last words as he faced the rifles were a courageous 'Viva México'.

Maximilian von Habsburg was the younger brother of the Austrian Emperor Franz Joseph. A well-meaning lightweight, he had been persuaded by Mexican reactionaries, French Emperor Napoleon III and his own ambitious wife Charlotte to accept the imperial crown of Mexico, a country mired in a ferocious civil war between extreme reactionaries backed by the Church and anti-clerical republicans.

Maximilian had thought to impose a 'liberal dictatorship' to restore order and stop the killing. Although so deeply conservative that he called his brother 'Your Majesty' even when the two were alone together, he could see that the priest-ridden society of the Mexican right, with few civil liberties, no religious freedom and a system of peonage that enslaved most of the peasants, should not continue. But he abhorred the Left's attack on aristocracy and the Church. So he accepted the poisoned imperial chalice and assumed control of a government held in power solely by a French army.

Napoleon III had invaded Mexico in 1861 for the putative reason of collecting the debts owed to France by the Mexican government, but his real ambitions were to establish French dominance in Latin America and to 'erect an insuperable barrier against the encroachments of the United States'. The timing had been ideal since the American Civil War precluded armed intervention to back up the Monroe Doctrine, which in effect banned European powers from intervening in the Western hemisphere. Napoleon saw Maximilian as little more than his puppet.

Maximilian tried to govern fairly and refused to rescind the confiscation of Church land executed by the republican government. But he was financially incompetent: Mexican debt rose from $81 million in 1861 to $202 million in 1866 and Maximilian's own imperial household expenses came to $1.5 million per year, 50 times the amount spent by his republican predecessor Benito Juárez. During his entire reign civil war continued as the republicans tried to regain lost power. In retaliation, in October of 1863 Maximilian issued the infamous Black Decree that permitted immediate execution of any captured 'rebel' soldiers, with no possibility to petition the Emperor or any other authority for mercy.

In April 1865 Maximilian's regime received a deathblow, although the Emperor was too complacent to recognise it: the American Civil War ended, and now it was only a matter of time before the Monroe Doctrine would be enforced. Within a year an army led by Philip Sheridan was massed on the Rio Grande, threatening to intervene. Napoleon III soon ordered his troops to sail for home, leaving Maximilian with a ragtag force of Austrians, Belgians and a few die-hard conservative Mexicans. He vacillated on whether to abdicate but was dissuaded by his wife, his mother and his ultra-conservative ministers who feared for themselves if the republicans should regain power. He took personal charge of the imperial army but soon was besieged, starved and finally betrayed at Querétaro, where he surrendered on 15 May 1867.

Tried within a month, Maximilian was found guilty of usurping the power of the legitimate government and using a foreign army to wage war against Mexico. Despite strong protests from Austria, France and Great Britain – and petitions from liberals like Victor Hugo and Garibaldi – Juárez refused to commute the sentence of death by firing squad.

On hearing of Maximilian's execution, Napoleon III waxed philosophical about his whole Mexican adventure: 'God did not want it; let us respect His decrees.' Republicans in Europe were jubilant. As future French Prime Minister

Georges Clemenceau wrote at the time, 'Between us and these people [royalty] there is a war to the death. They have tortured to death millions of us and I bet we have not killed two dozen of them.'

The decapitation of Piers Gaveston

1312 Had Piers Gaveston been born a woman, he probably would be remembered as one of history's magnificent mistresses, like Nell Gwyn or Madame de Pompadour. Handsome, athletic, wickedly witty and vain, this Gascon-born Englishman was first brought to the English court by Edward I. It was the King's son, however, who was drawn to Gaveston, so much so that when the son was crowned as Edward II, his Gascon lover carried his crown in the ceremony.

In the years immediately following the coronation, Gaveston's power increased in tune to the King's infatuation – to the fury of the nation's earls, who saw regal offices and jewels squandered on the insolent favourite.

Finally the earls revolted, and despite the King's desperate attempts to hide him, they captured Gaveston at Scarborough and imprisoned him in the castle there.

On 19 June 1312 the earls took the once proud favourite from his dungeon and marched him to Blacklow Hill, near the mighty castle of Warwick. There, despite his plea to his captor, Guy de Beauchamp, Earl of Warwick, 'O noble Earl, spare me!' Gaveston was rudely decapitated, and his head was presented to the King's cousin, the Earl of Lancaster.

To this day it is believed that Gaveston's malevolent ghost roams the ramparts of Scarborough Castle, hurling to their deaths any unwary enough to wander alone on the castle walls at night.

Also on this day

1623: French philosopher Blaise Pascal is born * 1829: The House of Commons passes Robert Peel's law establishing a police force

20 June

Europe is saved from Attila the Hun at the Battle of Châlons

AD 451 'They all have compact, strong limbs and thick necks and are so monstrously ugly and misshapen that one might take them for two-legged beasts ... By the terror of their features they inspired great fear ... They made their foe flee in horror because their swarthy aspect was fearful and they had, if I may call it so, a sort of shapeless lump, not a head, with pin-holes rather than eyes ... Like unreasoning beasts, they are utterly ignorant of the difference between right and wrong.' So did a contemporary historian describe the fearful Huns of Attila in the 5th century.

Although their origin is uncertain, the Huns were probably an Asian people called the Hsung-nu, barbarians of such ferocity that six centuries previously the Chinese had built the Great Wall of China to defend against them.

Attila himself was short and stocky with a wispy beard gracing his abnormally large head. He had become joint King of this Mongol horde in 433, sharing the throne with his brother Bleda. But by 445 he had murdered Bleda to take sole command.

The Western Roman Emperor at the time was Valentinian III, who normally paid Attila an annual tribute to keep him out of his realm. But in 450 his sister Honoria pleaded with Attila to rescue her from a marriage that Valentinian had arranged, sending him her ring as proof of her trust. Attila immediately declared Honoria to be his own wife, with half of Valentinian's empire as her dowry.

In early 451 Attila led a gigantic nomad force composed primarily of mounted archers across the Rhine and laid waste to every town he came upon: Reims, Metz, Amiens, Beauvais, Cologne, Strasbourg. The devastation he wrought justified his boast that 'grass never grows again where my horse has trod'. Even Paris was nearly destroyed, saved only by the miraculous intervention of St Geneviève, whose prayers inspired the defenders to hold the city walls. In like manner Orléans escaped destruction when its bishop Anianus (later St Aignan) restored the city's crumbling battlements by carrying holy relics around them.

With an army mounted on horseback, Attila used speed, surprise, mobility and above all ferocity rather than military strategy. The cruelty of the Huns and of Attila himself was extraordinary, even in this time of cruelty, as the Western Roman Empire was staggering towards its end.

But at last the Romans and their sometime allies the Visigoths combined forces under the command of the Roman general Aetius to meet this so-called Scourge of God. The two armies met on 20 June 451 on the fields near Châlons, in what today is the champagne country of France. Attila set the tone for the conflict by exhorting his men, 'Sunder the sinew, and the limbs collapse; hack the bones and the body falls. Huns of mine, rouse your rage and let your fury swell as of old!'

The battle lasted throughout the day, with terrible slaughter on both sides. At dusk the Visigoths finally smashed through the enemy's flank, threatening the Hun centre and almost killing their leader. Attila was forced to retreat, the first and only defeat in his marauding career.

The terrible Attila lived for only another year, spending that time laying waste to Italy. But the Battle of Châlons had turned the tide, saving much of western Europe from the ravages of the Huns. Attila's defeat also enormously boosted the prestige of the Church of Rome, which claimed much credit for resisting the heathen Huns at Paris and Orléans.

Such was the terror that Attila inspired that he appears in the legends of France, Italy and Scandinavia. He is also featured in the German *Nibelungenlied* under the name of Etzel, while he is called Atli in Icelandic sagas.

Raleigh and Essex capture Cadiz

1596 On this steamy Sunday two of England's best known adventurers, Robert Devereux, the Earl of Essex, and Sir Walter Raleigh, captured the city of Cadiz in southern Spain. Coincidentally, both men ended their lives on the block, Essex executed by Queen Elizabeth in 1601, Raleigh by James I in 1618. Along with them in their triumph at Cadiz was one man rather less known for his military exploits, John Donne, one of England's greatest poets.

Also on this day

1756: Over 140 British subjects are imprisoned in the Black Hole of Calcutta in India * 1791: Louis XVI and Marie Antoinette flee Paris – the 'flight to Varennes' * 1923: Mexican revolutionary leader Pancho Villa is assassinated

21 June

Galileo is condemned

1633 Today Pope Urban VIII issued his verdict: Galileo Galilei was guilty of having 'believed and taught' the pernicious doctrines of Copernicus that asserted that the Earth moves around the Sun.

Ironically, Urban had originally been both a supporter and personal friend of Galileo's, and the great scientist had once dedicated a book to him. But the steady pressures of militant Protestantism were eroding the influence of the Catholic Church, and the papacy was fighting back by reinforcing all the Church's most traditional dogmas. To make matters worse, Galileo's latest unorthodox book, *Dialogo Sopra i Due Massimi Sistemi del Mondo, Tolemaico e Copernicano* (Dialogue on the Two Great Systems of the World, Ptolemaic and Coperni-can), was written in Italian rather than scholarly Latin, making it accessible to a wide audience of readers.

Under pressure from the Dominicans who were in charge of the Inquisition, Urban condemned his old friend to house arrest for the remainder of his life and to public and private penance for his sins.

After hearing his sentence the 70-year-old Galileo knelt before the tribunal and devoutly recanted 'the false opinion that the Sun is the centre of the world and immobile, and that the Earth is not the centre of the world and moves'. But as he rose from his knees he muttered his celebrated denial, 'E pur si muove.' (But it *does* move.)

Galileo spent the remaining eight years of his life under house arrest in Arcetri on the outskirts of Florence, seeing only those visitors permitted by a watching Church. Even then, however, the great scientist could not be totally silenced, as he wrote one further book (this one on the less controversial subject of mechanics) which had to be published abroad because of the papal ban on Galileo's works.

Work starts on Sir Christopher Wren's St Paul's

1675 Although St Paul's Cathedral in London has stood for over 300 years, the current Baroque masterpiece is probably the fifth church to stand on that site, the first dating from the year 604.

In September 1666, the Great Fire of London destroyed the enormous Gothic St Paul's, which was by then already over 400 years old. Luckily there lived in London at that time one of history's greatest architects, Christopher Wren.

Only 34, Wren had already been a member of a commission studying ways to repair the old cathedral when the fire reduced it to rubble. Within a week of the disaster, he submitted preliminary plans for rebuilding the city of London, including St Paul's, but work was not started until 21 June 1675, when the foundation stone of the current church was laid.

St Paul's took 33 years to complete, although it was opened to the public on 2 December 1697. When Sir Christopher Wren finally died at the ripe age of 90 in 1723, he was buried within the walls of his greatest achievement. Today if you enter St Paul's and stand beneath the great dome, you will see spelled out in Latin on the floor Wren's own epitaph: 'Reader, if you seek his monument, look around you.'

Edward III and his greedy mistress

1377 Alice Perrers was young, beautiful, greedy and married to a complaisant husband, as such perfectly suited to be a king's mistress, which is what she was to England's bearded and aged Edward III.

Edward, who was crowned at fifteen, had had a long and brilliant reign, even though in his last years he sank into premature senility. His armies had destroyed the flower of France at Crécy and Poitiers, and England had become Europe's strongest nation. It was also while he was King that, for the first time, all proceedings in Parliament had to be in English instead of Norman French.

When Edward entered his seventh decade, his beloved wife dead, he fell completely under the spell of the calculating Alice Perrers. She stripped the treasury bare for her relatives, while the King's son, John of Gaunt, held the real power.

By 1377 it was clear that Edward's end was near. Still determined to bring rebellious Scotland to heel, he called for his son Edmund of Langley and exhorted, 'Carry my bones before you on your march. The rebels will not be able to endure the sight of me, alive or dead.'

On 21 June the once-glorious monarch was felled by a final stroke in his palace in Richmond. By his bedside was his mistress Alice, who saw the source of her wealth slipping away. Staying until only a few bribable servants were near, this loving companion slipped the rings from the dead man's cold fingers and a gold chain from around his neck.

Thus ended the reign of glorious Edward III, which had lasted for 50 years. Nimble-fingered Alice lived on in wealth for another 23 years.

Also on this day

1652: English architect Inigo Jones dies * 1813: The Duke of Wellington routs the French at the Battle of Vittoria in Spain

22 June

Niccolò Machiavelli dies outside Florence

1527 Old, frustrated and disappointed, Niccolò Machiavelli died this day at 58 on the outskirts of Florence, the city he loved so well, the city that had elevated, enriched, imprisoned, banished and forgotten him. Machiavelli had spent the last fourteen years of his life as a gentleman farmer, living in obscurity, writing his books. Clearly he had lost none of his worldly scepticism as death approached, commenting, 'I would rather go to hell than to heaven. There I will enjoy the company of popes, kings and princes, while in the other place are only beggars, monks and apostles.'

Ironically, it was during his time in the political wilderness that Machiavelli immortalised himself as the father of power politics. His most influential work is *The Prince*, a treatise based on his observations of that ruthless, treacherous, implacable and capable soldier and nobleman, Cesare Borgia.

The Prince sets out Machiavelli's ideas on what a ruler must do to succeed. His incisive cynicism is shown by one of the book's most famous passages. In advising how leaders should treat their subjects, he wrote, 'Men should be either treated with generosity or destroyed; because they will revenge themselves for small offences but for great ones they cannot.'

He also comments on how a prince should want others to see him. 'Is it better to be loved or feared? ... It is better to be both, but it is much safer to be feared than loved, if one has to choose between them.'

Future leaders who we know were influenced by Machiavelli's writings are numerous: Richelieu, Frederick the Great, Napoleon, Bismarck, Clemenceau. Hitler kept a copy of *The Prince* on his bedside table.

Napoleon abdicates – again

1815 Today at noon, a month short of his 46th birthday, the Emperor Napoleon abdicated for the second and final time, naming his son as successor to his empire. The son never ruled, of course, and Napoleon was shortly shipped off to St Helena to end his days.

With the exception of nine months in exile on Elba, Napoleon had ruled the

French since becoming First Consul in February 1800. Although chiefly remembered for his string of famous victories (and for his principal defeat at Waterloo, only four days before this abdication), he had achieved much that endures to this day.

Napoleon's legal code is still law in France, Belgium and Luxembourg, and it also became the model for the civil code in the state of Louisiana. He established the baccalaureate examination and the lycée and founded the Legion of Honour. His scientists discovered the Rosetta Stone during his campaign in Egypt. He laid the first pavements in Paris, founded the Bourse, introduced gas lamps and built the Arc de Triomphe and the rue de Rivoli. But perhaps his most enduring (and certainly his most endearing) monument comes from a law he passed in 1811 that decreed that all over France trees should be planted along the roads so that his soldiers could march in the shade.

Americans land on Daiquiri Beach

1898 Today should be observed as D-Day, and a generous-sized Daiquiri cocktail hoisted to honour the US forces that landed this morning on an enemy beach, the vanguard of a great invasion. It wasn't at Normandy or Iwo Jima or Inchon. It was at a remote spot on the long southern coastline of Cuba, where elements of the Army's V Corps went ashore at Daiquiri Beach, some eighteen miles east of Santiago.

This was amphibious warfare with a distinctly holiday air about it. From the deck of a troopship the correspondent Richard Harding Davis described the first wave going in:

> Soon the sea was dotted with rows of white boats filled with men bound about with white blanket rolls and with muskets at all angles, and as they rose and fell on the water and the newspaper yachts and transports crept in closer and closer, the scene was strangely suggestive of a boat race, and one almost waited for the starting gun.

A preliminary naval bombardment had evidently driven away any Spanish troops who might have been around to contest the landing site, which was just as well, for even a few hundred well-motivated defenders could have inflicted a terrible slaughter on the V Corps and changed the course of the war.

During this first day of invasion, 6,000 infantry, accompanied by a few reporters, got ashore in a continuous stream of launches and barges. Horses and mules for the artillery and pack trains were simply shoved out of cargo ports to swim ashore. Later, when cavalry dispatched by General 'Fighting Joe' Wheeler, who had once commanded troops of the Confederacy, raced up a hill behind the beach and raised their regimental flag, a reporter recorded that the entire invasion force, afloat and ashore, began cheering 'and every steam whistle on the ocean for miles about shrieked and tooted and roared in a pandemonium of delight and pride and triumph'.

With the advent of evening, the troops began pitching their tents above the beach. In the words of one historian, 'They were spending their first night in the field of war, in the near presence of the enemy. Whether or not they would even spend another they did not know.' So began the first ground operation of the Spanish–American War.

They don't make invasions like that any more. But you can make a Daiquiri by mixing four parts rum to one of lime juice, sugar to taste, and plenty of ice. Shake well before serving.

Also on this day

1535: Cardinal Fisher is beheaded on the orders of Henry VIII * 1699: French painter Jean Chardin is born

23 June

Robert the Bruce defeats the English at Bannockburn

1314 On this day near Stirling Castle outside Edinburgh, Robert the Bruce, King of Scotland, carefully positioned his infantrymen on a hillside above a stream called Bannockburn, taking advantage of cavalry-slowing bogs on one side of his front and an infantry-concealing forest on the other. Then he waited for the vanguard of the English army.

For almost twenty years now the Scots had fought to remain independent from English domination, in a seesaw struggle with England's King Edward I, the 'Hammer of the Scots'. Edward invaded Scotland for the first time in 1296, then again in 1306, after the Earl of Carrick, as Bruce was then, was crowned the Scottish King. So, Bruce as King became an outlaw, always on the run, at one point harried clean out of Scotland, his wife, daughters and sisters imprisoned, his youngest brother beheaded.

But Edward died at the beginning of the second invasion, and Edward II proved no match for his father in matters of war. The second campaign languished, and as victories came for Bruce and his growing forces, the Scottish nobility began to favour his cause. Now, however, for a third time, an English army, 25,000 strong, had come over the border, with the intent of relieving the siege of Stirling Castle, the last English stronghold in the north of the country.

On 23 June the English delivered their main attack, the sheer weight of which, Edward was sure, must prevail. The English cavalry crowded forward over the narrow front of stable footing, but it piled up in a congested mass, unable to get past the thick clusters of Scottish pikemen. In the confusion, the English archers rained down arrows on their own cavalry as much as on the Scots.

The brutal slogging match might have ended as a bloody draw but for an ingenious ruse that decided the day. A force of Scottish camp followers – grooms, priests, cooks and porters – emerged from the forest on the English left, waving banners and shouting in simulation of a counter-attack. The English, hesitating at what appeared to be a fresh army sent against them, began to withdraw, slowly at first, but soon in panic when it became known that King Edward had decamped.

Reinvigorated, the Scots drove their enemy from the field, leaving thousands dead and wounded and capturing hundreds more. Among the English dead were 21 barons and baronets, 42 knights and 700 gentlemen-at-arms. The ransoms paid for those captured would for a time make Scotland a rich country. The most important of the prisoners taken by the Scots was the powerful Earl of Hereford, whom Bruce exchanged for his wife, his daughters and his sisters.

The great victory at Bannockburn gave substance to the Scots claim of independence and to Bruce's leadership of his nation. It did not end the war, which dragged on until 1328, when Edward III signed the Treaty of Northampton, the main clause of which read: 'Scotland shall remain to Robert, King of Scots, free and undivided from England, without any subjection, servitude, claim or demand whatsoever.'

The Hundred Years' War begins at Sluys

1340 The problems all started in 1328 with the death of Charles IV. He was the last of three brothers who in turn had been kings of France, as none could produce a male heir. When Charles died, his cousin Philip VI took the throne, as there were simply no more brothers. There was a sister, Isabella, married to England's Edward II, but she was excluded by the Salic Law, which said that only males could inherit the throne.

Isabella's son Edward III himself conceded that 'the Kingdom of France was too great for a woman to hold, by reason of the imbecility of her sex'. But, claimed Edward, a woman could *transmit* inheritance, and therefore the crown of France should rightfully be his. Obviously Philip VI did not agree, and therein lie the origins of the Hundred Years' War.

Although there had been minor bloodshed since 1337, the Hundred Years' War's first major battle took place this day at sea near the port of Sluys, which lies north of Bruges near the present Belgian–Dutch border.

The Battle of Sluys was a great naval victory for Edward III, who was in personal command of the English fleet. In all, the French lost some 25,000 men.

After the battle no one dared tell Philip the outcome. Finally his frightened courtiers pushed forward the court jester, who said, 'Oh, the cowardly English, the cowardly English!' Asked to explain, the jester continued, 'They did not jump overboard like our brave Frenchmen.'

Thus the English won the first real battle, although in the end they lost the war. The end, however, came 113 years later.

Mutineers set Henry Hudson adrift

1611 Henry Hudson was one of England's greatest explorers, but his obsession to find a north-west passage through the Americas to the Orient proved to be his undoing.

Hudson first sailed to the Americas in 1607, but three consecutive attempts to find his way through to the East ended in failure. In the meantime, however, he explored much of the north-east of what is now the United States, ascending the river named after him as far as present-day Albany.

In 1610 Hudson mounted a fourth expedition, and this time he headed north. Passing between Labrador and Greenland, he reached Hudson Bay where, stymied by snow and ice, he was forced to winter. By June of the following year his wretched and starving crew were driven to mutiny when Hudson refused to sail for home. On 23 June the great explorer, his son and seven loyal companions were set adrift in the bay named after him, without food or water. They were never seen again.

Also on this day

AD 79: Roman Emperor Vespasian dies

24 June

Edward III creates the Order of the Garter

1348 Today at Windsor Castle, just a few miles west of London, King Edward III held the first ceremony for what has become the most celebrated order of chivalry in the world, the Order of the Garter.

For some time the King had planned to establish a noble order of knights based on the Round Table of King Arthur. The story goes that earlier in the year the exceptionally beautiful Joan of Kent, Countess of Salisbury, inadvertently lost a blue garter during an evening's dancing at court. Gallantly, Edward picked it up and attached it to his own sleeve. Then, thinking of the lady's reputation (and perhaps of his own, for he was known to have a roving eye), he remarked to his guests, 'Honi soit qui mal y pense.' (Ashamed be he who thinks evil of it.) This was the beginning of the Order of the Garter and its motto, which have lasted to this day as England's highest honour.

Initially, the Order had twelve members, but in 1805 the number was increased to 25. Most of its recipients have come from Britain's highest aristocracy or, more recently, highest political levels. Not all, however, have been faithful to their trust, as 36 have been beheaded.

In 1790 George III offered William Pitt the Younger the Order of the Garter, then a significant financial reward as well as an honour, but Pitt refused, requesting that it might be given to his less well-off brother instead. But in 1945

Winston Churchill turned down the award on the grounds that he had just been defeated in an election. As he told a friend, 'I can hardly accept the Order of the Garter from the king after the people have given me the Order of the Boot.'

Two emperors and a king slug it out at Solferino

1859 When a combined Piedmontese–French army met the forces of Imperial Austria at Solferino near Italy's Lake Garda today, the troops were commanded by two emperors and a king: Napoleon III of France, Franz Joseph of Austria and Victor Emmanuel, already King of Sardinia-Piedmont but soon to be the first King of a united Italy.

The battle was fought in almost unendurable heat, as some 270,000 men met to kill each other. In the end, the Piedmontese–French army prevailed, but the cost was frightful. Each side lost some 15,000 men killed or wounded, and some 8,000 Austrians were captured or went missing. Even the victorious Victor Emmanuel recoiled at the slaughter, aware of how near he had come to losing. 'Luck plays too great a role', was his view of war after this battle.

In addition to being a major step towards Italian reunification, the Battle of Solferino had other important effects. Because of French demands after the battle, Nice and Savoy were stripped from the Austrians and awarded to the French. One other result of Solferino was less apparent at the time. Among the appalled stretcher-bearers was a Swiss named Henri Dunant. So shocked was he by the savagery and suffering that he first wrote a book describing the horrors of Solferino and then went on to found the Red Cross.

Also on this day

1812: Napoleon and the Grande Armée cross the River Nieman into Russia

25 June

Pharaoh Ramses II begins the longest reign in Egyptian history

1279 BC My name is Ozymandias, king of kings:
Look on my works ye mighty, and despair!

Today the man whose statue inspired these famous lines by Percy Shelley became sole ruler of ancient Egypt, over which he reigned in unrivalled power for 66 years. We know him as Ramses II, but like all pharaohs he had many names, one of which was Usermaatre, corrupted over the millennia to Ozymandias.

Born a commoner, Ramses was the son of one of Egypt's leading generals who as Seti I became Pharaoh on the childless demise of the previous king. When Seti died, Ramses inherited the throne.

According to the hieroglyphics on his many monuments, Ramses was a great warrior king, principally against the Hittites, but modern scholarship suggests that the conflict was more of a stand-off. But he undoubtedly was an unparalleled builder. He built a new Egyptian capital which he called Pi Ramesse Aa-nakhta or House of Ramses Great of Victories. Today only traces remain, but there are gigantic statues of Ramses throughout Egypt, particularly at Luxor and Abu Simbel, where the four enormous statues all portray the Pharaoh.

Shelley mocks the vanity of kings, but these portrait statues were not entirely for self-glorification. Egyptians of Ramses' era believed the soul could go to 'heaven' – the Kingdom of Osiris – only if the body survived, a belief that inspired the process of mummification. But some thought that the soul could also survive through an image of the body, a statue.

Ramses' long rule ended when he died in August 1213 BC at almost 100 years of age. On his death his body underwent a 70-day embalming process. Clearly the embalmers did a good job, since in June 1886 a French archaeologist opened Ramses' bandages on the recovered body to uncover the still-intact face of an old man with red hair. Today you can see the mummy in the Cairo Museum.

Apart from the many colossal statues of Ramses in Egypt, there are other reminders of him in our daily life. One of his obelisks, originally in Luxor, today adorns the place de la Concorde in Paris, brought back from Egypt by Napoleon. The Washington Monument was inspired by it.

We can also read references to him in the Old Testament, as Ramses was the pharaoh referred to in the Bible at the time of Moses. It has been broadly established that Moses lived and worked in Egypt during Ramses' reign, and one French historian speculates that the two were actually friends. Finally, in America a leading brand of condom is called Ramses, rather inappropriately named after a ruler who fathered 46 sons and almost 50 daughters, including four whom he married.

Custer's last stand

1876 George Armstrong Custer was a tall, rangy man with a hard narrow face, a high forehead, flaxen hair worn long, and a droopy old-cowpoke moustache. Few remember today that he was also a noted soldier. In the American Civil War he was the youngest general in the Union Army, and at the war's close it was he who received the Confederate flag of truce and was present at the South's surrender at Appomattox.

By 1876 Custer was 37 years old and now, instead of Southerners, he was fighting a coalition of Indian tribes, including Sioux, Cheyenne and Arapaho. Leading the Indians was the great chief Sitting Bull.

On 17 June the combined Indian forces had defeated American troops in the Battle of the Rosebud in the Montana territory. Shortly after this victory

Sitting Bull had driven himself into a trance performing the Sun Dance, after which he reported having seen a vision of soldiers falling to earth like grasshoppers from the sky, accurately predicting the victory that was to follow in a few days.

Meanwhile Custer was leading the US 7th Cavalry when on 25 June he came upon the Indian encampment by a river called the Little Bighorn. Not realising the number of enemy he faced, he rashly divided his force of some 600 troopers into three groups – and attacked.

Custer was personally leading about 225 soldiers as the battle started. Of more than 1,000 waiting Indians was a 26-year-old chief named White Bull. Later White Bull told his story: 'When I rushed him, he threw his rifle at me without shooting. I dodged it. We grabbed each other and wrestled there in the dust and smoke … He tried to wrench my rifle from me. I lashed him across the face with my quirt … He let go … But he fought hard. He was desperate. He hit me with his fists on my jaw and shoulders, then grabbed my long braids with both hands, pulled my face close and tried to bite my nose off … Finally I broke free. He drew his pistol. I wrenched it out of his hand and struck him with it three or four times on the head, knocked him over, shot him in the head, and fired at his heart.'

The general and his force were killed to the last man at Little Bighorn in a battle known as Custer's Last Stand. It was a fitting end for the man who coined the odious phrase, 'The only good Indians I ever saw were dead.'

After his victory at Little Bighorn, Sitting Bull continued to resist American attempts to capture him until 1883, when, his followers devasated by hunger and disease, he finally surrendered and was sent to the Standing Rock Agency to live. Two years later, however, he was given his freedom to join Buffalo Bill's Wild West show. In 1890, amid fears of further Indian uprisings, American troops were sent to arrest him but killed him while his warriors were trying to save him.

Also on this day

1646: The surrender of Oxford to the Roundheads signifies the end of the English Civil War

26 June

The real Pied Piper

1284 Rats!
> They fought the dogs and killed the cats,
> And bit the babies in the cradles,
> And ate the cheeses out of vats,
> And licked the soup from the cooks' own ladles …

So did Robert Browning describe events in his 1842 epic 'The Pied Piper of Hamelin'. But what is the true story?

Today was the feast of St John and St Paul, a day when no one worked or went to school in the German town of Hamelin in Lower Saxony. No one knows for certain what happened that day, but records survive that show that 130 children disappeared. What is certain is that here lies the origin of the famous tale of the Pied Piper, the world's most famous ratcatcher.

Some believe the legend of the Pied Piper is purely symbolic, originating in the death of many children from the plague. In medieval times no one understood the connection between rats and the Black Death, but people must have observed the death of infected rats, followed by plague deaths of people.

Current theory concerning the substantial single-day disappearance in Hamelin, however, suggests that the children were actually led away. Their fate, however, was not Walt Disney's land of eternal youth but a German town in what is now the Czech Republic named Troppan. It seems likely that a German bishop of the period, a certain Bruno, enticed the children – who were probably teenagers – to follow him to colonise a new town. The rats were added to the tale only in the 16th century.

Did Peter the Great beat his son to death?

1718 The Tsarevich Aleksey was a weak and nervous young man of 28 who was terrified of his father Peter the Great – with good reason. For Aleksey wanted only peace and tranquillity, even offering to retreat to a monastery to get it, but Peter saw him as the inevitable inheritor of his realm, an inheritor who might undo the Westernisation that he had spent his life accomplishing.

So great was Aleksey's fear that eventually he fled in disguise, reappearing only in Vienna, begging the Austrian Emperor for sanctuary. But Peter sent emissaries to Aleksey, promising a full pardon should he return to St Petersburg. Duped by his father's apparent forgiveness, Aleksey headed back to Russia.

Once back in Peter's control, Aleksey was told he would have to renounce the rights to the Russian throne and denounce those who had helped him escape. Although he accepted these harsh terms, still his father was not satisfied. He arrested and tortured Aleksey's friends and then turned to Aleksey himself.

Imprisoned and tortured, Aleksey received over 40 lashes and was reduced to gibbering fright, admitting every conspiracy his father could conceive of. He was then forced to admit all his supposed crimes before the Russian Senate before being speedily sentenced to death by a special court that acted under orders from Peter.

Before the sentence could be carried out Aleksey died in prison on this day, possibly from the aftershock of torture or suffocated by the prison warders. Some historians believe his own father may have beaten him to death.

Whether Peter actually performed the deed is moot. He was certainly guilty of the murder of his son, which puts him in a class with his predecessor Ivan the Terrible, who killed his son with a poker.

Also on this day

AD 363: Roman Emperor Julian the Apostate is killed in battle in Persia * 1541: Spanish conquistador Francisco Pizarro is assassinated

27 June

Jeanne Hachette saves her city

1472 Jeanne Laisné was a simple butcher's daughter, raised in the handsome walled city of Beauvais just 50 miles north of Paris. It was her misfortune to live at the time when King Louis XI and Charles the Bold, Duke of Burgundy, were warring with each other for control of France.

In the spring of 1472 Charles's Burgundian army was on the rampage. The little city of Nesle had already surrendered when, during a truce, the Duke's men had burst into the town and massacred all the men, women and children who had fled to a church for refuge. On 27 June Charles arrived beneath the walls of Beauvais.

Knowing what would be in store for them if they surrendered, the citizens of Beauvais put up a mighty resistance, and none fought so fiercely as Jeanne Laisné. Armed with her father's butcher's hatchet, she cut down the Burgundian flag bearer, seizing the standard when her battered victim fell from the walls.

Twenty-five days after the siege began Duke Charles was forced to withdraw his depleted army. Beauvais had held out, and Jeanne became a heroine whose nickname would last for centuries – Jeanne Hachette. Her statue still stands in the city's old market-place.

Captain Joshua Slocum sails around the world alone

1898 In the midnight darkness a small vessel sailing close to shore made her cautious way towards the harbour of Newport, Rhode Island, recently mined against the possibility of a Spanish naval attack. 'It was close work,' wrote her captain, 'but it was safe enough so long as she hugged the rocks, and not the mines.' From a guard ship at the harbour entrance came a challenge. 'I threw up a light at once and heard the hail "*Spray*, ahoy." It was the voice of a friend, and I knew that a friend would not fire on the *Spray*. I eased off the mainsheet now, and the *Spray* swung off for the beacon-lights of the inner harbor. At last she reached port in safety, and there at 1.00 a.m. on June 28, 1898, cast anchor ...'

So ended one of the great sea voyages of history. Captain Joshua Slocum aboard his 37-foot sloop the *Spray* became the first man to sail around the world alone, a challenge he had undertaken simply because 'I was greatly amused ... by the flat assertions of an expert that it could not be done.' Slocum cruised more than 46,000 miles in the course of three years, two months and two days, during which time his progress was closely reported to the world by newspapers in his ports of call and by ships he encountered at sea.

The *Spray*, with a single mast and a net tonnage of nine tons, was 'an antiquated sloop which neighbors declared had been built in the year 1'. Slocum redesigned and rebuilt her for the long voyage at a cost of $553.62 for materials and thirteen months of his own labour. When the work was done, he was at once designer, owner, captain and ship's company. 'There never was a crew so well agreed', he wrote.

Slocum, an experienced ocean mariner, began his great adventure intending to sail eastward from Boston, Massachusetts, across the Atlantic Ocean, into the Mediterranean and through the Suez Canal. But after a narrow escape from Moroccan pirates off Gibraltar, he reversed course, sailing back across the Atlantic, down the east coast of South America, and through the Magellan Strait. His first port of call in the Pacific was Juan Fernandez, Robinson Crusoe's island. Reaching Samoa, he was greeted by the widow of Robert Louis Stevenson. At one stage in his long passage across the Pacific, he went 72 days without touching land.

Continuing westward through the Indian Ocean, he reached Cape Town, where the *Spray* spent three months refitting in dry dock. Slocum journeyed upcountry to Pretoria where he was introduced to Paul Kruger, President of the Boer Republic of Transvaal, as someone who was 'sailing around the world'. The phrase offended Kruger, who knew from his Bible that the world was flat. 'You don't mean "*round* the world"', growled the old president. 'It is impossible. You mean *in* the world.' No one argued the point.

Leaving South Africa in March 1898, Slocum sailed north-west on the last leg of his voyage. Only when he reached the Caribbean did he learn that the United States was at war with Spain. His famous account of the voyage, *Sailing Around the World Alone*, was published in 1900 and became a bestseller through many editions. Slocum was as good a writer as he was a sailor, combining a natural style with a vivid eye for detail. Here is how he described the very beginning of his voyage leaving Boston harbour:

> The day was perfect, the sunlight clear and strong. Every particle of water thrown into the air became a gem, and the *Spray*, making good her name as she dashed ahead, snatched necklace after necklace from the sea and as often threw them away. We have all seen miniature rainbows about a ship's prow, but the *Spray* flung out a bow of her own that day, such as I had never seen before. Her good angel had embarked on the voyage; I so read it in the sea.

Also on this day

1571: Italian painter and art historian Giorgio Vasari dies * 1787: Edward Gibbon completes *The History of the Decline and Fall of the Roman Empire*

28 June

Sarajevo

1914 Why the Archduke Franz Ferdinand, heir apparent to the throne of Austria, chose to visit the capital of Bosnia in this summer of Balkan discontent, we will never know for sure. 'To pay that visit', wrote Rebecca West, 'was an act so suicidal that one fumbles the pages of history books to find if there is not some explanation of his going, if he was not subject to some compulsion. But if ever a man went anywhere of his own free will, Franz Ferdinand went so to Sarajevo.'

Only eight years earlier Bosnia had been annexed by Austria-Hungary, infuriating the highly nationalist Serbs who constituted a large minority of Bosnia's population and hoped for eventual union with Serbia. Anti-Austrian feeling ran high, now exacerbated by Franz Ferdinand's decision to review military exercises in Bosnia in his role as inspector general of the Austro-Hungarian army.

When the trip was announced, the Serbian government, no friend of Austria, alerted Vienna to the strong likelihood of an assassination attempt by the secret Serbian irredentist group Crna Ruka or Black Hand, officially entitled Ujedinjenje ili Smrt, Unification or Death. This infamous organisation had become so powerful that in 1913 its leader was named head of intelligence for the Serbian General Staff.

Deaf to all advice, warnings and good sense, the ambitious and unpopular Franz Ferdinand determined to carry out the military inspection, perhaps viewing the visit as a rehearsal for his own emperorship. Whatever his motive, off he went, more arch-fool than archduke.

After attending two days of Austrian army manoeuvres, provocatively conducted near the Serbian border, Franz Ferdinand, now joined by his wife Sophie, started a processional drive through Sarajevo at 10.00 a.m. this Sunday morning – an offensive choice of date since it was Vidovdan, Serbia's national day.

You might have guessed that in such circumstances Austrian troops would have been posted along the route. But there were none, only local police. And surely the tour would have been cancelled after someone flung a bomb that glanced off the royal automobile and exploded under the next car, wounding an aide-de-camp. But the tour proceeded as scheduled to the Town Hall.

There the welcoming festivities were cut short and a route change agreed, but somehow no one informed the chauffeurs. At 11.15 a.m. the tour resumed. When the lead car with the deputy mayor of Sarajevo turned to follow the old route, there was confusion among the security detail. The second car, carrying the royal couple, came to a stop while things were sorted out. At this point, Gavrilo Princip, a nineteen-year-old Bosnian student and member of the Black Hand, stepped from the crowd of onlookers, drew a revolver and fired, one bullet hitting the archduke, another his wife who had thrown herself across the car to shield him. Both died within minutes. It was their fourteenth wedding anniversary.

Princip was instantly captured, tried within four months and sentenced to twenty years in prison, the maximum allowable for criminals under twenty. In less than four years he was dead of tuberculosis.

But one month to the day after the assassination, even before Princip was brought to trial, Austria declared war on Serbia, precipitating the First World War.

Catherine the Great's coup in St Petersburg

1762 Tsar Peter III suffered three great misfortunes. First, he was a grandson of Peter the Great and thus heir to the throne of Russia. Second, he married a hard-headed German named Sophia, who changed her name to Catherine. Third, he was a fool.

Peter had become Tsar at the start of 1762 with the death of his aunt, Empress Elizabeth. He had married Sophia/Catherine as a teenager in 1744 but had never truly lived with her as man and wife. Physically he was short, thin and frail, but his greatest weakness was his character. He idolised Frederick the Great of Prussia and generally held his Russian courtiers in contempt. He paid scant attention to Catherine but doted on his mistress. There were rumours he would replace Catherine – or worse.

On the morning of 28 June, the 33-year-old Catherine and her lover Grigory Orlov staged one of history's most successful coups. At dawn Catherine was brought to the capital of St Petersburg, while her husband was away on military manoeuvres. Proclaimed Empress by Orlov and other powerful nobles, she almost instantly won over the army, the Church and the rest of the nobility. All were delighted to rid themselves of the weak and irresolute Peter. The coup was so fast and so complete that Peter could mount no resistance. Not a shot was fired. As Frederick the Great said of Peter, 'He let himself be driven from the throne as a child is sent to bed.'

The coup was all but bloodless – except for Peter himself, who was murdered in prison a week later. His reign had lasted 124 days. Catherine's would last 34 years. She is known to history as Catherine the Great.

Also on this day
1491: Henry VIII is born in Greenwich Palace * 1519: Charles I of Spain is elected Holy Roman Emperor as Charles V * 1712: French philosopher Jean Jacques Rousseau is born * 1838: Queen Victoria is crowned

29 June

The Globe Theatre burns down

1613 The actual shape of London's Globe Theatre, where most of Shakespeare's plays were first performed, is still largely a matter of educated guesswork. It was probably a twenty-sided building cylindrical in shape, with a diameter of 100 feet. What is certain is that it had a thatched roof, which on this day was set on fire by a stage cannon, fired during a scene from *Henry VIII*. In less than an hour this seminal theatre of English drama was gone, burned to the ground.

The Globe was built in 1599 by two brothers, Richard and Cuthbert Burbage, of whom the former was a leading actor, the first to play Richard III, Romeo, Henry V, Hamlet, Macbeth, Othello and King Lear. The company of players who acted there was called the Chamberlain's Men, of which Shakespeare was a member. It is thought that Shakespeare and several other of the players owned shares in the Globe along with the Burbages.

Only eighteen months after its incineration the Globe had been rebuilt, this time with a tile roof. Although Shakespeare died just two years later, it continued as London's leading playhouse until 1642, when high-minded Puritans pulled it down, along with all of London's other theatres, in order to make room for housing for the poor.

For over three centuries what was left of the Globe was covered over and built over, but in 1970 an American actor named Sam Wanamaker established a project to recreate it. In 1987 the first work on the new Globe started some 200 yards from the original site, and two years later the foundations of the original Globe were discovered, although they could not be fully excavated since they lay beneath another building.

Even before the new Globe was completed, plays were held there, and on Thursday 12 June 1997 Queen Elizabeth II officially inaugurated the building, a close replica of the original where Shakespeare's plays are still performed in the round.

Also on this day
1577: Dutch painter Peter Paul Rubens is born * 1855: Trade unions are legalised in the United Kingdom * 1861: English poet Elizabeth Barrett Browning dies in Florence

30 June

King Henri II ignores his wife's astrologer

1559 Queen Catherine begged her husband not to joust. Ten years earlier her pet astrologer, Cosimo Ruggieri, had direfully predicted the King would die in a duel and he had repeated his prediction only a week before. But Henri II of France had never taken much notice of his wife's superstitions (or indeed of his wife). After all, she had been born in Italy with the name of Medici. So he ignored her pleas not to joust during the great 'Tournament of Queens' to be held at the Palais des Tournelles in Paris.

The tournament took place on a sunny Friday 30 June. All had gone well, and the knights and spectators were on the point of leaving when Henri sent word to Catherine that he would try one more bout 'for the love of her' (in contrast to his earlier bouts, possibly fought for the love of his mistress Diane de Poitiers, who was watching with the Queen).

As Henri prepared for the final clash a boy in the crowd called out, 'Sire, do not tilt!' Feeling the tension, another knight offered to joust for the King. But Henri insisted and prepared to charge his opponent, Gabriel de Lorges, comte de Montgoméry.

The trumpet sounded and the armoured figures met with a mighty crash. The impact snapped de Montgoméry's lance, and the sharp and shattered stump smashed into the King's face, penetrating his helmet and driving a splinter in over his right eye.

Rushed to bed, Henri endured the tortures of 16th-century medicine, as the splinter was painfully withdrawn. But all to no avail; after ten days the King died on 10 July. Catherine's foreboding had been right.

The greatest cosmic explosion in the history of civilisation

1908 It was already full daylight at 7.40 this morning when an enormous pale blue fireball trailed by a 500-mile tail of bright, shimmering, multicoloured bands hurtled across the Siberian sky and consumed itself in the greatest cosmic explosion in the history of civilisation.

This cataclysmic detonation occurred four miles above the Earth's surface over a huge, inaccessible and almost uninhabited pine forest near the Podkamennaya Tunguska River in central Siberia. Equal to 1,000 Hiroshima bombs, the blinding flash could be seen from 500 miles away.

This colossal blast produced no crater because it occurred so high above the Earth, but its shock wave flattened half a million acres of forest, and more than twenty miles from the epicentre scorched and splintered trees lay pointing radially outward in a vast circle of destruction. Almost 60 miles away at the trading post of Vanavara people were knocked to the ground by the force of the blast, and an hour later the seismic wave was picked up at the South Kensington Meteorological Office in London almost 4,000 miles away.

The debate still rages about the true nature of this titanic explosion. Most agree that some sort of extraterrestrial body, travelling at perhaps 60,000 miles an hour, detonated when it collided with the Earth's atmosphere. Some maintain that it was a 100,000-ton asteroid, others believe that it was a football-field-sized meteorite, and some insist it was a wayward comet fragment composed mainly of ice and dust. A more abstruse theory holds that the cataclysm was caused by a chunk of anti-matter, but a few assert that it was the explosion of the main drive reactor in a UFO manned by aliens bent on invading the Earth.

Also on this day

1520: Spanish conquistadors murder Indian chief Montezuma * 1934: Adolf Hitler orders the purge of his own party in the 'Night of the Long Knives' * 1936: *Gone with the Wind* is published

1 July

Teddy Roosevelt's Rough Riders storm San Juan Hill

1898 In the midday Cuban sun, thousands of American soldiers lay along the trough of the San Juan River, waiting for orders, sweltering in the riverbed, low on food, water and ammunition. Ahead of them, past the jungle fringe, they could see open ground leading to their objective, the strong defensive positions atop San Juan Hill and neighbouring Kettle Hill, from which Spanish rifle fire was having effect.

On the far right of the line was First US Volunteer Cavalry Regiment, a picturesque contingent of cowboys and college men who like thousands of their peers had joined the crusade to free Cuba from Spanish tyranny. An appreciative press had dubbed the regiment variously 'Teddy's Terrors', 'Rocky Mountain Rustlers', and finally, still alliteratively and most pleasing to its lieutenant colonel, 'Roosevelt's Rough Riders'.

Not too many weeks earlier, Theodore Roosevelt had been the Assistant Secretary of the United States Navy. But Roosevelt knew an absolutely bully opportunity when he saw one, and with war declared against Spain he resigned his office to raise a regiment of volunteers.

Around 2.00 p.m., Gatling guns were brought forward and went into action, clearing the Spanish soldiers from the top of San Juan Hill. Now, commanders shouted out orders to advance, and from the jungle beyond the riverbed a long line of blue-shirted figures emerged and started across the meadows. The Rough Riders were in reserve, but when Roosevelt got the message, 'Move forward and support the regulars', he decided it called for an all-out charge. Gesticulating with his hat, he led the way, mounted on his horse Texas, followed by a crowd of Rough Riders and black troopers from the Ninth and Tenth Cavalry. In a rush, they took Kettle Hill.

To his left, he could see the main advance stalled on San Juan Hill some 700 yards away, as American artillery, two miles to the rear and so far largely inactive, suddenly opened up on the summit. Frantic waving of hats and flags called off the firing, but the delay allowed Roosevelt time to join the attack for its final drive. In a few glorious minutes it was over, and all along the ridgeline American soldiers stood, firing at the backs of the retreating enemy and gazing down at the city of Santiago.

It was 4.00 p.m. Roosevelt brought order to the happy confusion of victory, formed up the soldiers on the summit, and prepared to meet the press. One historian wrote of the occasion: '... as the newspaper dispatches went off describing the heroism of the Rough Riders and their lieutenant-colonel, another military genius had been given to American history'.

Hostilities were over by August, and Secretary of State John Hay pronounced the outing 'a splendid little war'. And so it was for the United States, which in acquiring Puerto Rico, Guam and the Philippine Islands became a world power; for Cuba, which gained its independence after 400 years of Spanish rule; and for Colonel Roosevelt, his nation's newest hero, who went on to become governor of New York, vice president for President William McKinley, and on McKinley's death on 14 September 1901, President of the United States.

Slaughter at the Somme

1916 At 7.00 a.m., as the sun pierced the morning mists, 100,000 British soldiers climbed out of their trenches and marched into no man's land, confident they would fulfil their commander-in-chief's plan. Before nightfall, God willing and General Haig in command, they should have broken a large hole in the strongest, deepest and best-defended point in the entire German line.

But for these British soldiers along the Somme this day, most of them recent volunteers, it was not meant to be. History and technology were not on their side. Two years of war had given abundant proof that, in the absence of surprise, troops advancing against barbed wire, entrenchments in depth, machine guns and artillery had no chance of success. New technology was waiting in the wings in the form of the tank, but it was not ready to make its début. As for surprise, there could have been none after a week's preliminary artillery bombardment, which in any case failed to either cut the German barbed wire or destroy their frontline dugouts.

By nightfall, the British troops had advanced two miles but 20,000 of them lay dead, with another 40,000 wounded or captured, the greatest one-day loss ever sustained by an army in history. This was only the first day of an offensive that would last until mid-November. When it ended, both sides exhausted, the British had gained about seven miles. Tanks did make a brief appearance on 15 September and, before breaking down, achieved a spectacular local gain of some 3,500 yards – soon wiped out by strong German counter-attacks.

The rationale for the Somme offensive was to prevent the Germans from shifting troop strength away to fight in other sectors of the front. But Winston Churchill doubted the strategic contribution of the battle was worth the cost. 'We could have held the Germans on our front just as well by threatening an offensive as by making one', he advised the Cabinet on 1 August.

Total casualties for the battle were 420,000 for the British, 195,000 for the French, who fought alongside them south of the Somme, and a shocking 650,000 for the Germans, bled white by costly counter-attacks to regain lost ground.

Also on this day

1646: German mathematician and philosopher Gottfried Leibniz is born in Leipzig *
1863: The Battle of Gettysburg begins, in the American Civil War

2 July

Amelia Earhart, America's first and foremost aviatrix, vanishes in flight

1937 'KHAQQ calling *Itasca*. We must be on you but cannot see you but gas is running low ... unable to reach you by radio, we are flying at 1,000 feet ... one-half hour fuel and no landfall.'

At 7.42 this morning the US coastguard cutter *Itasca* received this short message from Amelia Earhart's Lockheed Electra as the great aviatrix tried to negotiate the last 2,556 miles from Lae in Papua New Guinea to the tiny coral atoll of Howland Island in the remote Pacific. Just over an hour later she briefly radioed her plane's position. She was never heard from again.

By 1937 Amelia Earhart was nearing 40, already the most celebrated woman pilot on Earth. She had been the first woman to solo across the Atlantic, the first to solo non-stop across the United States, the first to solo from Hawaii to California. She was determined to take up what she considered the ultimate challenge – flying 29,000 miles around the world.

On the first day of June she and her navigator Fred Noonan took off from Miami on the first leg of the trip headed for San Juan in Puerto Rico. From there she followed the north-east rim of South America, then headed north-east again to cross Africa at its widest point. Skirting the Persian Gulf, she proceeded on to Karachi and Calcutta and then to Rangoon, Bangkok, Singapore, Java, Port Darwin in northern Australia and finally Papua New Guinea. She now had covered over 22,000 miles.

Earhart knew the next leg flying eastward from New Guinea would be the most difficult one. Even with all inessentials removed from the plane to accommodate extra aviation fuel, she calculated that she had a safety margin of only about 10 per cent. But finding Howland Island would be challenging under the best of circumstances, a tiny dot in the wide Pacific just above the Equator, only a mile and a half long and half a mile wide.

The *Itasca* and three other ships were positioned as markers along her route. When they received her fuel shortage warning the *Itasca* changed its fuel mix to send heavy black smoke billowing upwards in the hope of providing the flyers with some sort of visual landmark, but the sky remained empty. As the hours ticked by it became certain that the plane had been lost.

President Franklin Roosevelt immediately dispatched nine ships and 66 aircraft to search 250,000 square miles of ocean, but no trace of the plane or its passengers was ever found.

Americans love conspiracies, and there were plenty put forward to explain Amelia Earhart's disappearance. Some claimed she had deliberately crashed into the ocean, while others maintained that she had been on a secret mission from President Roosevelt and had been captured by the Japanese. One bizarre notion was that she had been captured and then turned traitor, becoming the radio voice of Tokyo Rose during the war. For years there was 'hope' that she would be found on some isolated Pacific island, living with the natives.

Serious historians, however, are unanimous in their view that Earhart simply lost her way and crashed into the ocean when her fuel ran out. She had been well aware of the dangers she faced, writing to her husband shortly before her departure, 'Please know I am quite aware of the hazards ... Women must try to do things as men have tried. When they fail, their failure must be but a challenge to others.'

'Strangulatus pro republica': the murder of a president

1881 Today America's twentieth president, James Garfield, became the second to be mortally wounded by an assassin.

Garfield had been a brave soldier, attaining the rank of major general and fighting at Shiloh and Chickamauga during the American Civil War. He was first elected to the House of Representatives at the end of 1863, resigning from the army to take his seat. He later became a senator, and in March 1881 became President of the United States.

On 2 July, only four months after taking office, Garfield was standing quietly waiting for a train in the Baltimore and Potomac railway station in Washington when a disgruntled lawyer named Charles Guiteau shot him twice from behind at point blank range. Guiteau was a religious fanatic who claimed that killing the president was an act of high morality that would 'save the Republic'. In reality it seems that he was incensed because he had been refused the consular post he wanted.

Wounded in the arm and back, Garfield lay for weeks in the White House. By today's medical standards, his wounds would have been serious but not fatal, but in 1881 even surgeons had little true idea of hygiene, and Garfield contracted blood poisoning while doctors probed with unsterilised instruments.

By mid-July the president was clearly dying. Too weak to speak, he asked for pen and paper and scribbled, 'Strangulatus pro republica.' (Tortured for the republic.) He never spoke or wrote again.

In early autumn Garfield was moved to the New Jersey seaside to be with his family, but he died on 19 September, just two months before his 50th birthday. On 30 June the following year his assassin Charles Guiteau was hanged for the murder, his skeleton going to the Army Medical Museum.

Garfield was one of four American presidents who have been assassinated. The others were Abraham Lincoln in 1865, William McKinley in 1901 and John Kennedy in 1963. All were shot.

Also on this day

1566: Fortune-teller Nostradamus dies * 1644: The Roundheads defeat Prince Rupert and the Cavaliers at Marston Moor in the English Civil War * 1778: French philosopher Jean-Jacques Rousseau dies * 1850: British Prime Minister Robert Peel dies after being thrown from a horse * 1870: Italian King Victor Emmanuel II enters Rome on the unification of Italy

3 July

Birth of the Universal Spider

1423 Today in the city of Bourges the future Louis XI of France was born, a king remembered in history as 'the universal spider' for the plots he spun and the enemies he entrapped as he broke the feudal power of France's medieval barons.

Although fat and ugly, Louis was shrewd, intelligent, witty, devious and ruthless. He was informal at a time when pomp and ceremony were universally admired, and he had little respect for title or family. (He infuriated the nobility by sending his barber, the famous Olivier le Daim, as an ambassador.) Suspicious and superstitious, he suffered agonies from haemorrhoids and thought that lack of sex made them worse. Although devoutly religious, he still locked up the traitorous Cardinal Balue in an iron cage for over ten years.

During his reign of 22 years, Louis fought almost every powerful noble within reach. The list includes Holy Roman Emperor Frederick III, the Dukes of Bourbon, Armagnac and Brittany, Jean II of Aragon and his own brother, Charles of France. His most renowned enemy was Charles the Bold of Burgundy, who once held Louis prisoner but whom Louis eventually destroyed.

But the crafty Louis did not always have to do battle in order to best his foes. When England's Edward IV invaded France in 1475, Louis called for a parley and then arranged three days of sumptuous banquets and celebration with Edward and his captains before proposing a peace treaty. Then the cunning king offered Edward a pension in exchange for agreeing to recognise Louis's claim to all of France. Most pleased with this arrangement, Louis remarked to one of his courtiers, 'I have chased the English out of France more easily than even my father [Charles VII] did, for my father drove them out by force of arms, while I have driven them out with venison pies and good wine.'

Louis made the French monarchy more powerful than it had been since the time of Philip the Fair a century and a half before. He felt strongly about his rights and power as King of France and set the precedent for arrogance by French heads of state by telling his barons, 'I am France.' (In 1655 Louis XIV echoed this grand sentiment with his celebrated 'L'Etat c'est moi', and three centuries after that Charles de Gaulle proclaimed 'Je suis la France!' He subsequently maintained that 'When I want to know what France thinks, I ask myself.')

They gave the last full measure of devotion – the Battle of Gettysburg

1863 The Confederate General Robert E. Lee had heard that there were shoes to be found in the Pennsylvania town of Gettysburg and dispatched some troops to grab them. Unexpectedly, there they met a small contingent of Union General George Meade's army, and, rather by accident, the bloodiest battle in America's Civil War began.

When the Battle of Gettysburg finally bled itself to a halt two days later on 3 July, there had been a disastrous 23,000 Union casualties – but an even worse total of 28,000 Confederate killed, wounded or missing.

With 620,000 dead, the Civil War was America's bloodiest, although only a third died from battlefield wounds. The rest succumbed to sickness, principally dysentery, typhoid, pneumonia and malaria. In those days before much understanding of the connection between cleanliness and infection, any wound was likely to be fatal. More than 15 per cent of all wounded men died, compared with only 2 per cent in the Korean War and 0.25 per cent in Vietnam.

Death by disease, as frequent as it was, actually represented an improvement over previous wars. In the Crimean War four-fifths of all deaths were through disease, and, of the British who died in the Napoleonic Wars, eight men died of sickness for every victim of enemy fire.

Churchill wipes out the French fleet

1940 At 5.46 this evening, after a long day of unsuccessful negotiations, British Vice Admiral James Somerville gave his ships the order to open fire. Within ten minutes most of the powerful fleet anchored at the Algerian port of Mers-el-Kebir lay in ruins: one battleship blown up, two more beached, 1,250 sailors dead. Only a single battleship and a few destroyers managed to escape. What the British destroyed this day, however, was not the fleet of an enemy but that of their close ally, France.

Barely a month after Dunkirk and facing the prospect of imminent German invasion, Great Britain had to ensure that the fleet of recently defeated France would never fall into the hands of their common enemies, Germany and Italy. Despite assurances from Marshal Pétain, who had led his nation into capitulation to Germany, Prime Minister Winston Churchill ordered his fleet to issue this ultimatum to the French admiral at Mers-el-Kebir: Sail your ships to safety, in either England or the West Indies. Or scuttle them. Or Great Britain will sink them for you. Elsewhere British boarding parties seized French Navy vessels in Portsmouth and Plymouth and put their crews ashore. In Alexandria the French squadron disarmed itself under the orders of a British admiral.

Outraged by the humiliating loss of her fleet, France – now reduced by its armistice with Germany to the rump and puppet state of Vichy – broke off relations with Great Britain. Marshal Pétain complained to President Roosevelt of 'British aggression'. Many Frenchmen around the world now found themselves hating their former ally as much as they detested their conquerors. For General Charles de Gaulle, in London as the leader of the Free French, Mers-el-Kebir created a special problem. In the aftermath of Dunkirk, there were thousands of French soldiers and sailors in England. From among these and from among other Frenchmen in France's African colonies, he had been endeavouring to recruit a military force that would carry on France's fight alongside Great Britain. But after Mers-el-Kebir, could de Gaulle – could any Frenchman – remain on the side of his country's latest attacker?

De Gaulle was disheartened by the 'lamentable event', all the more so that the British treated it as a victory. Nevertheless, a few nights later when he spoke to his countrymen over the BBC, he told them this: 'Come what may, even if for a time one of them is bowed under the yoke of the common foe, our two peoples – our two *great* peoples – are still linked together. Either they will both succumb or they will triumph side by side.'

For his efforts, Vichy France sentenced de Gaulle to death for his 'refusals to obey orders in the presence of the enemy and inciting members of the armed forces to disobedience'. In the end, of course, it was a liberated France that sentenced Marshal Pétain to death for his role as a collaborator with Nazi Germany, a sentence commuted to life imprisonment by General de Gaulle.

Also on this day

1853: Russia invades Moldavia to start the Crimean War * 1866: Venice becomes part of a united Kingdom of Italy

4 July

Thomas Jefferson and John Adams die on Independence Day

1826 Today the United States reached its 50th birthday, firm in democracy, independence and progress. Instead of the thirteen original states, now there were 24, including two west of the Mississippi. The population had quintupled to 12 million, the country was at peace and one of its great selfless servants, John Quincy Adams, was President.

It had been hoped that celebrations in Washington would be embellished by two of the nation's surviving founders, John Adams, second president, signer of the Declaration of Independence and father of the current president, and Thomas Jefferson, America's greatest political thinker, author and signer of the Declaration of Independence and third president. But Adams was 90, living quietly in Quincy, Massachusetts, while Jefferson at 83 had long since retired to his beloved Monticello in Virginia.

So Washington had to celebrate without these two great men. It was only two days later that the news finally arrived: Jefferson had died quietly at one o'clock in the afternoon on 4 July, and John Adams followed him shortly

365: YOUR DATE WITH HISTORY

before six. A poignant aside, among Adams's last words were 'Jefferson survives'.

John Quincy Adams interpreted this strange and solemn marking of America's 50th birthday as a 'visible and palpable' indication of divine favour to the two departed founders and to the nation they had helped to create.

Saladin triumphs at the Horns of Hattin

1187 The Horns of Hattin, so named because of two large hills, lie just a few miles west of the Sea of Galilee in northern Palestine, and it was there that today that most famous Saracen, Saladin, totally destroyed the power of the Christian Kingdom of Jerusalem.

Like all the Saracen leaders, Saladin was a Kurdish Turk. He had once served as a young officer under Nur ed-Din, the ruler of Syria, and on Nur ed-Din's death in 1174, Saladin became the leader of Muslim orthodoxy in the Middle East.

During the evening of 3 July 1187 Saladin's great army completely surrounded the smaller Christian one under the command of the King of Jerusalem, Guy de Lusignan. An eye-witness tells the tale: 'As soon as they [the Christian army] were encamped, Saladin ordered all his men to collect brushwood, dry grass, stubble and anything else with which they could light fires, and make barriers which he had made all round the Christians. They soon did this, and the fires burned vigorously and the smoke from the fires was great; and this, together with the heat of the sun above them caused them discomfort and great harm. Saladin had commanded caravans of camels loaded with water from the Sea of Tiberias to be brought up and had water pots placed near the camp. The water pots were then emptied in view of the Christians so that they should have still greater anguish through thirst, and their mounts too ... When the fires were lit and the smoke was great, the Saracens surrounded the host and shot their darts through the smoke and so wounded and killed men and horses.'

By the next morning the Christians were dying and desperate. King Guy had no choice but to attack the larger enemy force. A division of knights 'charged at a large squadron of Saracens. The Saracens parted and made a way through and let them pass; then, when they were in the middle of them, they surrounded them. Only 10 or 12 knights ... escaped them ... After this division had been defeated the anger of God was so great against the Christian host because of their sins that Saladin vanquished them quickly; between the hours of tierce and nones [9 a.m. and 3 p.m.] he had won almost all the field.'

Most of the European nobles who survived, including the King of Jerusalem, were captured and held to ransom. The Christian army was totally destroyed, and 15,000 foot soldiers were sold into slavery. Of the Knights Templar and Hospitaller who were taken prisoner, all were slain, as they would never convert to Islam and had no hope of raising ransom.

Three months later Jerusalem fell to Saladin after 88 years of Christian rule.

When the news reached Europe, the Christian world went into shock. According to contemporary testimony, 'Pope Urban [III] who was at Ferrara died of grief when he heard the news. After him was Gregory VIII who was of saintly life and only held the see for two months before he died and went to God.'

Barbarossa the pirate dies in bed

1546 There would seem to be little poetic justice in the death on this day of history's most notorious pirate, Barbarossa, who passed away from an attack of fever in his opulent palace in Constantinople at the ripe old age of 82, wealthy and rich in honours.

Barbarossa, whose original name was Khidr, was a Turk from the island of Lesbos (then under Turkish rule). He seems to have been raised a Christian, but he first came to fame rallying the Moors of North Africa to scourge the coastal towns of Spain.

Later Barbarossa became de facto chief admiral for the Turkish navy under Suleiman the Magnificent, but his methods remained piratical. Barbarous Barbarossa (so named because of his bushy red beard) harried the coasts of Italy, Greece and France, plundering any town he entered, carrying off slaves and mercilessly slaughtering those who resisted or who were of no value for sale. In one Italian raid alone he sailed away with 10,000 captives to be sold in the slave markets of Constantinople. But Barbarossa was also extremely successful as an admiral, once defeating the fleet of Emperor Charles V and once conquering all of Tunis. At the height of his power he captured and sacked Nice.

Like pirates before and after him, Barbarossa had an eye for young virgins. But the famous pirate seemed concerned for their souls. It was said that he forced them to avow conversion to Islam before they were raped – and before their throats were cut.

The world's oldest republic is born

1776 Today the world's oldest republic came into being, as twelve of the thirteen American states formally approved the Declaration of Independence, freeing themselves from the yoke of British tyranny and creating the United States as a separate nation. The thirteenth state, New York, signed on eleven days later, when its representative received instructions from home.

Although the Declaration of Independence was approved and in force, it was not actually signed by the states' delegates until 2 August. Then, in Independence Hall in Philadelphia, the diminutive John Hancock of Massachusetts, who was President of the Continental Congress, stepped forward to be the first to sign. There are two versions of his comments, both full of patriotic bravado:

- 'There, I guess King George will be able to read that.'
- 'There! John Bull can read my name without spectacles and may now double his reward of £500 for my head. That is my defiance.'

Hancock then urged all the delegates to sign immediately, saying, 'We must be unanimous, there must be no pulling different ways; we must all hang together.'

'Yes,' replied Benjamin Franklin, 'we must indeed all hang together, or most assuredly we shall all hang separately.' Subsequently 55 other delegates added their signatures.

Sadly there is more than a suggestion that both of Hancock's comments are apocryphal, and the same can be said for Franklin's great reply – it was first related only in 1840.

Also on this day

1190: English King Richard the Lion-Heart and French King Philip Augustus leave together on crusade * 1807: Italian revolutionary Giuseppe Garibaldi is born

5 July

Napoleon's last victory

1809 A map of Paris is virtually a monument to the Emperor Napoleon. Almost 30 streets are named after his generals, the Avenue de la Grand Armée honours his army, the sixth arrondisement boasts a rue Bonaparte, a street where he lived was re-christened rue de la Victoire, and all Napoleon's military glory is commemorated together in the Arc de Triomphe. On top of that, twelve of his great victories are commemorated in place names: there are streets called Castiglione, Arcole, Rivoli, Pyramides (as well as a square), Aboukir, Marengo and Ulm. His most famous triumph, Austerlitz, has a street, a bridge, a port, a quay and even a railway station. Then comes Iéna with a walk, a square and a bridge and finally there are the avenues – Eylau (which is also a villa), Friedland and Wagram.

The last of these, Wagram, was fought today outside Vienna, and it was indeed the last, for Napoleon never won another major victory.

Wagram was a bloody, two-day battle fought by huge armies in terrible midsummer heat. It was especially notable for the massed artillery fire with which Napoleon buttressed the uncertain performance of his Saxon and Italian units; and for the extraordinary feats his engineers performed in bridging the Danube, which allowed the 188,000 soldiers and 488 guns of the Grande Armée to make a timely night crossing to the battlefield. The Austrian army, 155,000 soldiers under the command of Archduke Charles, was decisively defeated but withdrew intact. Six days later Austria asked for an armistice, which Napoleon granted.

Battle losses were extensive: over 32,000 killed, wounded or captured for the Grande Armée, almost 40,000 for the Austrian army. Among the Austrian casualties of war might be counted the great composer Joseph Haydn, aged 77, who died of shock and humiliation at the French occupation of his beloved Vienna.

In the peace treaty that followed the end of hostilities, the Austrian Emperor Franz I was forced to pay a heavy war indemnity and to cede huge tracts of territory – including Salzburg, part of Galicia, Trieste and the Dalmatian coast – to France and her allies.

Eager to celebrate his victory, Napoleon sent for his Polish mistress Marie Walewska, installed her in the Schönbrunn Palace outside Vienna, and to his delight – and relief – quickly impregnated her, thus demonstrating that he was not sterile. The happy news prompted him to consider the prospect of a new marriage, one that would produce an heir to his empire. The news was less happy for Marie and the Empress Joséphine, both of whom would be cast aside for a new empress. She turned out to be a daughter of the Austrian Emperor, the Archduchess Marie Louise, whom Napoleon married the following April.

Finally, the Russian Tsar Alexander I, on hearing of Wagram and its aftermath, drew the prescient conclusion that the Austrians had been too quick to capitulate. 'People don't know how to suffer', the Tsar remarked to an aide-de-camp. 'If the fighting went against me, I should retire to Kamchatka rather than cede provinces and sign, in my capital, treaties that were really only truces. Your Frenchman is brave; but long privations and a bad climate will wear him down and discourage him. Our climate, our winter, will fight on our side.' Paris boasts no rue de la Russie.

Also on this day

1810: American showman P.T. Barnum is born * 1853: British empire builder Cecil Rhodes is born * 1950: American forces engage the North Koreans for the first time at Osan, South Korea

6 July

The first Plantagenet king dies at Chinon

1189 The River Vienne runs just south of the Loire, and on its north bank stand the grey and forbidding remains of the fortress of Chinon. No renaissance jewel box this château, but 400 yards of impregnable defence from the Middle Ages, dominating the river below it.

Although the site has been fortified since Roman times, the oldest part of the fortress yet standing is the Fort St Georges, built by that great English King, Henry II, who died there on this day over 800 years ago.

When Henry retreated to Chinon for the last time, he was an old man by the standards of the day (he was 56) and he had just been humiliated by the young French King, Philip Augustus, who was allied with Henry's own son, Richard the Lion-Heart. Sick in body and spirit, Henry had had to be carried to the fortress in a litter, and there he learned that among his enemies in league with the French was also his youngest son, the treacherous John.

Lying on a rude bed, Henry turned to face the wall. 'Shame, shame,' he muttered, 'shame on a conquered king.'

So died Henry, the king who had ruled England and virtually the whole of western France for 35 years and who had founded the Plantagenet dynasty which was to last 332 years, longer than any other English dynasty before or since.

Sir Thomas More is beheaded

1535 On this day Sir Thomas More, writer, humanist philosopher and one-time Lord Chancellor to Henry VIII, met his end under the axe in the Tower of London. His crime had been double: he refused to support Henry's claim to supremacy over the Pope, and he refused to attend the King's marriage to Anne Boleyn, with the implication that Henry was still married to Catherine of Aragon.

Brought to trial for treason, More's conviction was never in doubt; three of the judges were Anne Boleyn's father, uncle and brother. For good measure, the prosecution used perjured testimony. Nothing better expresses the tyranny and callous injustice of Henry's reign than Sir Richard Riche's accusation condemning More's refusal to speak: 'Even though we should have no word or deed to charge against you, yet we have your silence, and that is a sign of your evil intention and a sure proof of malice.' But the ultimate cause of the conviction was the simple fact that Henry wanted it.

More kept his equanimity to the very end. As he walked to the scaffold on Tower Hill he said to his guard, 'See me safe up, and for my coming down let me shift for myself.' He then tied his own blindfold.

As he knelt to put his head on the block, More pushed aside his long beard, saying, 'it has never committed treason'. Then, turning to the executioner, he spoke for the last time. 'Pluck up thy spirits, man, and be not afraid to do thine office; my neck is very short; take heed therefore thou strike not awry, for saving of thine honesty.' And then the axe fell and one of the 16th century's noblest men was dead at the age of 57.

Four hundred years later, More, the man whom Erasmus had dubbed 'a man for all seasons', was declared a saint.

A tsar is strangled in his cell

1762 Only nine days earlier Catherine the Great of Russia had orchestrated a bloodless *coup d'état* with the help of her lover Grigory Orlov to become

Empress of Russia. Her hapless husband, Tsar Peter III, was sent under guard to a fortress prison at Ropsha, comforted only by his servants and his pet dog.

But Peter, although hopeless as a ruler, was deadly dangerous as a prisoner, an eternal threat to the usurper Catherine. So Orlov's brother Aleksei was sent to Ropsha.

Aleksei and two soldiers under his command entered the bedroom where Peter was held. The soldiers seized the Tsar and tried to smother him between two feather mattresses, but, although frail and small, the desperate Peter somehow threw them off and stood at bay, exhausted, in a corner of the room. Aleksei then threw himself on the royal prisoner and strangled him with his own huge hands.

The two soldiers who had been unable to smother Peter died the same day, not for their failure but to ensure secrecy of the deed. Both had been secretly poisoned just before they were ordered to execute the Tsar.

Catherine always claimed that she had no foreknowledge of this murder, but her plea of innocence sounds at best like that of Henry II about the murder of Thomas Becket – an expression of will, without a direct order. She publicly attributed the death to 'haemorrhoidal colic', clearly a fabrication that was believed by almost no one.

Peter III has the distinction of being the first Russian tsar to be murdered. But not the last. Four more were to be assassinated, including his own son 39 years later.

Also on this day

1415: Czech religious reformer Jan Hus is burned at the stake * 1685: The army of James II defeats the rebel Duke of Monmouth in the last land battle ever fought on British soil

7 July

The shot that started the Second World War

1937 The First World War began one morning in Sarajevo with the killing of an archduke. The Second World War began one night at a railway junction in China with the killing of a common soldier.

Twelve miles west of Peking, there is a place called Lukouchaio, where the railway line from Tientsin joins the Peking–Hankow line. It is in an area of northern China that had been ceded for commercial exploitation to Japan under a 1933 treaty. On the night of 7 July a brigade of the Japanese Kwantung Army was conducting night exercises in the area. At some point, a shot rang out, and not long afterwards Japanese troops discovered the dead body of one of their comrades lying near the ancient Marco Polo Bridge.

It has never been established who killed the soldier, but the Japanese government chose to make the China Incident, as it referred to the event, a *casus belli*. It presented China with an ultimatum: agree by 18 July to hand over the two northern provinces of Hopei and Chahar or Japan would act.

The only question now was what Chiang Kai-shek, the leader of Nationalist China, would do. Over the past decade the Generalissimo had shown reluctance to tangle with the Japanese over their numerous grabs of Chinese territory, preferring to pursue civil war against the Communists while waiting for the Western powers to help him defeat both of his foes.

Some seven months earlier, however, Chiang had experienced something rarely encountered by heads of state: he had been kidnapped by one of his own generals who wanted to force Chiang to abandon the civil war and form a united front against Japan. To preserve face, it was important for Chiang to avoid giving the impression of having secured his release by making a political bargain with his kidnapper. But there was no doubt that he had.

In the face of the Japanese ultimatum, there was initial silence from Nanking, the Nationalist capital. When at last Chiang responded, it was no ringing declaration, no call to arms for his people. He did nothing beyond stating that no more Chinese territory would be surrendered to Japan, but the implication of his words seemed clear: armed resistance would meet another incursion. At least that is how the residents of Peking interpreted the broadcast of Chiang's message, for they ran into the streets cheering and beating gongs.

A few days later Japan began the invasion of China, for which she had long planned, needing only a China Incident to begin it. Ten thousand of her troops crossed over the Great Wall and advanced into Hopei province. At first, the conflict was known as the Second Sino-Japanese War, but in a few years the world would come to see it as the first act of the Second World War.

Joan of Arc – innocent at last!

1456 When Charles VII finally expelled the English from France, he decided to cleanse the name of his kingdom by ordering a new trial for the girl who had saved it, Joan of Arc.

The new trial took six years, but finally on 7 July 1456 Joan was declared innocent of all crimes, body and soul. The new verdict was announced in the archbishop's palace at Rouen, where previously she had been condemned as sorceress, idolatress and relapsed heretic. Unfortunately for Joan, she had been burned at the stake 25 years earlier.

Also on this day

1860: Austrian composer Gustav Mahler is born in Kaliste, Czechoslovakia * 1887: Russian painter Marc Chagall is born

8 July

Peter the Great crushes the Swedes at Poltava

1709 The 8th of July brought mixed fortunes for Russia's Peter the Great. In 1695 when he was 23 he experienced his first real battle – and lost – against the Turks at Azov. In 1709 he was 37 and at war again, this time against one of the great soldier-kings of history, Charles XII of Sweden.

Charles had inherited Sweden's throne when he was just fifteen and ruled as an absolute monarch. By the time he was 27 in 1709 he had transformed Sweden into a great European power through a series of wars against Poland, Russia and various German states that came to be known as the Great Northern War.

On 8 July 1709 Charles's small army of only 17,000 men attacked a Russian fortified camp under Peter's command at Poltava in the Ukraine. The Swedes had two distinct disadvantages. First, their army, already tired and battle-weary, was massively outnumbered by Peter's 80,000 troops, and, second, Charles himself could not personally lead his army as was his custom because he had earlier sustained a wound in the left foot and had to be carried on a litter between two horses.

The Russians gave way before the initial Swedish assault, then launched 40,000 men in a devastating counter-attack that obliterated the Swedes. The shattered Swedish survivors retreated southwards and finally capitulated at the River Dnjestr outside the village of Perevolotjna four days later. Charles himself managed to escape with about 1,500 of his soldiers and took refuge in Turkey, where he was obliged to remain for the next six years.

Peter the Great's victory marked the start of Sweden's decline from the dominant nation of northern Europe to the lesser nation that it has remained ever since. Poltava also marked Russia's ascendancy, one that it has never relinquished.

Ernest Hemingway's wound inspires a great novel

1918 Shortly after midnight at Fossalta on the Piave front in northern Italy, an Austrian mortar shell exploded near a lonely farmhouse that was serving as a canteen for Italian soldiers. Among the casualties was an American Red Cross driver named Ernest Hemingway, severely wounded by shrapnel. An ambulance took him to a field hospital in Treviso, where he was transferred by train to Milan and the Ospedale Croce Rossa Americana. Here young Hemingway, just nineteen years old, underwent two operations, and then did what all wounded men at war are supposed to do: he fell in love with his nurse.

She was 26-year-old Agnes Korowsky, of Washington, DC. Their affair, such as it was, was enjoyable, but rather one-sided (his), and brief. Ernest went home to Oak Park, Illinois, in January 1919, and began the process of transforming himself into a war hero. Agnes stayed on in Italy as a nurse, and in March wrote him a 'Dear John' letter. For the world at large, however, it may have been the best way for things to turn out, because eventually Hemingway would write about his experiences – in Italy, being wounded, falling in love – and put them in a book that has one of the most memorable openings of any modern novel:

> 'In the late summer of that year we lived in a house in the village that looked across the river and the plain to the mountains. In the bed of the river there were pebbles and boulders, dry and white in the sun, and the water was clear and swiftly moving and blue in the channels. Troops went by the house and down the road and the dust they raised powdered the leaves of the trees. The trunks of trees too were dusty and the leaves fell early that year and we saw the troops marching along the road and the dust rising and leaves, stirred by the breeze, falling and the soldiers marching and afterward the road bare and white except for the leaves.'

It is the beginning of *A Farewell to Arms*.

Also on this day

1521: Ferdinand von Habsburg marries Anne of Hungary, leading to the incorporation of Hungary into the Austrian Empire * 1822: English poet Percy Bysshe Shelley drowns off Leghorn, Italy * 1839: American oil tycoon John D. Rockefeller is born

9 July

The end of the Medici

1737 For thirteen years Gian Gastone de' Medici had ruled as Grand Duke of Tuscany, but his few well-intentioned efforts to rebuild his state were washed away by his laziness, his alcoholism and his taste for bright young boys. Florence was now a bankrupt backwater, with only the jewels of its buildings and art treasures to remind the world of its vanished greatness, and Gian Gastone himself was the only reminder of the great Medici family that had been so vital in creating that greatness.

Since Cosimo the Elder had first dominated Florence in 1434, the Medici had produced a vast array of illustrious and prominent people. The most famous undoubtedly was Lorenzo the Magnificent, Cosimo's grandson, the greatest art patron the world has known. Lorenzo's son Giovanni became Pope Leo X, the first of the Medici popes. Later came Clement VII, the illegitimate grandson of Lorenzo's father, and finally Leo XI, Lorenzo's great-grandson.

Other illustrious Medici include Alessandro, Duke of Florence (the illegitimate son of the illegitimate Pope Clement VII), and two queens of France, first Catherine de' Medici (Lorenzo's great-granddaughter) and then Marie, a distant cousin.

By 1569 the Medici were so powerful that another Cosimo, descended from Cosimo the Elder's brother, became the Duke of Tuscany. He was followed by five more Grand Dukes, of which the last was Gian Gastone.

In 1737 Gian Gastone was a tired 65. Given his predilection for boys, it is not surprising that he was childless. He spent most of his days in bed, beard straggling and body unwashed. Thus it was almost expected when death came to him on 9 July. And so the great Medici family came to an end after 303 years of pre-eminence.

Also on this day

1497: Portuguese navigator Vasco da Gama leaves the River Tagus on a historic voyage to India via the Cape of Good Hope * 1553: Lady Jane Grey is proclaimed Queen

10 July

El Cid's last great (posthumous) victory

1099 Greatest of Spanish folk heroes, knight and conqueror, scourge of the Moors, faithful defender of Christian Spain. Such is the legend of Roderigo Díaz de Bivar, known to history as El Cid.

El Cid was in fact a mercenary warlord who fought for the Moors as well as against them. Even his popular name is revealing: El Cid comes from *Cid-y*, meaning 'my lord' in Arabic. But whoever's side he was on, El Cid was one of the most powerful figures in 11th-century Spain and undoubtedly its greatest general. He played an important role in saving his country from complete Moorish domination.

Although myth makes El Cid a noble knight on a par with King Arthur, the truth is less glorious. When he conquered Valencia from the Moors, he promised the Moorish commander Ibn Jahhaf that he would be spared. But as soon as he had fully taken over the town he had Ibn Jahhaf burned alive.

Many legends surround El Cid but none greater than that of his death on this day in Valencia, which he ruled.

Ailing and middle-aged (he was 56), El Cid died while the city was under siege from King Bucar and a vast Moorish army. But, following his deathbed instructions, El Cid's generals waited twelve days and then strapped his armoured body upright on his faithful horse Bavieca. At midnight, with El Cid in the lead, the entire army rode out through the city gates. Then, as the noble corpse moved forward with the baggage train, the Spanish knights turned and attacked the sleeping Moors from behind.

According to the *Chronica del Cid*, an almost contemporary account, 'it seemed to King Bucar that before them came a knight of great stature upon a white horse with a bloody cross, who bore in one hand a white banner and in the other a sword which seemed of fire and he made great mortality among the Moors ... And King Bucar and the other kings were so dismayed they never checked the reins until they had ridden into the sea.'

After the Moors had fled, El Cid's body was taken to the monastery of San Pedro de Cardeña, near Burgos, where for ten years it remained seated on an ivory chair before receiving proper burial. Not surprisingly, a superstitious cult soon grew up around the tomb.

El Cid's posthumous triumph in Valencia was not to last. The Moors reoccupied the city less than three years later and controlled it until 1238.

El Cid lives on in Spanish legend, and he is celebrated in the most famous Spanish epic poem, *El Cantar de mío Cid* (The Song of the Cid). Over 500 years later Pierre Corneille commemorated him again in his great drama *Le Cid*.

The Battle of Britain

1940 On this morning 70 German bombers with fighter escorts took off from airfields in France and Belgium to attack a convoy in the English Channel. So began the contest of air forces known as the Battle of Britain. Hitler, his air force commander Reichsmarschall Hermann Göring and other Luftwaffe commanders thought it would be a quick and easy knockout punch, four days to destroy the Royal Air Force – then on to Act Two, Operation Sea Lion, the invasion of Great Britain. Invasion barges were being collected, in French and Low Country ports.

Indeed, the Germans had good reasons to be optimistic, for in the last ten months the Wehrmacht had conquered Poland, Denmark, Norway, Holland, Belgium and France.

Only a month before, at Dunkirk, it had kicked the British army right out of Europe. As for the Luftwaffe itself, while the toll on its resources from the French campaign had been heavy, it was well blooded, its morale was high, and in fighter aircraft it outnumbered the RAF.

In this analysis, however, there were some factors the German high command did not – perhaps at the time could not – take into account. One was that the Luftwaffe's successes had been gained in support of ground operations, and it had never carried out a strategic air campaign. Then there was the matter of British technology: outnumbered as it might be in planes and pilots, the RAF had developed a radar-based air defence system far more comprehensive than anything the Luftwaffe had ever encountered. Finally, there was the quality of the pilots of RAF Fighter Command who would be scrambling in their Spitfires and Hurricanes to meet the invaders.

The German offensive began with daylight bomber attacks on coastal targets, such as ports, convoys and aircraft factories. The object was to lure the RAF fighters out over the Channel where German fighters could shoot them down in sufficient numbers to establish command of the air. When in early August it became clear that this strategy was not working, Göring gave new targeting orders: fly further inland and hit RAF airfields, radar stations, control centres and depots. This second phase, a battle of attrition fought between the two air forces at an absolutely furious pace, came near at times to putting the RAF out of business.

German losses, however, were also very heavy. In early September, just when it appeared that the Luftwaffe, if it persisted, might be close to achieving air superiority, Hitler gave orders to switch the main effort from airfields and radar stations to the city of London as a quicker way of bringing the British to their knees. The destruction and loss of life from these city raids was frightful, but British morale did not crumble. Moreover, the new orders simplified Fighter Command's task by giving it a chance to concentrate its forces in the defence of the new German objective. When on 15 September a large German raid over London lost 56 aircraft, it was apparent that the RAF was still very much in business. There would be no knockout punch. Luftwaffe losses began to increase. By the end of the month it switched from daylight to mainly night raids. On 12 October Operation Sea Lion, already postponed several times, was cancelled. Overall losses by the end of October were 1,733 German planes shot down against 915 British.

As the year drew to a close, it became clear the battle was won. The invasion barges were put away. Hitler, defeated for the first time, turned his gaze eastward. And Churchill, addressing the House of Commons, said of RAF Fighter Command: 'Never, in the field of human conflict, was so much owed by so many to so few.'

Also on this day

AD 138: Roman Emperor Hadrian dies at Baiae * 1509: Founder of Calvinism John Calvin is born * 1830: French painter Camille Pissarro is born * 1871: French novelist Marcel Proust is born

11 July

The most famous duel in American history

1804 Alexander Hamilton may have been the most influential American politician who never attained the presidency. His vision of America as a powerful and prosperous industrial nation governed by a strong central government formed the basis for the economic and political system that still exists.

But during his career, Hamilton made a bitter enemy of Aaron Burr, another New York politician who favoured a more pastoral, decentralised America.

In 1799 Hamilton's influence helped gain the presidency for Thomas

Jefferson, and Burr had to settle for the vice-presidency. Four years later Hamilton helped thwart Burr's hopes of becoming governor of New York.

Hating Hamilton for his influence – and for his attacks on his honesty – Burr challenged him to America's most famous duel.

At dawn on 11 July, the two adversaries and their seconds were rowed across the Hudson River to Weehawken in New Jersey – duels were illegal in New York. By morbid coincidence, it was the same spot where Hamilton's son had been killed in a duel three years before. Grimly they measured their positions, pistols in hand. The time was just 7.30.

Two shots broke the morning calm. Hamilton's was wide, but Burr's aim was true, and Hamilton fell, clutching his stomach, blood seeping through his fingers.

Although constantly attended by a surgeon, Hamilton died 28 hours later, at the age of only 49. Burr lived on another 32 years, the only American vice-president to fight a duel (although one president, Andrew Jackson, killed a man in a duel before he became president). The dead Hamilton had more influence over his nation than the man who shot him and survived.

The Battle of the Golden Spurs

1302 The people of Flanders were in revolt against their overlord, King Philip the Fair of France. To teach the Flemings a lesson, Philip dispatched 2,000 armoured knights plus a large troop of infantry under the command of his uncle, Robert of Artois, the greatest warrior in France.

Desperate, the Flemings formed a motley army of about 10,000 untrained workmen and artisans, mostly from the weavers' guild, armed with pikes and staves.

When the two forces met at Courtrai on this day, the Flemings, who knew the terrain far better than the French, took their stand on a patch of marshy ground surrounded by streams. The French cavalry tried to charge, but the horses could make no headway as their hooves sank into the soft ground. The Flemings then swarmed over the French knights before the French infantry could come forward.

The weavers and workmen had no use for the rules of chivalry; no prisoners were taken. At the end of the battle Robert of Artois was knocked from his charger. Dropping his sword, he cried, 'Prenez, prenez le compte d'Artois, il vous fera riches!' (Take him, take the Count of Artois, he will make you rich!) But he was instantly pierced by Flemish pikes.

In all, some 1,200 French knights were slaughtered. At the end of the day the Flemings gathered over 700 'golden' spurs from the field of battle and hung them in the vault of Our Lady's Church in Courtrai. Ever since, this mighty victory by Flemish artisans over the flower of French knighthood has been known as the Battle of the Golden Spurs.

Also on this day
1274: Scottish King Robert the Bruce is born * 1754: Language bowdleriser Thomas
Bowdler is born

12 July

The birth of Julius Caesar

100 BC Born today was Gaius Julius Caesar, the greatest man of ancient times,
perhaps of all time. He came from an aristocratic Roman family that fancied it
could trace its lineage back through Aeneas to his mother, the goddess Venus.
For all that, the Julian family was not particularly rich, and Caesar achieved what
he did through a combination of outstanding intelligence, brilliant generalship,
hard calculation and the ability to make men, especially his soldiers, love him.
He was an outstanding swordsman and horseman and totally fearless in battle,
always leading from the front, wearing a scarlet cape so that his men could see
him. The great Roman statesman Cicero called him 'an instrument of wrath,
terrifying in his vigilance, swiftness and energy'.

Caesar was tall, fair and well-built with brown eyes. His only physical defects
seem to have been that he suffered from epileptic fits and in later life started to
go bald.

Caesar demonstrated his cool courage and colder determination early in life.
Still in his teens, he was en route to Rhodes to study when he was captured by
pirates. He charmed the pirates and scolded them for setting his ransom too
low, telling them that he was worth far more than they imagined. In apparent
jest, he also promised that he would crucify them all when he was released, a
threat he carried out by raising a naval force at his own expense and hunting
them down. His only show of mercy was to have their throats cut before
crucifixion.

Although Caesar was an unparalleled womaniser, there were rumours that
he bedded men as well. These stemmed from time spent in his youth in
Bithynia in the company of the effeminate King Nicomedes. Later in life, when
Caesar had become a power in Rome, one of his political enemies jibed that he
was 'the Queen of Bithynia, who once wanted to sleep with a king and now
wants to be one'.

Caesar changed the course of history twice, once by conquering Gaul, where
for nine years he was the governor, thereby turning France into a Latin nation,
and once by assuming the dictatorship of Rome, ending for ever the Roman
Republic. Although he was never a Roman emperor, to this day derivations of
his name mean emperor, as in 'kaiser' in German and 'tsar' in Russian.

In 45 BC Caesar instituted the Julian calendar, which was in universal use
until 1582. (At the time Cicero joked, 'Even the stars now obey Caesar in his
commands.') Although the calendar itself has been superseded, we still have the

month of July, named after the great man who was born on the twelfth day of it. Contrary to common belief, however, Caesar was not delivered by Caesarean. Two thousand years ago such an operation was invariably fatal to the mother, and we know that Caesar's mother lived until he was an adult.

Also on this day

1536: Dutch humanist Desiderius Erasmus dies * 1730: American writer Henry David Thoreau is born * 1884: Italian painter Amadeo Modigliani is born

13 July

Charlotte Corday stabs Marat in his bath

1793 Although born in Switzerland to a Swiss mother and Sardinian father, Jean Paul Marat eventually became one of France's most fanatical and implacable revolutionaries.

Marat's early history suggested a more conventional life. In his 30s he moved to London, becoming an eminent physician as well as the author of a number of scientific books. At 34 he returned to Paris to become doctor to the personal guards of Louis XVI's brother, the future Charles X. He continued to conduct scientific experiments and publish learned tracts while attracting patients from the upper classes. He even corresponded with Benjamin Franklin.

Marat had an exaggerated view of his own achievements, considering himself superior to Sir Isaac Newton. But few shared this exalted opinion, and he was rejected by the Académie des Sciences. Over the years he came to feel not only unappreciated but betrayed by the world in which he lived and blamed it on the French aristocracy that set the standards. The more he considered the injustices done to him, the more he related them to social injustices done to the people. He became a revolutionary.

In the 1780s he turned to publishing, becoming the editor of the incendiary newspaper *L'Ami du Peuple*. By 1790 he was telling the public, 'Five or six hundred heads cut off would assure your repose, freedom, and happiness.'

Forty-nine years old in the summer of 1793, Marat was a dark, intense man who suffered terribly from open sores on his face and body, the result of prurigo contracted while hiding in the Paris sewers earlier in the Revolution. This affliction caused him great pain, and the only relief available to him was through soaking in the bath.

On this day in 1793 Marat was taking just such a therapeutic bath at his house at 30 rue des Cordeliers when a servant handed him a note. 'Have the goodness to receive me,' it read, 'I can help you to render a great service to France.' Intrigued, he agreed to see the visitor, a young aristocrat from Caen named Charlotte Corday.

Although of noble family, Charlotte Corday was a strong believer in democracy, but she thought Marat was leading France into radicalism and anarchy. Entering the room where he was bathing, she at first pretended to reveal secret information, naming putative royalists in Caen. Marat smiled and unknowingly guaranteed his own death with the response, 'They shall all go to the guillotine.'

Pulling a dinner knife from her bodice, Corday stabbed Marat to the heart, killing him instantly. Four days later she went calmly to the guillotine for her deed.

Jacques Louis David immortalised the murder in one of his greatest paintings. Like Marat, David was a radical member of the National Convention, and thus the painting is perhaps the only one of a murder painted by a great artist who actually knew the victim he portrayed.

In death Marat became a national hero, with 21 towns named in his honour (of which only one remains). In recognition of his revolutionary fervour, the Soviet Navy named one of its first battleships after him.

Bismarck starts a war with the Ems telegram

1870 This is a day to be noted by all editors, speechwriters, spin-doctors and the like for the splendid – or cautionary, if you prefer – example it provides of what a few word changes can do to the fate of nations.

The editor in this case was Otto von Bismarck, Prime Minister of Prussia, a kingdom on the verge of becoming an empire but needing just that foreign threat that would induce the remaining German states to join it. As it happened, the throne of Spain was vacant, and Bismarck had recently proposed a certain German prince, a cousin of King Wilhelm of Prussia, as a candidate. France, alarmed at the prospect of encirclement by Hohenzollerns, protested strongly. Wilhelm, having no wish for war – that would be a task for his grandson, he joked – instructed Bismarck to withdraw the candidate.

But bellicosity was in the Paris air, and the Second Empire desired more than a withdrawal from its rival, Prussia. Napoleon III, believing in the invincibility of French arms, wanted a brilliant coup – diplomatic or military – that would show the world who was top dog in Europe, thereby restoring his regime's reputation at home and abroad. So the French ambassador to Prussia, Count Benedetti, was instructed to press King Wilhelm not only for confirmation of the withdrawal but also for 'assurance that he will never authorise a renewal of the candidacy'.

Benedetti went to Bad Ems, where Wilhelm was taking the waters. The King treated him with his customary courtesy, but declined to offer such a guarantee. He also refused the ambassador's request for a further audience with him on the subject. Afterwards, the King had a telegram sent to Bismarck in Berlin giving him an account of the meeting.

Bismarck read the message. Attuned to French sensibilities in the matter, he revised the account, eliminating any hint of the consideration with which the

King had received Benedetti, thereby making it appear as if Wilhelm had delivered a humiliating snub. Then he released this edited version of the Ems telegram, as it is known to history, to the Berlin press, and thence to the world. It was the Merlin touch.

The next day was the sacred Bastille Day in France. French papers emblazoned the now-insulting telegram on their front pages. *A Berlin! Vive la guerre!* And so, on this flimsy *casus belli*, France declared war against Germany on the 15th.

France lost the war, an emperor, and Alsace-Lorraine. What France lost, Prussia won, and her King became Kaiser Wilhelm of Germany, crowned insultingly on French soil. A great editor, that Bismarck!

The last of the Stuarts

1807 At two in the morning on this day a frail, helpless Henry Stuart slipped from life at the exalted age of 82 at his castle in La Rocca near Rome. Henry was by profession a cardinal of the Church of Rome, by inclination a gentle but long-burnt-out homosexual and by heredity the theoretical King of England, the would-be Henry IX.

Grandson of James II who had been chased from England 119 years before, Henry was the last of the Stuarts, a family that had first come to Scotland from Normandy at the beginning of the 12th century. Although the Stuarts had ruled Scotland since a certain Robert became King in 1371, Henry himself had never visited Scotland or England, having been born and held in exile all his life.

Also on this day
1643: Lord Wilmot leads royalist troops to victory over the Roundheads in the Battle of Roundway Down in the English Civil War

14 July

The fall of the Bastille

1789 Over the centuries we have come to imagine the Bastille as a grim, grey fortress of cold stone in which innocents withered away and died, chained to the wall in bleak cells on the order of reactionary and contemptuous French kings. And when we think of 14 July – Bastille Day – we envision the heroics of a downtrodden people overcoming the King's heavily armed guards to free the hundreds of innocent prisoners inside.

The 'real' Bastille in Paris was indeed a massive medieval fortress. Built in the 14th century, it consisted of eight round towers connected by walls 100 feet high. In the summer of 1789 it was manned by 114 guards under the command of Bernard de Launay.

On Tuesday 14 July, a mob of some 800 revolutionary Parisians decided to assault the Bastille, a symbol of royal repression. Gathering outside the walls, they attacked with muskets and cannon captured in the Invalides earlier in the day. But it soon became apparent that the defenders could hold out indefinitely; some 100 of the mob had already been killed.

Although in no immediate danger, de Launay wished to avoid more bloodshed and offered to open the gates if his soldiers were spared. The attackers gave assurances of safety, and the drawbridge was lowered. Immediately the rioters rushed in and massacred the garrison, including its commander.

And so trickery rather than force of arms took the Bastille. Inside there were a mere seven prisoners.

The start of the French Revolution is generally dated to the fall of the Bastille, but it was another three years before the abolition of the monarchy. Even then it took a further 88 years before Bastille Day was established as a national holiday in France.

The reign of King Philip Augustus

1223 Although blind in one eye, Philip Augustus of France was a large and handsome man, once fair, who had become bald, it was said, from the heat of the sun encountered in the Holy Land when he was on crusade. His long reign of nearly 43 years was a great one in French history, as he more than doubled the size of his nation by conquering virtually all of the vast territories in France that had been under the control of the kings of England.

Beginning his rule in 1180 at the tender age of fifteen, Philip was a tough and intelligent realist. He played his rebellious barons off against each other to consolidate his own power and sent Simon de Montfort to crush the Albigensian heresy in the south of France.

Philip spent most of his time fighting against the Plantagenet kings of England. First he fought Henry II for a period of about two years. Although the redoubtable Henry lost no territory, in the end he was forced to do homage to Philip for his French lands, and then died two days after having done so.

Next Philip took on Henry's son, Richard the Lion-Heart. (For those fans of historical minutiae, Richard was not the only Lion-Heart; Philip's son Louis VIII was also called Coeur de Lion.)

Philip's relationship with Richard began in apparent harmony, as they joined forces on the Third Crusade. During the journey, however, Philip fell ill and used his illness as an excuse to return to France, whereupon he immediately made war on Richard's French territories. Although Richard set sail for France the moment he heard the news, he was captured and imprisoned in Austria for a year, giving Philip that much more time to consolidate his gains.

From 1194 to 1198 Philip and Richard were almost constantly at war, with Richard the predominant victor. Once more, however, fortune favoured Philip, for Richard was killed during an unimportant siege in 1199.

Philip's next opponent was Richard's brother, King John. Compared with Henry and Richard, John was militarily incompetent, and over fourteen years Philip took virtually all the Plantagenet territories in France.

Philip's other great victory was against the German Emperor Otto IV at the decisive battle of Bouvines, destroying Otto's plot to make France his fief and to dismember it for his vassals.

When Philip died on this day in 1223 he was a month short of his 60th birthday. Although remembered most for his military success, he also left two other enduring monuments. He paved the streets of Paris and built a large palace there that today we know as the Louvre.

The end of Billy the Kid

1881 Born in New York City as William H. Bonney, he had moved to New Mexico as a child and was already a murderer before he was a teenager. Cold, remorseless and without pity, he was dubbed by his contemporaries Billy the Kid.

Billy reputedly committed his first murder at the age of twelve. At nineteen he already headed a gang of cattle rustlers. He shot dead the first sheriff who opposed him.

In 1880 Billy was finally captured by Sheriff Pat Garrett and sentenced to hang, but, killing two sheriff's deputies, he made good his escape from jail. A few months later, on the evening of 14 July 1881, Garrett trapped him once again, but this time took no chances; he shot the Kid dead. On the day he died Billy the Kid was just 21 years, four months and five days old. He had killed 27 men.

Also on this day

1835: American painter James Abbott McNeil Whistler is born * 1933: Germany passes the Law for the Protection of Hereditary Health, the beginning of the Nazi euthanasia programme

15 July

The Crusaders conquer Jerusalem

1099 Today, with the aid of assault towers and scaling ladders, 15,000 crusaders stormed the walls of the holy city of Jerusalem crying, 'Help us, God!' The First Crusade had triumphed.

'Jerusalem is the navel of the world', had cried Pope Urban II at the Council of Clermont four years earlier. His call for a holy war might seem a trifle tardy – Jerusalem had been a Muslim city for over 400 years – but it was only in 1071 when the Seljuk Turks swept down from central Asia that the city was cut off from Christian travellers. So Urban called out, and the First Crusade was launched.

Perhaps as many as 50,000 knights, soldiers and camp followers started on this great adventure, including minor nobles seeking their fortunes and peasants seeking their freedom from the feudal ties that bound them at home. For three years the weary crusaders trudged across Europe and Asia Minor, attacked by hunger, thirst, disease, bandits and Turkish guerrillas. Finally reaching Palestine, they were roasted in their armour by the terrible heat, but still they came on. By the time they reached the Holy City in June 1099, more than half had died, deserted or simply wandered off.

When the inspired crusaders finally breached Jerusalem's walls, the Saracen defenders fled to the Temple of Solomon, but soon the attackers had smashed through its gates. There, according to an eyewitness, 'in this temple almost ten thousand were decapitated. If you had been there, you would have seen our feet splattered with the blood of the dead ... Not a single life was spared, not even women or children. You would have seen a wondrous sight, when our poorest soldiers, learning of the Saracens' cleverness, cut open the stomachs of the slain to take from their bowels the jewels they had swallowed while still alive. A few days later the bodies were piled up in a great heap and burned in order to find coins more easily in the burnt ashes.'

When at last the crusaders ran out of Muslims, they herded resident Jews into their main synagogue and burnt it to the ground.

Thus 15 July is the day of Christianity's greatest military victory. It resulted in the establishment of the Latin Kingdom of Jerusalem, of which the first ruler was Godefroi de Bouillon, the first Christian knight to stand on the conquered city's walls. He rejected the title of king, preferring Defender and Baron of the Holy Sepulchre, saying, 'I will not wear a crown of gold where my Saviour wore one of thorns.'

The Christian kingdom lasted for almost two centuries, although Jerusalem itself fell to the great Saracen leader Saladin in 1187. Ironically, the day the Christians took Jerusalem from its Muslim defenders was the exact anniversary of the Hegira, the day in 622 when Mohammed fled to Medina and which is considered the traditional beginning of the Muslim Era.

Monmouth faces the axe

1685 King Charles II of England had a lifelong passion for women, and one, Lucy Walter, who had been his mistress while he was still a prince in exile in The Hague, bore him a son named James. After the Restoration, Charles brought the thirteen-year-old James back to England and made him Duke of Monmouth.

At 36, Monmouth was all a royal bastard should be: attractive, arrogant, ambitious, and a trained soldier to boot. When Charles died, however, he explicitly left his throne to his brother, another James (II), rather than to his illegitimate son. King James immediately banished his nephew from England.

Monmouth understandably detested his uncle and was thirsting for power. Knowing King James's Catholicism to be highly unpopular with the English, he raised a small force to dethrone him.

With 82 followers, Monmouth landed at Lyme Regis in June 1685. Proclaiming his uncle a popish usurper, he announced that he was the rightful king. Marching north, he recruited an army of about 7,000 men, but on 6 July 1685 he was defeated and captured at Sedgemoor, near Taunton, by the Royalist army under the command of John Churchill, later Duke of Marlborough. (This was the last battle ever fought on English soil, although they were still fighting in Scotland until 1746.)

Taken to the Tower of London, Monmouth was quickly convicted of treason and condemned to the block. At first he entreated his uncle James for mercy, but when his letters received no reply he faced death bravely.

Only nine days after his capture at Sedgemoor, Monmouth faced the axe. Retaining his bravado till the end, he turned to his executioner Jack Ketch and commanded, 'Do not hack at me as you did my Lord Russell.' He then gave Ketch six guineas and laid his head on the block. But still fearing a botched job, he asked to feel the edge of the axe with his thumb and complained that it was too dull. Ketch reassured him that the axe was sharp and heavy enough to perform its function.

Despite his guarantee, the nervous executioner failed three times to sever Monmouth's neck and finally threw down his axe in despair, crying, 'God damn me, I can do no more. My heart fails me.' But the onlooking crowd bayed for blood, and once again Ketch lifted his axe to deliver the final terrible blow.

'It's a long time since I drank champagne'

1904 Today Anton Chekhov died from tuberculosis at the age of 44 in Bademweiler, Germany. Born in Taganrog in southern Russia of an impoverished middle-class family, he became a writer almost by chance, as he was forced to support himself while he studied medicine in Moscow.

Chekhov's works are often sombre, portraying the essential isolation and loneliness of humankind. Although initially a short story writer, his most lasting fame comes from his plays, especially his four masterpieces, *The Seagull, Uncle Vanya, The Three Sisters* and *The Cherry Orchard.*

Chekhov's life, too, was lonely. He married the actress Olga Knipper at the age of 41, but his chronic tuberculosis forced him to move to Yalta for the mild Black Sea climate while she pursued her career in Moscow. One can imagine him at work on *The Cherry Orchard*, this frail man with his high, intelligent forehead, his George V beard and his habitual pince-nez, melancholy with the absence of his wife and as nostalgic as his character Anya in the play.

Eventually Chekhov travelled to Germany in hopes of a cure, but the tuberculosis had him firmly in its grip. Typically, his last words were both memorable and wistful. Just before he died he murmured, 'It's a long time since I drank champagne.'

16 July

The threat of Muslim domination in Spain is extinguished at Las Navas de Tolosa

1212 Almost exactly half a millennium before – in 711 – a bold Arab chief named Tarik led some 12,000 warriors across the eight-mile channel that separates Morocco from Spain, to land at a point that still bears his name, Jebel-al-Tarik (meaning mount of Tarik), corrupted over the centuries to Gibraltar. For the next 500 years the Arabs (or Moors) continually advanced northward in Spain until they ruled most of it, in spite of Christian efforts to halt them.

In 1158 three-year-old Alfonso VIII inherited the throne of Castile and León. During his long years as King, Alfonso became increasingly determined to rid the peninsula of Moorish, that is to say Muslim, domination, and in 1212 he finally acted decisively.

First the King called on that redoubtable pope, Innocent III, to lend his spiritual (and political) support. Innocent was the instigator of two crusades to the Holy Land and another against the Albigensian heretics, so Alfonso felt confident that he would enthusiastically join any effort to attack the Muslims in Spain.

Innocent responded as anticipated; he proclaimed a crusade and urged the rulers of Aragon, Navarre and Portugal to join the Castilian army under Alfonso's leadership.

On 16 July Alfonso's formidable army met the Moors at the Battle of Las Navas de Tolosa (40 miles north of modern Jaén in Andalucía). Alfonso personally led the Christian forces into battle, and their victory was total. (Pope Innocent's fervent support for the campaign may have been noticed on high, for he was called to heaven precisely four years to the day after the battle.)

Las Navas de Tolosa was one of the decisive battles of European history. Although it took more than two centuries fully to defeat the Moors, from this day forward the Christians were predominant, the Moors in retreat. The threat of a Muslim Spain – or Europe – was over, until more than 300 years later, when the Muslim danger came from another direction, with the Turkish armies of Suleiman the Magnificent.

1796: French painter Camille Corot is born * 1918: Communist insurgents shoot Tsar Nicholas II, Alexandra and their four children in a cellar at Ekaterinburg * 1945: The first atom bomb explodes at Alamogordo, New Mexico, at 5.24 a.m.

17 July

The most calamitous marriage in French history

1388 Today, at the age of twenty, Charles VI, King of France since he was twelve, was married at last to an apparently suitable bride, young Elizabeth Wittelsbach of Bavaria, whom the French would call Isabeau.

When the royal wedding took place at Amiens, Isabeau had been in France for only a few days and spoke no French. But apparently her voluptuous allure was not lost on the blond and handsome king. Reporting on the wedding the chronicler Froissart commented, 'And if they spent that night together in great delight, one can well believe it.'

Little did anyone suspect on that hot July day what grief and tragedy was to come. The handsome Charles would gradually go insane, incapable of controlling his wife, much less his country. Isabeau would lose herself in her lust for power combined with her lust for men. Thirty-two years later she would deny her own son's paternity and sign a treaty making the infant Henry VI of England the legal heir to the throne of France.

Joan of Arc witnesses a coronation

1429 'And at the hour that the King was anointed, and also when the crown was placed upon his head, all those assembled there cried out "Noël!" And trumpets sounded in such a manner that it seemed the vaults of the church must be riven apart.' So reports an eyewitness to the coronation of Charles VII of France at Reims cathedral on Sunday 17 July 1429. Charles had already been King of France since his father's death in 1422, but insurrection at home and invasion by the English had prevented him from actually being crowned.

Coronations were long affairs in those days, this one lasting from nine in the morning until two in the afternoon. It was also a particularly poignant one. As the eyewitness testifies, 'During the said mystery the Pucelle was ever near the King, holding his standard in her hand. And it was a most fair thing to see.' The Pucelle, of course, was Joan of Arc, who only four months before had seen King Charles for the first time. In that short time she had forced the English to lift the siege of Orléans and had paved the way for the coronation.

In the few pictures we have of him, Charles looks rather like a tired and troubled monk, with his long nose, pessimistic mouth and wary, unblinking eyes. He was brought up in a court filled with passion and intrigue, with a mad father and a power- and sex-hungry mother, Queen Isabeau, who, under pressure from England's Henry V, agreed that Charles was a bastard and therefore not the true heir to the French throne. (Ironically, Charles's coronation took place on the anniversary of Isabeau's marriage to Charles's father.)

But Charles was to be one of France's most successful kings, although he needed help. His famous mistress Agnès Sorel gave him wise counsel, Jacques Coeur gave him and his kingdom money, and Joan of Arc started the defeat of the English. Yet Charles abandoned Joan to be burnt at the stake, and he allowed jealous courtiers to drive Coeur away in disgrace.

Slowly and skilfully Charles overcame resistance from his Burgundian and Armagnac vassals as well as a revolt largely orchestrated by his own son. He edged the English first out of Paris and at last out of France. It was on this same day in 1453 that Charles's army destroyed the English army at Castillon, the final battle of the Hundred Years' War, which brought Bordeaux back under French control for the first time in 300 years.

As he grew older, Charles grew increasingly suspicious of those around him, particularly of his son Louis, whose deviousness would be a lifetime hallmark. In 1461 he found himself at Mehun-sur-Yèvre, where he started to suffer stomach pains. Convinced Louis was trying to poison him, he refused to take nourishment and died (of poison or illness, no one knows) on 22 July. He had reigned for 38 years and eight months.

The end of the Hundred Years' War

1453 Today, as French cannon ceased firing on a vanquished English army at Castillon on the lower Dordogne, the Hundred Years' War – which actually lasted for 116 years – at last came to an end.

It had all started in 1337 when Edward III of England laid claim to the crown of France through the blood of his mother, Isabelle de Valois, daughter of King Philip the Fair of France. At first the English must have thought the war an enormous success with the great English victories at Crécy, Poitiers and Agincourt, but then the French had their turn with the stirring triumphs of Joan of Arc.

The defeat at Castillon left the kings of England no more of France than Edward III had controlled 100 years before.

But Britain did gain one lasting heritage from the war. During the century of fighting England's triumphs were primarily thanks to the longbow, the powerful weapon that could fire armour-piercing arrows two and a half feet long.

So formidable were the English longbows that the French cut off the first two fingers of any captured bowmen so they could no longer fire their bows. The bowmen's reaction to the French threat was to lift two fingers in contempt at the enemy, thus giving birth to the derisive two-fingered signal that the English use to this day to mock their opponents.

Also on this day

1674: The bones of two boys are found in the Tower of London, presumed to be the children of Edward IV * 1793: French patriot Charlotte Corday is guillotined * 1872: Mexican President Benito Juárez dies at his desk of a heart attack

18 July

Nero burns Rome

AD 64 On this night soldiers acting on the orders of their emperor touched off one of the great fires of history.

Among Rome's degenerate emperors, Nero grew to be one of the worst. Becoming Emperor at the age of sixteen, at first he modelled himself on his great-great-grandfather, the Emperor Augustus. During his first four years in power he reduced taxes, banned circus performances in which people were killed or injured and eliminated capital punishment. He even forgave writers of scurrilous criticism of himself and failed to put a single senator to death, a revolution in moderation for the time.

But as Nero became increasingly aware of his unlimited power, he began to change. He took to carousing in the streets at night and acting totally without restraint when it came to his own pleasure. He also fancied himself a great actor and scandalised the Roman nobility by appearing on stage, sometimes even taking the part of a woman. He wrote second-rate poetry and forced audiences to hear him recite it. As the historian Suetonius writes, 'No one was permitted to leave the theatre during his performances. We read of women in the audience giving birth ... and of men who were so bored they pretended they had died in order to be carried away for burial.'

Many of Nero's acts were those of insane egotism. He had one wife executed so he could marry someone else and kicked another wife to death while she was pregnant because she complained when he came home late from the chariot races. His most revolting deeds involved his revolting mother, Agrippina. (Agrippina was an interesting role model for Nero. She murdered her second husband so she could incestuously marry her own uncle, the emperor-to-be Claudius, having already contrived to murder Claudius's previous wife. Five years later she poisoned Claudius so that Nero could inherit supreme power, and four months after that poisoned Claudius's son by his first wife to eliminate a potential rival.)

Nero is reputed to have carried on an incestuous relationship with Agrippina, but when she interfered too much with his imperial powers he tried to drown her by putting her to sea in the Bay of Naples in a boat designed to sink. When she saved herself by swimming ashore, Nero gave orders for her execution, which was duly carried out in her own house. Before she died she cried out to her executioners, 'Strike my womb first!'

But of all Nero's acts of criminal insanity, the most famous is the burning of Rome, then a mighty city of some 900,000 inhabitants. Historians debate whether Nero really was responsible for the fire, but Suetonius claims that on 18 July 64, Nero had his troops wantonly fire the city.

The great conflagration lasted six days and seven nights, destroying huge parts of Rome and killing hundreds. Contrary to popular legend, however, Nero did not fiddle while Rome burned. Mostly he watched the blaze from the Tower of Maecenas, enchanted by what he called 'the beauty of the flames'. He then put on his actor's costume and sang his own composition, *The Sack of Ilium*.

Nero was only 27 at the time of the great fire. Four years later he was overthrown and driven to suicide, to the relief and joy of his people.

The Spanish Civil War begins

1936 The Spanish Civil War began at 5.15 this Saturday morning, when in a *pronunciamento* broadcast by radio from Las Palmas on Grand Canary Island, General Francisco Franco gave the order for the mainland garrisons of the Spanish army to rise against the republican government of Spain.

It was a rebellion in which an array of forces – landowners, monarchists, the Catholic Church, the army, the bourgeoisie, the fascist Falange party – sought to reclaim their country from an elected republican government they judged incapable of putting down the violent political disorder afflicting the nation. So it was that during the morning of 18 July, in city after city, garrisons seized public buildings, proclaimed a state of war, and arrested republican and leftwing leaders. In response, workers took to the streets, calling for a general strike and throwing up barricades.

The republican government of Spain faced a dilemma. It wished to put down the rebellion, but found the institutions of law and order – the army and the civil guard – in the hands of the rebels. On the other hand, the forces remaining loyal to the republic were the unions and the leftwing parties – Socialists, Communists and Anarchists – whose victory, if it came, promised proletarian revolution. Late in the day, the government made its decision: arm the workers. As trucks sped through the streets of Madrid carrying rifles to the headquarters of the unions, German and Italian transport planes airlifted the Spanish Army of Africa to mainland Spain. The fight was on.

At 10.00 in the evening, in a radio broadcast, Dolores Ibarurri, the Communist leader known as La Pasionaria, told her listeners, 'It is better to die on your feet than to live on your knees!' then echoed the old phrase from Verdun, 'No pasaran!' (They shall not pass!). It was to be the great rallying cry of republican Spain.

The war lasted almost three years, during which the world learned about such things as Guernica, the 'Fifth Column' and the Condor Legion. Nazi Germany and Fascist Italy supplied and reinforced Franco's Nationalists.

Soviet Russia sent aid to the republican Loyalists. The democracies – France, Great Britain and the United States – practised non-intervention. When Madrid fell in March 1939, after 28 months of siege, and Nationalist forces marched into the city, the crowds shouted, 'Han pasado!' (They have passed!).

Franco was by now El Caudillo – The Leader – a designation he shared with Der Führer and Il Duce. Pope Pius XII cabled him, 'Lifting up our heart to God, we give sincere thanks with your Excellency for Spain's Catholic victory.' The Nationalist Government now aligned itself with the Axis powers by joining the Anti-Comintern Pact and signing a five-year treaty of friendship with Nazi Germany. Only Russia among the great powers refused to recognise the Nationalist regime.

No precise estimates of the losses in the Spanish Civil War exist, but Hugh Thomas offered this tentative assessment: a total of 500,000 people perished in the conflict, of which perhaps 300,000 died in action, 100,000 died from disease or malnutrition, and 100,000 were executed or murdered. All in all, it was good practice for the Second World War, only five months away.

Also on this day

1610: Italian painter Caravaggio (Michelangelo Merisi) dies at Porto Ercole * 1811: English novelist William Makepeace Thackeray is born in Calcutta * 1817: English novelist Jane Austen dies * 1869: Pope Pius IX proclaims the doctrine of papal infallibility

19 July

The first feminist convention in America

1848 Today in the scenic Finger Lakes district of west-central New York State a crowd of about 250 women and 40 men met at Seneca Falls 'to discuss the social, civil, and religious rights of women'. Led by Elizabeth Cady Stanton and Lucretia Mott, who eight years earlier had been barred from the World Anti-Slavery Convention in London on the grounds of their gender, this was the first formal meeting in America of dedicated feminists. After two days of discussion they drew up a list of women's grievances and demands, including the contentious (some said preposterous) notion that women be allowed to vote.

Although American women had been permitted to stand for election since 1788, like their sisters in Great Britain they were long denied equality with men in the election booth.

In Great Britain women's suffrage had been an important cause since at least 1792 when Mary Wollstonecraft made a case for it in her *Vindication of the Rights of Woman*, but the first women's suffrage committee was formed in Manchester only in 1865, seventeen years after the American Seneca Falls Convention. Progress was slow, as even the backing of John Stuart Mill, whose wife was a strong 'suffragette', failed to get Parliament to enact favourable legislation due to the implacable opposition of Queen Victoria.

In 1903, two years after Victoria's death, a strident feminist named Emmeline Pankhurst and her two daughters founded the Women's Social and Political Union. Initially in favour of non-violent protest, in frustration the group turned increasingly militant, smashing Regent Street windows, burning postboxes and cutting telegraph wires. When suffragettes (a term coined by the newspapers) were sent to prison they responded with hunger strikes, and the authorities resorted to force-feeding.

In 1918 the British government finally caved in, but only women over 30 were enfranchised. Ten years later, in a society changed for ever by the war, women were at last given equal rights to men.

Back in the United States women had to wait until 1920 when on 26 August Congress passed the Nineteenth Amendment to the Constitution which stated: 'The right of citizens of the United States to vote shall not be denied or abridged by the United States or by any State on account of sex.'

Both the US and Great Britain were well behind several other nations. As early as 1893 the women of New Zealand had been enfranchised, and other countries that beat them in extending voting rights to women include Australia, Finland, Norway, Russia and Canada. Even Germany allowed women to vote before the United States, in spite of a Prussian law of 1851 that forbade women, along with mentally ill schoolchildren, even from attending meetings where political subjects were discussed.

Not all European countries were so hasty. In France women gained voting rights only in 1944 when the Free French leader in exile Charles de Gaulle issued a wartime decree, and in Italy Mussolini actually rescinded all women's voting rights, restored only after the end of the Second World War.

Also on this day

1374: Italian poet Petrarch dies near Padua * 1799: The Rosetta Stone is found in Egypt * 1870: Napoleon III declares war to start the Franco-Prussian War * 1903: Maurice Garin wins the first Tour de France cycle race

20 July

The plot to murder Hitler

1944 'I must go and telephone. Keep an eye on my briefcase. It has secret papers in it', whispered Colonel Claus von Stauffenberg to Colonel Brandt sitting next to him. Then he quietly rose from the crowded table and slipped from the conference room while Germany's top brass made their gloomy reports to their supreme leader in his fortified bunker at the Wolfsschanze (Wolf's Lair) headquarters in Rastenburg, in what is now north-eastern Poland.

Three minutes later, at 12.42, the bomb that had been concealed in a shirt in von Stauffenberg's briefcase exploded, killing four people including Colonel Brandt but doing little damage to its target, Adolf Hitler. Needing more leg room, the unfortunate Brandt had shoved the briefcase to the far side of a heavy table support, miraculously shielding Hitler from the worst effects of the blast.

The 36-year-old von Stauffenberg was a career army officer born to the Prussian nobility. An early supporter of Hitler, he had participated in all the Führer's major campaigns and had been severely wounded while serving with the 10th Panzer Division of Rommel's Afrika Corps in Tunisia. There in early 1943 Allied fighters had strafed his convoy, and von Stauffenberg had lost his left eye, his right hand, and the last two fingers of his left hand.

It was probably in Russia, after witnessing atrocities committed by the SS, that von Stauffenberg began to lose his faith in Hitler, and by mid-1944 it was clear to all but the most fanatical Nazis that Germany would lose the war. Von Stauffenberg became a key member of a conspiracy code-named Walküre (Valkyrie) whose aim was to seize control of the government and seek favourable peace terms from the Allies to save the country from total destruction.

The plotters searched for a way to get at Hitler, and on 1 June 1944 fortune smiled on them when von Stauffenberg was made chief of staff of the Reserve Army, giving him access to the Führer's most important military meetings. Then he was summoned to the Wolfsschanze conference on 20 July. By this time his earlier belief in Hitler had turned to loathing. 'Fate has offered us this opportunity,' he said, 'and I would not refuse it for anything in the world. I have examined myself before God and my conscience. It must be done because this man is evil personified.' Flying to Rastenburg in the early morning, he set the bomb's ten-minute timer just before entering the meeting. Immediately after the explosion he bluffed his way through three SS checkpoints and, believing his mission accomplished, flew back to Berlin to help take over the government.

Sadly, *Walküre*'s conspirators showed an incomprehensible lack of both planning and resolve, and the plot started to disintegrate the moment it became clear that Hitler, whose legs were burned, eardrums punctured and hair singed, was not dead after all. In fact, that same afternoon he conducted his final meeting with Mussolini and bragged that God had saved him to lead Germany's revenge on the world.

Hitler's vengeance was swift and savage. When von Stauffenberg arrived in Berlin late in the day, an SS countercoup was already rounding up most of the conspirators. At about midnight von Stauffenberg and three others were taken to a courtyard at the War Ministry and shot, the colonel shouting at the last, 'Long live our sacred Germany.' The bodies were buried nearby, but on Himmler's orders the corpses were dug up and burned, their ashes scattered to the winds.

Plotters all over Germany were arrested, tortured and executed. Eight were strangled with piano wire attached to meat hooks, their death agony filmed for Hitler's enjoyment. Some officers committed suicide, at least one by walking into no man's land at the front to be shot by the enemy, and Germany's most illustrious field marshal Erwin Rommel was forced to take poison to save his family. An estimated 4,980 people were executed while another 15,000, mostly relatives of conspirators, were sent to concentration camps. The killings continued into April 1945, even as Russians were in the streets of Berlin.

After the assassination attempt Hitler became even more morbidly suspicious and reclusive. He gulped pills offered by his doctors, his right hand suffered from severe tremors, and he rarely agreed to be photographed. Nonetheless, his determination remained undiminished. All hope of negotiation vanished. In December Hitler told his Luftwaffe aide, 'We'll not capitulate. Never. We can go down. But we'll take the world with us.'

Also on this day

1881: Sioux chief Sitting Bull surrenders to the US Army * 1917: Alexander Kerensky becomes the premier of Russia

21 July

Hotspur dies in battle

1403 Two stars keep not their motion in one sphere,
Nor can one England brook a double reign,
Of Harry Percy and the Prince of Wales.

So did Shakespeare comment on the bitter conflict between two of England's most celebrated medieval heroes, Henry Percy, called Harry by his friends and known to us by the picturesque name of Hotspur, and Prince Henry of Lancaster, the future Henry V, son of the usurper king Henry IV.

Hotspur came from the powerful and aristocratic Percy family that had come to England with William the Conqueror. By the 14th century the Percys were rulers of Northumberland, which formed a buffer against armed raids from Scotland. It was the Scots who gave Hotspur his nickname for his indefatigable patrolling of the Scottish/English border.

Hotspur and his father (also called Henry) initially backed Henry IV and battered the Scots while the King was trying to subdue the Welsh. The problem was, the Welsh resisted successfully and Henry IV refused to give the Percys his promised rewards. It was only then that the Percys, capable and honourable knights, rebelled against their king. But once the rebellion had started, the Percys determined to go all the way and take the throne of England for themselves.

It was on this day that the conflict reached its denouement, when Henry IV and his son decisively defeated the Percys at Shrewsbury. According to Shakespeare, Hotspur was struck down by the sixteen-year-old Prince of

Wales, but historians believe he died from a blow from an unknown hand when he lifted his visor to wipe sweat from his face.

> Ill-weaved ambition, how much art thou shrunk!
> When that this body did contain a spirit,
> A kingdom for it was too small a bound,
> But now two paces of the vilest earth
> Is room enough.

Hotspur's head was set on the gate of York to discourage further rebellion, while his brother Thomas Percy was decapitated after the battle so that his could decorate London Bridge. The Percys of the time seemed to have a knack for dying in battle. Hotspur's father Henry, who escaped from the field of battle at Shrewsbury, was eventually slain at Bramham Moor in 1408. His son died on the field at the first Battle of St Albans (1455), and his grandson was killed six years later at Towton.

The Battle of Shrewsbury greatly strengthened the Lancastrian hold on the throne of England and also proved an invaluable training ground for young Prince Henry, who only ever fought in one more full-scale pitched battle, against the French at Agincourt.

The Battle of the Pyramids

1798 'Soldats, songez que, du haut de ces pyramides, quarante siècles vous contemplent.' (Think of it, soldiers, from the top of these pyramids 40 centuries are looking down upon you.) So declaimed General Napoleon Bonaparte to inspire his troops just before they went into battle against a large Egyptian army spearheaded by 8,000 ferocious Mameluke horsemen.

In fact, the French needed little inspiration, as Napoleon's cannon as well as his tactics destroyed virtually the entire Egyptian force of 24,000 men in less than two hours, with a loss of only 200 Frenchmen. The only real opposition came from the cavalry, superb riders and fanatic in their intent, who had come close to routing a section of his infantry. After the battle Napoleon expressed his admiration: 'If I could have united the Mameluke horse with the French infantry, I should have seen myself as master of the world.' Such was the Battle of the Pyramids, fought this day.

The political results of Napoleon's invasion of Egypt have long since vanished in the mists of time, but two souvenirs remain. The first is the Rosetta Stone, the key to deciphering hieroglyphic writing, that was discovered in 1799 in the town of Rosetta near Alexandria by a French officer named Bouchard who was part of Napoleon's army. The second is the appearance of perhaps the world's most famous monument, the Sphinx. For 40 centuries the Sphinx had a prominent nose, but the flat-faced colossus we are all familiar with is the result of Napoleon's soldiers using it for target practice.

Bull Run – the first major battle of the American Civil War

1861 It was the hottest of July days in steamy Virginia when the Union Army attacked the Confederate Rebels in the first major battle of the American Civil War.

The Battle of Bull Run pitted a Union army 30,000 strong against a Southern force of only 22,000. The Northerners had taken victory so much for granted that civilian spectators had ridden the 30 miles from Washington to watch the sport.

As every American schoolchild knows, however, it was the Yankees' green, untrained troops who panicked under fire, who did the running at Bull Run. By the end of the five-hour conflict they had retreated all the way back to the capital.

It was at Bull Run that a famous Southern general earned his nickname. During the course of a Union attack General Thomas Jackson held his brigade firm in the face of fierce enemy fire. In an attempt to rally his own men, another Southern general, Barnard Bee, cried out, 'There is Jackson standing like a stone wall!'

From that time on, Jackson – who was killed later in the war after several years of brilliant generalship – has been known as Stonewall Jackson.

During Bull Run the Northern forces suffered about 2,900 casualties compared with only 2,000 for the South. More important than the body count, however, was the boost the battle gave to the Confederacy, demonstrating as it did that, in spite of their inferior numbers, Southern forces were at least a match for the Union.

Also on this day

1667: The Peace of Breda ends the Second Anglo-Dutch War * 1831: Leopold of Saxe-Coburg becomes the first King of Belgium * 1899: American novelist Ernest Hemingway is born

22 July

'Kill them all'

1208 Pope Innocent III had launched the Albigensian Crusade less than six months before, but already a sizeable army was marauding its way through southern France. Its aim was to extirpate the dangerous heresy known as Catharism, which not only denied the divinity of Christ, but also, in its non-authoritarian asceticism, stood in marked contrast to the corruption, worldliness and hypocrisy of the Church of Rome.

On this day the army reached the walls of Béziers in the very south of France, west of Marseille. Leading this band of opportunists, criminals seeking absolution, adventurers and religious fanatics were Simon de Montfort and his spiritual advisor, the papal legate Arnald-Amaury. At the city gates de Montfort handed the Bishop of Béziers a list of 222 Cathars to be handed over for execution. But the city leaders, not themselves Cathars, refused to provide the victims, saying, 'We had rather be drowned in the salt sea than surrender our fellow citizens.'

Now de Montfort ordered an assault, and the rampaging army began a brutal sack. There was to be no mercy for the heretics, but how, Arnald-Amaury was asked, can one tell a Cathar from the numerous devout Catholics in the population? 'Kill them all', said the Pope's representative. 'God will know his own.'

Except for those few who managed to flee, the entire population of Béziers – 15,000 men, women and children – were put to the sword, 7,000 alone in the vast Romanesque Church of Sainte-Madeleine where they had sought sanctuary.

The end of the Little Eagle

1832 Today in the exquisite Schönbrunn Palace just outside Vienna died Napoleon François Charles Joseph, Duke of Reichstadt, only son of Napoleon and his empress Marie-Louise.

Franzl, as his mother called him, had been born in the Tuileries in Paris in March 1811 when Napoleon was at the height of his power. Initially entitled 'the King of Rome' and heir to Napoleon's throne, the French Senate proclaimed him Emperor before it capitulated to the Allies after his father's first abdication in 1813. But although Tsar Alexander I preferred him to a restoration of the Bourbons, the other Allies would have no truck with further Napoleons and saw to it that he was soon demoted and taken to Vienna. He never saw his father again.

Franzl then became the 'Prince of Parma' when his mother was made the ruling duchess there, but Metternich vetoed this title on the grounds that one day the son of Napoleon might have a territory to rule. Eventually his grandfather Emperor Franz of Austria created him the Duke of Reichstadt, a Bohemian palatinate that he never ruled nor even visited. Many years after his death the romantic Victor Hugo christened him l'Aiglon (little eagle), the name by which he is often referred to today.

From 1813 onwards Franzl remained in Austria, where he was held in a sort of luxurious captivity, with all communication in German. Nonetheless, he became a Bonapartist, once writing to his mother that he was trying to live up to his father, asking, 'can there be a finer, more admirable model of constancy, endurance, manly gravity, valiance, and courage?'

By the time he was sixteen Franzl was already showing signs of the tuberculosis that would kill him. Bravely he carried on, always hopeful that he would be cured, but by the time he was 21 it was clear that death was near. Installed in the Schönbrunn Palace, he waited for the end in the same bedroom in which his father had dictated peace terms to the Austrians after his victory at Wagram 22 years earlier.

On Sunday 22 July it was hot and humid in Vienna, with thunder in the air. In the early hours of the morning he murmured, 'I am going under. Call my mother.' He then quietly slipped away, Marie-Louise at his side.

Franzl was buried in the traditional Habsburg burial crypt in the Kapuzinerkirche in Vienna, where he lay for 108 years. Napoleon III tried to persuade Austrian Emperor Franz Joseph to allow the remains to be sent to Paris to lie beside his father in the Invalides, but his requests were ignored.

By 1940, however, Austria had been integrated into Hitler's German Reich, and the Nazi government in Berlin wanted to persuade the Vichy French of Germany's good will. So on 12 December that year his coffin was shipped from Vienna to Paris, where he was buried near his father three days later.

Also on this day

1461: Charles VII of France dies * 1812: The Duke of Wellington defeats the French at Salamanca in the Peninsular War

23 July

Ulysses S. Grant: great general, terrible president

1885 Tortured by throat cancer and nearly broke, America's great Civil War general and eighteenth president Ulysses S. Grant died today in his cottage at Mount McGregor in the Adirondacks at the age of 63.

Grant had shown scant promise of greatness as a young man, graduating 21st in a class of 39 at West Point Military Academy. After fighting in the Mexican War, he left the army and was working in his father's leather goods store when recalled to service during the Civil War. Due to his strategic understanding, willingness to innovate and sheer tenacity in combat, he became the North's commanding general, eventually bringing the South to its knees.

In 1868 Grant at 46 became at the time the youngest man ever elected President. At first a popular success, he earned a second term in 1872, but his trusting and perhaps naïve attitude towards his subordinates allowed corruption to mushroom in the government, and he worsened the situation by accepting presents from admirers. Scandals in railroads, whiskey and gold and a Secretary of War who was impeached for accepting bribes all but destroyed Grant's reputation, although he was entirely honest himself.

Grant's last years were as full of failure as his middle ones had been of success. He joined his son in a brokerage firm that went bankrupt owing the colossal sum of almost $17,000,000 due to the fraudulent activities of one of the partners. By this time he was already suffering from the throat cancer that would kill him, no doubt the result of his lifetime habit of smoking 50 cigars a day. But despite his illness, he was determined to recoup at least some of his family's fortune by writing his memoirs.

Grant began writing in the autumn of 1884, with his oldest son Fred and another researcher checking facts, securing documents and reviewing the manuscript. In October his cancer was diagnosed as fatal, and the work became a race to the finish. As his health worsened and the pain increased, cocaine and morphine were prescribed. The manuscript of the first of two volumes of memoirs was sent to the compositor in April. In May he began dictating his narrative to a stenographer, but when he developed difficulty speaking, he huddled under a blanket in his library and laboriously wrote out his story by hand. So painful was the condition of his throat that to communicate he was reduced to writing notes.

In June Grant left his home in New York City on doctor's orders in the hope of being able to complete his memoirs before he died. (He had earlier signed a publishing contract with his friend Mark Twain, and the memoirs earned nearly $450,000, but by the time they were published he was dead.) A special train took him north, crowds gathering at stations along the route to wave. At Saratoga Springs, where he changed trains, veterans greeted him with cheers. Twenty years after the end of the Civil War, Grant remained a popular hero.

Settling into his cottage at Mount McGregor, he wrote his doctor a series of notes describing his deteriorating condition and the effects of the medicines he was taking. His very last note, written just a couple of days before his death, read: 'I do not sleep though I sometimes doze off a little. If up I am talked to and in my efforts to answer cause pain. The fact is I think I am a verb instead of a personal pronoun. A verb is anything that signifies to be; to do; or to suffer. I signify all three.'

Grant's funeral bore testimony to the respect in which he was held not only by comrades in arms but also by former enemies. Marching as pallbearers beside the Union generals William Sherman and Philip Sheridan were two Confederate generals, Joe Johnston and Simon Buckner. In his life Grant had defeated the South; in his death he helped to reconcile it with its Union conqueror.

Philippe Pétain – the hero who betrayed his country dies in prison

1951 Henri Philippe Benoni Omer Joseph Pétain, Marshal of France, died today at the age of 95 in prison on the lonely Ile d'Yeu. During the First World War he had been a very great hero of his country. In 1916 he was the 'Saviour of Verdun', and the next year, as Commander-in-Chief, he had performed a true miracle: in the perilous military situation after the disastrous Nivelle offensives, he had restored the mutiny-ridden French Army to discipline and battlefield efficiency, with the result that it fought valiantly and effectively through the remainder of the war. For these feats a grateful nation made him a marshal.

In the debacle of 1940, the hero of the last war was called upon once again to rescue his country from the Germans. This time, instead of rallying his forces, he negotiated the surrender of France, then ruled for the rest of the Second World War as the chief of the vassal state of Vichy. For these feats a dishonoured nation convicted the marshal of treason and sentenced him to death. Charles de Gaulle commuted the sentence to life imprisonment and later wrote of his old colonel: 'Monsieur le Maréchal! You who had always done such great honour to your arms, who were once my leader and my example, how had you come to this?'

Also on this day

1745: Bonnie Prince Charlie lands in Scotland * 1757: Italian composer Domenico Scarlatti dies * 1865: William Booth founds the Salvation Army

24 July

England snatches Gibraltar

1704 A narrow peninsula of only two square miles, with neither springs nor rivers, consisting mainly of a great barren rock that rises 1,400 feet: such is the tiny territory of Gibraltar one mile off the south coast of Spain that has been fought over for centuries.

In ancient times Gibraltar was thought of as one of the Pillars of Hercules (the other being Mount Hacho, across the Mediterranean on the African coast). In 711 the Moors crossed over from North Africa and took it, and in 1501, after the Spanish defeat of the Moors, Spain annexed it.

At the very beginning of the 18th century Spain found herself without a king. Then Louis XIV of France decided his grandson would do nicely and installed him as King Philip V. This decision was instantly challenged by the Holy Roman Empire, quickly joined by Holland and England, in what became known as the War of the Spanish Succession.

The war itself achieved very little, as Louis's grandson remained King of Spain, but during the conflict England made one enduring conquest. On 24 July 1704 a British force led by Sir George Rooke attacked and seized Gibraltar.

The Rock, as it is popularly known, has remained British ever since, but not without controversy.

Spain besieged Gibraltar from 1779 to 1783 but failed to oust its British occupiers. In the 1960s Spain again demanded its return, denouncing British colonialism as an anachronism from a bygone era. But the British organised a referendum in which Gibraltarians were asked to choose between a highly subsidised and tax-free existence under democratic Great Britain or absorption into the impoverished dictatorship of Francisco Franco. The result was no surprise: 12,138 voted to remain British versus 44 who wished to become part of Spain. Later Spain closed its borders with Gibraltar, depriving the community of Spanish workers and trade as well as access to Spanish beaches, but finally lifted the blockade in 1985.

Gibraltar today remains one of the last colonies in a post-colonial world.

Nelson loses his right arm

1797 En route to proving himself Britain's greatest admiral, Horatio Nelson survived illness and injury that would have put a lesser man out of the running.

He nearly died while on duty in the Indian Ocean through contracting malaria. He was so badly affected that the Navy sent him home to recover. Later the British force he was part of was decimated by yellow fever while attacking San Juan in Puerto Rico, and Nelson again was lucky to survive.

Nelson suffered his first serious battle wound in 1794 when his squadron was besieging Corsica in the hope of using it as a new base in the war against France. Infantry led the attack, supported by naval guns brought ashore to pound the enemy fortress. Nelson, then a 35-year-old captain, was in charge of the naval unit.

During the morning of 12 July the British guns were battering the enemy's positions at Calvi when suddenly a French shell exploded, showering the attackers with sand and broken rock. Something struck Nelson in the right eye, permanently clouding his vision.

Three years later the fleet was on the attack again, this time against the Spanish at Tenerife. On this day Nelson, by then an admiral, was trying to land when a musket ball tore through his right elbow. Immediately brought back to his flagship, he greeted his officers with astonishing nonchalance, refusing help in climbing aboard with the comment, 'I have got my legs left and one arm.' He said he knew his arm must come off, so the sooner the better.

In these days before anaesthetics, the amputation must have been painful in the extreme, but Nelson bore it stoically. Half an hour later he was back in his cabin giving orders and writing dispatches with his left hand.

Although fighting the French almost continually for the next eight years, Nelson managed to avoid injury or illness until October 1805 when he received his final, fatal wound at Trafalgar.

Also on this day

1783: South American liberator Simón Bolívar is born in Caracas, Venezuela * 1802: French writer Alexandre Dumas, author of *The Count of Monte Cristo* and *The Three Musketeers*, is born

25 July

'Paris vaut bien une messe'

1593 Technically Henri de Navarre had been King of France since 1589, when Henri III had died from stab wounds administered by a frenzied monk. But Henri was a Protestant in a country populated largely by Catholics, and he thus spent the first four years of his reign trying without success to conquer his own country. Ranged against him were the forces of the Catholic League, largely supported by that fanatical Catholic, Philip II of Spain, and much of the French population, particularly in Paris, which Henri had been unable to capture or control.

But Henri IV was a wise and tolerant man who put his people and his country above his sect, and he finally decided to turn Catholic to gain his kingdom.

On the morning of this day, Henri remarked to his beautiful mistress Gabrielle d'Estrées, 'It is today, my dear, that I take a perilous leap.' He then rode off to the gothic cathedral of St Denis just north of Paris, where France's kings are buried, where he abjured his Calvinism to join the Church of Rome. His real objective, however, was political rather than religious, as witnessed by his famous comment just before he entered the cathedral, 'Paris vaut bien une messe.' (Paris is well worth a Mass.)

By becoming Catholic Henri IV did indeed become King of France in fact as well as in name, and by his act he finally brought to a close more than 30 years of religious wars that had come close to destroying France.

A neurotic spinster queen marries a cold-eyed prince

1554 It was a splendid wedding on this warm day at Winchester Cathedral, as Mary Tudor, Queen of England, married the future Philip II of Spain, the heir to the largest, richest and most powerful empire in history.

Philip at 27 was already distant and austere, a bigoted Catholic who by now had been a widower for nine years. He would become King of Spain in 1556, to rule it for 42 years.

Mary was eleven years his senior, a neurotic virgin of 38 who looked even older than she was, having lost most of her teeth. Also an obsessive Catholic, she worshipped Philip as the man who would help her make Catholicism once more supreme in England and at the same time sire the child she so desperately craved. The cold-eyed and tireless Philip, on the other hand, had agreed to marry Mary for the same reason he did everything else: duty to his country and to his religion.

In the end, of course, neither got what they wanted. Mary died childless and virtually abandoned by her prince, Protestantism remained England's state religion, and Philip failed to bring England under Spanish domination, even when he sent his Armada against it 34 years later.

England and Scotland are united

1603 James Stuart had been crowned King James VI of Scotland at the age of fourteen months when Scottish nobles had revolted against the immorality, blind pride and stubborn Catholicism of his mother, Mary, Queen of Scots. Now, on the death of Queen Elizabeth, the 36-year-old James was crowned King of England as well, thus uniting these two neighbouring countries after centuries of conflict.

From this date forward all British sovereigns would wear both crowns of a United Kingdom. Each country retained its separate legislature until 1707. The Scottish Parliament was subsumed into the English one to become the British legislature during the reign of James's great-granddaughter, Queen Anne, who was the last Stuart monarch of Great Britain, as James had been the first.

At the close of the 20th century a Scottish parliament was once again established.

Also on this day

1394: Charles VI of France expels all Jews from the country * 1587: Chief Imperial Minister Hideyoshi bans Christianity and orders all Christians to leave Japan * 1848: British Prime Minister Arthur James Balfour is born * 1934: Nazis shoot and kill the Austrian chancellor Engelbert Dollfuss

26 July

The last execution of the Spanish Inquisition

1826 When he was hanged today in the town of Rizaffa, Cayetano Ripoll became the very last victim of the Spanish Inquisition, that holy office that had been hanging, burning and torturing heretics in Spain since its institution under Isabella of Castile in 1478.

Ripoll was a schoolteacher who was imprisoned for two years and then executed for the grievous crime of insisting that the only necessary religious teaching was the keeping of the Ten Commandments.

The original Inquisition was created by Pope Gregory IX in 1231. Initially the accused had ample opportunity to repent, and punishment (carried out not by the Church but by secular authority) ranged from simple prayer to life imprisonment. Only the secular arm could condemn to death.

The Inquisition came to Spain in the wake of the Spanish conquest of the Muslim Moors and reached its peak under the tender ministrations of the first

Grand Inquisitor, the Dominican Tomás de Torquemada. Torquemada probably condemned about 2,000 people to the stake, that gruesome process called by the remarkable euphemism *auto da fé* or 'act of faith'.

The Spanish Inquisition executed no more victims after Ripoll, and the institution itself was finally suppressed in 1834. The Spanish Inquisition's offspring, the Inquisition in Mexico, lived on, however, with the last *auto da fé* taking place in 1850.

The cheese of kings and popes

1926 The French have never been reticent about protecting their culinary superiority, as demonstrated today when the government established an *appellation d'origine* for Roquefort, the classic blue cheese made from ewes' milk. It was the first cheese ever so honoured. The effect of the new law was to ensure that only cheeses that have been aged in the limestone caves of Roquefort, a hamlet near Toulouse, may bear the name. But in truth the statute only confirmed what King Charles VI had already decreed in 1411 when he gave the Roquefort citizens the sole right to mature the cheese.

Roquefort is made by adding spores of the mould Penicillium roqueforti to the fresh cheese and then letting it mature for three months in damp caves where the humid air encourages the development of the cheese's blue veins. The result is a crumbly cylinder about eight inches across and four inches high that the French maintain should always be accompanied by other *appellation d'origine* products such as a good bottle of Châteauneuf-du-Pape (although in his *Mémoires* the free-spending Casanova recommends Chambertin).

Roquefort was a worthy candidate for the esteemed *appellation*, for it is the oldest known French variety, mentioned by Pliny the Elder in the 1st century AD and later known as Charlemagne's favourite. Not content with solely a royal pedigree, to this day French enthusiasts call it *le fromage des rois et des papes* (the cheese of kings and popes).

Eugene of Savoy escapes from France

1683 Today a young man who would become one of Europe's greatest generals fled his native city to find a career with his country's future enemies. His name was Eugene of Savoy.

Born and raised in Paris and of compelling title, nineteen-year-old Prince Eugene had been devastated to be turned down out of hand by his king, Louis XIV, when he sought to join the French officer corps. Small and horsefaced, Eugene was hardly prepossessing, but the real reason for his rejection was his mother. Niece of the great Cardinal Mazarin, she had once been Louis's mistress, but in 1680 was caught up in the great witchcraft scandal that rocked France, even touching the King's current *maîtresse en titre*, Mme de Montespan.

During the investigation Eugene's mother was accused of having poisoned her husband, and she had to flee to Brussels, where she remained. As no French officer could be so close to such a disgraceful incident, Eugene was denied his commission.

Crushed by Louis's dismissal, Eugene today fled from Paris without the King's permission. Stopped by French agents at Frankfurt, the young prince refused to return and shortly made his way to Vienna. There Emperor Leopold I welcomed him into the imperial service, where he remained until his death 53 years later.

Eugene of Savoy became the greatest general in imperial history. He scored crushing victories over the Turks, but most of his famous feats were victories over the French who had spurned him, including the battles of Blenheim, Turin and Malplaquet, fought in brilliant co-operation with the Duke of Marlborough, who led the forces of Austria's ally, England.

Also on this day

1529: Holy Roman Emperor Charles V issues a royal warrant authorising Francisco Pizarro to explore and conquer Peru * 1847: Liberia becomes independent, the first African colony to do so * 1856: Irish playwright George Bernard Shaw is born in Dublin

27 July

A cannonball kills a great soldier

1675 Today the man Napoleon considered the greatest military leader in history was killed by a stray cannonball as he reconnoitred his army's position.

Henri de la Tour d'Auvergne, vicomte de Turenne, had been born to the highest French aristocracy in 1611 and had already been entrusted with the command of an infantry regiment by the age of nineteen. For the next 45 years he was almost continuously on the battlefield, particularly during the Thirty Years' War.

Turenne successfully served Louis XIII and Louis XIV in turn. The first Louis's widow, Anne of Austria, was regent of France during her son's infancy, and it was she who made Turenne a marshal at the age of 31.

In 1675 Louis XIV was fighting yet another of his interminable wars, this one against the Austrians. Yet again Marshal Turenne was expected to save the day. On 27 July the French and Austrian armies clashed at Sasbach, and it was here that the fatal cannonball found its mark, prompting from a dying Turenne the plaintive remark, 'I did not mean to be killed today.'

As soon as the news was known in Paris, the court went into deep mourning, Louis declaring that the French had 'lost the father of the country'. Turenne's finest epitaph, however, comes from his contemporary Voltaire, who wrote,

'The virtues and abilities that he alone had made people forget the faults and weaknesses he shared with so many others.'

Turenne's final honour was to be buried among France's kings at St Denis, but during the Revolution the cathedral there was desecrated by the republican mob and his remains were transferred to the Musée des Monuments. Finally in 1800 an admiring Napoleon had the great general re-interred in the Invalides in Paris.

Philip Augustus triumphs at Bouvines

1214 Today King Philip Augustus firmly established France as the predominant European power by defeating a formidable combination of enemies at the Battle of Bouvines.

Holy Roman Emperor Otto IV thought he had found the perfect way to reward his barons and keep them loyal. He would conquer France and distribute its territories piecemeal to those who helped him do it. Fearful that he alone could not defeat Philip, he formed an international coalition with King John of England and two rebellious French vassals, the Count of Flanders and the Count of Boulogne.

Otto's plan called for John to land on the French coast and head for Paris, destroying as he went, while the two counts and the emperor would descend on Paris from the north.

Things first went wrong when Philip met the incompetent John and his army near Angers on 2 July and completely defeated them. Philip then moved north, gathering reinforcements from the local populace as he went. The armies met at Bouvines in Flanders, where Philip overwhelmed the surprised emperor and his remaining allies through the brilliant use of his cavalry against the enemy's infantry. Bouvines was the first battle in which the French nobility and army were joined by the merchants and middle-class citizens, thus representing a milestone in the development of French nationalism.

Also on this day

1694: The British Parliament founds the Bank of England * 1809: The Duke of Wellington defeats the French at the Battle of Talavera in the Peninsular War * 1946: American writer Gertrude Stein dies * 1953: The Korean War comes to an end

28 July

Robespierre gets poetic justice

1794 Maximilien Robespierre was born of good bourgeois stock in the town of Arras, where he once served as a choirboy in the local cathedral. Compulsively neat, righteous, ascetic (he was indifferent to both fine food and women), he later became the most feared man in France as head of the Committee for Public Safety, which initiated the Reign of Terror during the French Revolution.

The public called Robespierre 'the Incorruptible' for his apparently selfless revolutionary zeal, and he termed himself 'a slave of freedom, a living martyr to the Republic'. But in fact Robespierre was a mean and vindictive tyrant, who sent his political enemies to the guillotine more often than enemies of the state.

Eventually the bloody Reign of Terror Robespierre had done so much to create devoured him in its turn. In the early hours of 28 July 1794 he was seized by French troops at the Hôtel de Ville, and in the scuffle was painfully shot in the lower jaw. Later the same day he was arraigned before the Revolutionary Tribunal and sentenced to death, along with 22 of his supporters, including his brother. About eight o'clock that evening he was taken to what today is called the place de la Concorde, where the great guillotine waited. His face was wrapped in a bloodstained bandage, but he made no sound. Just before the final act the executioner ripped off the bandage and Robespierre's lower jaw fell open and blood poured from the gaping wound.

A witness reports that he 'let out a groan like a dying tiger, which could be heard across the square'. And then the blade whistled down, severing his head from his body in one of history's greatest cases of poetic justice. He was only 36 years old.

Vivaldi and Bach die on the same date

1741, 1750 To lovers of Baroque music, two of the most illustrious names are Antonio Vivaldi and Johann Sebastian Bach. They both died on this day, nine years apart.

Vivaldi spent virtually all of his life in Venice, where he became director of the Ospedale della Pietà, a conservatory for orphaned girls. Although he was an ordained priest, due to a severe asthmatic condition he was unable to celebrate Mass. Because of his red hair he was nicknamed Il Prete Rosso (The Red Priest). Today remembered primarily for his brilliant compositions, in his time he was known throughout Europe as a violin virtuoso.

Stern and unbending regarding his religion, Vivaldi was 48 when a pretty fifteen-year-old contralto named Anna Girò sang in one of his operas. Although her voice was not remarkable, she became part of his group, spawning the gossip that she was his mistress, but the rumour remains unproven.

Although Bach was undoubtedly the greater composer, he was an admirer of Vivaldi, arranging at least ten of Vivaldi's solo concerti for other instruments. Like Vivaldi, he excelled as a performer as well as a composer and was an outstanding harpsichordist and organist.

Bach lived in many German cities during his lifetime, was twice happily married and fathered twenty children. He was known to be modest about his music, once commenting, 'I have always had to work hard; anyone who works as hard could do what I did.'

Bach and Vivaldi were both born in the month of March and both died on the same date, 28 July. In 1741, when he was 66, Vivaldi travelled to Vienna for the production of his ninetieth opera but fell ill and died before it opened. When he died some 450 of his works remained unpublished, finally making their way to the Turin Library where they were first edited and performed in the late 1990s.

We do not know exactly what killed Bach except that he was sick for several months prior to his death in 1750 in Leipzig at the age of 65.

Henry VIII marries Catherine Howard

1540 It was a June and December wedding when on this day 44-year-old King Henry VIII took to the altar in a private ceremony his fifth wife, nineteen-year-old Catherine Howard. Henry was enamoured, calling her his 'rose without a thorn', although looking at her portrait today we see a large-featured, coarse and rather dim-looking woman. Catherine had first come to his notice when she was a maid of honour for Henry's previous wife, Anne of Cleves, when they had married only six months earlier, on 6 January. Henry divorced Anne on 9 July (it was rumoured that the marriage had never been consummated) and dashed off to marry Catherine eighteen days later.

History does not state if Henry's wedding to Catherine was a festive occasion, but perhaps a few spirits were dampened by the fact that Thomas Cromwell, for nine years Henry's closest advisor, was beheaded on the very same day. Cromwell had served Henry loyally and well. He had largely emasculated the Church's power in favour of the King and had overseen the destruction of the monasteries, bringing the treasury (i.e. Henry) enormous wealth.

But Cromwell had made one principal error. Mistakenly thinking that England needed alliances with German principalities, he had persuaded the King to marry Anne of Cleves, to whom Henry took an immediate and visceral dislike. Within a month of their marriage it became clear that Henry had no need of German allies and that therefore the marriage to Anne had not been necessary after all.

Cromwell had inevitably made enemies during his years of power, and they quickly circled like vultures on seeing Cromwell's position weaken, persuading Henry that he was in truth a traitor and a heretic. Henry condemned him to the block without a hearing.

Cromwell's execution that day turned out to be an omen for those who cared to read it. Catherine Howard herself went to the axe only nineteen months after her wedding day.

Also on this day

1914: Austria declares war on Serbia, starting the First World War * 1920: Mexican outlaw and revolutionary Pancho Villa surrenders

29 July

The birth of Benito Mussolini

1883 Predappio – a small town just a few miles from Ravenna, once the proud capital of the Western Roman Empire – perhaps a fitting place for the birth today of Benito Mussolini, the last Italian leader ever to try to build an empire of his own.

Mussolini was the son of a poor blacksmith who doubled as a socialist journalist and a schoolteacher mother. He inherited his parents' brains and perhaps the violence of the forge, as bullying his classmates marked his school years, and he twice assaulted other pupils with a knife.

As a young man he became a violent socialist, spending some time in prison in Switzerland, where he was a full-time journalist and part-time rabble-rouser. He later started an affair with Rachele Guidi, the daughter of his father's mistress (but not of his father). The couple eventually married shortly before Mussolini was sent to prison for the fifth time.

In his 20s Mussolini had been a dedicated Socialist Party member, opposed to all wars and a committed internationalist. But slowly his views became narrower, and by the time he was 30 he had become a xenophobic warmonger, strongly backing Italy's entry into the First World War. Joining the Italian Bersaglieri, during the war he was wounded in a training accident, although later the incident was blown up into a heroic action on the front line. He returned home totally opposed to the Socialist Party that had by then expelled him. He was convinced that he was the great leader he believed Italy so desperately needed.

In 1919 Mussolini formed a new party in Milan, christening it the Fasci de Combattimento, harking back to the glories of ancient Rome with reference to the fasces or wooden staves carried by Roman lictors as symbols of authority as they guarded Rome's magistrates. Soon his followers were wearing the famous black shirts to distinguish them from the crowd, no doubt inspired by Garibaldi's Red Shirts of the Risorgimento.

By 1920 Italy was becoming increasingly chaotic, and Mussolini's posturing as a man of destiny and his open call for authoritarian leadership had strong appeal for a populace fed up with riots in the streets and the unceasing strikes paralysing the nation. At a Fascist rally in Naples on 24 October 1922 he openly threatened the government, 'Either the government will be given to us or we shall seize it by marching on Rome.' A week later the King appointed him Prime Minister, at 39 the youngest in Italy's short history.

Once in power, Mussolini did not make the trains run on time although he made the world think he did. A neurotic who wouldn't shake hands because he thought it unhygienic, he did build the first *autostrada*, temporarily crush the Mafia and excavate the Roman Forum. He also took complete dictatorial control of his country.

Mussolini considered Adolf Hitler 'a terrible sexual degenerate' (presumably because of Hitler's apparent lack of sex life) and Germany 'a racist insane asylum'. But when Hitler invaded Poland and then rolled up the rest of Europe, Mussolini was consumed by jealousy of his military success after Italy's costly failure in Ethiopia. And so, half for reasons of envy, half to protect Italy from German aggression, Mussolini committed himself to the Axis and declared war on an already defeated France. In explanation he portentously announced, 'One moment on the battlefield is worth a thousand years of peace.'

The rest, as they say, is history – Italy's catastrophic defeat in the war and Mussolini's ignominious end. He was executed with his mistress by his own people.

The Armada

1588 To Philip II of Spain the situation had finally become intolerable. The heretic English were supporting Dutch rebels against Spanish rule, and that famous admiral-buccaneer Sir Francis Drake was raiding Spanish ports in the Caribbean, severely damaging the Spanish economy. Even worse, England's Queen, the bastard Elizabeth, persisted in allowing Protestant heresies rather than continuing her sister Mary's return to the true Catholic faith. The only answer was invasion.

For two years King Philip assembled his attacking force: over 130 ships, 19,000 soldiers, 8,000 sailors, 2,000 galley slaves, 1,000 noblemen and some 600 priests and monks. In July this enormous Armada set sail for England.

On 29 July the English first sighted the Armada off the coast of Cornwall. Sir Francis Drake was enjoying a leisurely game of bowls at his home near Plymouth Hoe when Thomas Fleming, captain of his flagship *Golden Hind*, came galloping to report the Spanish approach. On hearing the news, Drake refused to be hurried, replying, 'We have time enough to finish the game and beat the Spaniards, too.'

Battle was soon joined. The English had faster and more manoeuvrable ships and superior cannon, allowing them to bombard the Spanish at long range, but the Spaniards had superior numbers. The battle seemed stalemated, and for a week the opposing fleets drifted up the Channel, neither side gaining a decisive victory. Then the Spanish anchored off Calais with the intent of picking up more troops coming from the Spanish Netherlands. At midnight on 7 August Drake changed the whole course of battle when he cut loose eight blazing fire ships to drift down upon the Spanish fleet. In panic the Spaniards cut their cables to flee, at the very moment the English fleet launched its attack.

What followed was the decisive moment in the English defence against the Armada. The Spanish fleet was completely disorganised, its formation destroyed. The English cannon started to take a heavy toll, largely without response since many of the Spanish heavy guns had been dismounted during the night. By the end of the day the Spaniards knew they were beaten, and the dispersed fleet sailed north, the only way to avoid the English warships and to return to Spain.

Up around Scotland and finally off the Irish coast sailed the Spaniards but the north Atlantic gales (what Protestant Drake called 'the Winds of God') further dispersed the fleet, causing many ships to founder.

Eventually only 66 ships returned to Spain, and some 15,000 Spanish soldiers and sailors had perished, including the Prince of Ascoli, Philip II's illegitimate son. England was safe for ever from the threat of Spanish invasion.

To celebrate the victory Queen Elizabeth ordered struck a commemorative medal bearing the inscription *Deus flavit, et dissipati sunt* (God blew, and they were scattered).

A Confederate ship is born in Liverpool

1862 In Liverpool this morning, an unfinished steam-powered vessel, bearing hastily drawn papers identifying her as the British merchantman *Enrica*, left her dockyard slip draped in bright bunting and headed down the Mersey for a 'trial run'. In addition to her crew, she had on board a number of well-dressed guests with a picnic lunch suitable for the festive occasion. But at noon a tugboat came alongside onto which all supernumeraries were speedily off-loaded. Then *Enrica* turned north and disappeared into the Irish Sea.

Three weeks later, in the Azores, outfitted for war, she was reborn as the Confederate States' Ship *Alabama*, the most successful commerce-raider of the Civil War, in fact the most successful in all naval history. In the next 21 months, the CSS *Alabama* became the scourge of Northern shipping around the world. With a Southern captain and officers and an Anglo-Irish crew, she cruised some 75,000 miles, capturing, ransoming or destroying over 60 Union merchant ships, for a combined loss of $6,500,000. In all her travels, she never once put into a Confederate port, but revictualled and refuelled at places like Cape Town, Singapore and Bahia, usually with the permission of local British authorities.

Reflecting his nation's outrage, the American ambassador in London, Charles Francis Adams, strongly protested to the British government – officially neutral in the American Civil War – about the lax security that had allowed the ship to escape into enemy hands. But British dockyards had already begun producing other raiders, like the *Shenandoah* and the *Florida*, which collectively, by war's end, would destroy over 200 vessels and cargoes valued at as much as $25 million and sank more than half of the American merchant fleet.

Alabama's spectacular string of depredations ended off the French port of Cherbourg in June 1864, when the USS *Kearsarge* caught up with her and sank her in a 90-minute battle. Among the witnesses who thronged the shore to see the clash was Edouard Manet, who painted the well-publicised event.

The genius behind the purchase and escape of the *Alabama* and other Confederate raiders was James D. Bulloch, a Georgian and experienced naval officer whom Jefferson Davis had sent to England early in the Civil War to acquire ships for the South. After the war he remained in Liverpool, but his celebrated exploits made him a hero, not only to Confederate sympathisers but also to his asthmatic – and very pro-Union – young nephew in New York City in whom he inspired a lifelong interest in naval affairs. Some years later, when the nephew began writing his first book, Bulloch provided valuable advice on matters of naval combat. The book, *The Naval History of the War of 1812*, appeared in 1882. Its author, only 23 years old but already an up-and-coming New York politician, was Theodore Roosevelt.

Also on this day

1830: The 'Citizen King' Louis-Philippe usurps the French throne * 1900: King Humbert of Italy is assassinated by anarchists at Monza

30 July

Bismarck the Iron Chancellor dies

1898 On this day died Prince Otto von Bismarck, a resentful and bitter old man of 83.

Bismarck had indelibly changed the face of Europe during his 28 years as Prime Minister of Prussia and nineteen as Chancellor of a united Germany. What once had been a hodgepodge of mini-kingdoms was now the single greatest power, industrial and military, in Europe. The theoretical Germanic hegemony once based in Vienna was now true domination controlled from Berlin.

Autocratic but brilliant, Bismarck had once famously said that 'die Politik ist die Lehre vom Möglichen' (politics is the art of the possible). But later he had told the Prussian House of Deputies that the great issues of the day could be settled only 'durch Blut und Eisen' (through blood and iron).

In domestic policy the mighty chancellor was an extreme reactionary who had fought for years to eradicate all forms of social democracy, especially the Socialist Party. In his mind he grouped together all liberals, from socialists to anarchists, terming them 'this country's rats [who] should be exterminated'. But in 1890 a group of leftist parties gained control of the Reichstag, and the 21-year-old Kaiser Wilhelm II felt compelled to ease the ageing, inflexible chancellor from office.

Although out of office and bitter towards the Kaiser and the government, Bismarck retained his acute political insight to the end. One of his last predictions was that, 'If there is ever another war in Europe, it will come out of some damned silly thing in the Balkans.'

The First Defenestration of Prague

1419 We've all heard of the 'Defenestration of Prague', such a bizarre title for a historical event, but how many of us know what it actually was? Well, there were two of them; the first happened today.

The early 15th century was a period of religious turmoil. Two popes reigned during the Great Schism (sometimes three), reformers like Jan Hus were burnt at the stake, and the Catholic world was already pregnant with the Protestantism to be born in the next century. There was no place of greater ferment than Bohemia, where the well-meaning but weak King Wenceslas IV ruled from Prague.

Unfortunately for Wenceslas, the religious unrest soon turned into a full-scale rebellion. Rioting broke out in Prague, and on this hot and humid 30 July the mob broke into the town hall and hurled several of the King's councillors out of the window to their deaths. No doubt this rather minor bloodletting is remembered solely because of its peculiar name, although there was a second more famous defenestration 199 years later on May 23.

Luckily for King Wenceslas, he wasn't in the town hall to be thrown out, but the shock of it all did him in, as he died of chagrin only seventeen days later.

Also on this day

1818: British novelist Emily Brontë is born * 1857: American economist Thorstein Veblen is born * 1865: American automobile tycoon Henry Ford is born * 1898: British sculptor Henry Moore is born

31 July

Etienne Marcel is hacked down

1358 Beside the Hôtel de Ville in Paris sits a great statue of Etienne Marcel, who ruled that city for almost two years and who forced the Dauphin, the future Charles V, into desperately needed reforms.

Marcel was provost of Paris's merchants, and he had grasped power when the English captured the King, Jean le Bon, at Poitiers in 1356. But being just a burgher, Marcel eventually found himself caught between the competing forces of the Dauphin and the King of Navarre, known as Charles the Bad, both of whose armies wished to enter Paris.

As the Dauphin had already broken his earlier promises of reform, Marcel decided to admit the bad Charles even though this king had well earned his nickname through treachery and double-dealing with principalities all over Spain and France. At midnight on the last night in July Marcel crept secretly to open one of Paris's gates to the Navarrese and their king. But there he was caught with the keys in his hand by one of his oldest supporters, Jean Maillart.

Maillart, however, had resolved to support the Dauphin, realising that Marcel was now acting more from his own ambition than to help his fellow Parisians. Seeing Marcel about to open the gate, Maillart challenged him, to which Marcel coolly answered, 'Jean, I am here to take care of the city of which I have charge.'

But Maillart, sensing that Marcel was about to betray the city, instantly felled his old friend with an axe. So ended the life of Etienne Marcel at the age of 40, the first Parisian who had successfully (for a while) stood up to royal power and forced through changes that helped the common man rather than the nobility.

Jean Jaurès is shot

1914 On this day a shocking event occurred in Paris. While lunching at his favourite restaurant, the Café du Croissant in the rue Montmartre, the revered French Socialist leader Jean Jaurès was shot to death by a crazed young patriot-extremist. The assassin evidently hoped to prevent a general strike by French workers that would disrupt France's imminent mobilisation for war against Germany. Ironically, Jaurès was a patriot in his own right who had just two days earlier called for his followers to join their regiments should France be attacked.

It was a moment of crisis for the French nation, divided as it was on the eve of war by political feuds and rivalries. There was no time for deliberation, for Germany had already ordered her mobilisation in response to that of France's ally, Russia. The war was expected to be a quick, decisive affair, surely to be lost by any country that failed to call up its reserves in time.

With their most trusted leader dead, would the working classes answer the mobilisation order, set for the next day? Or, feeling they had nothing to lose but their chains, would they go on strike and refuse France's call to arms?

President Poincaré's government had no idea what to do, how seriously to take the pacifist rhetoric spouted so noisily by the leaders of the anti-militarist left. As to the leaders, Clemenceau's advice to the government was 'Crack down!' But for the workers themselves, the prediction of the chief of the Sûreté proved accurate: 'They will follow the regimental bands.'

And so they did, Jaurès's death notwithstanding. The mobilisation went calmly, the army was deployed, and the Great War began two days later on 3 August. The expectation that the war would be quick and decisive turned out to be quite wrong: it lasted four years, three months and eight days.

The soldier who founded the Jesuits

1556 Although a diminutive man of less than five feet two inches, Ignatius Loyola had been a proud soldier of 26 in the service of Spain when Martin Luther nailed his famous theses challenging the Catholic Church to a church door. Loyola gave little thought to religion at that time, later describing himself as 'a man given to the vanities of the world, whose chief delight consisted in martial exercises, with a great and vain desire to win renown'. But four years after Luther's pronouncements, Loyola's leg was crushed by a cannonball during the siege of Pamplona in one of the unending conflicts between Holy Roman Emperor Charles V and François I of France.

Then all was changed. First Loyola underwent unspeakable tortures on the operating table and the rack as surgeons tried to heal his leg without a resultant limp. The surgeons failed, and Loyola determined that if he could no longer fight for his king he would fight for his church.

Later Loyola attended the University of Paris where he made his first recruits into his army for Christ, and by the time he was 49 his society, the Jesuits, received official blessing from the Pope.

The Jesuits were moulded after the personality of their founder: militant and activist, believing that, in the name of God, the end justifies the means.

Loyola himself never ceased in his battle for the Church. He was a work-aholic, indifferent to his surroundings and personal comfort. He established the Jesuits' headquarters in a Roman slum and lived on a diet of bread, water and chestnuts. All the while he directed his order. The number grew of trained 'soldiers of the Church', and when he died in Rome on this day at the age of 65 some 1,500 Jesuits were spread throughout Europe.

Loyola was canonised in 1622.

Also on this day

1886: Hungarian composer and piano virtuoso Franz Liszt dies

1 August

Nelson wins the Battle of the Nile

1798 Napoleon Bonaparte had left his fleet of seventeen ships in Abu Qir Bay near the mouth of the Nile, while he stormed through Alexandria and Cairo. He was not to know that Rear Admiral Horatio Nelson was closing in. Today the British would score a crushing victory at the Battle of the Nile.

Nelson was determined to make his mark. The day before the battle he affirmed: 'Before this time tomorrow I shall have gained a peerage, or Westminster Abbey.'

A few hours before nightfall Nelson attacked. In a brilliant tactical thrust he sent five British men-o'-war between the French ships and their shore batteries, opening fire from both sides of his ships at once. When the French fired back they were in danger of overshooting the British fleet and hitting each other.

At about ten at night the battle reached its climax when the French admiral's 120-gun flagship *Orient* exploded, killing most of its crew and the admiral himself. The British continued to attack the remains of the French fleet, finally capturing or sinking all but two of the enemy's ships of the line.

The Battle of the Nile was exceptionally bloody; French losses approached 10,000, while the victorious British sustained almost 1,000 casualties, including Nelson, who suffered a minor head wound. But later that year Nelson gained his peerage as he had predicted.

This was Nelson's first great triumph against Napoleon, but oddly enough the battle was most famously commemorated by a contemporary bit of English doggerel that celebrates the French, not the English. The English poetess Felicia Hemans immortalised the heroism of the son of the captain of the French flagship, who tried to halt the flames of his father's foundering ship:

> The boy stood on the burning deck
> Whence all but he had fled;
> The flame that lit the battle's wreck
> Shone round him o'er the dead.

Sadly, the boy failed and went down with the ship.

Hindenburg's departure clears the path for Hitler

1934 Today Paul von Hindenburg, President of Germany and the nation's enduring hero for his great 1914 victories at Tannenberg and the Masurian Lakes, died at the age of 87 at Neudeck, Germany. It is ironic that this old Junker, anti-democratic and monarchist to the end, was the last best hope of the liberal Weimar Republic. In the final months of his life, he was all that stood between Adolf Hitler and total power in Germany.

As Supreme Commander during the last two years of the First World War, Hindenburg, aided by his Quartermaster-General Erich Ludendorff, had been virtual ruler of Germany, and in that capacity had led his nation to defeat and revolution. Mainly as a dignified symbol of the nation's former stability, of its better days and past glories, the old soldier was called from retirement and elected President of the German republic in 1925. 'Better a zero than a Nero', one observer wrote.

When his five-year term was up he was re-elected. But despite the enormous respect and admiration in which he was held in Germany, Hindenburg was no bulwark against the ominous trend of events. He loathed Hitler and the Nazis – '*That* man a chancellor? I'll make him a postmaster and he can lick stamps with my head on them' – but the army chiefs finally prevailed upon the President to send for Hitler because they thought they could do business with him if they brought him to power. Hitler took office as Chancellor on 30 January 1933.

The next year when it was clear that Hindenburg was dying and that a successor as President would have to be found, the army leaders once more chose Hitler in the mistaken belief that they could control him and their future. Within hours of Hindenburg's death, Hitler announced that the functions of President would be combined with those of Chancellor, and that from now on he would be 'Führer und Reichskanzler'.

The very next day, anxious to cement the bargain with their new leader, the German armed forces, from the highest commanders to the newest recruits, swore their unconditional obedience to the Führer, their supreme commander, as once they had done to the Kaiser. It would prove a tragically misplaced act of fealty.

At Hindenburg's funeral service on 6 August, his coffin was borne down the aisle to the strains of the funeral march from *Götterdämmerung*. It was appropriate music with which to mark the death of a field marshal – and that of the German republic.

Eleanor of Aquitaine marries her first king

1137 As befitted a royal second son, Louis Capet was reared in the cloisters of Notre Dame in Paris while his elder brother was groomed to reign. When Louis was ten, however, his brother was killed in a riding accident, and suddenly the second son had become the heir to the throne of France.

By the time Louis was sixteen it was time for him to marry – particularly when there was a brilliant, beautiful duchess on the market, a year younger than he, the greatest heiress in France. Her name was Eleanor, her duchy Aquitaine, and Louis's father King Louis the Fat (sixth of his name) claimed her for his son.

On 1 August 1137 the couple were wed in Eleanor's capital of Bordeaux and immediately headed for Paris. But even before they arrived, fate struck, and Louis the Fat lay dead at 56. Young Louis and his bride had started their journey as prince and princess but entered the capital as King and Queen.

Louis VII and Eleanor perhaps should have earned historical immortality as King and Queen of France, but while they remained together for almost fifteen years, their marriage eventually collapsed. Although a prolific producer of daughters, Eleanor produced no son. And when the royal couple went on crusade, her dalliance with her own uncle proved the final straw. King Louis divorced her.

Only then did Eleanor gain her greatest and lasting fame, for she married the future Henry II of England and mothered two famous kings, the storied Richard the Lion-Heart and the feckless John.

Poor Louis gained some historical renown as a royal cuckold, the man who relinquished half of France when he divorced his wayward wife. But his most permanent claim to fame came through his love of flowers. He chose the iris as his emblem and used a stylised version for his escutcheon. The simple iris thus became known as the *fleur de Louis*, later corrupted to *fleur-de-lis*. Louis's flower remained the symbol of the French monarchy for over 700 years.

Also on this day

10 BC: Roman Emperor Claudius is born * 1498: Christopher Columbus discovers South America * 1714: Queen Anne dies, bringing George I and the Hanoverian dynasty to the English throne

2 August

Hannibal destroys the Romans at Cannae

216 BC Today the great Carthaginian general Hannibal Barca totally annihilated a huge Roman army at the Battle of Cannae.

Six hundred years earlier, in 814 BC, Phoenician traders from Tyre had founded a new city on the north coast of Africa (where today's Tunis stands), calling it simply 'Kart-Hadasht', or 'new town'.

Over the centuries Carthage developed into a powerful and prosperous Mediterranean power, a rival of Rome, with colonies in Spain, Sicily and Sardinia, but in 264 BC a minor encounter in Sicily grew into the First Punic War with Rome, a conflict that gained its name from the Roman word for Carthaginians, *Punici*, which itself comes from Phoenician, the language of ancient Carthage.

Hannibal was born in Carthage of noble parents during this war in 247 BC. When the conflict ended six years later, victorious Rome stripped Carthage of much of its wealth and territory. Brought up in Carthage-controlled Spain, he learned to hate the Romans for the humiliation and impoverishment of his country, and vowed revenge.

Hannibal was an arresting man. Tall, clean-shaven, handsome and athletic, he was an outstanding swordsman and a fearless rider. His appearance revealed his Phoenician (Semitic) bloodlines, with a slightly hooked nose, curly hair and dark eyes (one of which he later lost during his fight against Rome). By 26 he was already a general.

At 29 Hannibal embarked on one of the most daring military exploits in all of history to achieve his goal of a decisive victory on Roman soil. To avoid having to challenge Rome's naval dominance of the Mediterranean, he marched his huge force – Carthaginian and Iberian foot soldiers, Numidian cavalry and 37 elephants – north from Carthago Nova ('New Carthage', today's Cartagena in Spain) and across southern Gaul. It was nearing winter when he reached the Alps, but, despite severe losses of men and pack animals, in only fifteen days he led his army through the mountains and down into Italy. Somehow all the elephants survived.

Even in his first battles against the Romans Hannibal displayed his military genius in a series of devastating victories. He was a master of deception, one night tying lighted faggots to the horns of cattle to convince his enemies that his army was on the move when in fact they were waiting in ambush. Within two years he had covered much of Italy, leaving Rome terrified but not beaten.

In the spring of 216 BC, Hannibal moved south to capture a Roman supply depot at Cannae, a small village on the Achilles Heel of the Italian boot. Determined to rid Italy of the Carthaginian invader, the Roman consuls Lucius Aemilius Paulus and Gaius Terentius Varro advanced with a huge army of about 80,000 men to do battle with an enemy force of only half their size. Hoping to break the Carthaginian line with a heavy attack in the centre, the Romans massed their infantry and charged. Hannibal ordered his line to bow backward under the weight of the Roman assault, encouraging Varro to pile more infantry into the centre. Then the Carthaginian sent his two wings to envelop the concentrated Roman infantry on both sides, and his cavalry, which had already bested the Roman horse, completed the encirclement by attacking from the flanks and rear. The battlefield became a killing ground.

Up to 50,000 Romans perished in the slaughter (the near-contemporary historian Polybius says 70,000). Whatever the true number, it represented the greatest one-day loss in all of Rome's history, a massacre that was unsurpassed in any battle anywhere until the 20th century.

So great was the terror inspired by Hannibal's triumph that for centuries Roman parents would frighten mischievous children with the words 'Hannibal ad portas!' (Hannibal at the gates!).

King William Rufus is slain in the New Forest

1100 Today Walter Tirel was riding with his king, William Rufus, through the New Forest in the south of England, enjoying a day's deer hunting. Suddenly a stag bounded between them. 'Shoot, Walter, shoot, as if it were the devil', cried the King. Tirel loosed an arrow, but, glancing off the stag's back, it impaled the King, who tumbled from his horse and lay dead in the silent forest.

William II was a heavy-set man with sharp eyes, an occasional stammer and a fiery red complexion, from which he gained the nickname of Rufus. Second son of William the Conqueror, he inherited his father's ruthlessness but added to it an opportunism and brutality of his own. He inherited the English throne on his father's death in September 1087, while his elder brother received the preferable inheritance, the Duchy of Normandy. In his thirteen years as king, William Rufus had maintained order in troubled times, further consolidating his father's conquest, but never shrank from cruelty or bloodshed to achieve his ends.

Ever since William Rufus's fatal accident there have been rumours that it was murder. Also hunting in the New Forest that day was William Rufus's younger brother Henry, who stood to inherit the throne. And Walter Tirel, who shot the deadly arrow, immediately fled the country to hide across the Channel.

Murder has never been proved, but Henry did become King as Henry I. As for William Rufus, he was buried in Winchester but was refused religious rites by the clergy there because of his bloody career.

Also on this day

1589: Friar Jacques Clément stabs King Henri III of France to death * 1776: The American Declaration of Independence is signed * 1788: British painter Thomas Gainsborough dies of cancer * 1876: Wild Bill Hickok is shot dead in the Number Ten Saloon, Deadwood, South Dakota

3 August

Columbus sets sail with three good ships

1492 Ever since he was 23 (in 1474), Christopher Columbus had been trying to persuade someone to finance a voyage to the West, to seek a route to the Indies. Son of a wealthy weaver from Genoa, his first appeals had been to the Florentine geographer Paolo Toscanelli, and by 1483 he was seeking help from King John II of Portugal, but all to no avail.

Finally in 1486 Columbus approached the Catholic Majesties, Ferdinand and Isabella of Spain. At first he was rejected, but in 1492 he was called back to the Spanish court and the project was agreed.

So, on the fateful morning of 3 August 1492 Christopher Columbus sailed from Palos de la Frontera in Andalucía with a crew of 88 on his three good ships, the *Niña*, the *Pinta* and the *Santa María*, on history's greatest voyage of discovery.

Two months and nine days later the little convoy first sighted land in the New World. Two months after that the *Santa María* ran aground and was lost on the coast of present day Haiti. Today there exist neither pictures nor descriptions of any of Columbus's ships, so the myriad depictions and reconstructions to be found may represent typical 15th-century ships but cannot show us the way the originals really looked.

Jesse Owens humiliates the Nazis at the Olympic Games

1936 So far it had been a good year for the Third Reich. In February Germany hosted the fourth winter Olympic games at Garmisch-Partenkirchen, where her athletes finished a highly creditable second behind the Norwegians. In March German troops reoccupied the Rhineland unopposed. And in June in New York City, Max Schmeling knocked out Joe Louis in the twelfth round at Yankee Stadium.

This morning, however, in a Berlin made resplendent for the summer Olympics, something occurred to take the edge off the notion of Aryan invincibility. Before 110,000 spectators jam-packed into the new Olympic Stadium, with Adolf Hitler and the Nazi brass in attendance and Leni Riefenstahl's camera crews set to film the scenes of German triumph, an American sprinter burst from the starting line like a rocket and streaked down the cinder track to win the finals of the 100-metre dash in a world record time of 10.2 seconds. For the victor, a tall, graceful black man named J.C. Owens – hence Jesse – this victory would be the first of four he would accomplish at the Berlin games.

In a towering performance, acclaimed even by the German crowds, Owens in the next six days went on to win gold medals for the United States in the 220-metre dash, the 400-metre relay, and the long jump, setting or equalling Olympic records in each event. The Führer was disgruntled. He told Baldur von Schirach, the Hitler Youth leader: 'The Americans ought to be ashamed of themselves for letting their medals be won by Negroes. I myself would never even shake hands with one of them.'

In the end, however, despite American domination of the track and field events, Germany 'won' the 1936 Olympics with 181 points, the United States coming in second with 124 points, and Italy third with 47 points. Some 4 million spectators, including thousands of visitors from overseas eager to see the 'New Germany', witnessed the Berlin games. As both mass pageantry and sports triumph, the eleventh Olympiad proved an extraordinary propaganda victory for Hitler and the Nazi leadership. 'The generous congratulations he and his lieutenants received for their Olympic successes', wrote the historian of the Nazi Olympics Richard D. Mandell, 'were both emboldening to them and deceiving to their opponents'. Indeed, even as the games got under way, Hitler had begun his fateful meddling in the Spanish Civil War. In the aftermath, with the world's attention still held by the glamour of Olympic feats, he turned his eyes towards Austria.

Also on this day

1876: British Prime Minister Stanley Baldwin is born * 1914: Germany declares war on France

4 August

Queen Philippa saves the burghers of Calais

1347 In his endless quest to claim the crown of France, England's Edward III needed a deep-water port to ensure transport of supplies from England, and the logical choice was Calais, a strongly fortified town that Edward claimed by right in his role as Count of Ponthieu. Encircling the city with his army on 3 September 1346, he determined to starve it into submission.

For month after month the good citizens of Calais resisted, devouring first their horses, then their dogs and finally their cats and rats. But still no French army came to the rescue, and although their defences held firm against the English attack, at length starvation forced them to surrender on this day after eleven months of siege.

Furious at Calais's long resistance, Edward demanded that the six most important men of the town come to him barefoot, clothed only in their shirts, with ropes around their necks. Six of the richest burghers appeared as ordered, sweating from the heat and shivering in their fear of the King's wrath.

But just as Edward was about to signal their execution, his beautiful wife Queen Philippa, who had accompanied her husband throughout the siege, knelt before the King. 'Gentle Sire', she begged, 'I humbly beseech you in the name of the son of Holy Mary and for your own love of me to show mercy to these men'.

Impressed by the goodness of his noble wife, Edward relented and let the burghers go free. Such is the touching story of the burghers of Calais, a tale so moving that over half a millennium later the great sculptor Auguste Rodin created one of his most famous statues based on the event.

Calais remained English until the reign of Mary Tudor, when France seized it back permanently.

German cavalry invade Belgium to start the First World War

1914 Today at 5 a.m., just 35 days after Austrian Archduke Franz Ferdinand had been assassinated at Sarajevo, German cavalry units swept over the frontier into neutral Belgium in the first fighting of the First World War, ending 43 years of peace among the Great Powers of Europe.

Although the great Bismarck had completed the unification of Germany in 1870, the country in truth was an amplified Prussia; the Kaiser was the Prussian king, and the German army was loyal to him alone. The Prime Minister, too, was responsible only to him, not to the Reichstag. Furthermore, the country had a three-tier voting system giving disproportionate weight to the rich and powerful. The most populous European nation, this military autocracy was determined to be reckoned among the greatest of powers, and alarmed its neighbours by its military and naval build-up. Yet Germany felt itself a victim, encircled by France on the west and Russia on the east, two countries that had allied themselves solely from fear of German might. When Germany launched its attack, most of her citizens felt they were only defending themselves.

Germany's northern sweep through Belgium was a central element in the 1905 plan developed by the Prussian General Alfred von Schlieffen. His aim was to destroy the French with a massive attack while fighting a holding action against Russia. But heavy fortifications on the German–French border precluded direct assault, so von Schlieffen advocated sending a massive army on a quick enveloping dash through neutral Belgium. The Germans would storm past Brussels and down into France at Lille and along the coast, then swing around below Paris to catch the main French army from the rear. He thought France would be defeated in 40 days, too short a time for backward Russia to get more than a few token troops to the eastern front, or for Great Britain, tied by treaty to Belgium, to get its troops across the Channel. Once the French had been defeated, the German army would swing east to crush the Russians.

But nothing went according to plan. The Germans met fierce Belgian resistance at Liège, which slowed down their attack, and when they reached France in early September they found themselves facing the French army and the British Expeditionary Force. In the opening clashes of the war, at the Ardennes, the Sambre, Mons, Le Cateau, and Guise, the Germans continued their inexorable advance. But at the Marne in early September, the Allies managed to hold the line and mount a counter-attack, stalling the German onslaught and forcing them back into positions that would not change much over the next four years. In like manner, war against Russia proved far more difficult than anticipated. Despite early German victories at Tannenberg and the Masurian Lakes, by the autumn the two sides were stalemated in the horrors of trench warfare on both the eastern and western fronts. Instead of 40 days, the war had another four years to run.

By the time the conflict finally ground to a halt, Germany had committed some 11 million men, of whom 1,774,000 had been killed and an additional 4 million had been wounded. Perhaps luckily for General von Schlieffen, he died in January 1913, too early to see how disastrous his great plan would turn out to be.

Also on this day

1792: British poet Percy Shelley is born at Horsham, Sussex

5 August

Farragut damns the torpedoes at Mobile Bay

1864 Today American Admiral David Farragut earned his place in naval history, as well as in all future books of quotations.

Farragut commanded a Union fleet of eighteen ships during the American Civil War. As the mists evaporated on this hot August morning, the admiral led his fleet past Fort Morgan, a Confederate stronghold that guarded Mobile Bay on the Alabama coast of the Gulf of Mexico. Immediately the enemy opened fire, and the intrepid Farragut had a sailor lash him to the mast so he could use both hands to hold his telescope and see above the swirling smoke.

In addition to firing their cannon, the Confederates had laced the channel with mines (then called torpedoes), and the leading Yankee warship, the *Tecumseh*, blew up and sank with all hands. Near panic, the *Brooklyn* hove to, and Farragut's whole line hesitated, uncertain whether to attack or retreat, as the guns of Fort Morgan continued their deadly cannonade.

Refusing to be intimidated, Farragut cried, 'Damn the torpedoes! Full speed ahead', and led his fleet safely through the minefield to destroy the Southern fleet waiting within the bay and forcing the surrender of Fort Morgan.

This famous victory effectively closed the last Confederate port still successfully defying the Union naval blockade, and made a major contribution to the North's march to victory.

The first English English king since the Saxons is crowned

1100 When the 31-year-old Henry I was crowned at Westminster Abbey today, he became the first English king since the Saxons to be born on English soil. He inherited the monarchy from his brother, William Rufus, who had been killed only three days before in a hunting accident that may have been a murder – and may have been instigated by Henry.

Henry was the fourth son of William the Conqueror. Like his father, he was thickset and strong, though inclined to fat. Also like his father, he was a capable leader, but he added his own brand of savagery to William's severity. (He once ordered a poet to be blinded for having written satirical verse about him, and the poet, Luke de la Barre, escaped the penalty only by committing suicide.)

Where Henry differed totally from his father was in his ideas concerning marital fidelity. William was apparently a loyal husband, but Henry openly acknowledged over twenty bastards, by a variety of women.

Henry I ruled England for over 35 years until his death in 1135. Some years before he died he arranged for his only surviving child, Matilda, to marry a young French count named Geoffrey Plantagenet, so Henry's blood flows down in English royalty through the Plantagenet line of kings.

The first American income tax

1861 To fight a war you need money, a principle well understood by Salmon P. Chase, Secretary of the Treasury for the North during America's Civil War. With that same principle in mind, and with the encouragement of Chase and other Republican leaders, the 37th Congress today enacted the very first federal income tax in American history: a 3 per cent levy on incomes over $800, thus exempting most wage earners. (Chase's innovation was in fact no innovation at all, for Great Britain had introduced the world's first income tax in 1799 to finance the Napoleonic wars.)

One reason an income tax was needed was to pay the interest on the war bonds the federal government was now so actively selling, not just in large denominations to bankers, but for as little as $50 to ordinary people – another Chase innovation.

There was of course opposition to the new income tax, as the US Constitution prohibited a direct tax on American citizens, but Chase easily persuaded the Supreme Court to OK the idea.

Although Chase's income tax was repealed in 1872, future generations of Americans have suffered more than Northerners did in 1861. On 3 February 1913 the states ratified the 16th Amendment to the US Constitution, authorising the collection of income tax broadly in its current form, but even then the maximum rate reached only 7 per cent. During the Second World War the top bracket was set at 94 per cent, and although rates have declined ever since, by 2001 the annual revenue raised by the tax reached $994 billion for the government.

Also on this day

1850: French writer Guy de Maupassant is born * 1858: Queen Victoria exchanges greetings with US President James Buchanan when the first transatlantic cable is opened

6 August

The last Holy Roman Emperor resigns his title

1806 According to Voltaire, it was neither holy nor Roman nor an empire, yet that amorphous political entity known as the Holy Roman Empire influenced and often dominated European affairs after Charlemagne revived the idea of Augustan Rome in the year 800. But Charlemagne had constructed a very different empire from that of the Romans. It included most of modern Germany, France, Belgium, Switzerland and Holland, extending from the Elbe River in the east to the Atlantic Ocean and including most of Europe south of Denmark to central Italy. His capital was at Aachen rather than in Rome.

Charlemagne's successors soon let his empire disintegrate into chaos, but in 962 it was restored with the coronation of Otto I, the first of an unbroken line of emperors to stretch over eight centuries.

The Holy Roman Empire is of course much associated with the house of Habsburg. The first Habsburg emperor was Rudolf I, known as Rudolf the

Founder, who assumed the title in 1273. Once or twice after that a non-Habsburg wore the crown, but from 1438 onwards every Holy Roman Emperor was a Habsburg.

In 1806 another Habsburg, Franz II, was Emperor, but he lived in a Europe dominated by Napoleon, who controlled much of the Empire's theoretical territorial sphere of influence. Believing the imperial title an unrealistic anachronism (and willing to keep a lesser title rather than lose a grander one), Franz renounced it on this day, henceforth styling himself the Emperor of Austria.

Thus came to an end the Holy Roman Empire, an idea whose time had gone after 844 years and 67 emperors.

The first coronation in Reims's new cathedral sets a six-century trend

1223 Today when Louis VIII and his wife Blanche of Castile were crowned in the new cathedral at Reims, north-east of Paris, they set a precedent that was to last for 602 years.

Reims Cathedral was then only twelve years old, built to replace an earlier church ruined by fire. Although the building required over 80 years to complete, even by Louis's time it had reached a suitable state of glory to justify a coronation. Larger than its two most renowned predecessors, Chartres and Notre Dame, Reims has an interior length of 496 feet, with two glorious towers soaring to a height of 270 feet. Although the cathedral's stained glass windows are perhaps marginally inferior to those of Chartres and Sainte-Chapelle, it remains one of the architectural and artistic gems of the French High Gothic.

Over the centuries Reims Cathedral was the site of 25 French coronations, including Charles VII's in 1429, witnessed by Joan of Arc. The last French king to be crowned there was the 68-year-old reactionary Charles X, who was booted into exile five years later in the Revolution of 1830.

Also on this day
1623: Shakespeare's wife Anne Hathaway dies * 1637: English dramatist Ben Jonson dies in London * 1680: Spanish painter Diego Velázquez dies in Madrid * 1809: English poet Alfred, Lord Tennyson is born

7 August

The Marines storm ashore at Guadalcanal

1942 'Now hear this! Now hear this! Stand by to disembark! …' This was the sound you would have heard aboard Navy transports lying in Ironbottom Bay at 0600 hours on this calm, clear, tropical morning. It was the sound of the First

Marine Division going to war. Over the side, down the cargo nets, into the Higgins boats they went, company by company, battalion by battalion, as the division landed on the beaches of Guadalcanal Island. For American forces, it was the first offensive ground operation of the Second World War.

The Marines took the beaches unopposed, but that was a condition that did not last for long. Guadalcanal would prove to be the longest battle of the entire Pacific war. It was a laboratory of warfare for the Marine Corps and Army troops who fought there – and for the naval and air forces that provided crucial support – where they learned the techniques of joint combat operations required to defeat the Japanese in the excruciating jungle terrain. And learn they did, for despite the blunders and losses of the ensuing months, they survived, prevailed, and finally forced the remaining 16,000 Japanese off the island in February 1943.

Historian Robert Leckie, who was a machine-gunner and scout with the First Marine Division on Guadalcanal, estimated that as many as 28,000 Japanese soldiers may have died in the battle, while American losses in the ground combat were about 1,600 deaths and some 4,200 wounded. Combined naval and air losses may have reached a similar total. Next to the Japanese, the toughest foe the Americans faced was the female of the anopheles mosquito: over 5,000 troops were incapacitated with malaria.

In the Marine cemetery on Guadalcanal someone scratched the following epitaph on a mess kit left by one of the graves:

And when he gets to heaven
To St Peter he will tell:
'One more marine reporting, sir —
I've served my time in hell.'

A papal candidate fakes his way to election

1316 For over two years there had been no pope, as the cardinals grappled for power and to keep the papacy in Avignon or to return it to Rome. In June the cardinals met in Lyon but still failed to agree, so Prince Philip of Poitiers (later King Philip V of France) invited them to meet in the Church of the Jacobins for one more deliberation. But as soon as the cardinals were inside, Philip's men slammed the doors and bricked up all the entrances except for one narrow doorway. A pope must be elected, declared Philip, and no one would leave until one was. And so the days started to pass.

Among the horrified holy men was a small, slight cardinal with a pallid complexion and a large store of hidden ambition. He was Jacques Duèse, son of a cobbler from Cahors, now 72 years of age. Seeing his chance, Duèse feigned increasing weakness and ill health, planting the idea that if he were elected, his reign would be a short one. Finally, after more than a month incarcerated in the church, the 24 cardinals came to an agreement. The feeble and ancient Duèse would be their choice. On 7 August 1316 he was duly elected, and at last the imprisoned Conclave was released.

How the rival cardinals would regret their pick. John XXII (as he was subsequently called) was both dictatorial and pig-headed. He was also a world-beater in the art of nepotism; twenty of the 28 cardinals he created were also from southern France and three were his own nephews. Worse, the crafty Duèse outlived almost all his rivals, reigning for eighteen years and dying at the ripe age of 90.

A great historian changes camps

1472 Philippe de Commynes was perhaps the first 'modern' historian. In his writing he tried to draw lessons or morals from the events unfolding around him, and only when he could blame neither human foolishness nor stupidity would he credit the influence of the hand of God. His reports are colourful and full of irony, reflecting Commynes's great zest for life and his sceptical outlook.

Both diplomat and historian, Commynes was godson to Philip the Good, Duke of Burgundy, and was brought up in court. He became counsellor to Philip's son Charles the Bold, and it is thanks to Commynes that we have so clear a picture of the Burgundian ducal family. But the astute Commynes soon realised that Charles was no match for his sworn enemy, Louis XI of France, nicknamed the Universal Spider for the intricate webs of deception he wove. And so it was that on 7 August 1472 Commynes furtively slipped from the great duke's household to join the camp of his foe.

Charles's loss was history's gain, as Commynes remained with and reported on the French court until his death in 1511 at the age of 64. And Commynes's judgement was sound; five years after his defection, Charles the Bold lay dead before Nancy and the Universal Spider was in the process of dismembering his territories.

Also on this day
1485: Henry Tudor (the future Henry VII) lands at Milford Haven to challenge Richard III * 1815: Napoleon is exiled to St Helena * 1819: The Spanish surrender to revolutionary Simón Bolívar at Boyaca, Colombia

8 August

Hadrian, Rome's great builder emperor, rises to power

AD 117 Late tonight Hadrian, Rome's most peripatetic emperor, assumed imperial power when his adoptive father Trajan was felled by a stroke in Selinus (in modern Turkey) at the age of 63.

Trajan had ruled nineteen years, six months and fifteen days, during which time he enlarged the empire to its greatest extent with his conquests in Parthia and Dacia and directed a massive construction programme in Italy and Spain. Today, however, he is most kindly remembered for his tolerance to Christians, a policy that earned him a place in Dante's *Paradiso*, the sole pre-Christian emperor so honoured. According to the 2nd-century Roman historian Cassius Dio, his only flaw was his excessive fondness for wine and young boys.

The new emperor Hadrian preferred improving his empire to expanding it and spent the next 21 years roving across his vast territories, building as he went. He left us four of the most renowned Roman monuments that we can still visit today.

Although the Pantheon in Rome was initially constructed in 27 BC by Augustus' great general Agrippa, Hadrian completely rebuilt it, adding the mammoth dome 141 feet in diameter that was the largest ever built until the 20th century. Today the Pantheon is a church where Italy's first two kings and many great artists such as Raphael are buried, but the massive building with its heavy bronze doors remains much as it was when Hadrian ordered its construction almost two millennia ago.

Also in Rome on the banks of the Tiber is a huge brick drum over 60 feet high crouched on a square base that today we call the Castel' Sant'Angelo but which originally was built as Hadrian's tomb, started about two years before the Emperor's death in AD 138. Hadrian's Tomb received its current name in 590 when, during a procession to pray for the end of an outburst of plague, Pope Gregory the Great saw a vision of St Michael hovering over the building, sheathing his sword. The plague instantly abated, and the Pope renamed the tomb Castel' Sant'Angelo (Castle of the Holy Angel). In 1752 a bronze statue of St Michael was placed on top. Over the centuries Hadrian's Tomb has served as a place of sanctuary for popes under siege and later, until 1901, as a prison. (In Puccini's *Tosca*, set in 1800, Angelotti is locked up there and Tosca leaps from its battlements.) It is now a military history museum.

Another of Hadrian's monuments was his fabulous villa at Tivoli, eighteen miles east of Rome. The Emperor spent about ten years constructing this vast 750-acre complex of gardens, pavilions, dining halls, baths, libraries and theatres to create the most magnificent villa of Roman times.

The fourth great Hadrianic monument is his huge wall in northern England, started in 122. Designed to keep barbarous Picts and Scots from invading Roman Britain, the wall originally stretched 73 miles from coast to coast with forts every five miles. Up to ten feet wide and fifteen feet high, it continued to serve as a defensive barrier until the Romans pulled out of Britain in the early 5th century. It is the largest construction project in the history of Great Britain and today, even after having been used as a quarry for centuries, it remains formidable testimony to Roman power and construction skills.

Hadrian's ceaseless travel ended at Baiae on the Bay of Naples at his seaside villa that had been built by Julius Caesar. He had been ill and suffering for some weeks, and had begged to be put out of his misery, but his adopted son

Antoninus Pius forbade such an impious act. 'How miserable a thing it is to seek death and not to find it', complained the Emperor. On 10 July 138 he finally expired at the age of 62, probably of dropsy.

Also on this day

1883: Mexican revolutionary leader Emiliano Zapata is born * 1925: The first national congress of the Ku Klux Klan opens

9 August

Caesar defeats Pompey at Pharsalus

48 BC On the hot, arid plain of Pharsalus in central Greece the direction and fate of the Roman Empire was determined today when Julius Caesar annihilated the army of his long-standing rival, Pompey the Great. The battle guaranteed his dominance of the Roman state but hastened the end of the Roman Republic that had been established almost five centuries before, in 509 BC.

Caesar and Pompey had once been firm allies, both opposed to the clique of knights who dominated the Roman Senate and obstructed all progress to reform a creaking Roman government. But Caesar's alarming military success in Gaul made Pompey fear that he would lose his position as the first man in Rome, and he was persuaded to side with the knights when in 49 BC Caesar and his battle-hardened legions crossed the Rubicon and entered Roman Italy.

Pompey fled the capital, accompanied by consuls, conservative senators and some of his army. Caesar now faced a two-front war, as two of Pompey's lieutenants commanded legions in Spain, while Pompey himself had holed up in Greece. Caesar showed his scorn for his adversaries with the comment: 'I am going to Spain to fight an army without a general, and then to the East to fight a general without an army.'

In Spain, Caesar persuaded the enemy legions to join him rather than fight him and then pursued Pompey to Greece, repeatedly offering compromise rather than battle. Perhaps because he had defeated Caesar at Dyrrhachium, Pompey underestimated his opponent's military genius. When Pompey failed to capture him during that battle, Caesar dismissively concluded that Pompey 'has no idea of how to win a war'.

When the armies faced each other at Pharsalus, Pompey initiated the battle, confident of victory with some 50,000 troops compared to 30,000 under Caesar's command. He planned to roll up Caesar's right wing with his cavalry and then crush the enemy with his superior numbers. But Caesar had hidden 2,000 of his most experienced legionnaires behind his front lines. When the Caesarean wing fell back under Pompey's onslaught (as Caesar had planned that it should), Caesar's legionnaires suddenly attacked the cavalry, using their javelins as spears to stab the enemy horses. Confounded by the attack, the cavalry fled from the field, enabling Caesar to outflank Pompey and start a general massacre. Knowing victory to be his, Caesar attempted to diminish the killing, calling out to his troops: 'Spare your fellow Romans!' He allowed his men to save one enemy soldier apiece.

At the close of the battle Caesar had lost just 200 men killed, but 15,000 of Pompey's troops were dead or missing, with another 23,000 captured. Surveying the enemy dead after the battle, Caesar remarked bitterly, 'Hoc voluerunt' (This is what they wanted), referring to the knights' and Pompey's refusal to compromise.

Pompey escaped, but not for long. Caesar pursued him to Egypt, where an officer of King Ptolemy murdered him. When Caesar reached Egypt he was presented with Pompey's preserved head.

After Caesar's dictatorship and the civil wars that followed his assassination, Rome became an empire under Caesar's protégé Octavian (Augustus) and remained under the command of Roman emperors for 500 years in Europe and 600 in the east, from Constantinople.

The French and Indians conquer Fort William Henry

1757 On this late summer morning, Fort William Henry, the British bastion at the head of Lake George, fell after six days of siege in which 'the cannon thundered all day, and from a hundred peaks and crags the astonished wilderness roared back the sound'.

The attackers, a mixed force of 8,000 French regulars, Canadian militia and their Indian allies, were commanded by the marquis de Montcalm. They had sailed up the lake from their stronghold at Fort Ticonderoga with the aim of driving the British military forces out of central New York.

A drum was beaten, a white flag was raised above the fort, and a mounted officer rode out towards Montcalm's tent. There it was agreed that under the civilised custom of European warfare the British garrison consisting of regulars and colonial militiamen, after swearing to be non-combatants for eighteen months, would march out with the honours of war for their brave defence, leaving their dead and wounded behind, and receive safe passage under guard to Fort Edward, on the Hudson River fourteen miles distant.

Montcalm's Indian allies, however, did not care for such a settlement, preferring instead a chance to plunder their defeated foe. The next day, as the British column, which included many wives and children of militiamen, began the march to Fort Edward, the Indians struck, demanding rum, baggage, clothing, money and weapons. Anyone who resisted or ran was tomahawked. Children and women were seized and dragged into the forest. When the French finally restored order, 185 people had been killed and some 500 or 600 wounded, mistreated, or dragged away, although of this last category Montcalm's men eventually recovered 400 from the forest.

Now, the Indians cleared out for Montreal, taking with them their plunder and some 200 captives. The following day, the French successfully escorted the survivors of the British column to Fort Edward.

The French withdrew down the lake to Fort Ticonderoga on 16 August, leaving Fort William Henry a smoking ruin in the wilderness. Then, as Francis Parkman wrote: 'The din of ten thousand combatants, the rage, the terror, the agony, were gone; and no living thing was left but the wolves that gathered from the mountains to feast upon the dead.'

The fall of Fort William Henry, described by James Fenimore Cooper in *The Last of the Mohicans*, was not the last French victory in the bloody conflict called the French and Indian War. The very next year the French under Montcalm inflicted an even greater defeat on a British force at Fort Ticonderoga. At the same time, however, the British strategy began to prevail with the capture, first of the French fortress at Louisbourg, and then of Fort Duquesne at the forks of the Ohio River. Finally, in the culminating effort of the war, General Wolfe took the great French stronghold at Quebec in 1759, and North America was fairly won to British arms.

Also on this day

AD 378: The Visigoths defeat and kill Roman Emperor Valens at Adrianople * 1595: Izaak Walton, author of *The Compleat Angler*, is born

10 August

A victory on the Feast of St Lawrence inspires the building of a palace

1557 Of the thousands of battles fought throughout history, most are now forgotten, but the one fought this day at St Quentin in Picardy left a memorial over 600 miles away that stands in gloomy splendour to this day.

At the Battle of St Quentin, Spain's new king, Philip II, utterly routed a French army, killing over half its number. Being of a grave religious bent, Philip was aware that 10 August is the Feast of St Lawrence, that unfortunate Roman deacon who was roasted on a gridiron for his Christian beliefs. Hence, in commemoration of the great victory on St Lawrence's Day, King Philip sent orders to Spain that a great palace in the shape of a gridiron should be built in the Guadarrama mountains north-west of Madrid.

Philip intended the building to serve as a monastery for Hieronymite monks, a palace for himself and a grand burial place for the kings of Spain. To symbolise its royal and religious importance, it was constructed entirely of blue-grey granite and would be one of the largest religious buildings in the world. Its ground plan covers almost 377,000 square feet. This sombre memorial has 86 stairways, 1,200 doors and 2,710 windows.

Twenty-seven years after Philip's victory at St Quentin the palace-monastery was finally completed. It is called El Escorial. Philip died there in his spartan bedroom in 1598.

The mob butchers Louis XVI's Swiss Guard

1792 The Bastille had fallen three years earlier and France was in turmoil as revolutionaries tried to extend the Revolution while émigrés abroad did everything to stop it. King Louis XVI was virtually a prisoner in the Tuileries, but retained some royal powers. In April the government had declared war on Prussia and Austria which insisted on the full restoration of the monarchy, but French forces had suffered ignominious defeats as the Austro-Prussian army crossed the French border and advanced towards Paris.

Believing that King Louis was behind the foreign intervention, revolutionary fanatics in the Paris Commune ordered the Legislative Assembly to bring the monarchy to an end by depriving the King of his few remaining powers. When the Assembly dithered, on 10 August 1792 militants recruited a huge crowd of 20,000 marching and chanting peasants. Threats exploded into violence.

The gigantic crowd approached the Tuileries, defended only by Louis's Swiss Guard, the last troops loyal to the King. Suddenly shouts became rocks and small-arms fire, and the mob swept through the buildings, massacring all 800 Guards. Louis looked on helplessly, finally saving himself by fleeing to the Assembly and pleading for protection. The monarchy was doomed, and the King had only five months to live.

Most historians see poor Louis as a hapless and powerless victim of an unstoppable revolutionary explosion. But one observer of the massacre of 10 August did not agree. In the crowd watching the assault on the Tuileries was another absolute ruler-in-waiting, a 23-year-old soldier named Napoleon Bonaparte. Shortly after the event he expressed his own ideas about leadership in a letter to his brother. 'If Louis had mounted his horse', he wrote, 'the victory would have been his'.

Also on this day

1810: Italian patriot and unifier Camillo Benso, Count Cavour, is born * 1874: US President Herbert Hoover is born

11 August

The story of the most beautiful chapel in France

1239 Louis IX of France was not only a king but also a saint, so not surprisingly he was an avid collector of religious relics. In the year 1239 he learned that

Christ's Crown of Thorns could be had from Venetian traders, and he instantly dispatched his agents to buy it.

On 11 August of that year the Crown was brought into France, and King Louis determined to build for it a shrine worthy of housing such a holy treasure. He conceived of a church designed as a reliquary, with stone in place of metal and stained glass instead of gems and enamel.

Work on the chapel-reliquary was started immediately and completed in a mere 33 months. What became of the Crown is uncertain, but fortunately that gem of a building with all its deep-toned glass is still with us today, every bit as beautiful as Saint Louis intended. It is located on the Ile de la Cité in Paris and is fittingly called the Sainte-Chapelle.

A Borgia becomes Pope

1492 This was a watershed year for Europe: King Ferdinand and Queen Isabella finally conquered the last Moorish stronghold in Spain (and three months later expelled the Jews) to unite the country under Christian rule; Christopher Columbus discovered America; and Lorenzo the Magnificent died after 23 years of leading Florence, Europe's most civilised city-state. It was also the year that the papacy moved into its most worldly, cynical and corrupt period with the election of Roderigo Borgia, who on this day became Pope Alexander VI.

Roderigo was 61 at his elevation and had long been a highly capable Vice Chancellor of the Church. Nonetheless, he assured his election by appropriate bribes, including four mule loads of silver to one of the more influential cardinals.

Even at his election there were many who feared what was to come. 'Now we are in the power of the wolf', said the young Cardinal de' Medici (later Pope Leo X). 'The most rapacious perhaps that this world has ever seen; and if we do not escape, he will inevitably devour us.'

Perhaps the cardinal was too apprehensive, although Alexander was certainly one of the most venal of all popes. During the course of his eleven-year pontificate he appointed 47 cardinals primarily for their political support and willingness to turn a blind eye to his depredations. He also schemed with his three sons and his daughter to create a Borgia dynasty with enormous temporal power in Italy. But he spent most of his reign ministering to his mistresses and patronising the arts. Among other achievements, he persuaded Michelangelo to draw up plans for the rebuilding of St Peter's Cathedral.

Also on this day

AD 117: Hadrian is acclaimed Roman Emperor by his troops * 1495: Flemish painter Hans Memling dies

12 August

Castlereagh commits suicide

1822 At 53 he was exhausted, despondent and so paranoid that he imagined his long-time friend and political ally the Duke of Wellington was intriguing against him. On this day Robert Stewart, Lord Castlereagh, Great Britain's Foreign Secretary and one of his nation's greatest diplomats, slit his own throat at Cray Farm, his country retreat in Kent.

Son of an Anglo-Irish peer, Castlereagh had been educated at Cambridge and at 21 elected to the Irish Parliament, soon rising to the position of Lord Lieutenant of Ireland. An early supporter of Pitt the Younger, he resigned his office with Pitt when Parliament refused to grant Catholic emancipation in Ireland, but on Pitt's return to power was appointed as Secretary of State for War in 1805. One of his most perceptive acts was to use his influence to have Sir Arthur Wellesley – later the Duke of Wellington – given the command of the British expeditionary force sent to Spain to fight the Peninsular War against Napoleon.

In spite of his apparent success, Castlereagh found an implacable enemy in the then Foreign Secretary George Canning. Discovering that Canning was conniving to have him dismissed from his post, he challenged him to a duel during which Canning was slightly wounded, and both men were forced to resign from government.

But by 1812 Castlereagh was back as Secretary for Foreign Affairs, and after the assassination of Prime Minister Spenser Perceval he became leader of the House of Commons as well. And here he performed with brilliance. His astute diplomacy created the coalition that finally defeated Napoleon and he, along with Metternich, became the driving force at the Congress of Vienna after Napoleon's downfall, where he successfully established the principle of 'balance of power', resisting the territorial ambitions of Russia and Prussia.

But peace brought Castlereagh more problems than war ever had, as England fell into depression and rebellion was in the air. When soldiers killed eleven protesters and injured more than 500 at the Peterloo Massacre in Manchester in 1819, Castlereagh was widely condemned by English liberals for his known repressive beliefs. In his famous poem *The Mask of Anarchy*, inspired by the massacre, Shelley wrote:

> I met murder on the way —
> He had a face like Castlereagh —
> Very smooth he looked, yet grim;
> Seven bloodhounds followed him.

After an abortive plot to assassinate the Cabinet in 1820, Castlereagh always carried a pistol in case he was attacked. Held in contempt by England's liberals and hated by the lower orders, he began to develop the paranoia that would destroy him.

During the summer of 1822, Castlereagh revealed to an astonished Duke of Wellington that he was being blackmailed both for entering a brothel three years earlier and for an unspecified homosexual act. (It remains unclear whether Castlereagh was actually being blackmailed or whether he in reality committed either of these acts. He had been supposedly devotedly married to the beautiful Emily Hobart for 28 years, but the couple had no children.)

In August Castlereagh was residing at his Kent estate, so edgy, depressed and suspicious that his wife clandestinely removed his razor and pistols. On Monday 12 August in an explosion of distrust, he wildly accused his wife of joining a conspiracy against him, then, apparently realising that he was unbalanced, called for his doctor named Bankhead.

When Bankhead arrived he found that Castlereagh had retreated to his dressing room, where he stood with his back to the door facing the window, looking upwards as if to inspect the ceiling. 'My dear lord, why do you stand so?' asked the doctor. Turning, Castlereagh cried in anguish: 'Bankhead, let me fall upon your arm; it is all over.' As the doctor caught the collapsing man he saw blood spurting from his throat, a small pearl-handled knife gripped in his right hand. Castlereagh fell forward, slipped from Bankhead's grasp and crumpled face downwards on the floor. In moments he was dead.

Earlier, another of Castlereagh's liberal foes, Lord Byron, had penned this dreadful epitaph:

Posterity will ne'er survey
a nobler grave than this.
Here lie the bones of Castlereagh:
Stop, traveller, and piss.

Also on this day

1827: English poet and painter William Blake dies * 1896: Gold is discovered near Dawson City, Yukon Territory, Canada * 1898: Hawaii is formally annexed by the United States

13 August

How Blenheim Palace got its name

1704 A few miles north-west of Oxford in the rolling Cotswold hills stands the great palace of Blenheim, a gift by the grateful English nation to John Churchill, first Duke of Marlborough.

The bloody battle after which Blenheim is named took place on this day near the small Bavarian town of Blindheim, anglicised in English history to Blenheim. The battle was part of the War of the Spanish Succession, a struggle by a coalition of European nations to prevent Louis XIV's grandson from becoming King of Spain, thus setting the stage, they feared, for France and Spain to come together under the rule of a single king.

Blenheim was the first decisive battle of Marlborough's career, although he was already 53 at the time. It was also his first collaboration with that other celebrated general, Prince Eugene of Savoy.

During the course of this long day 56,000 French soldiers were overwhelmed by combined forces of 52,000 Austrians, Prussians, Dutch, Hessians, Danish mercenaries and English. Although Marlborough was in overall command, only 12,000 troops were from his own country.

When the battle finally ended at nightfall, 12,000 of the victors lay dead or wounded. But Marlborough and Eugene between them had killed or wounded 20,000 of the enemy while taking 14,000 prisoners, 5,400 supply wagons, 40 cannon and 34 coaches filled with French officers' women.

Although a glorious triumph, the Battle of Blenheim hardly settled the war, which dragged on for another ten years. And at the end Louis XIV's grandson was still King of Spain, although France and Spain were never united under a single monarch. Almost a century later the English poet Robert Southey penned his famous satirical lines:

Now tell us about the war,
And what they fought each other for ...
'And everybody praised the Duke,
Who this great fight did win.'
'But what good came of it at last?'
Quoth little Peterkin.
'Why that I cannot tell', said he,
'But 'twas a famous victory.'

The Edict of Nantes establishes freedom of religion in France

1598 Ever since the Protestant Jean Vallière was burned at the stake in Paris in 1523, France's Protestants, or Huguenots, had suffered from the most calamitous religious persecution as Catholic and Protestant alike resorted to murder and mayhem in defence of God's true faith, as they saw it. But then Henri of Navarre, the nation's first Bourbon monarch, came to the throne as Henri IV, a nominal Protestant who outwardly turned Catholic to consolidate his power.

On this date, nine years after assuming the throne, Henri signed the Edict of Nantes in the ducal château in the city of that name in Brittany. The Edict's 92 articles gave France's Protestants the religious freedom that had been denied them so long, including the right to worship openly, except in Paris where Catholic feeling was still too strong. Protestant pastors, along with Catholic priests, would be paid by the state. The Religious Wars that had torn the nation apart for 36 years had come to an end at last.

Sadly for the nation, Henri's great edict would stay in force for less than a century. On 18 October 1685 his grandson Louis XIV revoked it, once more denying the Huguenots both religious and civil rights. In the years that followed almost half a million of them left the country for the more welcoming Protestant regimes in Holland, England and Prussia, where their talent, wealth and industry helped their new homelands to the detriment of France.

Also on this day

1521: Spanish conquistador Hernán Cortés recaptures Tenochtitlán (Mexico City), and overthrows the Aztec empire * 1624: Louis XIII appoints Cardinal Richelieu as chief minister * 1863: French painter Eugène Delacroix dies * 1923: Kemal Atatürk is elected the first President of Turkey

14 August

Portugal fights to keep its independence

1385 João o Bastardo he was called, John the Bastard, not for his personality but because of his illegitimate birth as son of Portugal's King Pedro I. In his early years he kept a low political profile befitting his station, especially after his half-brother inherited the throne. But then the half-brother died, and his widow Queen Leonor was manoeuvred into recognising John I of the neighbouring kingdom of Castile (in north central Spain) as Portugal's new king.

Even in the 14th century Portuguese patriotism was strong, and soon a group of fervent Portuguese nationalists, led by a 25-year-old soldier named Pereira Nuno Alvares, persuaded João to assassinate Leonor's chief minister and seize power for himself. Fearing for her own life, Queen Leonor fled from Lisbon, imploring John of Castile to put down João's coup.

Soon John of Castile was on the march with a large army. They succeeded in entering Portugal, but on this day João and Pereira, reinforced by a small contingent of English archers, met them on the road to Lisbon at Aljubarrota and inflicted a devastating defeat. So thankful was João for the English support that the following May he signed the Treaty of Windsor with England, pledging 'an inviolable, eternal, solid, perpetual and true league of friendship'. The alliance is still in force today, the oldest in European history.

Two years after the battle, João married the English duke John of Gaunt's daughter Philippa, with glittering results. Philippa not only created a court of high culture in Portugal but also produced highly talented children, one of whom was the famous explorer Henry the Navigator.

Thus the Battle of Aljubarrota ensured independence for the Portuguese and a throne and glorious reign for João. Pereira's rewards were even greater, although it took a little longer for him to collect them all. Because of his military achievements, João made him constable of the kingdom, and Pereira became rich enough to found a Carmelite monastery in Lisbon, where he became a friar in 1423. Five hundred years later he was declared a saint.

The most cultivated pope

1464 Although not a patron of the arts, Enea Silvio Piccolomini, who died today, was perhaps history's most cultivated pope. Early in his career Holy Roman Emperor Frederick III made him poet to the court in Vienna, and later Piccolomini became acknowledged throughout Europe as a diplomat, historian, geographer, propagandist and orator. He also wrote at least one scandalous novel, entitled *The Tale of Two Lovers*, and was the father of several bastard children.

During his early career Piccolomini served as secretary to several ecclesiastical figures, including the anti-pope Felix V, but then Emperor Frederick took him under his wing, moving him to Vienna. There, frightened by a serious illness, he abandoned his dissolute life, disavowed the anti-pope and received sacred orders at the advanced age of 41. Only a year later he was made a bishop.

At 53 Piccolomini was elected Pope as Pius II. It was said that he selected his papal name because his own was Enea (Aeneas), and one of his favourite heroes, Virgil, had made reference to 'pious Aeneas'.

The great issue of the day was the conquest of Constantinople, which had fallen to the infidel Turks just five years before the start of his pontificate. Pius spent most of his six papal years trying unsuccessfully to persuade the princes of Europe to launch a crusade to recapture the city. By June 1464 he was ailing but nonetheless left Rome for the Adriatic port of Ancona personally to lead the campaign. To his chagrin, he arrived to find no one to lead, as Europe's Christian princes refused his call. After two months of anxious waiting, on the evening of 14 August Pius took to his bed and succumbed to his illness. His heart was left in Ancona for burial, a symbol of the crusade he had hoped to lead. His other remains were transported back to Rome for interment in St Peter's.

Although he failed in his struggle to launch a crusade, if Pius looked down on us today he would still no doubt feel satisfied that his literary pre-eminence remains intact. In the 2,000 years of the papacy, he is the only pope to write his autobiography.

Also on this day

1900: A British-led international military force captures Peking to put down the Boxer Rebellion * 1945: Japan announces its unconditional surrender in the Second World War

15 August

Napoleone is born

1769 Ajaccio was a small, dusty port on the island of Corsica, only recently part of France, having been purchased by Louis XV from the Republic of Genoa. But now, fifteen months later, the people still followed Italian customs, including the celebration of *ferragosto* or the feast of the Assumption on 15 August. So young and beautiful Letizia Buonaparte, still not yet twenty, insisted on going to Mass although she was heavily pregnant.

Returning home immediately after the service, she lay down on the living room sofa and, just before midday, gave birth to a black-haired son. There was joy in the household as Letizia and her husband Carlo celebrated the birth of a living child. Their six years of marriage had produced three previous births, but only one baby, a boy they named Giuseppe, had survived.

The proud parents named their new child Napoleone, a good Italian name in a family that had originally come from Tuscany two centuries before. In spite of his name and language (his native tongue was Italian), Napoleone was born a French citizen thanks to Louis XV's timely purchase of Corsica. But it was only when he was 27 and already firmly established as a French general that he frenchified the spelling of his name to Napoléon Bonaparte, eventually persuading his elder brother to convert from Giuseppe to Joseph.

During the next half-century Napoleon would win 60 of the 70 battles he fought, conquer most of Europe, and honour his family in an orgy of nepotism, sprinkling glorious titles among his brothers and sisters. Joseph became King of Spain, Louis King of Holland, Jerome King of Westphalia, and Lucien Prince of Canino. Sister Caroline became Queen of Naples by virtue of her marriage to Napoleon's cavalry commander, 'King Joachim' Murat, and even Napoleon's stepson by his first marriage was made Viceroy of Italy. Napoleon himself, of course, famously crowned himself Emperor, lost all that he had won, and arguably became the most famous man in history.

Loyola founds the Jesuits

1534 Today a lame, middle-aged Spanish soldier named Ignacio de Loyola led a small band of six followers to the Chapel of the Auxiliatrices in the rue Yvonne-Le-Tac on the Left Bank in Paris. There they formally swore to serve the Catholic Church with vows of chastity, poverty and obedience. In time this new organisation would become the Jesuits.

It had started three years earlier at the University of Paris where Loyola was studying. He had been crippled by a cannonball thirteen years before and now, unable further to serve his king, he had decided to dedicate himself to God. He soon recruited two younger disciples, a Frenchman named Pierre Lefèvre and another Spaniard, the future saint Francisco Javier. As a mark of their devotion, they fixed a picture of Jesus on the door to their room. On seeing this ostentatious display of piety, other students derisively called the three the *Societas Jesu*, and the name stuck – and has now for almost 500 years.

Loyola was the driving force behind the new organisation, and within three years he had enlisted four more followers. The members continued to proselytise new converts, and six years later Pope Paul III recognised the order. The Jesuits were well on their way to becoming the spearhead of militant intellectual Catholicism combatting the Protestant Reformation.

Loyola died 22 years after founding his order, but the Jesuits grew in number and influence over the centuries. But the society has always provoked controversy, especially in Catholic countries where it was strongest.

The Jesuits' devotion to the Pope sometimes ran counter to the absolutist ambitions of kings and queens, while their passion for ecclesiastical reform infuriated Church leaders. The order has been expelled by virtually every European country, and came close to extinction in 1773 when Pope Clement XIV suppressed it. It was saved only by the intervention of Frederick the Great of Prussia and Catherine the Great of Russia, admirers of the society's erudition and educational zeal, who refused to publish the Pope's ban.

Pius VII, who had himself been educated by Jesuits, finally re-established the society in 1814. Since that time the order has generally flourished, combative, intellectual, proselytising – just like its founder Ignacio de Loyola.

Also on this day

778: Charlemagne loses the Battle of Roncesvalles, inspiring the legend of the *Song of Roland* * 1057: Macbeth, King of Scotland, dies * 1771: Scottish writer Walter Scott is born

16 August

Eugene of Savoy's greatest victory

1717 The Turks had controlled most of the Balkans since the 16th century, and Suleiman the Magnificent once reached the gates of Vienna. It was only in the late 17th and early 18th centuries that Austria (or, more properly, the Holy Roman Empire) wrested the territory away, and much of this success was due to one man, Prince Eugene of Savoy, who inflicted one defeat after another on the Turks.

Eugene's first great victory was at Zenta in 1697, and on this day twenty years later he achieved his last and greatest triumph at Belgrade.

Eugene had been besieging the city when a massive Turkish army came to its relief, trapping the Prince's forces between the city walls and the Turkish host. Eugene commanded some 60,000 men, many weak from disease, and the Turks had four times that number. Some of his commanders begged him to withdraw to save the army, but Eugene held his position and waited for nightfall. Then, under cover of darkness and a thick fog, he launched his attack.

The battle was fierce and brutal, but when the fog lifted at daylight, the Prince's forces annihilated the Turkish army, which broke and fled. The Austrians gave no quarter, killing all the stragglers unable to escape.

Today the battle is largely forgotten, except in the famous German song 'Das Prinz Eugen Lied'. Probably written by a Bavarian trooper who fought at Belgrade, the song is still sung by German soldiers.

Also on this day

1819: Police in Manchester fire on a crowd demanding suffrage at the so-called Peterloo Massacre

17 August

The passing of Frederick the Great

1786 Frederick the Great of Prussia died today in the early morning, sitting up in an armchair. He had lived for 74 years, five months and 24 days, and was 46 years a king.

Frederick was one of history's most extraordinary rulers. He was highly cultured, an accomplished musician and poet. He neither smoked nor drank and paid no attention to women, including his wife, whom he totally neglected. He may have been homosexual, but essentially this mocking, detached man had little affection for people. 'He has no heart whatever', said a contemporary. Although a German, he almost invariably spoke French.

Frederick's greatness was in his supreme military ability. In reference to the Seven Years' War, when Prussia was attacked by Austria, France and Russia together, no less an authority than Napoleon said of him: 'It is not the Prussian army that for seven years defended Prussia against the three most powerful nations in Europe, but Frederick the Great.'

Frederick not only established Prussia as a major European power but also ensured the dominance of his family – the Hohenzollerns – who ruled Germany until defeat in the First World War.

Frederick died at Sans Souci, the exquisite palace he built in Potsdam, just outside Berlin. Knowing death was imminent, he spoke to his valet Strutzki for the last time: 'La montagne est passé, nous irons mieux.' (We're over the hill, we'll be better now.) He had planned to be buried in his beloved palace and had ordered an inscription carved on the base of a statue there: 'Quand je serai là, je serai sans souci.' (When I shall be there, I shall be without care.) But his heirs had him buried in the Garrison Church nearby. Almost two centuries later an admiring Adolf Hitler kept a portrait of him on the wall of his bunker in Berlin.

A magnificent château dooms a French minister

1661 Today Nicolas Fouquet thought to impress the young King Louis XIV with a magnificent house-warming at his extraordinary new château of Vaux-le-Vicomte, some 35 miles south-west of Paris. But instead of the glory he sought, he found life imprisonment.

The son of a wealthy ship-owner, in 1653 Fouquet had been appointed *surintendant des finances*, roughly finance minister, under Cardinal Mazarin. There he had helped both the government and himself, as he became excessively wealthy. On Mazarin's death he hoped to climb even higher in the King's service, in keeping with his family motto 'Quo non ascendet' (What heights will he not scale?).

Hence the lavish fête. Apart from the King, Fouquet invited some 6,000 guests, to whom he distributed favours such as diamond brooches and thoroughbred horses. He arranged a spectacular display of fireworks that dazzled his visitors as they wandered through almost 100 acres of manicured gardens studded by 250 fountains, and he even commissioned Molière to write a ballet-comedy, *Les Fâcheux*, for the occasion.

What Fouquet did not know was that Mazarin's confidant, Jean-Baptiste Colbert, was determined to discredit him and place himself on the King's right hand – and thanks to Colbert's secret briefings, Louis now believed that Fouquet had enriched himself through misappropriation of royal funds. The spectacular house-warming at Vaux-le-Vicomte was the last straw; appalled by his minister's 'luxe insolent et audacieux', Louis then and there decided that no man should surpass the King. As Voltaire later wrote: 'Le 17 août à 6 heures du soir, Fouquet était le roi de France: à 2 heures du matin, il n'était plus rien.' (On 17 August at 6 in the evening, Fouquet was King of France; at 2 in the morning, he was nobody.)

Only weeks after the fête Fouquet was accused of embezzlement (he was arrested by a commander of Musketeers named d'Artagnan) and brought to trial. The case continued for almost three years, Louis hoping for the death penalty, but most of the judges wanted only to banish the former minister. Then, for the first and last time in French history, the head of state overruled the court's decision, not to lighten the sentence, but to increase it. Fouquet was imprisoned in the château-fort of Pigneroles, from which he never emerged. There he died after sixteen years of captivity.

King Louis would never again see one of his subjects outshine him. From this evening sprang his determination to build the greatest of all royal châteaux, Versailles. He even engaged Fouquet's architect and landscaper to work on it.

Also on this day

1786: Legendary American frontiersman Davy Crockett is born * 1850: French novelist Honoré de Balzac dies * 1876: The first performance of Wagner's *Götterdämmerung* is given in Bayreuth

18 August

The last of Genghis Khan

1227 When Genghis Khan died on this day at about 65, he had created the greatest land empire in history through his great generalship and utter, barbaric ruthlessness.

Genghis Khan's given name was Temujin. He was born holding a clot of blood in his hand, a sure sign of great military prowess.

The main weapon with which Genghis Khan defeated and united the numerous Mongol tribes was his formidable cavalry. According to legend, its pungent stench signalled the approach of death even before you could see the dust or hear the drumming of hooves. These fearsome warriors could fire an arrow with deadly accuracy from a distance of 200 yards. One Persian account claims that Genghis Khan's soldiers were so filthy that lice covered them 'like sesame growing on bad soil'.

In victory Genghis Khan was totally merciless, once ordering the massacre of all those taller than the height of a cart axle. In 1206 the conquered Mongol tribes awarded him the title of Genghis Khan, which probably means universal leader.

When Genghis Khan conquered an enemy city he either annihilated the population entirely or sold it into slavery. At Herat in Afghanistan after a full week of carnage his army is said to have slaughtered 1,600,000 people. He told his chiefs to 'show no clemency to my enemies without a direct order from me. Rigour alone keeps such spirits dutiful.' People were not the Great Khan's only victims; he sacked major cities and razed important cultural centres such as Samarkand and Bukhara.

But no one could deny the effectiveness of his draconian methods: by the time of his death he had destroyed the Chin dynasty of China and his empire extended from Peking to the Caspian Sea.

A Borgia pope dies addressing God

1503 On this day died Roderigo Borgia after 72 years on this earth, eleven of them as Pope under the papal name of Alexander VI. Apparently addressing the God he had so often ignored during his pursuit of secular power, his final words are reported to have been: 'I come. It is right. Wait a minute.'

Alexander had been born Spanish in the town of Játiva but had easily progressed through the ranks of the Church through the patronage of his uncle, Pope Calixtus III, who created him a cardinal when he was still only 25.

Alexander's career was famous for ambition, treachery, simony, nepotism and lust for power, and the number of his mistresses (three) and illegitimate children (nine) was high, even for a priest. But he also had his accomplishments, embellishing much of the Vatican. One of his decisions left a lasting mark on history when, in 1494, he negotiated the Treaty of Tordesillas that divided South America into Spanish and Portuguese zones of influence.

It is likely that Alexander died of what the Italians called *mal aria* (bad air – they had no idea the disease was borne by mosquitoes), a constant menace of Roman summers 500 years ago. But such was the ruthlessness of the age and the reputation of the man that there are still suspicions that he may have been poisoned. The most dramatic (and improbable) account is that Catarina Sforza, whom Alexander had imprisoned, sent him a bamboo cane inside which was a secret letter that had been rubbed with the shirt of a man who had died of plague, leading to Alexander's grisly death.

Also on this day

1587: Virginia Dare, the first English child born in what would become the United States, is born in the Roanoke Island colony * 1830: Austrian Emperor Franz Joseph I is born

19 August

Caesar Augustus, Rome's first and greatest emperor – was he murdered?

AD 14 Today died Rome's first and greatest Emperor, Caesar Augustus, who had ruled the civilised world for 44 years, greatly enlarging and enriching his empire while creating such firm underpinnings that it would last, in one form or another, for another 462 years in the west and 1,439 years in the east.

Augustus died in Nola, just north-east of Naples, only a month short of his 76th birthday, after several days of severe stomach aches and strong diarrhoea. Suetonius tells us his last words were addressed to Livia, his wife of 52 years: 'Livia, do not forget our marriage. Farewell!' But was this the natural passing of an ageing man or was it murder?

According to Tacitus, tongues wagged that Livia did him in. She had married Augustus under duress – she was already married and pregnant when he forced her to divorce her first husband and marry him. Although all reports suggest they lived contentedly together, he is known to have been flagrantly unfaithful, perhaps including young men among his conquests. And Livia was desperate for one of her sons by her first marriage (she had none by Augustus) to inherit the empire. Rumours insinuated that she had already arranged the deaths of three of Augustus's grandsons from his earlier marriages, and she had managed to persuade him to name her own son Tiberius as joint inheritor along with his sole surviving grandson, Agrippa Postumus. But as the great man aged she was tormented by the fear that at the last he would drop Tiberius in favour of Agrippa Postumus, because he was linked to Augustus by blood.

The story relates that a few days before his death Livia offered Augustus some grapes that she had poisoned, carefully leaving several clean ones for herself to avert suspicion.

Whatever the truth, Augustus's corpse was taken to Rome and cremated on the Campus Martius. And his stepson Tiberius duly became Emperor. Livia lived on for another fifteen years and died at the glorious age of 87. Her grandson, the Emperor Claudius, later deified her.

Allied disaster at Dieppe

1942 This morning at 4.45 Operation Jubilee commenced: Allied troops landed at the French port of Dieppe to launch a daring attack on Nazi-held Europe, the first such operation since the all-triumphant Wehrmacht had kicked the British Army off the continent at Dunkirk two years earlier. By early afternoon it was all over, a terrible disaster in which of the 5,100 men who went ashore – two brigades of the Canadian Division supported by British commando units – 3,684 did not make it back, either killed or captured. Among those killed was Lieutenant Edwin Loustalot, one of 50 US Rangers taking part in the attack. He was the war's first American battle death in the European theatre.

Operation Jubilee suffered from inadequacies in almost every aspect: objective, planning, intelligence, communications, tactics, and strategy. Loss of surprise also contributed to the mission's failure. Only courage among the attackers was not in short supply, but alone it could not prevail. The Royal Navy lost a destroyer and 33 landing craft, while the RAF lost 106 planes to the Germans' 48.

The raid at Dieppe was meant to be a practice run for the great cross-Channel attack that would establish the Second Front and reclaim Europe from German occupation. In its two strategic purposes, however, the raid failed either to draw off German units from the Eastern Front, where Soviet Russia was reeling under Operation Barbarossa, or to inflict heavy losses on the Luftwaffe units sent to defend the port. Finally, the utter failure of the raid went a long way to bring US war planners around to the British contention that the time was not yet right for a full-scale invasion of the Continent.

The German High Command described the Dieppe raid as 'an amateur undertaking', but Winston Churchill was also right when he called it a 'mine of experience'. Among the valuable lessons the Allies learned this day was that for such an operation air dominance is vital; another was that the initial landings should be made not at a port, where urban warfare would be the order of the day, but on a long stretch of open beaches providing adequate room for the fast build-up of an invasion-sized force. Like Normandy, for instance.

Emperor Maximilian acquires a wife – and a country

1477 She had inherited the great Duchy of Burgundy, he was the son of the Holy Roman Emperor, so it should have been a purely political marriage.

Indeed, when Mary of Burgundy wed Maximilian von Habsburg on this day in 1477, she was searching desperately for protection; her father, the reckless Charles the Bold, had been killed before Nancy only seven months earlier, and the wily Louis XI of France was poised to invade.

But the marriage proved a love match between the eighteen-year-old prince and twenty-year-old Mary. The wedding took place in Ghent in today's Belgium, where the couple had met only a few days before. In a letter to a friend, the eager Maximilian wrote: 'She has skin as white as snow, brown hair, a little nose, a small head and face, grey-brown eyes, beautiful and light. Her lower eyelid droops a little, as if she had just been asleep, but you hardly notice it. Her lips are a little strong, but pure and red. She is the most beautiful woman I have ever seen.'

It was a romantic beginning, but tragedy stalked the marriage. Mary was killed in a hunting accident only five years later.

Politically, however, the union bore precious fruit. It brought together the great Burgundian domains and the Holy Roman Empire. Descendants of this couple were to rule in Spain until 1700 and in Austria for four and a half centuries, until after the First World War.

In other ways the effects of the romance between Mary and Maximilian are with us still. Until their time, only kings wore diamonds, but the enamoured prince gave his bride a diamond engagement ring and so started a custom that shows no signs of disappearing after half a millennium.

Also on this day

1631: English poet John Dryden is born * 1662: French mathematician, philosopher and writer Blaise Pascal dies in Paris * 1692: Six 'witches' are executed during the Salem witch trials in Massachusetts * 1871: Aviation pioneer Orville Wright is born in Dayton, Ohio

20 August

The Spartans defy the Persians at Thermopylae

480 BC Mighty Xerxes, King of Persia, the greatest empire the world had known, had resolved to conquer the stubborn Greeks, who had defeated his father Darius at Marathon ten years before. So great was his army that it took them seven days and seven nights to cross the Hellespont. (Herodotus tells us that the Persians numbered two and a half million men, but modern estimates suggest a more reasonable 200,000.) Knowing that all Greece was in mortal danger, a force of 7,000 hoplites (infantry) from several Greek city-states was rushed to meet the invaders under the leadership of the Spartan king, Leonidas. Indifferent to the odds against him, Leonidas declared: 'If you reckon by number, all Greece cannot oppose even a part of that army, but if by courage, the number I have with me is enough.' The armies clashed at Thermopylae in one of history's most heroic defences.

Thermopylae means 'hot gates', named for the hot sulphur springs nearby. It is a narrow mountain pass only 50 feet across at its widest, accommodating just a single wagon track. On one side tower high cliffs while on the other is a precipitous drop to the sea. It was through this restricted defile that the Persian army had to pass to enter central Greece. Even before the battle the location had dramatic connotations for every Greek, for it was on nearby Mount Oeta that Heracles had died, poisoned by the blood of a dead centaur.

Upon seeing the tiny Greek force, Xerxes demanded that Leonidas lay down his arms, to which the Spartan king tersely challenged, 'Come and take them'. As the defenders waited for the onslaught, one fearful soldier speculated that the Persian archers were so many that their arrows would hide the sun. 'Good', answered the Spartan Dieneces, 'then we shall fight them in the shade'.

To open the battle the Persian king ordered his Medes and Cissians to lead the charge. But the Greeks, armed with long spears and protected by large round shields, crested helmets and lower-leg greaves, were more than a match for the invaders, who had shorter spears and weaker armour, better suited to warfare on the open plains than to the narrow defile of Thermopylae. Soon Xerxes was forced to call on his élite infantry, the Immortals, but even they could make no progress against the ferocious defenders, who slew thousands of the enemy during the first two days of battle. So many Persians were killed that the front ranks had to be driven into battle with whips.

But then came treachery. A Greek traitor, Ephialtes, hoping for a rich reward, told Xerxes of a mountain path through which the Persians could send an encircling force. On the night following the second day of battle the Immortals started working their way behind the Greek position.

Once Leonidas learned that the Persians were closing in from behind, he sent all the Greek warriors except his own 300 Spartans home to defend their cities. Then he settled down with his men for a last meal, bleakly ordering, 'Breakfast well, for we shall have dinner in Hades'. He was determined to fight to the last.

At nine o'clock on this third day of battle, the resolute Spartans marched out for the final confrontation to the sound of their flutes. Although fighting with ferocity, they were soon overwhelmed, Leonidas among the first to fall. Finally the last defenders were surrounded on a small hill. Herodotus relates that 'they fought in a frenzy, without concern for their lives ... Most had already lost their spears, and they cut down Persians with their swords ... [they] defended themselves with daggers ... and with their hands and teeth ... while those [Persians] who had come round the mountain completed the circle.' But, despite their fanatical struggle, soon all 300 Spartans lay dead. In his anger at the stubborn Spartan resistance, Xerxes had Leonidas's lifeless body crucified, his severed head stuck on a pole.

Herodotus says that the Spartans killed 20,000 Persians at Thermopylae, no doubt an exaggeration but in any case not enough to prevent Persian invasion of the Greek mainland and the capture of Athens. Greece was saved not by Thermopylae but by the naval victory of Salamis the next month.

On the small hill where the Spartans made their last stand the Greeks erected a monument, now long vanished, with the inscription from Simonides of Ceos:

Go, stranger, and to listening Spartans tell
That here, obedient to their laws, we fell.

Richard the Lion-Heart slaughters his prisoners

1191 Over the centuries England's King Richard the Lion-Heart has come to symbolise the virtues of knightly valour and chivalry. His reputation is based largely on his famous adventures during the Third Crusade, when he matched armies and wills with that pinnacle of Saracen honour and courage, Saladin. Nothing displays Richard's true character better than the story of his triumph at Acre.

Saladin had been supreme in the Holy Land since the destruction of the main Christian army in 1187. But in the fiery summer of 1189 the King of Jerusalem, Guy de Lusignan, gathered his small remaining forces to lay siege to Acre, a key Saracen fortress and seaport. Saladin soon arrived with his army to relieve the siege but was unable to dislodge King Guy, and before long Christian reinforcements arrived. First came the French under King Philip Augustus, then the remains of the army of German Emperor Frederick Barbarossa (Barbarossa himself had drowned while crossing a river). Then came the Austrians under Duke Leopold, and finally the English commanded by Richard.

The siege, which lasted for two years, was fierce, with casualties high on both sides. Eventually Saladin's commanders inside the fortress could see that their lord could not relieve them, and they surrendered on 12 July 1191.

When the Crusaders took possession of the fortress they captured some 3,000 surrendering Saracen soldiers whom Richard was anxious to barter for Saladin's Christian prisoners and the True Cross that Saladin was reputed to have in his possession. But the days passed and no final agreement could be reached.

On 20 August Richard's patience came to an end. All 3,000 Saracens, bound with ropes, were marched outside the city walls so that they would be well in view of Saladin's nearby army. Then Richard ordered one of history's most barbarous slaughters. All the prisoners were to have been beheaded, but, finding this method too slow, Richard ordered his soldiers in with lance, sword and mace. To a man the Saracens were murdered where they stood.

The conquest of Acre was the Crusaders' only important victory during the Third Crusade; they never reached Jerusalem. But in 1192 Richard concluded a treaty with Saladin that guaranteed the rights of Christian pilgrims in Jerusalem.

Also on this day
1625: French playwright Pierre Corneille is born * 1940: Leon Trotsky is assassinated in Mexico on orders from Stalin

21 August

Napoleon's marshal Bernadotte becomes Crown Prince of Sweden

1810 Two years earlier, Napoleon had made his favourite cavalry commander, Joaquim Murat, King of Naples. Today Jean-Baptiste Bernadotte became the second of the Emperor's marshals to take a royal title when he became Sweden's Crown Prince, taking the name of Charles John.

Born in the foothills of the Pyrenees and son of a lawyer, Bernadotte joined France's republican army at the age of seventeen, displaying his zeal by having 'Death to tyrants!' tattooed on his arm. He first met Napoleon in Italy in 1797, after he had already become a brigadier general. The two generals impressed each other, and in 1798 Bernadotte even married one of Napoleon's former sweethearts, Désirée Clary, who was also a sister-in-law of Napoleon's brother Joseph.

A strong republican, Bernadotte condemned Napoleon's rise to absolute power, but he finally offered his support when Bonaparte declared himself Emperor in 1804. A few months later Bernadotte's loyalty, military skill, and family connections were fully rewarded when the Emperor made him a marshal, and a year later he received the title of Prince of Ponte-Corvo for his heroic participation in the great French victory at Austerlitz.

Although not a brilliant commander, Bernadotte always scrupulously obeyed the rules of war, treating both his troops and his enemies with generosity and good sense. Thus, when Sweden found itself ruled by the ageing, childless King Charles XIII in 1809, the Riksdag invited Bernadotte to become Charles's successor.

Much to Napoleon's chagrin, the new Prince's loyalties were now to Sweden rather than France, and he joined the allied forces at the Emperor's bloody defeat at Leipzig in 1813.

On 5 February 1818 old King Charles finally died, and the once staunchly republican general became a conservative and autocratic king who restricted the press and put a stop to liberal reforms. Unlike Napoleon's other marshal-king – Murat was deposed and shot after seven years as King of Naples – Bernadotte ruled for 26 years until he died in bed at the worthy age of 81. Shortly before his death he smugly but accurately murmured, 'No one living has made a career like mine'. To this day his descendants still wear the crown of Sweden.

Catherine the Great marries the heir to the throne of Russia

1745 The groom was sixteen, the bride a year younger. Both had been born and raised in Germany, but now, in St Petersburg, he was heir to the throne of Russia and she was his loving wife, mother of future Romanov tsars.

The bride and groom who married today would each rule Russia, he as Peter III for a scant six months, she as Catherine the Great for 34 years.

According to her autobiography, Catherine was such an ignorant bride that, until her mother informed her on the day before the wedding, she had no concept of her expected wifely duties. Not that it mattered much – Peter was also a virgin and made no demands on their wedding night.

In fact, we know that the marriage was still unconsummated seven years later, perhaps never consummated, although by then Catherine was far from the fifteen-year-old virgin she had been. She had already started on her string of lovers, one of whom was probably the father of the heir to the throne.

Perhaps Peter should have been more passionate. Seventeen years after their wedding, he finally inherited the throne, but only six months later Catherine staged her famous *coup d'état* and had her husband strangled in his prison cell.

Also on this day
1872: English illustrator Aubrey Beardsley is born

22 August

Richard III dies at Bosworth Field

1485 This is one of the most significant dates in all of English history. In defeating Richard III today in the Battle of Bosworth Field, Henry Tudor accomplished more than he knew. His victory ended the Wars of the Roses, that periodic and bloody rivalry for the English crown that had afflicted the country since 1455. Moreover, Bosworth Field, resulting as it did in the death of King Richard, brought to an end the great Plantagenet dynasty which had supplied every English king for the past 332 years, starting with Henry II in 1154. Finally, when Henry Tudor took the crown as Henry VII he began his own dynasty that lasted for 118 years and sent to the throne such notables as Henry VIII, Bloody Mary and Elizabeth I.

At the time of the battle, Richard III had been King for only two years and two months, having usurped the throne from his twelve-year-old nephew Edward V, whose murder in the Tower of London he had ordered. His opponent Henry Tudor also had only the flimsiest of claims to the English crown. Through his mother he could trace his blood back five generations to King Edward III, and his entitlement to royalty on his father's side was even thinner.

His paternal grandfather had (perhaps) been married to Catherine de Valois, the widow of Henry V.

But Henry Tudor was the only living male member of the House of Lancaster and so became its champion in the Wars of the Roses. Gathering an army in France, he landed at Milford Haven in Wales on 7 August and headed north until he met Richard's forces at Bosworth Field, twelve miles west of Leicester.

Richard might have defeated Henry had not some of his most important barons defected at the last moment, guaranteeing a Tudor victory. But even when defeat was certain, Richard challenged his fate. 'I will not budge a foot', he swore to his lieutenants, 'I will die king of England'. A few minutes later he was unhorsed and killed.

Richard was only 32 when he fell at Bosworth Field, the last English king to die in battle.

Why the French heir to the throne is called a dolphin

1350 Although he is little known today, Philip VI, who died on this date at the age of 57, established some landmarks in the history of France.

First, he was France's first Valois king (he had inherited the throne from the last of the Capetians, his first cousin Charles IV), and the Valois would rule the nation for 261 years.

Second, he started the longest war in history, the Hundred Years' War pitting France against England, which began in 1337 and actually lasted 115 years.

Third, he instituted the most hated tax, the *gabelle*, which eventually became a tax on salt but in Philip's time was the first sales tax on consumer goods.

Fourth, he created the title of Dauphin for the heir to the French throne. The Dauphiné was an area of France near Lyon. It was thus called because its sovereign lords wore a dolphin (*dauphin* in French) on their coats of arms. When the Dauphiné became an integral part of the King's territory in 1349, Philip agreed that from that time forward the eldest son of the King would bear the title Dauphin.

These accomplishments apart, Philip's reign was notably unsuccessful, as he suffered catastrophic defeat by the English at the Battle of Crécy, and later the Black Death killed perhaps a third of his people. Philip himself met his maker after 22 years, six months and 21 days as King.

Also on this day

1642: The English Civil War begins when Charles I raises his standard at Nottingham * 1806: French painter Jean-Honoré Fragonard dies in Paris * 1864: The International Red Cross is founded by the Geneva Convention

23 August

William Wallace pays the price for treason

1305 For the crime of treason there was only one penalty in England. First the traitor was hanged but cut down while still alive. He was then emasculated and disembowelled and his entrails were burned before his eyes. Finally, he was decapitated and his body cut into four parts, to be hung in public places as a reminder of the fearsome wrath of the King. On this day in London the Scottish patriot William Wallace suffered such a death. His left leg was displayed in Aberdeen, his right one in Perth, and his left arm in Berwick, his right one in Newcastle. His head was impaled on a spike and put on view at London Bridge.

In the late 13th century, Scotland was in leaderless turmoil. When eight-year-old Queen Margaret died, there were thirteen claimants to the throne, and competing Scottish lords ravaged the country. At length the Scottish leaders asked England's King Edward I to arbitrate, and the Scottish crown finally went to John de Balliol, who promptly swore fealty to Edward. For this act, John earned from his subjects the name 'Toom Tabard', Empty Coat. But then John refused to send troops for Edward's wars in France, rejected his demand to cede three border castles, and renounced his homage to England. This provided all the excuse Edward needed to invade the country.

Into this confusion stepped a member of the lesser Scottish gentry, William Wallace, a giant of a man (about six feet six inches), who, according to a near-contemporary historian/hagiographer, was 'all powerful as a swordsman and unrivalled as an archer'. Furthermore, 'his blows were fatal and his shafts unerring; as an equestrian, he was a model of dexterity and grace; while the hardships he experienced in his youth made him view with indifference the severest privations incident to a military life'.

By 1296, when Wallace was about 27, he was leading what amounted to a guerrilla band against the invading English. Initially successful, he was once captured and left to starve in a dungeon but subsequently rescued by local villagers. After recovering his strength, he recruited another band of about 30 rebels and continued his attacks. Drawing ever more Scots to his banner, in 1297 he became the scourge of the English and scored a major victory at Stirling Bridge where, although heavily outnumbered, he slaughtered some 5,000 English as they crossed the river. For this triumph Wallace was knighted, probably by Scotland's future king, Robert the Bruce.

But Wallace's great triumph had been against Edward I's lieutenants rather than against the redoubtable English king. The following year Edward himself led an army of 25,000 deep into Scotland and annihilated Wallace's force at Falkirk. Wallace escaped the rout and spent the next few years alternately hiding from the English and keeping his revolt alive, at one point slipping off to France to seek aid.

Edward never relented in his search for Wallace, whom he regarded as a traitor for his resistance to his feudal overlord, which Edward considered himself to be. In August 1305 Wallace was captured near Glasgow and brought to London, where he was tried for treason and the murder of civilians (the indictment claimed he spared 'neither age nor sex, monk nor nun'). Although Wallace claimed that he was wrongly accused because he had never sworn fealty to Edward, under Edward's vengeful eye only one verdict was possible. The man the English considered a treacherous outlaw and the Scottish a national hero was condemned to be hanged, drawn and quartered.

With Wallace dead, Edward believed he had cowed the Scots, but in fact, by his barbarous method of execution he had turned Wallace into a martyr. By the time of his own death in 1307 Edward was already facing a new and far more dangerous enemy, Robert the Bruce. By 1314 Robert had reasserted Scottish independence by totally destroying the army of Edward's son Edward II at the Battle of Bannockburn, only two miles from Wallace's great triumph at Stirling Bridge seventeen years before.

Scotland retained its autonomy for centuries to come, although in 1603 its king, James VI, became James I of England, thus uniting the crowns if not the two countries. Finally in 1707 England and Scotland were formally brought together under the name of Great Britain.

Stalin and Hitler celebrate a pact

1939 Reflecting the celebratory mood of the occasion, Joseph Stalin rose and offered an extraordinary toast: 'I know how much the German nation loves its Führer. I should therefore like to drink his health.' Around the Kremlin conference table, all glasses were drained in an instant. Stalin's gesture honoured one of the unholiest alliances ever created, for earlier that day a non-aggression pact had been signed between Nazi Germany and Soviet Russia.

In their treaty, the two signatories – so recently adversaries in the Spanish Civil War – promised to refrain from aggressive action against one another, but also, in a secret side agreement signed at the same time, they agreed on the imminent carving up between them of the nations of Eastern Europe, from the Baltic to the Black Sea. For Germany, with its eyes on the west, the treaty was insurance against a two-front war. For Russia, it bought time.

Churchill described the treaty as 'an unnatural act'. Its spirit, however, was best caught by the great English political cartoonist David Low, who drew the two dictators standing over the corpse of Poland bowing to each other elaborately, and offering fulsome greetings: 'Scum of the earth, I believe?' says Hitler. 'Bloody assassin of the workers, I presume?' replies a cordial Stalin.

Just nine days later, Nazi Germany invaded Poland. On 15 September, Soviet Russia advanced from the east to take her share.

The non-aggression treaty was stipulated to last ten years. In fact, it lasted just 22 months, until 22 June 1941, when the German army launched Operation

Barbarossa, the invasion of Russia, thus lending strength to the old adage that there is no honour among thieves.

Also on this day

1244: Jerusalem falls to the Muslims and the armies of the Sultan of Egypt seize Damascus * 1839: The British capture Hong Kong * 1944: Free French and American troops enter Paris during the Second World War

24 August

The Massacre of St Bartholomew

1572 At dawn today, the feast of St Bartholomew, the great bell of Paris's Saint-Germain-l'Auxerrois church began to toll, signalling the start of the greatest religious massacre in European history. Fired by holy fanaticism, Catholic bands roamed the streets, killing Huguenots and putting their houses to the torch. Over 3,000 were slaughtered, men, women and children.

The real spark-plug for the massacre had come nine years earlier when, in an attempt to bolster the power of the Huguenots, Admiral Gaspard de Coligny had ordered the assassination of the arch-Catholic leader, François de Guise. Guise's murder had produced the desired results, for within a decade Coligny had become the most trusted advisor of France's neurotic King Charles IX, and Protestant power was at its zenith. But Coligny had made two miscalculations. He had neglected Guise's son Henri, who swore to avenge his father's death, and, worse, his influence with King Charles had appeared threatening to Charles's devious and power-mad mother Catherine de' Medici, who feared losing her control over the King.

Henri de Guise bided his time until both he and Coligny were in Paris during the steamy days of August 1572 for the wedding of the King's sister. Then he struck.

Guise's first attempt to murder the Admiral failed when, on 22 August, his hired marksman merely wounded the Huguenot leader. The following day a bandaged Coligny was again closeted with the King, but here he made his last, fatal blunder. He warned King Charles not to trust his mother, saying that she lusted only for power. Later that day poor weak Charles repeated this to Catherine, and Coligny's fate was sealed.

Summoning the King, his brother and several Italian courtiers, Catherine soon persuaded them that Coligny had to die. 'Kill the Admiral if you want', screamed Charles hysterically. 'But you also have to kill *all* the Huguenots, so that not one is left to reproach me. Kill them all! Kill them all! Kill them all!' Quickly the Queen Mother authorised Guise to try again.

The final attempt began at 2.30 the next morning, on the feast of St Bartholomew. Guise and a band of followers stormed Coligny's house (located where today stands number 144 rue de Rivoli) and cornered the Admiral in his bedroom. Coligny seemed resigned to death. He addressed one young assailant with the words: 'Young man, you should respect my grey hairs, although you can shorten my life but little.'

Attacked with daggers, the Admiral quickly fell dead, and his corpse was thrown from the window for the waiting crowd of Catholics to dismember and hang for all to see. Then the general massacre began, first in Paris and then spreading throughout the rest of France, leaving in its wake over 8,000 dead Protestants. Fanatical Catholics everywhere applauded, and in Rome Pope Gregory XIII ordered a *Te Deum* to celebrate the slaughter.

In the end, the great loser was France itself as religious war continued for the next seventeen years and many Huguenots, among France's most successful merchants, left the country for England and Holland. King Charles spent his remaining two years on Earth racked with guilt, and Henri de Guise was assassinated in his turn by Charles's brother sixteen year later. The only winner was the sinister Catherine de' Medici, who continued to dominate her sons for another seventeen years.

Rome falls to 'the licentious fury of the tribes of Germany and Scythia'

AD 410 Today the city of Rome, inviolate and unconquered for 800 years, fell to the troops of the Visigoth leader Alaric.

Alaric was a Visigoth nobleman by birth who had once commanded the Gothic troops in the Roman army, but when he was 25 he left the Romans and was elected chief of the Visigoths. From the moment he took power he was constantly at war with his former masters, first in Turkey, then in Greece and ultimately in Italy itself.

Twice he tried and failed to conquer Rome, still a great city even though the Emperor of the Western Roman Empire had moved his capital north to Ravenna in AD 402. In 410 he tried once more, demanding land and gold from Emperor Honorius in return for leaving the city in peace. The Emperor unwisely refused, and in August Alaric besieged the city. The defiant Romans threatened to send their army out to fight him, to which Alaric made the famous reply: 'The thicker the hay, the easier it is mowed.'

At first it seemed that Alaric would be stymied by the city's monumental walls, but the Romans had forgotten their own slave population that was ready to welcome Alaric as liberator. Edward Gibbon describes the scene: 'At the hour of midnight, the Salarian gate was silently opened [by disaffected slaves] and the inhabitants were awakened by the tremendous sound of the Gothic trumpet. Eleven hundred and sixty-three years after the foundation of Rome, the Imperial city, which had subdued and civilised so considerable a part of mankind, was delivered to the licentious fury of the tribes of Germany and Scythia.'

In fact, Alaric, a Christian, spared the city's churches and, by the standards of the time, restrained his soldiers from mass murder, although Saint Augustine tells us of some killing and arson. Gibbon informs us that 'the matrons and virgins of Rome were exposed to injuries more dreadful, in the apprehension of chastity, than death itself'. After having occupied the city for six days, Alaric and his army marched away laden with plunder, leaving Rome poorer but intact. He died in Cosenza in Calabria just a few months later at the age of 40 and was buried, together with his looted treasure, in the riverbed of the Busento.

King John marries an ambitious wife

1200 King John of England was 32 when he first met the ravishing Isabella of Angoulême, and he instantly determined to marry the fifteen-year-old beauty. No matter that he already had a wife of thirteen years, or that Isabella was betrothed to a neighbouring baron named Hugues le Brun of Lusignan; John was King of England and controlled much of France, and he was not to be denied.

Quickly finding a complaisant priest to dissolve his first marriage on grounds of consanguinity (his first wife was a very distant cousin), John brushed aside the protests of the outraged Hugues le Brun and married the ambitious Isabella in Bordeaux Cathedral on this day.

The marriage was not a complete success, for both King and Queen had a roving eye. John, however, like many husbands since, felt that extramarital adventures were a prerogative of the man alone, and thought to teach his wife a lesson. One day she returned to her bedroom to find the body of her current lover hanging at the foot of her bed, strung up with the elaborate hangings of the canopy.

Despite such tiffs, the marriage lasted until John's death in 1216. Shortly thereafter the still beautiful Isabella, then only in her early 30s, returned to Angoulême to marry none other than Count Hugues le Brun, whom she had jilted years before.

Although Isabella and Hugues had nine children, her primary interest was in advancing her family's position. In 1241, when she was 56, she watched with anticipation when her husband mounted a revolt against the French king, Louis IX. The rebellion was short-lived and disastrous, and the Count was forced to throw himself on the mercy of the King. But although the good Louis kindly forgave Hugues, Isabella continued to carry a grudge. Two years later she bribed two of the King's cooks to poison their lord, and when this plot also failed, the woman who had once been Queen of England was consigned to spend her last years in a dark and tiny cell in the abbey at Fontevrault. Since Louis was later canonised, Isabella's final distinction comes from being the only Queen of England who ever tried to murder a saint.

Also on this day
1724: English horse painter George Stubbs is born in Liverpool * 1812: The British burn Washington during the War of 1812

25 August

The last days of Pompeii

AD 79 'Although it was daybreak, the light was still pale and weak. Around us the buildings were trembling ... Our carriages ... rolled about first in one direction, then in another, even though the ground was completely flat, and would not stop even when blocked with stones. We saw the sea sucked away ... by the earthquake, ebbing from the beach so that great numbers of sea creatures were left on the dry sand. Inland great bursts of forked and tremulous flame burst through a forbidding black cloud, which opened to reveal great tongues of fire, like enormous flashes of lightning.'

So reported Pliny the Younger, an eyewitness from the nearby port of Misenum to today's colossal eruption of Mount Vesuvius, during which his uncle, the admiral, naturalist and writer Pliny the Elder, perished from the fumes.

The eruption had started about noon on the previous day when the volcano started spewing out an enormous black cloud which, according to Pliny, rose to a great height like a massive umbrella pine, probably not dissimilar to the mushroom cloud of a nuclear explosion. Below, at the south-eastern base of the mountain, the city of Pompeii was buried in pumice and ash to a depth of nine feet. But worse was yet to come.

The following morning, surges of pyroclastic material accompanied by toxic gases rolled over Pompeii's walls and asphyxiated most of the city's remaining inhabitants who had survived the ash and volcanic debris of the day before. By the time the eruption was over, the city and some 20,000 of its citizens were covered with over twenty feet of pumice and the nearby town of Herculaneum had been overwhelmed by a gigantic mud-flow.

Vesuvius has erupted many times since the year 79 and is still active today. Its crater now measures 2,000 feet across and 1,000 feet deep, and on its slopes is grown a sweet fizzy wine known as Lacrima Christi, the Tears of Christ.

St Louis dies of plague

1270 Louis IX was one of France's good kings and great men. Born in 1214, he inherited the throne at the age of twelve and was initially guided by his formidable mother, Blanche of Castile. Although Blanche remained regent until he was twenty, Louis was an assiduous student of kingship, and at the age of fifteen he personally commanded his army in the field.

France was largely prosperous and at peace during Louis's reign, but his real fame comes not from the excellence of his governance but from the quality of his character. He was highly religious, purchasing the Holy Lance, parts of the True Cross and the Crown of Thorns to enshrine them in his greatest monument, the breathtaking Sainte-Chapelle in Paris. He heard Mass twice a day, often fasted and surrounded himself with priests chanting the hours even when he was on horseback. On one occasion he must have left his courtiers somewhat bemused when he gave each a present of a hair shirt.

On a more practical level, Louis had hospitals built, including the 'Quinze-Vingts' for 300 knights who had been blinded by the Saracens. Sometimes he cared for the sick himself, and he felt strong responsibility for the poor of his realm. By his order, 100 beggars were given food or alms from royal provisions every day.

His piety notwithstanding, Louis was also a courageous knight, undaunted by adversity and (between prayers, at any rate) a good companion, the ideal king of the Middle Ages.

In August 1248 Louis embarked on his first crusade, setting sail for Egypt with his wife Marguerite and 35,000 soldiers. Unfortunately, it was a disastrous adventure. Louis's brother was killed, and plague struck the army. Louis almost died of dysentery and was captured by the Saracens. He returned to France only four years later.

On 1 July 1270 Louis once more set out on crusade, leaving France from a Mediterranean port he had ordered built some 30 years before, the small walled town with the ominous name of Aigues-Mortes, derived from 'aquae mortuae' or dead waters, after the surrounding saline marshland.

Seventeen days later Louis landed in Tunis, near the ruins of ancient Carthage. Initially his army gained some painless victories, but the summer heat was frightful, and soon plague appeared, first ravaging the army and then striking the King himself. Knowing he was dying, Louis instructed his son and successor Philip (III) to take special care of the poor.

Louis died on 25 August 1270 at the age of 56, having reigned for 43 years. His body was brought back to France in one long funeral procession, with mourners lining the roads as it passed through Italy, over the Alps and on to Paris. This great king was buried in the Abbey of St Denis just north of Paris, historic last resting-place for the kings of France.

From the moment of his burial Louis was thought a saint, and people prayed for miracles at his tomb. He was canonised in 1297, only 27 years after his death, by Pope Boniface VIII. He is the only French king ever declared a saint.

The only pope ever to resign

1294 At the close of the 13th century the struggle of the Guelph and Ghibelline factions for papal power was at its height. On the death of Pope Nicholas IV, however, it became clear that neither Guelph nor Ghibelline would be elected, and after two years of wrangling, the College of Cardinals turned to a compromise candidate, a Benedictine ascetic named Pietro Angeleri dal Morrone, who chose the papal name of Celestine V.

Celestine was a far cry from the worldly, political popes to which Europe had become accustomed. Over 80, he had been a hermit for twenty years, living in solitude in a cave on Monte Majella in the Abruzzi.

Celestine's first act was to break tradition by choosing Aquila instead of Rome for his coronation, which duly took place on this day in 1294. Later he continued his pious ways. He travelled mounted on an ass rather than with normal papal splendour. Worse, he appointed another hermit as head of the rich abbey of Monte Cassino, perhaps an inspiration to the wild-eyed and hairy in clerical ranks but an indication to others that the spoils of the Church might go to those unable to appreciate them.

The forces of power and politics were soon ranged against Celestine, finally forcing him to do the unthinkable – to resign the papacy. This he did in December 1294, only 161 days after his election. He was the only pope in all 2,000 years of Church history to resign.

Celestine's successor Boniface VIII quickly banished the ex-pope to an isolated castle at Fumone, where he died, practically a prisoner, eighteen months later. Subsequently the Church thought highly enough of Celestine's selfless ignorance to make him a saint, with direct passage to heaven. Not everyone agreed. Dante, a Guelph supporter, found a place for him in his *Inferno,* just inside the gates of Hell, referring to Celestine as 'him who from cowardice made the great refusal'.

Also on this day

1530: Ivan IV ('the Terrible') is born * 1688: Welsh buccaneer Sir Henry Morgan dies in Jamaica * 1830: The Belgian revolution starts, resulting in modern Belgium

26 August

The Battle of Crécy

1346 If you drive north from Paris to Calais, just beyond Abbéville you pass by the small town of Crécy. There on this day over six centuries ago the age of knightly chivalry received a mortal wound from which eventually it would die.

Here on this showery Saturday afternoon England's King Edward III took on the might of France during the Hundred Years' War with a force of some 11,000 men, including 7,000 longbowmen.

The French army was nominally under the command of King Philip VI, but in fact it was composed of too many undisciplined knights who thought of themselves as allies rather than subjects and were determined to win glory (and ransom from noble English prisoners). The number of the French force is reckoned somewhere between 35,000 and 60,000, but by any estimate far larger than the English. Among the French were 8,000 Genoese crossbowmen.

The difference in bows and bowmen was critical to the battle. The crossbow had first been used in Europe in the 10th century. It fired a heavy, armour-

415

piercing bolt, but the rate of fire was no more than two per minute. The longbow, first developed in Wales, fired a metal-tipped armour-piercing arrow three feet long that required a strong bowman, as the longbows of the time required a 100-pound force to draw. But the English longbowmen could fire five arrows a minute and more.

The French sent their crossbowmen to open the attack, but before the Genoese came within effective range the English longbowmen responded with a murderous shower of arrows, overwhelming their enemy in a matter of minutes and sending them into full retreat. Seeing the slaughter, the French mounted knights rode down their own bowmen in their haste to attack the English, but once again a deadly shower of arrows brought down men and horses in thousands. Once the knights had been unhorsed, the English men-at-arms quickly finished them off with swords and maces. It has been estimated that in all the English bowmen fired some 500,000 arrows at the French.

The battle had its pathetic moments of 'honour'. Blind King John of Bohemia asked his captains: 'Gentlemen, as I am blind, I request you to lead me so far into the engagement that I may strike one stroke with my sword.' He then charged into battle with a French knight guiding him on each side – and was almost immediately slaughtered. (His crest of three ostrich feathers with the motto 'Ich dien' was taken by Edward's son, the Black Prince, and is still used today by English Princes of Wales.) But each new charge was met by another lethal flight of arrows, and the cavalry could not attack the longbowmen whose positions were protected by rows of sharpened stakes. Eventually darkness brought the grisly slaughter to a close.

The following day the English counted the casualties. Fewer than 100 English had lost their lives but 15,000 French and Genoese soldiers lay dead on the field and a further 1,500 French knights had been captured or killed.

With the introduction of the longbow, a new type of warfare had been invented. Never again was the charge of knights in armour to determine the course of victory. The Battle of Crécy did not, however, have much effect on the Hundred Years' War, which continued spasmodically for another 107 years.

The Habsburgs take control of Austria for 640 years

1278 From this day on, the Habsburgs ruled Austria for the next 640 years. Five years previously Rudolf I von Habsburg had been the first Habsburg elected Holy Roman Emperor, but he still found Austria out of his control, ruled as it was by Ottocar Przemysl, King of Bohemia.

Determined to add Austria to his domain, Rudolf invaded the country and soon starved Vienna into submission. But just as he was celebrating his victory, Ottocar appeared on the other side of the Danube with a far superior force. Because of his greater numbers, the Bohemian king expected to starve Rudolf out in turn.

Rudolf waited in Vienna, trying to lull Ottocar into believing that all he had to do was remain where he was for the fruit to fall into his hands. Then on this day he managed to cross the Danube unseen and attacked the surprised Ottocar near his camp at Dürnkrut, about 30 miles north-east of Vienna. The rout was complete, and King Ottocar was cut down on the field of battle.

From that day onwards the Habsburgs ruled Austria until the young Emperor Karl abdicated in November 1918 in the aftermath of the First World War.

Catherine the Great gives Poland to her lover

1764 Catherine the Great of Russia was famous for her lovers – she had at least sixteen of them, perhaps modest by today's standards but scandalous for a woman in the 18th century. She also rewarded her lovers generously, none more so than an ineffectual but handsome and intelligent Pole named Stanislaw Poniatowski, who had struck the Empress's fancy in the mid-1750s.

When the Polish king died in 1763, Catherine wanted 'a weak and pliant successor. Under enormous pressure from Catherine's troops (sent to Poland to 'ensure stability'), the Polish Sejm (parliament) today unanimously pronounced in favour of none other than Stanislaw, who became the new king under the grand name of Stanislaw Augustus. It was Catherine's greatest gift to a lover – an entire country.

Stanislaw turned out to be a thoughtful and progressive ruler, although he lacked the grit and determination the job required. During his eleven years on the throne he introduced a remarkably forward-looking and democratic constitution, but nonetheless the nation was partitioned three times by Russia and Prussia and finally ceased to exist as an independent country in 1775. Poland remained the pawn of other nations, frequently reshaped and repartitioned, until the restoration of the Polish Republic in the aftermath of the First World War in November 1918.

Also on this day

55 BC: Julius Caesar lands in Britain * 1666: Dutch painter Frans Hals dies * 1676: First English Prime Minister Robert Walpole is born * 1819: Prince Albert is born in Coburg, Germany * 1920: In the United States, the 19th Amendment is proclaimed by the Secretary of State, enfranchising women on an equal basis with men

27 August

Lope de Vega, the Spaniard who wrote 1,500 plays

1635 Lope de Vega was not only Spain's greatest playwright and the founder of modern Spanish drama, he was also one of the most prolific writers who ever put pen to paper. He wrote lyric poetry, some prose (including his auto-biography) and more than 1,500 plays. Almost 500 of his works are still extant.

Given his incredible output, it is a wonder he had time for anything else, but Vega also led a tempestuous life enlivened by two wives and innumerable mistresses.

At fifteen he entered the university at Alcalá de Henares outside Madrid to study for the priesthood, but soon left to pursue a married mistress. In need of work, he established himself as secretary to various Spanish nobles, with the essential role of finding women for them. All the while he continued his adventures with the fair sex, but at one point ended up in prison for issuing libels against a mistress who had deserted him for another man.

On top of these entertaining activities, Vega was also a fighting man. At 21 he participated in an expedition against the Azores and five years later sailed with the Spanish Armada.

When not fighting or seducing, Vega was busy writing plays. His work revolutionised Spanish theatre, abandoning the classical 'rules' of place and time and introducing the real life of ordinary people as fit subject matter for drama. The public flocked to his work, and he became a national hero. Because of his extraordinary output his contemporary Cervantes called him a 'prodigy of nature'.

In his early 50s Vega suffered terrible tragedy when in a few short years his wife, his son and his favourite mistress all died. Understandably depressed, in 1614 he entered the priesthood, although continuing to provide young women for his patron, the Duke of Sessa. Fearing that Vega's religion might interfere with his services as procurer, the Duke persuaded one of Vega's former mistresses to seduce him, thereby forcing Vega to return to the secular world.

Towards the end of his life Vega entered a quiet monastery in Madrid, dying on this day at the age of 72. His death evoked mourning throughout the nation he had entertained so well for so long.

Krakatoa erupts

1883 The volcano on the uninhabited island of Krakatoa had been rumbling ominously since May, telling the natives of Java that Orang Aljeh, the mountain devil, had been disturbed. About midday today, a Sunday, the volcano started its titanic eruption.

All that day rock, steam and smoke were spewed high into the air, blotting out the sun. The ocean churned wrathfully and winds blew at hurricane force. Through the night it continued, and at ten o'clock the next morning suddenly the great cone-shaped mountain literally exploded, producing the loudest noise in history, clearly heard over 3,000 miles away. The eruption discharged nearly five cubic miles of rock fragments.

The island of Krakatoa vanished completely, leaving in its place a submarine cavity 1,000 feet deep. The gigantic explosion created a tsunami or giant tidal wave 120 feet high, moving at 300 miles per hour, which crashed into the coast of Java, completely obliterating the town of Anger and travelling some fifteen miles inland. In all, about 36,000 people were killed, and for days afterwards the straits around Java and Sumatra were jammed with hideous debris – the corpses of humans, cattle, fish, snakes, tigers and pigs floating together.

Although the cataclysm of 1883 is the most famous of Krakatoa's eruptions, one over a millennium earlier, in 535, probably killed even more people, as scientists believe it triggered an onslaught of the bubonic plague in 542, which killed over 250,000 inhabitants of Constantinople and subsequently millions more in the rest of Europe.

The bubonic plague originated in Africa, and is carried by fleas. When Krakatoa erupted, the enormous cloud of debris covered much of Africa, shielding the land from the sun and causing temperatures to drop. But at lower temperatures the flea's gut becomes blocked, dooming the flea to starve to death for lack of blood in its own intestines. This drives the flea to seek new sources of blood at a voracious rate, thereby spreading the plague at exponentially increased speed.

During the 6th century Constantinople enjoyed a thriving ivory trade with Africa. Ivory traders and vermin hosting infected and hungry fleas were carried by ship from Africa to the Gulf of Suez, crossed the isthmus and then sailed across the Mediterranean to Constantinople, igniting the epidemic there. Once Constantinople was struck, its fleeing citizens spread the plague all over Europe.

In sheer explosive force, however, the eruption of Krakatoa in 535 was far smaller than that of 1883, which was long considered the greatest explosion, natural or otherwise, in the recorded history of man. Recent scientific research, however, suggests that the eruption of the Greek island of Thera (today's Santorini) in about 1470 BC might have been two to four times more powerful, destroying the Minoan civilisation on Crete with its gigantic tsunami.

Also on this day

551 BC: Chinese philosopher Confucius is born * 1576: Italian painter Titian dies * 1770: German philosopher Georg Wilhelm Hegel is born in Stuttgart

28 August

Goethe – the greatest Renaissance Man since the Renaissance

1749 Born this day in Frankfurt am Main was arguably the greatest Renaissance Man since the Renaissance. Although trained as a lawyer, he became an accomplished scientist, an expert in biological morphology; he conducted orchestras as well as opera performances; a gifted painter, he was chief minister to his German state of Weimar and was an occasional journalist; he spoke German, French, English, Italian, Latin, Greek and Hebrew, and translated Cellini,

Voltaire and Byron into German. He appreciated all forms of art, and once defined architecture as 'eine erstarrte Musik' (frozen music). He was also a talented and successful womaniser, but above all he was a great poet and dramatist, who practically created the literary movement known as *Sturm und Drang* (storm and stress). His name was Johann Wolfgang von Goethe.

Goethe's talent and fame was so great in his own day that even heads of state clamoured to be introduced to him. When Napoleon met him at Erfurt in 1808, he remarked: 'Voilà un homme!' (What a man!)

Goethe lived to a grand old 82. Strangely enough, today he is best known for his great poetic drama, *Faust*, but the second half of *Faust* was published only after his death.

King John founds Liverpool

1206 King John of England is so well known for his treachery, duplicity and shifty opportunism that it's a surprise to find that on rare occasions he showed foresight and vision.

In the summer of 1206 John was travelling in the west of England and picked out one spot of barren coast as particularly appropriate to become a port. On his instructions a town charter was drawn up, which was officially granted on 28 August.

The spot that John chose is where Liverpool now stands, and he is rightly known as its founder. Some people still consider the place a barren coast, of course, but it's possible to conjecture that without John's foresight we would never have had the Beatles.

Also on this day

1640: The Indian War in New England ends with the surrender of the Indians * 1808: Russian novelist Leo Tolstoy is born * 1850: Richard Wagner's *Lohengrin* is performed for the first time at Weimar

29 August

Great Britain takes Hong Kong

1842 On this day the Chinese and British signed the Treaty of Nanking, which not only ended a war but also ceded Hong Kong Island to Great Britain.

During the century and a half since the Treaty was signed, Hong Kong has represented the ultimate in unfettered trade and tax-free wheeling and dealing that made its businessmen rich and eventually financed the spectacular Hong Kong skyline. The foundation of Hong Kong's thriving economy and frenetic business life was opium.

In the early 19th century, freewheeling British traders realised there was a fortune to be made in selling opium to the Chinese. And these men were just in the right position to grasp the opportunity, since opium was grown in abundance in British-controlled India. The Chinese objected (not so much to the sale of opium but to foreign traders garnering all the profits), but the British continued illegally to import the drug.

In 1839 the Chinese government decided to act, and launched an anti-opium campaign in Canton that culminated in the military take-over of a British factory and the confiscation of some 20,000 chests of opium. While the British were angrily demanding a return of their property, some inebriated British sailors killed a local Chinese, and the British government refused to hand over the culprits to the Chinese authorities. Deemed an insult to national sovereignty, the killing sparked the first Opium War, principally a naval conflict in the sea around Hong Kong.

The war lasted three years, and the British were easily victorious. But they could see that they now needed a safe and insulated base from which to trade. The result was the Treaty of Nanking.

This should have ended the problem of opium trading, but it did not. In 1856 the British, this time joined by the French, fought a second Opium War, won it, and as a result took over Kowloon, across the bay from Hong Kong. Finally, in 1898 Britain leased the New Territories (partly mainland, plus over 200 islands) for 99 years.

Britain built Hong Kong into one of the great trading and commercial cities of the world, but was forced to return it to China on 1 July 1997 when the lease on the New Territories expired and the Communist Chinese made it clear that they intended to take back all of Hong Kong, not just the part under lease.

Suleiman the Magnificent conquers Hungary

1526 Mohács lies on the west bank of the Danube, straight south from Budapest. It was there on this day that the great battle took place that was to change Hungary's history for over a century.

The Turkish sultan Suleiman the Magnificent had been demanding tribute from the Hungarians, and when they foolishly refused to pay, he invaded with an enormous army of 100,000 men. King Louis II of Hungary hastily gathered whatever troops he had at hand, and, without waiting for reinforcements from other parts of his kingdom, marched down from Buda to engage the Turks.

When he reached Mohács, Louis found Suleiman's vast army waiting for him and immediately ordered his 4,000 cavalry to charge. Briefly it appeared that the Hungarians' insane attack might rock the invaders into panic as the Turkish line buckled under the weight of so many tons of armour plate. Immediately the Hungarian infantry, another 21,000 men, followed the mounted knights into the assault.

But not even mad courage could defeat odds of four to one, and the Turkish counter-attack produced an appalling slaughter. Hungarians fell and died, as the Turks gave no quarter, routinely massacring their prisoners. Seeing that catastrophic defeat was inevitable, King Louis tried to escape but was crushed by his own war-horse when it fell on him.

In all some 24,000 Hungarians died on the plain of Mohács. After the battle, Suleiman marched up river to Buda and then withdrew from the country, taking 100,000 Hungarian captives with him. Hungary was finished as a fighting force, and the nation was absorbed into the Turkish empire for a century and a half.

Passage of the Factory Act

1833 Today the British Parliament passed the Factory Act, the first government intervention into the plight of factory workers and as such the first recognition that the common labourer needed state protection from the full might of unbridled capitalism.

The Industrial Revolution is generally considered to have started about 1760, but it was in the early 19th century that it got up to speed. It changed the lives of almost everyone in the country. The big winners were the middle classes who could afford the flood of new manufactured goods, but those who paid the price for progress were largely the country's factory workers, especially women and children, who were subjected to a gruelling workload and inhuman conditions. But as output grew, conditions deteriorated, and finally the British Parliament resolved to put a stop to some of the most heartless conditions.

The Factory Act became law in spite of heavy opposition from the Tories and from some *laissez-faire* Whigs. It was unambitious in its scope, applying only to the textile industry, and the restrictions imposed seem hardly extreme today.

Children under nine were forbidden to work in factories, and those between nine and thirteen were restricted to a meagre 48 work hours a week. Older children from thirteen to eighteen also had their working time reduced, to 69 hours a week. But in spite of its mildness, the Act set a precedent for the responsibility of governments to look to the conditions of the common workman.

Also on this day
1789: French painter Jean-Auguste Ingres is born in Montauban * 1835: The city of Melbourne is founded in Australia

30 August

Cleopatra clasps an asp to her bosom

30 BC Today amid the delicacies of a royal feast the last pharaoh of Egypt died by her own hand. She was the fabulous Cleopatra, the original femme fatale, lover of Julius Caesar and Mark Antony and extolled by Shakespeare for her 'infinite variety':

> ... other women cloy
> The appetites they feed, but she makes hungry
> Where most she satisfied.

Ever since Menes 3,000 years before, Egypt had been ruled by pharaohs, and since 323 BC by the dynasty established by Alexander the Great's general Ptolemy. Cleopatra was the last in Ptolemy's line. Her first language was Greek, but she spoke eight other languages as well, her voice 'an instrument of many strings', according to Plutarch.

Cleopatra had first beguiled Mark Antony at Tarsus, sailing up the Cydnus River in her opulent barge that 'like a burnished throne, burned on the water'. During eleven years they produced three children and hoped to rule the world together, Mark Antony as the new Caesar, Cleopatra as his partner and Queen of Egypt. But ever since Julius Caesar's death, his heir Octavian (the future Emperor Augustus) had laid claim to imperial power and resolved that Egypt should be just another Roman province rather than an independent kingdom.

In 31 BC Octavian crushingly defeated Mark Antony's and Cleopatra's fleets at Actium, and within a year his legions were marching towards Alexandria. Mark Antony led his army out of the city to do battle, but first his fleet defected and then his cavalry followed suit. His infantry was soon overwhelmed, and Mark Antony fled back into the city.

Dreading the fate awaiting her, Cleopatra secreted herself in her new mausoleum and had the rumour spread that she was dead. On hearing this direful news, Mark Antony attempted suicide but succeeded only in stabbing himself in the stomach, fainting on his couch. When he came to, one of Cleopatra's servants informed him that she was not dead after all, and summoned him to her presence. Carried by litter to her mausoleum, he was hoisted through a high window by Cleopatra's serving women, too frightened of Octavian's imminent arrival to open the gates. There, stretched out on his lover's couch, Mark Antony died of his wounds.

A few days later Octavian arrived at the head of his army. When Cleopatra refused him entry into the mausoleum, he sent soldiers in through the windows to disarm her before she could stab herself.

Octavian allowed her to arrange a splendid funeral for Mark Antony, who was interred in her mausoleum. But all the while he kept her surrounded with guards. In a desperate attempt to use her seductive charms one more time, she dressed in her most transparent garments and threw herself at her conqueror's feet, but he was immune to her allure. Now realising that her fate was to be paraded in chains through the streets of Rome, a prized captive, Cleopatra determined on suicide. Legend has it that she ordered condemned prisoners to be executed with various poisons to establish which would cause the least painful death.

On 30 August she returned to her mausoleum on the pretext of visiting Mark Antony's tomb. There she bathed and ordered a sumptuous feast. Among the delicacies delivered was a basket of figs in which was secreted an asp, an Egyptian symbol of divine royalty but more importantly for Cleopatra, deadly poisonous.

Her banquet completed, the Queen wrote to Octavian, pleading to be buried with her lover. The Roman instantly sent soldiers to prevent her suicide, but when they arrived they found her lying dead on her golden bed, two of her servant girls expiring at her feet. According to tradition, she had pressed the asp to her breast, but other reports suggest that two puncture wounds from the snake's fangs were found on her arm. She was still just 39 and had been pharaoh for 22 years.

On his return to Rome Octavian proudly announced to the Senate: 'I have added Egypt to the Empire of the Roman people.' His achievement lasted over six centuries, until the Arab conquests in 639, but through the magnificent drama of her life and death Cleopatra had become immortal, the most famous of all the queens of history.

The king who brought France out of the Middle Ages

1483 When Louis XI was born 60 years earlier, France was still a medieval country, a feudal nation of semi-independent and warring baronies where the English ruled large chunks of its territory. Louis himself at the age of eight had actually met that final glory of medieval French mysticism, Joan of Arc.

But during Louis's lifetime the world changed. When he was thirteen, Gutenberg invented mobile type. In Italy the Renaissance, although not yet at high noon, was in the ascendant (Leonardo was born when Louis was 29). The classic symbol of the end of the Middle Ages, the fall of Constantinople to the Turks, had occurred when he was 30. The Hundred Years' War ended the same year. Martin Luther was born in the year that Louis died.

Louis also changed his world. He broke for ever the feudal power of his barons, manoeuvring Charles the Bold of Burgundy to destruction. Perhaps more than any other king, he brought France into the modern era, as a Frenchman's primary loyalty was now to the crown rather than to the local feudal lord.

Oddly, Louis in temperament remained medieval. Suspicious in the extreme, he spent his last years in his fortress of Plessis, guarded by 40 crossbowmen day and night on the castle towers, plus 400 archers on patrol. Highly superstitious as well, Louis collected religious icons and relics, endowed churches, and seemed to think he could bargain with God.

Louis died at eight in the evening on this day, a Saturday, at Plessis-les-Tours in Touraine at the age of 60, probably of a cerebral haemorrhage.

Also on this day

1748: French painter Jacques-Louis David is born * 1797: *Frankenstein* writer Mary Wollstonecraft Shelley is born

31 August

Caligula – the story of a monster

AD 12 Born today at Antium, near modern Anzio on the Mediterranean coast of Italy, was history's prototype monster of despotic cruelty, the future third Roman emperor, Gaius Caesar Germanicus, commonly known as Caligula.

Caligula was related to the most powerful figures of the Roman Empire. Augustus was his great-grandfather (as was Mark Antony), and Tiberius, who became Emperor when Caligula was two, his great-uncle. His father Germanicus was a great military leader who took his young son on campaign with him, dressing him as a miniature soldier. From this he acquired the nickname of Caligula, or Little Boots, from his father's adoring soldiers.

When Caligula was seven, Germanicus died in Syria, many believed poisoned on orders from Tiberius, who was jealous of his reputation for bravery, generosity and military leadership. Ten years later the half-mad emperor exiled Caligula's mother Agrippina (the Elder) to the island of Pandateria, supposedly for plotting against him, and summoned Caligula, then eighteen, to live in the royal palace on Capri.

It was on Capri that Caligula first displayed his love of torture, eagerly attending executions. By that time he had also (according to that old gossip, Suetonius) enjoyed incestuous relations with all three of his sisters. A year after his arrival on the island, the paranoid Tiberius had Caligula's two elder brothers executed on flimsy charges of treason, and two years later Agrippina was forced to starve herself to death. This brought to four the number of immediate family members who died at Tiberius's hands, but Caligula continued to play the sycophant at court. It seems, however, that the Emperor was not fooled, once boasting that he was 'rearing a viper for the Roman people'.

When Caligula was 25, Tiberius died at the age of 78, some say smothered on the orders of his impatient great-nephew intent on inheriting the throne. For the first seven months of his rule Caligula was both just and generous, but he then fell severely ill, emerging from the sickness as the ogre of legend.

A huge spendthrift, he soon went through the three billion sesterces left by Tiberius, and started wholesale executions in order to confiscate rich men's property. He even initiated a tax on prostitutes, opening a brothel in a wing of the imperial palace to collect more fees.

Caligula's love of inflicting pain was notorious. He often witnessed the killings he ordered, telling the executioner to kill his victim slowly in order to 'make him feel that he is dying'. When one man cried out that he was innocent of the charges against him, Caligula halted the execution to have his tongue cut out, then proceeded to put him to death. He even had convicted criminals slaughtered to feed his collection of wild animals. When the prisoners were lined up before him, Caligula ignored the charge sheet specifying their crimes, simply commanding the executioner to 'kill every man between that bald head and that one', indicating two bald criminals on either end of the line.

Tall and ungainly with only a fringe of hair around the ears, Caligula was so sensitive about his baldness that he made it a capital offence for anyone to look down on him. Even his family was not safe from his vindictive cruelty, as he forced his father-in-law to cut his own throat with a razor and probably poisoned his grandmother Antonia.

Caligula eventually concluded that he was a god, and ordered the Senate to treat him as one. On moonlit nights he would invite the moon goddess to join him in bed, and he talked openly to Jupiter, once threatening: 'If you do not raise me up to heaven I will cast you down to hell.' He even built a temple for himself on the Palatine Hill.

The most famous story about Caligula concerns his favourite horse Incitatus, which he housed in an ivory stall in a marble stable and adorned with a collar of precious stones and blankets of royal purple. He suggested, perhaps in jest, that he would make Incitatus consul, but never actually did so.

At the age of only 28, after less than four years as Emperor, Caligula was assassinated by two of his imperial guards on 24 January 41.

Henry V dies at Vincennes

1422 One of the few extant portraits of England's Henry V now hangs in London's National Portrait Gallery. It shows the King in profile, at first glance looking somewhat monkish, as the hat that conceals his blond hair gives him the air of a medieval canon. His face is strong, long and bony, with a large straight nose and contemplative brown eyes that would offer more justice than mercy. The anonymous artist read his subject well.

Stern Henry, England's last great warrior monarch, victor of Agincourt and de facto ruler of France, died today, less than a month after his 35th birthday. He was, according to his brother, 'too famous to live long'. Although the cause is uncertain, it seems likely that he died of dysentery, the scourge of medieval soldiers.

Henry had been ill for some months and was forced to leave his final campaign on a litter, returning to his headquarters at the château of Vincennes, just east of Paris. There he spent his last three weeks putting his dominions in order and securing the royal inheritance for his infant son (the future Henry VI), whom he had never seen.

In his day, Henry was seen as a hero who as a youth had been a boisterous scapegrace but as King became renowned for his determination, bravery and justice. He could also be brutal, contemptuous of men's lives and piously priggish as well. He spent most of his nine years as King in a largely successful attempt to crush a France already riven by civil war and saddled with a lunatic monarch. But within seven years of Henry's death, France's Charles VII was crowned at Reims with the help of Joan of Arc and the claims of Henry's son were discarded.

When Henry died, his flesh was boiled from his bones to preserve it, and both flesh and bones were placed in his casket which made a stately return to London over the next two months. There Henry enjoyed a great pageant of a funeral, when even his horses were led to the altar in Westminster Abbey for a final farewell to their illustrious master.

Also on this day

1688: English writer John Bunyan dies in London * 1867: French writer Charles Baudelaire dies in Paris * 1888: The first victim of Jack the Ripper, 'Polly' Nichols, is found dead and mutilated in Buck's Row, London

1 September

Kublai Khan and the Divine Wind

1281 The Mongol Empire of Kublai Khan was the greatest the world had known, extending from Hungary in the west to Korea in the east. But one country not yet conquered was Japan, and the great emperor, grandson of the fearsome Genghis Khan, was determined to add it to his territories.

In August 1281 Kublai Khan assembled a huge invading force of 140,000 battle-hardened soldiers aboard a vast fleet. The Mongols landed on the coast of Japan at Hakata Bay but were fought to a standstill by Japanese samurai, who denied them a beachhead. Withdrawing to their ships, the invaders planned another attack.

But while the Mongols planned a second D-Day, unknown to them an ominous date arrived, 1 September, the 210th day of the Japanese lunar calendar, famous for storms. And so it was, before the Mongols could mount their next assault, a massive typhoon struck, wreaking havoc with the Mongol fleet, destroying hundreds of ships and drowning thousands – some say over 100,000 – of the invaders.

The remaining Mongols sailed away or were captured and butchered. Ever since that day the Japanese have referred to the great enemy-destroying typhoon as the divine wind, or Kamikaze.

The Napoleonic dreams are crushed for ever at Sedan

1870 The first of September marks the beginning and the end of Napoleonic glory. It was on that date in 1785 that Napoleon Bonaparte first received his commission as an artillery officer, the true start of his military success and the Napoleonic saga. Exactly 85 years later to the day came the battle that ended the Napoleonic story, as the army of his nephew, Emperor Napoleon III, crashed to defeat at the hands of Prussia at Sedan.

For 22 years Napoleon III had been the master of France, first as President of the Second Republic, then as Emperor. During that time he had helped his country to prosper, but now France's position in Europe was threatened by the potential unification of the German states under Prussia's Iron Chancellor, Otto von Bismarck. In July 1870 the crafty Bismarck, who wanted the conflict as a means of drawing together some reluctant German principalities, cunningly manoeuvred Napoleon into war.

After some early French successes, the larger and better trained Prussian army quickly got the measure of the French, culminating on 31 August in the surrounding of a French army of 130,000 men in Sedan, where Prussian artillery mercilessly pounded the city. Leading the beleaguered French was Napoleon himself, the last emperor ever to command in the field. Accompanying the Prussian army was Crown Prince Wilhelm Friedrich, soon to become Emperor of the combined German states as Kaiser Wilhelm I.

By 1 September Napoleon could see that the situation was desperate. The Prussians had completely encircled Sedan, cutting off all hope of reinforcements, and the most senior French general, Marshal Mac-Mahon, had been seriously wounded. Knowing that he could never continue as Emperor after such a disastrous loss, Napoleon spent the day riding where the action was hottest, apparently hoping for a stray shell to end his reign in dignity. He survived unscathed, but his army was completely shattered, with 17,000 dead or wounded against half that number of Prussian casualties. On the afternoon of the following day he sent this message to Crown Prince Wilhelm: 'Monsieur mon frère; Not having succeeded in dying in the midst of my troops, nothing remains for me but to deliver my sword into your majesty's hands.' He thus became one of almost 100,000 French prisoners of war.

On 3 September his captors took Napoleon to Prussia, never to see France again. After a few months in regal confinement with Crown Prince Wilhelm Friedrich, he went into exile in England where he died in January two years later at the age of 64.

The setting of the Sun King

1715 'J'avais cru plus difficile de mourir' (I had thought it would be more difficult to die), said France's Louis XIV to his wife as he lay on his deathbed in the great château he had built at Versailles. He seemed remarkably composed for a man who had been suffering for weeks from gangrene in one of his legs and the fever that attended it. On this Sunday France's most glorious king finally passed from the world just four days short of his 76th birthday.

Louis had been monolithic and unchanging throughout his life, embodying the idea of the divine right of kings. As he wrote in his memoirs: 'God, who has given kings to men ... [reserved] to Himself alone the right to examine their conduct.'

He cared only for the glory of France and for his own, and could sometimes not distinguish between them. He kept his country almost constantly at war, his cannon inscribed with the motto 'Ultima ratio regum' (the last argument of kings), but with varying degrees of success. But his cultural achievements were of a high order. He founded the Comédie Française and backed France's two greatest classical playwrights, Racine and Molière. He initiated the three great French academies – of Painting and Sculpture, of Architecture and of Science. He also turned Paris into Europe's grandest city by razing the old city walls and building the Invalides and the Champs Elysées.

In the millennium between Charlemagne and Louis-Philippe, of 49 French kings – Carolingians, Capetians, Valois and Bourbons – only Louis reached the age of 70, and his reign of 72 years, three months and seventeen days remains the longest of any monarch in European history.

History's only English pope

1159 Today at Anagni south-east of Rome, Nicholas Breakspear died at the age of 59, the only Englishman ever to become Pope. As pontiff he assumed the name of Adrian IV.

Breakspear was born in Abbots Langley, just north of London. As Pope Adrian, apart from his unique nationality, he succeeded in two other rare achievements during his five-year reign.

First, while Pope he placed Rome itself under interdict, an ecclesiastical censure that withdrew most sacraments, including baptism and marriage. This happened during his struggle with Arnold of Brescia, an Italian monk who had made himself master of the city and who stood against the temporal power of the papacy. Sadly for Arnold, although he had previously managed to exile one pope, he was no match for Adrian, who called on the German king Frederick Barbarossa to capture the recalcitrant monk. This Barbarossa did, whereupon Adrian had him hanged.

Adrian's second distinction was his crowning of Barbarossa as Emperor, in return for the King's help with Arnold of Brescia. Barbarossa was the first Holy Roman Emperor crowned by a pope since Charlemagne.

Also on this day

AD 70: Roman Emperor Titus orders the destruction of Jerusalem * 1339: England's King Edward III declares war on France to start the Hundred Years' War * 1939: Germany invades Poland and captures Danzig, starting the Second World War

2 September

Octavian crushes Mark Antony at Actium

31 BC Today at the Battle of Actium, Octavian became master of the civilised world through his decisive victory over Mark Antony. The Augustan age had begun.

First there were three who controlled the Roman Empire: Octavian, Mark Antony and Lepidus. Together they avenged the murder of Julius Caesar, crushing the army of Marcus Junius Brutus at Philippi in 42 BC, a victory that left Brutus no way out but suicide. Then slowly Marcus Lepidus was moved aside until, in desperation, he raised an army in Sicily in an attempt to regain his authority. But even Lepidus's soldiers knew he was a lost cause and deserted, and Octavian sent him into forced retirement. Now there were only two, Mark Antony controlling the East, Octavian the West of the empire.

At first Mark Antony and Octavian maintained an uncomfortable alliance, cemented by Mark Antony's marriage to Octavian's sister, Octavia. But soon Mark Antony was openly living with Egypt's Queen Cleopatra, comporting himself in the style of an Oriental potentate. He then repudiated Octavia and married Cleopatra, an act contrary to all Roman laws under which no Roman could marry a foreigner. Together he and Cleopatra followed a licentious lifestyle in ostentatious luxury, proclaiming themselves incarnations of Dionysus and Aphrodite.

Meanwhile Octavian had been winning the propaganda war, inciting fury in Rome when he read to the Senate what he claimed to be Mark Antony's will in which he left all to his children by Cleopatra, stated his wish to be buried in Egypt and revealed his intent to relocate the capital from Rome to Alexandria. This gave Octavian all the justification he needed to declare war on Cleopatra, although his real target was Mark Antony.

The two armies came together near the bay of Actium (modern Punta), on the west coast of Greece. Both Octavian and Mark Antony commanded about 75,000 troops, and each had 400–500 ships. On the advice of Cleopatra, Mark Antony decided to launch a naval attack instead of an assault by his army.

Mark Antony drew up his fleet facing west, with Cleopatra's 60 galleys behind in reserve. At first the battle was furious, with neither side able to take a decisive advantage, but then some of Octavian's ships struck through the centre of Mark Antony's line. Fearful of capture, Cleopatra ordered her squadron to turn and row for safety, although she might have saved the day had she committed her reserve. Seeing the Queen in full retreat, Mark Antony turned and followed with a few of his galleys, leaving the rest of his fleet and his land army to surrender to Octavian.

Within fourteen months both Mark Antony and Cleopatra had committed suicide, while Octavian soon received the title Augustus and ruled the Roman Empire for another 45 years.

Nine days that never existed

1751 If you look for historic events in Great Britain between 3 and 13 September 1751, you won't find any – because those days never existed.

Until 1751, Britain had stuck to the Julian calendar, instituted by Julius Caesar in 46 BC. Caesar's calendar worked very well except that it reckoned the year to be eleven minutes, fourteen seconds longer than it actually is. Thus by 1751 Britain was eleven days behind, and on 2 September the Gregorian calendar was adopted. To catch up, the day following 2 September was declared to be 14 September, and the dates in between vanished from history.

Britain's adoption of the Gregorian calendar (instituted by Pope Gregory XIII) once more demonstrated the country's long-standing wariness of things from continental Europe. Most of the rest of Europe had started to use it 169 years earlier, in 1582.

Also on this day
1666: The Great Fire of London starts in a baker's shop in Pudding Lane * 1898: Lord

Kitchener leads British troops to defeat the Sudanese at the Battle of Omdurman, with the last cavalry charge in British history * 1910: French painter Henri Rousseau dies

3 September

Geronimo surrenders

1886 Today at Skeleton Canyon, cornered and outnumbered, the last great war chief of the Apaches agreed to surrender himself and his desperate band to the United States Army. Some 5,000 soldiers and 500 Indian auxiliaries and trackers had been pursuing Geronimo's tiny group of only 35 warriors for the past five months. Here, in this remote corner of the Arizona Territory near the Mexican border, the squat, broad-shouldered Geronimo conversed briefly with the tall soldierly figure of General Nelson A. Miles before returning to his encampment to collect his people for the march north to Fort Bowie and captivity.

For almost a century, Apache tribes had fiercely resisted the intrusion of European settlers into their territory. The chiefs who led them in this long guerrilla struggle of raids and retreats became legendary: Mangus Colorado, Cochise, Victorio, Nana – and finally Geronimo. But the cavalry, employing mobile columns, Indian trackers and the heliograph, proved relentless and ultimately successful. Over the years, band by band, the Apaches were hunted down, killed when they resisted, and sent away to reservations. Now it was the turn of Geronimo and his Chiricahua Apaches, whose elusiveness General Miles declared had 'never been matched since the days of Robin Hood'.

Arriving at Fort Bowie four days after their surrender in the canyon, the Apaches were herded into railroad cars for their journey to Florida and exile. They were never again to see their homeland. A thoughtful farewell touch was provided by the 4th Cavalry band, which played 'Auld Lang Syne' as the train pulled away. So at last the Apache war – the 'Geronimo war', the cavalry had begun to call it – was over; there was peace in the desert.

Still, a residual bit of resistance occurred many years later, as reported in this wire-service story filed from Tucson on 22 April 1930: 'Riding out of their wilderness hideout, high in the Sierra Madre Mountains, a band of wild Apache Indians scalped three persons, April 10, in a settlement near Nacori Chico, Sonora, Mexico, it was reported by V.M. White, a mining engineer. ... Armed parties immediately set out to trail the painted savages and attempt to engage them in battle before they reached their impregnable and historic cliffs. The Apaches are believed to have been led, White said, by Geronimo III, the grandson of the Geronimo who was chased by the U.S. Army for three years during the '80's in Arizona.'

The crowning of the Lion-Heart

1189 On this date, just five days short of his 32nd birthday, Richard I, the Lion-Heart, was crowned in Westminster Abbey. But the ceremony was ill-omened, marred by the presence of a black bat that swooped about the church. Indeed, although Richard was one of England's most storied kings, in truth he was a disaster for the country.

Richard's interests included war, glory, France and England, in that order. He considered his new kingdom as nothing more than a milch cow to finance his dreams of crusade, selling numerous titles and positions to raise money. He claimed, 'I would sell London if I could find a bidder', a sentiment uttered in French, as he never learned to speak English. In less than a year after his coronation he was off to the Holy Land.

En route to Palestine, Richard dropped by Cyprus to wed a princess from the Kingdom of Navarre named Berengaria, to whom he brought no more luck than he did to England. Once married, he left his wife to join the crusade, was captured in Austria returning home and didn't see Berengaria again for over four years. The couple had no children, and when Richard was killed in 1199, Berengaria retired to her own convent in Le Mans, where she lived for 30 more secluded years. She was the only English queen who never set foot in England.

While on crusade Richard failed to achieve his acclaimed objective, the liberation of Jerusalem from the Saracens. Worse, the ransom paid to free him from his Austrian captors virtually bankrupted England.

Richard spent the last few years of his life fighting in France, until his death from gangrene caused by a wound from a crossbow bolt during the siege of Châlus. Although his reign lasted for nine years and nine months, he spent only 179 days of it in England.

Also on this day

1650: Oliver Cromwell defeats the Scots at the second Battle of Dunbar * 1651: Oliver Cromwell defeats Royalist troops under Charles I at Worcester, ending the English Civil War * 1658: Oliver Cromwell dies * 1939: Britain declares war on Germany

4 September

The last Roman emperor

AD 476 History – or at least tradition – tells us that Romulus and Remus founded Rome on 21 April, 753 BC, from which small beginning it came to dominate the known world.

On this day, 1,229 years, four months and fourteen days later, the last Roman emperor, a sixteen-year-old also named Romulus – Romulus Augustulus – abdicated his imperial office, bringing to an end the Roman Empire (although its eastern half continued as the Byzantine Empire for another 977 years).

Romulus Augustulus was forced to resign by his own German mercenaries, who had revolted in August, killing his father. Eleven days later young Romulus Augustulus too was gone. He was replaced by Odoacer, the chief of the mercenaries and son of one of Attila the Hun's lieutenants, who took the title of King of Italy. In the words of Edward Gibbon: 'Odoacer was the first barbarian who reigned in Italy, over a people who had once asserted their just superiority above the rest of mankind.'

In the beginning Rome had been a kingdom, but in 509 BC the city's nobility revolted against the tyrannical Tarquinius Superbus and established the Roman Republic. Initially dominated by the Etruscans, Rome gradually grew in power and dominion with its conquests of neighbouring kingdoms in the early 5th century BC.

For the next four centuries Rome was an empire without an emperor, ruled by the Roman Senate, which annually elected two consuls to serve for a single year. In times of crisis the Senate appointed dictators to rule for six months, although later ones, notably Sulla and Julius Caesar, forced the Senate to accept them on a more or less permanent basis. The first leader of Rome to be called Emperor – *imperator* – was Augustus, who awarded himself the title in January of 42 BC.

In all there were 90 Roman emperors, most of whom came to unpleasant ends. Five committed suicide, six were killed in battle, three more were executed after having been captured in war, and 35 were murdered. One, Petronius Maximus, was lynched by a Roman mob, but perhaps the unluckiest was Carus, who was struck by lightning.

Queen Elizabeth's favourite dies

1588 At ten o'clock on this Wednesday morning Queen Elizabeth's favourite, Robert Dudley, Earl of Leicester, died peacefully near Oxford at the age of 55.

Although Leicester came from England's highest aristocracy, the fifth son of the Duke of Northumberland, he was thrown into the Tower of London at 22 when his father was executed for attempting to place his daughter-in-law Lady Jane Grey on the throne of England. Leicester's grandfather had also previously been beheaded for treason.

Leicester was twice lucky in his time in the Tower; first that he survived, second that a fellow prisoner at the time was the future Queen Elizabeth, who was just a few months younger than he.

Leicester was a bold and handsome man, an exceptional horseman and so dark that he was mockingly referred to as 'the gypsy'. After Elizabeth's ascension in 1558, he soon became a court favourite. She affectionately called him Robin, and if she was not the Virgin Queen of common legend, he would certainly have been the reason why. She made him Master of the Horse, and later a Privy Councillor, Knight of the Garter and Constable of Windsor Castle.

When he was 27, Leicester's wife Amy died falling down some stairs, and the Earl was widely rumoured to have given her a push to clear the way for marriage to the Queen. Despite Leicester's entreaties, however, Elizabeth refused to marry him, although they remained close friends until the end of his life.

Even after Leicester's death two family traditions were maintained. His stepson Robert Devereaux, Earl of Essex, replaced him as Queen Elizabeth's favourite – and was executed for treason in his turn, just as Leicester's father and grandfather had been.

Also on this day

1260: Tuscan Ghibellines supporting Holy Roman Emperor Rudolf I defeat the Florentine Guelphs, who support Pope Alexander IV, at the Battle of Montaperto * 1870: Léon Gambetta, Jules Favre and Jules Ferry proclaim the Third Republic from the Hôtel de Ville in Paris * 1907: Norwegian composer Edvard Grieg dies

5 September

The lucky conception of Louis XIV

1638 This story really starts nine months earlier, in December 1637, when King Louis XIII of France was caught in a driving thunderstorm after visiting a convent near Paris. Louis had already ordered his household to a château some distance away, but the cold, wet weather made it impossible for him to reach it that night. Where then to sleep?

Louis's quick-thinking captain of the guard urged him to go to the nearby Louvre, where his wife Anne of Austria lived. They had been married for 23 years but estranged for fifteen.

Louis hesitated. No doubt he remembered his wife's affair with the Duke of Buckingham and the famous diamonds (on which Dumas later built his tale of musketeers). But at last he grudgingly agreed. Even his wife's hospitality would be better than camping out in the storm.

It seems his wife's hospitality proved exemplary, as on 5 September 1638, exactly nine months later to the day, she gave birth to a son at the royal château at Germain-en-Laye. Like his father, the son would be called Louis, the fourteenth of that name, and he would reign for 72 years, longer than any other monarch in European history.

Suleiman the Magnificent dies in the field

1566 Suleiman the Magnificent, greatest of all Turkish sultans, died today while attempting to put down a revolt in one of his many conquered territories.

Suleiman ruled Turkey and its empire with an iron hand for 46 years. He added Hungary to his domains and twice nearly conquered Austria. Domestically he was known as a great law-giver, and he ordered built many of the finest buildings in Constantinople, Baghdad and Damascus. But as he grew older he became increasingly megalomaniac, perhaps even paranoid, to the point that (on separate occasions) he ordered two of his three sons strangled for imagined treason, as well as a number of their children.

Even at 71, sick and ageing, Suleiman thought primarily of consolidating his power. When revolt broke out in Hungary he personally led the avenging army.

By mid-summer of 1566 Suleiman was camped outside the Hungarian castle of Sziget, his enemies under siege within. Eventually Turkish sappers would blow a fatal gap in the castle's walls, but the great Sultan was not there to see his final triumph. On the night of 5 September he was stricken by either a heart attack or a stroke, dying in his tent.

Suleiman's body was brought back to Constantinople where he was buried outside the great mosque he had built, known as the Suleiman mosque, one of the largest and most beautiful in the world.

Also on this day

1569: Flemish painter Pieter Bruegel the Elder dies * 1857: French philosopher and founder of sociology Auguste Comte dies in Paris * 1877: American Indian chief Crazy Horse is killed in a scuffle with his prison guards

6 September

François I orders the building of the Château de Chambord

1519 On this day 25-year-old King François I gave orders for work to begin on 'a beautiful and sumptuous edifice' in the valley of the Loire. The result was France's most grandiose Renaissance building, the Château de Chambord, a grand palace 170 yards long with 440 rooms and 356 sculpted chimneys. This breathtakingly beautiful building also contains a magnificent double staircase built of two superimposed spirals, so constructed that people ascending one spiral can see the people descending the other but never meet them. Such playful architecture perfectly suited this rakish king who kept a number of mistresses and welcomed high-class prostitutes at his dissolute court.

François was as passionate about Chambord as he was about women, committing funds for its construction even when he himself was a prisoner, captured at the Battle of Pavia by Holy Roman Emperor Charles V. Later, however, François invited Charles to Chambord as his guest, suitably impressing the Emperor with the château's lavishness and taste.

On François's death the château was passed on to his son Henri II and subsequently down the line of French kings. But no other owner quite shared François's enthusiasm for Chambord. Louis XIV visited it only nine times during his reign of 72 years (although during one visit Molière staged the first performance of *Le Bourgeois Gentilhomme*). Eventually it was plundered during the Revolution and finally bought by the state.

Chambord today stands virtually empty, a colossal and beautiful monument for wide-eyed tourists, brought to wonderful false life only by the *son et lumière* on summer evenings. Inside is François's study, where a brief verse is engraved on a window, purportedly cut by the King himself with his diamond ring:

Souvent femme varie,
Bien fol qui s'y fie.
(A woman is very fickle; he who trusts her is a fool.)

Barbara Frietchie defies General Robert E. Lee

1862 Today we remember the importance of winning hearts and minds.

When, on the heels of the great Confederate victory at the second battle of Bull Run, Robert E. Lee brought his Army of Northern Virginia splashing across the Potomac fords into Maryland – Union territory – he had a strategy in mind. First, he expected his forces to be greeted as liberators by a Southern-sympathising population that would eagerly rebel against the Union and join the Confederate cause. He also counted on resupplying his forces from the rich harvest of a grateful countryside. Then the army would proceed into Pennsylvania, well ahead of any pursuit, and for the first time bring the experience of war to Northern states. Finally, in Lee's grand strategic vision, these moves might offer the opportunity for some dazzling military triumph – before Philadelphia, perhaps, or near New York City – which would induce a demoralised Federal government to sue for peace.

The first sign that things might go wrong occurred today as the Confederate army wound its way through the streets of Frederick. There, in a very public act of defiance, a woman displayed a United States flag from the attic window of her house and then loudly disputed the right of the Confederate troops to shoot it down. According to John Greenleaf Whittier's war ballad, it was 95-year-old Barbara Frietchie who showed the Stars and Stripes that day and uttered the words: 'Shoot if you must this old grey head, but spare your country's flag.' Whittier's famous account is, however, poetic licence based on a real incident: a Mrs Quantrill, another resident of Frederick, did stand with her daughter before their gate that day and insultingly wave a Union flag at the Southern soldiers in the street.

At this time, the Army of Northern Virginia, 55,000 strong, was starving, exhausted, shoeless, and inclined towards pillage – 'a most ragged, lean, and hungry set of wolves', one observer called them. Despite the heavy posting of provost guards along the route of march, a third of the troops would disappear over the next few days. Nor were the army's invading presence and the prospect of its resupply welcomed by the citizens of Maryland. Farmers left their crops unharvested in the fields and drove their cattle to safety in the mountains; merchants and tavern keepers locked their doors. The army remained famished; Maryland stayed in the Union.

None of the other goals of Lee's invasion was realised. Surprised by the alacrity of the Union pursuit, the Army of Northern Virginia never got as far as Pennsylvania, never found its dazzling war-ending victory. Instead, reduced to fewer than 40,000 through straggling and desertion, it went to ground at Sharpsburg, Maryland, fought a sanguinary draw with 75,000 Federals, and retired to war-ravaged Virginia and another two and a half years of conflict.

Given the way the Civil War divided families, it is not perhaps so surprising that Mrs Quantrill, the staunch Union patriot who became Whittier's 'Barbara Frietchie', turns out to have been a relative of William Quantrill, the bloodiest of the Confederate guerrillas.

Also on this day

1522: Ferdinand Magellan's seventeen surviving crew members reach Spain for completion of the first round-the-world voyage * 1620: The British ship *Mayflower* sails from Plymouth to North America * 1901: Leon Czolgosz shoots and fatally wounds American President William McKinley * 1944: The Germans fire the first V-2 missile at Paris

7 September

'Voilà le soleil d'Austerlitz!' 'Voilà le commencement de la fin'

1812 Today the meteoric career of Napoleon Bonaparte reached its apogee and started its precipitous descent towards catastrophe as the Emperor fought the Russians in one of the bloodiest battles of the 19th century.

At the end of June Napoleon had marched into Russia with an army of 530,000, the greatest concentration of troops in Europe since the Persian king Xerxes had invaded Greece in 480 BC. With this vast array came over 1,000 guns, 30,000 supply wagons and 28 million bottles of wine.

For weeks the army marched through the vast emptiness that was Russia, as the Tsar's army refused to be drawn into a major battle. Slowly Napoleon's front-line force was reduced, mostly to guard his ever-lengthening lines of communications but also owing to sickness, accident and the occasional guerrilla ambush. By early September the Emperor's forces ready for battle were only about 130,000.

On 6 September the French army (which in fact was only one-third French, the rest being conscripts from Napoleon's empire) arrived at the town of Borodino, a little over 60 miles west of Moscow. There at last the Russians turned to fight, 120,000 strong under the command of 67-year-old General Prince Mikhail Kutuzov, a fat and heavy-drinking noble who had lost an eye fighting the Turks but who possessed the cunning, determination and ruthlessness to match his adversary.

On the morning of 7 September Napoleon rose early and, remembering the brilliant weather at his most famous victory seven years before, he welcomed a glorious sunrise with the optimistic exclamation: 'Voilà le soleil d'Austerlitz!' (Look, the sun of Austerlitz!) At six he ordered his cannon to open fire to start a day of frightful carnage.

By nightfall the stubborn Russians had lost some 45,000 men killed or wounded, but these could be replaced. Napoleon had suffered 30,000 casualties of irreplaceable troops 1,500 miles from home. (For a compelling if slightly fictionalised narrative of the battle, try Tolstoy's *War and Peace*.)

The following morning Kutuzov ordered a retreat, enabling the French to claim a victory and to begin the march on Moscow. But the Battle of Borodino was in fact Napoleon's greatest defeat. During the next three months his soldiers occupied a deserted Moscow which burnt to the ground around them, and then struggled back to the Polish border in the dead of Russian winter, attacked by Cossacks, guerrillas, the bitter cold and starvation. Only about 10,000 of the original force of over half a million survived the campaign. As Tsar Nicholas I later remarked: 'God punished the foolish; the bones of the audacious foreigners were scattered from Moscow to the Nieman.'

After the Battle of Borodino Napoleon's sun had passed its zenith and the Emperor's days in power were numbered. As the crafty old Talleyrand said on hearing of the battle: 'Voilà le commencement de la fin.' (There is the beginning of the end.)

Queen Elizabeth is born

1533 She said of herself: 'I am more afraid of making a fault in my Latin than of the kings of Spain, France, Scotland and the House of Guise and all their confederates.' Her chief minister Robert Cecil said of her: 'More than a man but sometimes (by troth) less than a woman.'

She was of course Queen Elizabeth I, born this Sunday morning at Greenwich Palace just outside London exactly seven months and thirteen days after the hasty and secret marriage of her parents, Henry VIII and Anne Boleyn.

Elizabeth's reign was to be one of the greatest in British history, and one of the longest – 44 years, four months and eleven days. Of Britain's 41 monarchs since the Norman Conquest of England, only three kings and one queen reigned longer, and many believe that none ruled better.

Also on this day
1901: The Boxer Rebellion in China ends with the signing of the Peace of Peking

8 September

The slap at Anagni

1303 King Philip the Fair of France was young, blond and handsome, while Pope Boniface VIII was over 60, with a pinched, suffering face that reflected both his character and the torments of gallstones. Like Philip, he was cunning, ruthless and arrogant, with a strong will to power. 'It is necessary to salvation', he said, 'that every human creature be subject to the Roman pontiff'. Boniface's ambitions had been clearly revealed when still a cardinal. Then he had manoeuvred Pope Celestine V into an unprecedented resignation that allowed for his own elevation to the papacy, and he then imprisoned his predecessor until he died.

Conflict between King and Pope was inevitable, especially since Philip greedily eyed the riches of the Church in France and decided to tax the clergy. Later he even imprisoned a French bishop on patently trumped-up charges in an attempt to gain secular control of the clergy. Boniface's response was to draw up a bull excommunicating the French king.

Reacting with cold fury, Philip dispatched his Keeper of Seals, Guillaume de Nogaret, with a small army to seek out the Pope and formally charge him with papal misconduct. Nogaret headed for the Pope's summer residence in Anagni, 45 miles south-east of Rome. Along the way he picked up an ally in Sciarra Colonna, leader of the pope-producing family that had largely been disenfranchised by Boniface.

On the night of 7 September Nogaret and Colonna attacked Anagni and quickly overcame all resistance. Boniface had barricaded himself in his palace, but Colonna smashed down the doors the following morning. The Pope was now the prisoner of the King. Fearing assassination, he boldly if somewhat melodramatically declared: 'Here is my neck, and here is my head. Betrayed like Jesus Christ, if I must die like him, at least I will die a pope.'

But Nogaret was intent on inflicting humiliation rather than death. First he and his lieutenants openly discussed in front of Boniface whether or not to execute him on the spot, without trial. Then he presented the frail old man with a list of charges: heresy, idolatry, nepotism, simony, sorcery and sodomy. The recitation of accusations was accompanied by a ringing slap across the face.

It mattered little that the next day the loyal citizens of Anagni finally rescued their pontiff. Boniface was a broken man, mortified and treated with contempt by his enemies. A few days after his humiliation he seemed to forget the excommunication of Philip and returned to Rome in a daze. Only a month later, on 11 October, Boniface expired in the Vatican. Tradition says he died of shame and rage.

Huey Long is assassinated

1935 On this warm Sunday evening in Baton Rouge, a man stepped out from behind a pillar in the state capitol building and fired a revolver. What he hit – and destroyed – was a true force of nature on the American political scene: Huey Pierce Long, Jr, United States Senator from the state of Louisiana, the great Kingfish himself.

Flamboyant in dress and personality, with a face ready-made for cartoonists – and dubbed 'Kingfish' by his cronies after a character in a popular radio show of the era – Long was often called a demagogue, a breed he resembled in his campaign oratory but departed from by actually keeping the promises he made to get elected. In 1927, at the age of 34, he won the governorship of Louisiana and proceeded to finance his extensive public works programme – free schoolbooks, bridge and road construction, and a state hospital offering free medical care to all – by raising taxes on the wealthy and on the corporations doing business in the state. In so doing, he won the support of the state's rural population but the undying enmity of Standard Oil and the planter class.

Long had an intuitive genius for political leadership. For all his country-bumpkin manner, he was shrewder and tougher than any of his rivals. On his way to unsurpassed power in the state, he smashed all opposition.

With his Louisiana base secure, Long charged onto the national scene, taking up a seat in the US Senate in 1932. Now he encountered a rival of a very different sort: President Franklin Delano Roosevelt, whom he initially supported, then hoped to dominate, and finally came to distrust. In a nation gripped by economic depression, Long's 1934 Share Our Wealth programme – his Louisiana programme writ large, with its captivating slogan 'Every Man a King' – proved so attractive to voters around the country that it appeared Long might hold the balance of political power in the 1936 presidential election. He determined to run for President as a third-party candidate and deny Roosevelt a second term.

Long was now at the top of his form. He even wrote a book, published in 1935, called *My First Days in the White House* – 'a mixture of nonsense and wisdom, frivolity and gravity', one historian called it – recounting the early actions of 'President Long', including his Cabinet selections, among which was FDR as Secretary of the Navy.

But if Long's supporters around the nation were numerous, his enemies – 'polecats', he called them – were legion. For those on the right he was a radical socialist; for those on the left an American Hitler or Mussolini; and for many in between an unclassifiable but diverting political phenomenon. Visiting America, H.G. Wells admired Long as a 'Winston Churchill who had never been at Harrow'. Rebecca West took a dimmer view and found him 'the most formidable kind of brer fox'.

If others were puzzled by Huey Long, one man in Baton Rouge, Dr Carl Austin Weiss, a respected ear–nose–throat specialist and son-in-law of one of Long's Louisiana adversaries, seemed to have made up his mind. For motives that are still unclear, Dr Weiss took matters into his own hands and fired the shot from which Long died two days later. The Kingfish's last words were: 'God, don't let me die. I have so much to do.'

Also on this day

1157: Richard the Lion-Heart is born * 1886: After gold is discovered nearby, the city of Johannesburg is founded

9 September

William the Conqueror dies in France

1087 Today died the last man successfully to invade England, William the Conqueror, at the age of 59.

For the past twenty years William's main concern had been his subjugated kingdom in England, but he had in no way forgotten his original patrimony, the Duchy of Normandy. Thus when a French army started to pillage his duchy in the summer of 1087 he quickly crossed the English Channel with his own troops.

William soon routed the enemy near the town of Mantes, but during the fight his horse stumbled and he fell forward onto the hard iron pommel of his saddle, receiving severe internal injuries.

Five weeks later the injured king was moved by litter to the outskirts of his Norman capital of Rouen. On Thursday morning, 9 September, the tolling of the bells of Rouen Cathedral awakened him. Construing this as a divine signal, he commended himself to God and died instantly.

During his 21 years as King of England this illegitimate issue of a Norman duke and a tanner's daughter had ruled his conquest with a hand of steel. Indeed, one Norman monk's account says that on his deathbed he bitterly repented the brutal repression he had visited upon the conquered land.

William left much that is still with us today. He built the White Tower in the Tower of London and he created a vast deer preserve in what is still called the New Forest in Hampshire. But most of all he introduced into Saxon England the values of Norman France, along with its triumphalist Gothic cathedral architecture.

William is buried at the monastery he founded of St Stephen at Caen.

Captain Bligh and the other mutinies

1754 In 1932 Charles Nordhoff and James Norman Hall published a spectacularly successful novel entitled *Mutiny on the Bounty* that was shortly followed by an Academy Award-winning film starring Clark Gable. Between them, the book and the movie created the image we have today of British

Captain William Bligh as the cruel and tyrannical bully who drove his men to history's most famous mutiny on HMS *Bounty*.

Bligh, who was born today, was a disciplined master who had gone to sea at the age of seven and who had later sailed with Captain Cook. Cook had been so impressed by Bligh's seamanship that he named an island after him. Although not the tyrant of legend, Bligh undeniably was intolerant of error and gave vent to his anger in abusive terms. In his career he managed to play a role in no fewer than three mutinies.

The first and best known was in 1789 aboard the *Bounty*, when he was 35 years old, having already been a ship's officer for thirteen years. His magnificent seamanship was put to the test when he and eighteen others were cast adrift in an open longboat. Some 41 days later Bligh brought them to a safe landing near Java.

When Bligh returned to England the Admiralty treated him as hero and victim rather than villain, and soon gave him a new command. But in 1797 once again he was involved in a mutiny. The ship he commanded was anchored with the rest of the British fleet at the Nore, off the coast of Kent. His crew joined a fleet-wide mutiny of sailors, and Bligh was put ashore.

Once more the Admiralty found no fault with the captain and in 1805 sent him to New South Wales as Governor. Three years later came the third mutiny, this time led by an English major who put Bligh under arrest, but again the captain escaped with honour when a court found the mutineers guilty of conspiracy.

In Great Britain's long naval war with Napoleonic France, Bligh distinguished himself at the battles of Camperdown and Copenhagen. The Admiralty clearly considered his fighting record more important than his involvement in three mutinies, for it promoted him to Rear Admiral in 1811 and to Vice Admiral in 1814. Bligh died in London in 1817 at the age of 63.

Also on this day

1585: French 'Eminence Rouge' Cardinal Richelieu is born * 1828: Russian novelist Leo Tolstoy is born * 1901: French painter Henri de Toulouse-Lautrec dies

10 September

The English enter France through the hole in the Duke of Burgundy's head

1419 Today the treacherous murder of the Duke of Burgundy plunged France into chaos, leaving the country defenceless against the invading forces of Henry V of England.

France was being torn apart by the bitter rivalry between Burgundians and Armagnacs, two great feudal houses each struggling to grasp power from the mad French king, Charles VI. The Burgundians were led by their formidable duke, known as Jean Sans Peur for his valour. Their trump was insane King Charles whom they virtually held captive.

But the Armagnacs held the King's sixteen-year-old son, Dauphin Charles. And already leading a marauding army across northern France was England's Henry V, who claimed the French throne as part of his inheritance.

Recognising the danger from the English, the Burgundians and Armagnacs finally agreed to meet in the hope of reaching some sort of power-sharing agreement. On 10 September Jean Sans Peur and the young Dauphin met at Montereau, where a bridge spans the Seine about 40 miles from Paris.

Dauphin Charles, surrounded by his bodyguards, was already at the bridge when Duke Jean arrived. The Duke knelt to show his obeisance, but as he rose his hand accidentally brushed his sword handle in a movement that one of the guards found threatening. 'Would you put your hand on your sword in the presence of My Lord the Dauphin?' he cried. Instantly another Armagnac noble, Tanneguy du Châtel, struck Jean full in the face with a small axe, and the Duke fell dead on the bridge.

His Armagnac bodyguards quickly led the frightened Dauphin away, paralysed with shock. The most powerful man in France had been murdered, and chaos was certain. Fearful for their lives and hungry for revenge, the Burgundians quickly signed an alliance with the English king, and eight months later the French were forced to sign the Treaty of Troyes by which Henry would marry mad King Charles's daughter and become heir to the French throne. As a French prior from Dijon later famously said: 'The English entered France through the hole in the Duke of Burgundy's head.'

Commandant Perry defeats the British on Lake Erie

1813 The British had burned Washington and the governor of Detroit had surrendered the town during the War of 1812 when the American naval officer Master Commandant Oliver Hazard Perry attacked the enemy fleet on Lake Erie on this day.

Perry was a young (28) and courageous officer who was determined to regain not only the lake but Detroit as well from the conquering British. His fleet of ten vessels outnumbered the enemy almost two to one, and his firepower was greater. Hostilities began at noon. At first the battle went badly, as the American flagship, the brig *Lawrence*, was severely hit, but Perry quickly transferred to the *Niagara* and led his fleet directly into the British line so that his short-range firepower could take full effect.

By three o'clock the British had surrendered, and Perry was able to earn his place in the American book of famous quotations by sending a message to General William Henry Harrison that 'We have met the enemy and they are ours'. The British suffered 40 dead with another 94 wounded, while of Perry's force 27 were killed and 96 wounded.

With the British fleet out of the way, American ships controlled Lake Erie and Harrison was able to take the offensive, soon retaking Detroit. Perry became something of a national hero in America for his exploits and was soon promoted to captain. Sadly, only five years later he died from yellow fever contracted on a voyage to South America.

Also on this day

1823: South American revolutionary Simón Bolívar is named President of Peru * 1898: On a quay in Geneva an Italian anarchist stabs to death Elisabeth of Bavaria (Sisi), the estranged wife of Austrian Emperor Franz Joseph

11 September

Eugene of Savoy's greatest victories

1697, 1709 On this date twelve years apart Prince Eugene of Savoy, one of Europe's greatest generals, gained two of his most momentous victories. By far the more important was the first one at Zenta, when Eugene was 34 and had only recently received his command in the Imperial (Austrian) army.

Ever since the mid-16th century the Turks had been threatening Austria, and more than once had come to the very walls of Vienna. Thanks to a great Austrian victory there in 1683 the Turks had retreated into the Balkans, but the threat of their return was always there.

In 1697 the Austrian Emperor Leopold I ordered Eugene vigorously to attack the Turks in an attempt to end the constant menace. On this day Eugene caught up with the army of Sultan Mustafa II near Zenta (in present-day Yugoslavia) where the Danube meets the Tisza. Discovering that Mustafa had already crossed the smaller river with his artillery – but had left his infantry for the moment on the other side – Eugene ordered an immediate attack, even though his force was far smaller than the Turk's.

Without cannon the Turkish soldiers were helpless. Many ran in panic, and mutinous Janissaries (élite soldiers who were kidnapped as boys from Christian families and converted to Islam) murdered the Turkish general on the field of battle. When the rout finally ended at ten o'clock that night, 20,000 Turks lay dead with 10,000 more drowned in the river trying to escape. Austrian losses amounted to only 300 killed.

The victory was enormous, and the resulting peace treaty ceded all of Hungary and Transylvania to the Austrian Emperor. Zenta was Eugene's first major victory.

Twelve years later to the day Eugene and the Duke of Marlborough cele-brated another major triumph, this against the French at Malplaquet. Although undoubtedly a victory for the Austrians and English (in the end the French retreated), it was hardly as glorious, as the allies suffered 22,000 casualties against only 12,000 for the French. After the battle the beaten French commander, the duc de Villars, wrote to his king, Louis XIV: 'If God should grant us another such defeat, our enemies would be destroyed.' And the War of the Spanish Succession in which the battle was fought continued for another five years.

Also on this day

1297: Scottish rebel William Wallace defeats the English at the Battle of Stirling Bridge * 1855: During the Crimean War the Russian city of Sevastopol falls to British, · French and Piedmontese forces after a siege of almost a year * 1885: English writer D.H. Lawrence is born

12 September

Vienna is saved from the Turk as croissants and cappuccino are invented

1683 Today we celebrate a famous victory that saved Vienna for ever from the threat of Turkish conquest and gave the rest of the world two recipes for the perfect Continental breakfast.

Ever since the reign of Suleiman the Magnificent a century before, the Turks had lusted for the great capital of Vienna, and now a vast Ottoman army a quarter of a million strong was camped around the city. Every day for two long months the guns of Grand Vizier Kara Mustafa crashed against the walls; the outer fortifications had been captured and the Turks were tunnelling through to the inner walls. It was only a matter of time before the Austrian defences would collapse, the barbarously cruel Turkish brand of murder and rapine would begin and the nation's Christianity would be extirpated for the glory of Islam.

So confident was the Grand Vizier that he complacently ignored the camp fires twinkling down from the Kahlenburg Heights only a few miles north of the city. But there the Polish King John Sobieski, who had come to Vienna's rescue in return for a huge subsidy from Pope Alexander VIII, joined the Austrian army under the command of Charles of Lorraine. Acting as the Pope's emissary was the Capuchin monk Marco d'Aviano, whose job it was to ensure co-operation among the various Christian commanders.

At first light on 12 September some 80,000 Christian soldiers thundered down into the mass of Turks. The battle lasted for fifteen hours, but in the evening a devastating charge by the Polish horse completely routed the invaders, who left their guns, vast stores of food, Kara Mustafa's fabulous jewels and tens of thousands of corpses on the field. In his dispatch to the Pope, the Polish king modestly paraphrased Caesar, reporting: 'I came, I saw, God conquered.'

What remained of the Vizier's army fled through Hungary towards Turkey, but Kara Mustafa reached only as far as Belgrade, where he was ceremoniously strangled with a silken cord, sent on orders from the Sultan at first news of the defeat.

Vienna was saved, Christianity remained triumphant and Ottoman rule in the Balkans was badly shaken. Among the victorious troops who celebrated that evening was a nineteen-year-old prince named Eugene of Savoy who would utterly crush the Turk fourteen years later at Zenta and who would become the greatest general ever to serve the Holy Roman Empire.

This tale of Vienna's salvation also has two remarkable culinary addenda. The first comes from Vienna's bakers, who commemorated the Austrian victory by creating a new roll in the shape of the crescent moon from the Turkish flag and christened it a *Kipfel*, German for crescent. The Kipfel gained immediate popularity in Vienna, and in 1770 Marie Antoinette (daughter of Empress Maria Theresa of Austria) introduced it to France when she married the future Louis XVI. Today we usually call it by the French word for crescent, *croissant*.

The second gastronomic creation of the battle perfectly complements the first. Among the supplies abandoned by the Turks as they fled the field was a vast store of coffee. Finding it too bitter for their tastes, the Christian soldiers sweetened it with milk and honey, some say at the suggestion of the friar Marco d'Aviano. In any case, the tasty drink, whose colour resembled the friar's habit, was named Cappuccino in honour of the Capuchin order to which he belonged. For this, and other holy deeds, Marco was beatified in 2003.

France's great Renaissance king, François I

1494 In the west of France, north of Bordeaux and the Dordogne River, is the town of Cognac, famed for its exquisite brandy and as the place where on this day France's great Renaissance king, François I, was born.

Although François was the great-great-grandson of King Charles V of France, at his birth there was no reason to suspect that he would one day be King. On the throne sat a distant uncle, Charles VIII, then only 24 with two infant sons and ample time to produce more. In the improbable event that something should happen to Charles and his family, another of François's uncles, Louis, duc d'Orléans, then only 32, was next in line.

But both of Charles's sons died within two years of François's birth and, although he became King on Charles VIII's death in 1498, uncle Louis never produced an heir in spite of three marriages, so the unlikely François inherited the throne of France at the age of twenty.

Ambitious, generous and dissolute, François was the French Renaissance Man embodied. His first love was women. 'A court without women is a year without spring and a spring without roses', he said, and he became famous for his gallant escapades. He also was a patriot, and fought for years without success against Holy Roman Emperor Charles V's attempts to dominate Europe, once being captured and imprisoned by Charles after he personally led a cavalry charge at the Battle of Pavia.

But François was also a man of enormous culture, and his impact on France was huge. Andrea del Sarto was his court painter, as was, for a time, Leonardo da Vinci, who died with François at his bedside. Raphael and Titian both portrayed him, Benvenuto Cellini was his jeweller, and he was a patron to Rabelais. The library he collected would one day form an important part of the Bibliothèque Nationale.

But when we think of François I, most of all we think of his glorious châteaux, especially Fontainebleau, which he transformed from a luxurious royal hunting lodge into a magnificent palace. But at the same time François owned Amboise, Plessis-les-Tours, Vincennes, Coucy, Chenonceau, Azay-le-Rideau, the magnificent Chambord, which he built, and Rambouillet, where he died after a reign of 32 years.

Peter the Great starts to transform Russia

1689 Today seventeen-year-old Peter the Great took personal control of his country to start Russia's momentous transformation from a priest-ridden Byzantine backwater to a formidable European power.

Peter had been Russia's anointed co-Tsar in 1682 along with his weak-minded brother Ivan, but the country had in fact been ruled by his older half-sister Sophia, who was technically regent but who was determined never to relinquish her power. By the time he reached seventeen, Peter felt himself ready to supplant Sophia but feared that if he failed, she and her lover Fedor Shaklovity would put him to death.

When Sophia tried to take advantage of a revolt by the palace guard to consolidate her position, Peter fled the Kremlin to hole up in a monastery outside Moscow and commanded his army generals to come to him, the legal ruler of the country. The generals vacillated between brother and sister. Sophia tried everything from bribes to threats to keep them on her side, while Peter attempted to persuade them to support their Tsar. When he succeeded, Sophia was instantly entombed in a local nunnery, but she fared far better than her lover, who received sixteen lashes of the knout and was subjected to the strappado before being decapitated.

Peter allowed his half-brother to remain as nominal co-Tsar, but Ivan's health, never strong, deteriorated further until he became partially paralysed and died. Peter continued to rule for 35 dictatorial years until his death in 1725.

Peter was a man of immense contradictions. In turning his country westward he established it as a military power and largely broke the traditionalist stranglehold of the Orthodox Church. He forced his nobles and churchmen to adopt the European custom of shaving (which many considered a mortal sin), and founded the first hospital in all of Russia, as well as the Russian navy. But his rule was both despotic and capricious, and Peter himself was one of history's most cruel and violent monarchs. He often executed his enemies personally, and not only approved of judicial torture but supervised it in person.

Yet this same man created a European Russia. He fought Turkey to gain access to the Baltic and Black Seas, defeated Persia to secure the southern and western shores of the Caspian Sea, and moved the capital to St Petersburg.

Also on this day

1852: British Prime Minister Henry Herbert Asquith is born * 1943: Italian dictator Benito Mussolini is rescued by German troops

13 September

General James Wolfe dies while winning Quebec

1759 Early this morning, after nearly three months of frustration, British Major General James Wolfe finally outwitted the French defenders of Quebec and under cover of darkness snuck an advance party up the steep heights above the St Lawrence River and onto the Plains of Abraham. He had finally discovered the unlocked back door to the great bastion. By first light his seven battalions – 4,800 men – were deployed in a battle line stretching across the mile-wide tract of open land. Now he awaited the French response.

Since his expedition had arrived by ship in front of Quebec in late June, Wolfe had probed up river and down but found no way to crack the stout defences behind which lay the marquis de Montcalm and a force of 12,000. Now time was running out: with winter in the offing, the British fleet would soon retire down river, and with it all chance of taking the city this year. But at last he spotted a route up the cliffs.

When the French emerged onto the Plains at 9.00 a.m., the British held their fire until the enemy was within 60 yards, then unloosed volley after volley, halting the attackers and routing them back inside their fortifications. That evening the French regulars left Quebec and retreated up river. The fortress surrendered on the 18th. Thus, the glorious deed was done. But in the doing, Wolfe was shot three times and bled to death. His adversary, Montcalm, also severely wounded, died the next day.

The battle of Quebec was decisive. The French retreated to Montreal, which fell the next year. Canada was now British.

The battle on the Plains of Abraham became a celebrated event for many in that and later times. It inspired Benjamin West's 1776 painting, *The Death of Wolfe*. It may have added to the popularity of Thomas Gray's 'Elegy in a Country Churchyard', known to be Wolfe's favourite poem, whose famous line seemed to capture both his exploit and his fate: 'The paths of glory lead but to the grave.'

Finally, we know that in the dire military situation of Korea in the summer of 1950, General Douglas MacArthur drew inspiration from Wolfe's surprise manoeuvre at Quebec to plan his brilliantly successful backdoor landings at Inchon.

Philip II dies at El Escorial

1598 Today died one of history's most sombre monarchs, Philip II of Spain. Heir to half of Europe and much of South America, he had seen his father, Holy Roman Emperor Charles V, abdicate his throne and retire to a monastery in an age when kings abdicated only with death. Philip's deep-seated sense of duty ruled out any early retirement on his part, and he ruled Spain and its enormous territories for 42 years before his demise.

Philip fought doggedly and tirelessly to maintain his heritage and his empire's Catholic faith, once writing: 'Rather than permitting any harm to come to religion and the service of God, I would relinquish all my territories and a hundred lives, if I had them, for I could never accept or wish to be the ruler of heretics.' But throughout his reign he saw the inroads of Protestantism grow ever greater and his Dutch/Belgian subjects rise in open revolt.

In his battle against 'heretics', Philip made full use of the Inquisition and his own armed forces. Once, when attending an *auto da fé* ('act of faith', the euphemism for burning at the stake carried out by the Inquisition) in Valladolid, he told a condemned prisoner about to be chained to the stake: 'If my own son were such a wretch as you, he should suffer the same fate.'

Philip married four times, once to the fanatical Mary Tudor, and was four times widowed, living the last eighteen years of his life with neither wife nor mistress. His first-born son, Don Carlos, revolted against him, certainly was a sadist and was probably insane. It seems likely that Philip condoned his murder to prevent his inheriting the empire.

As he grew older Philip retreated ever more into solitude, distrustful of all his advisors, with work and prayer as his sole occupations. From the age of 32 he never left the Iberian Peninsula, ruling his empire from his palace in Madrid or from the Escorial, that cheerless monastery-cum-palace outside the city that he had built.

In some ways Philip was a great king – fair and just, with great concern for what he deemed to be the interests of his subjects. He gave his life to them, and worked right up to the end, despite great pain from gout and an ulcerated skin. He died in his austere bedroom in the Escorial at the age of 71, stricken by cancer and gangrene of the leg caused by his gout. His final words were appropriately sombre: 'I die like a good Catholic, in faith and obedience to the Holy Roman Church.'

A brave defence against a British attack inspires 'The Star-Spangled Banner'

1814 Today an unsuccessful British attack on an American fort gave birth to the country's national anthem, 'The Star-Spangled Banner'.

In 1814 Baltimore was America's third largest city, with a population of some 45,000. It had been a particular thorn in the side of the British, as privateers based there had seized or sunk over 500 British ships. Now at war with the United States, the British fleet was determined to pound it into submission.

The plan was to sail into Baltimore harbour and attack the city with cannon fire, but the entrance to the harbour was protected by a star-shaped fortress named Fort McHenry, so the first assault came against the fort.

At 6.30 in the morning the schooner *Cockchafer* opened fire, and during the next 24 hours British warships and bomb vessels fired about 2,000 shells and 800 rockets at Fort McHenry, which was defended by only 1,000 men and 57 guns, commanded by Major George Armistead. Over the fort flew an enormous American flag measuring 42 feet by 30 feet, hand made by Mary Pickersgill, whose mother had made flags for George Washington.

From eight miles away an American lawyer named Francis Scott Key observed the firing from the deck of a British flag-of-truce ship, where he was negotiating the exchange of an American prisoner. As he watched the battle and the flag, Key rejoiced when the British finally pulled back at dawn the next day, the Americans undefeated. Based on what he saw he wrote the words to 'The Star-Spangled Banner', scanned to go to an old English drinking song called 'To Anacreon in Heaven'.

'The Star-Spangled Banner' was immediately published in newspapers around the United States, an instant success. But even its popularity couldn't rush the American Congress, which waited until 1931 before declaring it the American national anthem.

Uncle Sam is born

1767 Today, in the small city of Troy in northern New York state, Uncle Sam was born in the person of Sam Wilson, who grew up to become a prosperous meat-packer.

During the War of 1812 Wilson was appointed inspector of provisions for the American Army. His assignment was to check the meat furnished by Elbert Anderson, and he stamped each barrel that passed muster 'EA-US', the EA representing the supplier Elbert Anderson and the US for the buyer, the United States.

Many of the soldiers had been recruited in Troy, and they had known Sam Wilson for years. When asked the meaning of the 'US' stamped on the barrels, they claimed it referred to 'Uncle Sam', their friendly inspector.

The nickname spread, and by the end of the war 'Uncle Sam' was commonly being used to designate the US government. In the beginning 'Uncle Sam' was only a name, but in 1832 he made his first visual appearance in political cartoons, dressed in stars and stripes. Uncle Sam's appearance is commonly thought to be an amalgam of two earlier American figures, Yankee Doodle and Brother Jonathan.

Uncle Sam Wilson died at the ripe age of 87 in 1854. Over 100 years later the United States Congress made his grave an official national shrine.

14 September

'Onorate l'altissimo poeta'

1321 Today, during the black hours of pre-dawn, the first great modern poet, Dante Alighieri, died in exile in Ravenna at the age of 56.

In some ways Dante was the precursor of the versatile Renaissance Men who were to spring forth from his native Florence a century and more after his death. Philosopher, dashing cavalryman (he had fought for Florence against Arrezo at the battle of Campaldino), councilman, servant of princes, ambassador – Dante was all of these as well as the creator of arguably the greatest single poem ever penned.

Dante spent the last nineteen years of his life in exile from Florence, banished by the pro-pope faction, the Black Guelphs, whose views Dante opposed. During that time he composed his masterpiece, *The Divine Comedy*, an epic of 100 cantos written in *terza rima*, with a rhyming pattern of aba bcb cdc, etc. Originally he called it simply *La Commedia* (The Comedy) because of the happy ending with Dante being guided through Paradise. Only two centuries after his death did the epic have the word 'divine' added to its title.

In the centuries since Dante's death, *The Divine Comedy* has inspired many other great artists. Botticelli, Michelangelo, Blake and Doré all produced illustrations for it, and Rossini, Schumann and Liszt used it as a basis for their compositions. Longfellow translated it into English, and because of it T.S. Eliot placed Dante on a par with Shakespeare as one of the two greatest of all poets.

Dante himself was also an admirer of previous poets, most notably the Roman Virgil, whom he selected to be the guide in his voyage through the Inferno. Most would consider the words Dante used to describe Virgil as equally suitable for Dante himself: 'Onorate l'altissimo poeta.' (Honour the greatest poet.)

Douglas MacArthur lands at Inchon

1950 Early this morning, in darkness off the Korean coast, the United States X Corps, 40,000 strong, prepared to launch one of the boldest amphibious assaults in all military history. Its purpose was to reverse an impending military disaster at Pusan, where United Nations forces defending the Republic of Korea were facing almost certain annihilation by the Communist North Korean Army.

With X Corps and directing the entire operation was General Douglas MacArthur, Commander-in-Chief of United Nations forces, whose intention it was to land his force behind enemy lines at the port of Inchon, cut the North Korean Army's supply line, and strangle the invasion that the Communists had launched so savagely on 25 June.

MacArthur's plan was extremely hazardous. It required complete surprise, and in addition the enormous tides at Inchon would allow only two hours for the initial landings. When he first proposed the operation, the Joint Chiefs of Staff opposed it as too hazardous. But at a strategic conference in Tokyo, MacArthur countered Washington's assessment with a forceful argument in which he incorporated this history lesson:

'Surprise is the most vital element for success in war. ... On the Plains of Abraham [in 1759], Wolfe won a stunning victory that was made possible almost entirely by surprise. Thus he captured Quebec and in effect ended the French and Indian War. Like Montcalm, the North Koreans would regard an Inchon landing as impossible. Like Wolfe, I could take them by surprise.'

On 29 August the Joint Chiefs cabled their approval.

In the tense pre-landing atmosphere, MacArthur, aboard his command ship *Mount McKinley*, stared into the darkness. 'Then I noticed a flash', he wrote, 'a light that winked on and off across the water. The channel navigation lights were on. We were taking the enemy by surprise.' By 8.00 a.m. the Marines carrying out the first wave of the assault had secured a beachhead without losing a man. With the evening's tide most of X Corps was ashore, moving inland.

As their author predicted, the Inchon landings forced the Communist invaders out of South Korea. The military scene in Korea went from almost certain disaster to what seemed like war-ending victory. But MacArthur's feat, unlike Wolfe's, did not end the war. When United Nations forces moved north to destroy what was left of the retreating North Korean Army, they suddenly encountered half a million Chinese Communist 'volunteers'. A new phase of the war began in which the front line see-sawed back and forth for another eighteen months. In the end, the invasion of South Korea was decisively defeated, but that success was obscured by military stalemate, endless armistice negotiations, and the heavy cost in lives: 142,000 deaths in the UN forces (including over 33,000 Americans), 415,000 in the South Korean army, and perhaps 1,500,000 Chinese and North Koreans.

Also on this day

1516: French King François I wins the Battle of Marignano * 1812: Napoleon enters Moscow * 1852: The Duke of Wellington dies at Walmer Castle in Kent * 1901: Theodore Roosevelt becomes the 26th President of the United States on the death of the assassinated President McKinley

15 September

The first day of the Congress of Vienna

1814 Vienna. In Roman times it was a frontier outpost called Vindabona, but it must have had some importance, for the Emperor Marcus Aurelius chose it as his military headquarters in his fight against barbarian German tribes, and he died there in AD 180. Centuries later it became the Habsburg capital of the Holy Roman Empire and three times withstood the siege of the Turks. Later Napoleon crushed the Austrian army at Wagram, 110 miles west of the city, entered Vienna in triumph and forced the Austrian Emperor to offer him his daughter in marriage.

But in all its varied history, never had Vienna, that magical and beautiful city on the Danube, been as much at the centre of history as it was on this day in 1814, which marked the formal opening of the Congress of Vienna.

Organised to restore peace and the balance of power in Europe after the Napoleonic wars, the Congress was possibly the greatest gathering of political power in history. It was hosted by Emperor Franz II of Austria (whose daughter Napoleon had married) at a cost in today's terms of $50,000,000. A tsar, three kings, eleven princes and over 90 ambassadors and plenipotentiaries attended it. In the cast were Castlereagh from Great Britain, as well as the illustrious Duke of Wellington, the famous Russian Foreign Minister Nesselrode and the two greatest masters of diplomacy and intrigue of the century, Talleyrand, representing the restored French monarchy, and Metternich, Austria's arrogant Foreign Minister. (This wily and aristocratic pair had much in common. Both became princes, and Talleyrand's most recent mistress was Dorothea, Duchess of Dino, while Metternich had formerly been the lover of her elder sister, Wilhelmina, Duchess of Sagan. Not surprisingly, the two men worked well together.)

The Congress lasted six months, marked by a brilliant succession of entertainments, including a concert of Beethoven's Seventh Symphony conducted by Beethoven himself. But most of all it is remembered for its endless series of balls. Indeed, some questioned that any progress was being made. As the Belgian Prince de Ligne famously punned: 'Le congrès ne marche pas, il danse.' (The Congress doesn't walk [i.e. work], it dances.)

Distracted by waltzes as it may have been, the Congress of Vienna accomplished its stated task of carving up Europe and establishing a peace that lasted for nearly 40 years until the Crimean War. Most of the boundaries established in 1815 remained for almost a century, until the First World War.

Also on this day

1613: French aphorist François, duc de La Rochefoucauld is born in Paris * 1917: Russia is proclaimed a republic with Alexander Kerensky as Prime Minister

454

16 September

The death of Torquemada, the implacable fanatic of the Spanish Inquisition

1498 Today in the quiet of the Monasterio de Santo Tomás in Avila died a frail 78-year-old Dominican monk, weary from a life dedicated to God. No one has ever less deserved a peaceful death; he was the first and worst Grand Inquisitor of the Spanish Inquisition, Tomás de Torquemada, whose name appropriately means 'burnt tower'.

In 1483 Pope Sixtus IV had chosen Torquemada to head the Spanish Inquisition, but even the Pope had no inkling of the demented zeal with which his appointee would perform his task of cleansing Spain of heretics. Torquemada's special target was the so-called Marranos, Jews who claimed to have converted to Christianity but who secretly still followed the Jewish faith. Using unspeakable torture to extract confessions and punishing the guilty with execution at the stake, this fanatical monk used a network of spies to ferret out suspects and crossed the country attended by 50 armed knights and 200 foot soldiers to enforce his will.

Historians still debate how many 'heretics' Torquemada burned in the name of God, but the minimum suggested is 2,000, with another 25,000 convicted and punished less harshly.

In his persecution of the Jews, Torquemada was a chilling forerunner of the Nazis half a millennium later. His ultimate goal was to establish nothing less than *sangre limpia* (pure blood) in Spain – that is, Christian blood. He made the Marranos forfeit their property, forced them to wear the *sambenito*, a yellow shirt sewn with crosses, and had them flogged in public at the entrance to a church. He even issued a set of tell-tale signs by which good Christians could detect secret Jews, e.g. 'If on Saturday your neighbours wear clean clothes, they are Jews.'

After ten years of religious cleansing of the secret Jews, Torquemada stepped up his efforts to persuade King Ferdinand and Queen Isabella to expel all Jews. But then some wealthy Jews offered 30,000 ducats if the Jews could remain, and the King and Queen were sorely tempted.

On hearing of the offer, Torquemada hurried to the palace and, holding his crucifix before him, confronted the royal pair. 'Judas sold Jesus Christ for thirty pieces of silver', he admonished. 'You would sell Him for thirty thousand. Here, take Him and sell Him, and I will leave my office and you will explain your agreement to God.' He then turned and left the room. Not surprisingly, in the face of such holy intransigence, on 31 March 1492 the King and Queen ordered all Jews to leave the country no later than 1 July or face execution. More than 160,000 fled.

Many have wondered over the centuries what drives a man like Torquemada to such extremes of relentless persecution. Some believe that, like Hitler's notorious SS officer Reinhard Heydrich, Torquemada was subconsciously compelled by the knowledge of his own tainted bloodline: his grandmother had been a converted Jew.

Also on this day

1387: Henry of Monmouth (Henry V of England) is born at Monmouth Castle, Wales * 1701: British King James II dies in exile at Saint-Germain in France

17 September

A bridge too far – the largest airborne operation ever

1944 With Paris liberated, Antwerp captured, and the Germans everywhere on the run in north-west Europe, an intoxicating optimism ran through the Allied camp. Imbibing this spirit, the normally cautious Field Marshal Montgomery advanced a bold strategic plan that gave promise of ending the war by Christmas.

It called for a great thrust northward through Holland to get past the Siegfried Line, Germany's formidable frontier defences, and then a swing eastward towards Berlin and final victory. Not everyone among the Allied brass agreed, but General Eisenhower, the Supreme Commander, was willing to give Monty's plan a try, at least the first part, a combined ground and airborne operation to get forces across the Lower Rhine River, the last great water barrier before Germany itself. The operation bore the deceptively pastoral codename Market Garden.

Accordingly, on this sunny late summer morning, from airfields across southern England, a great armada of transport planes and gliders took off for Holland carrying 20,000 paratroopers from three Allied divisions. The mission was to 'lay an airborne carpet' behind German lines along a 65-mile corridor running north from the Allied front line to the town of Arnhem on the far side of the Rhine. The paratroopers would seize key bridges along the corridor, then hold them until the ground forces of XXX Corps came through on their way to Arnhem.

Allied planners viewed the retreating enemy as demoralised and incapable of strong resistance. They discounted intelligence indicating a formidable concentration of German units in the very area through which Market Garden would pass. At a top-level briefing for Market Garden commanders, the general commanding the British 1st Airborne Division asked how long his men would have to hold Arnhem before XXX Corps got through to them. 'Two days', Monty told him confidently. 'They'll be up with you by then.'

On the ground it was very different. The Germans met 1st Airborne's drop near Arnhem with unanticipated quickness and ferocity. Only one battalion of British paratroopers managed to reach the town. The rest came under heavy fire and by nightfall went to ground west of town. At the southern end, as the

Guards Armoured Division leading XXX Corps got under way its lead units were ambushed by heavy fire from anti-tank guns. The column halted while infantry was brought up to flank the ambushers and bulldozers cleared away the wreckage of vehicles. The tanks resumed their advance, but the pattern was set for a painfully slow, stop-and-go advance. When the Guards reached Eindhoven, just eleven miles from the start line, they were already 24 hours behind schedule.

In seizing their assigned bridges, the paratroopers of the 101st and 82nd US Airborne Divisions had done a remarkable job; but so had the German defenders in attacking the Allied columns that jammed the single roadway north. At the town of Nijmegen it took XXX Corps two days of heavy fighting, including an amphibious assault by the 82nd, to clear the bridge across the River Waal.

The advance continued, but time was running out. With one isolated battalion desperately holding the north end of the Arnhem bridge against 9th SS Panzer Division, the rest of 1st Airborne was pinned in a shrinking pocket, backs to the Rhine. An attempt to fly in reinforcements went disastrously awry when anti-aircraft fire forced Polish paratroopers to jump early, putting them on the wrong bank of the river.

Reduced to 2,200 from the 10,000 paratroopers who had landed eight days earlier, the division was almost out of food, ammo and medical supplies, and could no longer care for its growing number of wounded. Montgomery, finally realising that XXX Corps, close as it was, would not reach Arnhem in time, gave 1st Airborne the order to withdraw. During the night and under intense fire, the survivors were ferried or swam to safety across the Rhine.

Market Garden failed utterly. In the gallant effort, 17,000 Allied troops had been killed, wounded or captured. Arnhem proved to be, in a phrase that would become famous, 'a bridge too far'. Critics of the operation compared it to Dunkirk and the Dardanelles. The Allies would need to find a different strategy from Monty's single thrust. There would be one more Christmas at war.

The king who discovered Velázquez

1665 Today in Madrid Philip IV of Spain died at the age of 60, one of history's most feckless monarchs.

In his 44 years as King, Philip's only lasting accomplishment was the appointment of Diego Velázquez as court painter in 1623. Ironically, it is thanks to Velázquez that we have such a complete and accurate record of what Philip looked like. Through the great artist's work we can see the arrogant face with a petulant, full-lipped mouth, the high, intellectual forehead, the jutting Habsburg jaw, the silly upturned moustache and the baggy, debauched eyes.

In life Philip was just as Velázquez presented him in art – intellectual but weak, a man of great place and little consequence, who let his nation slide steadily downhill.

During the first half of his reign, Philip left the running of the country to his ambitious and greedy minister the Conde de Olivares, while he devoted himself to his mistresses, by whom he had over 30 bastard children. Eventually Philip felt compelled to dismiss Olivares, especially after Portugal, ruled by Spain since the time of Philip's grandfather Philip II, revolted and won its independence.

But without his first minister Philip still felt the need for guidance, and turned to a mystical nun named Sor María de Agreda, with whom he regularly corresponded, seeking her advice on critical matters of state.

Sor María's counsel was as unproductive as Olivares's. By the time of her death in 1665, Spain, once the greatest power in Europe, had become a second-class power both economically and militarily. Just four months later Philip followed the mystical nun to the grave.

Also on this day

1630: John Winthrop founds the town of Boston * 1631: Protestant Swedes and Saxons under King Gustavus Adolphus defeat forces of the Holy Roman Empire at Breitenfeld * 1787: The Constitution of the United States of America is signed * 1796: President George Washington delivers his 'Farewell Address' to Congress * 1862: The Battle of Antietam is fought in the American Civil War, the bloodiest single day in US history

18 September

Another Roman emperor is done in by his wife

AD 96 Today one of Rome's more loathsome emperors met his death at the hands of his own wife and servants, to the contentment of the Senate and the joy of dozens of his subjects who feared for their lives.

Domitian was the son of a great emperor, Vespasian, and the brother of a good one, Titus, against whom Domitian ceaselessly plotted during the two years that Titus ruled. When Domitian was 29, Titus fell seriously ill, and Domitian ordered his attendants to leave him for dead even while he was still alive, thus accomplishing passive fratricide.

On inheriting his brother's imperial rank, Domitian was at first a competent ruler, but he soon showed his inherent sadism by frequently sequestering himself in his office to catch flies and stab them to death with his pen. As he grew older, despite his athletic frame, he grew paunchy and bald, for he took no exercise except sex, which he jocularly referred to as 'bed wrestling'. One of his mistresses was his own niece (Titus's daughter) Julia. He also became increasingly autocratic, insisting on being addressed as *dominus et deus* (master and god).

According to the historian Suetonius (who was 30 when Domitian was murdered), the Emperor's 'lack of funds made him greedy, and fear of assassination made him cruel'. Whatever the cause, as time went by Domitian increasingly condemned people to death on the flimsiest of pretences, convinced that all were plotting against him and eager to appropriate their wealth.

Domitian could also be maniacally vindictive. Before becoming Emperor, he had forcibly taken and married Domitia Longina, who was the wife of another man, one Aelius Lamia. Shortly afterwards Aelius had been joking with Domitian's brother Titus, who encouraged him to remarry. 'What?' asked Aelius, 'Are you looking for a wife too?' For this idle repartee, years later Domitian had Aelius executed.

Domitian's irrational malevolence was also demonstrated when his wife entered an affair with an actor named Paris. The Emperor first banned her but later took her back ('recalled her to my divine bed', was how he described it). But subsequently he had one of Paris's student actors executed purely on the grounds that he was Paris's pupil and apparently much resembled him physically.

According to Suetonius, a number of augurs foretold that Domitian would be assassinated, one even predicting the exact date. Terrified by the threat, the Emperor proscribed or executed so many people that even those with no guilty secrets lived in mortal terror of the imperial summons.

Among those living in dread were his wife Domitia Longina, who feared further imperial retribution, and Stephanus, the steward of the Emperor's niece Domitilla, whom the Emperor had sent into exile. Stephanus had been accused of embezzlement and, afraid for his life, sought out several equally panicky members of Domitian's household staff. Together they hatched a murderous plot.

For several days Stephanus went everywhere with his arm in a bandage, beneath which he concealed a dagger. Then, on the morning of 18 September, Domitian's attendants announced that the steward had arrived to warn the Emperor of an assassination plot. When Stephanus entered the royal bedchamber he handed Domitian a scroll supposedly containing the details of the scheme, but when the Emperor reached for it, the steward stabbed him in the groin. Suetonius relates that 'Domitian wrestled Stephanus to the ground, where the two men fought long and hard, Domitian trying to grab the dagger and to claw out his attacker's eyes with his torn and bleeding fingers'. Before either man could subdue the other, four of Stephanus's confederates joined the fray and stabbed the Emperor seven more times, leaving him dead on the floor. It was just four days after he had celebrated his fifteenth anniversary as Roman Emperor, the most powerful man in the world.

Two royal dynasties get started

1517, 1714 The 18th September seems to be a day of dynastic arrivals, as it marked the start of two great royal families, the Habsburgs in Spain and the House of Hanover in England.

On this day in 1517 a blond, strapping seventeen-year-old named Charles von Habsburg landed at a point called Tazones in Asturias on the north coast of Spain. Charles's father was dead and his mother Juana was morbidly and incurably insane. Since his maternal grandfather King Ferdinand had died the previous year, Charles arrived as King Charles I on this, his first visit to Spain. (Two years later he would be chosen Holy Roman Emperor as well, becoming Charles V for the Empire while confusingly remaining Charles I for Spain.) As well as being Spain's first Charles he was also the country's first Habsburg monarch, and the House of Habsburg would rule the country until the death of his imbecilic great-great-grandson, the hapless Charles II, on 1 November 1700, some 183 years later.

Just fourteen years after the Spanish Habsburgs died out, 18 September once again became a day of dynastic arrival, as towards evening on that date in 1714 a fat, 54-year-old prince landed in the fog at Greenwich on the Thames. George was his name, and he arrived as King George I, the first Hanoverian king of England.

George's line proved even more durable than Charles's, as the House of Hanover held the throne until 1901 for a run of 187 years. It was then succeeded by the house of Saxe-Coburg-Gotha (the family name of Queen Victoria's consort Prince Albert). In 1917 George's great-great-great-great-great-grandson, George V, rechristened the family Windsor in a fit of patriotic fervour during the First World War. The same sentiment also caused all wicked German shepherds in England to be renamed Alsatians.

Also on this day

AD 324: Roman Emperor Constantine defeats Licinius at Chrysopolis, becoming the sole emperor of the whole Roman Empire, east and west * 1709: Samuel Johnson is born in Lichfield, Staffordshire * 1851: The first issue of *The New York Times* appears

19 September

The Black Prince captures a French king

1356 The Hundred Years' War had already been running for nineteen years when the English routed their French foes today at the Battle of Poitiers.

In early September the English heir to the throne, Edward, the Black Prince, led a raiding party of only 7,000 men out of English-held Bordeaux, but he soon found himself pursued by King Jean II of France with a vastly superior force. The armies fought briefly on 17 September but arranged a truce for the following day, a Sunday. This day of rest gave the Black Prince the time he needed to organise his army in a damp marshland where the Clain and Miosson Rivers come together near the town of Poitiers.

Ten years earlier, at Crécy, the French had found themselves in a very similar situation – outnumbering the enemy but stymied by bogs that gave their war-horses no footing. Lack of discipline plus the accuracy of English longbows had destroyed the French then, just as happened today at Poitiers.

The French charged repeatedly, each time losing dozens of knights to England's lethal arrows, and when they pushed their advance further their horses bogged down in the marsh and English foot soldiers quickly dispatched their riders, helpless on the ground.

Poitiers was a particular disaster for the French because King Jean, who had quixotically led the final charge against the English, was captured and carried off to London for four years of luxurious captivity.

The battle may have seemed decisive at the time, but it was in truth just another blip in this seemingly endless conflict that dragged on for another 97 years.

Also on this day

1777: The US wins the Battle of Saratoga in the American Revolution * 1812: Founder of the House of Rothschild, Mayer Amschel Rothschild, dies in Frankfurt

20 September

How the Great Papal Schism began

1378 Pope Gregory XI had died shortly after bringing the papacy back to Rome, ending the so-called Babylonian Captivity, that period of almost 70 years when popes lived in Avignon under the thumb of French kings. Now the Neapolitan Bartolomeo Prignano sat on St Peter's throne, having taken the name of Urban VI. He was stubborn, dictatorial and difficult, wildly accusing his cardinals of lasciviousness and simony, seeing vice in every corner. But to a large group of French cardinals, his greatest crime was his refusal to return the papacy to Avignon after having gained their votes by his promise to do so.

At first the furious cardinals tried to depose Urban, calling him 'anti-Christ, devil, apostate, tyrant, deceiver' and other mild condemnations. But Urban stubbornly clung to power.

Moving to Fondi, near Naples, the cardinals held their own conclave and on 20 September 1378 elected another Frenchman, Robert of Geneva, as their new pope and whisked him back to Avignon. Robert styled himself Pope Clement VII, but the problem was, Urban VI remained Pope in Rome.

Popes and anti-popes were nothing new in the Church. A certain Hippolytus was the first anti-pope way back in the year AD 218. Clement VII was rather a late-comer to the trade, the 34th anti-pope since St Peter founded the Church.

But the split (called the Great Schism) that started with Clement and Urban was much the most serious disruption in the Church's history. During the next four decades there were five 'legitimate' popes and four anti-popes, with at least two and sometimes three enthroned simultaneously, one in Rome, one in Avignon and occasionally one in Bologna.

Eventually, on 26 July 1417 Martin V became the sole Pope when the Council of Constance deposed one of the pretenders, Benedict XIII. The Great Schism had lasted 38 years and 309 days.

Unfortunately, the papacy's papal problems were far from over at the end of the Great Schism, as there were still two more anti-popes to come. But the last of these, Felix V, abandoned his claim in 1449.

Garibaldi reunites Italy

1870 Ever since the disintegration of the Roman Empire in the 5th century, Italy had been divided into different principalities and territories, never a single state. Even in the mid-19th century, Austria ruled in Venice, dukedoms such as Tuscany, Modena and Parma were independent, southern Italy consisted of the Kingdom of the Two Sicilies, the King of Sardinia ruled from Turin, and the Pope governed the Papal States.

The Risorgimento (or 'rising again') has no specific starting date, but this nationalist movement initially began in the early 1800s.

The first real gain for reunification came in 1859, when the Kingdom of Sardinia (which was really Piedmont) annexed Lombardy. The following year, thanks to the brilliant generalship of Giuseppe Garibaldi and the equally brilliant policies of the Sardinian minister Camillo di Cavour, Sicily, Tuscany, Bologna, Parma and Modena joined Piedmont under King Victor Emmanuel. In 1866 Austria was finally forced to cede Venetia, and that left only Rome, ruled by the defensive and reactionary Pope Pius IX.

Pius had been sheltering behind the power of Napoleon III's France, but when the Emperor surrendered to Prussia at Sedan on 2 September 1870, Victor Emmanuel's government was quick to take advantage, dispatching Garibaldi and his army into the Holy City. On 20 September Garibaldi's troops entered Rome through the Porta Pia, following a purely symbolic defence by the Pope's few soldiers.

The reunification was at last complete (although the 78-year-old Pius retreated to the Vatican and refused to recognise the new Italian state, a posture continued by his successors until 1929). Italy was again whole, for the first time in fourteen centuries.

'Duke by the grace of God'

1455 Today Philip the Good of Burgundy achieved his lifetime's ambition of becoming independent from his suzerain, King Charles VII of France, by virtue of a treaty that granted him the title of grand duc d'Occident. From this day forward Philip styled himself 'duke by the grace of God' rather than by the grace of the King of France.

Philip's territory consisted not only of the wine-growing Burgundy around Beaune and Dijon that is now part of France, but also most of what today is Belgium, Holland and Luxembourg. Philip himself had added much of this area through wars, diplomacy and marriage. The great cities of Brussels, Ghent and Bruges were among the richest in the world, and Philip's court promoted a civilisation of sophistication, taste and high artistic merit.

The Duke was a great patron of the arts, a highly cultured man with a narrow but strong and intellectual face. In his youth he had been an exceptional athlete, not only a fine horseman and jouster but also a talented archer and tennis player. His other sporting interest was women, as he fathered so many illegitimate children that he was publicly criticised by the Bishop of Tournai.

In 1429, when Philip was 32, he founded the famous chivalric Ordre de la Toison d'Or (Order of the Golden Fleece) to rival England's Order of the Garter that had been created almost a century before. He named his order after the heroic quest of Jason and his Argonauts, but by using the word 'fleece' he also made a complimentary reference to the flourishing wool industry of his duchy. The order was originally restricted to 24 noblemen but was later enlarged.

After Philip died, the Ordre de la Toison d'Or's leadership was inherited by his son and then descended to the Habsburgs (Philip's granddaughter married the Holy Roman Emperor Maximilian von Habsburg). It became predominantly a Spanish order when Philip II of Spain inherited it, but when the Spanish Habsburgs petered out in 1700, both the Spanish Bourbons and the Austrian Habsburgs claimed the order, and so two branches continued to exist.

In Austria the Ordre de la Toison d'Or disappeared with the Habsburgs in 1918, but it continued in Spain until it was abolished by the Spanish Republic in 1930 after a run of 501 years.

Sadly for Philip the Good, his great Duchy of Burgundy proved far less durable, once again becoming part of France when Philip's son, Charles the Bold, was killed in battle on 5 January 1477.

Also on this day

356 BC: Alexander the Great is born * 1519: Ferdinand Magellan starts his round-the-world voyage with five ships and 280 men * 1857: The siege of Delhi ends, leading to the collapse of the Indian Mutiny

21 September

The Greeks annihilate the Persians at Marathon

490 BC The mighty Persian empire stretched from the edge of India to the Aegean, and King Darius the Great had set his sights on the still independent city-states of Greece.

Two years earlier Darius's first attempt had ended in failure when his fleet was storm-wrecked off Mount Athos, but now he was armed with a secret weapon, what amounted to a fifth column, in the Alcemaeonidae family in Athens who secretly favoured a Persian victory, hoping it would restore their political power. If the Athenian army could be drawn away from the city, perhaps Athens would fall by insurrection rather than costly invasion.

In September of 490 BC Darius landed an army of 15,000 men on the Bay of Marathon, which lies about 26 miles north-east of Athens. Frantic, the Athenians immediately sent a messenger, Pheidippides, to plead for reinforcements from the Spartans. Although Pheidippides covered 150 miles in less than two days, his mission was fruitless, for the Spartans announced they could not march before the completion of certain religious festivals, still ten days away. The Athenians would have to face the Persians alone.

In mid-September 10,000 Greeks, including the poet Aeschylus, reached Marathon, and there for eight days uncertainly faced the invading Persians, the Athenians fearful of Persian military might, the Persians hoping to hear that, with the Greek army out of Athens, the Alcemaeonidae were overthrowing the government.

On 21 September the Greek commander Miltiades saw that the Persian cavalry had re-embarked, probably to mount a direct attack on Athens. He also learned that Persian reinforcements were on their way. He chose this moment to strike.

The Athenian infantry charged forward and were immediately counter-attacked by the Persian front line. The Greek centre bowed backwards under the assault, as the Persians hurled themselves forward, thinking the Greeks were in retreat. Then Miltiades brought his two reinforced wings around in a double envelopment, smashing into the Persian flanks.

The result was massacre. The Greeks lost only 192 men, but 6,400 Persians died on the Plain of Marathon. What was left of the Persian army fled to their ships and headed for home.

Now the Persian threat had been stymied, what of the threat of revolt in the city? Knowing that the Alcemaeonidae could not act without Persian military support, the Greeks immediately dispatched a messenger (some say Pheidippides again) to herald the great victory. Without pause for rest or water, he ran the 26 miles between Marathon and Athens, announced the Athenian triumph ('Nike' in Greek, meaning victory) and then fell dead from exhaustion.

Almost two and a half millennia later, the Greeks commemorated this famous run by instituting the first 26-mile 'marathon' race in the 1896 Olympics, held in Athens. Appropriately, it was won in two hours, 58 minutes and 50 seconds by Spyridon Louis, a Greek.

The French abolish the monarchy and replace the calendar

1792 The Bastille had fallen three years earlier, but Louis XVI still lived, a captive king restricted to the Temple in Paris, a 12th-century construction once the headquarters of the Templars.

But the members of the National Convention were becoming daily more revolutionary, and on this day they formally abolished the monarchy in France, marking the start of the First Republic.

Not content with initiating a new political era, the representatives decided to get a truly fresh start – by abolishing the Gregorian calendar altogether and starting anew. So the following day, 22 September, became Day One of Year I. The new calendar still contained twelve months but specified that each would have 30 days, with five days left over for Republican holidays. The seven-day week was also gone, replaced by one of ten days with the sensible but boring names of Primidi, Duodi, Tridi, Quartidi, Quintidi, Sextidi, Septidi, Octidi, Nonidi and Décadi.

Even the months of the year gained a more rational nomenclature, with names based on the weather thought to be characteristic of the season. For example, winter months were called Nivôse (snowy), Pluviôse (rainy) and Ventôse (windy). Other months included Germinal (in the spring) and Thermidor (indicating the heat of late July and August).

Having abolished the monarchy and the calendar, the Convention rested for precisely four (old-fashioned) months and then abolished poor Louis XVI with the guillotine.

It's probably a good thing that today the Revolutionary calendar is long forgotten. How would we feel about Bastille Day were it on 26 Messidor? About the only legacy that remains from this great French calendarial innovation is Lobster Thermidor, said to have been named by Napoleon after the month in which he first tasted it, and Emile Zola's novel *Germinal*, the title of which echoes the hopes of the republican Revolution, suggesting that mankind is on the verge of a new spring.

'I speak Spanish to God, Italian to women, French to men and German to my horse'

1558 The words above come from Emperor Charles V, and even in that list he omitted Flemish, which he spoke fluently as well. (Apparently he made the quotation in French.) No doubt he found his five languages useful to rule his vast realm – six modern nations (Spain, Italy, Belgium, Austria, Luxembourg and Holland) claim him as a past sovereign. He was truly an emperor (perhaps the only emperor) without nationality, as he lived in and ruled more of Europe than anyone since the Romans.

During his 36 years as Holy Roman Emperor, Charles stopped the Turks in the Balkans and threw the French out of Italy, but he failed in his greatest quest, to reunite Europe's Christian lands in the Catholic faith. Worn out and disillusioned at 55, he took the unprecedented step of abdicating his powers and retired to the monastery of San Jeronimo at Yuste, in the loneliness of

Extremadura in Spain. There he lived for two quiet years, not in monastic poverty but royal opulence, pained by gout, in constant touch with his son, austere Philip II who was now King of Spain.

Charles might have continued in splendid retirement for many years had he not built a small pool near his rooms in San Jeronimo. For in that pool may have bred the very mosquitoes that gave him the malaria of which he died this day, when he was still just 58.

Sultan Selim the Grim

1520 When he died today at 50, Turkey's Sultan Selim I had propelled his country to pre-eminence in the world of Islam through his conquest of Egypt, Palestine and Syria. He also helped set the stage for a bitter Islamic confrontation that has continued to this day when he crushed the Shi'ite Muslims of Iran who he felt threatened Turkey's Sunni branch of the religion.

Even for a Turk, Selim must have been ferocious, as his own people called him Yavuz (the Grim). Rumour had it that he had his father poisoned, and what is certain is that he consolidated his position as Sultan by having his two elder brothers strangled. Taking no chances, he then rounded up his brothers' five children and had them strangled too, while he listened to their gurgling from the adjoining room.

Selim reigned for only nine years, but his death brought even greater glory to Turkey as his son, the incomparable Suleiman the Magnificent, greatest of all Ottoman rulers, inherited his empire.

Also on this day

19 BC: Roman poet Virgil dies * 1452: Fanatical preacher Girolamo Savonarola is born in Ferrara * 1832: British writer Sir Walter Scott dies

22 September

The most barbarous royal murder in history

1327 Today three henchmen of the Queen of England and her lover committed the most barbarous royal murder in history. The victim was the Queen's husband, King Edward II.

Handsome, silly, weak and dominated by male favourites, Edward II had been overthrown by Queen Isabella and her paramour Roger de Mortimer. He was now a prisoner and had been moved from London to the more remote Berkeley Castle in Gloucestershire under the guard of Sir Thomas Gurney, Sir John Maltravers and William Ogle. But no matter how securely the King was imprisoned, he still represented an intolerable threat to the usurpers of power.

Perhaps hoping Edward would succumb to natural causes, his jailers locked him in a small, cold room and fed him with scraps, but his constitution was rugged, and he showed no signs of sickness or deterioration. Something had to be done.

During the night of 21 September the three henchmen entered Edward's cell while he slept and pinned him to the bed with a table. Then one of them thrust a red-hot spit up through his anus, burning out his internal organs. This indescribably agonising method of execution both served as an evil parody of the King's homosexuality and left his body outwardly unmarked, so that it could later be laid out in state for inspection.

Edward's death – publicly explained as due to sudden illness – permitted Queen Isabella to control the state as regent for her fourteen-year-old son, now Edward III, with her lover Mortimer acting as unofficial co-ruler. Neither the Queen nor Mortimer understood young Edward's hatred for their usurpation or his steely determination as he grew older. When he reached his majority three years later he sent his mother to forced retirement while ordering a traitor's execution for Mortimer, to be hanged, drawn and quartered.

Although Edward II had accomplished little during his lifetime, his horrible death produced one of England's great buildings. The monks at Gloucester treated him as a martyr, and soon his tomb became a focus for pilgrimage. The enormous offerings left behind by pious visitors enabled the monks to rebuild the cathedral in Perpendicular style, the first and greatest example in England.

'I only regret that I have but one life to lose for my country'

1776 Next time you are in New York, go to the corner of 63rd Street and 3rd Avenue. You will be standing on the spot where Nathan Hale, one of America's greatest Revolutionary heroes, was executed.

Hale was born in Connecticut in 1755 and, after attending Yale, became a schoolmaster. When the American Revolution broke out, he joined his state militia and soon rose to the rank of captain.

In the autumn of 1776 General George Washington's troops were sparring with the British around New York. On 21 September young Hale volunteered for the dangerous mission of going behind enemy lines to learn the British strength and position. Once his assignment had been accomplished, Hale intended to return to the American lines, but fires started by Washington's soldiers blocked his route. Unable to rejoin his own forces, he took refuge in a local tavern, where British soldiers picked him up during a routine sweep.

Hale openly admitted his mission, and a British officer sentenced him to hang the next day, without further trial. Remarkably composed throughout, just before his execution he pronounced his famous words: 'I only regret that I have but one life to lose for my country.' He then climbed the ladder that would be pulled from beneath his feet.

Hale became much more famous after the Revolution than he ever was during it, so it is possible that his celebrated words have been embellished by history. They bear a remarkable resemblance to the hero's speech in Joseph Addison's play *Cato*: 'What a pity is it that we can die but once to serve our country!'

Also on this day

1692: Six women and one man are hanged during the Salem witch trials in America * 1862: US President Abraham Lincoln issues the Emancipation Proclamation, freeing America's slaves, which comes into force the following 1 January

23 September

The Greeks save the Western world at Salamis

480 BC Persia's mighty King Xerxes had sent his heralds throughout Greece demanding earth and water, symbols of submission, but the Athenian general Themistocles responded with a brutal symbol of his own: he had the messenger put to death for daring to make his barbarian demands in the Greek language. Enraged, Xerxes resolved to conquer those foolish enough to resist him.

Soon Xerxes had assembled a huge army, estimated by Herodotus at 2,641,610 men, but assumed by modern historians to be a more modest 200,000. To cross from Asia Minor into Greece he constructed two boat bridges across the Hellespont, and when waves destroyed them during a storm, he ordered the sea scourged with 300 lashes. He then threw a pair of shackles into the water, grandly pronouncing: 'Ungracious water, your master condemns you to punishment for having injured him without cause. Xerxes the king will pass over you, whether you consent or not!' By then the storm had abated, and his army easily crossed over on a new bridge.

In spite of the defensive league formed by the Greek city-states, the Persians rolled irresistibly forward. In August of 480 they defeated the heroic Spartans at Thermopylae, opening the route to Athens, which the Athenians then abandoned, leaving only a heavily fortified Acropolis. Soon that too had fallen, with all defenders slain.

The assembled Greek generals as ever bickered interminably over tactics. Some wanted to withdraw to Corinth, while Themistocles argued vehemently for a naval engagement. At length it seemed that the Athenian had won the dispute, but only by threatening to withdraw his ships and men. But on 22 September yet another debate erupted, and this time Themistocles took an even greater gamble. He sent a slave with a secret message to Xerxes: Themistocles is on your side, and the rest of the Greeks are ready to run away. Attack now while they are still arguing what to do and you shall have a great victory.

Having heard from his own spies about dissension in the Greek camp,

Xerxes believed Themistocles' message and launched his attack. The Greeks suddenly had no choice but to stay and fight.

Themistocles' brilliant plan was to lure the Persian fleet into the narrow straits between the port of Piraeus and the island of Salamis, where the enemy would have no room for manoeuvre. Outnumbering the Greeks more than two to one, on this day some 1,000 of Xerxes's galleys fell into the Greek trap. According to Herodotus, Themistocles delayed the final action 'until the time when there is regularly a strong breeze from the open sea that brings a high swell into the straits, which presented no difficulty to the low-built Greek ships but was harmful to the slow and cumbersome Persians, with high sterns and decks, as it made them vulnerable to the quick attacks of the Greeks'.

For seven long hours the Greeks harried the Persians. Greek triremes ran up alongside the enemy galleys, shearing off their oars, and then returned to ram or board. When day became evening, some 300 Persian galleys lay shattered on the seabed, against losses of only 40 for the Greeks.

Xerxes had remained on dry land, sitting in his golden throne high upon a promontory to watch his inevitable victory. As more and more of his ships went down, his ally Artemisia, Queen of Helicarnassus, rammed and sank an enemy trireme, at which the King lamented: 'My men have become women, my women, men.'

Defeated and fearful of being cut off in Greece, Xerxes scuttled back to Persia, leaving behind an army to achieve on land what he had so conspicuously failed to do by sea. But in August the following year that army was destroyed at the Battle of Plataea.

The Battle of Salamis was much more than the first great naval battle in history. With the victory at Plataea, it ended the Persian threat for a century and a half, until Alexander the Great finally conquered the Persian Empire in 331 BC. More than that, it prevented Greece from being crushed by Oriental despotism, leaving it free to develop its systems of democracy and the philosophical ideals that have pervaded Western civilisation ever since. In the words of historian Will Durant: 'It made Europe possible.'

The first and greatest of all Roman emperors

63 BC Just before sunrise on this day was born the first and greatest of all Roman emperors, Gaius Octavius Caesar, later known as Augustus. He grew to be a handsome man with light brown hair and blue eyes, although slight in stature, only five feet seven inches tall.

Octavian, as he was known before becoming Emperor, had the great good fortune to be the child of Julius Caesar's niece, and that relationship, together with Caesar's high regard for his abilities, caused Caesar to adopt him as his son when Octavian was eighteen. When Caesar was assassinated, Octavian inherited not only his colossal wealth but also the fidelity of some of his legions.

For the next thirteen years Octavian shared power in uneasy alliance with

Lepidus and Mark Antony. Lepidus was the first to be sidelined, and after Mark Antony was finally defeated at the Battle of Actium in 31 BC, Octavian ruled alone for the next 44 years. From 27 BC he began to style himself 'Augustus'.

Augustus could be utterly ruthless to achieve his ends. He once starved the town of Perusia – today's Perugia – into submission, executing 300 prisoners of equestrian rank, and after the downfall of Antony and Cleopatra he had Caesarion, Cleopatra's son by Julius Caesar, executed even though he was Augustus's brother by adoption. But generally he ruled by clever compromise, careful to give the appearance that Rome was still a republic governed by the Senate when in fact he had total autocratic power.

Augustus added huge areas to his empire, including Egypt, northern Spain, Switzerland, Austria, Hungary, and parts of Yugoslavia. He completely changed the empire's administrative systems and gave it over 40 years of uninterrupted peace and prosperity. He established Rome's first standing army and then set up armed camps throughout the empire that subsequently became some of Europe's greatest cities. In Rome itself he made vast improvements. As Augustus himself accurately boasted: 'I found Rome built of bricks; I leave her clothed in marble.'

In his private life Augustus was devoted to his wife Livia. In order to marry her he had compelled her to divorce her first husband while still pregnant by him. He passed rather puritanical laws against adultery and banished his own daughter for scandalous conduct, although he kept a string of mistresses himself.

Although essentially a simple man with little regard for his own appearance, Augustus did have one slightly narcissistic moment of which the effects are with us still. Because, according to Suetonius, 'in the month of Sextilis he won his first consulship and his most decisive victories', Augustus renamed Sextilis 'August' after himself.

John Paul Jones has not yet begun to fight

1779 Not all battles of the American Revolution were fought in North America. On this fine late summer evening, at Flamborough Head on the Yorkshire coast of England, 1,500 people gathered at cliffside, drawn by the rumble of cannon from a spectacular naval battle taking place six miles out to sea. There, commanding a 40-gun rebuilt French merchantman renamed the *Bon Homme Richard*, the Scottish-born American John Paul Jones, the best fighting captain in the Continental navy, was taking on the British ship *Serapis*, a 50-gun frigate built for war.

For hours the ships traded murderous broadsides, Jones seeking to close for boarding, *Serapis* manoeuvring away. Outgunned, the *Richard* got the worst of the exchange. At one point the British captain called out: 'Has your ship struck?' To which Jones gave his immortal answer: 'I have not yet begun to fight!' As night fell, however, Jones managed to bring the two vessels together, and then in an extraordinary effort helped his crew swing around a nine-pounder cannon from his unengaged side so it trained on the enemy's mainmast.

Finally, with both ships severely damaged and on fire, a sailor on the *Richard* managed to toss a grenade through a hatch into the *Serapis*'s gun deck, where it ignited the powder bags and blew up her main battery in an enormous explosion that brought down the mainmast. Shortly afterwards, in the moonlight, the *Serapis* surrendered, three and a half hours after the action began.

With the *Bon Homme Richard* sinking, Jones transferred his command to the *Serapis* and, eluding British patrols, sailed her as a prize of war into a neutral Dutch port. When he reached Paris he was a hero, the symbol of French–American victory over the common foe. A grateful Louis XVI made Jones a *chevalier* of France.

It was a memorable encounter, and not only because of Jones's indomitable reply. Like the battle of Bunker Hill, the victory off Flamborough Head served notice that the American rebels were able to meet the best that Britain could throw at them. In England, the shock of the event, occurring as it did in home waters, called into question British naval invincibility and lent force to the anti-war sentiments of Fox, Pitt and Burke.

Finally, the dramatic outcome of the battle and the style of Jones himself, while soon forgotten in the young American republic that had won its independence, served in time as a source of inspiration for advocates of a strong professional navy, among them President Theodore Roosevelt. In 1906, at the President's direction, Jones's remains were taken from an unmarked grave in Paris and brought to the Naval Academy at Annapolis, where with great public ceremony they were interred near the inscription: 'He gave our navy its earliest tradition of heroism and victory.'

Also on this day

1938: British premier Neville Chamberlain flies to Munich to meet Hitler * 1939: Austrian founder of psychoanalysis Sigmund Freud dies

24 September

Isabeau of Bavaria – France's worst queen?

1435 France has had its share of dreadful queens – Catherine de' Medici comes to mind. Today died a lesser known one, Isabeau of Bavaria, who harmed her nation as much as any invader.

She was born Elizabeth, daughter of the Duke of Bavaria. But when she married Charles VI of France her name was gallicised to Isabeau, a distinctive name for a distinctively depraved and selfish woman.

Beautiful and intelligent as well as exceptionally sensual, she was married to Charles at the age of fourteen, but after seven years of marriage it became clear that the King was going mad. During the next 30 years he suffered 45 fits of insanity, some lasting several months, when often he could not recognise her.

Although Isabeau bore the King six children, she also took a series of lovers, including both the King's brother and his cousin. In between titled paramours she entertained strapping soldiers of the palace guard. According to legend, she would also have her soldiers bring handsome men in off the streets, make love to them, then have them tied up in sacks and thrown into the Seine.

All of this could have been just good fun, but Isabeau also wielded power. Her most disastrous act was to sign the Treaty of Troyes by which King Henry V of England became heir to the French crown in place of Isabeau's own son Charles, who was to be sent in exile from France.

As she grew older Isabeau's beauty vanished and she grew increasingly fat, until she finally had to be carried everywhere in a litter. During her last years she witnessed the heroic deeds of Joan of Arc and the recognition of her son Charles (VII) as the rightful King of France. She died at the age of 64, held in contempt equally by the English she had helped and the French she had betrayed.

The second conquest of England?

1326 It is common knowledge that no one since William the Conqueror has ever successfully invaded England – but is it really true?

Take the case of Queen Isabella, wife of England's Edward II. Bored, insulted and generally fed up with her feckless and homosexual husband, Isabella manoeuvred herself into a diplomatic mission to the court of France. Once there, she openly lived with her paramour, one Roger de Mortimer, an English baron whom she had helped to escape from the Tower of London.

With great energy and resource, Isabella and Mortimer moved on to Holland where they raised an army and borrowed a Dutch nobleman, John of Hainault, to share command of the troops.

On this day the invasion force landed on the Suffolk coast and within four months had captured poor, pathetic Edward, forced his abdication and imprisoned him. Nine months later Mortimer, with Isabella's knowledge, had Edward hideously murdered in his cell. Isabella then took power as regent for her teenage son with Mortimer at her side.

Does this constitute a conquest? The army was Dutch, as was one of its two commanders. And the driving force of the invasion was Isabella, who, although Queen of England, was in fact French, the daughter of King Philip the Fair. So French was she that she was known then and since as the She-Wolf of France.

Marlborough's early start

1667 Today a seventeen-year-old court page was gazetted as an ensign in the Guards of King Charles II of England, largely because his sister Arabella was the mistress of Charles's brother, the future James II. The young ensign who thus took up his first military position through backstairs nepotism was named

John Churchill, one day to be Europe's most illustrious general with the title the Duke of Marlborough.

If Churchill had any second thoughts about the influence that had obtained for him his first posting, no doubt he subsequently took some subtle pleasure in seducing one of King Charles's own mistresses, the Duchess of Cleveland, a few years later.

But even such a 17th-century sophisticate as Churchill must have wondered at the system when, as he later fought Louis XIV of France, he found one of his enemy's principal generals to be his own nephew, the Duke of Berwick, the result of his sister's liaison with James II, the same relationship that had gained for Churchill his very first position.

Also on this day

1541: Swiss physician and alchemist Paracelsus dies * 1896: American novelist F. Scott Fitzgerald is born

25 September

Another calamitous crusade

1396 A mission to save the Christian world from Muslim domination had first been proposed in 1095 with Pope Urban II's impassioned call for the forces of Christendom to join the First Crusade. During the next two centuries Europeans launched seven more great campaigns, gradually ceding dominance of the Middle East to the Turks. Today another crusade, even more futile than its predecessors, reached its unhappy denouement at the Battle of Nicopolis in Bulgaria.

By the late 14th century the Ottoman Turks had reduced the once mighty Byzantine Empire to little more than the city of Constantinople itself. And now the Turkish Sultan was the fearsome Bayezid, called the Thunderbolt for his sudden and devastating attacks. Determined to widen his rule yet further, in 1395 he marched west, to the alarm of Christian Europe. By the beginning of July he had reached Nicopolis, a Bulgarian fortress on the banks of the Danube. There, after a brief siege, he shattered the defenders, killing the Bulgarian Tsar Ivan Shishman in the process.

Now Christian Europe was in panic. This time Pope Boniface IX led the call for a crusade to halt the Muslim threat. In July 1396 the Duke of Burgundy's son Jean de Nevers set out with a motley army of 10,000 Frenchmen, 2,000 Germans, 1,000 Englishmen and assorted soldiers from Poland, Austria, Lombardy and Croatia, as well as a contingent of Knights Hospitallers. As they marched east they were joined at Buda by a huge army of 30,000 Hungarians under the command of their king Sigismund. The crusaders' aim was nothing less than to turn the Turks out of the Balkans and then to march through

Anatolia and Syria to Jerusalem to recapture the Holy City. Their first major target would be the recently conquered Nicopolis, now occupied by the Turks.

Throughout the centuries, crusader courage and determination had been far stronger than their planning and preparation. The crusade of 1396 was no exception, for the European armies had brought no siege equipment and so were forced to surround and isolate Nicopolis rather than overpower it. This error gave the defending Turks several weeks to hold the fort and wait for help.

Reinforcements were not long in coming. Resolved to save Nicopolis, Bayezid the Thunderbolt marched out from Turkey at the head of a large army, including the feared Janissaries, infantry composed of Christian boys kidnapped from their families, forced to convert to Islam and (perhaps worse) to remain celibate. Joined by loyal Serbian allies, Bayezid soon arrived at Nicopolis and took up defensive positions on the city road with his flanks protected by deep gullies.

Lusting for blood, the impatient French knights immediately launched an attack, in spite of pleas for caution from King Sigismund. At first they met with success, routing the Turkish infantry and light cavalry and launching themselves at the Janissaries. Then suddenly the French cavalry were forced to halt; they had charged into a field of sharpened stakes planted in the ground and had to dismount or disembowel their horses. But even on foot they were formidable fighters, breaking the Janissary line while killing thousands.

Now the French and their allies charged up a small hill in the hope of looting the Sultan's quarters, only to find the Ottoman heavy cavalry massed there. Cut off from the rest of the Christian army, they were surrounded and slaughtered or captured.

Meanwhile the crusaders' Hungarian infantry initially fared better, routing the Turkish force before them until Bayezid's Serbian soldiers emerged from ambush to stampede the whole crusader army into panicky retreat.

Only a few of the crusaders escaped. Sigismund fled to the Danube and got away by ship, and Jean de Nevers was captured and later ransomed. But the day after the battle, Bayezid, incensed by his heavy losses, massacred most of his prisoners. The few survivors were given to his soldiers as slaves.

Once again, Islam was triumphant. For five centuries the Bulgarians were plunged into the Dark Ages under oppressive Islamic domination, what they refer to as the 'Turkish yoke'. The Bulgarian nobility was destroyed – aristocrats were coerced either to accept Islam and 'Turkicisation' or face execution. The peasants were turned into serfs while the Turks instituted what Bulgarians call 'the blood tax', as thousands of young boys were compelled to convert and pressed into the Janissary Corps. Only in 1878 did the Bulgarians at last regain their freedom.

Also on this day

1066: English King Harold II defeats Harald Hardrada of Norway at the Battle of Stamford Bridge * 1534: Medici Pope Clement VII dies * 1897: American novelist William Faulkner is born

26 September

A conquistador discovers the Pacific

1513 Today a Spanish conquistador discovered a gigantic new ocean, the Pacific. Three centuries later John Keats celebrated the event with his stirring lines:

> Or like stout Cortez when with eagle eyes
> He stared at the Pacific – and all his men
> Looked at each other with a wild surmise –
> Silent, upon a peak in Darien.

Fortunately Keats was a better poet than historian, since the man who sighted the Pacific was not Cortés but Vasco Núñez de Balboa.

Balboa was born and raised in the Extremadura of western Spain, that flat, arid province whose very name means 'extremely hard'. He was the first of the tough and uncompromising conquistadors from that area, a list that includes Cortés and Pizarro.

At 25 Balboa first came to the New World on a voyage of exploration to Colombia. Later he tried to settle down in Hispaniola (current Haiti), but by the time he was 35 he was mired in debt and fled the island as a stowaway, landing at Darién on the north coast of the Isthmus of Panama where it joins South America. There at last he began to prosper, and had soon taken command of the Spanish settlement.

Balboa was shortly leading expeditions into the interior in search of gold and slaves. Although he never resorted to the wholesale slaughter of the Indians as some of his Spanish contemporaries did, he used bribes, force where necessary, and occasionally terror, once having 40 Indians torn to pieces by Spanish war dogs.

In 1513 Balboa heard rumours of vast hoards of gold somewhere in the interior and determined to find it. Selecting 190 men and several hundred Indian guides and bearers, on 1 September he set out to cross the stifling rain forests of the Isthmus of Panama, jungle so thick that for days he and his men could never see the sky.

For 25 days the rugged and indefatigable Spaniards slogged their way through virtually impenetrable jungle and foetid swamp, finally emerging on the south coast of the isthmus to see a mountain peak looming before them. Ordering his men to halt, Balboa climbed to the top and in the distance saw the ocean.

According to Balboa's own account, he immediately dropped to his knees to give thanks to God and the saints and then called his men to join him at the summit, where they carved the name of the Spanish king (Ferdinand) on tree trunks to establish possession.

Four days later Balboa reached the ocean itself. Plunging into the water in full armour, he brandished his sword and claimed it for Spain.

Discovering the Pacific was Balboa's crowning achievement. Only six years later he became embroiled in a terminal conflict with Pedrarias Davila, who was both his father-in-law and technically his superior, in charge of the Spanish colony. Davila was jealous of Balboa's achievements and hated him for his reports to Spain condemning Davila's performance. When news arrived in the colony that Davila was being replaced, he summoned Balboa and had him tried on trumped up charges of treason. The great explorer and three of his comrades were beheaded in the main square of Darién, their corpses fed to vultures.

Also on this day

1791: French painter Théodore Géricault is born in Rouen * 1820: American frontiersman Daniel Boone dies * 1888: American (later British) poet T.S. Eliot is born * 1898: American composer George Gershwin is born in Brooklyn

27 September

Cosimo de' Medici is born

1389 Today marks the birth of one of Florence's great patricians and bankers, Cosimo de' Medici, whose family claimed descent from a stalwart knight named Averado who served the Emperor Charlemagne in the 9th century. They maintained that their coat of arms proved it.

According to the Medici tradition, one day Averado was riding north of Florence when he met a cruel giant who was terrorising the local peasantry. Taking up arms for the victims, Averado slew the giant and in the fight received three dents on his shield from the giant's mace. Hearing of his courageous victory, Charlemagne allowed him to add to his escutcheon a gold field bearing three red balls symbolising the dents. From that time forth the Medici used this insignia. (Historians have a more prosaic explanation, that the balls represent three Byzantine coins, symbols for money-changing.)

Historical evidence suggests that the Medici origins were somewhat more humble. The family were originally Tuscan peasants from Cafaggiolo, 16 miles north of Florence. In the 12th century they moved into Florence itself and within a hundred years had become one of the city's great banking families.

Cosimo de' Medici was born in Careggi just outside Florence, the son of Giovanni di Bicci de' Medici. Giovanni had come from moderate wealth, made much more and married well. A supporter of the arts for his city, he had been one of the backers for Ghiberti's magnificent doors for the Baptistery, although they were not finished until well after his death.

Cosimo was 40 and rich when his father died. But his path to real dominance over Florence was sometimes difficult. The city's ruling Albizzi family feared him and coveted his wealth in equal measure, and had him arrested on the capital charge 'of having tried to raise himself up higher than others'. Cosimo bought first his life and then his freedom with Medici cash and went into exile for a year, only to return and become the de facto ruler of the city, banning the Albizzi for ever. He was so powerful that Pope Pius II described him as 'a king in everything but name'.

As well as Europe's richest and most influential banker, Cosimo was also a scholar, an early humanist and one of history's most eminent art patrons, supporting many of the great artists of his day, including Fra Angelico, Donatello, Ghiberti, Filippo Lippi and Gozzoli. He encouraged Brunelleschi to complete his great dome for Florence's cathedral, and ordered the construction of the Medici Chapel at Santa Croce and the convent of San Marco. He built the Palazzo Medici and established the ascendancy of the Medici family that was to last for 200 years.

Cosimo had a sceptical mind and a mordant sense of humour. As he grew older, he was aware that death was closing in on him. Once, when his wife asked him why he sat so long with his eyes shut, he answered simply, 'To get them used to it'.

His foreboding was accurate. Feverish, frail, sorely afflicted by the family disease of gout, he died on 1 August 1464 at the age of 75. The sad but grateful citizens of Florence named him *Pater Patriae* (father of his country) after his death.

Also on this day

1826: The world's first passenger railway opens from Stockton to Darlington * 1917: French painter Edgar Degas dies * 1944: French sculptor Aristide Maillol dies

28 September

The real King Wenceslas is murdered

929 Good King Wenceslas looked out
On the Feast of Stephen,
When the snow lay round about
Deep and crisp and even.
Brightly shone the moon that night,
Though the frost was cruel,
When a poor man came in sight
Gathering winter fuel.

This merrie carol was written in 1853 by an English preacher named Neale to a 16th-century Swedish tune. Even today we still sing about that good king of Bohemia (who was actually a duke), who was assassinated today on the way to church.

477

Wenceslas's father died young, but the boy was raised a good Christian by his saintly grandmother Ludmila. Unhappily, Wenceslas's mother Drahomira remained a pagan and soon had her mother-in-law murdered so that she could hold power as regent for young Wenceslas.

When Wenceslas came of age he took over the reins of government, instantly showing he had all the right instincts during the wrong time in history. He took vows to remain a virgin, encouraged the spread of Christianity in Bohemia and, much to his soldiers' disgust, made peace with the German Emperor, Henry the Fowler. He infuriated his nobles by his Christian rectitude, particularly his desire to help the poor.

In the year 929 the 22-year-old duke left his capital of Prague to visit his brother Boleslav. After an evening of magnificent entertainment, Wenceslas rose early to attend matins. But as he was about to enter the church, henchmen sent by his brother brutally struck him down.

Boleslav got what he wanted: to become Duke. But Wenceslas got to be the patron saint first of Bohemia and then of Czechoslovakia.

Clemenceau le Tigre *is born*

1841 This should be an occasion worth celebrating for all small-d democrats and small-r republicans, wherever they may be, for on this day was born Georges Clemenceau, a member of both species. Known and feared as *le Tigre* for the Jacobin ferocity he brought to the arena of French politics, Clemenceau defended the Third Republic for almost half a century against all threats, whether launched by the Catholic Church, royalist plotters, bonapartists, the army, anti-dreyfusards, defeatists of every persuasion, or foreign enemies.

Early on, Clemenceau studied medicine. He had strong intellectual interests – he translated John Stuart Mill into French – and a special fascination with ancient Greece, which he called 'a republic of islands'. During the Paris Commune of 1871, he was mayor of Montmartre. Later, as a journalist and newspaper owner, he championed the cause of Captain Dreyfus. His marriage to a young woman from America failed, in part no doubt because she was out of her depth in his surroundings, but mostly because, as Clemenceau himself admitted, his only true love was *la belle France*.

A loner at heart and opposed to the élitist nature of French politics, Clemenceau understood the fragility of the Third Republic's parliamentary system, which produced a seemingly endless stream of governments, one of which he had headed as premier early in the new century. But in his unremitting pursuit of the causes he believed in, he became known as a wrecker of governments, and accordingly his enemies far outnumbered his supporters.

On 17 November 1917, with France reeling from the blows of war and with the voices of defeat and despair growing louder, President Poincaré asked Clemenceau, now 76, to form a government. Winston Churchill was in Paris at the time and described the dire situation: 'The last desperate stake had to be played. France had resolved to unbar the cage and let her tiger loose upon all foes, beyond the trenches or in her midst. With snarls and growls, the ferocious, aged beast of prey went into action.'

Clemenceau's policy was, 'I wage war!' While the French armies confronted the Germans in the field, his government rallied the nation at home and crushed every form of opposition. His end was victory, not surrender, and every means was justified: civil liberties were curtailed, secret dossiers consulted, dissidents arrested.

Victory came in November 1918. Afterwards, Clemenceau presided over the Versailles Peace Conference, but a France at peace no longer needed her great war leader, and his government fell in 1920. He died on 24 November 1929. He is in the pantheon with Lincoln, Churchill, and Roosevelt.

A future French emperor is sentenced to life imprisonment

1840 Prince Louis Bonaparte had always been open about his ambition to reclaim the crown of France for the Bonapartes, particularly for himself.

In 1840 Louis was only 32 and clearly still young and foolish. Inspired by the news that his uncle Napoleon I's body was to be returned from St Helena to France for splendid burial, Louis mounted a force of 56 men and set sail for France from England, where he had been living in exile.

Within a day Louis's force had been routed and he had been captured in an example of history realised as farce. But the French King Louis-Philippe failed to see the joke, and on 28 September Louis was sentenced to life imprisonment.

Yet Louis never gave up. During the five and a half years he spent in jail, he managed to father two sons. He then made his escape disguised as a prison workman. And only twelve years after his conviction he had achieved his impossible dream of becoming the Emperor of France.

Also on this day

48 BC: Roman general Pompey the Great is assassinated * 1573: Italian painter Caravaggio (Michelangelo Merisi) is born * 1864: Karl Marx founds the First International in London * 1895: French scientist Louis Pasteur dies

29 September

The first Habsburg emperor

1273 Today Herzog (Duke) Rudolf von Habsburg was elected Holy Roman Emperor by his fellow German princes, the first Habsburg to hold that office. With the election, his family was well on the way to becoming the most powerful in Europe for most of the next 600 years.

The Habsburg family took its name from their fortress perched high among the crags in what today is Switzerland – the Habichtburg or Hawk Castle. Over the centuries the name was shortened to Habsburg. In the second half of the 13th century Rudolf inherited his father's dukedom. He was an intelligent and enterprising warrior whose family was too weak to be a threat to other German princes. In fact, Rudolf's weakness became his cardinal strength, as his fellow nobles elected him Emperor largely on the grounds that he represented no danger.

Although Rudolf proved to be a fine emperor (he defeated both the powerful Bohemians and the French), he was unable to persuade the electors to grant the imperial throne to his son. But the fact that he had become Emperor set a precedent that helped Habsburgs to gain the crown intermittently until 1438, when they pretty well gained it for good, until Napoleon finally forced Emperor Franz II to resign his title in 1804, bringing the Holy Roman Empire to an end.

The saint who hurried towards death

1582 Visiting the convent at Alba de Tormes that she had founded, St Teresa of Avila found death on this day at the age of 67.

St Teresa was a rather ominous combination of mystic and autocrat. She wrote of her visions and founded an order of Carmelite nuns who ate no meat, slept on piles of straw and remained strictly cloistered. She called them Descalzadas, or bare-foot ones, to contrast their poverty and discipline with the parent order, the Calzadas (shod ones). Eventually she founded seventeen convents. Her passion for austerity, discipline and reform was so great that she was once forced to retire to a convent in Castile for two years and was occasionally investigated by the Inquisition.

Disappointed with the imperfections of life, St Teresa wished to hurry towards death, writing: 'Me muero porque no muero.' (I am dying because I don't die.) After she died, the smell of violets is said to have issued from her tomb, and one of her hands, lopped off by a fervent monk, continued to work miracles.

Also on this day
1758: British admiral Horatio Nelson is born * 1910: American painter Winslow Homer dies

30 September

Richard II becomes the first English king to abdicate

1399 Today before Parliament in Westminster Hall, hard by the cathedral where he had been crowned 22 years earlier, Richard II, King of England, calmly declared his abdication to the benefit of his first cousin Henry Bolingbroke, whose land Richard had previously confiscated. Bolingbroke was now King Henry IV.

At the age of ten Richard had inherited the throne from his grandfather, Edward III, and for the next seven years was content to let his uncle John of Gaunt rule the kingdom while he grew into a tall, blond and handsome young man with a strong interest in culture but little in the normal kingly pursuits of jousting and war.

In the years after he started to rule in his own right, Richard became increasingly selfish and extravagant, while entertaining a number of favourites, first Robert de Vere and later Edmund, Earl of Rutland. As his liaisons became more open, Richard grew increasingly authoritarian, paying scant regard to Parliament, first packing it with his supporters, then dismissing it altogether. In his megalomania he even tried (unsuccessfully) to be elected Holy Roman Emperor.

Among the nobles who resented Richard's spendthrift ways and court favouritism was his cousin Henry Bolingbroke, son of John of Gaunt. At one point Bolingbroke and four confederates forced the King to banish de Vere and thus earned Richard's undying enmity. The King's revenge was not long in coming. In 1398 he exiled Bolingbroke and subsequently seized his property to distribute to his friends.

A year later Richard made the misjudgement of going on an expedition to Ireland, giving Bolingbroke (now, after John of Gaunt's death, the Duke of Lancaster) the opening to invade England as champion of all the dispossessed nobles. On 4 July 1399 Bolingbroke landed at Ravenspur in Yorkshire and soon took control of most of England. Hurrying back from Ireland, Richard found every hand turned against him and was forced to surrender to Bolingbroke's supporters, who incarcerated him in the Tower of London. There he was threatened and demoralised until, fearing for his life, he finally agreed to renounce his throne. On 30 September he abdicated before Parliament, and on 13 October Bolingbroke was crowned King Henry IV.

King Henry imprisoned Richard in Pontefract Castle in Yorkshire, and four months later he was dead, possibly a suicide from starvation but more probably murdered on the orders of the new king.

Richard II was one of four English kings to abdicate; the others were Edward II, James II and Edward VIII.

Birth of a great editor

1884 This should be an important day of observance for writers – especially for novelists – because the great book editor Maxwell Perkins, of Charles Scribner's Sons, was born this day in Windsor, Vermont. When we think of Perkins, the names of F. Scott Fitzgerald, Ernest Hemingway and Thomas Wolfe come to mind. But we forget that there were so many other distinguished writers for whom he was editor: among them, Ring Lardner, Marcia Davenport, Douglas Southall Freeman, John P. Marquand, S.S. Van Dine, Allen Tate, Edmund Wilson, Dawn Powell, Erskine Caldwell, Marjorie Kinnan Rawlings, Alan Paton and James Jones.

What was it his authors thought Perkins did for them? Well, among other things he urged every one of them to read – and reread – *War and Peace*, his favourite book. He was also a good listener and, perhaps because of a reticent manner face-to-face, a remarkable letter-writer.

He was a creature of habit. When the Western writer Will James (*Smoky, Lone Cowboy*) came to New York, Perkins admired his ten-gallon hat. James sent him one, and after that Perkins was rarely seen without some sort of hat on his head, indoors or out.

He always drank a martini or two at lunch, usually at Cherio's on 53rd Street between Fifth and Madison. The drinks were invariably followed by roast breast of guinea hen. How many aspiring authors have dreamed of lunching over martinis and guinea hens and hearing Perkins say: 'Go ahead and write it. We will publish it.' That's what he told Marcia Davenport before she had written a word of her Mozart biography.

After Cherio's it was back to the office. For many years Perkins lived in New Canaan, Connecticut, so his evening procedure was to leave Scribners before five, stop off for 'tea' at the Ritz bar (46th and Madison), and then on to Grand Central, just in time for the 6.02.

With a routine like that, who wouldn't want to be an editor?

Also on this day

1520: The rule of Suleiman the Magnificent in the Ottoman Empire begins * 1791: The first performance of Mozart's *The Magic Flute* takes place in Vienna

1 October

Alexander the Great conquers the Persians at Gaugamela

331 BC Today the man who was perhaps history's greatest general destroyed the Persian Empire in his greatest victory at Gaugamela, in what is now northern Iraq.

Alexander the Great had been taught by his father Philip of Macedon and his tutor Aristotle to hate the Persians, who had been invading and harrying Greece since the time of Xerxes a century and a half before. But Alexander had also developed revolutionary ideas of his own. He was a fervent believer in the superiority of Greek civilisation and thought he had a mission to spread it to the barbarian world.

When Alexander succeeded to the Macedonian throne on his father's assassination, he inherited a kingdom, a superb army and a fledgling plan to invade the great Persian Empire that ruled from Anatolia to the plains of India. In the spring of 334 BC he crossed the Dardanelles with an army of about 50,000 men, including some 7,000 cavalry, determined to conquer. 'Heaven cannot support two suns, nor the earth two masters', he portentously announced.

Within three years Alexander had defeated many of the Persian Emperor Darius III's satraps (governors of his provinces), and Darius attempted to buy him off, promising to cede substantial territory and pay 10,000 talents in gold if Alexander would return to Greece.

When told of the offer, Alexander's most senior general Parminio advised, 'I would accept it were I Alexander', to which the haughty Alexander replied, 'And so truly would I if I were Parminio.'

Forced at last to fight, Darius now massed near the town of Arbela a vast army of perhaps 200,000 that included vicious scythe-chariots and at least fifteen elephants.

Darius picked his ground carefully. Nearby lay the Plain of Gaugamela, perfect terrain for cavalry and chariots. To ensure his victory, the Emperor ordered trees felled and the ground roughly flattened in order to give his superior force a better chance of surrounding the invading Greeks.

When Alexander arrived on the high ground before Gaugamela his generals urged immediate action, but instead he ordered his troops to rest for the night while giving the impression that attack was imminent, thus fooling Darius into keeping his men up all night awaiting the assault. By the next morning the Persians were already exhausted when they went into battle.

Once the battle began, the Persian cavalrymen moved forward to charge, leaving a gap in their line into which Alexander led his own horsemen and drove them directly at Darius. When the Emperor fled, Alexander wheeled to attack the enemy's flank, starting the general disintegration of the Persian army.

There are various estimates of battle casualties, none reliable, but what is certain is that the Persians suffered grievous losses, perhaps 40,000 killed, while only a few hundred of Alexander's Greeks died on the field.

Following the battle Alexander pursued Darius, but before he could catch up with him the Emperor was murdered by one of his own generals. Alexander's victory at Gaugamela gave him control of what to that time was the greatest empire the world had known, but perhaps an even more important result was the spread of Greek values and Alexander's own concept, unique in his era, that the good men of the world, Greek or barbarian, should unite to rule the world for the benefit of mankind.

Henry III – king of England and France, ruler of neither

1207 Today Henry Plantagenet was born at Winchester, first son of John of England and his queen Isabella. Only nine years later King John would be carried off by dysentery and his young son would become Henry III, a weak and vacillating monarch who would reign for 56 years, a period exceeded among English sovereigns only by Queen Victoria (64 years) and George III (60 years).

Although Henry reigned long, he often did not rule. For his first thirteen years as King a council of barons ran the country, led by the venerable knight William Marshal. But even when Henry came of age, powerful barons continued to rule until 1234 when the King was 27.

When Henry finally took charge of the government himself, he ruled capriciously and badly, spending outrageous sums in unsuccessful efforts to reclaim English territories in France and gain the Kingdom of Sicily for his infant son. So unhappy did these expensive failures make his barons that in 1258 they forced on him what are called the Provisions of Oxford that effectively allowed the barons to oversee (and overrule) all of Henry's decisions. Three years later Henry reasserted himself, only to face another baronial uprising under the leadership of the powerful Simon de Montfort in 1264. Montfort easily captured Henry and controlled England for the next fifteen months.

Luckily for Henry, his son Edward, now 26, defeated and killed Montfort at the Battle of Evesham in August 1265. Even then, however, poor Henry had no opportunity to regain personal command, as his son took charge of the government while the King relapsed into senility, dying seven years later.

In all, poor Henry ruled for only 24 of the 56 years of his reign. His accomplishments as monarch were less than nothing, but he did leave one great memorial, Westminster Abbey, which he transformed from the Romanesque church of Edward the Confessor to the Gothic masterpiece we know today.

Also on this day

1066: William the Conqueror lands at Pevensey in Sussex * 1684: French playwright Pierre Corneille dies * 1936: Francisco Franco becomes Head of State in Spain

2 October

Saladin retakes Jerusalem

1187 Today the holy city of Jerusalem fell to the forces of Islam after less than a century of Christian rule.

When European Christians had first captured the city from the infidel during the First Crusade, they had established there a kingdom, but by the close of the 12th century the royal house was in steep decline. When King Baldwin IV died of leprosy, the throne should have passed to his young nephew, but Baldwin's sister Sibylla had other ideas. With her husband Guy de Lusignan she seized the crown for herself and had Guy declared King.

But Guy had neither the intelligence nor the ruthlessness of former Christian rulers, and their Saracen adversary was the formidable and experienced Sultan Saladin, who had already been Commander-in-Chief of the Saracen army for sixteen years.

Born in Mesopotamia (modern Iraq), Saladin was a devout Muslim, totally committed to the idea of jihad against the Christians and the recapture of Jerusalem. In July 1187 he completely routed the Crusader army at Hattin and then marched on the holy city. After only a short siege, it fell to the Muslim host. To the delighted astonishment of the conquered Christians, Saladin and his men treated them with kindness and courtesy rather than the indiscriminate slaughter that followed the Crusaders' capture of the city.

Nonetheless, for Christians in Jerusalem and all over Europe, the fall of the holy city was considered a major catastrophe. To the Saracens, however, the date itself must have confirmed their belief in the divine righteousness of their cause, for it was also on 2 October over half a millennium before that Mohammed had ascended to heaven from that self-same place, Jerusalem.

Jerusalem had been Christian for exactly 88 years, two months and seventeen days.

Birth of the Mahatma

1869 Today at Porbandar, the capital of a small principality in Gujarat in western India, was born one of the greatest men that India has ever produced, Mohandas Gandhi.

Although educated as a lawyer in London, Gandhi became to Western eyes the archetypal Indian. Gnomelike and bespectacled, he was a fervent Hindu dressed in a loincloth who ate no meat. He became the most important person in India's battle for independence from Great Britain and was so greatly admired by his fellow Indians that he was called Mahatma, or great-souled.

Gandhi grew up in a strongly religious Hindu family, whose beliefs included commitment to non-violence and vegetarianism, but despite their religious

485

zeal, Gandhi and his family were equally tolerant of other faiths if sincerely held.

Gandhi virtually invented passive resistance as a political tool and used his moral pre-eminence to great effect both in persuading the British to free India and in quelling the Muslim–Hindu riots that followed the partition (which he opposed) of India and Pakistan. He became famous for his principled fasting, used to put unbearable pressure on both the British and varying factions within India.

Gandhi was, by Western standards, something of a religious mystic. He believed Western medicine was evil since it healed bodies sick from wrong living and considered hospitals as institutions for propagating sin. At the age of 36 he renounced sex, observing the Hindu practice of Brahmacharya (celibacy). He sorely tested his commitment (successfully, by all reports) by sleeping naked in the same bed as young women. He lived in poverty and, some believe, retarded India's ability to escape it by the example he set.

Despite his ascetic lifestyle, Gandhi could occasionally share a joke. Once when asked his opinion of Western civilisation, he responded, 'I think it would be a very good idea.'

On 30 January 1948 a disgruntled fellow Hindu who blamed him for the partition shot Gandhi to death at a prayer meeting in New Delhi. He was 78.

Also on this day

632: The Prophet Mohammed ascends to heaven from Jerusalem * 1968: French artist Marcel Duchamp dies

3 October

St Francis dies at Assisi

1226 Among the rolling hills of Umbria lies a medieval jewel called Assisi, now damaged by earthquake and tacky souvenir shops but nonetheless much as it was three-quarters of a millennium ago when its most famous citizen expired nearby at the monastery of Porziuncola.

When St Francis of Assisi died today at the age of 44, he was already widely recognised as a saint for his personal piety, various miraculous healings he brought about and his founding of the Franciscan order for men and the Poor Clares for women. In spite of his total dedication to God and the Church, he was one of history's more likeable saints, with his love for animals, which he referred to as 'brothers' and 'sisters'.

When Francis was 42 he experienced a dramatic vision. St Bonaventure, leader of the Franciscan order later in the 13th century, describes it: 'As it stood above him, he [Francis] saw that it was a man and yet a Seraph with six wings; his arms were extended and his feet conjoined, and his body was fixed to a cross.' When the seraph vanished, Francis found the wounds of the stigmata on his body. Later he became almost completely blind, probably from an infection he had picked up on an earlier trip to the Middle East.

Francis was a mystic who loved life but hated property, so much so that during his last hours he requested his fellow Franciscans to lay him on the bare ground to die. Knowing that he was *in extremis*, he murmured, 'Welcome, sister death.'

So venerated was he that only two years later he was named a saint, and only 27 years after his death the majestic cathedral in Assisi that was built to honour him was consecrated.

Pierre Bonnard, painter of warmth

1867 Slight, bespectacled, serious and colourless in appearance, Pierre Bonnard reserved his verve, energy and colour for his paintings. These were highly emotional, warm, and often intimate in their examination of a bedroom, a living room or a nude in the bath. 'You can take any liberty with line, with form, with proportions, with colours, in order that the feeling comes through', he said.

Bonnard was born today in Fontenay-aux-Roses a few miles south of Paris. After spending most of his life in Paris, he moved to Cannes in the south of France when he was 58. There he painted glorious sun-drenched landscapes and intense and colourful still lives, joining the tradition of great painters like Cézanne, Matisse and Picasso, who had also been drawn by the Mediterranean sun. He died at his home in Cannes at the age of 79 in 1947.

Also on this day

1656: Myles Standish, leader of the Plymouth Colony (the first permanent settlement in North America), dies * 1896: English artist William Morris dies * 1910: Leading republican Miguel Bombarda is murdered by a maniac, igniting the Portuguese revolution

4 October

The Crimean War begins

1853 Russia's Tsar Nicholas I had contemptuously called Turkey 'the sick man of Europe' and in May had marched into the Danubian principalities (now Romania) that in theory were under joint Russian and Turkish 'protection'.

France, Austria and Great Britain protested loudly, and by September crowds were rioting in Constantinople against the Russian incursion. The tension was palpable, as two corrupt and dying empires, Ottoman Turk and Romanov Russian, eyed each other for the main chance.

Knowing that they had the principal European powers behind them, the Turks enthusiastically declared war on this day in 1853 to begin the Crimean War.

By March of the following year France and Britain had thrown their lot in with the Turks, and eventually even the Kingdom of Sardinia would send a regiment.

The Crimean War dragged on in appalling conditions for almost two and a half years, men dying of war wounds, of cold and most of all from diseases that ravaged all sides. In the end Russia conceded a few trifling border changes and fighting ground to a halt. The war witnessed some legendary if futile heroics such as the Charge of the Light Brigade, and Florence Nightingale became a British heroine for ministering to the wounded during the conflict. But in total some 250,000 men died in the Crimea, one of the most purposeless wars in history.

Tsar Nicholas, the man who had started the war, did not survive to see the end of it, dying on 2 March 1855, some eleven months before the finish. Some historians maintain that he committed suicide in despair over Russia's mounting losses, but it seems more likely that he succumbed to pneumonia, his exhausted body too weak to resist.

Perhaps the sole beneficial result of the Crimean War was the enrichment of the English language regarding apparel. From it came the balaclava helmet, invented to combat the murderous cold and named after the 1854 Battle of Balaclava, the raglan sleeve, originally designed to be worn by the one-armed British commander Field Marshal Raglan, and the cardigan sweater, named for its inventor, British General Sir James Cardigan.

'Thy necessity is yet greater than mine'

1586 Today died Sir Philip Sidney at the age of 31, knight, courtier, poet, soldier, diplomat, scholar, friend and supporter of artists and scientists, a man widely admired in his time not so much for any particular accomplishment but as the quintessence of what an Elizabethan gentleman should be.

Sidney was one of the best-connected young men in England. His grandfather was the Duke of Northumberland, one uncle was the Earl of Warwick and another was Queen Elizabeth's favourite, Robert Dudley, the Earl of Leicester. He was godson to King Philip II of Spain and son-in-law to Sir Francis Walsingham, Queen Elizabeth's Secretary of State.

In spite of these spectacular relations, Sidney failed to get the state appointments he wanted after he had shown poor judgement in an early ambassadorial assignment. Fortunately for posterity, this gave him the time to pursue his literary career and other intellectual interests.

Sidney's chance to serve the Queen came in 1585 when Elizabeth decided to come to the aid of Dutch Protestants in their struggle with Catholic Spain. She sent a small force under the command of Sidney's uncle Leicester, and Sidney was put in charge of a company of cavalry.

By the autumn of 1586 the rebellious Dutch and their English allies were besieging the town of Zutphen, trying to prevent the Spanish resupplying the small garrison within. Suddenly an enemy supply train was spotted. Sidney was about to lead his cavalry into attack when he noticed that one of his men had been caught without full armour. The gallant commander threw across his own thigh piece and then thundered off into the assault.

Three times Sidney charged the enemy, but on his last attack a musket ball smashed into his leg just above the knee, shattering the bone. Seriously wounded, he managed to retain his mount and escape from the field of battle to a nearby field filled with English casualties. As he lay injured, he saw a common soldier stretched out near him, clearly on the point of death. In a moment of conspicuous gallantry, Sidney handed the soldier his own cup of water, saying, 'Thy necessity is yet greater than mine.'

Sidney's men then carried their stricken leader to nearby Arnhem, his wound already showing signs of infection. Eleven days later, on 4 October, he died. Subsequently he was given a state funeral in St Paul's Cathedral in London, the last to be so honoured until Nelson over two centuries later.

Pope Gregory launches his new calendar

1582 One of Julius Caesar's most enduring memorials was the calendar that he introduced to the Western world in 46 BC. In his honour it was called the Julian calendar. But over 1,600 years later, in 1582, another Italian, Ugo Buoncompagni, decided to modify Caesar's legacy and insert his own name into history.

Ugo was in fact Pope, having taken the name of Gregory XIII. He knew that the trouble with the Julian calendar was the reckoning that a year lasts 365 days and six hours, when in fact it is only 365 days, five hours, 49 minutes and 46 seconds. By 1582 this discrepancy, cumulated for over 16 centuries, had put the world more than a week out of whack.

On 4 October 1582 Gregory instituted his new (or Gregorian) calendar so that the following day was 15 October. Julius Caesar had already introduced the concept of a leap year every four years, but Gregory's new calendar dictated that century years, even though they are always divisible by four, are not leap years, with the exception of those that can be divided by 400, which explains why 2000 was a leap year while 1900 was not. Finally, he ordered that the year throughout Christendom would always begin on 1 January.

Within a year of the introduction of his new calendar, the Italian states, Spain, Portugal and the German Catholic states adopted it, but not everyone was so hasty. Great Britain retained the Julian calendar until 1752, and Greece made the change only in 1923.

The birth of Belgium

1830 Belgium became an independent country today, which was something of a geopolitical wonder, because, unlike the other emerging nations of the day such as Poland and Greece, its inhabitants spoke three different and mutually incomprehensible languages, French, Flemish and German.

For centuries Belgium had suffered from ever-changing foreign domination. Over two millennia ago Germanic and Celtic tribes fought each other for control until the Romans conquered them in the first century BC. When Rome faded, the French Merovingian and then Carolingian kings ruled the land until separate principalities started to emerge. Then, in the 14th century, Philip II of Burgundy gained control of Flanders, and subsequently the country passed to the Habsburgs when Philip's granddaughter married Holy Roman Emperor Maximilian I. Eventually the Habsburgs of Spain took over, but they later ceded the country to their Austrian cousins. After a brief rule by Napoleon's France at the turn of the 19th century, the House of Orange from the Netherlands took command.

But the Netherlands' William I was a firm believer in monarchical power as well as a strong Protestant. By 1830 Belgium was ripe for revolt, as all of Europe yearned for more democracy, and the country's Catholics, the majority of the population, resented William's attempts to impose Protestantism.

Finally in 1830 revolutions broke out across Europe, in Poland, Greece, some German principalities and France, where Charles X was toppled. Soon the Belgians had joined the trend, and in October they created their own provisional government that on this day declared the country's independence.

Although King William started gearing up for war, the European great powers warned him off, and Belgium finally won full international recognition as an independent nation on 20 January 1831. So the modern Belgium that we know today came into existence.

Also on this day
1669: Dutch painter Rembrandt van Rijn dies in Amsterdam * 1720: Italian artist Giambattista Piranesi is born * 1814: French painter Jean François Millet is born

5 October

Napoleon gives the rabble a whiff of grape

1795 It was 13 Vendémiaire, An IV, according to the French republican calendar. Both Louis XVI and Robespierre had already been fed to the guillotine, but hard-eyed monarchists and fanatical revolutionaries still roamed the streets of Paris. Now royalist agitators, bizarrely backed by their former enemies on the hard left, were marching at the head of a mob of 30,000 armed and excited protesters. Their goal: the Tuileries, where the Convention was meeting. The government must fall, no matter who was there to pick up the pieces.

In charge of security was vicomte Paul Barras, a brawny provincial nobleman who had helped bring about the executions of both Louis XVI and Robespierre. As commander of the Army of the Interior and the police, he was one of the most powerful men in the country. He had recently begun a new affair with a tempting 32-year-old widow from Martinique named Joséphine de Beauharnais.

Realising that only military force could quell the mob, Barras called on a young unemployed brigadier general named Napoleon Bonaparte and put him in charge of the Convention's defences. Bonaparte instantly recognised the need for artillery and ordered Major Joachim Murat, whom he now met for the first time, to commandeer 40 cannon and place them at key points around the Tuileries.

In mid-afternoon the excited rabble approached. Bonaparte held fire until the crowd reached point-blank range, then commented contemptuously, 'We'll give them a whiff of grape.' The cannon spat out murderous grapeshot, instantly cutting down over 200 and wounding twice as many more. The mob fled in panic, and the government was saved.

In an uncanny way, the lives of many of the principal players from 13 Vendémiaire would be intertwined in the years to come. A year later Bonaparte married Joséphine de Beauharnais, whom he had met at Barras's house. Barras went on to even greater power in the government but was precipitously driven from office and eventually exiled from France by Bonaparte, the general he had drafted. Murat became one of Bonaparte's most successful marshals, ultimately becoming the King of Naples. And of course in his *coup d'état* of November 1799 Bonaparte also destroyed the republican government that he had so well protected.

Grigory Potemkin – larger than life

1791 Today died the most influential minister in Russia's history, Prince Grigory Potemkin, the manic and sybaritic genius who was the lover and possibly the husband of Catherine the Great.

Potemkin was larger than life both literally and figuratively. He stood well over six feet tall and, after his more athletic youth was past, was gigantic in girth as well. He was also endowed with a mountainous flow of energy, with ambition to match. Given incomprehensible sums by the Empress – some say over 9 million roubles at a time when a field marshal earned about 1,000 roubles a year – he spent all of this and more, making no distinction between his own almost unlimited funds and those of the government.

Potemkin helped Catherine greatly to enlarge her empire, adding Lithuania, Belorussia and the Ukraine through conquest and treaty. He was also responsible for Russia's take-over of the Crimea from Turkey, but in this project he failed in his even more ambitious goal of restoring the Byzantine Empire under one of Catherine's grandsons. He also built innumerable splendid palaces for himself and lived in a more regal fashion than any monarch.

Born in a time when Russia boasted only about 20 million inhabitants, of whom almost half were serfs, Potemkin came from a family of minor nobility. At sixteen he joined the horseguards in Moscow and played a minor role in Catherine's *coup d'état* seven years later. But his participation gave the voracious Empress the chance to notice the then handsome soldier ten years her junior, and he was rewarded with a small estate. For the next twelve years he served Catherine in various ways and was finally taken on as the Empress's official lover. The affair lasted for two years, during which time he and Catherine may have been secretly married. The relationship was too stormy to last – both he and Catherine probably had other lovers during the affair – but Potemkin probably continued intermittently to sleep with Catherine for the rest of his life.

Potemkin was an insatiable seducer of women, with an endless string of mistresses, including three of his own nieces. He was reputed to be so robustly endowed that Catherine ordered a mould taken of his powerful appendage and cast a copy in porcelain.

Also on this day

1889: The Moulin Rouge opens in Paris * 1910: Portugal is proclaimed a republic as King Manuel II is driven from the country

6 October

The execution of the man who wrote the English Bible

1536 William Tyndale was the sort of religious fanatic whom religious fanatics hate. Ordained a Catholic priest, he joined the faculty at Cambridge University and there was converted to the idea that the Bible rather than the Church hierarchy should be the authority for religious doctrine. He also became committed to providing a Bible that was accessible to all worshippers. His life's work became the translation of the Bible into English.

Tyndale completed his version of the New Testament in 1525, and a decade later 50,000 copies had been printed, the first English text of the New Testament to be published.

But Tyndale's views were too hot for England to hold. Another fanatic, Sir Thomas More, condemned his religious beliefs, his criticism of divorce drew the wrath of King Henry VIII, and Henry's Chief Minister Thomas Wolsey tried to have him arrested even after he had fled England for Germany.

Tyndale eventually made the tragic error of trying to hide in Antwerp, then part of the Spanish Netherlands. There the greatest fanatics of them all, the administrators of the Spanish Inquisition, condemned him to a heretic's death.

On this day Tyndale was brought forth from his cell and led to the *quemadero*, the burning place. As he was roped to the stake he is reported to have prayed, 'Lord, open the eyes of the King of England.' Then he was strangled by the hooded executioner and his body burned.

It is nice to think that William Tyndale may be looking down on us, for if he is, he has seen the triumph of his efforts. The men who persecuted him and the Inquisition have long since vanished, but his translation still forms the basis for the King James Version of the Bible.

Also on this day

AD 105: At Arausio (now Orange in Provence) the German Cimbri and Teutoni tribes rout the Roman armies of Caepio and Mallius, killing 80,000 * 1887: Swiss architect Charles-Edouard Le Corbusier is born, La Chaux-de-Fonds * 1891: Irish nationalist Charles Stewart Parnell dies at Brighton * 1892: Alfred, Lord Tennyson dies

7 October

Christian Europe defeats the Turk at Lepanto

1571 It is fitting that this day was a Sunday, the Lord's Day, when the Christian forces of Spain, Venice and the papacy combined to destroy the Turkish fleet at the Battle of Lepanto, ending for ever the danger of Islamic conquest of Europe.

The two fleets met at dawn off the west coast of Greece. The huge European armada with 316 vessels outnumbered the Turks, who had only 245 ships. But in the 16th century naval battles were won primarily using heavily manned rowing galleys carrying soldiers who fired on enemy ships and then boarded them, and the Turks had a critical advantage in number of galleys.

In command of the Christian flotilla was Don Juan of Austria, the dashing illegitimate son of retired Holy Roman Emperor Charles V and thus half-brother to Spain's King Philip II. Although only 24, he had already proved himself against Barbary pirates. As the fleets approached each other he ordered the attack. His captains urged caution, to which Don Juan replied, 'Gentlemen, it is no longer the hour for advising, but for fighting.'

The battle lasted four hours and was decided not by the galleys and soldiers but by the Christians' sailing ships – galleons, frigates and galleasses heavily armed with cannon. The Europeans' superior firepower proved decisive, slaughtering enemy troops and sinking their galleys before they could bring their soldiers into play. When his galley was overrun, the Turkish commander dropped to his knees, offering a huge ransom in return for his life. Disdainfully a Spanish soldier lopped off his head as he knelt, then displayed it on the end of his pike.

This was the first engagement in naval history where sailing ships supplanted galleys as the primary weapon. When the battle ended, over 8,000 Christians had perished, but almost 30,000 Turks had been cut down or drowned. In addition, about 15,000 Christian galley slaves had been set free from the Turkish vessels.

The Battle of Lepanto marked the end of Turkish domination of the seas and destroyed the myth of Turkish invincibility that had been created earlier in the century during the reign of Suleiman the Magnificent. It was also a decisive experience for a 24-year-old Spanish soldier wounded in the left hand by a Turkish bullet. He abandoned his military career, perhaps believing that a pen in his good right hand would prove mightier than the sword. His name was Miguel de Cervantes.

Also on this day

1769: Captain Cook discovers New Zealand * 1777: American revolutionaries defeat the British at the Second Battle of Saratoga * 1849: American writer Edgar Allan Poe dies of drink

8 October

Backwoods hero – Corporal Alvin York

1918 Of all the American heroics of the First World War, none are more celebrated than those of Corporal Alvin York, a backwoodsman from the Tennessee mountains who single-handedly put 35 German machine guns out of action, killed over twenty machine gunners and captured 132 enemy soldiers in a single morning.

York's platoon was part of a 328th Infantry Battalion attack against heavily fortified enemy positions in the Argonne forest. At dawn on 8 October the assault began, but the Americans were almost immediately riddled with machine gun fire, pinned down and seemingly helpless. German machine guns continuously raked their position, and American casualties were heavy. In desperation, seventeen men including York's squad determined to work around behind the enemy through a concealed gully.

Miraculously they succeeded in getting behind the Germans, only to have the enemy machine gunners turn around to face them, immediately killing six of them.

By now York was the most senior man left. Here is his own account of what happened next. 'As soon as the machine guns opened fire on me, I began to exchange shots with them. There were over thirty of them in continuous action, and all I could do was touch the Germans off as fast as I could. I was sharpshooting. I don't think I missed a shot ... In order to sight me or to swing their guns on me, the Germans had to show their heads above the trench, and every time I saw a head I just touched it off ... Suddenly a German officer and five men jumped out of the trench and charged me with fixed bayonets. I changed to the old automatic and just touched them off too. I touched off the

494

sixth man first, then the fifth, then the fourth, then the third, and so on. I wanted them to keep coming. I didn't want the rear ones to see me touching off the front ones, I was afraid they would drop down and pump a volley into me.'

Terrorised and bewildered by this American killing machine, the remainder of the Germans surrendered to York, who marched them to the rear holding a pistol to the senior German officer's head.

For his spectacular heroism York was promoted to sergeant and received the Medal of Honor directly from General Pershing, the commander of all American forces in Europe.

Napoleon's last trip to Paris

1840 On this day the Emperor Napoleon entered Paris for the first time since his famous Hundred Days 25 years before, but this time he came in a coffin.

In an attempt to curry popular favour, French King Louis-Philippe had laboured for seven long years to gain British agreement to allow the return of Napoleon's body to France. It was only now, some nineteen years after the Emperor's death, that the corpse was brought back from St Helena aboard a frigate with the glorious name of *La Belle Poule*. Accompanying the coffin was Louis-Philippe's son, the Prince of Joinville.

When the Prince and the defunct Emperor arrived in Paris, the coffin was opened for two minutes. All those present testified that, like some medieval saint, Napoleon had remained in a state of perfect preservation.

Despite his return, however, Napoleon had to wait another 21 years to reach his final resting place, for it took until 1861 for Visconti's great tomb in the Invalides to be completed.

Also on this day
1085: St Mark's Cathedral in Venice is consecrated * 1754: British novelist Henry Fielding dies in Lisbon * 1871: The Great Chicago Fire starts in Patrick O'Leary's cowshed, killing over 250 people and making 95,000 homeless

9 October

The man who wrote Don Quixote

1547 Today is the first trace we find of Miguel de Cervantes – the day of his baptism in the small town of Alcalá de Henares about 20 miles from Madrid. We do not know the day of his birth, but a good bet is 29 September, the feast day of San Miguel. We think we know the date he died (23 April 1616), although it is disputed. We do not know where he was buried. That, like the details of much of his life, has vanished in the haze of passing centuries.

No portrait of Cervantes exists, but we have one verbal description, written by Cervantes himself when he was in his mid-60s: 'of aquiline countenance, with dark brown hair, smooth clear brow, merry eyes and hooked but well-proportioned nose; his beard is silver though it was gold not 20 years ago; large moustache, small mouth with teeth neither big nor little, since he has only six of them and they are in bad condition and worse positioned, for they do not correspond to each other; the body between two extremes, neither tall nor short; a bright complexion, more pale than dark, somewhat heavy in the shoulder and not very light of foot'.

Cervantes led an unexpectedly exciting life for a man most of us know only as the author of the world's first novel, *Don Quixote*.

He was probably raised in Madrid, the son of an itinerant barber who doubled as an apothecary-surgeon. Before he took up writing he was a courageous soldier, at 24 fighting against the Turks at the great naval battle of Lepanto, where he received three gunshot wounds, the last of which crippled his left hand for life. Four years later he was captured by Barbary pirates, who held him as a slave in Algiers for five years, waiting for his family to produce 500 gold escudos for his ransom.

At 40 he was living in Seville where he was temporarily excommunicated for having stolen supplies from the cathedral, and he was later twice imprisoned for shady dealings at his job as ship's purveyor for the Spanish crown.

Cervantes almost certainly wrote *Don Quixote* for money. Part I was published when he was already 58, and Part II did not appear until nine years later, just two years before his death. Today, almost 400 years later, the world still considers *Don Quixote* the greatest novel ever written in Spanish, and the Spanish of course think it the greatest novel in any language.

The Lion-Heart heads for home

1192 On this day King Richard the Lion-Heart sailed for home from Acre on the Palestinian coast, after sixteen months of bloody but profitless fighting during the Third Crusade.

In the beginning the Crusade had been full of promise. Pope Gregory VIII had called for action, offering absolution to the warriors of Christianity who would fight for the reconquest of Jerusalem, fallen to the Saracens of Saladin at the end of 1187. Europe's most powerful monarchs agreed to join forces, and preparations were soon under way. From France came the scheming but intelligent Philip Augustus, from Germany the Emperor Frederick Barbarossa, now almost 70, from England the redoubtable Richard the Lion-Heart and from Sicily Richard's brother-in-law, King William the Good. A massive force was gathered to crush the Saracens and return the Holy Land to the control of Christians.

But all had not gone according to plan. William of Sicily, still only 35, died even before setting off, and Barbarossa was tragically drowned crossing a river in Turkey. Richard and Philip succeeded in conquering Acre, but the victory was sullied by Richard's brutal slaughter of several thousand Saracen prisoners, men, women and children.

After Acre, on the excuse of illness, Philip returned to France to plot with Richard's brother John in dismembering Richard's French possessions. Richard continued southward towards Jaffa and finally met Saladin in battle at Arsuf in 1191, where his heavy cavalry drove Saladin's lighter horse into panicky retreat. Then the English King took Daron and led his army to within twelve miles of Jerusalem.

But there Richard had to stop. His force was so depleted that he had little chance of taking the city, and even if he had succeeded, he could not have garrisoned it sufficiently to keep it.

Reluctantly, Richard turned back for Acre. On 2 September 1192 he and Saladin finally agreed a five-year peace treaty that gave Christian pilgrims free access to Jerusalem. But the only territory now in Christian hands was a thin strip of coastline 100 miles long from Acre to Jaffa. Saladin controlled everything else.

So, a month after peace had been agreed, Richard boarded ship. The Third Crusade was over, with little achieved and much lost. Richard found only further disaster on his route home, captured and held for ransom in Austria.

Also on this day

1000: Scandinavian explorer Leif Erikson lands in North America * 1779: The first Luddite riots, against the introduction of machinery for spinning cotton, begin in Manchester * 1835: French composer Charles Camille Saint-Saëns is born in Paris

10 October

Charles the Hammer earns his name

732 Charles Martel – Charles the Hammer – earned his nickname today.

In the 8th century the most aggressive and successful military power in the world was militant Islam, intent on endless conquest for the glory of Allah. In 711 the Moors crossed from North Africa into Spain to begin an occupation of almost eight centuries. Twenty years later they were again on the march, this time into France.

Abd ar-Rahman, the Moorish governor of Spain, led his invading cavalry into Aquitaine in south-west France. There he easily defeated Aquitaine's Duke Eudes and headed towards Tours in search of the city's reputed vast wealth.

Desperate, Eudes fled to Paris to beg for support from his one-time enemy, Charles, the de facto ruler of the Franks. Charles welcomed him with caution and agreed to help only on the condition that Eudes swear fealty to him, something that the distraught duke was only too happy to do.

Assembling an army perhaps 30,000 strong, Charles and Eudes headed for Tours. Somewhere between Tours and Poitiers they met the forces of Abd ar-Rahman, numbering about 80,000 mounted men.

For seven long days the two armies nervously watched each other. The Moors trotted on their horses, magnificent with lances and scimitars but without body armour, depending on the will of Allah and their own ferocious courage to defeat their enemy. The Franks were primarily on foot but lightly armoured and equipped with axes, swords and javelins.

At last Abd ar-Rahman gave the order to charge, and several thousand horsemen swept down on the waiting Franks. But Charles had formed his men into impenetrable squares that, in charge after charge, the Muslim cavalry could not break. The Moors knew no other battle tactic than the wild cavalry charge, and their casualties began to mount under the rain of javelins and thrown axes.

Suddenly a cry went up among the Moors. Their treasure – all they had plundered since leaving Spain – was under attack. They would lose it all. Several squadrons of cavalry turned to protect their goods. They soon discovered that the cry was false, but by then it was too late. The Franks had cut down Abd ar-Rahman, and other Muslim troops were turning from the field. The battle was effectively over.

The remaining Moorish horsemen fled back towards Spain, and the Muslim threat to western Europe was over until Suleiman the Magnificent marched into Austria in the 16th century.

Ever after this battle Charles was known as Charles Martel for his hammering defence that broke the Moorish onslaught. Two years later Eudes died, allowing Charles to march into Bordeaux to take direct control. By 739 he had also taken possession of Burgundy, substantially enlarging his Frankish domain. Charles died in 741 at the age of 53, leaving behind a virtual kingdom that was to be enlarged into an empire 50 years later by his grandson, Charlemagne.

Also on this day

1469: Italian painter Fra Filippo Lippi dies in Spoleto * 1684: French painter Jean-Antoine Watteau is born in Valenciennes * 1813: Italian opera composer Giuseppe Verdi is born in Le Roncole * 1911: China's Imperial Dynasty abdicates, and Sun Yat-Sen proclaims a republic

11 October

A militant Protestant falls in battle

1531 When one thinks of militant Christians, the first name that comes to mind may be John Calvin, that unforgiving founder of Puritanism, or perhaps even more readily that of Ignatius Loyola, a former soldier who structured his Jesuit order on military lines. But perhaps the most militant of all was Huldrych

Zwingli, a 16th-century military chaplain and Church reformer who largely established the basis for Protestantism in Switzerland.

Born in St Gall, Zwingli became a priest at the age of twenty, and before he was 30 was acting as chaplain to a group of Swiss mercenary soldiers. He fought on the losing side at the Battle of Marignano when the Swiss were hired to defend Milan against the troops of France's François I.

In between wars Zwingli fought for 'protestantisation' of the Catholic Church. He had images removed from churches and destroyed organs. Among his most important teachings were that Christ alone, not the Pope, was at the head of the Church, that there is no biblical foundation for the idea of purgatory, and that dead saints cannot intercede for the living. He also strongly disputed the idea of transubstantiation and made an enemy of Martin Luther by his stand. When he was 36 Zwingli's preaching helped incite revolts against religious fasting and priestly celibacy, and two years later in 1524 he set the style for clerical marriage by contracting his own.

In 1531, when he was 47, Zwingli once more marched out as chaplain with his Swiss soldiers, this time defending the Protestant community of Zurich from five Catholic Swiss cantons that wanted to stop the spread of Protestantism, if necessary by force of arms. On the border between the cantons of Zurich and Zug, at the monastery of Kappel, the two armies clashed, and Zwingli was seriously wounded during the mêlée. On the point of death, he professed his faith with the stoic remark, 'What does it matter? They can kill the body but they cannot kill the soul.' A few minutes later he was dead. Today an engraved boulder sits on the spot where he was cut down.

The Pope honours Henry VIII

1521 In retrospect, this is one of the greatest days of historical irony, for on this date King Henry VIII of England at last received from the Medici Pope Leo X the most coveted title of Defender of the Faith.

In January Leo had finally excommunicated Martin Luther for his sacrilegious Protestantism. Henry fully approved the punishment and later that year published his own book entitled *Assertio septem sacramentorum adversus Martinum Lutherum* in which he bitterly attacked the heretic. Henry's reward for this display of Catholic piety was the coveted new title.

Only two months after proclaiming Henry Defender of the Faith, Leo died suddenly in Rome just ten days before his 46th birthday. Fortunately for him he could not see into the future.

Twelve years later Leo's cousin, Clement VII, wore the papal crown. Largely in deference to Holy Roman Emperor Charles V, Clement steadfastly refused to grant Henry an annulment of his marriage to Catherine of Aragon, who was Charles's aunt. Henry's only recourse was rupture with Rome, and in 1534 at Henry's behest the English Parliament made Henry head of the English Church, severing ties with the papacy for ever.

Since Henry's time two British sovereigns have been Catholic but all the rest have been Protestant. Nonetheless, the title of Defender of the Faith has remained hereditary to the British crown and is still proudly held today by Queen Elizabeth II, although her heir Charles has said with great political correctness that he would wish to be defender of all the faiths.

Also on this day

1689: Russian Tsar Peter the Great takes personal control of the government, to which he will dictate for the next 35 years * 1899: The Boer War begins

12 October

Edith Cavell before the firing squad

1915 At 7.00 this morning, in the city of Brussels, an English nurse was marched before a German firing squad. Before stepping to the execution post she pinned her skirt tightly around her legs to prevent it from flaring up on the impact of the bullets. Moments later four shots were fired, and she died instantly.

When the German army entered Brussels in August 1914, Edith Cavell, 49 years old, was working as a matron at a Red Cross hospital. The Germans offered her and other nurses safe conduct to Holland, but she chose instead to remain tending the Allied soldiers wounded in the opening days of the First World War. She was arrested in August 1915 and taken before a German military court, where she admitted the charges brought against her: that she had helped some 200 British and French POWs and Belgian civilians to escape to neutral Holland.

The night before her execution, she told a British chaplain that 'Patriotism is not enough. I must have no hatred or bitterness towards anyone.' Her words became famous, but public reaction in Great Britain and the United States was not so Christian in attitude. A celebrated war poster soon appeared showing a nurse's corpse on the ground and standing above it a German officer wearing a spiked helmet, a smoking pistol in his hand. The poster's legend was 'Gott Mit Uns' (God with us).

At war's end her body was brought home to England. In May 1919 her memorial service at Westminster Cathedral was thronged, the streets around lined with mourners. A statue was erected just north of Trafalgar Square.

There was also a memorial to Cavell in Paris, but on 23 July 1940, after an early morning's tour of the vanquished capital, Adolf Hitler, with a veteran's bitter memories of the last war, ordered the monument torn down, along with other offensive reminders of French victory.

Also on this day

1492: Columbus sights his first land in discovering the New World, calling it San

Salvador * 1822: Brazil gains independence from Portugal * 1870: Confederate general Robert E. Lee dies in Lexington, Virginia

13 October

Emperor Claudius is poisoned by his wife

AD 54 The Roman Emperor Claudius was murdered today by his wife Agrippina. Some men never learn.

Claudius had become Emperor almost by accident when he was 40. His nephew, the schizophrenic Caligula, had been assassinated by his own officers, and a member of the guard had found Claudius cowering behind a curtain in the imperial palace. Taken by force to the army barracks, he was proclaimed Emperor, a decision the Roman Senate was in no position to dispute.

Tall and white haired, Claudius was considered little more than a clumsy clown by his family. He stammered, dribbled and occasionally suffered fits of uncontrollable laughter. (Modern science suggests that he had cerebral palsy.) He spent his early years writing history under the tutelage of the great Roman historian Livy. And he married.

Claudius divorced his first wife Plautia Urgulanilla on the grounds of scandalous behaviour and suspicion of murder. He divorced his second wife for what the historian Suetonius calls 'minor offences'. Then he married wife number three, the infamous Messalina, whose adulteries ranged from minor actors to prominent senators. Worse, to destroy her enemies and rivals, she persuaded her husband that they were plotting against him. Between her enemies and Claudius's own, some 35 senators, over 300 knights and Claudius's own niece were put to death. Another victim was Appius Silanus, who had recently married Messalina's mother but unwisely rejected the advances of his lascivious new stepdaughter. Finally, however, Messalina went too far; although already wed to the Emperor, she openly married one of her lovers. Claudius had both of them killed. Messalina was still only 26.

But hope sprang eternal within Claudius's breast. Within a year of disposing of Messalina, he married for the fourth time. His new wife was his niece Agrippina, who had been accused of poisoning her husband only a few months before. She persuaded the Emperor to give her son (the future Emperor Nero) preference over his own son Britannicus, but she soon became apprehensive, on hearing Claudius's claim that it was 'his destiny to suffer and finally to punish the infamy of his wives'.

Claudius unwisely kept an official poisoner named Locusta on the palace payroll. On the evening of 12 October, Agrippina bribed Locusta to spice some fresh mushrooms with a delicate poison and then enlisted the aid of Halotus, the official taster, to offer them up to the Emperor. When Claudius was seized with diarrhoea but showed no signs of dying, Agrippina brought on Xenophon, the court doctor. Most sources agree that Xenophon administered the fatal dose, but there are different versions of his method. One historian says that, on the pretence of making Claudius vomit, he put a feather that he had poisoned down the Emperor's throat. Another version says the good doctor added poison to an enema.

In the small hours of the following morning Claudius died in agony at the age of 63, after fourteen years as the most powerful man in the world.

Agrippina succeeded in her aim of securing the throne for her son Nero, who deified the dead Claudius, whimsically claiming that mushrooms must be the food of the gods, since Claudius had become a god by eating them. A year later Agrippina struck again, this time poisoning Claudius's son Britannicus, leaving Nero without a rival. Four years after that, Nero rewarded his loving mother by having her put to death.

A usurper is crowned King

1399 Today Henry Bolingbroke, so called because of his birth in Bolingbroke Castle, was crowned in Westminster Abbey to become King Henry IV.

Henry was the son of John of Gaunt and grandson of King Edward III, but in spite of his royal antecedents he had not inherited the throne – he had usurped it from his cousin, the egotistical and feckless Richard II.

In 1398 Henry became embroiled in a bitter quarrel with the Duke of Norfolk and denounced him to King Richard as a traitor. When Henry and Norfolk were on the point of fighting a duel, Richard intervened and exiled both of them for five years, promising to protect their estates until their return. But in February 1399 Richard confiscated Henry's inheritance while he was still abroad. Bent on revenge, Henry wasted no time in collecting an army and invaded England in July, just when Richard was on a punitive operation in Ireland. Richard hurried back to meet the invader, but soon found that most of his support had melted away. By August he had surrendered and then was forced to abdicate on the last day of September. Henry then confined the ex-king to a cell in Pontefract Castle in Yorkshire (where eventually he was murdered).

Henry has three unrelated distinctions. He was the first king since the Conquest to have been born on English soil of an English father and English mother. He was England's first king from the Lancaster branch of the royal family, so his usurpation of the crown was a root cause of the Wars of the Roses that started under the reign of his grandson, Henry VI. He also passed the law that permitted the Church to burn heretics and sanctioned the first such execution in English history.

As he grew older Henry began to suffer from some disfiguring disease, which his contemporaries thought to be leprosy but which may well have been syphilis. Too incapacitated to rule, he finally died on 20 March 1413 at the age of 47.

1775: The United States Navy is founded * 1792: President George Washington lays the cornerstone of the White House * 1815: King and Marshal Joachim Murat is executed trying to regain his Kingdom of Naples

14 October

Rommel the Desert Fox is forced to commit suicide

1944 In the old photographs we see him in a weathered leather field coat, sporting goggles on the brim of his battered officer's cap. Nazi Germany's most coveted medal, the Iron Cross, hangs from a ribbon around his neck. He is Field Marshal Erwin Rommel, who today was forced to take his own life.

Rommel was born in 1891, son of a schoolmaster. He chose a military career, and at the age of twenty, fresh out of Cadet School, he joined an infantry regiment. After war broke out in 1914 his regiment fought in France, Romania and Italy. He won his first Iron Cross in September 1914 when he was wounded in France, and another in 1915, but his highest medal of the war was for action in Italy, where he won the Pour le Mérite, then the highest award for gallantry in action given by the Imperial German Army.

After the First World War Rommel remained in the military, just another infantry officer in a defeated army. It was only in 1933 with the rise of Adolf Hitler that his star began to rise. In 1937 he published *Infanterie greift an* (*The Infantry Attacks*), a military textbook based on his combat experiences, and came to be considered a superior military thinker. Hitler was impressed and made him commander of his bodyguard.

At the outbreak of the Second World War Rommel, by this time a major general, was commander of Hitler's field headquarters during the invasion of Poland. From this special vantage point in the fast-moving campaign, where he accompanied Hitler both in the field and at conferences, he grasped the potential that tanks offered to the determined attacker. Even though his experience was in infantry, he now asked for an armoured division, and, with Hitler's intervention smoothing the way, received command of the 7th Panzer Division in time for the invasion of the Low Countries and France.

Once France had been subdued, Rommel was sent to North Africa as commander of the Afrika Korps. There he gained fame for his brilliant tank attacks across wide expanses of open desert, earning the nickname used by both Germans and the Allies, the Desert Fox.

Rommel used speed and surprise to outwit the British, driving them 600 miles back into Libya. He was also a master of deception, once having brooms and rags tied to the back of his tanks to raise clouds of desert dust, making the enemy believe he had superior numbers. In June 1942 he reached his greatest success with the capture of Tobruk.

In October of 1942, however, superior British numbers and firepower – plus the careful planning of the British Field Marshal Montgomery – defeated the German force at El Alamein. On learning of the Afrika Korps' imminent defeat, Hitler ordered its commander to hold to the last man, but, knowing the cause was hopeless, Rommel ignored the order. The British captured 230,000 Germans and Italians.

Returning to Germany, Rommel was still a national hero. His next assignment was to defend Normandy against Allied invasion. He wanted a mobile defence with 1,500 tanks positioned behind the beaches, but he was overruled in this disposition, and the result was just what he feared: the landings weren't met with sufficient German strength to stop the attackers on the shore and drive them back into the sea.

On 4 June 1944 he left on leave to celebrate his wife Lucie's 50th birthday. Two days later the Allies landed in Normandy. Hurrying back to the front, he was wounded when an RAF fighter strafed his staff car. The injured field marshal was sent home to convalesce.

The following month Colonel Claus von Stauffenberg led a group of senior army officers in an attempt to assassinate Hitler, but the bomb he placed in Hitler's headquarters succeeded only in wounding the dictator. Hitler's vengeance was swift, terrible and all-encompassing.

The Gestapo suspected that Rommel might have been involved in the plot, but although he had been approached, he had refused to participate. But any connection to the bungled assassination was enough for Hitler, who ordered Rommel's death.

The only obstacle to a quick trial and execution was Rommel's stature as one of Germany's most heroic field marshals. Therefore two army generals were dispatched to call on him at his home, there to offer him a grim choice: either to commit suicide or to be disgraced in a public trial and executed, leaving his family at the mercy of the Gestapo.

On this day the generals arrived at his home in Herrlingen, near Ulm. To save his wife and son Rommel left with the generals and took poison in the staff car. The public was told he had died of war wounds, and the government arranged a solemn state funeral, which Hitler refused to attend. Goebbels, Göring and other top Nazi leaders, all of whom knew that Rommel had in effect been executed, sent odious notes of condolence to his widow. Hitler's, dated 16 October 1944, read: 'Accept my sincerest sympathy for the heavy loss you have suffered with the death of your husband. The name of Field Marshal Rommel will be forever linked with the heroic battles in North Africa.'

How William the Conqueror won at Hastings

1066 In January King Edward the Confessor died childless, and the throne of England was up for grabs. First came Edward's brother-in-law, Harold Godwine, who asserted that Edward had named him on his deathbed. But the English barons had no sooner agreed to Harold's suzerainty than his exiled brother Tostig, supported by the Norwegian King Harald Hardrada, claimed the crown. And of course there was a third claimant, a certain Norman duke called Guillaume le Bâtard because of his illegitimate birth. Guillaume, or William, swore that Edward the Confessor had promised the throne to him.

The first invasion of England came in September, launched by Tostig and Harald Hardrada, who landed in Scotland and came down over the border. On hearing of the incursion, King Harold marched his men almost 200 miles in five days and crushed the intruders at Stamford Bridge (near York), killing both his brother and the Norwegian King. But just as his soldiers were recovering from this hard-fought battle, Harold heard that William had landed with another invading force at Pevensey on the Sussex coast. Desperately he turned his army south for another forced march.

On the evening of 13 October Harold caught William by surprise six miles from the coast, near the town of Hastings, but it was already growing late and too dark to fight.

The following morning the two armies faced each other, Harold's soldiers protected by great war shields and armed with axes, William's infantry better armoured and equipped with swords and crossbows. But William's trump was his cavalry, some 2,000 strong.

At first William's assaults made little progress against Harold's wall of shields, and William himself was nearly slain, with three of his horses killed under him. After repeated failure to break the enemy line he finally resorted to ruse, ordering his men to pretend to panic and break to the rear. In spite of Harold's efforts to restrain his troops, the English line broke in triumph, eager to pursue what they saw as a defeated enemy.

With the English streaming towards his retreating men in a chaotic charge, William unleashed his cavalry, who ploughed into the disorganised enemy, cutting them down in hundreds.

Harold still held part of his original line, but many of the English were dead or dying. Resolutely he pulled his men behind their wall of shields, but now Norman arrows constantly bombarded them, and they could not return fire as the English archers had all been routed. Before the battle could reach a final conclusion, a Norman arrow struck Harold in the eye and killed him.

William the Bastard had vanquished the English, and in the years ahead he would subjugate the Welsh and Scottish, too. Enthroned in Westminster Abbey on Christmas Day in 1066, he was known henceforward as William the Conqueror.

Also on this day

1806: Napoleon defeats the Prussians at the Battle of Jena * 1890: American President Dwight Eisenhower is born * 1947: American pilot Chuck Yeager becomes the first man to break the sound barrier

15 October

Scipio overwhelms Hannibal at Zama

202 BC Today was fought one of history's pivotal battles, when two of antiquity's greatest generals faced each other at Zama to determine hegemony of the Mediterranean world.

After the calamitous annihilation of the Romans at the Battle of Cannae in 216 BC, it looked as if the formidable Carthaginian general Hannibal would force Rome to sue for terms, restoring Carthage to the pre-eminence lost in the First Punic War 39 years before. But the obdurate Romans simply refused to be defeated. As Livy wrote two centuries later, 'No other nation could have suffered such a tremendous disaster and not been destroyed.'

This was Hannibal's problem. In spite of his victories, he could not force his enemies to submit. He continued to roam Italy for another thirteen years, once coming within three miles of Rome, but with no siege machinery, he could not attack the great city.

Then Hannibal's problems got worse. A young Roman patrician named Publius Cornelius Scipio had escaped the slaughter at Cannae. Now he had become a general, and, in a series of brilliant tactical engagements, he reconquered virtually all of Carthage's vast territories in Spain. Then, in 204 BC, he embarked for North Africa with an army of 35,000 to strike at Carthage itself.

Scipio brilliantly defeated the Carthaginian forces at Bagbrades, reportedly killing 40,000 men, while destroying enemy towns and cutting off Carthage's food supply. As Scipio knew it must, the Carthaginian government ordered Hannibal to return from Italy to protect the home front.

Two years later these two illustrious generals met on this day at Zama (five miles south of today's Tunis) to determine the fate of the Western world.

Hannibal's army of 45,000 infantry and 80 elephants looked stronger than Scipio's force of only 34,000. But the Carthaginian troops were largely raw and untrained, and Roman and allied Numidian cavalry came to 9,000 horse, three times the mounted strength Hannibal could put in the field.

In the early stages of the battle the Romans managed to panic the Carthaginian elephants with the deafening blare of trumpets and horns. Then the Roman horse put the Carthaginian cavalry to flight, apparently leaving the battle to be settled by the lines of infantry. At first it appeared that the larger Carthaginian force would prevail, but while the Roman soldiers held, their cavalry came charging back into the conflict, taking the enemy from the rear. Some 20,000 Carthaginians died on the field. The defeat of Carthage opened the way for complete Roman domination of southern Europe and North Africa for over half a millennium.

A magnanimous victor, Scipio permitted Hannibal to remain in Carthage, where he was elected the country's ruler. When the two generals met shortly afterwards, Scipio, perhaps fishing for compliments, asked Hannibal who he thought were the three greatest generals in history. The Carthaginian named Alexander the Great, Pyrrhus and himself. 'And what if you rather than I had won the Battle of Zama?' asked the Roman. 'Then I would be the greatest of all', answered the confident Hannibal.

In gratitude, the Roman Senate awarded Scipio the title of Africanus. In 25 years of warfare this remarkable commander never lost a battle.

Hannibal was not so fortunate. A few years after Zama the Roman Senate decided it wanted revenge, forcing him to flee for a secret life in exile. Finally, when he reached the age of 64, his enemies found him in Bythnia. As Roman soldiers surrounded his house to capture him for return to Rome and execution, the great general escaped their clutches in the only way possible, by taking poison. 'Let us relieve the Romans of their continual dread and care,' he said, 'who think it long and tedious to wait for the death of a hated old man.'

Money doesn't buy happiness

961 For over two centuries Moorish Spain had been far more advanced in culture, riches and martial ferocity than the northern, Christian region of the country. Its greatest leader was the urbane and powerful Abd ar-Rahman III of the Umayyad Arab Muslim dynasty, who died today after 49 years of absolute power. (His only misfortune may have been his name, which in full was Abd ar-Rahman ibn Muhammad ibn Abd Allah ibn Muhammad ibn Abd ar-Rahman ibn al-Hakam ar-Rabdi ibn Hidham ibn Abd ar-Rahman ad-Dakhil.)

Abd ar-Rahman's capital was Córdoba, where he completely renovated and greatly expanded the Great Mosque, which still today enthrals visitors from around the world. This remarkable caliph was ferocious in war – defeating Muslim rebels, Christians and usurping North African Fatimid contenders alike. But he was also a man of taste and intelligence who lived in unparalleled splendour. Three miles from Córdoba at vast expense he built a new royal city, Madinat az-Zahra, complete with a marble palace whose roof was supported by 4,000 pillars. For a quarter of a century some 10,000 labourers toiled on this magnificent complex, while Córdoba itself became one of the great cities of the world, with its 3,000 mosques and 100,000 houses and shops.

To guard his royal presence, Abd ar-Rahman maintained a guard of 12,000 horsemen armed with gold-studded scimitars. To top it off, he kept a seraglio of 6,000 concubines. As he wrote of himself, 'In victory and in peace I have been beloved by my subjects, dreaded by my enemies and respected by my allies. Riches and honours, power and pleasure, have waited on my call, nor does any earthly blessing appear to have been wanting to my felicity.'

Abd ar-Rahman was 70 when he died, still adored by his people and surrounded by unimaginable riches. Yet among his papers was found this mournful note, apparently his last before his demise: 'I have diligently numbered the days of pure and genuine happiness that have fallen to my lot; they amount to fourteen. O man, place not thy confidence in this present world!'

The tale of Mme Tussaud

1795 Today in Paris a 34-year-old sculptress named Marie Groshlotz married a young Frenchman eight years her junior named François Tussaud, thus gaining the name that she would make world famous.

Born in Strasbourg, Marie moved first to Switzerland and later to Paris, where she learned the art of wax modelling from her uncle, who owned two wax museums. She must have been an excellent pupil for, by the time she was twenty, she had already been engaged by King Louis XVI's sister to teach her the art.

When revolution exploded in France in 1789, Marie was accused of royalist sympathies and flung into prison. Fortunately, she convinced the authorities of her republicanism, but she was nonetheless given the macabre job of moulding death masks from newly severed heads. She often found herself working on the heads of friends.

Just before the end of the Revolution Marie's uncle died, and she inherited his wax museums. The following year she married François Tussaud, by whom she had two sons. Ultimately, however, the marriage failed, so Marie left France for England, bringing her sons and wax models with her.

For over three decades Marie – or Madame Tussaud as she now was – travelled around England displaying her wares and creating new models. Finally at the grand old age of 80 she established her own museum in Baker Street in London and continued to work there until she died eight years later. Some 34 years after her death her museum – now world famous – was moved to the Marylebone Road, where it has remained until this day.

Also on this day
70 BC: Roman poet Virgil is born * 1764: Edward Gibbon, in Rome, first gets the idea of writing his monumental history of the Roman Empire * 1839: Queen Victoria proposes marriage to Prince Albert * 1917: Mata Hari is executed by the French after being convicted of passing military secrets to the Germans

16 October

Marie Antoinette's last ride

1793 Marie Antoinette, raised in the court of her mother Empress Maria Theresa of Austria and now Queen of France, rose early this morning and dressed in a white piqué gown, a white bonnet, a muslin shawl and plum-coloured high-heeled shoes. Then she drank a cup of morning chocolate.

Shortly after eleven she found herself en route for what today is called the place de la Concorde. Her arms were tied as she sat in the tumbrel. She was headed for her own execution.

Marie Antoinette's husband, fat Louis XVI, had already faced the guillotine with dignity nine months before. Her children had been taken from her and she was imprisoned first in the Temple, then in the Conciergerie in an eleven-foot-square cell. The cell was damp and dark, and it contained three beds, one for the Queen, another for her female attendant and a third for the two gendarmes who never left, even when the women had to satisfy the needs of nature. As Marie Antoinette said to her daughter the last time she saw her, 'God Himself has forsaken me – I no longer dare to pray.'

Now the tumbrel clanked through the Parisian streets, crowds jeering from every side. When it pulled up at the scaffold, the Queen was trembling so badly that she had to be helped from the cart. At the top of the steps she tripped and stepped on the executioner's foot. 'Monsieur', she apologised. 'Excuse me, I didn't do it on purpose.' She never spoke again, and a few minutes later the blade swept down, neatly severing her head from her body. She was still only 37.

Napoleon demolishes the walls of Vienna

1809 Its massive city walls had protected Vienna since the Middle Ages and before, but by the early 19th century they no longer had any real military value. Nonetheless, when he left the city on this day, the Emperor Napoleon spitefully ordered the walls demolished, and at four that afternoon great explosions shook the city as commanding gates and high ramparts were blown up.

To the Viennese of the time, this was a humiliating spectacle, especially since the day marked the anniversary of the Turks' withdrawal after failing to overcome these walls in 1529.

Later, sections of the walls were rebuilt, but their fate was truly sealed. Perhaps Vienna's inhabitants would have been less saddened could they have known that, when all the walls finally vanished for ever some 60 years later, they would be replaced by Emperor Franz Joseph's beautiful Ringstrasse, the most spectacular street in what remains one of Europe's most enchanting cities.

Also on this day

1555: Bishops Hugh Latimer and Nicholas Ridley are burned at the stake * 1815: Napoleon is defeated at the Battle of Leipzig * 1854: Irish playwright Oscar Wilde is born in Dublin * 1946: Eleven Nazi war criminals are hanged after the Nuremberg trials

17 October

The start of the Spanish Inquisition

1483 On this day Pope Sixtus IV established the most brutal, feared and loathsome institution in European history prior to the creation of the Third Reich – the Spanish Inquisition.

Sixtus was a classic Renaissance pope. A scion of the ducal house of Urbino, he meddled incessantly but ineffectively in politics, was notorious for his nepotism and contributed significantly to the culture of his and our times. It was Sixtus who built the Sistine Chapel with its delicate frescoes by Botticelli, Perugino, Pintoricchio and Ghirlandajo. (Michelangelo's great work was commissioned in a later pontificate, under Sixtus's nephew, Julius II.) Unfortunately, his solutions for the spiritual ills of the time were as disastrous as his culture was refined.

At this time Spain was the only European country with a substantial population of *conversos*, Jews and Muslims who had converted to Christianity. Spain's Catholic Monarchs King Ferdinand and Queen Isabella feared that many *conversos* were really only feigning their belief in Christ while secretly following their old faith. To help root out these dangerous heretics, on this day Pope Sixtus issued a Bull establishing the Consejo de la Suprema y General Inquisición or Supreme Council of the Inquisition in Spain, appointing a 63-year-old Dominican monk named Tomás de Torquemada as the first Grand Inquisitor.

Torquemada had been a prior in a monastery in Segovia for 22 years when he took up his new post, but he already had the confidence of Ferdinand and Isabella. He had known the Queen since her childhood and was the confessor and sometimes advisor to both.

Torquemada served as Grand Inquisitor for fifteen terrifying years, during which time he encouraged the use of torture to extract confessions, including such Spanish delicacies as the *toca*, in which water is forced down your throat, the *garrucha*, in which your hands are tied behind your back and you are then lifted by the wrists and let fall to dislocate your joints, and the *potro*, a form of the rack.

Torquemada was also active in widening the scope of crime for which the unhappy victims could be accused. Although the Inquisition was established to combat heresy, only a year after taking office he extended its range to include sodomy, blasphemy, usury and sorcery.

Torquemada did not introduce Spain to the *auto da fé* – a technique of persuasion first employed in Granada in February 1481 – but he brought it to new heights of glory, ordering about 2,000 souls to be burnt at the stake during his tenure.

Pope Sixtus was shaken when he learned of the Inquisition's excesses and issued a Bull deploring the rigged trials, torture and horrors of the *auto da fé*, but it had no effect on the fanatical monk, who continued diligently at his task. Finally, on 16 September 1498, Torquemada died in the Monasterio de Santo Tomás in Avila at the age of 78. But the Spanish Inquisition lived on, finally suppressed only on 15 July 1834 after 351 years.

Chopin's finale

1849 If you step out of the front door of the Ritz Hotel in Paris and look diagonally across Place Vendôme, you will see number 12, where Frédéric

François Chopin coughed himself to death of tuberculosis on the morning of 17 October 1849. Mozart's Requiem was played at his funeral as Chopin had requested.

Chopin was just 39 when he died, yet his life had been an extraordinarily full one: first concert at eight, fame in his native Warsaw by nineteen, Paris by 21, where he was quickly recognised as the musical genius he was. In all, he wrote some 200 pieces, and during his lifetime his audience and patrons were of the highest French society. In fact, even his mistress of eight years was a baroness named Aurore Dudevant, although her readers knew her better as the writer George Sand.

In the autumn of 1848 Chopin visited London on a playing tour, and it was in the Guildhall there that he played his last concert. He had already been ill for some time, and after the exertions of foreign travel he returned to Paris. Fearing the worst, he wrote in his last letter, 'The earth is suffocating. Swear to make them cut me open, so I won't be buried alive.'

He died a few weeks later, on 17 October. On the morning of his death a doctor asked him if he was in pain, to which Chopin replied 'Plus' ('No more'), his last word. Although buried in Paris's Père-Lachaise cemetery, he is interred in Polish soil, scattered over his coffin from a supply the farsighted composer had brought with him from his native country twenty years before.

Today Chopin is still considered one of history's greatest composers and pianists. In fact, his music is still with us on a more pedestrian level than he would ever have dreamed. Apart from classical concerts, it endures in debased form in songs like 'I'm Always Chasing Rainbows'.

Gambetta escapes from Paris by balloon

1870 Fat, one-eyed and dishevelled, Léon Gambetta was an unlikely candidate to become a national hero, but today he defied a conquering army by one of the most famous escapes in history, earning huge popularity with the French people and creating a memorable moment in French history.

Only three months earlier France had been considered the great power of Europe, securely directed by Emperor Napoleon III. Then had come the Franco-Prussian War with the crushing German victory at Sedan, and suddenly Napoleon was gone and Léon Gambetta, Jules Favre and Jules Ferry proclaimed the birth of the Third Republic.

But despite the new and would-be-democratic government, the German army pressed on to force France to submit, and soon had ringed Paris and started a heavy bombardment.

Inside the city the new government refused to surrender, and young Gambetta (he was only 32), who was the Minister of the Interior, decided on desperate action. Determined to break out in order to inspire further French resistance, he ordered the construction of a hot air balloon and on this day made his legendary escape, soaring over the Paris rooftops and the encircling German troops.

Once free, he helped to raise more armies, but France was shortly forced to come to terms, ceding Alsace and Lorraine to the now unified Germany. But Gambetta's Third Republic survived until another German subdued France in 1940.

Also on this day

1651: England's Charles II flees to France * 1777: The British under General John Burgoyne surrender to American forces at the Battle of Saratoga, causing France to recognise the new nation and openly give military aid

18 October

Napoleon retreats from Russia

1812 Today the 90,000 men remaining from Napoleon's Grande Armée trooped out of Moscow to begin the most famous retreat in military history.

Thirty-five days before, Napoleon and his army had at last reached the Russian capital after twelve long weeks of plodding across 500 miles of empty and desolate Russian countryside, laid waste by Russian peasants before they abandoned it.

Yet Moscow, too, was ominously quiet and empty. Indeed, only 15,000 of its quarter of a million inhabitants remained, mostly foreigners, vagabonds and criminals. The rest had deserted the city on orders from its governor.

Then came the fires, deliberately set by the Russians, which razed four-fifths of Moscow. No word came from the Tsar, no surrender, no discussion of terms. Each day food became scarcer; each day there was less left to burn to fight the murderous cold.

Recognising that his plight was desperate, Napoleon appealed to Alexander I for a truce, but the Tsar refused even to answer the Emperor's letter. Later he wrote to an ally, 'We would rather be buried beneath the ruins of the empire than make terms with the modern Attila.'

Finally Napoleon understood that his only hope was withdrawal, and he gave the order to abandon the city.

Now the army tramped 500 miles in retreat, numbed with fatigue, frozen by the terrible Russian winter, with regular frosts of −25° centigrade. As described by future American President John Quincy Adams, who was in Moscow at the time as his country's ambassador, 'The invader himself was a wretched fugitive and his numberless host was perishing by frosts, famine, and the sword.'

Badgered by guerrillas and marauding Cossacks, tracked by the main Russian armies, Napoleon's men and horses fell and died, left equally for the howling wolves. For seven weeks the army struggled on, at last reaching sanctuary in Vilna (now Vilnius in Lithuania). By then perhaps 20,000 were left, and Napoleon could only repeat his now-famous observation, 'Du sublime au ridicule il n'y a qu'un pas.' (From the sublime to the ridiculous is only a step.) The days of the Empire were numbered.

Farewell to Lord Cupid

1865 Harry Temple was born to the richest and proudest in England, succeeding his father as Viscount Palmerston when only eighteen years old. From then on this brash, calculating, jingoistic and somewhat mediocre man devoted his life to politics. He won a seat in the House of Commons when he was 23 and retained it with one break of a few months until he died today of fever, just two days before his 81st birthday. He had served as Secretary of War, Foreign Minister, Home Secretary and for nine years as Prime Minister, an office he held at his death.

After politics, Palmerston's overriding interest was women, whom he pursued with insatiable appetite throughout his long life, earning the sobriquet 'Lord Cupid'. Among his conquests were Lady Jersey, the Princess Lieven and Lady Cowper, the last of whom he finally married at the age of 55 when she was widowed, after years of scandalous affair. At the time a contemporary wrote, 'There will be nothing new about it except the marriage vow which they both know does not bind them.'

By 1865 Pam, as he was universally known, had attained the great age of 80 and his energies both political and sexual were spent. On 18 October he lay frail and feeble on his sumptuous bed at Brocket Hall in Hertfordshire, clearly approaching the end.

But even then his brashness and wit did not desert him. Gravely his doctor told him that he must die. 'Die, my dear doctor,' Pam whispered, 'that's the last thing I shall do!' He then closed his eyes – and did.

Also on this day

1520: Portuguese explorer Ferdinand Magellan finds a strait to the Pacific – now the Straits of Magellan * 1663: Eugene of Savoy is born in Paris * 1685: Louis XIV revokes the Edict of Nantes * 1859: French Nobel-Prize-winning philosopher Henri Bergson is born * 1931: American inventor Thomas Edison dies

19 October

The American Revolution ends with a victory at Yorktown

1781 With no way out by land or sea, and no prospect of timely relief, General Cornwallis today surrendered his 8,000 British troops to General Washington and an allied army at Yorktown, Virginia, bringing to an end major military operations in the War of the American Revolution. The victory was the result of a combined American–French land–sea campaign that remains a model of timing and co-operation.

Throughout six years of war in America, the British had always enjoyed the considerable advantage of command of the sea. But suddenly – and only briefly – a window of naval opportunity opened for the rebels. With his army around New York City, Washington received word in August that Admiral de Grasse and his French fleet in the West Indies were sailing north for Chesapeake Bay, where he could be available for operations until mid-October. The presence of a French fleet in such a position would cut communications between the British armies in Virginia and New York, leaving the southern army especially vulnerable to blockade and attack.

Washington set his army moving southward from New York in forced marches, accompanied by a French army under the command of General Rochambeau. Arriving in Virginia in mid-September, the joint force was joined by another American army under General Lafayette. The French fleet, with 3,000 more troops and siege artillery, had already arrived off Chesapeake Bay and driven off a British fleet. On 28 September, with 17,000 allied troops on hand, half of whom were French, Washington began siege operations at York-town. Cornwallis soon recognised his position as hopeless and on 17 October requested a truce.

And so, the Americans, with crucial help from their French allies, beat the mightiest military power in the world. It seemed an amazing turn of events, at least as amazing as the examples offered in the old tune to which (legend has it) the British soldiers marched out from Yorktown this morning to lay down their arms:

If ponies rode men, and if grass ate the cows,
And cats should be chased into holes by the mouse …
If summer were spring, and the other way 'round,
Then all the world would be upside down.

King John loses his treasure and then his life

1216 King John of England quarrelled with everyone – his father, Henry II, his brother, Richard the Lion-Heart, the kings of France, the Pope, and most of all his own barons. He was cunning, vengeful and vicious; he had murdered his nephew Arthur of Brittany (some say with his own hand) and once starved to death the wife and son of a mutinous baron.

The autumn of 1216 found him in an ever-worsening position. The French had been conquering John's once vast Angevin territories for over a decade, and Normandy, the traditional 'home' fief of all British kings since William the Conqueror, was now gone as well. Only the previous year his rebellious barons in England had forced him to sign the humiliating Magna Carta that restricted his power to tax or seize property and ended with the humiliating provision that a council of 25 barons would have the right to make war on him if he failed to follow the agreement.

Now John was marching with his army across England, revenging himself on his barons one by one. Because he trusted no one, he carried with him the great royal treasure, a vast hoard of gold and precious jewels, including the crown and sceptre of England.

John and his forces were about 85 miles north of London, near the part of the North Sea known as the Wash. Here there was a small river to be forded, but it was running fast with the autumn floods. With typical rashness, John ordered his men forward. Suddenly the current gripped the treasure wagons. In a flash they were overturned, and England's invaluable treasure was lost for ever to the waters, swept down into the sea.

Thunderstruck by this disaster, the king pushed on to the nearby abbey at Swineshead, where he feasted in despair, consuming a heavy meal followed by peaches mulled in wine. Immediately severe dysentery struck, but still he pushed on the same night, carried on a litter to the palace of the Bishop of Lincoln in Newark.

The next day John collapsed completely and in a few hours lay dead, tradition has it in the midst of a howling gale. On 19 October 1216 England's worst king was no more. Treacherous, lecherous, murderous and cruel, John had ruled for seventeen years, dying at only 48.

'Sheridan's Ride'

1864 On this Indian summer morning Major General Philip Sheridan made a celebrated ride from Winchester, Virginia, to Cedar Creek and turned the rout of his Army of the Shenandoah into a timely victory for the Union.

Returning to his command from Washington, DC, Sheridan, having spent the night at Winchester, woke to the sound of heavy gunfire from the army's encampment twenty miles away. Riding out to investigate, he encountered 'the appalling spectacle of a panic-stricken army ... all pressing to the rear in hopeless confusion.'

With two aides and twenty troopers, 'Little Phil' Sheridan began the gallop to the battlefield over roads choked with wounded soldiers, stragglers and transport. As he rode through, he shouted to them: 'About face, boys! We are going to lick them out of their boots.' They began to cheer. When a hysterical infantry colonel yelled at him: 'The army's whipped!' Sheridan replied, 'You are, but the army isn't.' An officer who accompanied him wrote: 'Sheridan, without slowing from the gallop, pointed to the front; men cheered and shouldered arms and started back.'

The diminutive Sheridan arrived at Cedar Creek at 10.30. Riding up and down on his big, black horse Rienzi, he began to restore order to his battered army, exhorting men and officers, ordering breastworks thrown up, directing returning units back into the line, and establishing a new headquarters. At 4.00

he sent off the counter-attack that swept Jubal Early's Confederate forces from the field and carried the day.

His spectacular victory had political as well as military significance. In the war-weary North, the 1864 presidential election was only days away, with Republican President Lincoln running against his former general George B. McClellan of the anti-war Democrats, known as 'Copperheads'. With Atlanta fallen to Sherman the month before, Horace Greeley could now write, 'Sheridan and Sherman have knocked the bottom out of the Copperheads.'

For his ride and victory, Sheridan was the hero of the hour and the toast of the Union army. President Lincoln said he had always thought that a cavalryman should be about six feet four, but 'now five feet four seems about right', unwittingly reducing the general's true height by an inch.

Like another famous rider, Paul Revere, Sheridan became the subject of an immensely popular poem. Here is the first stanza of 'Sheridan's Ride' by Thomas Buchanan Read:

Up from the south at the break of day,
Bringing to Winchester fresh dismay,
The affrighted air with a shudder bore,
Like a herald in haste to the chieftain's door,
The terrible grumble and rumble and roar,
Telling the battle was on once more,
And Sheridan twenty miles away.

Isabella marries Ferdinand

1469 Of all the dates connected with the development of Spain as a nation, few are as significant as this one, the day that eighteen-year-old Isabella of Castile married Ferdinand of Aragon, uniting Spain's two largest kingdoms. Combining their strength, the Catholic Monarchs, as Ferdinand and Isabella are known, spent the next twenty years driving the Moors from the peninsula, finally succeeding in 1492, the same year they dispatched an adventurous Genovese sailor named Christopher Columbus to find a passage to the Indies.

Ferdinand and Isabella's path to marriage was far from easy. Her brother Enrique of Castile favoured the King of Portugal, while the French had also proposed a matrimonial candidate. Worse, Ferdinand and Isabella were cousins, creating possible problems of consanguinity in the eyes of the Church.

Legend has it that the seventeen-year-old Ferdinand was truly enamoured of his cousin and so made his way to her court in disguise, delighting the enraptured Isabella. To persuade her to go through with the wedding he came bearing a papal bill of dispensation regarding their bloodlines. Unknown to the bride, the bill was a convenient forgery, but by the time it was discovered the two were blissfully wed.

Also on this day
1745: Irish satirical writer Jonathan Swift dies in Dublin * 1872: The Holtermann nugget, weighing 630 pounds, is mined at Hill End, Australia, the largest gold-bearing nugget ever found

20 October

The Long March that changed Chinese history

1935 Today some 8,000 bedraggled survivors of Mao Tse-tung's Communist army reached safe haven in Communist-controlled Shensi Province in north-western China after one year and four days of retreat from the repeated attacks of Chiang Kai-shek's Kuomintang troops. The Long March was over, and over 90 per cent of the Communist army had perished, but Mao had survived, achieving in the process de facto leadership of China's Communist Party.

The previous October Mao, his pregnant wife and 100,000 soldiers of the Red Army had abandoned their capital of Juichin in Kiangsi province to start a trek of over 6,000 miles from one side of China to the other. During the next twelve months they covered some of the world's most inhospitable terrain while constantly pursued by Chiang Kai-shek's forces. It was the longest – and fastest – infantry march made under combat conditions by any army in history.

Since the Red Army had no motorised transport, the Long March was indeed a march, every man afoot except Mao himself, who was so ill from malaria that he rode the army's solitary horse. When the terrain was too difficult for him to stay in the saddle, four soldiers would carry him in a wooden litter.

Every soldier had to march with his own supplies. According to Mao's chief artillery engineer, 'Each man carried five pounds of ration rice and each had a shoulder pole from which hung either two small boxes of ammunition or hand grenades, or big kerosene cans filled with our most essential machinery and tools. Each pack contained a blanket or quilt, one quilted winter uniform, and three pairs of strong cloth shoes with thick rope soles tipped and heeled with metal.'

The army had little ammunition, less food and virtually no medical supplies. Sometimes forced to go several days without eating, many fell by the wayside due to weakness while even more died of disease.

Almost insuperable obstacles barred the Red Army's progress. At Luting the soldiers had to haul themselves over a river on a chain suspension bridge from which all the wooden slats had been removed. Later they had to cross seven high mountain ranges crested with snow, and in the heat of August they tramped across the Grasslands of Chinghai, a high plateau that was boggy with rain and infested with swarms of malaria-carrying mosquitoes. The wet ground prevented the soldiers from making fires to cook the little food they carried, and many suffered from severe dysentery from eating raw rice and vegetables.

Although China's Communists were on the point of annihilation, the Long March not only provided a stirring example of revolutionary zeal and commitment, it also gave Mao time for the political situation to change. China had already been under attack from Japan, but Chiang Kai-shek had decided to cleanse the country of Communists as his first priority. The Long March showed that total victory against the Communists was unachievable, and by September 1937 the Kuomintang and the Communists had (temporarily) joined forces to fight the common enemy. Once the Japanese were defeated, however, the civil war was re-ignited almost immediately, and in 1949 Mao's armies took over the country, forcing Chiang to flee to Taiwan and amply demonstrating his famous maxim that 'political power grows out of the barrel of a gun'.

Eddie Rickenbacker gets his last kill

1918 Today, with the First World War drawing to a close, Captain Eddie Rickenbacker, commander of the 94th Aero Pursuit Squadron, flew his Spad high above the trenches of the Western Front and shot down his 26th – and final – German aircraft of the war. Over the past six months, he had become America's best combat pilot, her 'ace of aces'.

Rickenbacker was a natural in the air. Before the war, he had won fame – as well as money and influence – as one of the world's top racing car drivers, but he had never flown a plane. When the United States entered the war in March 1917 he joined the Army with the hope of organising a flying squadron of former racing drivers, counting on their experience operating powerful engines at high speeds to make them first-rate pilots. When the War Department proved resistant, he managed to get to France as a driver, first for General John J. Pershing, then for Colonel 'Billy' Mitchell, head of the recently formed American Air Service. Eventually, with Mitchell's help, Rickenbacker got assigned to a flying unit as an engineer, then to pilot training and an officer's commission, and finally, in March 1918, to the 94th Squadron, the famous 'Hat-in-the-Ring' Squadron. He took his first combat flight on 25 April and four days later, piloting a Nieuport, downed his first enemy plane. At the end of May, Rickenbacker was a five-victory ace.

In the course of the long war, there were plenty of aces who had more kills than Rickenbacker – Billy Bishop, the Canadian ace flying for the British, had 72, for instance, and on the other side Manfred von Richthofen had 80 – but no other pilot ever matched Rickenbacker's rate of 26 in just six months. For his feats he received the Croix de Guerre, the US Distinguished Flying Cross, and the Congressional Medal of Honor.

Three weeks later, on 11 November 1918, Rickenbacker took his plane out over the front lines to see the war end. 'It was a foggy morning at the base,' he wrote years later, 'and I wriggled my way out just a half minute before eleven o'clock. I was flying down no-man's land, between the trenches of the opposing forces, and they were shooting at each other just as madly as they could. And then the hour of eleven struck. The shooting stopped, and gradually men from both sides came out into no-man's land and threw their guns and helmets into the air. They kept talking to each other and shaking hands and doing something for the men who had been hit. ... I was only about a hundred feet over no-man's land. I got out to see what I went out to see and went back home and that was it.'

Also on this day

1632: English architect Christopher Wren is born * 1818: Britain and the United States agree on the 49th parallel as the boundary between Canada and the USA * 1854: French poet Arthur Rimbaud is born

21 October

Trafalgar

1805 Atop his column in London's Trafalgar Square stands one-armed Admiral Horatio Nelson, who won a battle and lost his life on this day in 1805 at the age of 47.

Nelson joined the navy at the age of twelve, so he had been serving for over twenty years before his years of greatness during the French Revolutionary and Napoleonic Wars. He lost an eye at Calvi helping to capture Corsica in 1797 and four years later his right arm at Tenerife. A year after that he destroyed Napoleon's fleet at the Battle of the Nile.

On this day Nelson, with only 27 ships, completely outmanoeuvred a French/Spanish fleet of 33 warships at Cape Trafalgar on the south coast of Spain. It was before this battle that he issued his famous signal, 'England expects that every man will do his duty.'

Nelson certainly did his. Ordering what amounted to a frontal assault on the French line, Nelson in his flagship *Victory* led one column of ships directly at and through the French fleet, raking the enemy's flagship with crippling cannon shot.

Even when *Victory* became entangled with a French warship, Nelson remained fully exposed to enemy fire, walking resolutely on the quarterdeck with his captain Thomas Hardy. At 1.15 in the afternoon a sniper's bullet fired from the rigging of the enemy ship caught Nelson in the shoulder, passed through his lungs and shattered his spine.

In indescribable pain, Nelson was carried below, to survive for another three hours. Knowing he was about to die, he beseeched Hardy 'to take care of my poor Lady Hamilton' (Nelson's mistress). At the end he murmured, 'Kiss me, Hardy.' The captain knelt and kissed his cheek, and the great admiral expired, according to legend dying with the famous words, 'Now I am satisfied. Thank God I have done my duty.'

The Battle of Trafalgar was one of the truly decisive naval encounters in history. The French lost 19 ships and 14,000 men killed or captured, including their admiral. British losses were only 1,500, and not a ship was lost. Napoleon's last hope of invading England had been denied for ever.

Nelson's body was brought back to England to receive an imposing funeral in St Paul's Cathedral. There he was buried in a coffin that he himself had ordered, made from timber taken from the French warship *Orient* that he had destroyed at the Battle of the Nile.

An author in search of a title

1940 He had started writing the novel in Cuba the year before and was up to Chapter 35 in April 1940 when he decided he needed a title. He came up with many possibilities – *The Undiscovered Country* was the best of them, he thought – before turning to Shakespeare and the Bible. Searching further, he consulted *The Oxford Book of English Prose*, where at last he found just what he was looking for. He sent his editor the first draft of the manuscript with his proposed title, and got this cable in reply: ALL KNOCKED OUT. THINK ABSOLUTELY MAGNIFICENT. TITLE BEAUTIFUL. CONGRATULATIONS.

When the final longhand draft was completed in July, he took it up to New York for typing before handing it over to his editor. All signs were favourable. The publisher had set an October publication date and a first printing of 100,000 copies. In August the Book of the Month Club made the novel its main selection for November. From Hollywood came the news that Paramount Pictures wanted the film rights.

And so it was that on this date Charles Scribner's Sons published Ernest Hemingway's fifth novel, a story of the recently concluded Spanish Civil War. It bore the title *For Whom the Bell Tolls*, drawn from one of John Donne's *Devotions* that begins, 'No man is an Island, entire of itself ...' and ends with, 'And therefore never send to know for whom the bell tolls; it tolls for thee.'

The critical reception seemed to bear out what his editor Max Perkins had written to him in April: 'I think this book has greater power, and larger dimensions, greater emotional force, than anything you have done ...' In *The Atlantic*, Robert Sherwood called the book 'rare and beautiful'. Clifton Fadiman in *The New Yorker* said, 'I do not much care whether or not this is a "great" book. I feel that it is what Hemingway wanted it to be: a true book.' Edmund Wilson in *The New Republic*, J. Donald Adams in the *New York Times Book Review* and Lionel Trilling in the *Partisan Review* all followed suit. Only on the left were there voices of dissent complaining of a misportrayal of the war in Spain and of the Loyalist leaders. Among them was Alvah C. Bessie writing in the *New Masses*, who objected that Hemingway was concerned only with the fate of his characters and that 'the cause of Spain does not, in any *essential* way, figure as a motivating power, a driving, emotional, passional force in this story'.

At least as good as the critical reception were the sales. By the end of 1940

Scribners had sold 189,000 copies. Three years after publication 785,000 copies of all editions had been sold in the United States, not far below the sales of *Gone with the Wind*. The only sour note came when the judges of the Pulitzer Advisory Board unanimously chose *For Whom the Bell Tolls* as the best novel of 1940 but were overruled by the conservative President of Columbia University on the grounds that the university would not wish to be associated with 'an award for a work of this nature'. There was no Pulitzer award for fiction that year.

Hemingway dedicated *For Whom the Bell Tolls* to Martha Gellhorn with whom he had been living for three years in what she described as 'contented sin'. Learning just two weeks after publication that his divorce from Pauline Pfeiffer had come through, he married Gellhorn in late November in Cheyenne, Wyoming.

Also on this day

1680: Louis XIV signs a decree establishing the Comédie Française * 1760: Japanese printmaker Katsushika Hokusai is born * 1772: English poet Samuel Taylor Coleridge is born * 1918: The Great Influenza Epidemic, which will kill 30 million people, begins

22 October

The mad Emperor Commodus takes power in Rome

AD 180 Still only eighteen years old, in March Commodus had been campaigning on the Danube with his father the Emperor Marcus Aurelius when Marcus was carried off by plague. After arranging for burial and deification, young Commodus, now the most powerful man in the world, slowly travelled with his army the 700 miles to Rome, there to put his own malign imprint on history. Today in a spectacular triumphal procession he and his troops entered the Eternal City to take control of the government. He would rule supreme for the next twelve years.

Before Commodus's succession to power, Rome had enjoyed 83 uninterrupted years of peace and prosperity under five benevolent emperors, Trajan, Hadrian, Antoninus Pius, Lucius Verus and Marcus Aurelius. Initially Commodus, too, ruled generously and well, but the omens were unfavourable: born on 31 August, he shared a birthday with his psychotic predecessor Caligula.

Within five years Commodus began to show signs of the brutal insanity that would consume him. He assumed a lifestyle of enormous depravity and expense, organising orgies with his harem of 300 women and 300 boys and revelling in luxuries. Soon he was running short of money, a problem he resolved by executing rich senators on trumped up charges of treason, and seizing their property.

In 186 he executed one chief minister in order to placate the army, and three years later allowed the Roman mob to lynch another one. Meanwhile the unfettered power he enjoyed only fed his megalomania. He changed the name of Rome to Colonia Commodiana (Colony of Commodus) and he renamed the months after the many names that he had given himself. Starting from January, they were now to be known as Lucius, Aelius, Aurelius, Commodus, Augustus, Herculeus, Romanus, Exsuperatorius, Amazonius, Invictus, Felix and Pius. He ordered that henceforth every Roman citizen should carry the name Commodianus.

Even more bizarre, Commodus began to imagine that he was Hercules. Dressed in a lion skin and bearing a club, he now entered gladiatorial contests against both men and beasts. According to the historian Herodian, 'He defeated his opponents with ease, and he did no more than wound them, since they all submitted to him, but only because they knew he was the emperor, not because he was truly a gladiator.' The animals he faced fared less well. Another historian, Dio Cassius, reports that he once killed five hippopotami in a single combat and also cut down various elephants, rhinoceroses, leopards, lions and deer, 'always killing them with a single blow ... he cleanly shot the heads off countless ostriches with crescent-headed arrows. The crowd cheered as these headless birds continued to run around the amphitheatre.'

Convinced that he was Rome's greatest gladiator, Commodus forced the gladiatorial fund to pay him 1 million sesterces every time he appeared in the arena. He also brooked no competition, once executing another gladiator merely for having skilfully killed a lion with a javelin.

This playing at gladiator scandalised the Roman people and appalled the Senate, as the arena featured condemned criminals and other dregs of society. The authority of the Emperor was draining away, while both senators and members of the imperial household lived in fear for their lives.

Inevitably, a plot against the Emperor developed. His chamberlain, his Praetorian Prefect and his favourite concubine Marcia swore to bring him down.

On the last day of AD 192 Marcia surreptitiously slipped poison in his wine, but Commodus's delicate stomach rejected the toxin. The conspirators then called in a professional wrestler named Narcissus, who strangled him in his bath.

Joyful at this unexpected end to Commodus's tyranny, the Senate expunged his name from all state documents and ordered his statues destroyed.

A Frenchman makes the first parachute jump

1797 The first balloon flight had taken place only fourteen years earlier, when two French brothers, the Montgolfiers, launched an unmanned hot air balloon that reached a height of only 90 feet. Later the same year two other Frenchmen, Jean-François Pilâtre de Rozier and his aristocratic friend François Laurent, marquis d'Arlandes, achieved the first manned flight when they soared over Paris in a Montgolfier balloon, staying aloft for almost half an hour. Now, however, the challenge was not so much how to go up but how to come down.

The idea of the parachute may have originated in ancient China, and it had certainly been explored as early as the 15th century, when Leonardo da Vinci experimented on paper with the idea. But it was three centuries later when yet another Frenchman, Louis-Sebastian Lenormand, became the first man ever to descend with something like a parachute. Holding two parasols, he climbed a tall tree and jumped – and made it safely to the ground. Lenormand made several other experimental jumps, envisaging the contrivance as a safety apparatus with which to escape from burning buildings.

Finally, on this day in 1797, the first true parachute came into being, once more with a Frenchman in the lead. Twenty-eight-year-old Jacques Garnerin took off from Paris in a hot air balloon, rose to 3,200 feet and then leaped into space. His parachute opened and he landed safely in the Parc Monceau. Man's first parachute jump had been accomplished.

Also on this day

1746: Princeton University receives its charter * 1811: Hungarian composer and pianist Franz Liszt is born * 1906: French painter Paul Cézanne dies in Aix-en-Provence

23 October

America's first combat in the First World War

1917 At 6.05 in the morning on this day C Battery of the 6th Field Artillery fired a round from its French 75mm gun towards the German trenches a few hundred yards to the front. America had truly entered the Great War at last.

Ever since 1914 the Allied powers had attempted to persuade the United States to join in the conflict against Germany, and finally, on 6 April 1917, President Woodrow Wilson had declared war. But now American troops were for the first time actually engaging the enemy.

By the time the Germans collapsed seven months later the United States had increased the strength of the American Expeditionary Force to just under 2 million men, an incredible feat of planning and logistics. Commanding US forces in Europe was General John 'Black Jack' Pershing, aged 57 when he took command but still tough and energetic, as he proved on arriving in Paris when he took a 23-year-old French mistress.

Pershing was originally dubbed 'Black Jack' by fellow officers in a derisory reference to his command of a black cavalry unit, but later it came to represent his dark, hawk-like looks and stern discipline. He had climbed the ranks of the military in part through unimpeachable connections. He had become a great friend of Teddy Roosevelt when Roosevelt was Police Commissioner of New York, and his father-in-law was the head of the Senate Military Affairs Committee. No doubt there was also tremendous sympathy for him because his wife and three daughters had all perished in a fire in San Francisco a few years before the war. Nonetheless he was a fine soldier, as he had demonstrated in searching out and almost killing the Mexican revolutionary and bandit Pancho Villa.

Pershing deserved and received much of the credit for the great fighting success of the American forces in Europe. In all they fought in thirteen battles and turned the tide of the war from stalemate to victory. Although light compared with the European nations that had fought since 1914, American casualties were still significant. In all over 116,000 were killed in action while another 200,000 were wounded.

Charles V becomes the most powerful man since Charlemagne

1520 A contemporary describes Charles V as 'a lonely figure, not prone to laughter', and his portraits invariably depict his minor deformity, the famous 'Habsburg jaw', by showing him with his mouth slightly open. Today young Charles, still only twenty, was anointed German King and Holy Roman Emperor-elect in the ancient cathedral of Aachen, where Charlemagne himself had held his capital seven centuries previously and where his ancestor, the first Habsburg Emperor Rudolf, had been crowned precisely 274 years, minus one day, before.

Charles had all the right ancestors. His mother was Queen of Spain, his father, now dead, had been Prince Regent. His maternal grandparents were Spain's Catholic Monarchs, Isabella and Ferdinand, and his paternal grandfather was Holy Roman Emperor Maximilian I. But in spite of his antecedents (and the fact that he was already King of Holland and Regent of Spain, standing in for his demented mother) Charles's election was far from certain, as there was stiff competition from Henry VIII of England and especially from France's François I. In the end, Charles's superior virtues were made clear to the elector princes through his gift of 850,000 florins.

Charles became the most powerful Holy Roman Emperor of them all, suzerain of Spain, most of Italy, the Netherlands and Belgium, Austria and the German principalities.

Also on this day
42 BC: At the Second Battle of Philippi Octavian and Mark Antony defeat Brutus and Cassius * 1642: The first battle of the English Civil War at Edgehill * 1707: The First Parliament of Great Britain

24 October

The end of the Thirty Years' War

1648 At last the Treaty of Westphalia was signed, and the Thirty Years' War – the most destructive in European history until 1914 – staggered to a close.

The Thirty Years' War was really a series of wars, fought chiefly over religious differences between Catholic and Protestant, but eventually broadened by grasping kings who saw in the chaos of war an opportunity to seize someone else's territory.

The war's prime instigator was Jesuit-educated Ferdinand II of Austria. Recognised as King of Bohemia by the Bohemian Diet, he started forcibly converting his predominantly Protestant population to Catholicism. By all accounts, he was a kind and gentle man, a roly-poly monarch who dressed as a Spanish courtier, but when it came to religion, his devotion to Romish absolutism was too much for his new subjects, who, led by the nobles, rose in open revolt and deposed him.

Following five years of armed conflict Ferdinand finally regained his royal authority, but by this time the war had spread, involving Poland, Russia, Denmark, Sweden, the Netherlands and dozens of the semi-autonomous German principalities over which Ferdinand had gained theoretical overlordship on becoming Holy Roman Emperor in 1619. In addition to the religious battle, the Thirty Years' War was exacerbated by the underlying struggle between the Habsburg Holy Roman Empire and France led by Cardinal Richelieu.

Most of the combat took place on German soil, and some 350,000 were slain on the field of battle, as the contending powers relied increasingly on mercenaries to do the fighting. Caring nothing for the civilians in their path, armies on all sides destroyed whole villages and ravaged the countryside as they went, burning, looting and sweeping it clean of farmers and food. Some 8 million people are thought to have perished.

The winners, if there were any, were France, now Europe's strongest power, the Netherlands, which had gained independence from Spain, and Sweden, which now dominated the Baltic. The biggest loser would have been the man who started it all, Ferdinand II, except that he had died eleven years before the end. But his cherished idea of a dominant Holy Roman Empire with an emperor at its head and the Pope at its heart was as dead as the hordes of people cut down by sword, famine and pestilence during the war.

Catastrophe at Caporetto

1917 Between 1915 and 1917 on the Italian front there were eleven battles of the Isonzo, a series of costly and mostly inconclusive assaults by the Italian army on Austrian positions north of Trieste. The twelfth battle began on 24

October 1917, and it is usually called the Battle of Caporetto, after the place where the breakthrough occurred, 'a little white town with a campanile in a valley'. The battle was anything but inconclusive, but this time it was the Austrians who launched the assault, and it proved to be a disaster for Italy.

The attacking forces, greatly bolstered by the presence of German divisions, knocked a fifteen-mile hole in the Italian line and then kept moving, infiltrating their forces into the rear of the Italian strong points. 'The further we penetrated into the hostile positions, the less prepared were the garrisons for our arrival, and the easier the fighting', wrote a young German infantry leader named Erwin Rommel, whose exploits during the offensive won him the Pour le Mérite.

The Italian Second Army crumbled in panic, forcing the armies on either side to pull back. When the Italians finally stopped retreating eleven days later at the Piave River, they were some 80 miles to the rear of their former line on the Isonzo. The Austrians were now in a position to threaten Venice but, mercifully, had outrun their supplies. The Piave line held. In the retreat, the Italians had lost some 40,000 men killed and wounded and another 275,000 taken prisoner.

A few good things came out of the catastrophe at Caporetto. General Count Luigi Cadorna, an unimaginative martinet, was sacked as the Italian Commander-in-Chief. Then, Great Britain and France, at long last recognising that the informal and haphazard direction of the Allied war effort was proving inadequate to the task of defeating the Central Powers, called a meeting of the Allies in Locarno on 5 November at which the parties agreed to establish a Supreme War Council.

Finally, a man who wasn't even in Italy at the time of Caporetto left a vivid account of the retreat that ranks with the very best war fiction: he was Ernest Hemingway, who wrote of it in *A Farewell to Arms*.

Also on this day

1273: The first Habsburg emperor Rudolf von Habsburg is crowned at Aachen * 1537: English Queen Jane Seymour dies twelve days after the birth of the future Edward VI * 1725: Italian composer Alessandro Scarlatti dies in Naples * 1929: Share values on the Wall Street stock market crash on 'Black Thursday', starting the Great Depression

25 October

Agincourt

1415 Shakespeare tells us that today was the feast day of Saint Crispin and Saint Crispian when an exhausted, bedraggled English army met a French force at least four times its size at Agincourt, a hamlet a little south-east of Boulogne amid the rolling countryside of Normandy. Here England's King Henry V achieved enduring fame in one of the great victories of medieval Europe.

Convinced that his Angevin inheritance entitled him to great swathes of France, Henry had resolved to invade in order to enforce his claims, knowing that France was in turmoil, ruled by mad King Charles VI. In early autumn of 1415 he led his army across the Channel.

In September he successfully captured Harfleur, but battle casualties and disease substantially reduced his strength to perhaps 6,000 men, and he turned to find shelter in English-held Calais. But before he could reach safety, a huge French force of 20,000 to 30,000 men caught up with him at Agincourt. Determined to redress the humiliating defeats at Crécy and Poitiers over half a century before, the French blocked the English line of retreat. There was no escape.

Henry positioned his slender force along a narrow, 1000-yard front, flanked by dense forest on both sides. At about eleven in the morning French men-at-arms advanced on the English line.

'Cry "God for Harry! England, and Saint George!"' called out the English King to inspire his men (or at least so says William Shakespeare).

And the line held, as English archers devastated the advancing enemy infantry. Then heavily armoured, dismounted French knights moved forward through the churned mud. Henry urged his men to one more effort:

Once more unto the breach, dear friends, once more:
Or close the wall up with our English dead!

So narrow was the field of battle that the French could not bring their superior numbers to bear. Soon the crush was so intense that the knights could scarcely raise their swords to strike. They became easy targets for English archers who, when not skewering the enemy with arrows, finished off fallen knights with axes and mallets.

In half an hour the battle was over, the French in full retreat. But now, fearing that he lacked the troop strength both to guard the prisoners taken in the battle and to withstand an expected renewal of the French attack, Henry ordered the killing of all prisoners. When his soldiers refused, he ordered his own guard of 200 to carry out the grisly massacre.

In all the French lost three dukes, 90 counts, over 1,500 knights and about 4,000 men-at-arms, plus an uncounted number of archers, servants and fighters of low station. France would remain at the mercy of the English until the miraculous appearance of Joan of Arc some fifteen years later.

The Charge of the Light Brigade

1853 Theirs not to reason why,
Theirs but to do or die,
Into the valley of death
Rode the six hundred.

So wrote Alfred, Lord Tennyson of the famous Charge of the Light Brigade, which took place today during the Battle of Balaclava in the Crimean War.

Early in the battle the British commander Lord Raglan sent orders to the Light Brigade to attack an isolated Russian outpost on the Vorontsov Heights. In transmission to the Brigade's commander, General James Cardigan, the message became muddled. Cardigan was a wealthy earl, a quarrelsome martinet of an officer just a few days short of his 56th birthday. At first he tried to question the confused order, but then commanded his cavalry to charge down the valley between the heights rather than towards the enemy outpost.

Some 607 British horsemen swept forward over a mile of open ground, but a battery of 30 Russian guns opened fire, scything down the attackers. Nevertheless, the British managed to reach the Russian guns and temporarily put them out of action. They then galloped back down the same valley, always under fire. Only 198 survived.

The Charge of the Light Brigade remains one of the most senseless and horrifying displays of proud courage in all of military history. Nothing sums it up better than the comment of the French general Pierre Bosquet, who witnessed the heroic debacle: 'C'est magnifique, mais ce n'est pas la guerre.' (It's magnificent, but no way to fight a war.)

Also on this day
1400: English poet Geoffrey Chaucer dies * 1825: Austrian composer Johann Strauss the Younger is born in Vienna * 1881: Spanish painter Pablo Picasso is born in Malaga

26 October

A date with a political orientation?

1759, 1879, 1916 Is it possible for a date to have a political orientation? It seems implausible, but consider this.

On this day in 1759 the great (and corrupt) French revolutionary Georges Jacques Danton was born in Arras in the Champagne country. A leader in overthrowing the monarchy, he voted for the execution of Louis XVI and later was head of the notorious Committee of Public Safety that rooted out anyone with even the smallest royalist (or indeed moderate) leaning. Towards the end of the Revolution he seemed to turn more conservative and paid for it with his head, disdainfully crying at his execution, 'Let me be led to death, I shall go to sleep in glory.'

Precisely 120 years later another dedicated revolutionary was born, this time in the Ukraine. His name was Lev Bronshtein, but he is better known to us as Leon Trotsky, a pseudonym he adopted from a forged passport when he escaped from a tsarist prison in Siberia when he was 23. Shortly afterwards he fled to London where he first encountered a certain Vladimir Ilich Ulyanov, who would adopt the pseudonym of Lenin.

When he returned to Russia, Trotsky became a leading member of Lenin's drive to overthrow the Tsar. Although he was in jail at the time, he was elected to membership of the Bolshevik Central Committee and later, after the Reds had seized power, became commissar of war. As number two man to Lenin, he was one of five charter members of the Politburo. Eventually, of course, Trotsky was undermined, toppled and exiled by yet another pseudonymous Russian, one Iosif Vissarionovich Dzhugashvili, who styled himself Joseph Stalin (derived from the Russian *stal*, steel). Like Danton before him, Trotsky was eventually consumed by the revolution that he had helped to create. On Stalin's orders an assassin buried the point of a pickaxe in his head while Trotsky was living in exile in Mexico in 1940.

While Trotsky was fomenting revolution in Russia, another wily left-winger was born. On this day in 1916 a stationmaster and his wife in Jarnac, France, celebrated the birth of a boy who would one day become his country's first Socialist president. His name was François Mitterrand.

As a socialist stalwart in the years before his presidential triumph, Mitterrand made much of his valour as a wartime member of the French Resistance. It emerged only shortly before he died that his time in the Maquis had been less than heroic and that he had previously laboured for the collaborationist Vichy government.

In Mitterrand's first foray into presidential politics he represented both the Socialists and Communists in opposing de Gaulle in 1965. By the time he had finally achieved office in 1981, his initial measures were to nationalise a large number of banks and key industries, most of which had to be reversed when the French economy stalled. He managed to avoid both execution and assassination, dying of cancer in 1996.

When the world began

4004 BC That's when it all began – the entire Universe, that is – according to the elaborate calculations of the Anglo-Irish prelate James Ussher who, in 1654, published the conclusions of a lifetime's work with biblical and Semitic texts.

Ussher was not the first to identify the date of creation, or *Annus Mundi*. The Byzantine Church had declared it to be 5509 BC, while the Jewish calendar fixed it at 3760 BC.

But Ussher's reckoning was so persuasive that much of the Christian world came to accept it as accurate, concurring as it did with the widely believed biblical assertion that God had created Heaven and Earth in a mere six days. And Ussher was no minor priest; he had risen from professor and then vice-chancellor of Trinity College, Dublin, to Archbishop of Armagh by the time he was 44. He later moved to England where he advised King Charles I and, after Charles's execution, continued as a noted preacher at Lincoln's Inn in London. He collected such a fine library that it is now in the University of Dublin.

Ussher died an admired and respected figure just two years after the publication of his definitive findings. His chronology of the Creation was largely accepted until the 19th century. So precise were Ussher's calculations that he was able to establish the very hour of Creation as 9.00 in the morning. Amen.

Also on this day

1764: English caricaturist William Hogarth dies in London * 1860: Italian unification leader Giuseppe Garibaldi proclaims Victor Emmanuel King of Italy * 1881: The 'Gunfight at the OK Corral' takes place at Tombstone, Arizona * 1905: Norway and Sweden sign a treaty of separation, making Norway an independent state

27 October

A flaming cross inspires Emperor Constantine at Milvian Bridge

AD 312 Few battles are true turning points in history, but the one fought today at Milvian Bridge near Rome was one of them.

Early in the 4th century several rivals were jockeying (and fighting) for control of the Roman Empire. Two of the most powerful were Constantine, who held sway over Gaul, England and parts of Germany, and Maxentius, who was master of Italy, Spain and Africa. In 310 Constantine took over Spain and now was determined to seize the rest of Maxentius's territories. (The fact that the two were brothers-in-law apparently made no difference in their bloody rivalry.)

At noon on 26 October, the day before the battle, Constantine saw suspended in the sky a flaming cross brighter than the sun inscribed with the words *In hoc signo vinces*. (By this sign thou shalt conquer.) Understanding this as a message direct from God, he ordered a cross interwoven into the imperial standard and attached to the helmets and shields of his soldiers.

The following day the two contending emperors met at Milvian Bridge, where Constantine's inspired troops scored an overwhelming victory, and Maxentius was drowned in the Tiber when a bridge collapsed while he was fleeing the field. So convinced was Constantine that he had received divine aid that he immediately erected a triumphal arch in Rome which credits his success to the inspiration of God.

The first result of the Battle of Milvian Bridge was the eventual reunification of the Roman Empire under a single ruler (another regional Caesar, Licinius, still had to be overcome first, which he was in 324). But of far more lasting consequence was Constantine's confirmed commitment to Christianity. The year after the battle he and Licinius published the Edict of Milan that established toleration of Christianity throughout the Empire.

For the remainder of his reign Constantine actively and continually tried to Christianise his subjects. Numerous laws supported Christianity while (usually mildly) suppressing paganism. He abolished crucifixion as a punishment because of its symbolic significance and imposed the observance of religious worship on Sundays. He even went to war with a portable altar and commanded that his soldiers recite a special Christian prayer that he himself had written.

In 326 his mother Helena, long a committed Christian, travelled to Jerusalem where she discovered the Holy Sepulchre. Constantine ordered the construction of a great basilica on the spot.

It was largely through the efforts of Constantine that the Western world was converted to Christianity as early and as completely as it was. Oddly, the emperor himself waited until a few days before his death to be baptised into the Church.

Burned to death by slow fire

1553 The fact that bigotry knows no borders was perfectly demonstrated today when the unorthodox Christian theologian Michael Servetus was burned to death by slow fire, not by the Catholic fanatics of his native Spain but by the obsessive Calvinists of Switzerland.

Servetus (Miguel Servet in Spanish) had been born in Villanueva but as a young man had studied medicine at the University of Paris, the university where both John Calvin and Ignatius Loyola had studied only a few years before. Loyola went on to found the Jesuits to spearhead the Counter-Reformation while Calvin launched the joyless, militant brand of Protestantism that eventually would bear his name.

Servetus was in theory a Catholic, but at nineteen he attended the coronation of Emperor Charles V at Bologna, where he was deeply shocked by the worldly ostentation of the Pope and his retinue. This led him to doubt the whole faith in which he was raised, and two years later he published his own views, denying the Trinity and the concept of original sin.

Later Servetus became a physician and found a position in the French town of Vienne, near Lyon, where he published his discovery of the pulmonary circulation of the blood. Here he continued his religious explorations and wrote several books stating his convictions. He then began writing to Calvin, perhaps hoping for a kindred spirit who challenged the established beliefs of the Catholic Church.

Calvin took no notice of Servetus's correspondence, but, unfortunately for the Spaniard, some of his letters were sent to the inquisitor general of Lyon, who immediately imprisoned both Servetus and the printers of his books on charges of heresy.

Terrified of what penalty the French inquisitors might impose, Servetus managed to escape, leaving the ecclesiastical authorities with the small satisfaction of burning him in effigy. Fearing recapture, he fled across the border to Calvin's City of God in Geneva, under the delusion that Calvinist Puritanism would be more understanding than inquisitorial Catholicism.

Upon his arrival in Geneva, one of Servetus's first acts was to go to church. During the service he was seized once more, this time by uncompromising Calvinists. Once again he was tried for heresy, with John Calvin himself playing a prominent role in the prosecution. When Servetus was convicted, Calvin urged his execution but displayed his moderation by suggesting decapitation. His sterner co-religionists, however, demanded a more draconian end, and Servetus was led to the stake.

Also on this day

1466: Dutch humanist Erasmus is born in Rotterdam * 1728: English explorer Captain James Cook is born * 1782: Italian composer and violin virtuoso Niccolò Paganini is born in Geneva * 1858: American President Theodore Roosevelt is born

28 October

Catherine de' Medici marries a future king

1533 Unmarked at the time, today was one of the most calamitous days in French history.

On this day the future Henri II, still a gangling fourteen, married a Tuscan orphan of the same age. Black-haired and bug-eyed, the bride's primary attraction was the temporal power of her uncle, Giulio de' Medici, now Pope Clement VII, and the eminence of her forebears, for she was the great-granddaughter of Lorenzo the Magnificent.

The Pope himself performed the wedding rites, which took place in Marseille, with King François I and his Queen in attendance. And so, if Florence lost a daughter, France gained a future queen, in the person of Catherine de' Medici.

Catherine spent the next 26 years playing second fiddle to her husband's famous mistress, Diane de Poitiers, who was nearly twenty years older than her lover. Despairing of attracting her own husband while he enjoyed Diane's favours, Catherine ingested a number of so-called magic potions, including mule's urine, a sure cure for sterility, to boost her sexual allure. When all else failed, she even drilled a spy hole in the floor so that she could watch Henri and Diane in action, in the hope of learning her rival's secrets.

But in 1559 when Henri died from wounds suffered in a joust, Catherine was quick to take control, ruling France for 30 years through the destructive incompetence of her three dismal sons. 'She had too much wit for a woman, too little honesty for a queen', said a contemporary, and even her closest foreign ally and son-in-law Philip II of Spain called her 'Madame la Serpente'. Indeed, her method of keeping tabs on her court was to establish a group of beautiful women (the *Escadron Volant* or Flying Squadron) who dallied with her friends and enemies alike to prise out their secrets.

Catherine's shallow intelligence, malevolent deviousness and lust for power combined to add fuel to France's terrible religious wars, culminating in the Massacre of St Bartholomew. Over this period the population was decimated and France reduced to a second-rate power.

Surprisingly, Catherine also made some positive contributions to her country. Tradition has it that she introduced the fork to France, the nation that today knows best how to use it, and she created one lasting monument for which all tourists to France have been eternally grateful, the exquisite château of Chenonceaux. Henri II had originally confiscated Chenonceaux from a rebellious baron and had given it to his mistress Diane, but when Henri died, Catherine forced Diane to relinquish it to her. It was Catherine who then built the remarkable gallery that crosses to the left bank of the Cher River, making Chenonceaux the most hauntingly beautiful of all the châteaux in the Loire Valley.

The story of the Statue of Liberty

1886 Originally her name was 'Liberty Enlightening the World', a colossal woman holding a torch. Conceived to commemorate the French and American revolutions and the friendship between the people of France and America, she eventually was christened the Statue of Liberty, officially dedicated by American President Grover Cleveland on this day in 1886.

The idea was French, dreamed up by a historian named Edouard de Laboulaye and financed by the Franco-American Union. The sculptor Frédéric-Auguste Bartholdi modelled the face on his mother's, and the original statue reached a height of nine feet, but the lady who welcomes visitors to New York is now 151 feet high, standing on a 150-foot pedestal. The seven spikes in the crown on the statue's head symbolise the seven seas and continents.

Formed of hammered copper sheets, the Statue of Liberty requires an enormous underpinning to support the weight. The ingenious engineer who designed the internal framework was Gustave Eiffel, the man who later built the eponymous tower in Paris.

Also on this day
1636: Harvard University is founded * 1828: French novelist Victor Hugo is born

29 October

Sir Walter Raleigh goes to the block

1618 'Fain would I climb, yet fear to fall', scratched Sir Walter Raleigh on a window pane with his diamond ring. His patroness Queen Elizabeth noticed the scribble and cut beneath it, 'If thy heart fail thee, climb not at all.'

In all the years that followed, Raleigh's heart never failed him, whether he was colonising Virginia, attacking the Spanish, exploring the Orinoco, battling for the Queen's favour or seducing ladies at court.

For 22 years Raleigh was supported by Queen Elizabeth (even though he was periodically banned from court for his misbehaviour). His only serious mistake was to impregnate and secretly marry one of Elizabeth's ladies of court, Elizabeth Throckmorton, for which both Raleigh and his wife were briefly confined to the Tower of London.

After the Queen died in 1603, Raleigh found himself at odds with her successor, James I, who had no interest whatever in Raleigh's swashbuckling adventurism. Worse, Raleigh's enemies spread false rumours that he was plotting to dethrone the King, so he was once more imprisoned in the Tower, where he spent some thirteen years. But even this second imprisonment failed to damp his spirit, for there he began his *History of the World*.

At last released in 1616, Raleigh was sent on another expedition to the Orinoco to search for gold, but with strict orders that no Spanish possessions must be molested.

Sadly for Raleigh, his co-commander defied orders and burned a Spanish town. Returning to England, Raleigh was immediately imprisoned and, on 29 October 1618, the 66-year-old courtier-poet-adventurer was led to the block in the yard of the Old Palace at Westminster. There, encircled by officials and some 60 guards, the Queen's favourite who had feared to fall, fell at last.

But even at the very end Raleigh's spirit did not desert him. Standing with the masked executioner, Raleigh reached to touch the axe and punned, ''Tis a sharp remedy, but a sure one for all ills.' Then, turning to the solemn witnesses, he addressed them with his final words, 'I have a long journey to take, and must bid the company farewell.'

In a gruesome coda to the execution, Raleigh's head was given to his wife in a red leather bag.

Birth of the greatest biographer

1740 Born in Edinburgh today was James Boswell, one of history's most convivial, entertaining and amiable characters, who would leave his mark on English literature with his *The Life of Samuel Johnson, LL.D.*

Son of a Scottish lord, Boswell was a well-meaning but feckless man with a passionate interest in women. His first known conquest was when he was an eighteen-year-old student at Edinburgh University. His paramour had three scandalous defects in the eyes of Boswell's father: she was married, a Roman Catholic and an actress. His father quickly shipped him off to the University of Glasgow to end the liaison. By the time he was twenty he had already tasted the fleshpots of London and contracted gonorrhoea for the first but hardly the last time in his adventurous life. He also managed two illegitimate children by two different mistresses before he finally married at 29.

A genial man with a taste for a good drink, Boswell was fascinated by people of all sorts, including himself, but particularly by famous ones. He met Samuel Johnson for the first time in 1763 when he was 22 and the good doctor already 54. At the first encounter he found the great man 'of a most dreadful appearance', 'slovenly in his dress', with 'a most uncouth voice' and a 'dogmatical roughness of manner'. But the two men got on famously, and in time, as Christopher Morley observed, 'Each became, for the other, the son or father he had never had.' Boswell soon knew Johnson's associates such as Sir Joshua Reynolds and Oliver Goldsmith. He was also on familiar terms with Hume, Voltaire and Benjamin Franklin, and once shared a mistress with Jean-Jacques Rousseau.

Johnson died at the end of 1784, but it was almost seven years before Boswell published his great biography on 16 May 1791, 28 years to the day after he first met the great doctor. With typical insouciant self-assurance, Boswell described his work as 'without exception, the most entertaining book you ever read'.

Boswell himself died at the age of 54 on 19 May 1795 at his house in Great Portland Street in London.

Also on this day

1628: French Cardinal Richelieu conquers La Rochelle, ending Protestant independence in France * 1787: In Prague, Mozart's opera *Don Giovanni* is performed for the first time * 1863: Swiss philanthropist Henri Dunant founds the International Red Cross * 1923: The Turkish Republic is proclaimed

30 October

John Adams, America's second president

1735 Among his enemies, from time to time he counted Benjamin Franklin, Alexander Hamilton, James Madison and Thomas Jefferson, a virtual galaxy of supernovae of the American Revolution. Yet he, too, was a revolutionary hero, America's first ambassador to Great Britain, his nation's first vice-president (a position that he derided as 'the most insignificant office that ever the Invention of man contrived or his Imagination conceived'), and America's second president.

He was John Adams, born today in Braintree (now Quincy), Massachusetts, the first child of Deacon John Adams and his wife Susanna.

Raised in a simpler time when the population of the American states was only two and a half million, Adams was a stout, irascible, round-faced man who was one of the last American politicians to eschew political parties on the idealistic if impractical belief that each member of government should simply do what he thought right for his country rather than support a particular faction.

As a 35-year-old lawyer, Adams demonstrated his determination to live by his own high principles when, in the face of popular outrage, he successfully defended British soldiers accused of murder during an incident known as the 'Boston Massacre'. Later, as President, he avoided a potentially ruinous war with France when the majority of congressmen were baying for blood.

Some of Adams's most valuable contributions to the building of an independent United States were seemingly minor actions with significant consequences: it was Adams who nominated George Washington for Commander-in-Chief of the revolutionary army; he also chose Jefferson to draft the Declaration of Independence.

Despite his success, during his long career in government Adams managed to rouse the ire of many of the nation's most influential leaders. Benjamin Franklin, who preceded Adams as American representative in Paris, thought him mentally unbalanced for his insistence on speaking his mind to his French hosts rather than kowtowing to advance American interests.

Adams and Thomas Jefferson had been firm allies during revolutionary days, but Jefferson and his great supporter James Madison were two great states-righters, who distrusted what they saw as Adams's belief in strong federal government, leading to an acrimonious break with Adams. On the other hand, Alexander Hamilton thought Adams not federalist enough, while Adams thought Hamilton to be planning a coup to make himself king.

Happily, after years of estrangement, Adams was finally reconciled with Jefferson and initiated a brilliant series of 158 letters between the two former presidents, who died on the same day, Adams with Jefferson's name on his lips.

The last Muslim invasion of Spain

1340 What chance did a poor sultan of Morocco have against two Alfonsos, one from Castile called the Just, and one from Portugal called the Brave? As it turned out, not much.

When he succeeded to the Moroccan sultanate in 1331, Abu al-Hasan dedicated himself to a familiar Muslim goal, to cleanse all Spain of Christian infidels. To that end he crossed from North Africa with a vast army, captured Gibraltar and Algeciras, and then utterly destroyed the Castilian fleet in the Strait of Gibraltar when the Spaniards tried to reclaim the Rock. The entire Iberian Peninsula looked ripe for the picking, for its two principal Christian states, Castile and Portugal, were enmeshed in deadly rivalry. The sultan marched his divisions north, towards Seville.

Abu al-Hasan's mistake was to forget that the Christian powers hated the Muslims just as much as the Muslims hated them. Although the two Alfonsos had long been at loggerheads about disputed territory, Abu al-Hasan's victory at Gibraltar inspired them to forge an alliance to combat the Moorish threat.

And so it was that on this day the combined forces of Alfonso the Just and Alfonso the Brave met Abu al-Hasan's Saracen army at Rio Salado just outside Seville. The Christian victory was quick, complete and merciless. It was such a disastrous defeat for Abu al-Hasan that he was forced to flee for North Africa, never to return. This was the last Moorish attempt to conquer Spain. The Muslim jihad was over, and, little by little, the forces of Christianity would reconquer all of Spain until that day in 1492 when Granada, the last Moorish stronghold, would open its gates to the army of Ferdinand and Isabella.

Also on this day

1821: Russian novelist Fyodor Dostoyevsky is born in Moscow

31 October

The building of St Peter's inspires Luther to ignite the Protestant Reformation

1517 Today has been called the first day of the Reformation, when, on the eve of All Saints' Day, a 34-year-old Augustinian monk named Martin Luther nailed his famous 95 theses to the door of the Schlosskirche at the Saxon city of Wittenberg.

What triggered Luther's historic challenge to the Church of Rome was Pope Leo X's decision to complete the rebuilding of Rome's ancient and crumbling St Peter's Cathedral – or rather, how Leo proposed to pay for the work.

St Peter's had been one of Christianity's holiest places since the putative burial there of the apostle St Peter in about AD 67. The first known monument, an *aedicule* or shrine for a small statue, was constructed in around 170, and later Emperor Constantine built a basilica over the *aedicule*. Over the centuries several more churches were built there, but by the 15th century they had fallen into disrepair, and Pope Nicholas V determined to build a cathedral without rival to be named the Basilica of St Peter in honour of the founder of the Church.

Nicholas died in 1455, and construction on St Peter's began only in 1506 under the pontificate of Julius II, and when Leo X became Pope in 1513, the great building was still only partly finished. Leo resolved to continue the project, and with artists like Raphael to hand, he had only one problem – money. So, to raise the cash for the new basilica, he took to selling indulgences to deliver souls from Purgatory.

Leo's call went out to bishops throughout Europe, urging them to find buyers. One particularly energetic salesman was Johann Tetzel, a German Dominican friar who was assigned by the Archbishop of Mainz to get to work.

The Church had been awash with simony, nepotism, venality and corruption for a century, but when Luther, then a monk lecturing at the University of Wittenberg, learned of Tetzel's cynical sales programme, it was the final straw. In reaction to this last impiety, he hit back at the offending Church, starting with Tetzel, about whom he swore, 'God willing, I will beat a hole in his drum!' Then on this day he nailed his famous 95 theses to the church door at Wittenberg.

Luther's theses, written in Latin, only indirectly criticised papal policy, while emphasising spiritual life within the Church. Luther contended that divine grace cannot be easily acquired but must be gained through true belief and tribulation. But to ensure that someone beyond a junior acolyte would read the theses, he sent copies to the Archbishop of Mainz. Thanks to the recently developing art of printing, further copies were then circulated across much of Europe.

Thus it was that the building of its greatest monument touched off the blast that sundered the Catholic Church for ever.

Jan Vermeer

1632 On this day in his family's tavern in the market-place of Delft was born Jan Vermeer, that reclusive Dutch painter who gave such exquisite beauty and frozen silence to simple Dutch household interiors.

We know very little about this quiet genius. Son of an innkeeper/art dealer father, he married Catharina Bolnes at 21 and fathered eleven children. Earning his living as an art dealer, he remained in Delft all his life, and his paintings consist almost entirely of beautifully constructed interiors. Even his two known landscapes were painted from a window. Only 35 paintings are unquestionably attributed to him, and only three of these are reliably dated.

When Vermeer died at 43 he left his wife and family bankrupt, as he had never sold a single one of his own paintings.

The feast of the naked courtesans

1501 The time: Sunday evening, All Saints' Eve. The place: the Apostolic Palace in the Vatican in Rome. The most honoured guest: the Pope, Alexander VI. Such was the virtuous setting for one of history's more debauched parties.

According to an eyewitness, a papal secretary named Johannes Burchard, the evening's entertainment was 'a supper, participated in by fifty honest prostitutes of those who are called courtesans. After supper they danced with the servants and others who were there, first clothed, then naked ... lighted candelabra were placed on the floor and chestnuts thrown among them which the prostitutes had to pick up as they crawled between the candles ... At the end they displayed prizes ... which were promised to whoever should have made love to those prostitutes the greatest number of times.'

The host for this ennobling soirée was none other than the Pope's illegitimate son, Cesare Borgia, who was giving the party to honour the forthcoming marriage of his sister Lucrezia.

Also on this day

1795: English poet John Keats is born * 1902: The first telegraph cable across the Pacific Ocean is completed * 1940: The Battle of Britain ends * 1952: The United States detonates the first hydrogen bomb at Eniwetok Atoll in the Pacific

1 November

The pope who asked Michelangelo to paint the Sistine Chapel

1503 When Giuliano della Rovere was elected Pope on this day, he was a month short of his 60th birthday. In the eleven years of his reign, this headstrong and irascible pontiff achieved the worldly greatness of a Renaissance prince.

Giuliano's uncle was Pope Sixtus IV, who made him a cardinal and granted him nine bishoprics in Italy and France as well as numerous prosperous abbeys. While enjoying his riches and generally ignoring his flock, the sophisticated cardinal managed to father three illegitimate daughters. But in 1492 he was forced to flee to France when the spectacularly corrupt Alexander VI became Pope, whose election Giuliano had vigorously opposed.

Still trying to bring about Alexander's downfall, Giuliano twice joined foreign invasions of Italy, first with the French King Charles VIII and subsequently with his successor, Louis XII. Enraged, the Pope ordered the cardinal's assassination, but Giuliano remained in safety in the French court.

Alexander died in 1503, and after the seventeen-day reign of Pius III, Giuliano finally managed to buy enough votes to assure his own election, taking the name of Julius II. One of his first acts as Pope was to declare that in the future any papal election won by simony would be invalid.

During the next eleven years Julius fought two wars to strengthen the temporal powers of the Vatican, often taking the field himself, the last of the warrior popes. During the second of these he unsuccessfully attempted to force his former French allies to leave Italy. In spite of his own shady rise to power, he worked hard to cleanse the Church of much of its nepotism and corruption.

But Julius's greatest contribution was artistic. He ordered the construction or refurbishment of countless buildings and churches in Rome, and he laid the foundation stone for the new St Peter's basilica, commissioning Bramante and Michelangelo to work on it. He was a patron of Raphael and formed a virtual partnership with Michelangelo in the creation of the great frescoes in the Sistine Chapel.

Pope Julius died on 21 February 1513 and lies buried in St Peter's, but the tomb he commissioned, never completed, is in the Church of San Pietro in Vincoli, guarded by Michelangelo's statue of Moses.

The worst earthquake in European history devastates Lisbon

1755 Every year there are some 50,000 earthquakes that can be detected without the aid of scientific instruments, but most of these frighten the local population while causing little damage. Occasionally, however, the earth is subject to a far greater shock.

Today in Lisbon people were quietly attending Mass to celebrate All Saints' Day when at 9.40 a massive quake struck the city. Although it lasted for only fifteen minutes, it is believed to have measured an enormous 9.0 on the Richter scale, only slightly below the maximum ever recorded (9.2 in Alaska in 1964). More than 12,000 houses collapsed into rubble, along with a large number of public buildings. Worst hit were the many churches packed with believers during the morning services.

Desperate, people scrabbled from the collapsed churches only to find fires raging across the city, and worse was yet to come, as a 40-foot wave smashed into the city, drowning many who had escaped from falling and burning buildings. So powerful was the wave that when it crashed into Martinique, almost 4,000 miles away, it still maintained a height of twelve feet.

About two-thirds of Lisbon was destroyed that day, and almost 80,000 people are believed to have perished.

The last Habsburg king of Spain

1700 Carlos el Hechizado they called him, Charles the Bewitched. Weak-brained and slightly deformed, he had been carried around like an infant until the age of ten – but had inherited the throne of Spain as Charles II when he was only four. He died today in Madrid, just five days short of his 40th birthday, the last king of the Habsburg dynasty that had ruled Spain for 196 years. His last (and perhaps only) significant act as King was to leave his throne to a new dynasty that would be even more durable than the Habsburgs.

Charles was rational if dim, but his prognathous Habsburg jaw made his speech nearly unintelligible and prevented him from chewing, so he subsisted on soups and slops. And if that were not enough, he was also impotent, which may have been a blessing for his two wives.

During the last years of his 35-year reign, he was constantly in ill health, and Spain was impoverished and depopulated during a period of constant minor warfare and emigration to Spanish colonies abroad. Since the King had no heirs, competing European powers jockeyed to put forward their favourites to inherit the throne on his death or to dismantle Spain's empire by depriving Spain of its possessions in the Netherlands and Italy.

Even Charles was aware of the problems likely to follow on his death and became determined to settle his inheritance while he was still alive. Having convinced himself that only France would leave Spain and its possessions intact, he willed his throne to a Frenchman, Philippe, duc d'Anjou, grandson of France's Louis XIV.

In his determination to put things right, the unfortunate Charles succeeded in putting things wrong, as his testament ignited the bloody fourteen-year War of the Spanish Succession. Louis XIV clearly favoured Charles's choice, but other European powers feared it would lead to a union of Spain and France under a single king.

In the end Charles's will was honoured and Philippe became Spain's Philip V, founding Spain's Bourbon line, which still holds the crown today, over three centuries later.

Also on this day

1500: Italian sculptor and jeweller Benvenuto Cellini is born * 1757: Italian sculptor Antonio Canova is born * 1800: The White House becomes the residence of American presidents as John Adams spends the first night there

2 November

The prince in the tower who became the monarch with the shortest reign in British history

1470 Today was born the future Edward V of England, who twelve years later would inherit the throne and reign a mere 79 days, the shortest rule of any British monarch from William the Conqueror to Elizabeth II.

On 1 May 1464 Edward's father, 22-year-old King Edward IV, had secretly married a ravishing widow five years his senior named Elizabeth Woodville. The English court was appalled by this misalliance, as Elizabeth came from a family of only modest gentility, but the marriage seemed to work, in spite of the King's flagrant promiscuity. Six years later a son was born, shortly followed by another.

When the elder Edward died on 9 April 1483, young Edward inherited the throne. As he was still only twelve, his uncle Richard, the capable but ambitious Duke of Gloucester, was made protector of the realm.

In order to 'ensure their safety', Richard first moved the young King and his brother to the security of the Tower of London. Then, citing his brother Edward IV's licentious adventures and his secret marriage to Elizabeth, he persuaded the court that the marriage had in fact never taken place, making young Edward V illegitimate – and therefore not King at all.

On 25 June an assembly of lords duly declared Richard King Richard III, while Edward and his brother were still held in the Tower of London. And, as every schoolchild knows, neither of the young princes was ever seen again.

In all probability, in August that same year Richard's agents secretly smothered the two brothers in their room, but to this date debate has raged concerning their fate. Two centuries later the skeletons of two young boys were found buried in the Tower, presumed to be the princes, but historians still debate who killed them. Some claim it was their traitorous paternal uncle Richard, others nominate their equally unscrupulous maternal uncle, Richard's supporter Henry Stafford, Duke of Buckingham, while a few maintain it was the King who supplanted Richard III, King Henry VII.

Which American president gained the most territory for his country?

1795 These days few people remember much about America's eleventh president James Polk, who was born today. Austere and distant, he served only one term in the White House, leaving office a sick man with only three months to live. But in that single term, he gained more territory for the United States than any other American president before or since, increasing the size of the country by two-thirds.

Even in 1844 when Polk ran as the Democratic Party's candidate for the presidency he was a colourless and anonymous character. Despite having served fourteen years in Congress, he was so obscure a figure on the political scene that his Whig opponents thought they could beat him by raising the derisive cry 'Who is James Polk?'

But in his campaign Polk adopted the alliterative slogan of 'Fifty-four Forty or Fight', a reference to his determination to seize disputed territory from the British even if it meant a war.

'Fifty-four Forty' referred to the northern boundary of an enormous parcel of land on the west coast of North America between the Mexican territory of California and Russian-held Alaska. Known as the Oregon country, this land had been occupied jointly by the United States and Great Britain for the last 35 years. But American settlers were streaming into it, and many believed in their country's 'Manifest Destiny', the supposedly inevitable march of the nation westward to the Pacific. American annexationists wanted the entire Oregon territory, right up to its border with Alaska at 54 degrees, 40 minutes north latitude. Great Britain, however, wanted the line drawn at the 47th parallel, along the Columbia River. Such was the appeal of Polk's bellicose slogan that it overcame his previous obscurity and he won the election.

Once in office, however, Polk renounced war for negotiation and offered a compromise line at the 49th parallel, accepted by Great Britain in June 1846. With that agreement, the United States took sole possession of land that would eventually comprise the states of Washington, Oregon, Idaho and parts of Wyoming and Montana. Great Britain received what is now the Canadian province of British Columbia and Vancouver Island.

That was only part of Polk's enlargement of his country. In May 1846 he brought on war with Mexico over Texas, already annexed to the United States, which resulted not only in military victory but also in the addition of territory that would eventually become the states of California, Nevada, Utah, most of Arizona, and parts of New Mexico, Colorado and Wyoming.

When he wasn't busy expanding the United States, Polk managed to create the Department of the Interior, establish the Naval Academy at Annapolis and authorise the founding of the Smithsonian Institution. All in all, a very creditable performance for a one-term president no one much remembers.

Also on this day

1734: American pioneer Daniel Boone is born * 1755: Future French Queen Marie Antoinette is born in Vienna

3 November

Rome's April Fools' Day

BC In ancient Rome today was a festival called the Hilaria, a sort of Roman April Fools' Day when believers were permitted to play practical jokes on each other. It was a special holiday of celebration and gaiety observed by the cult dedicated to Isis and Osiris, two deities the Romans had adopted from their Egyptian colony. The Hilaria honoured the murdered god Osiris, who had been resurrected on 3 November.

The full tale was pretty grim stuff, and pretty confusing, too. Osiris, who was both the god of fertility and king of the underworld, married his sister Isis, a great magician. The two of them had a brother named Seth, who was a formidable fellow with a curved, fox-like snout, slanting eyes and a dog's body with a forked tail. He was also the god of storms, warfare and chaos.

Seth hated Osiris and was desperate to usurp his position as king of the underworld. One day he tricked his brother into climbing into a chest, slammed the lid shut and hurled the chest into the sea. He then sliced his drowned brother's corpse into fourteen pieces and scattered them all over Egypt. But Seth hadn't counted on Isis, who retrieved her husband's bits and buried them, all except for his penis. She then magically brought Osiris back to life and, no doubt with the help of that one unburied member, miraculously produced a son, Horus. Horus was a god who looked like a falcon, whose eyes were the sun and the moon. He spent most of his life fighting with his uncle Seth and finally defeated him, but during the battle he received a wound to his left eye. The injury accounted for the waning and waxing of the moon.

Stanley finds Dr Livingstone

1871 'I noticed that he was pale, looked worried, had a gray beard, wore a bluish cap with a faded gold band round it, had on a red-sleeved waistcoat, and a pair of gray tweed trousers ... I did not know how he would receive me, so ... I walked deliberately up to him, took off my hat, and said, "Dr Livingstone, I presume." "Yes," he said, with a kind smile. Lifting his cap slightly ... and we both grasped hands.'

So wrote Henry Stanley, intrepid reporter sent out by the New York *Herald* to find Africa's most famous explorer, Dr David Livingstone, who had seemingly vanished into the Dark Continent. Leading a small caravan of native guides and bearers, Stanley tramped through the African bush for over six months, encountering disease and hostile tribes along the way, but eventually made his way to Ujiji, on Lake Tanganyika, where on this day he found Livingstone living among the natives. The doctor had seen no other white man for six and a half years. Resolutely refusing to return to England, he died two years later at the age of 60 without ever seeing another one.

4 November

Montgomery defeats Rommel at El Alamein

1942 Make sure you drink a Montgomery cocktail (recipe below), for today marks the completion of a tremendous two-week battle at El Alamein, Egypt, in which the British Eighth Army, under the command of General Bernard Law Montgomery, defeated the Italian-German Panzerarmee Afrika led by General Erwin Rommel.

If you were in England and read the next day's *Daily Telegraph*, you would have seen this headline: 'AXIS FORCES IN FULL RETREAT: OFFICIAL. Rommel's disordered columns attacked relentlessly. 9,000 prisoners; 260 tanks destroyed.' In America, on the eve of congressional elections, news of the victory swept politics off the front pages.

El Alamein was a most welcome feat of arms, coming as it did after the British debacles at Singapore and Tobruk, and went a long way to cement relations between the British and American military chiefs. Montgomery's victory saved Egypt and the Suez Canal. Churchill, in handsome overstatement, said, 'Before Alamein we never had a victory; after Alamein we never had a defeat.' In truth, the battle marked a turning of the tide of war, a shift that would be entirely confirmed three months later by the German defeat before Stalingrad.

Monty always had his detractors, however, who found his style of warfare too cautious and deliberate. Some years later in Harry's Bar in Venice, Ernest Hemingway invented the Montgomery cocktail, a martini made up of fifteen parts of gin to one of vermouth. This mixture, its inventor swore, was based on the ratio of his own troops to those of the enemy that Monty required before ordering an attack. Serve very cold.

Howard Carter finds the tomb of Tutankhamen

1922 Today a 49-year-old Englishman named Howard Carter made the most spectacular archaeological discovery in history when he and his excavating team found the nearly intact tomb of the 14th-century BC Egyptian Pharaoh Tutankhamen.

Carter had been digging in Egypt off and on since he was seventeen, at one time serving as inspector general of the Egyptian antiquities department. When he was 24 he was contacted by the noted Egyptologist Lord Carnarvon, who wanted him to supervise further excavations in the Valley of the Kings. From that time forward the two men worked in close collaboration.

In late October 1922 Carter was once again in the field exploring an area near the tomb of Ramses VI, where he had found a large number of ancient workman's huts. Suspecting something might lie beneath, he decided to have his workers clear away some of the huts. Then, in Carter's own words, 'Hardly had I arrived at work next morning (4 November) than the unusual silence, due to the stoppage of the work, made me realise that something out of the ordinary had happened, and I was greeted by the announcement that a step cut in the rock had been discovered underneath the very first hut to be attacked.' It was the first sighting of the entrance to Tutankhamen's tomb.

Working 'feverishly' for all that day and the next, Carter and his team soon were certain that what they had found was indeed the tomb entrance, with its seals intact. Although they continued to clear away rubble, since Carnarvon was away, they waited until his return on 26 November to open the tomb itself. Then, Carter reports, 'With trembling hands I made a tiny breach in the upper left-hand corner [of the door] ... I inserted a candle and peered in ... At first I could see nothing, the hot air escaping from the chamber causing the candle flame to flicker, but presently ... details of the room within emerged slowly from the mist, strange animals, statues and gold – everywhere the glint of gold.'

When Carter's team finally entered the tomb, they found Tutankhamen's mummy encased in three coffins, the innermost one of solid gold. Covering the king's face was the now world-famous inlaid gold funerary mask. The burial chambers were stuffed with beautiful statuary and furniture, the king's weapons and a magnificent gold chariot.

Carter's find ignited a Tutankhamen mania throughout Europe and America – there was even a brand of cigarette called King Tut. Eventually most of the tomb's contents were transferred to the Cairo Museum, where today you can gaze with awe at the large and exquisite collection of artefacts that lay buried with the young king for almost three and a half thousand years.

Also on this day
1847: German composer Felix Mendelssohn dies in Leipzig

5 November

Guy Fawkes

1605 London was smaller then, the population only a few hundred thousand, and November nights were cold and black, the only lighting seeping from a few unshuttered windows. But tonight there were bonfires in the streets, the crowds around them rejoicing to the sound of church bells ringing across the city. England's Protestant King James I and his young son Prince Henry had been saved from a murderous Catholic plot.

A nobleman named Robert Catesby, frustrated in his efforts to gain from the King greater tolerance for the Catholic faith, was at the heart of the conspiracy. Drawing together a group that finally included thirteen others, he planned to blow up the Houses of Parliament on their opening day on 5 November 1605, killing not only the King and his son but also virtually the entire parliament and the Protestant churchmen in attendance. Among the plotters was a certain Guy Fawkes, an English mercenary soldier just returned from the Spanish Nether-lands after ten years of fighting Protestants. Fawkes was the group's technician; thanks to his military experience he knew how to build and detonate bombs.

In early 1605 one of the conspirators leased a house across the street from Parliament with a cellar that extended directly under the building. Soon the cellar was filled with 36 barrels of gunpowder, each weighing 100 pounds. After the explosion, Catesby would ride north to incite a Catholic uprising.

Ten days before the target date, however, probably in an attempt to save Catholic members of parliament, one of the plotters sent an anonymous letter to his brother-in-law warning of a forthcoming 'blow'. The brother-in-law promptly turned it over to the King, who proclaimed, 'It smells of gunpowder.'

King James now alerted his security services under the command of his redoubtable First Minister Robert Cecil. At exactly midnight on 4 November, the King's men pounced, catching Fawkes in the cellar about to light an eight-hour fuse that would detonate the powder the following morning just as the King opened Parliament.

Taken to the Tower, Fawkes was first interrogated by the King himself, then tortured on the rack, soon revealing all he knew. Troops were dispatched to apprehend the other plotters, who were surrounded in a house in Warwickshire where they had fled on hearing of Fawkes's arrest. The soldiers shot down two. Then Catesby and one remaining ally, armed only with swords, charged out through the front door like Butch Cassidy and the Sundance Kid. His companion was killed immediately, but Catesby, wounded, managed to crawl into the chapel before dying.

The remaining conspirators were incarcerated in the Tower with Fawkes until their trial in Westminster Hall. Quickly found guilty, all were dragged through the streets on sledges to Old Palace Yard where they were hanged, drawn and quartered, their heads displayed on pikes around the Tower.

Remember, remember the fifth of November
Gunpowder, treason and plot.
I see no reason why gunpowder treason
Should ever be forgot.

So chant the children to this day, as the British light bonfires on the evening of 5 November, burning Guy Fawkes in effigy amid a celebration of fireworks commemorating the explosion that never took place.

Also on this day

1854: During the Crimean War British and French armies defeat the Russians at the Battle of Inkerman * 1955: French painter Maurice Utrillo dies

6 November

Russia loses Catherine the Great

1796 Catherine the Great died today, having lived for 67 years, Empress of Russia for the last 34 of them.

Catherine had been born in Germany and brought to Russia at the age of fourteen to marry the future Tsar, Peter III. By the time this ineffectual prince finally gained the throne, Catherine was 33 and entirely estranged from her husband. She had already taken at least three lovers, of whom one was probably the father of her son, future Tsar Paul I. Six months after Peter's succession, Catherine seized power and engineered her husband's murder by her current lover's brother.

From then on Catherine ruled as the most absolute monarch in Europe, while taking a succession of increasingly younger lovers whom she lavishly rewarded when she tired of their services. She had at least nine favourites while she was Empress, the youngest being twenty-year-old Alexander Lanskoy, whom she took up when she was 51.

It was rumoured that Catherine's lovers were all market tested by ladies of the court before being invited to attend the Empress. No doubt the candidates needed both stamina and imagination, since the licentious Catherine grew increasingly fat as she grew older. Her last paramour, Platon Zubov, must have been particularly resolute: he was only 22 when the Empress engaged him at the age of 60.

Although a scandal across Europe (Frederick the Great called her the Messalina of the North), Catherine changed Russia for ever. Claiming to be a liberal, in most things she was actually an extreme reactionary. She made the plight of Russia's serfs even worse by increasing the power of landowners, stripping the serfs of any state protection and strictly prohibiting any appeal for relief to the sovereign. She also imposed serfdom on the Ukrainians, who had hitherto been free.

Even so, she fancied herself an enlightened ruler, corresponding with intellectuals such as Voltaire and Diderot. She volunteered herself and her son for the first tuberculosis inoculations in Russia in order to set an example for her suspicious and recalcitrant people. She also enormously increased the size of her country by appropriating over 200,000 square miles of new territory, equivalent in size to California and New York State combined, and more than twice as large as Great Britain.

On 5 November 1796 Catherine was felled by a stroke. Like George II before her and Elvis Presley after, she was sitting in her privy closet when she was stricken. It took six strong men to carry her unconscious body to her bedroom, where, too heavy to be lifted onto her bed, she was laid on a mattress on the floor. In spite of the efforts of her doctors to revive her, she never regained consciousness, dying at 9.45 the following evening.

No sooner was Catherine dead than her son Paul had his putative father's body exhumed. He then turned Catherine's state funeral in the cathedral of Saints Peter and Paul into a double ceremony, the still fresh corpse of the bloated Empress lying beside the desiccated remains of the husband she had murdered 34 years before.

Philippe Egalité to the guillotine

1793 Philippe, duc d'Orléans carried royal blood in his veins; he was the great-great-great-grandson of Louis XIII. Nonetheless, he professed to be a democrat and styled himself Philippe Egalité upon giving up his title during the French Revolution. Although he was probably the richest man in France, he felt radical enough to vote for the execution of his cousin, Louis XVI, in January of 1793.

Philippe Egalité may have been sorely disappointed, then, when in November the same year he himself was tried by the Revolutionary Tribunal, largely because his son had fled to the safety of Austria and the Habsburg court.

Convicted of treason, he went to the guillotine on this day at the age of 46. Apparently he was unmoved by the proceedings and died calmly, with a smile on his lips. Could he have guessed that men of his blood would rule France again one day? Thirty-seven years later the son who had fled to Austria would become King Louis-Philippe.

Also on this day

1860: Abraham Lincoln is elected 16th President of the United States * 1893: Russian composer Peter Ilyich Tchaikovsky dies * 1924: British Tory leader Stanley Baldwin is elected Prime Minister

7 November

The October Revolution – the Bolsheviks take over Russia

1917 Today one of the most improbable events in history took place. It was announced with this message at 10.00 a.m., composed by Lenin only minutes before: 'TO THE CITIZENS OF RUSSIA! The Provisional Government has been deposed ...' But what had occurred during the night was no glorious uprising of workers, no pitched battle in the streets, no storming of a Bastille, only a mild and bloodless coup carried out so quietly that almost nobody resisted and very few knew it had even happened. When it was over, however, the city of St Petersburg and the government of Russia lay in Bolshevik hands.

The slightest resistance might have saved the day. The Bolsheviks had taken over the instruments of power simply by walking in and dismissing those on duty: post offices, railway stations, banks, bridges and telephone centres changed hands without a shot. When morning came, only the Winter Palace remained under the control of the Prime Minister, Alexander Kerensky, and the Provisional Government.

Leaving his Cabinet ministers behind, Kerensky departed St Petersburg by car and in disguise, looking for troops who would defend the government. At Pskov he persuaded some Cossack units of the Third Cavalry Corps to accompany him, but when the soldiers discovered that no other units would join them, they quit two hours from the capital.

Lacking sufficient forces to take the lightly defended Winter Palace by assault, the Bolsheviks ordered the artillery of the Peter and Paul Fortress to fire on the building. Of 35 shells fired, two hit their target with minimum damage. The 'storming' of the Palace, later portrayed by Bolshevik historians as the epic event of a great popular rising (called the October Revolution because in Russia the old Julian calendar still prevailed), came about that night only after most of the discouraged defenders – teenage cadets – sensing that reinforcements were not going to turn up, had slunk away, and only then because, as George Kennan wrote, '... someone had inadvertently left the back door open'.

In the capital of Russia, at least, the first day of their bid for power ended successfully, if not heroically, for the Bolsheviks. In other places it was not always so easy – where there was resistance, it often prevailed – but authority, whether military or civil, showed little determination to save itself. So the improbable became reality. Within weeks, in most of the cities of central Russia, the Bolsheviks, with barely 25,000 members around the country, had taken power in the name of 100 million Russian people, most of whom had never heard of the Bolsheviks.

No one mourned the death of the Provisional Government. It had come to uncertain power in the vacuum left by the fall of the monarchy in February. It could not govern a Russia grown unmanageable under the multiple burdens of war, shortages, inflation, strikes and mutiny.

One eyewitness to the day's events was John Reed, who liked what he saw. Later, in *Ten Days That Shook the World*, he remembered how he felt the next morning: 'Now there was all great Russia to win – and then the world! Would Russia follow and rise? And the world – what of it? Would the peoples answer and rise, a red world-tide? Although it was six in the morning, night was yet heavy and chill. There was only a faint unearthly pallor stealing over the silent streets, dimming the watch-fires, the shadow of a terrible dawn grey-rising over Russia ...'

The last man hanged at Tyburn

1783 Today a convicted forger named John Austin gained unfortunate fame by becoming the last man ever to be publicly hanged at Tyburn Tree, the famous London gallows that stood at the north-east corner of what is now Hyde Park, near Speaker's Corner.

The first execution at Tyburn may have taken place as early as 1196, and the Scottish rebel William Wallace may have met his end there in 1305. What is certain is that Roger de Mortimer, the lover of Queen Isabella who arranged the murder of her husband Edward II, was hanged, drawn and quartered at Tyburn in 1330.

It was in 1571, however, that Tyburn became the official venue of choice for execution, its first client being a certain Dr John Story. By now, though, the method had, except for treason, been reduced to simple hanging. In the intervening years thousands went to the gallows there; in the 18th century alone about 1,300 died on the Tyburn gibbet, including at least four children under fourteen.

Most criminals condemned to death were held in Newgate Prison. On the day of their execution they were carried by open horse-drawn carts along the three-mile westward trek that ended with a long pull down today's Oxford Street to the gallows at Tyburn. Some of the more flamboyant convicts wore their wedding suits in order to leave the world with a splash. Along the way spectators cheered and jeered, and prisoners were much admired if they could banter with the crowd as they headed for their deaths. The carts would usually stop so that the criminals could enjoy one last drink of ale at the Bowl Inn at St Giles in the Fields.

At Tyburn huge throngs would wait in holiday mood, including anatomists who would fight for the dead bodies at execution's end. Normally some 10,000 people would attend, but for a particularly famous execution like the Cato Street conspirators' in 1820, approximately 100,000 watched. Among those who enjoyed a good hanging were the diarist Samuel Pepys and the biographer James Boswell. William Hogarth even painted the scene.

The condemned men (and 90 per cent of those executed were men under 21) were either hooded or blindfolded and their wrists tied behind their backs before the noose was placed around their necks. Some died quickly with broken necks, but others dangled, choking, until a friend or relative hurried forward to pull on their legs to bring their suffering to an end.

It is no surprise that the rowdy crowds, fuelled by drink, often erupted in riot. Therefore after John Austin's hanging in 1783, Tyburn was never used again for executions. The venue was moved to Newgate Prison, where (for a fee) the public could still watch men being put to death, but in 1868 public executions were ended for ever in Great Britain. Finally, on 9 November 1965, capital punishment was abolished altogether.

Also on this day

1805: Explorers Lewis and Clark become the first American men to travel across North America and reach the west coast * 1867: Polish scientist Marie Curie (née Sklodowska) is born in Warsaw * 1900: Heinrich Himmler, head of the Nazi SS and organiser of extermination camps in Eastern Europe, is born * 1913: French philosopher and novelist Albert Camus is born

8 November

'O liberté! Que de crimes on commet dans ton nom!'

1793 'O Liberty, what crimes are committed in thy name!' The woman who spoke these famous words faced the guillotine today in Revolutionary Paris.

In 1780 25-year-old Manon de La Platière married an inspector of manufactures in Amiens named Jean-Marie Roland, who was twenty years her senior. Eleven years later, after the outbreak of the French Revolution, the couple moved to Paris, where she soon established a salon for like-minded liberals who eventually became known as the Girondins, a relatively moderate bourgeois faction that opposed the Revolution's most radical elements. Both striking and intelligent, Manon Roland, as she now was, masterminded her husband's career and helped him to rise to the post of Minister of the Interior.

In the early stages of the Revolution Manon Roland had sounded a bloodthirsty note, insisting that 'Il faut du sang pour cimenter la révolution.' (It takes some blood to cement the revolution.) Later, although still fervent democrats, both Rolands had become more moderate, and, at the instigation of his wife, Jean-Marie launched an attack on Danton and Robespierre before the Convention. Then, two days after the execution of Louis XVI, which he had vigorously opposed, he resigned his ministerial post.

Less than six months later Robespierre had become the most powerful man in France and expelled all Girondins from government. Then, in May 1793, began the awful butchery called the Terror. Jean-Marie fled, but on 31 May Manon was arrested and thrown into prison, where she occupied her time by writing her memoirs. After five months of incarceration she was led to the place de la Révolution for execution.

Ignoring the taunts shrieked by the brutal mob surrounding the scaffold, Manon hesitated before mounting the steps. Bowing in mockery in front of a giant statue of liberty at whose base stood the guillotine, she uttered her famous apostrophe.

Jean-Marie had evaded arrest, but on learning of his wife's execution, a week later he fell on his sword.

The Battle of the White Mountain

1620 It all started with that famous farce, the Second Defenestration of Prague, during which three agents of the Holy Roman Emperor were tossed out of the first-floor window of the Hradcany Palace by Bohemian Protestants in protest against the Catholic Habsburgs. No one was hurt, but imperial dignity was badly bruised, and Catholics and Protestants were further polarised.

Two years later Ferdinand II, who had been elected King of Bohemia in 1617 only to be deposed by the largely Protestant Bohemian Diet (parliament) a year later, became the new Holy Roman Emperor. Educated by Jesuits, he was a fervent Catholic and determined to restore the true faith, if necessary by force.

Then some Protestant Bohemian nobles rose in revolt under the leadership of the 24-year-old Frederick V, the very man who had replaced Ferdinand as King of Bohemia. This gave the Emperor all the excuse he needed to send in his army.

On this day in 1620 imperial troops under the command of Johann Tserclaes, Graf von Tilly annihilated the rebel Bohemians on the outskirts of Prague in what is known as the Battle of the White Mountain.

Prior to this battle the Bohemians had been semi-independent. When it was over they had become an integral part of the Holy Roman and later the Austrian Empire, not to regain their independence for three centuries until the creation of Czechoslovakia in the aftermath of the First World War.

Also on this day

1656: English astronomer Edmond Halley is born * 1674: English poet John Milton dies * 1895: William Röntgen discovers X-rays at the University of Wurzburg * 1923: Hitler leads the unsuccessful Beer Hall Putsch in Munich * 1942: British and American forces commanded by General Dwight Eisenhower invade North Africa

9 November

Napoleon's coup d'état

1799 In revolutionary France, today was 18 Brumaire, An VIII, the first day of Napoleon Bonaparte's *coup d'état.*

Just back from his battles in Egypt, the diminutive Napoleon (he was just five feet six) was seen as a national hero. Backed by a few powerful members of government (notably Talleyrand), he donned his splashiest general's uniform – white breeches, blue coat with gold-embroidered lapels and a flamboyant red, white and blue sash at the waist – and paraded through the streets of Paris to tumultuous applause. He then entered the Tuileries to swear allegiance to one chamber of the government (the Elders) and next promptly sent 300 soldiers to 'protect' the other chamber, the Council of the Five Hundred.

The following day Napoleon boldly addressed each group, but the Council of the Five Hundred in particular turned on him savagely, and a pale and stammering Napoleon had to be accompanied from the chamber by four soldiers.

Having failed to charm the government with words, Napoleon did what he always did best. He sent in troops. His soldiers charged into the Orangerie, forcing the 500 members to flee through the windows.

On the evening of 10 November Bonaparte was declared First Consul; the Republican government known as the Directory was over. From that day until his abdication Napoleon held supreme power in France. Six years earlier to the day the revolutionary government had abolished the worship of God, and on that anniversary they instituted a replacement.

Piero de' Medici flees Florence

1494 The first Medici to gain official power in Florence was a certain Ardingo, who in 1296 became *Gonfaloniere* (standard bearer) of the Florentine Republic. Two centuries later the family was by far the dominant force in the state. Thus today was a black and shocking day for the Medici, when 22-year-old Piero de' Medici was forced to flee the city, never to return.

Only two years earlier he had assumed the leadership of his family (and of Florence) on the death of his father, Lorenzo the Magnificent. But from the first his arrogance had annoyed his fellow citizens, and then he found himself caught between the messianic zeal of the fanatical prelate Savonarola and the threat of invasion by Charles VIII of France. Hoping to placate the French King, he hurried to meet him as he descended on Italy with his army. The Florentines saw this attempt at diplomacy as abject capitulation, giving them all the excuse they needed to revolt. They sacked the Medici palace and drove a desperate Piero from the city. From then on Piero was known as *Il Fatuo*, the Fatuous.

Now Piero had no recourse but to join King Charles, but after nine years of service as courtier and soldier, he was drowned in the Garigliano River in southern Italy. It looked as if Medici power in Tuscany was gone for good.

Fortunately for the family, however, Piero's brother Giovanni had all the guile and toughness that Piero lacked. A cardinal by the age of thirteen, with the tacit backing of Rome he re-established Medici ascendancy by 1512, and a year later was elected Pope as Leo X. The family reigned supreme until the Medici magic was stilled for ever in 1737.

Also on this day
1918: Germany's Kaiser Wilhelm abdicates and flees to Holland * 1925: Adolf Hitler establishes the SS (Schutzstaffel or 'Protection Squad') as his personal bodyguard

10 November

The US Marine Corps is born

1775 Today, just six months after the first shots of the American Revolutionary War were fired at the Battle of Lexington, the Continental Congress authorised the creation of the Continental Marines, now known as the United States Marine Corps. The first Marines signed up in the Tun Tavern in Trenton, New Jersey, and in March the following year they executed their first amphibious assault when they captured a British island in the Bahamas. Since then they have conducted over 300 amphibious landings on foreign shores.

Deactivated at the end of the war in 1783, the Marine Corps was re-instituted fifteen years later. Marines have fought in all of America's major wars, and in most cases were the first troops to see combat.

In the early 1800s Marines fought Barbary pirates from North Africa and crushed an enemy force in Tripoli, in what is now Libya. During the Mexican War they won a major victory at Chapultepec Castle, later fancifully referred to in a Marine Corps song as 'the halls of Montezuma'.

During the American Civil War the Marines' best-known assignment was a minor one, the apprehension of abolitionist John Brown at Harper's Ferry. Their commander was an Army general named Robert E. Lee. In 1898 28 Marines were among the 260 killed when the USS *Maine* blew up in Havana Harbour, igniting the Spanish–American War. During this same war the Marines established the American base at Guantanamo Bay in Cuba.

In the First World War the Marines' most famous battle occurred in 1918 when the 4th Marine Brigade attacked the German line at Belleau Wood. Both before and after that war, American presidents used the Marines to quell revolutions (and support American business interests) in the 'banana wars' of South and Central America.

During the Second World War the Marines were the country's primary ground assault force in the Pacific, fighting in bloody battles such as Guadalcanal, Tarawa, Saipan, Guam and Okinawa. The bloodiest of all was Iwo Jima in early 1945, when the Marines suffered 6,000 dead and 17,000 wounded while killing some 20,000 Japanese defenders.

Marines played a prominent role in the Korean War, especially in MacArthur's surprise amphibious attack at Inchon. They were the first American ground troops to fight in Vietnam and saw combat in the Gulf War, Afghanistan and the war against Iraq.

Today the Marine dress-blue uniform still includes a standing collar, evolved from the leather one that was part of the original 18th-century uniform. From this distinctive if uncomfortable feature comes the Marine nickname of 'leatherneck'.

Marines like to think that 'Semper Fi', their shorthand version of the Corps motto 'Semper Fidelis' (always faithful), is their most famous slogan, but perhaps even better known is a word they coined during the Second World

War, snafu, an acronym denoting confusion and chaos. It stands for 'Situation Normal, All Fucked Up'.

Draconian persuasion leads to the shortest reign in papal history

1241 When Pope Gregory IX was felled by the August heat, there was an urgent need to replace him. The short-tempered, headstrong Gregory had led the Church for fourteen years, during which time he had proved to be one of the strongest (and perhaps most misguided) popes in history, famous for his turf battles with Holy Roman Emperor Frederick II and for establishing the papal Inquisition. The Church sought an equally dynamic successor.

As always, the election of a new pope was fraught with politics. In Rome the Orsini and Colonna families were fighting desperately for their candidates, while Emperor Frederick had actually captured two cardinals en route to the papal conclave, in the hope of influencing the outcome. The result was a sharply divided group of prelates – and no conclusion. And so the weeks went by.

Growing impatient, Matteo Orsini (a powerful senator from Rome) had the assembled cardinals locked into the decrepit Septizonium Palace, where guards were instructed to use the leaky roof as a lavatory. Occasionally the electors were even shackled together, and conditions were so terrible that the English cardinal fell ill and died. In fury at the continued indecision, Orsini threatened to dig up the decomposing corpse of Pope Gregory and lock it in with the bickering churchmen.

Finally on 25 October the cardinals chose a compromise candidate, Goffredo Castiglione, who was cardinal bishop of Sabina and came from a powerful Church family (his uncle had been Urban III). Castiglione selected the papal name of Celestine IV.

Sadly, Celestine did not turn out to be the forceful successor to Pope Gregory that the Church so desired. On 10 November, just sixteen days after his election, he died before he could even be consecrated, Pope for the briefest reign in papal history.

Martin Luther, the man who splintered the Church

1483 Born this day in Eisleben in Saxony was Martin Luther, the single man most responsible for the splintering of the Church of Rome and the development of Protestantism.

At seventeen Luther entered the University of Erfurt, where his earnest discussions earned him the sobriquet of 'the Philosopher'. He had not then decided on a life of religion, but at 21 he was caught in a violent thunderstorm near the village of Stotternheim. Fearing for his life, he swore to become a monk if he survived. Two weeks later he entered the Augustinian monastery at Erfurt.

Luther continued to study and pile up degrees, but the true turning point in his life may have been a trip to Rome when he was 27. There he saw at first hand the worldliness and corruption of the Catholic clergy. Seven years later he nailed his 95 theses to the church door in Wittenburg.

But Luther's disagreement with Rome went far beyond scandalous behaviour in the Vatican. He came to believe that you cannot buy your way into heaven with good works, that salvation can be attained only by faith. He also preached that man can be saved only by God's mercy, and that therefore believers can find salvation without clergy or sacrament.

Luther continued to convert others to his views until he died at the age of 62, in spite of his famous confrontation with Emperor Charles V at the Diet of Worms, whose unappetising name has provoked giggles from schoolchildren ever since.

Also on this day

1697: English painter and caricaturist William Hogarth is born * 1759: German poet and dramatist Friedrich Schiller is born in Marbach

11 November

The eleventh hour of the eleventh day of the eleventh month

1918 At the eleventh hour of the eleventh day of the eleventh month an armistice, signed six hours before in French Marshal Ferdinand Foch's railway carriage at Compiègne, France, took effect between the Allies and the Central Powers, bringing the First World War to a close after four years, three months and nine days of fighting.

By July the Allied armies, greatly strengthened by 42 American divisions, had contained the German spring offensives and then launched a series of powerful counter-offensives that rolled the German army back towards the Rhine.

From far-flung fronts in Italy, the Balkans, Palestine, Mesopotamia and the Caucasus, and on the seas, the war news was at last favourable for the Allied cause.

For Germany, the news was correspondingly bad. During recent weeks, the Supreme Command had acknowledged that the war could not be won, the fleet had mutinied at Kiel, and revolution was in the streets. The Kaiser had fled to Holland the day before the Armistice, and the Reichstag declared a republic. Meanwhile, Germany's allies – Bulgaria, Turkey and Austria-Hungary – had all left the war.

Across the world, the news of the armistice was electrifying. Parisians sang and cheered in the boulevards. In New York 1 million people thronged Broadway. In London one observer recalled the event: 'I stood at the window of my room looking up Northumberland Avenue towards Trafalgar Square, waiting for Big Ben to tell that the War was over … And then suddenly the first stroke of the chime … From all sides men and women came scurrying into the streets. Streams of people poured out of all the buildings. The bells of London began to clash … All bounds were broken. The tumult grew … Flags appeared as if by magic … Almost before the last stroke of the clock had died away, the strict, war-straitened, regulated streets of London had become a triumphal pandemonium.'

For all the celebration, the costs of the war were staggering. An estimated 65 million people were mobilised during the war, of whom 8.5 million had died, another 21 million had been wounded and 8 million were being held prisoner when the war ended. Another 6 million civilians also died.

As well as human beings, four imperial dynasties perished during or in the aftermath of the chaos. Had they tombstones they would read:

Habsburg 1282–1919
Hohenzollern 1415–1918
Romanov 1613–1917
Ottoman 1290–1922

For the Germans the end of the war brought still further losses. By the terms of the Versailles Treaty of 1919 they were made to relinquish large swathes of territory, their colonies and enormous quantities of war *matériel*. One of the few things the Germans gained during the peace process was the myth created by their generals that the German army were 'undefeated in the field' and had been 'stabbed in the back' by their own civilian government at the peace table. As the American commander General 'Black Jack' Pershing bitterly but presciently observed, 'They never knew they were beaten in Berlin. It will have to be done all over again.'

Louis XIII fools his mother on the Day of Dupes

1630 Today is known in French history as the Day of Dupes, for on this date King Louis XIII fooled everybody in his court by doing what no one – especially his mother – expected him to do and thereby changed the course of history.

France stood at a crossroads, having to choose between reverting to the spirit of pre-Reformation Europe, allied to the Church and the reactionary Holy Roman Empire, and thrusting forward as an independent nation that would lead the world rather than follow.

Urging consolidation with the forces of Catholicism and the powers of the Habsburgs in Spain and Germany was Louis's mother, Marie de' Medici, backed by a restless nobility itching for a return to a feudal society in which their ancient privileges would be restored.

Opposing her was the great cardinal Armand-Jean du Plessis de Richelieu, a playwright and musician of some ability, who contended that France's natural role was to lead the world not only politically but also in the arts, firmly believing that the cultural shape of civilisation should be defined and moulded by France.

In previous years, Marie's incessant scheming had earned her repeated exile from court, but in the end she always managed to re-ingratiate herself, thanks largely to the intercession of her chief advisor Richelieu, then still a bishop. She later rewarded Richelieu by using her influence to gain for him a cardinal's hat and persuaded young Louis to make him his Chief Minister.

Shallow, selfish and stupid, Marie never understood that Richelieu would always put the *gloire* of France ahead of any lingering gratitude to her. As the years passed, the astute cardinal increasingly dominated King Louis, while progressively pushing the Queen Mother even further from the centre of power. By 1630 Richelieu had been First Minister for six years, and Marie, now hating the cardinal whom once she had befriended, resolved to act.

On 11 November, bidden by his mother to the Palais de Luxembourg, Louis heard yet another venomous attack on Richelieu. But the cardinal, hearing of the meeting, boldly broke into their private conversation by slipping in through a side door. Exploding in hysterical rage, Marie demanded that Louis choose between the cardinal and herself, and Richelieu, for once abashed, left the room in tears.

Almost instantly the whole court buzzed with rumours as to what had happened, fully convinced that Richelieu's ascendancy was over, the cardinal disgraced and perhaps even in mortal danger. Richelieu himself seems to have believed that all was lost and planned to flee from Paris as his enemies prepared themselves to take over the reins of government.

But Louis wanted above all else to be a great king. It took him only a few hours to decide that only Richelieu could give him the canny advice he so urgently needed to guide him through the labyrinth of European politics. That evening he commanded the cardinal to his hunting lodge in Versailles and there informed him he would keep his post as First Minister.

Aghast at her son's incomprehensible decision, Marie de' Medici fled first the court and then France, never to return. The courtiers allied to her were disgraced and in one case executed. In the twelve years left to him before he died, Richelieu became the architect of French national glory. He set France on the path to political and cultural pre-eminence to which it has aspired ever since, from the time of Louis's son, Louis XIV, to the 20th century and Charles de Gaulle.

Also on this day

1855: Danish philosopher Søren Kierkegaard dies in Copenhagen * 1868: French painter Edouard Vuillard is born in Cuiseaux

12 November

Gustavus Adolphus takes the Swedish throne

1611 Gustavus Adolphus was still only sixteen when on this day he was crowned King of Sweden, having inherited the throne – and innumerable problems – from his unspeakable father, King Charles IX.

Charles had usurped the throne from his nephew, becoming a tyrant to his subjects, irascible, foul-mouthed and vicious. Worse, at the time of his death, he had involved Sweden in three wars simultaneously, against Russia, Poland and Denmark. But from this unpromising stock sprang Gustavus Adolphus, one of Sweden's very greatest kings.

The new king formed a remarkable partnership with his Chancellor Axel Oxenstierna. Together they not only reformed the government of Sweden but also had a profound impact on all of northern Europe through Sweden's decisive involvement in the Thirty Years' War.

Gustavus Adolphus first settled the wars he had inherited, largely through diplomacy but also through occasional battles. Here he first learned the art of war and then became the foremost European general of his generation.

Domestically, Gustavus Adolphus and his Chancellor radically modernised their government, making it more efficient than any other in Europe. Through his charm, good sense and more concrete economic benefits, he persuaded the Swedish nobility to serve the nation, even if it meant losing some of their ancient privileges. He also completely reformed the educational system of the country, supporting universities and virtually creating a new and superior system of secondary education.

Although Gustavus Adolphus had settled the wars inherited from his father, a new and much larger conflict, the Thirty Years' War, broke out in 1618 when the Holy Roman Emperor Ferdinand II tried to suppress the Protestant Reformation in the German principalities. For a dozen years Gustavus Adolphus watched and waited, no doubt hoping for a Protestant breakthrough that never materialised. By 1630 the Protestant cause looked all but lost as Ferdinand's great general Wallenstein recorded victory after victory.

When Gustavus Adolphus finally intervened, he launched a bold attack through northern Germany, almost immediately sweeping through Frankfurt and Mainz. That same year Ferdinand had made the cardinal error of replacing Wallenstein with Count Johann von Tilly, a highly capable soldier but no match for a military genius like Gustavus Adolphus. In September 1631 the two armies met at Breitenfeld, where the Swedes completely routed the imperial forces. They also roared through Bavaria, taking Munich, Augsburg and Nuremberg.

Only a year after Breitenfeld, in November 1632, Gustavus Adolphus defeated a recalled Wallenstein at Lützen, although the courageous Swedish King was killed during the action.

Gustavus Adolphus died just a month short of his 38th birthday. Although the Thirty Years' War continued for another sixteen years, during the last two years of his life the great Swede had saved the cause of Protestant Reformation, with ramifications that are still with us today, almost four centuries later.

An army major general publishes Ben-Hur

1880 Today Harper & Brothers published a historical novel set in the time of Christ. The plot concerned a young Jew, falsely accused of plotting to kill the Roman governor of Palestine, who escapes his imprisonment, becomes a Roman officer, avenges himself on his betrayer in a climactic chariot race, and at the end, with the aid of Jesus, is converted to Christianity. The novel, titled *Ben-Hur: A Tale of the Christ*, became one of the greatest American bestsellers of the 19th century.

Printed through the years in countless editions and translations, *Ben-Hur* also spawned many versions in other media: an 1899 play ran for some 6,000 performances in New York and on tour around the world; a 1907 one-reeler featured only the spectacular chariot race; a 1925 film starring Roman Novarro as Ben-Hur and Francis X. Bushman as his nemesis Messala cost $4 million but helped establish MGM as a major studio; and the 1959 version starring Charlton Heston in the title role won eleven of the twelve Academy awards for which it was nominated.

The author of the bestseller that spawned this string of box-office successes wrote his novel while resident in the Governor's Palace in Santa Fe, serving as governor of the lawless frontier territory of New Mexico. He was Lew Wallace, Indiana native, sometime lawyer, newspaper reporter, artist, veteran of the Mexican War, and in the Civil War a major general in the Union Army. At war's end he was a member of the court-martial that convicted the conspirators in the assassination of President Lincoln. He also presided over the military trial of Henry Wirz, commandant of the notorious Confederate prison camp at Andersonville, Georgia.

Wallace had written an earlier novel, *The Fair God: A Story of the Conquest of Mexico*, published in 1873, that enjoyed a substantial sale. In 1875 he began to 'shape the Jewish story', as he called it, which he originally intended as an illustrated serial for magazine publication on the subject of the journey of the Three Wise Men to Bethlehem. After he began the writing, he seems to have undergone a religious conversion, and the work turned into a fully-fledged biblical epic.

Shortly after publication, Wallace sent a copy of *Ben-Hur* to President James Garfield, a fellow Union Army veteran, who read it and replied, 'With this beautiful and reverent book you have lightened the burden of my daily life and renewed our acquaintance which began at Shiloh.' When a few weeks later Garfield named Wallace Minister Resident of the United States to the Ottoman Empire, it was widely assumed that the appointment was made on the strength of the President's enthusiasm for the novel.

For all Wallace's popularity as a novelist in an earlier era, his novels – a third one, *A Prince of India*, was published in 1893 – inevitably lost their appeal to more modern tastes. Edmund Wilson, commenting on the 'romantic trappings' of Wallace's style, concluded that 'In the novels of Lew Wallace … we usually find Walter Scott at his worst.'

Also on this day

1035: King Canute dies at Shaftesbury in Dorset * 1840: French sculptor Auguste Rodin is born * 1948: Former Japanese Prime Minister Hikedi Tojo and seven other war criminals are sentenced to hang

13 November

Talleyrand finally calls it a day

1834 Today at last Charles-Maurice de Talleyrand, who had backed winning horses over six decades, resigned his last diplomatic post as French ambassador to Great Britain at the age of 80, thus ending the most spectacular and arguably the most successful career of all of history's diplomats.

This nimble careerist served first the Catholic Church, then the doomed monarchy of Louis XVI, followed by the Republic, the Emperor Napoleon, the restored monarchy of Louis XVIII, and finally the regime of King Louis-Philippe after the July Revolution of 1830.

Talleyrand entered the seminary of Saint-Sulpice in Paris at sixteen, received minor orders five years later and by 34 was a bishop. A year later, on the eve of Revolution, he was elected to represent the clergy at the National Assembly. Astutely reading the republican wind, he celebrated a Mass in commemoration of the fall of the Bastille and earned for himself the nickname of 'l'Evêque de la Révolution' (the Bishop of the Revolution). For this escapade, as well as for democratising the French Church, he was excommunicated by Rome and left the Church.

Talleyrand's next post was as envoy to Great Britain in 1792, representing the French monarchy in spite of his known republicanism. But the execution of Louis XVI and the failure of his peace mission left him no safe haven in either France or Britain, so he fled to the United States, where he spent two years.

By 1796 he was back in France, and a year later he was appointed Foreign Minister by the republican Directory. An early triumph was his negotiated peace with Austria after Napoleon's victories, taking home for himself over a million francs in bribes. He continued as Foreign Minister under Napoleon's Consulate, and in 1804 Napoleon, now Emperor, made him Grand Chamberlain. Even though he shortly resigned this office, he was pivotal in arranging Napoleon's dynastic marriage to Marie-Louise of Austria.

Alarmed by Napoleon's hubris, when the Emperor rashly invaded Russia

Talleyrand began secretly negotiating with allied powers (most of whom were either emotionally or actively France's enemies) for the restoration of France's Bourbon kings. When Napoleon's first abdication led to the occupation of Paris, Tsar Alexander I stayed at Talleyrand's luxurious town house. (Talleyrand's easy change of loyalties caused Napoleon to refer to him as 'a shit in silk stockings'.)

In some measure due to Talleyrand's persuasive powers, the allies agreed to support the ageing Louis XVIII to replace the exiled Napoleon, and Louis expressed his gratitude by appointing Talleyrand once again as Foreign Minister. Sent to represent his country at the Congress of Vienna, he remained there when Napoleon escaped from Elba but returned to Paris after the former emperor's defeat at Waterloo. This time, however, Louis's ultra-royalist court forced him into retirement because of his revolutionary past.

By this time Talleyrand was 70, and the unwary believed he was retired, living in quiet luxury, writing his memoirs. But the old fox recognised Louis's successor Charles X for the reactionary bigot that he was, famously observing that the Bourbons 'have learned nothing and forgotten nothing'. He soon was scheming for Charles's removal, a job accomplished by the July Revolution of 1830, when Talleyrand, already in secret talks with Louis-Philippe, helped him to gain the throne. His reward? Once again to become an ambassador, this time to Britain, where he remained until his retirement on this day.

The king who started the Hundred Years' War

1312 On this day at the great medieval fortress of Windsor was born a baby boy who one day would become the seventh king in the Plantagenet line, the future Edward III of England. His parents were the inept and homosexual Edward II and his implacably ambitious Queen, Isabella of France (who eventually acquiesced to the murder of her husband).

Tall, blond and handsome, young Edward was crowned in the January before his fifteenth birthday while his mother's lover Roger de Mortimer held his father in prison. Eight months later his father was brutally murdered in his cell.

In 1330, when Edward was King in fact as well as name, he avenged his father by executing Mortimer as a traitor and sending his mother into permanent retirement, eventually to join the Poor Clares order of nuns.

Edward is known as one of England's great warrior kings, with famous victories over the French at Sluys and Crécy. His contemporaries considered him an exemplary knight, chivalrous, good-tempered and brave in battle. Even his extravagance and taste for the ladies endeared him to his court and his people. Today he is perhaps best remembered as the founder of England's highest chivalric honour, the Order of the Garter.

Unfortunately, Edward's most important legacy was his obsessive claim to the throne of France, based on historic Plantagenet holdings in Gascony and his insistence on the rights of his mother, despite France's Salic law that excluded females from the throne. Edward made his first claim when he was still only sixteen and a dozen years later in January 1340 he added the title of King of France to his own. He repeatedly tried to invade France, igniting the Hundred Years' War. So persistent was Edward's belief in his right to the French crown that his successors continued the claim for half a millennium. Every English king called himself King of France until George III finally abandoned the claim in 1801.

England's Model Parliament

1295 The very first English parliament – when common men sat down with nobles and churchmen to debate the laws of the land – took place in 1265, but the form of parliament as it exists today stems from what is called the Model Parliament, assembled at Westminster on this day in 1295.

Gathered together were some 50 earls and barons plus two knights from each shire. The Parliament also included representatives of the common people plus a sampling of bishops. Unlike the earlier assembly of 1265, in the Model Parliament each of the three groups met and debated separately, and it was this form, later reduced to only two groups, that so clearly foreshadowed the British government of the present day.

Also on this day

1850: British novelist Robert Louis Stevenson is born in Edinburgh * 1868: Italian composer Gioacchino Rossini dies in Passy, France * 1903: French painter Camille Pissarro dies in Paris

14 November

How a Dutchman became King of England

1650, 1677 Today in 1650 in The Hague was born a brown-haired Dutch boy who was brought up speaking French and who would one day be King of England. His name was William of Orange.

Although of royal stock (he was the son of the Prince of Orange and Dutch Stadholder (Prime Minister elected by the States General), and grandson of England's Charles I), William's early years were difficult. His father died when he was just eight days old, and Dutch nobles, remembering his father's imperious ways, debarred the House of Orange from holding office. Meanwhile the bloodlines linking him to Charles I provided no help since Charles had been executed the year before William was born, leaving England in the tender care of Oliver Cromwell.

Perhaps what gave William his first boost to power came in 1671 when Louis XIV of France decided to invade the Netherlands. Appointed captain general, William led a band of largely untrained Dutch soldiers in combat against the French. Desperately searching for leadership that might halt the invaders, the States General shortly elevated him to Stadholder, and, although unable to overcome the French militarily, William managed to ally himself with Spain and the Holy Roman Emperor, thus bringing the conflict to a stalemate that could be settled by negotiation.

Now a man of consequence, on 14 November 1677, his 27th birthday, William married his cousin, Princess Mary of England, then a fifteen-year-old girl, daughter of the future James II.

In 1685 James inherited the throne on the death of his brother Charles II, but his militant Catholicism alarmed his Protestant subjects. In June 1688 the English Parliament invited William to invade their own country, and William landed at Brixham on the Devon coast on 5 November 1688, the day after his 38th birthday. By December the feckless James was in exile in France, and on 12 February 1689 Parliament invited William and Mary to become joint King and Queen, the only time in English history that a husband and wife have reigned together. Although Mary died after five years as Queen, William ruled until his death in 1702.

Emperor Justinian dies after 38 years in power

565 Today in Constantinople the Byzantine Emperor Justinian died at the age of 82. He had ruled for 38 years in a time of unusual turmoil, as during his reign the bubonic plague killed perhaps two-fifths of the population of his empire.

Justinian was an unusual man by any measurement. Historian Joan Mervyn Hussey describes him as 'a man of large views and great ambitions, of wonderful activity of mind, tireless energy, and an unusual grasp of detail'. But he could also be petty and vindictive, as witnessed by his shameful treatment of his great general Belisarius whom he continually (and unfoundedly) suspected of treason and whom, according to some accounts, he eventually blinded.

Justinian also had the courage and the judgement to marry an actress named Theodora at a time when actresses and prostitutes were virtually synonymous and the Church denied them the sacraments. Theodora eventually shared Justinian's rule and saved his throne if not his life when the Nika insurrection in Constantinople threatened to overturn the government.

Although Justinian successfully defended his empire against the Persians in the east and conquered parts of North Africa, his attempts to reunite the eastern and western parts of the old Roman Empire were doomed to failure. Those against whom he battled make a list of long-vanished tribes, including the Vandals, the Ostrogoths, the Bulgars, the Slavs, the Kotrigur Huns and the Avars.

Some historians believe that, in spite of his generally laudable ambitions,

Justinian set the stage for the turmoil of the Middle Ages. They maintain that his attempt to reconquer the Western Empire only ensured its final and irrevocable split, a division made worse when he abandoned Latin as the language of government in Constantinople. They also claim that his failure to fully defeat the Persians left them in a position to weaken the Byzantine Empire so much after his death that the eventual triumph of Islam became inevitable.

Whatever your judgement on Justinian, he left two enduring monuments. The first is the Great Church in what is now Istanbul, today called the Hagia Sophia. The second is his contribution to Europe's fashion industry. During his time China carefully guarded its lucrative monopoly on the production of silk. Justinian bribed two monks who had lived there to return and steal silkworm eggs. These they secreted in hollow bamboo canes and brought back to Constantinople, allowing the Emperor to develop a thriving silk industry. Today all of Europe's silk-producing caterpillars descend from those smuggled worms.

Also on this day

1687: Charles II's mistress Nell Gwyn dies * 1716: German mathematician Gottfried Leibniz dies in Hanover * 1840: French painter Claude Monet is born in Paris * 1862: Lewis Carroll begins writing *Alice in Wonderland* * 1940: German bombers devastate Coventry, killing 1,000

15 November

Louis XIV opens Versailles

1684 Of all the palaces in the Western world, the most magnificent is surely Versailles, which took over half a century to build. Even twenty years after work had first begun, the palace was still being constructed by a force of 36,000 labourers and 6,000 horses. Within Versailles, surely the grandest room is the Galerie des Glaces, which on this day proud King Louis XIV opened to his court.

The Galerie des Glaces is 225 feet long, pierced by seventeen huge windows, each reflected by an equal-sized wall mirror. The hall was in its greatest glory at night, when it was lit by hundreds of candles glittering in 32 enormous silver chandeliers.

The Galerie des Glaces was often the scene of great events, like the marriage of the hapless Louis XVI to Marie Antoinette, but two centuries after its first opening, this great hall was used for a more sombre purpose. It was there that a victorious Bismarck proclaimed King Wilhelm of Prussia to be Kaiser of a united Germany after having humiliated the French in the Franco-Prussian War.

Louis XIV might have been better pleased half a century after that, however, when the Treaty of Versailles, humiliating the Germans at the end of the First World War, was signed in the Galerie on 28 June 1919.

Sherman's march through Georgia

1864 This morning advance units of the Union Army began moving out of Atlanta heading south-east in two columns. Behind them the city lay 'smouldering and in ruins', as their commander General William Tecumseh Sherman later described the destruction he had ordered. Grown tired of chasing his Confederate opponent General Hood and of having to protect a supply line stretching all the way back to Louisville, 'Uncle Billy' Sherman had decided to cut his force loose against the heartland of the Confederacy. For over a month the North would have no news of Sherman and his troops. 'I know the hole he went in at,' said his brother, the senator from Ohio, 'but I can't tell you what hole he will come out of.'

The hole he came out of was Savannah, Georgia, on 22 December. In the intervening weeks his two columns, with a combined strength of 62,000 and for the most part unopposed by rebel forces, destroyed much of what the Confederacy needed to keep fighting: crops, industry, transportation, infrastructure and morale. Foraging far and wide, helped immensely in their task by growing thousands of bummers and runaway slaves who accompanied the army, the Union soldiers stripped Georgia bare. No army on either side had eaten so well. And what the troops didn't take, they let rot or they burned.

Sherman's march could not have been a pretty sight, but as military strategy it worked by shortening the war. It also produced one of the greatest marching songs of this or any war, 'Marching through Georgia':

Hurrah, hurrah, we bring the jubilee.
Hurrah, hurrah, the flag that makes you free.
So we sang this chorus from Atlanta to the sea,
As we went marchin' through Georgia.

Also on this day

1708: British statesman William Pitt the Elder is born * 1787: Austrian composer Christopher Gluck dies in Vienna * 1802: English painter George Romney dies

16 November

A king dies incarcerated in the Tower of London

1272 Henry III, son of the iniquitous King John and fourth Plantagenet king of England, breathed his last on this day in the Tower of London. He was 65 years old and had been King for 56 years, a record reign among European monarchs that would survive for 450 years until France's Louis XIV surpassed it with the all-time record of 72 years.

Sadly, length of reign was Henry's sole achievement. It is calculated that this ambitious but cowardly and incompetent monarch actually ruled during only 24 of the years that he was King. First he was dominated by his courtiers, then he was overthrown by the redoubtable Simon de Montfort, Earl of Leicester, and when Leicester was finally defeated and killed, Henry's son Edward I took over the reins of government from the now faltering and senile old King.

Although Henry's 56-year reign is impressive, two non-European monarchs before him had reigned longer, the Byzantine Emperor Basil II for 62 years in the late 10th–early 11th centuries and the Egyptian Pharaoh Ramses II for 66 years in the 13th century BC.

Today Henry ranks eighth in length of reign, surpassed not only by Louis XIV, Basil and Ramses but also by:

Louis XV – 59 years
George III – 60 years
Hirohito – 63 years
Victoria – 64 years
Franz Joseph – 68 years

Papal reigns of course cannot compete, as popes are invariably at least middle-aged when elected. But Pius IX lived until he was 88, Pope for a record 32 years.

In terms of longevity of title (if not of reign), queen consorts put the kings to shame. Elizabeth Bowes-Lyon, the Queen Mother of England, died at almost 102, a queen for 66 years (the last 50 of them a widow), and the remarkable Eleanor of Aquitaine managed 67 queenly years, 15 as Queen of France, 52 as Queen or Queen Mother of England, before dying at 82 in 1204. But the all-time champion was Zita von Bourbon-Parma, wife of Charles, the last kaiser of Austria and King of Hungary. She was titularly a queen for a magnificent 75 years, although she was widowed for 67 of them, dying in exile in Switzerland at 96.

The battle that saved the German Protestants

1632 Today Europe's two greatest generals, King Gustavus Adolphus of Sweden and Prince Albrecht von Wallenstein, met near the Saxon town of Lützen in a battle whose outcome prevented the destruction of Protestantism in Germany. The victor died on the field.

Gustavus Adolphus's portraits show a man of high and noble brow, calm, speculative eyes and a long, strong nose above his moustache and narrow, pointed goatee. He was intelligent and enlightened, an inspiring leader and brilliant commander.

He had inherited the Swedish throne in 1611, seven years before the outbreak of the terrible Thirty Years' War between Germany's Protestant principalities and the reactionary Catholic Holy Roman Emperor Ferdinand II of the House of Habsburg.

Wallenstein was an altogether different animal. Eleven years Gustavus Adolphus's senior, he was born in Bohemia, orphaned at thirteen and raised a Protestant by his uncle. But at 23 he cynically converted to Catholicism to strengthen his position with the Emperor of the day, and three years later married an elderly but fabulously rich widow, whose money he inherited five years later. His wealth enabled him to provide an army at his own expense in the service of the Emperor, and by 1625 he had become the head of all imperial forces, while grabbing for himself enormous swathes of Germany and Denmark. As his power grew, so did his ambitions, as he then started to trade alliances like any unscrupulous king, negotiating for advantage with Protestants and Catholics alike, finally causing Emperor Ferdinand to sack him in August 1630.

But only weeks later, seeing the cause of Protestantism in danger of collapse, Gustavus Adolphus joined the German principalities in their conflict against the Emperor. Supported financially by France's crafty Cardinal Richelieu, the 34-year-old king swept across northern Germany, utterly crushing the imperial forces under the command of Wallenstein's replacement, Johann von Tilly, at Breitenfeld, earning himself the sobriquet of 'The Lion of the North'. Desperate, Emperor Ferdinand was now forced to recall the arrogant, ambitious but supremely talented Wallenstein.

The morning of 16 November 1632 was cold and misty as Gustavus Adolphus launched his assault against Wallenstein's army at Lützen. His Swedish soldiers rushed to the attack singing Martin Luther's hymn 'Eine feste Burg ist unser Gott' (A Mighty Fortress is Our God) and another hymn composed by the King himself. The fate of Protestant Germany rested on the outcome.

All day long the two forces battled, with the Swedish King leading his own cavalry. But in one fierce charge Gustavus Adolphus became separated from his men and was cut down by encircling imperial horsemen. According to the mythmakers, his last words were a noble 'I seal with my blood my religion and the liberties of Germany.'

In spite of his death, Gustavus Adolphus's army continued to batter Wallenstein's, capturing the enemy artillery and forcing Wallenstein to retreat in defeat. At the close of battle the King's body was found on the field and the spot was marked with a stone. Later the German people raised a monument there.

In bringing about the death of the Empire's most capable enemy, Wallenstein performed a great service for the Emperor, but it also meant he was no longer vital to the Emperor's cause. Unwisely, he kept his army at the ready but failed to bring it to Ferdinand's support. Now considering his one-time favourite a traitor, the Emperor ordered his assassination two years later.

The final death scene of Old Russia

1920 Today, if you had been in the Black Sea port of Sevastopol, you would have witnessed the final death scene of Old Russia, as the last White army began its evacuation from the Crimea. Greatly outnumbered and facing annihilation by the victorious Red Army, some 35,000 troops of the counter-revolutionary forces of Baron Peter Wrangel withdrew to ships that would carry them from the Crimean peninsula to Turkey. Under their protection were three times as many civilians seeking escape from revolutionary Russia. Those left behind faced firing squads, labour camps or forcible incorporation into the Red Army. The Russian Civil War had come to an end.

When, after the Communist coup of November 1917, it became clear that a police state was emerging from the political chaos and that it intended to carry out its revolutionary justice by means of a Red Terror, hundreds of thousands of Russians fled the Bolshevik north for Siberia, the Ukraine or southern Russia. Counter-revolutionary – White – armies were raised to fight the Bolshevik regime. The war lasted for three years, fought on both sides mainly by hastily assembled, ill-trained and poorly motivated troops. Fluid fronts stretching for hundreds of miles defied logistics. The Whites came closest to winning in 1919 when five of their armies advanced on Moscow and St Petersburg, offering the prospect of capturing both capitals. But by October the Red Army rose to the occasion and turned them all back in defeat. Now the only White force left intact was Wrangel's army, which was forced to retreat to the Crimea.

The White cause failed for many reasons but mainly because it pursued a simple military solution to a very complex problem. It appeared to be a reactionary movement bent on restoring the old order, offering no political or economic programme with which to win the allegiance of the populations across whose lands its forces waged war. Wrangel, the Whites' best and most perceptive commander, recognised the flaw: 'We had not brought pardon and peace with us, but only the cruel sword of vengeance.'

Late in the day, the ships took Wrangel's army out of Sevastopol, once the playground of the old regime, and steamed for Gallipoli, scene of another military debacle. There the soldiers would reside in old Allied camps awaiting their dispersal around the world. As they left the harbour, Wrangel must have spoken the thoughts of many when he wrote, 'God has helped me to do my duty. He would bless our journey into the unknown ... The stars are gleaming in the darkening sky; the sea is all a-twinkle. The lonely lights on my native shore grow fainter, and then vanish all together, one after another. And now the last one fades from my sight. Farewell, my country.'

Also on this day

42 BC: Roman Emperor Tiberius is born * 1913: French novelist Marcel Proust publishes the first volume of *Remembrance of Things Past*

17 November

Bloody Mary is gone at last

1558 At seven o'clock this morning Bloody Mary, one of the saddest and most disastrous monarchs in all of England's history, died of influenza at the age of 42.

Mary lived a miserable and unrewarding life from the age of seventeen, when her father Henry VIII, after six years of effort, finally forced through the annulment of his marriage to her mother, Catherine of Aragon, so that he could marry Anne Boleyn. The annulment made Mary a bastard, a status with which her father concurred.

With Anne as Queen, Mary's life became even worse, for she lost her title of Princess and was forced to defer to her newly born half-sister, Elizabeth. Moreover, Henry sent Catherine into retirement, and Mary was never allowed to see her mother again.

Over the years Mary was a pawn to Henry's political ambitions, betrothed to a long list of European royalty ranging from her cousin Holy Roman Emperor Charles V, fifteen years her senior, to Charles's son, Philip II, eleven years her junior, whom she finally married in a loveless and childless union.

Finally, on the death of her teenage half-brother, Edward VI, at the age of 37 Mary became England's first queen regnant. During the five and a half years of her reign, her Catholic fanaticism made her one of her country's most hated monarchs, as she had over 300 Protestants burnt at the stake, including her father's chief advisor Archbishop Thomas Cranmer and Bishops Ridley and Latimer. About 60 of her Protestant victims were women. While Mary was Queen, France wrenched back Calais, the last scrap of territory that England possessed in continental Europe.

On Mary's death several of her courtiers rode out to Hatfield House just north of London to announce the news to Elizabeth. They found the new queen contemplating the Bible beneath an oak tree in the garden, in spite of the damp chill of the season. She is said to have responded to the courtiers' news with a quotation from the 118th psalm, 'This is the Lord's doing; it is marvellous in our eyes.'

Indeed, the day of Mary's death was a day of celebration for the English, and in a sense it has remained a day of celebration for all of us ever since, as it was the first day of that glorious period that we now call the Elizabethan Age.

The Suez Canal opens for business

1869 The Suez Canal finally opened today, after ten years, six months and 24 days of backbreaking labour by Egyptian workmen led by a stubborn but charming and generous French aristocrat, Ferdinand de Lesseps. Attending the ceremony were a mixed lot of Middle Eastern potentates and European literati such as Théophile Gautier, Emile Zola and Henrik Ibsen, plus a smattering of royalty, including Austrian Emperor Franz Joseph and French Empress Eugénie, who happened to be a cousin of de Lesseps's.

De Lesseps was already 54 when he ceremonially delivered the first blow of a pickaxe to start construction on 25 April 1859. He had already pursued a successful diplomatic career, including several stints in the Middle East. But when he was only 27 he had been stationed in Alexandria, where he studied plans for a canal drawn up by one of Napoleon's engineers.

The Suez Canal connects the Mediterranean and Red Seas, but its real achievement is to allow ships to sail between the Mediterranean and the Indian Ocean and even on to the Pacific. Its route meanders for 101 miles, taking advantage of several lakes, instead of driving straight across the isthmus, a distance of only 75 miles as the crow flies. The original wedge-shaped canal was just 26 feet deep and 190 feet wide at the surface, reducing to 72 feet wide at the bottom. (In subsequent years it was significantly deepened and further widened.)

Originally the canal was jointly owned by the French and the Egyptian Khedive Isma'il Pasha, but in 1875 Benjamin Disraeli persuaded the British Parliament to buy out Isma'il Pasha, a purchase which inadvertently led to the Suez Crisis of 1956 when Egyptian President Gamal Abdel Nasser nationalised it.

The grand opening of the canal on this day should probably be called a grand re-opening. The first canal across the Isthmus of Suez had been built in the 19th century BC and subsequently restored by rulers such as the Egyptian Pharaoh Ptolemy II, the Persian King Xerxes and the Roman Emperor Trajan.

Also on this day

1800: The US Congress meets for the first time * 1912: Woodrow Wilson is elected President of the United States * 1922: Kemal Atatürk deposes the last sultan of Turkey

18 November

Urban II launches the First Crusade

1095 The huge crowd outside Clermont Cathedral in the Auvergne region of France shivered with cold, wept with religious fervour and smiled inwardly with greedy anticipation when Pope Urban II made his dramatic appeal today for a holy crusade.

'Jerusalem is the navel of the world,' declared the Pope, 'a land more fruitful than any other, a paradise of delights. This is the land which the Redeemer of mankind illuminated by his coming, adorned by his life, consecrated by his passion, redeemed by his death, and sealed by his burial. This royal city, situated in the middle of the world, is now held captive by his enemies … It begs unceasingly that you will come to its aid.'

Such was the call to arms that today launched the First Crusade to reclaim Jerusalem from the heathen Muslims and return it (and all the riches between it and Constantinople) to Christian domination.

Urban had been strongly influenced by an ascetic monk called Peter the Hermit who had visited the Holy Land the year before. His descriptions of the miseries of the Christians and the sacrilegious insults offered to Jerusalem's holy Christian shrines inspired Urban to unite the faithful into one vast effort to overthrow the Seljuk Turks who controlled Palestine.

Offering remission of all penance for sin to all who helped the Christians in the east, Urban provoked an immediate and overwhelming response. Soon a massive force of some 4,000 mounted knights and 25,000 infantry, principally from France, Italy and the Germanic states, was headed towards Constantinople en route to the greatest Christian adventure in history.

Wearing the symbolic white cross on their breasts, the crusaders were soon pillaging and sacking their way to the Holy Land, encouraged by their battle cry of 'Deus le volt!' (God wills it!)

In June 1099 the Christian army, which had dwindled to perhaps 1,500 mounted knights and 12,000 foot soldiers, reached Jerusalem. On 15 July the great walled city fell to the crusaders for a triumphant massacre and sack. The First Crusade had reached its jubilant conclusion.

Peter the Hermit, however, fared less well. He and another rabble-rousing friar, Walter the Penniless, led a 'People's Crusade' of unattached soldiers, fervent peasants, adventurous youths and unemployed criminals to Constantinople. Evicted from the city as a threat to its civilian population, this ragtag army was ambushed at Cibotus and annihilated by the Turks.

Jerusalem remained in Christian hands for less than a century, falling to Saladin in 1187. In all there were nine crusades aimed at conquering or retaining Jerusalem, the last in 1365.

Nathaniel Palmer discovers a new continent

1820 Further and further south the seal hunters sailed, as each successive breeding ground was discovered – and depleted – in the unending search for profitable pelts.

In October 1820 American Captain Nathaniel Palmer headed south from the Falkland Islands in command of the tiny sloop *Hero*, just 45 tons and only 47 feet long. Palmer was still only 21 but had already made his mark, first as a blockade runner during the War of 1812, then as an outstanding navigator in southern waters.

Palmer's course first took him to the South Shetland Islands, but once again he found few seals, so he determined to probe yet further south.

Sailing past immense icebergs, *Hero* continued through uncharted waters.

Early on the morning of 18 November Palmer came to inhospitable land, a shore of massive icy cliffs dropping straight to the sea. After following the coast for some hours and finding neither landing place nor sight of seals, the captain finally turned his ship north. Only later would he come to realise that he had discovered a vast continent of over 5 million square miles for which explorers had been searching for 200 years. He had discovered Antarctica.

The Sun King is attended by doctors

1683 A curiosity of 17th-century life in Europe was that life expectancy for the peasant, living in extremes of poverty, squalor and hunger, was as long as that of the noble, coddled in splendid châteaux, fed with the best food available and tended in luxury by dozens of servants. The most likely explanation is the 17th-century doctor, who attended only the rich.

At that time doctors bled their noble patients profusely, forbade them fresh air, wrapped them warmly when in fever and had them swallow medicines of fantastic variety, including mixtures of animal dung. Hygiene was an unknown concept.

Even kings were not free from their ministrations. Witness Louis XIV, whose long life was miraculous testimony of his physical robustness.

Louis almost died of smallpox at nine and again of an unspecified fever at twenty. Later his doctors pulled out all his upper teeth, cauterising each wound with a red-hot coal.

On this day Louis was operated on for an anal fistula. During the surgery he underwent two lancings and eight incisions without uttering a cry. Subsequently the 45-year-old king was bled and then heard Mass, after which he conducted his daily business exactly according to schedule. He sat with his council until seven, the sweat of pain pouring down his face.

Such was the Sun King, who overcame the Dutch, the Habsburgs, his own nobles and his doctors to live to the respectable old age of 77.

Also on this day
1626: St Peter's in Rome is consecrated * 1922: French novelist Marcel Proust dies

19 November

The second Medici pope

1523 Elected on this day as Pope Clement VII was that vacillating schemer, Giulio de' Medici, whom history remembers primarily for his refusal to allow England's Henry VIII to annul his marriage.

Giulio had been born both illegitimate and posthumously, for his father had been assassinated in Florence's great red-domed Duomo a month before his birth. Fortunately for Giulio, he was immediately taken into the household of his uncle, Lorenzo the Magnificent, where he learned the life of a Renaissance prince. He also grew up with his cousin, Lorenzo's son Giovanni, two years his senior.

Since Giovanni was Lorenzo's second son, he was destined for the Church, receiving his tonsure at the early age of eight. And as he rose in the hierarchy of Rome, Giulio followed in his footsteps.

By 1513 Giovanni had achieved his ultimate ambition of becoming Pope, taking the name of Leo X. Once enthroned, he lived (and spent) more like the prince he was than a man of the cloth. He wanted to elevate his cousin Giulio, but Giulio's illegitimate birth was a seemingly insurmountable barrier. First Giovanni/Leo gave his cousin a special dispensation and then he accepted a formal declaration that Giulio's parents had really been secretly married, therefore making Giulio legitimate. He then promoted Giulio to the rank of cardinal, all within his first year as Pope.

When Giovanni/Leo died at the end of 1521, the College of Cardinals turned to Adrian VI, history's only Dutch pope, no doubt believing that two Medici cousins back to back would be more than decency (or the papal treasury) could bear. But ten years later Adrian died, and at last Giulio was elected at the age of 51, taking the name of Clement VII.

During his eleven papal years Giulio/Clement used most of his energies grasping for temporal power for himself and his family while commissioning great artists such as Michelangelo and Raphael. He completely failed to come to grips with Catholicism's greatest challenge, the emergence of Protestantism. Although usually supporting Holy Roman Emperor Charles V, he once made the serious error of signing a treaty with Charles's rival, François I of France. Charles sent his army into Rome for its worst sack since Alaric over a millennium before, and Guilio/Clement escaped only by barricading himself in the Castel' Sant'Angelo. Later the Pope made amends by agreeing to crown Charles, making Charles the last Holy Roman Emperor ever crowned by a Pope.

Giulio/Clement's dependence on Charles caused one of his few historically important acts. When England's Henry VIII petitioned for an annulment of his marriage to Catherine of Aragon, Giulio/Clement turned him down, not for doctrinal reasons but because Catherine was Charles's aunt. The Pope's refusal was the trigger that forced Henry at last to break for ever with the Catholic Church.

Also on this day

1600: British King Charles I is born in Dunfermline Castle * 1828: Viennese composer Franz Schubert dies of syphilis at the age of 31 * 1863: American President Abraham Lincoln gives the Gettysburg Address

20 November

The death of Leo Tolstoy

1910 Today died the man once hailed as the greatest of all novelists, Count Leo Nikolayevich Tolstoy, famous, rich and probably unhappy.

Tolstoy was born at his aristocratic family's estate in Yasnaya Polyana, about 130 miles south of Moscow. As a young man he fought with the army both in the Caucasus and in the Crimean War, and later he married and fathered ten children who survived infancy.

Tolstoy wrote his first novel when he was 24, but he was over 40 when he published his masterpiece of realism *War and Peace*. In it the experience he had gained in battle served him well in describing scenes of combat. The British poet Matthew Arnold maintained that a novel by Tolstoy was not a work of art but a piece of life.

Eight years later saw the publication of Tolstoy's other undoubted master-work, *Anna Karenina*. While he was at work on this book he began to suffer bouts of depression and even considered suicide. At this time he was also developing his own religious and moral beliefs that led him to part from the Russian Orthodox Church (in the end he was excommunicated). He became a dedicated pacifist and came to believe that he should abandon material possessions.

A noble who gave up his own riches, Tolstoy soon found himself giving up his large family as well, as his wife and children, except for one daughter, became estranged from this dogmatic man with the air of an Old Testament prophet. Thus he was to experience his own famous first line from *Anna Karenina*, 'All happy families resemble each other; but each unhappy family is unhappy in its own way.' After years of increasing hostility, he finally decided to leave home for good. On his travels he caught pneumonia and he finally succumbed to heart failure in the small railway station of Astapovo at the age of 82. His last words were a bewildered, 'The truth ... I care a great deal ... how they ...'

Tolstoy's great novels are still widely read, although modern critics tend to rate the works of his Russian contemporary Fyodor Dostoevsky more highly for their psychological insights. But Tolstoy's influence still lives with us today. Mohandas Gandhi put into practice Tolstoy's ideas about pacifism and passive resistance in ousting the British from India, and Gandhi's principles in turn influenced the thinking of Martin Luther King.

Also on this day

1818: Simón Bolívar declares Venezuela to be independent of Spain * 1945: The Nazi war crime trials begin at Nuremberg

21 November

Man's first free flight

1783 Earlier in the year the Montgolfier brothers had sent the first unmanned balloon aloft near Lyon. A few months later the French physicist Pilâtre de Rozier became the first man to ascend with a balloon, but Rozier's flight had been in a balloon made fast to prevent free flight, and he had risen a mere 90 feet. (At the time even this ascent was considered so hazardous that local authorities decreed that two criminals sentenced to death should be forced to undertake it. Only the intervention of King Louis XVI allowed Rozier and a colleague, the marquis d'Arlandes, the honour of manning the first flight.)

But a few months later, on 21 November, Rozier and the marquis lifted off in Paris's Bois de Boulogne and floated free for 25 minutes, crossing the Seine and landing some five miles from the Bois. For the first time in history man had flown.

In the audience that day was the American ambassador to France, Benjamin Franklin. When asked by a friend what good a balloon flight would do, Franklin replied, 'And what good is a new-born baby?'

In 1785 Rozier and a colleague attempted to be the first to cross the English Channel in a balloon, but they unwisely used a hot-air balloon tucked under a hydrogen balloon. When this double balloon reached a height of about 3,000 feet, fire used to produce the hot air reached the hydrogen, and the upper balloon exploded, killing Rozier and his companion in the fall.

Napoleon appoints Talleyrand

1799 On this date, just eleven days after he staged his *coup d'état* to take control of the French government, Napoleon Bonaparte appointed Charles-Maurice de Talleyrand as Foreign Minister. In choosing the 45-year-old diplomat he knew exactly what he was looking for. 'I needed', he later wrote, 'an aristocrat, and an aristocrat who knew how to handle things with an entirely princely insolence.' Talleyrand fitted the bill perfectly; son of a count, he had entered and left the Church (excommunicated at the end) and had already served as Foreign Minister under the Directorate.

Unquestionably Talleyrand entirely agreed with Napoleon's assessment of the sort of man required. 'A monarchy', he wrote, 'should be governed by democrats and a republic by aristocrats.'

Talleyrand served Napoleon skilfully but not faithfully, conniving with the Russians for the restoration of Louis XVIII when Napoleon lost most of his Grande Armée on his retreat from Moscow. Later the Emperor reflected, 'I have two faults with which to reproach myself regarding Talleyrand. The first was not to have followed the wise advice he gave me; the second was not to have hanged him.'

Louis Napoleon gains a dictator's majority – 97 per cent of the vote

1852 Dictators love elections. Hitler was appointed German Chancellor after his Nazi party gained 37 per cent of the popular vote, thus setting the stage for his eventual dictatorship, and later was supported by over 90 per cent of the electorate in a plebiscite. Franco conducted a referendum in 1947 that confirmed his lifetime dictatorial powers in Spain, and Fidel Castro regularly stages elections in his one-party Cuban state. Even Louis Napoleon Bonaparte, in the middle of the 19th century, felt the need for a popular mandate.

In 1848 Louis Napoleon had been elected President of France, but the law decreed that he could not succeed himself at the end of his four-year term. The result was his successful *coup d'état* of 2 December 1851, which made him effectively the nation's dictator. Having not only a taste for power but also a grasp of popular politics, he decided to put the final choice to the French people.

Thus on this day in 1852 the French came to the polls. The results were overwhelming. Some 97 per cent of the voters – 7,824,189 to 253,145 – voted Louis Napoleon Emperor, a title that he took officially on 2 December that year, the anniversary of his own coup and of the crowning in Notre Dame of his uncle, Napoleon I, in 1804.

Also on this day

570: The Prophet Mohammed is born * 1694: French writer Voltaire is born in Paris * 1898: Belgian surrealist painter René Magritte is born * 1916: Austrian Emperor Franz Joseph I dies

22 November

Warwick the Kingmaker

1428 Today is the birthday of the man who was called by one of those magic names that echo down the centuries from medieval England: Warwick the Kingmaker, the man who made two men King of England.

The kingmaker's name was Richard Neville. The son of an earl, he attained his own earldom not by inheritance but by marriage to the richest heiress in England, daughter of the previous Earl of Warwick. Thus Neville gained not only a title but also the greatest fortune in the land, not excluding the King's.

Warwick's first venture at kingmaking came in 1461, when he stage-managed the defeat of poor Henry VI, as young Edward of York took over as Edward IV.

Warwick virtually ruled the country for several years, but when Edward showed signs of independence, he daringly switched sides and, in a matter of months, invaded England with a force from France and restored the hapless Henry to the throne.

Six months later, however, Edward gathered his own army and defeated Warwick at the Battle of Barnet on Easter Sunday 1471. At the battle's end two foot soldiers seized the fleeing Warwick. One forced open his visor with an axe, the other plunged in his sword.

Sadly, no likeness of Warwick remains, so we can only imagine the no doubt shrewd and forceful face of the most daring and adventurous man of 15th-century England.

Frederick II, a most unusual Holy Roman Emperor

1220 Today in Rome Pope Honorius III crowned Frederick II Holy Roman Emperor a month before his 26th birthday, thus confirming another Hohenstaufen in an office the family had held (with one four-year interruption) since 1138. Because Frederick was already King of Sicily (which included most of southern Italy as well as the island), the appointment put the Church's papal territories in the midst of Frederick's, creating a geographical anomaly that kept the Emperor and future popes in conflict for the next 30 years.

Frederick hardly improved relationships with the papacy by his unorthodox behaviour. He kept Jewish and Muslim scholars at his court, maintained a harem and corresponded with non-Christian rulers in Egypt. (He even sent one a polar bear as a present.) But his greatest sin was in denying papal suzerainty over temporal rulers. He claimed to believe that the Church should return to the conditions of poverty and prayer of the first Christians. The Church's response was to excommunicate him, comparing him to the Antichrist.

Frederick did go on crusade, after years of papal urging, but he did it while excommunicated. Worse, he managed to negotiate the rights to Jerusalem, Bethlehem and Nazareth without spilling a drop of Saracen blood. He then arranged for his own coronation as King of Jerusalem in the Church of the Holy Sepulchre.

In fact, Frederick set a record of sorts for Holy Roman Emperors in that he was excommunicated three times in all, twice by Gregory IX and once by Innocent IV. Innocent even declared a crusade against Frederick, the first time any pope had used this device against a political enemy rather than an enemy of the faith.

This righteous effort failed to dislodge Frederick, who ruled the Empire until his death in 1250. Even then rumours arose that he was not really dead but entombed alive in a mountain or volcano, waiting to return to Earth to scourge the worldly Church.

John Churchill changes sides

1688 If ever a man knew which side his bread was buttered on, it was John Churchill (later Duke of Marlborough), and never did he demonstrate it better than today.

Churchill was brought to favour and elevated to the rank of lieutenant general by King James II largely through the good offices of Churchill's sister, who was James's mistress. But by 1688, if Churchill's star was rising, James's was fast sinking, as his fervent Catholicism was seen as an increasing threat by England's largely Protestant population. So strongly did James's opponents distrust the King that on 20 July a group of disgruntled English nobles issued an invitation to the Dutch Stadholder William of Orange and his wife Mary – who was James's daughter – to seize the English throne. By mid-November William, Mary and their army had landed on the English coast in Devon.

On this day Churchill was riding with James to meet this threat, but, correctly sensing James's lack of any real support, he rode from his camp early in the evening to join the invading William, thus guaranteeing that James could only flee for his life instead of fighting.

Although Churchill's motives were largely opportunistic, this desertion of his benefactor probably saved England from another civil war.

Also on this day

1774: Robert Clive of India commits suicide * 1819: English novelist George Eliot (Mary Ann Evans) is born * 1869: French author André Gide is born * 1890: French general and President Charles de Gaulle is born

23 November

Queen Isabeau sends her lover to his death

1407 At first his subjects called Charles VI of France le Bien-Aimé for his kindly nature, but when he was 24 he suffered the first of the bouts of madness that continued throughout the rest of his life, and Charles the Well-Loved was now called Charles l'Insensé (Charles the Mad). Although he had occasional periods of rationality, his spells of insanity rendered him unfit to govern and thus loosed a bloody and ferocious power struggle for control of France.

The primary contenders were the King's brother, Louis, duc d'Orléans and his nephew, the powerful Duke of Burgundy, Jean Sans Peur (John the Fearless). But behind the scenes was Charles's wife, the beautiful, debauched and scheming Isabeau of Bavaria.

In the early years of Charles's madness, Isabeau had welcomed his brother Louis to her bed, and together they had ruled the kingdom. But it soon became clear that Jean Sans Peur had the support of most of France's powerful nobles, and Isabeau decided to switch sides.

On the evening of this day in 1407 the 36-year-old Queen invited Louis to sup with her in her apartments and then led him to her bedchamber. Suddenly the enraptured couple were disturbed by the arrival of an urgent summons from the King requiring Louis's immediate presence on the other side of Paris. He hurriedly dressed and left the Queen's quarters with a light escort to make his way through the darkened streets of the city.

Louis had ridden only a few hundred yards when he was suddenly attacked by a group of cut-throats who came at him from all sides. A sword severed his right hand as he held the reins.

'I am the Duke of Orléans', he shouted desperately. 'Just the one we wanted', came the reply, and Louis was knocked to the ground and savagely slain.

The next day it became clear that both the 'king's messenger' and the assassins had been sent by Jean Sans Peur, a charge the fearless duke readily acknowledged. His willing helper in the murder had been the heartless Isabeau, who had lured Louis to her boudoir to set the trap. Jean's position was now as unassailable as Louis's had been previously, for now he was sharing Queen Isabeau's bed as well as the rule of France.

For almost twelve years Jean Sans Peur remained a power in the land, but Louis's supporters had neither forgotten nor forgiven. In 1419 he was treacherously murdered during a diplomatic parley on a bridge in Montereau, about 50 miles from Paris.

As for Isabeau, she remained a power behind the throne until poor mad Charles died in 1422. Although her son Charles VII then became King, Isabeau found common cause with England's invading Henry V and married off her daughter Catherine to him. The fruit of that marriage was England's Henry VI, to whom Catherine passed on her father's feeblemindedness. Isabeau lived on until 1435, dying at the age of 64.

Also on this day

1876: Spanish composer Manuel de Falla is born in Cádiz

24 November

Charles Darwin publishes On the Origin of Species

1859 Today Charles Darwin published the most important scientific work of the 19th century, *On the Origin of Species by Means of Natural Selection, or The Preservation of Favoured Races in the Struggle for Life*. In it he wrote, 'I have called this principle, by which each slight variation, if useful, is preserved, by the term of Natural Selection.' Although one reviewer called the book 'so turgid, repetitive, and full of nearly meaningless tables, that it will only be read by specialists', it sold 1,250 copies on the first day and has never since been out of print.

On the Origin of Species elicited admiration from scientists, dismay from God-fearing Christians and fury from the Church hierarchy, enraged at its denial of the story of Genesis and the creation of the world in seven days. But in this work Darwin focused primarily on the evolution of animals, only lightly touching on the implications of his hypothesis for mankind. Twelve years later he remedied this omission with the publication of *The Descent of Man and Selection in Relation to Sex*, which filled out his theory of evolution.

Here Darwin describes man's primordial ancestors as 'a hairy quadruped, furnished with a tail and pointed ears, probably arboreal in its habits'. He concludes his book with the claim that man 'still bears in his bodily frame the indelible stamp of his lowly origin'. The Church was hostile in the extreme, for, in positioning humans as descendent from other primates rather than created separately in God's image, the book specifically refutes the biblical account of man's origin. As Darwin's theories became more widely known, the public reacted with bemusement; one no doubt apocryphal story tells of a vicar's wife who, on hearing of Darwin's contentions, exclaimed, 'I hope it is not true that we are descended from apes, but if it is true, I hope it does not become generally known.'

A year after the appearance of *The Descent of Man*, Darwin published yet another contentious theory in *The Expression of the Emotions in Man and Animals*. Here he once again positioned human beings as simply a more highly developed form of animal, showing that animals experience many of the same emotions as human beings and use the same facial muscles to express emotions such as fear, anger, love and grief.

In spite of his conviction that his books revealed nature's truth, Darwin always felt somewhat guilty for his heretical theory, referring to himself as 'the Devil's Chaplain'. He declined to comment publicly on his own views on a Christian God, writing to a friend, 'I feel most deeply that the whole subject is too profound for human intellect. A dog might as well speculate on the mind of Newton.'

Darwin's angst about his own ideas manifested itself in extreme poor health that started about the time he first began to commit his theories to paper in 1837. For the next 35 years he suffered from a whole raft of unpleasant symptoms – nausea, heart palpitations and insomnia – and became a semi-invalid. No specific cause was ever diagnosed, and many believe his illnesses were psychosomatic, brought on by the stress of developing ideas so totally in conflict with the religious teachings with which he had been raised.

Darwin continued to write at his house in Kent, his last work the rather less controversial *The Formation of Vegetable Mould, Through the Action of Worms, with Observations on Their Habits*. He died at home on 19 April 1882 at the age of 73. Today virtually the entire civilised world has come to accept his revolutionary evolutionary theories, as Christians and Jews now accept the story of Genesis as symbolic rather than literal. But his brilliant discoveries are still denied in some backward parts of Borneo, the Congo, rural Pakistan and the United States.

The king who never joined a battle

1542 The most famed English kings gained their renown primarily on the field of battle – witness William the Conqueror, Richard the Lion-Heart, Edward III, Henry V and Henry VII to name but a few. But the exception to the rule is perhaps the most famous of them all, King Henry VIII.

The English fought only two serious battles during Henry's reign. Both were against Scotland, both were victories, both resulted in the death of a Scottish king, and both left an infant behind to inherit the Scottish throne. And Henry was at neither of them.

The first, the Battle of Flodden, was fought on 9 September 1513. During the fighting Scotland's King James IV was killed on the field. But the victory was due to the generalship of Thomas Howard, Earl of Surrey, as Henry was in France at the time. On James's death his son of just seventeen months inherited the crown as James V.

On this day 29 years after Flodden came the second major battle, at Solway Moss, fought while Henry was in London, once again leaving the combat to his barons. Here a small force of only 3,000 Englishmen met a Scottish army of 15,000, but most of the Scots turned and ran without a fight. The victors captured 1,200 prisoners, including 500 gentlemen, five barons and two earls, thus eliminating Scotland as a military threat for the remainder of Henry's reign.

This time the Scottish King, the same James V who had inherited the crown on his father's death after the Battle of Flodden, survived the battle – just. But although he escaped the English, the defeat brought on a mental breakdown, and he died just twenty days later. Shortly before he died, his wife Mary of Guise gave birth to a daughter, named Mary after her mother, who on her father's death became Mary, Queen of Scots.

Henry lived on for another five years, never imagining that his then thirteen-year-old daughter Elizabeth and five-year-old Mary would never meet but would in their turn become mortal enemies.

Also on this day

1713: Novelist Laurence Sterne is born in Clonmel, Ireland * 1864: French painter Henri de Toulouse-Lautrec is born

25 November

A remarkable woman stages a coup

1741 Although Tsarina Elizabeth was the daughter of Russia's Peter the Great, it required sixteen years and the death of five sovereigns before she could gain the throne – and then she had to take it herself. On this day she executed a successful *coup d'état* while the reigning Tsar Ivan VI was still only a year old.

Elizabeth was just sixteen when her father died. By the standards of her day or any other, she was remarkably beautiful, with a beauty evenly matched by vanity. She dyed her hair and eyebrows jet black (she was actually fair), never wore the same dress twice and smothered herself in ostentatious jewellery. She reputedly owned 15,000 pairs of shoes, with dresses to match. She was also believed to be licentious in the extreme, preferring lovers from the lower social orders, including coachmen and household servants. In spite of her promiscuity (or perhaps because of it), she was extremely religious, attending Mass regularly.

By the time Elizabeth was 32, she had watched four rulers come and go – her father Peter the Great, his wife Catherine, his grandson Peter II, and his niece Anna. Now Anna's great-nephew, the year-old Ivan VI, was Tsar, under the control of his ferocious mother, another Anna.

But when the second Anna threatened to banish Elizabeth to a convent, Elizabeth displayed the ruthlessness she had inherited from her father. Gathering her allies in court, she imprisoned Anna and the infant Tsar and seized the crown for herself.

Elizabeth was a complex mixture of European sophistication and Tartar barbarism. She established Russia's first university and built St Petersburg's fabulous Winter Palace. She abolished the death penalty but did not shrink from torture. She once discovered a treasonous plot involving two noble women whom she hated anyway for their beauty. She spared their lives but had their tongues cut out.

Elizabeth ruled Russia for twenty years, leaving her weak-minded predecessor Ivan VI languishing in prison. On her death, although Ivan was still alive, the throne went to the first Anna's son Peter III, who made the colossal blunder of marrying a German princess named Sophia von Anhalt-Zerbst, known to history as Catherine the Great. In 1762 Catherine took over Russia in a *coup d'état*, and had her husband locked away and subsequently murdered in his cell. Two years later, poor Ivan, who had never been released, met the same grisly fate.

Disraeli buys the Suez Canal

1875 Isma'il Pasha, Khedive of Egypt, was one of history's great government spenders. When the Turkish sultan placed him in the job in 1863, Egypt's national debt stood at a modest £7,000,000. Twelve years later it had ballooned to a gargantuan £100,000,000. Hence the need for cash.

The Suez Canal had finally been completed in 1869 after ten years of labour, its ownership split between the Egyptians and the French, who had engineered its construction. But by 1875 Isma'il was desperate for money and so offered Egypt's shares for sale. News of Isma'il's plight was picked up by a British newspaperman, who immediately sent it on to the British Foreign Office.

In a moment of myopia, the Foreign Office recommended against the acquisition, but Britain's Prime Minister Benjamin Disraeli had a broader understanding of the canal's strategic value for the Empire and the remarkable opportunity it offered for shipping and trade, especially with the jewel of the Empire, India. But where to get the money? He could probably persuade Parliament to go along with the deal, but that would take time, and in the interim some other foreign power might snatch up the shares.

Without a word to Parliament, Disraeli went straight to the richest man in the country, Lionel Rothschild, who coughed up the then staggering sum of £4,000,000 within a few hours. On this day the Prime Minister quietly purchased the shares, later persuading Parliament to ratify the transaction.

This was Great Britain's first step into Egypt, a step that led inexorably to the British occupation of the country in 1882. In 1922 an Egyptian monarchy was established, still largely under British control, but 30 years later Egypt finally completely freed itself from British domination when Gamal Abdel Nasser ousted the last Egyptian king, the fat and licentious King Farouk.

Also on this day

1562: Spanish dramatist Lope de Vega is born in Madrid * 1616: Cardinal Richelieu joins the French government for the first time

26 November

Death of the formidable Blanche of Castile

1252 Today died Blanche of Castile, one of history's most forceful characters, even if not the most appealing. She was born in Spain in 1188, but at the age of eleven was taken to France by her grandmother, Eleanor of Aquitaine, to marry the future Louis VIII. Tradition has it that Blanche kept such a sharp eye on her husband that he remained impeccably faithful for their 26 years of marriage, something of a miracle for a king in an arranged marriage in the Middle Ages (or perhaps in any age).

Blanche was twice regent of France, the first time on her husband's death when their son, Louis IX, was only twelve. Sensing weakness with a boy king on the throne, France's barons rose in revolt, with clandestine support from England. The barons had sadly underestimated the indomitable Blanche, who, dressed entirely in white, personally led her armies to eventual victory.

Blanche attempted to dominate her son even more than she had his father, particularly in his private conduct. When Louis reached maturity and married, court gossip had it that her attempts to regulate his sex life forced the young King to meet his wife in secret on the staircase between their rooms.

By the time Blanche reached 60, she had developed a worrying heart condition, but nonetheless agreed to take charge of the country once again when Louis and his wife embarked on a crusade to the Holy Land. Four years later she was struck down by a fatal heart attack when Louis was still in Jaffa.

There is some debate about the exact place where she died. One source claims that she left the world from an abbey in Melun just south of Paris, having intended to renounce it to become a nun. Another contends that she suffered a heart attack en route to the abbey but was brought back to the Louvre in Paris where she was improbably laid on a bed of straw to repent her sins and receive the last rites. A third maintains that she breathed her last in a palace located on the current site of Paris's Bourse de Commerce in the area of Les Halles.

George Washington proclaims Thanksgiving

1789 During his first year as President, George Washington proclaimed today a National Day of Thanksgiving in honour of the new American Constitution. In so doing he gave prominence to a holiday that Americans had first celebrated in 1621 and had continued to celebrate sporadically over the intervening years.

But Thanksgiving has always been a moveable feast. The famous first one was celebrated sometime in early October by the 56 Pilgrim colonists who still survived from the 102 who had landed with the *Mayflower* the previous November. They invited 90 members of the Wampanoag Indian tribe to join them in a three-day harvest festival.

During the ensuing years Thanksgiving was mostly not held at all, and when it was, it was a local affair on varying dates. In 1777 for the first time all thirteen of the nation's states agreed on a single Thanksgiving Day in October, but this was really to commemorate the American victory over the British at Saratoga the month before, rather than a harvest festival.

In spite of Washington's declaration, Thanksgiving did not become an official American institution, but in 1827 a 39-year-old New Englander named Sarah Josepha Hale initiated her tireless campaign to have it formally recognised. The next year she became America's first female editor of a magazine when she was asked to take charge of the *Ladies' Magazine* and, later, *Godey's Lady's Book*. She used both publications as forums for continuing her crusade (while on the side penning the children's verse 'Mary Had a Little Lamb', a poem that became so famous that in 1877 Thomas Edison recorded himself reciting it for the first public demonstration of his gramophone).

Finally, after 36 years of writing to presidents, governors and senators, Sarah Hale was rewarded when, in 1863, Abraham Lincoln made Thanksgiving an official national holiday, specifying that it should always take place on the last Thursday in November.

Even then there was one more change to come. In 1939 the United States found itself in the midst of a worldwide depression and wanted to boost consumer purchases. Therefore President Franklin Roosevelt proclaimed Thanksgiving Day a week earlier – on the fourth, not the last, Thursday of November – to give American consumers one more week of shopping before Christmas. It has been celebrated on the fourth Thursday in November ever since.

Also on this day
1504: Queen of Castile and Aragon Isabella I dies at Medina del Campo in Spain
* 1607: Founder of Harvard University John Harvard is born

27 November

Clovis, the first French king

511 Clovis, the Frankish king whom the French regard as the founder of France, died today in Paris at the age of 45. So revered was he that a derivation of his name – Louis – was used for eighteen future kings.

French claims notwithstanding, Clovis was really a Belgian, born a prince of the Salian Franks, whose capital was around Tournai and whose native language was Frankish German.

At only fifteen Clovis inherited his father's small kingdom and immediately set out to expand it. By his death he had quadrupled its size to form an 'r'-shaped realm that covered most of western France, south as far as Toulouse, east almost to the Rhône, and in the northern part, covering today's Belgium and parts of what is now western Germany.

Clovis's take-over of the Rhineland Franks was a good example of his cunning and ruthlessness. Knowing of bad blood between King Sigebert and his son Chlodoric, he persuaded Chlodoric to murder his father to put himself on the throne. After the assassination Chlodoric was searching through his father's treasure chest for a gift for Clovis when one of Clovis's knights crept up behind him and split his skull with an axe. Clovis then reported to the remaining Rhineland Franks that Chlodoric had murdered his father but had received a mortal blow in the process. Now leaderless, the gullible Rhinelanders then accepted Clovis as King.

Later he defeated his cousin Ragnacaire, the King of Cambrai, who was taken prisoner and brought before Clovis with his hands chained behind his back. 'Why', asked Clovis, 'have you permitted our blood to be humiliated by allowing yourself to be put in chains? Better that you should die.' Whereupon Clovis hacked his prisoner down. Then, turning to Ragnacaire's brother, who had also been taken prisoner, he said, 'Had you but helped your brother, they would not have chained his hands', and promptly executed the brother as well.

Clovis was the only French king ever to wed a saint. At about 30 he married Clothilde, the Catholic daughter of the King of Burgundy. At first he ignored her pleas to become a Christian, but in 496 he found himself threatened with defeat by the Alemanni. Desperate for help from any quarter, he offered a prayer to Christ for victory. After his triumph in the ensuing Battle of Tolbiacum, he led 3,000 of his army to Reims for a mass baptism on Christmas Day.

According to legend, just as the ceremony began it was discovered that the consecration oil was missing, but a dove descended from heaven with a full ampoule carried in its beak. This so-called Sainte Ampoule of Reims was miraculously preserved in Reims cathedral and used for the coronation of every French king from Philip Augustus in 1179 until Charles X in 1824, even though the cathedral itself burned down at the beginning of the 13th century, to be replaced by the one that stands there today.

After the baptismal ceremony the presiding bishop, St Remi, famously characterised Clovis's change from paganism to Christianity with the remark, 'Henceforth we must burn what we have worshipped and worship what we have burned.'

Although Clovis's decision to push his people towards Christianity changed the direction of religion in France for ever, his faith was manifested in some rather unchristian ways. After one battle a knight snatched a vase from a church, prompting the local bishop to plead for its return. Shortly Clovis met with his men at Soissons to divide the spoils of war. There he asked for the vase, but the knight refused, shattering it with his axe. Without a word the King took the pieces and returned them to the bishop.

A year later Clovis saw the same knight at a military assembly. Before the gathered warriors, the King accused him of carrying a dirty axe and threw it to the ground in front of him. When the knight stooped to pick it up, Clovis brought his own axe down on the offender's head, sneering, 'Thus didst thou serve the vase of Soissons.'

Later in his reign Clovis established Paris as his capital, a useful central location to keep an eye on his various conquests. There he and Clothilde built the church that ultimately became Sainte-Geneviève, where they were buried side by side. During the French Revolution their tomb was desecrated and their ashes scattered to the winds.

Roger de Mortimer establishes a grisly tradition at Tyburn

1330 Stroll through London and stop at Marble Arch, at the north-east corner of Hyde Park. Where now stand the handsome houses of Connaught Square and the shops of the Edgware Road once was England's most famous place of execution, Tyburn. Its name derives from the Tyburn River, a small tributary of the Thames that formerly went through London's West End before it was culverted.

There is some evidence that Tyburn's first gallows was erected as early as 1190, but most historians believe that the execution of Roger de Mortimer on this day in 1330 was the start of a grisly tradition (although some maintain that the Scottish rebel William Wallace, who was hanged, drawn and quartered in 1305, was executed at Tyburn).

The darkly handsome, arrogant Mortimer was one of England's premier villains. A powerful baron who joined a minor rebellion against King Edward II, he was imprisoned in the Tower of London but shortly escaped and fled to

France. There he seduced Queen Isabella, Edward's French wife, who was home for a visit to escape the humiliation of her husband's homosexual lovers.

Queen and paramour soon returned to England, but this time leading an army. They captured and foully murdered the King and ruled the country for three years until the King's son, Edward III, escaped from their care and captured them in turn.

Although shielding his adulterous and murderous mother, young Edward had no qualms about her lover and ordered the once supreme Mortimer to be hanged, drawn and quartered at Tyburn before an assembled multitude of ghoulish onlookers.

From that day Tyburn became England's location of choice for executions, which it remained until 1783.

A twelve year old joins the Navy

1770 A frail twelve-year-old boy entered the British navy today, enrolled as a midshipman aboard HMS *Raisonable*, a 64-gun ship of the line that had been captured from the French twelve years earlier.

This was the navy of legend that pressed most of its seamen to service, as conditions were so vile and pay so low that few volunteered. Crews routinely spent years afloat without chance of leave. Quarters were impossibly cramped and discipline was fierce, enforced by the cat-o'-nine-tails. The food was unspeakable, featuring maggot-infested biscuits among other delicacies. Indeed, this was the navy that Winston Churchill later referred to as 'nothing but rum, sodomy, and the lash'.

Despite these hardships, this twelve-year-old midshipman was determined to make his name and fortune. In this he succeeded, owing much to the eternal conflict with France and Spain that continued throughout his life. His name was Horatio Nelson, the greatest admiral produced by England since Drake.

Also on this day

43 BC: Octavian (future Augustus), Lepidus, and Mark Antony form the second Triumvirate * 1582: William Shakespeare marries Anne Hathaway * 1953: American playwright Eugene O'Neill dies

28 November

The story of the 'Eleanor Crosses'

1290 Throughout 36 years of happy marriage King Edward I had been devoted to his wife Eleanor, and during that time she had borne him no fewer than seventeen royal children. So when she died this day of a persistent fever, the King was sorely stricken.

Although originally Spanish (her father was the King of Castile), Eleanor might just as well have been English. She married Edward (then still a prince) in Spain when she was only eight years old and immediately went with him to his lands in Gascony and then came to England, still only ten years old.

When Eleanor was 26 (and already married for eighteen years), she became Queen of England on the ascension of her husband. That same year she accompanied him on crusade. When the royal couple were at Acre an assassin nearly killed him by attacking him with a poisoned knife. Tradition has it that Eleanor saved his life by sucking the poison from the wound. Whatever the truth of the matter, when they returned to England Edward was more devoted than ever to his wife, who was a moderating influence on his sometimes arrogant and even brutal behaviour.

In 1290 the couple were visiting Harby in Nottinghamshire when the Queen fell sick and died. Edward had her body brought to London for burial, and as a special demonstration of his love, he ordered built a beautiful stone cross at each place along the way where her body had rested for a night.

In all, eleven 'Eleanor Crosses' were carved, a few of which are still standing. The last was placed at a town near London called Charing. The town is no more, nor is its cross, but the place where it stood is still known as Charing Cross.

Also on this day

1680: Italian sculptor and architect Giovanni Bernini dies in Rome * 1757: English poet and painter William Blake is born * 1820: German Communist philosopher Friedrich Engels is born in Barmen

29 November

Cardinal Wolsey dies just in time

1530 Cardinal Thomas Wolsey was the son of a butcher and cattle dealer in Ipswich, but had become the second most powerful man in England through intelligence, diligence and an uncanny ability to give Henry VIII what he wanted. He was a short, corpulent man of earthy humour who was known for his arrogance, his vanity and his greed. But he was an outstanding administrator, and such talent, combined with his all-consuming ambition, had helped him to run England successfully for almost twenty years.

But now Wolsey had been cast out from the court he served, charged with high treason and summoned for trial. His first mistake had been building Hampton Court and staffing it with over 400 servants. His master King Henry simply took it over as far too good for a cardinal but just about right for a king.

But Wolsey's fatal error was his failure to gain Henry an annulment of his marriage to Catherine of Aragon. The Pope sided with the Queen under pressure from her nephew Holy Roman Emperor Charles V, the most powerful man in Europe.

On 28 November Wolsey arrived at Leicester Abbey in the custody of Sir William Kingston, the lieutenant of the Tower. Sick at heart but also in body, he lamented his fate, 'Had I but served God as diligently as I have my king, He would not have given me over in my grey hairs.' He died the next day at the age of 55.

The king who moved the papacy

1314 On this day Philip the Fair of France died where he was born, in the royal hunting lodge at Fontainebleau. King of France for 29 years, he was a ruthless, enigmatic figure described by a contemporary as 'ni un homme ni un bête. C'est un statue.' (Neither man nor beast, he is a statue.)

Philip's mother had died when he was only three, and his father Philip III had quickly remarried. Then, when Philip was eight, his elder brother succumbed to a mysterious fever, and rumours grew that he had been poisoned by his stepmother, who intended to remove all the King's children by his first wife to give primacy to her own. Although Philip's stepmother was almost certainly innocent, the trauma made Philip silent, introverted and suspicious.

He grew up to be tall, handsome and blond (hence his sobriquet 'the Fair'). Deeply religious, he idolised the memory of his grandfather St Louis, whom he could hardly have remembered, for he died on crusade in Tunisia when Philip was only two years old.

Philip's passion was to increase the power of the throne of France, something he achieved through judicious warfare and intimidation of the papacy. To fund his plans he taxed the Church, destroyed the Templars to gain their wealth, and expelled both the Jews and Lombard bankers from France in order to confiscate their property.

Philip was largely responsible for the start of the famous 'Babylonian Captivity' when he pressured his pocket pope, the Gascon Pope Clement V, to move the papal seat from Rome to Avignon.

During the last years of his life Philip occasionally wore a hair shirt beneath his royal garments as a form of religious dedication. He died as the result of a hunting accident at the age of 46, an appropriate end for a king whose secret seal had been a ring engraved with a galloping deer.

A future saint is crowned in France

1226 It was St Andrew's Eve on this day in 1226 when Louis Capet was crowned King of France at Reims, three weeks to the day after the death of his father, King Louis VIII. Only twelve years old, he was blond and handsome but with a delicate and sensitive face. He would grow up to become one of

Europe's very greatest kings, and the only king of France ever to be judged a saint by the Roman Catholic Church.

At first Louis was carefully guided by his formidable mother, Blanche of Castile, who brought him up to be strongly but tolerantly religious. But by the time he was fifteen, although constantly and sometimes well advised by his mother, he was largely taking his own decisions, and personally led his troops in the field. Fortunately, the enemy (the perfidious English, as usual) fled before battle was joined, and the young King saw no combat.

Indeed, during the 44 years of Louis's reign, he won no great wars, conquered no territory and twice led disastrous crusades to the Holy Land. During the first he commanded a force of 35,000 men, but after attaining a victory at al-Mansurah, plague struck his army and he was forced to retreat. Thousands died and the expedition ended in ruinous failure, as Louis and his chief barons were captured and had to be ransomed. Louis's second crusade was even less successful, as plague struck once again, this time killing the King.

Unlike other famous medieval kings, Louis earned his enduring fame through his character rather than conquest. He was known for the justice of his decisions, which he often handed down personally, gathering his subjects at the foot of an oak tree in the grounds of his palace in Vincennes. But Louis was not simply 'good'. He was a cheerful, affable man who talked easily and frequently with those around him.

One of Louis's lasting marks on history came through his firm religious beliefs. His private confessor was a priest named Robert de Sorbon, a man of poor family who had made his own way through devoutness and hard work.

By 1253 Sorbon had started instructing students as well as the King. Four years later he bought some land and, with the King's backing, founded a seminary for impoverished students called the Maison de Sorbonne. The Maison de Sorbonne soon grew into the core of the University of Paris, which to this day bears his name.

Immediately upon Louis's death his subjects took to considering him a saint, a judgement confirmed by the Church only 27 years later.

Also on this day

1780: Austrian Empress Maria Theresa dies * 1797: Italian composer Domenico Donizetti is born * 1864: American cavalry units kill over 150 disarmed Cheyenne and Arapaho Indians during the Sand Creek massacre * 1924: Italian opera composer Giacomo Puccini dies

30 November

Oscar Wilde's last quip

1900 At the turn of the 21st century in the rue des Beaux Arts on Paris's Left Bank is one of Europe's most sophisticated hotels, somewhat self-consciously called simply 'L'Hôtel'. Each room is different, each impeccable in its décor.

At the turn of the 20th century, however, the hotel that occupied the same site was a far more humble establishment, and it was here that a poor and demoralised Oscar Wilde took lodging.

Almost twenty years before, Wilde had established himself as England's leading wit and playwright, over the years producing masterpieces such as *Lady Windermere's Fan* and *The Importance of Being Earnest*. He was also an inveterate traveller, which provoked a typical Wildean witticism, 'I never travel without my diary. One should always have something sensational to read in the train.' He married at 30 and had two children.

But Wilde's sexual preferences were homosexual, and in one of the great scandals of the time, at 41 he was convicted of sodomy and served two years in jail, his career and reputation entirely destroyed.

So Wilde fled to Paris, weak and prematurely aged. No doubt he wondered about his famous claim that he put only his talent into his books but his genius into his life.

Installed in the rue des Beaux Arts, Wilde this day was dying and he knew it. But he kept his celebrated wit to the end. His last words were, 'Either that wallpaper goes, or I do.'

The apex and nadir of Sweden's Charles XII

1700, 1718 On this date eighteen years apart occurred both the greatest triumph and the untimely end of Sweden's warrior king, Charles XII. In between these events fell a far-ranging conflict known to history as the Great Northern War.

When his father died of stomach cancer on 5 April 1697, Charles became an absolute monarch at the age of fourteen. Despite his youth, he was exceptionally strong willed, not to say obstinate, with a fervid belief in his country's destiny and his own moral duty to serve it. Fearless in the face of danger, he shot his first bear at eleven, and became an outstanding horseman. Later in life he developed an interest in painting and architecture, could quote Swedish poetry and relished philosophical arguments. But his real genius was war.

In February 1700, when Charles was still seventeen, Denmark, Poland and Russia launched an attack against Sweden to start the Great Northern War, which was to last for 21 years. First turning his attention to the Russians, Charles led his army into what today is Estonia where on this day he annihilated the army of Peter the Great at the Battle of Narva.

Rain was pouring down when Charles's army reached the battlefield, but it shortly turned to snow. Although the 40,000 Russians far outnumbered the 10,000 Swedes, Charles managed to split the enemy's forces and destroy them piecemeal.

Charles himself was always where the action was hottest. When his fifth horse was shot out from under him, he laconically commented, 'These people seem disposed to give me exercise.' At one point he fell into a swamp and lost his boots and sword when his men pulled him free. Cheerfully he continued to fight in his socks.

Soon the Russians were fleeing in panic, thousands surrendering while others threw themselves in the Narva River in an attempt to escape. In all some 15,000 Russians perished against only 667 Swedes. So many Russians were captured that the Swedes couldn't guard them and had to let them go after confiscating their guns and equipment. The high point for many Swedish soldiers came after the battle when they celebrated their extraordinary triumph with a huge store of captured Russian vodka.

Charles continued to crush his enemies for the next nine years. He defeated the Danes, the Saxons and the Poles, capturing Krakow. Convinced of his righteous cause, he had little mercy for his defeated enemies, commenting, 'Rather let the innocent suffer than the guilty escape.' He instructed his troops to 'ravage, singe, and burn all about! Make the whole district a wilderness!'

But in 1709 Charles made the mistake of attacking a vastly superior Russian force at Poltava, and his army was obliterated. Charles escaped and fled to Turkey where he remained for the next six years.

In 1715 Charles finally returned to Sweden after an absence of fifteen years for reasons of battle or exile. Extraordinarily, during all of this time he had continued to rule his kingdom in absentia. And the Great Northern War ground on without final result.

In 1718 Charles launched a new campaign to conquer Norway (then a Danish province) to force the Danes to sue for peace. In November he brought his army before the enemy fortress at Fredrikshald (today's Halden) and surrounded the town with trenches. On this day Charles entered the trenches to get a better look at the enemy's positions. As he peeped over the parapet suddenly a bullet smashed into his head, killing him instantly.

Almost immediately rumours began to spread that someone from his own side had shot him – anyone who had kept his country in a state of war for eighteen years was bound to have enemies. The question will never be definitively answered, but most historians now believe he was killed by a lucky shot from the enemy.

The Great Northern War continued for another three years, reducing Sweden to the minor power that it still is today. Charles remains a contentious character. Some blame him for Sweden's precipitous decline from major power status, but many celebrate him as a great general and leader. More ominously, both Napoleon and Hitler looked to his example as a guide for their own invasions of Eastern Europe and even now he is extolled by Sweden's right-wing extremists for his chauvinism.

Also on this day

1508: Italian architect Andrea Palladio is born in Padua * 1667: Irish writer Jonathan Swift is born in Dublin * 1835: American writer Samuel Clemens (Mark Twain) is born * 1874: British Prime Minister Winston Churchill is born at Blenheim Palace

1 December

King Henry I dies of a surfeit of lampreys

1135 Today King Henry I, William the Conqueror's youngest son, died at Lyon-la-Forêt in eastern Normandy, the French duchy he ruled along with England. The legend is that his cook served him a dish of lampreys beyond their sell-by date, and the King expired of food poisoning. His body was returned in state to England, where it was buried in Reading Abbey, which Henry had founded.

Most contemporaries were not sad to see Henry go. As one of them wrote, 'God endowed him with three gifts, wisdom, victory and riches, but these were offset by three vices, avarice, cruelty and lust.'

Henry certainly had the last-named vice, as he fathered over twenty bastard children. As for avarice and cruelty, the case is proved by his treatment of his two brothers.

In 1100 Henry had inherited the throne of England from his elder brother William II (Rufus), who had been killed in a mysterious hunting accident that many believe Henry instigated in order to gain the crown.

Later he invaded his brother Robert Curthose's duchy of Normandy, captured Robert in battle, imprisoned him for the last 28 years of his life, and took over the duchy for himself.

Of Henry's many children, the only legitimate one surviving at the time of his death was a daughter named Matilda, to whom he left the throne of England. But Henry's favourite nephew, Stephen of Blois, was just as ruthless as his uncle. He ignored Matilda's rights and seized power. This usurpation eventually led to a mini civil war when Matilda unsuccessfully invaded the country. Stephen finally died in 1154 and England returned to Henry's direct bloodline in the person of his grandson, Matilda's son Henry Plantagenet, who founded the Plantagenet line.

Lady Astor becomes the first woman to sit in the House of Commons

1919 In the 654 years since Simon de Montfort, Earl of Leicester, had organised the very first British parliament in 1265, not a single woman had been a member. Today that changed for ever when Lady Nancy Witcher Astor took her seat in the House of Commons as MP for the Sutton division of Plymouth, becoming the first ever woman MP. (As a measure of her achievement, women in England had only been given the vote the previous year, and in America they were not enfranchised until 1920.)

Born of the rich Langhorne family near the sleepy town of Danville, Virginia, Nancy married richer, divorced her first husband and married yet richer still, to Waldorf Astor of the fabulously wealthy Astor clan. Waldorf's American great-great-grandfather John Jacob had made most of the money, and in 1890

Waldorf's father William had moved to England. After giving generously to the British war effort during the Great War, William had been rewarded with a title in 1917.

Waldorf had been a Member of Parliament but had given up his seat in 1919 when he succeeded to his father's viscountcy. This opening inspired Nancy, then 40, to stand in his place. To the astonishment of many, she was elected by a wide margin, and so an American (by birth anyway) became the first female member of the British Parliament. When someone suggested that her marriage to an Astor had helped her, she jokingly retorted, 'I married beneath me. All women do.'

Intelligent, quick-witted and afraid of neither man nor beast, Nancy Astor had a particular interest in what today we would call women's liberation. 'We are not asking for superiority [to men],' she said, 'for we have always had that. All we ask is equality.' Once while visiting the Churchill family's ancestral home at Blenheim Palace she started to harangue Winston Churchill about her favourite cause, a subject Churchill considered much of an irrelevance. After several minutes of disagreement, she finally exclaimed, 'Winston, if I were married to you, I would put poison in your coffee!' 'And if you were my wife,' the great man replied, 'I'd drink it.'

Nancy Astor served in Parliament for 26 uninterrupted years, retiring only when she was 66. (Or, as she once told a friend, 'I refuse to admit that I am more than fifty-two, even if that makes my children illegitimate.') She lived on in luxury for another nineteen years, to die in the bosom of her family. During her final illness she showed she had lost none of her wit. Waking to find her relatives grouped around her bed, she asked, 'Am I dying or is this my birthday?'

Also on this day

1455: Lorenzo Ghiberti, the sculptor who created the 'Gates of Paradise' bronze doors for the baptistery of the cathedral of Florence, dies

2 December

American abolitionist John Brown is hanged

1859 It is said that fanatics make good martyrs, and John Brown, who was hanged today, was a perfect example. Hawk-nosed, hard-eyed and bearded, he even looked the part he played.

Born in Connecticut in 1800, he had failed at numerous trades: tanner, land speculator, drover and travelling salesman. Moving his large family from place to place, he became a fanatical abolitionist, once demonstrating his ardour by living in a free black community in New York State. Later he moved to the Kansas Territory and led a night-time guerrilla raid against a pro-slavery community in which five men were dragged from their cabins and beaten to death.

In October 1859 Brown led a ragtag bunch of sixteen whites and five blacks on a raid on Harper's Ferry, Virginia (today West Virginia). After an early exchange of shots in which two bystanders were killed, he set up headquarters in the federal armoury that his men had captured. For two days and nights he holed up there with some 60 hostages, waiting for nearby slaves to rise up to claim their freedom. By then state militia had surrounded the armoury, and on the morning of 18 October a company of US Marines under the command of Colonel Robert E. Lee stormed it. A Marine lieutenant beat Brown to the ground with his sword, and ten of Brown's men were killed in the action, including two of his sons.

Brown was quickly taken to Charleston (now in West Virginia), tried, convicted of murder, treason against the state and inciting slave insurrection, and sentenced to be hanged.

About eleven o'clock this morning he was brought to the field of execution, where a crowd of 1,000 waited in anticipation, along with 1,500 soldiers. He arrived riding in a furniture wagon, sitting on his own coffin, his arms tied at the elbows.

The shabbily dressed prisoner was calm and courteous. He mounted the scaffold without resistance and offered his neck for the noose. His head was then covered with a white hood.

The sheriff asked Brown if he wanted to signal the drop himself by throwing a handkerchief, but the tired old man replied, 'No, I don't care. I don't want you to keep me waiting unnecessarily.' These were his last words, spoken civilly, without emotion. Then a hush fell over the crowd until there was total silence, and the sheriff cut the rope with a sharp blow from his hatchet.

Within eighteen months Brown's cause was vindicated; the Civil War had begun, and 'John Brown's Body' soon became a favourite marching song of Northern troops.

Napoleon Day

1804, 1805, 1851, 1852 Today should be called Napoleon Day, as it commemorates the greatest triumphs of the Napoleons, uncle and nephew.

The first notable 2 December was a Sunday in 1804 when Napoleon Bonaparte, once Napoleone Buonaparte, shed his last name altogether to become Emperor Napoleon I. A crowd of 8,000 jammed Notre Dame to witness the coronation. There Pope Pius VII officiated but did not crown, as Napoleon reserved that honour for himself, famously placing the iron crown of Charlemagne and the old Lombard kings on his own head, then solemnly repeating their challenge, 'Dio me la diedes, guai a chi la tocca!' (God gave it to me; woe to him who touches it.) He then crowned his wife Joséphine Empress of France.

Precisely one year later, on 2 December 1805, 62,000 Frenchmen under

Emperor Napoleon utterly routed a combined Russian–Austrian army of 80,000 commanded by Alexander I of Russia and Franz I of Austria. Fought near a Moravian town called Austerlitz (now Slavkov u Brna in the Czech Republic), this seismic victory was called the Battle of the Three Emperors.

Napoleon split the enemy force with a determined assault by Marshal Soult against the centre and then vigorously pursued both enemy halves. Allied losses came to 15,000 killed and wounded and 11,000 captured, compared with Napoleon's loss of only 9,000 men. Because of the unusually bright sunshine on this winter day, the battle is remembered as 'the sun of Austerlitz'. It was Napoleon's greatest military victory and the apogee of his career, as France now became the dominant power in Europe.

By 1851 the first Emperor Napoleon was long in his grave, but his nephew Louis Napoleon added to the Napoleonic mythology of 2 December.

When Louis Napoleon had been elected President of France in 1848, his term of office had been limited to four years, and the constitution forbade him from succeeding himself. In July 1851 he tried and failed to persuade the Assembly to revise the constitution, and this failure had set his resolve to seize by force what he could not gain by persuasion.

Working closely with his half-brother the duc de Morny, Louis Napoleon chose 2 December for his *coup d'état*. On the previous evening his men placed posters throughout Paris proclaiming him Emperor, and his confederate Maupas, the Prefect of Police, secretly arrested 78 troublemakers at dawn on 2 December. (Ironically, one of those taken into custody was Adolphe Thiers, who nineteen years later would become the President of France on Napoleon's downfall.)

Later in the day Louis Napoleon rode through the streets of Paris accompanied by a glittering troop of splendid soldiers, including most of France's generals. And so it was done. There was no bloodshed that day and little resistance. Louis Napoleon was now the nation's dictator, although his imperial position had been gained by force and had yet to be endorsed by the French Senate. (Karl Marx's reaction to Louis's coup was his famous dictum, 'Hegel says somewhere that all great events and personalities in world history reappear in one fashion or another. He forgot to add: the first time as tragedy, the second as farce.')

The final 2 December in the Napoleonic legend occurred one year later, in 1852. On that day the Senate passed a resolution confirming that the French Empire was restored and Louis Napoleon its Emperor, with the title of Napoleon III.

President James Monroe bans more European colonies in the Western hemisphere

1823 'The American continents, by the free and independent conditions which they have assumed and maintain, are henceforth not to be considered as subjects for future colonisation by any European powers.'

These are the opening words of the famous doctrine issued this day by President James Monroe, effectively banning Europe from establishing additional colonies in the Western hemisphere.

The Monroe Doctrine was aimed at Russia, France and especially beleaguered Spain, which had once owned Chile, Colombia, Mexico, Peru and La Plata (Argentina), all of which had been recognised as independent countries by the United States in 1822. There were rumours that Russia, Austria and Spain might form an alliance to retake these territories. What's more, Russia's Tsar Alexander I had recently laid claim to the entire north-west coast of North America as far south as Oregon.

Although named after Monroe, the Doctrine was both conceived and partially written by his intellectual Secretary of State, John Quincy Adams (who would succeed him as President). It became a central part of America's foreign policy, although in the early years the country had neither the strength nor perhaps the temerity to exercise it. In 1833 the American government sagely averted its eyes when Great Britain occupied the Falkland Islands in the south Atlantic.

In the 1840s, however, President James Polk used the Doctrine to warn off Spain and Britain from setting up colonies in California, Oregon and the Yucatan. During the 1860s France took advantage of American preoccupation with the Civil War to establish the Habsburg Maximilian as Emperor of Mexico but was forced to pull out in 1867 when American troops were massed on the Rio Grande, threatening to intervene. (The Emperor was executed by a Mexican nationalist firing squad.)

Later President Theodore Roosevelt conceived what is called the Roosevelt Corollary to the Doctrine: that in cases where a foreign nation has justified claims against a Western hemisphere country, the United States can bar foreign intervention while itself pursuing those claims. This was the justification he used to take over Santo Domingo in 1904, when that nation was staggering under a foreign debt of $18,000,000. Later in the same year he solved similar problems in Venezuela, succinctly explaining his motives in a private letter to his Secretary of State: 'It will show these Dagos that they will have to behave decently.'

Also on this day

1547: Spanish conquistador Hernándo Cortés dies in Seville * 1697: The newly rebuilt St Paul's Cathedral in London reopens * 1814: French writer, philosopher and pornographer the marquis de Sade dies

3 December

The first French dauphin

1368 Born on this day was King Charles VI of France, known as Charles l'Insensé for the 44 fits of insanity that he suffered during the last 30 years of his life.

King for 42 years, Charles was one of the longest reigning and most disastrous monarchs in French history. His madness – attacks that lasted up to nine months – permitted his greedy cousins, the Dukes of Burgundy and Orléans, to usurp his power while battling each other. Meanwhile his sensuous wife, Isabeau of Bavaria, was trying to gain influence for herself, simultaneously cuckolding the King with a legion of lovers. Into this chaos marched England's King Henry V, who smashed the French at Agincourt and became de facto co-ruler of the country.

Charles has one unique distinction. On his birth he was given as his apanage (the grant of land given by his father, Charles V) the Dauphiné, a region in south-eastern France, thus becoming the first royal dauphin, the title given to all subsequent heirs to the French throne.

Although the French word dauphin also means dolphin, the title has no real aquatic origins. It is a personal name that appears as early as the 4th century, apparently derived from a family's coat of arms featuring a dolphin (*dauphin* in French). In the 12th century a certain Guigues IV Dauphin was ruler of what was then called Viennois, and most of his successors also used the name until it became a title and the territory began to be called the Dauphiné.

The Council of Trent sets Church doctrine for centuries to come

1545 Today in the northern Italian town of Trent the 19th Ecumenical Council of the Roman Catholic Church began its deliberations. Known for ever after by the name of the town in which it was convened, the Council of Trent met on and off for eighteen years and defined Church dogma and doctrine for centuries to come.

In the 16th century Christianity was in turmoil. Luther had posted his theses on a church door in 1517, Calvin fled to Basle in 1533, the same year Henry VIII effectively took England out of the Church of Rome, and trouble was brewing throughout Germany and Holland. In response, Pope Paul III, still vigorous at 78, issued a bill proclaiming the Council.

Among the issues decided, confirmed or set in motion at Trent were: only Catholics could enter heaven; Latin should be the only language of prayer; priests should be celibate; the Index of Forbidden Books was drawn up; faith and good works plus the seven sacraments were proclaimed as the sole means to salvation; the nature and consequence of original sin were defined.

The Council of Trent both shaped the future Church and created some much-needed reforms. But it failed in its original purpose – to bring all of Christianity into one church.

Also on this day

1857: Polish-born English writer Joseph Conrad is born in what is now Berdichev, Russia * 1894: Scottish writer Robert Louis Stevenson dies of a stroke in Samoa

4 December

Death of the great Cardinal Richelieu

1642 Cardinal Richelieu, Duke and First Minister to King Louis XIII, had virtually ruled France for eighteen years. Brilliant, calculating, pragmatic and unrelenting, he had the clearest of visions of the greatness and glory that he thought his country deserved.

When he was still young, Pope Paul V had said of him, 'He will prove a great rascal.' At least in the eyes of Richelieu's adversaries, that prediction proved true, as the mighty cardinal crushed his enemies at home and confounded them abroad to make France the greatest power in Europe.

But the all-powerful Richelieu had a history of ill health. He had been afflicted with migraines since the age of 25 and also suffered from those classic symptoms of over-stressed executives, ulcers and haemorrhoids. Further, he had a tubercular osteitis on his right arm that was evidenced by a festering sore. His constitution was weak, and he was prey to frequent fevers.

By 1642 Richelieu was 57, sick and weary. In November he was stricken with pneumonia compounded by pleurisy. After persuading King Louis to appoint Cardinal Mazarin as his successor, the great cardinal waited for death in the Palais Cardinal. At midday on 4 December he summoned his favourite niece to bid farewell. She told him that she had heard of a vision that predicted that he would not die at this time. 'My niece,' said the cardinal who had dealt in worldly power his entire career, 'there are no truths except those in the gospel; it is only in them that you should believe.' He died that afternoon.

On hearing of Richelieu's death, the sceptical old Pope Urban VIII commented, 'If there is a God, Cardinal Richelieu will have much to answer for. But if not – well, he had a successful life.'

The first Spanish Bourbon king

1700 Charles II, the last Spanish Habsburg, had died two months earlier, deranged and childless, finally leaving his great empire to his first Bourbon cousin twice removed, Philip, duc d'Anjou, grandson of Louis XIV of France.

Louis emphatically agreed that Philip was the man for the job, hoping to turn mighty Spain into a docile appendage of France. To the French court he grandly announced, 'It was the command of Heaven, and I have granted it with pleasure.'

On 4 December the seventeen-year-old Philip set off from France for his new kingdom. Asking his grandfather for a final word of advice, he may have been somewhat dampened in spirit to receive the reply, 'Never form an attachment for anyone.'

Philip V, as he was, remained King of Spain for 46 years until his death, in spite of the fourteen-year War of the Spanish Succession fought by Austria, England and France disputing his right to wear the crown. Philip himself remained resolutely French, building the beautiful La Granja palace near Madrid in French architectural style. During his last years he suffered fits of insanity, leaving control of the state largely to his wife. He was the first Spanish Bourbon, the royal house that has reigned on and off to this day, for over three centuries.

Also on this day

1154: The only Englishman to become Pope, Nicholas Breakspear, is elected Pope Adrian IV * 1795: Scottish author Thomas Carlyle is born * 1892: Spanish dictator Francisco Franco is born in El Ferrol

5 December

Requiem for Mozart

1791 At five minutes to one o'clock on this cold, damp December night died the composer many consider to be supreme in the history of Western music, Wolfgang Amadeus Mozart.

In the last months of his life Mozart completed some of his very greatest works. His clarinet concerto was published on 29 September, and the most loved of all his operas, *Die Zauberflöte* (*The Magic Flute*), premiered in Vienna the very next day. At the time of his death he was finishing his magnificent Requiem.

At the end of November Mozart had taken to his bed in his apartment in the Rauhensteingasse in Vienna, but he continued to work on his Requiem. The day before he died part of it was sung at his bedside. Undoubtedly aware of his coming end, the composer remarked, 'Didn't I tell you that I was writing this Requiem for myself?' He then slipped into unconsciousness.

The exact cause of Mozart's death is still debated. At the time it was attributed to 'severe miliary fever', but later diagnoses have included heart disease, rheumatic fever, typhus, trichinosis, kidney failure, broncho-pneumonia caused by a streptococcal infection and the fearful-sounding Schönlein-Henoch syndrome. Perhaps it was the uncertainty of the cause that immediately engendered speculation that his demise had not been so natural after all but the result of poisoning by the rival composer Antonio Salieri. One source maintains that in his final illness Mozart complained to his wife, 'Surely someone has poisoned me.' Most historians consider this no more than a plaintive description of how unwell he felt. Salieri, the Emperor's distinguished *Hofkapellmeister*, is said to have admitted to poisoning Mozart from professional envy, but at the time of the supposed confession he was already unhinged.

Mozart died two months before his 35th birthday. He was buried with scant ceremony in an unmarked multiple grave, and, at his wife's request, his Requiem was completed by the minor Austrian composer Franz Xaver Süssmayr.

Frederick the Great's greatest victory

1757 During the Seven Years' War Prussia's population totalled only four and a half million while the opposing alliance of Austria, France and Russia could draw their armies from over 100 million inhabitants. But Prussia had Frederick the Great.

Frederick was the greatest general of the 18th century, perhaps the greatest of any century. On this day he proved it and saved his nation from extinction.

The town of Leuthen lies just west of the Oder in land that Frederick had seized from Austria only a few years before. Here his force of just 36,000 men would face an Austrian army of 60,000–80,000. Aware of the enormous odds against his success, Frederick offered his officers the chance to leave before the battle, but none defected. The evening before the battle he laconically remarked, 'Shortly we shall either have beaten the enemy, or we will never see one another again.'

The next day, through a brilliant flanking manoeuvre, Frederick utterly routed the Austrians. Although Prussia lost some 6,000 killed and wounded, the enemy lost 10,000 killed, plus another 21,000 captured. And within two weeks another 17,000 dispirited Austrian soldiers surrendered almost without a fight at Breslau.

The war dragged on until 1763, sometimes favouring Frederick's enemies, but the great general always managed to extricate himself from disaster with a timely victory. As Napoleon remarked in the following century, 'It is not the Prussian army which for seven years defended Prussia against the three most powerful nations in Europe, but Frederick the Great.'

In the years ahead, the Battle of Leuthen became a totemic victory for the German people, a symbol of German superiority that would play its role in the eventual unification of the country, reverberating through the centuries to the First World War and culminating in the militarism of the Third Reich. As Frederick's contemporary the comte de Mirabeau commented, 'La guerre est l'industrie nationale de la Prusse.' (War is the national industry of Prussia.)

Also on this day

63 BC: Roman consul Cicero denounces the agitator Catiline in the Roman Senate * 1926: French Impressionist painter Claude Monet dies * 1933: Prohibition is repealed in the USA after more than thirteen years of privation

6 December

The true story of St Nick

AD 343 Today in the small town of Myra on the Mediterranean coast of Lycia (now Demre in Turkey) a popular local bishop named Nicholas died, whose legend would enthral millions for centuries to come. Nicholas had been born a pagan in the Lycian seaport of Patara, but converted to Christianity in his youth. After travels in the Holy Land he returned to become Bishop of Myra, only 50 miles from his birthplace. There he was imprisoned during Emperor Diocletian's ferocious persecution of the Christians but released when Constantine came to power.

Nicholas gained a saintly reputation by generous deeds for the poor and despondent, including the miraculous reassembling and reviving of three small children who had been carved into pieces by a greedy butcher trying to pass them off as spring lamb.

His most famous charitable deed concerned three sisters who were on the point of being forced to sell themselves into prostitution because their father could not afford dowries. Hearing of their plight, Nicholas dropped bags filled with gold coins down their chimney, one of which landed in a stocking that had been hung up by the fireplace to dry.

When the good Bishop Nicholas died in 343, he was buried in Myra, where his tomb quickly became a shrine. We do not know if he was ever officially canonised, but nonetheless he was soon considered the patron saint of some seemingly conflicting groups: prisoners and judges, sailors and virgins, pirates and merchants, and charitable guilds and pawnbrokers. So celebrated was he that in 1087 some Italian sailors filched his bones and transported them to Bari on Italy's Adriatic coast. There they remain, enshrined in the Basilica di San Nicola, built especially to house them.

During the Middle Ages the cult of St Nicholas was widespread in Europe, where he was depicted with a full beard, wearing the red robes of a bishop. The cult gradually died away except in Holland, where he was known as Sinterklaas (a Dutch corruption of Saint Nicholas). The Dutch in turn took the tradition with them to the New World when they colonised New Amsterdam (New York) in the 17th century. There Sinterklaas soon evolved into Santa Claus.

Today in Great Britain and America Santa Claus still wears red, is still full-bearded and is known to drop down the chimney on Christmas Eve to fill deserving children's stockings hung by the fireplace. In much of Europe he appears on his feast day on 6 December, the anniversary of his death, when children put their shoes outside their bedroom doors in the hope that they will be filled with fruit and sweets.

In spite of the evidence from millions of small children around the world, some remain sceptical. In 1969 Pope Paul VI had the Feast of St Nicholas dropped from the Catholic calendar, citing the lack of documentation of St Nick's life and deeds.

Marshal Ney is executed in the gardens of the Palais Luxembourg

1815 Today Michel Ney, one of Napoleon's most illustrious marshals, was shot by firing squad in the gardens of the Palais Luxembourg in Paris.

Ney was a beefy, red-haired, tobacco-chewing man of the people. Although his mother tongue was German (he was of Alsatian origin), he was exactly the kind of soldier Napoleon most valued: brave under fire to the point of recklessness, intimate with his troops, and intensely loyal.

Ney's blacksmith father had hoped for a genteel future for his son and had found him a position as apprentice to a lawyer, but at nineteen the adventurous young man ran away to join a regiment of hussars. He had already risen to the rank of general by the time he was 32, when he first met Napoleon.

Promoted to marshal three years later, Ney served the Emperor loyally, participating in the great victories at Jena, Eylau and Friedland and heroically commanding the rearguard in Napoleon's retreat from Moscow, for which the Emperor created him Prince de la Moskowa. He also fought courageously in the crucial defeat at Leipzig, where he was wounded.

When Napoleon was packed off to Elba, Ney allowed fat King Louis XVIII to persuade him to remain a marshal of France, and when the ex-emperor escaped, Ney vowed to 'bring him back in a cage'. But on seeing Napoleon again, he returned to his original loyalties, rejoined him for his 100 Days and commanded the left wing at Waterloo. There he had five horses shot out from under him, and at the battle's end tried to stop the rout, crying to his soldiers, 'Venez voir comment meurt un maréchal de France!' (Come and see how a marshal of France can die!)

This reversal of loyalties engendered the special hatred of King Louis. Soon after Waterloo Ney attempted to escape from France but was captured and returned to Paris in chains.

Tried for treason, he was sentenced to death, and on the cold, clear morning of 6 December, the bold marshal bravely faced the firing squad. Refusing a bandage over his eyes, he addressed his executioners, 'Don't you know that for twenty-five years I have learned to face both cannonballs and bullets? Come on, soldiers, straight to the heart.'

Ney died a criminal in the eyes of his government but a hero in the eyes of the French people. In 1853 sculptor François Rude's vigorous statue of the great marshal was placed around the corner from the Luxembourg Gardens in the Avenue de l'Observatoire in front of what today is the Closerie des Lilas, the café so beloved by Ernest Hemingway.

Also on this day
1779: French painter Jean-Baptiste-Siméon Chardin dies * 1882: British novelist Anthony Trollope dies * 1917: Finland declares independence from Russia

7 December

Cicero faces his executioners

43 BC 'At least make sure you cut my head off properly', he said to the soldier seconds before his death, and then leaned out of the litter in which he was being carried to offer his throat to his executioner. So on this day died 63-year-old Marcus Tullius Cicero, the Roman world's greatest orator, sometime philosopher, occasional poet, senator, consul and backer of wrong horses.

Cicero had been born in the Roman provinces of a rich and influential family. During his early years in Rome he became one of the city's greatest trial lawyers, when he perfected his rhetorical style. First a senator, later consul, Cicero was a strong believer in the old values of the Roman Republic at the very time when the expansion of the state was making its labyrinthine systems of checks and balances an unworkable way to run an empire. As consul he thwarted the Catiline conspiracy to overthrow the government and summarily executed some of the plotters, dramatically proclaiming their death to the waiting crowd with the single word *vixerunt* (they are dead). But some of the conspirators came from exalted families, and their relations never forgave Cicero for executing them without trial.

Later Cicero backed Pompey as representative of the 'legitimate government' in his fight against Caesar and survived Caesar's triumph only because Caesar spared all his opponents. But after Caesar's assassination, in which he took no part, Cicero praised the murderers, while repeatedly haranguing the Senate against the unrestrainedly ambitious Mark Antony, who claimed to be Caesar's political heir. In one fiery speech he blamed all of Rome's troubles on Mark Antony, calling him an embezzler and a criminal, a drunken lecher who spent his time with outlaws and prostitutes.

Worse, Cicero seriously underestimated Octavian (the future Augustus), suggesting to his colleagues that 'the young man should be given praise and distinctions – and then be disposed of'. When his remarks were reported, Cicero had gained another mortal enemy.

In 43 BC Mark Antony, Octavian and Lepidus formed an alliance against Caesar's assassins, taking the opportunity to cleanse the state of other undesirables as well. Cicero's name was added to the proscribed list, which stripped him of all property and meant that any Roman citizen could kill him without fear of state reprisal.

Cicero refused to flee from Italy, dramatically vowing, 'I will die in the country I have so often saved.' He headed south by boat to his estate in

Formiae, on the Mediterranean coast about 90 miles from Rome, but his servants, aghast at seeing him in so much danger, forced him into his litter to escape. But they were too late. A force of Roman soldiers caught up with him on the road and dispatched the venerable statesman. His head and hands were cut off, to be nailed to the speakers' platform at the Forum in Rome, but not before Mark Antony's wife Fulvia had pierced his tongue with a long hairpin, symbolising the lies he had told about her husband.

Bernini, the man who created the Baroque

1598 Today was born the man who more than any other created the Baroque style and transformed 17th-century Rome, Gian Lorenzo Bernini. Sculptor and architect extraordinaire, he was also a stage set designer, painter, playwright and creator of fireworks displays.

Although born in Naples, Bernini spent almost his entire life in the Eternal City. Learning his trade from his sculptor father, he was a child prodigy who was already working in marble at the age of twelve.

A fervent Catholic who went to church every day, Bernini served eight popes during the 50-odd years that he dominated the artistic life of the city. His work represents his own strong religious views and reflects the triumphant militancy of the Church during the Counter-Reformation. Of all his work his sculpture is the most distinctive, characterised by a feeling of movement and strong emotion.

Bernini's first commission was remodelling the Church of Santa Bibiana, but he was simultaneously appointed to design the baldachin, an enormous bronze canopy supported by columns, that stands over the tomb of St Peter in St Peter's Cathedral, which took almost ten years to complete.

Other Roman landmarks created by the great sculptor include the fountain in the Piazza Barberini with its four dolphins supporting a giant seashell holding Triton, and two magnificent fountains in Rome's Piazza Navona, the Fountain of the Moor and the Fountain of the Four Rivers.

The Fountain of the Four Rivers includes four huge human figures, one of which has his right hand raised as if to ward off a blow. Legend has it that this was Bernini's comment on the work of the rival architect Francesco Borromini, who created the façade of the church opposite. The figure raises his hand to protect himself not from a blow but from falling masonry from the church, which Bernini was sure would collapse.

Of all of Bernini's works, his greatest masterpiece is undoubtedly the giant encircling colonnade of 96 columns in the Piazza San Pietro before St Peter's, designed to accommodate the large crowds that gather before the cathedral to receive the Pope's blessing on special religious occasions.

On 28 November 1680 Bernini died in Rome shortly before his 82nd birthday, recognised as the greatest artist of his time.

1709: Dutch landscape painter Meindert Hobbema dies in Amsterdam * 1837: Benjamin Disraeli makes his maiden speech in the House of Commons * 1941: Japanese warplanes launch a surprise attack on the American base at Pearl Harbor

8 December

Horace the poet (and soldier)

65 BC Today in Venusia (now Venosa) in the ankle of southern Italy was born Quintus Horatius Flaccus – known to us as Horace – one of the greatest poets of the Roman world. He came from low estate (he was the son of a freed slave) but rose to become poet laureate and friend to the Emperor Augustus. Much of his success was due to his father, who was devoted to his son and gave him a first-class education, including a time in Athens, then the cultural capital of the world.

While Horace was a twenty-year-old student in Athens, Julius Caesar was assassinated by a cabal of Roman republicans who feared he would make himself king. Shortly two of the leading conspirators, Marcus Junius Brutus and Gaius Cassius, found themselves under attack from Caesar's vengeful heir Octavian and Caesar's sometime protégé Mark Antony. Horace, then the young student liberal, hurried to enlist with the republican cause. Although short, podgy and unathletic, he radiated enthusiasm and was appointed *tribunus militum* (a junior officer) and given co-command of a legion.

The two armies met in Greece for the two battles of Philippi. Horace held his ground in the first battle, but when Brutus's army was overwhelmed in the second, the poet-to-be dropped his shield and ran from the field, an experience that may have temporarily slipped his mind when he later wrote, 'Dulce et decorum est pro patria mori.' (Lovely and honourable it is, to die for your country!)

Making his way back to Italy, Horace was broke and without resources, except for his poetical genius, which he used to earn a living. Fortunately, his brilliant work soon brought friendship with the established poet Virgil, who introduced him to Maecenas, a friend and political adviser to Octavian (soon to become the Emperor Augustus).

Maecenas not only became Horace's devoted friend but also bought him a country retreat near Tivoli. There he composed many of his greatest works, often reflecting his own buoyant nature and love of life. 'Misce stultitiam brevem: / Dulce est desipere in loco', he writes. (Mix a little foolishness with your serious plans: it's lovely to be silly at the right moment.) Most famously, he advises, 'Dum loquimur, fugerit invida / Aetas: carpe diem, quam minimum credula postero'. (While we talk, time will have meanly run on: Seize the day, don't count on the future in the slightest.)

In time Maecenas presented Horace to Augustus, against whom he had fought at Philippi. The open-minded Emperor admired his work and, on the death of Virgil, made him virtually poet laureate of the Empire.

Horace expired in Rome on 27 November in the year 8 BC, naming Augustus as his heir. Years earlier he had written, 'Non omnis moriar.' (I shall not die completely.) That we still enjoy his poetry to this day is proof that he was right.

Pius IX promulgates the first new dogma in 291 years

1854 In 1846 54-year-old Giovanni Mastai-Ferretti had been elected Pope, calling himself Pius IX. Eight years later he promulgated a new Catholic dogma, the first since the Council of Trent in 1563.

Thus it was that on this day Pius declared in the bull *Ineffabilis Deus* the dogma of the Immaculate Conception of the Virgin that holds that the Virgin Mary was free from original sin, making this long-held Catholic belief an article of faith.

Christians had celebrated the Immaculate Conception as early as the 5th century, and although opposed by luminaries such as St Bernard of Clairvaux and St Thomas Aquinas, by the mid-19th century it had become a widely accepted belief. Now, with Pius's declaration, there would be no doubting the doctrine – especially after 1880, when Pius promulgated another new dogma, that of papal infallibility.

Also on this day
1542: Mary, Queen of Scots is born, Linlithgow Palace, Scotland * 1813: Beethoven's Seventh Symphony is performed for the first time, with Beethoven as conductor * 1914: A British force sinks the German cruisers *Scharnhorst, Gneisenau, Nuremberg* and *Leipzig* in the Battle of the Falkland Islands * 1941: The US and Great Britain declare war on Japan

9 December

Gladstone becomes Prime Minister

1868 Today William Gladstone began the first of his four terms as Prime Minister, an office he held for fifteen years. About this man of lofty principles and stern moral probity, his great rival Benjamin Disraeli once commented, 'He has not a single redeeming defect.'

Gladstone was first elected to Parliament in December 1832 as a Tory but progressively moved to the left, claiming towards the end of his career that 'I will back the masses against the classes.' By the time he became Prime Minister in 1868, he was leading the Liberal Party. Although undoubtedly highly principled, he was seen by his enemies as humourless and sanctimonious, as demonstrated by his comment, 'I think [the clergy] are not severe enough on congregations. They do not sufficiently lay upon the souls and consciences of their hearers their moral obligations, and probe their hearts and bring up their whole lives and actions to the bar of conscience.'

Until he died in 1881, Disraeli was not only Gladstone's most formidable opponent but also a man of wit and charm. When asked to define the difference between a calamity and a misfortune, Disraeli innocently answered, 'If, for instance, Mr William Gladstone were to fall into the river, that would be a misfortune. But if anyone were to pull him out, that would be a calamity!'

A woman who happened to sit next to Gladstone one night at dinner and next to Disraeli the next encapsulated the difference between the two men: 'When I left the dining room after sitting next to Mr Gladstone I thought he was the cleverest man in England, but after sitting next to Mr Disraeli I thought I was the cleverest woman in England.'

Gladstone was on the side of history; he espoused a long list of liberal causes, almost all of which are common practice today. He fought for free trade, better working conditions for London dock workers, the admission of Jews to Parliament, reduced defence spending, Irish home rule, women's right to own their own property, free elementary education, and the secret ballot in voting. He was also highly influential in broadening the franchise to include a much wider range of working men.

Gladstone's reforming zeal extended even to his private life. He and his wife famously established a 'rescue' home for prostitutes and at night he would occasionally trawl the London streets for fallen women in an attempt to persuade them to take up a different life.

As Gladstone grew older, he became increasingly insufferable with his ponderous air of noble rectitude. Fellow politician Henry Labouchere once famously remarked that 'he did not object to the old man always having a card up his sleeve, but he did object to his insinuation that the Almighty had placed it there'.

Even Gladstone's wife occasionally seemed overawed by her husband's righteousness. On one occasion several guests at the Gladstone house found themselves in debate over the meaning of a biblical text. 'Well,' a guest commented, 'there is One above who knows all things.' 'Yes,' replied the earnest Mrs Gladstone, 'and Mr Gladstone will be coming down in a few minutes.'

When the Liberals won the general election of 1892, Gladstone became Prime Minister for the fourth time at the age of 82, a record among British Prime Ministers. Among those who both objected to his liberal policies and detested his demeanour was Queen Victoria, who complained that he 'addresses me as if I was a public meeting'. When she heard the results of the election she insisted that it was 'a defect in our much-famed Constitution to have to part with an admirable government like Lord Salisbury's for no question of any importance, or any particular reason, merely on account of the number of votes'. It was with great reluctance that the Queen, who was herself 73, entrusted the government 'to the shaking hand of an old, wild, incomprehensible man of eighty-two and a half'.

In 1893 Gladstone suffered the indignity of having the House of Lords reject his Irish Home Rule bill by a vote of 419 to 41, the greatest majority ever recorded. He then found himself in total disagreement with his own Cabinet over the navy's budget and resigned, using his failing hearing and eyesight as an excuse. Retiring to his country house in Wales, he developed cancer of the palate and died on 19 May 1898.

During Gladstone's last years in Parliament, Randolph Churchill had described him as 'an old man in a hurry'. His son Winston had a more acerbic summing up: 'Mr Gladstone read Homer for fun, which I thought served him right.'

The Index of Forbidden Books

1565 Today died Pius IV, who had served as Pope for just under six years, since his election on Christmas Day 1559. He was a good but unexceptional pope and a cultured one, a patron of Michelangelo. Today he would probably be little remembered except for one activity – the creation of a register of books forbidden by the Church, considered necessary to fight against emergent Protestantism.

In 1545 a beleaguered Church convened the Council of Trent to map plans for Church reform and the counter-attack against Protestantism. The Council continued intermittently until 1563, but at its conclusion not all the agreed tasks had yet been carried out. Pope Pius was given several assignments for completion, including drafting the catalogue of banned books.

Since at least AD 496, when Pope Gelasius I issued a list of both prohibited and recommended reading, the Church had been periodically proscribing books deemed inimical to the faith or morals of believers. Pius's list, christened Index Librorum Prohibitorum (Index of Forbidden Books), was more permanent. It would stay in force, continually amended, for the next 400 years.

The Index came to include works by a virtual Hall of Honour of distinguished writers. Included were obvious opponents of Catholicism such as Calvin, Luther, Erasmus and Descartes. Sexually explicit books also fared badly, ranging from Boccaccio's *Decameron* to Casanova's *Memoirs* to the notorious *Justine* by the marquis de Sade.

Not too surprisingly, free thinkers such as Montaigne, Voltaire, Rousseau and Thomas Paine were added to the list, and 19th-century French writers seemed to be there en masse with the prohibition of novels by Hugo, Balzac, Dumas, Flaubert and Stendhal.

It took the Vatican only seven years after publication to ban Gibbon's *Decline and Fall of the Roman Empire* for the gentle mockery with which he describes the rise of the Church, but Charles Darwin's great work *On the Origin of Species* was not banned until 1937, 78 years after it first appeared.

Not that the Catholic Church had a monopoly on banning books; virtually every country in the world has at some point prohibited works that were deemed too radical, too irreligious or too sexy. D.H. Lawrence's *Lady Chatterley's Lover*, which seems virtually prudish by today's standards, was banned in Great Britain until 1960. Nazi Germany and Soviet Russia took the censoring of books to the logical totalitarian extreme; all books were outlawed unless specifically approved.

In 1948 the Vatican published the final edition of the Index Librorum Prohibitorum, prohibiting over 4,000 titles. This list of suppressed books was itself suppressed in June 1966.

Also on this day

1608: English poet John Milton is born * 1641: Flemish portrait painter Anthony Van Dyck dies

10 December

Death of the man who gave birth to the world's greatest prize

1896 Aged 63 years, one month and nineteen days, Alfred Nobel this day quietly passed away in the beautiful resort of San Remo on the Mediterranean coast of Italy. Five years later the anniversary of his death was turned into a celebration of excellence.

Nobel was a Swede who had studied chemistry in St Petersburg and had been further educated in Paris and the United States. His family's company in Heleneborg manufactured explosives for use in torpedoes and mines, but when Nobel was 31 his younger brother was killed in an accidental nitro-glycerine explosion that destroyed the factory. When the Swedish government refused the company permission to rebuild, Nobel set up a laboratory on a barge where he started searching for a way to make explosives safer to handle.

At length Nobel discovered that nitro-glycerine combined with a chalk-like material called kieselguhr would form a stable substance that could be safely handled until its intended detonation. His invention, which was patented in 1867 as 'Dynamite, or Nobel's Safety Blasting Powder', promptly established his fame and fortune. In the years that followed, he established factories throughout Europe, and his invention was used in the construction of canals, tunnels and railways around the world.

When Nobel died he left $9,000,000, an enormous sum at the time, to be invested to create a fund from which the interest would be 'annually distributed in the form of prizes to those who, during the preceding year, shall have conferred the greatest benefit on mankind'. There were to be awards in chemistry, literature, peace, physics and physiology or medicine. A sixth discipline, economic sciences, was added in 1969.

The first Nobel Prizes were awarded exactly five years after the day Nobel died and to this day are given on the anniversary of his death. Two each of the first year's winners came from Germany and France and one each from Holland and Switzerland. They ranged from still famous men such as Henri Dunant, who founded the Red Cross, and Wilhelm Röntgen, the discoverer of the X-ray, to a now obscure French poet named Sully Prudhomme.

During its first century the Nobel Foundation recognised many outstanding authors but also managed to ignore some of the best. In early 2001 literary critics around the world opined about the finest writers of the 20th century. Almost all agreed that the two greatest were James Joyce and Marcel Proust, neither of whom was ever awarded a Nobel Prize.

The first British recipient was Sir Ronald Ross who won the Nobel Prize for Physiology or Medicine in 1902 for his work on malaria. A year later Randal Cremer became the first Peace Prize winner for the UK, honoured for his contributions to international arbitration. In total almost 90 Britons have won the Nobel Prize, including six who were awarded the Prize for Literature. The first of these was Rudyard Kipling in 1907, followed by John Galsworthy (1932), the American-born T.S. Eliot (1948), Bertrand Russell (1950), Sir Winston Churchill (1953) and William Golding in 1983.

The most remarkable British achievement was by the biochemist Frederick Sanger, who in 1980 became only the fourth person ever to win two Nobel Prizes (his first was in 1958 for his work on the structure of the insulin molecule).

The abdication of Edward VIII

1936 If you had listened to the BBC this evening at 10.00, you would have heard a thin voice saying, 'You must believe me when I tell you that I have found it impossible to carry the heavy burden of responsibility and to discharge my duties as King, as I wish to do, without the help and support of the woman I love.'

It was the voice of the former King Edward VIII – the man who would *not* be King – speaking from Windsor Castle to inform a stunned nation that he was giving up the British crown. Just hours before the broadcast he had signed the instrument of his abdication in favour of his younger brother who was now King George VI.

Edward's reign had lasted 325 days, since the death of his father, King George V, on 20 January. At the end, he had to choose between marriage and the throne. He chose Wallis Simpson, whose two divorces, the second granted only weeks earlier, had rendered her unsuitable as a wife for a monarch, at least in the eyes of those in the British establishment who knew of the King's intention to marry her. Among the powerful opposition to the marriage were the King's mother, the Archbishop of Canterbury, the Prime Minister Stanley Baldwin, the Cabinet ministers, and the Prime Ministers of the largest dominions in the British Empire. At last it became clear to Edward that if he persisted in his plan to marry Mrs Simpson, the Government would resign, bringing on elections in which the main issue would be the King's personal affairs, with all the attendant damage to the monarchy such a debate would create.

Some hours after the broadcast, HMS *Fury* slipped out of Portsmouth harbour bearing the Duke of Windsor, as Edward would now be known, to France where Wallis waited. Of that moment of departure from crown and country, he later said, 'So far as I was concerned, love had triumphed.'

For many, however, it appeared that what love had triumphed over was duty, responsibility and national tradition. In Britain, where a press ban had kept the public ignorant of the events leading up to the abdication, the reaction was restrained, the mood one of regret, of shame for some. Among many people, there was resentment, not only towards the woman who had wooed away their King, but also towards the King who deserted them for her.

Edward married Wallis the following year in France shortly after her divorce decree became final. It was a small ceremony, held in the Château de Cande in the Loire valley, with only sixteen guests. Wallis became Duchess of Windsor, but in their displeasure at the marriage the British royal family had withheld from her the expected title of Her Royal Highness. Snubbed, the Windsors chose thereafter to live abroad, glamorous irrelevancies in luxurious exile.

Also on this day

1475: Florentine painter Paolo Uccello dies * 1848: Louis Napoleon is elected President of France * 1898: Spain and the United States sign a peace treaty to end the Spanish–American War

11 December

James II flees from London, never to return

1688 On this day King James II of England hurried from St James's Palace in London to sail down the Thames before his son-in-law William of Orange and his daughter Mary could arrive and usurp the monarchy. As he raced down the river the enraged King petulantly dropped the Great Seal of England over-board, determined that no one but he should have this symbol of authority. No doubt his rage was even greater when he later learned that, by an incredible stroke of luck, a fisherman caught the Seal in his net and turned it over to William, now William III of England.

In his younger years James (the Duke of York at the time) showed both mettle and ability. When he was just fifteen, a year before his father Charles I was beheaded, James had evaded zealous Roundheads and escaped to France during the English Civil War. At 21 he joined Louis XIV's army under the legendary general Turenne, and proved to be an able commander, fighting in four campaigns. Later, when his brother Charles (II) gained the British throne to start the Restoration, James fought valiantly at the Battle of the Dunes. Then, back in England during Charles's reign, he became Lord High Admiral and planned the British seizure of New Amsterdam from the Dutch, renaming it New York in his own honour.

Although capable, James was stubborn, humourless and arrogant. Worse, he became a devoted Catholic during a period when Catholicism was virtually illegal in England. He had been admitted to the Church in 1669 but at first, on his brother's insistence, continued outwardly to practise Protestantism. But in 1673 he refused to take an anti-Catholic oath and the same year he married the staunchly (and publicly) Catholic Mary of Modena, causing near hysteria among the country's devout Protestants, who feared James's ascension should his childless brother die. Wild rumours grew that Catholics had developed a 'Popish Plot' to murder Charles so that James could inherit the throne.

Then, on 6 February 1685, Charles II did die (of kidney failure, not assassination) and James, Duke of York, became King James II.

High on principle but low on common sense, the haughty new King grandly informed his subjects that 'our Kings derive not their rule from the people but from God; that to Him only are they accountable, that it belongs not to subjects, either to create or censure, but to honour and obey their sovereign'. For just such sentiments had these same subjects removed the head of James's father some 39 years before. Worse, James started to bring Catholics into important government positions, formed new army regiments with Catholic officers and even directed that Magdalen College, Oxford, should be given over to Catholics. In the meantime, the always suspicious James became almost paranoid about real and imagined plots against him.

In late autumn 1687 what should have been joyful news proved to be the last straw for the country's uncompromising Protestants – the 30-year-old Queen was pregnant, and the British monarchy might soon have a Catholic heir. (Previously the direct heirs had been James's two daughters, Mary and Anne, who had been raised as Protestants on the insistence of their uncle, King Charles, but if the new baby was a boy, he would stand first in line to the throne.)

Then, in May of the following year, James ordered read aloud in churches throughout the kingdom a Declaration of Indulgence that, in effect, established freedom of religion for Catholics. Next, in June Queen Mary produced a young son (James Edward, in the future to be known as the Old Pretender). By the end of the month leading Protestants had written to William of Orange inviting him to invade the country and seize the crown. On 5 November William landed at Brixham, and after a month of desertions among his own army, James fled London, was briefly intercepted in Kent but then allowed to leave for France on 23 December. That was the last England would see of James II, the man whom his brother's mistress Nell Gwyn had mockingly christened 'dismal Jimmy'.

Leo X, the first Medici pope

1475 The expectant mother's dream had been wild and unnerving. She dreamt that she was giving birth not at home but in Florence's great red-domed cathedral, and when the baby arrived, it was not in human form but a large and powerful lion. It was a prophetic vision because the child born today was to become master of the Church of Rome and the most powerful man in Italy. He was Giovanni de' Medici, son of the great Lorenzo the Magnificent.

Second son in the family, from birth Giovanni was earmarked for the Church. Through his father's influence he became a cardinal at only sixteen, and his family's position and his own hard work enabled him to become Pope as Leo X at only 37.

Short, round-faced and corpulent, Leo ruled well as pontiff, but his fore-most interests were temporal. As he had commented to his brother Giuliano on his elevation, 'God has given us the papacy. Let's enjoy it.'

Leo became the most powerful man in Italy. As Pope he was ruler of both the Church and the Papal States and, as head of the Medici family after the deaths of his father and brother, he was also de facto ruler of Florence.

Powerful as he was, Leo dreamt of elevating his family yet higher and planned to create a kingdom in central Italy for his younger brother, who unfortunately died before Leo's ideas could be put into effect.

Like many men in command, Leo could be ruthless. When he was 42 and had been Pope for five years, an attempt was made to assassinate him. Discovering several cardinals among the plotters, he had some tried and executed for their crime and one strangled in his prison cell.

Leo spent extravagantly of both his own and the Church's treasures as a great patron of the arts. He was instrumental in furthering the construction of the new St Peter's Basilica that his predecessor Julius II had started, and commissioned Raphael to create the magnificent series of tapestries that today hang in the Vatican.

Leo died just ten days before his 46th birthday. He was one of the better Renaissance popes, but, sadly for his reputation, today he is best remembered for having excommunicated Martin Luther.

Also on this day

1803: French composer Hector Berlioz is born * 1941: German dictator Adolf Hitler declares war on the United States

12 December

Robert Browning dies at 77

1889 'Fear death? – to feel the fog in my throat, / The mist in my face.'

So had Robert Browning evocatively described the coming of death, which came to him today in Venice, as he was struck down by what looked to be a simple cold but which the 77-year-old poet could not withstand.

The son of a clerk in the Bank of England, Browning was born and brought up in London, showed little interest in formal education and lived at home with his parents until he was 34, writing poems and plays. By most accounts he was attractive and entertaining, and he is praised by one biographer for 'the perpetual boyishness, the hearty enthusiasm, the noisy ebullience, the invincible optimism, the graciousness and personal charm' that everyone found in him.

In his early years Browning's poetry was only marginally successful. One of his better-known works was the narrative poem *Sordello*, which became famous for its obscurity. When the editor of *Punch* tried to read it while recuperating from an illness, he became so confused that he feared he had suffered brain damage. Later in life Browning was asked for the meaning of a particularly bewildering passage. The poet reread his own lines aloud and then replied, 'When I wrote that, God and I knew what it meant, but now God alone knows!'

When he reached 33 Browning was still a bachelor, but then he met the woman of his life. Living with her parents in Wimpole Street was a 39-year-old spinster named Elizabeth Barrett. Since the age of fifteen she had been a semi-invalid suffering from some sort of bone disease, but she was also a poet – in fact, a better-known one than Browning. But she had read some of his poems, and in her work *Poems* included words of praise for Browning. In January 1845, although he had still not met her he responded with a telegram saying, 'I love your verses with all my heart, dear Miss Barrett. I do, as I say, love these books with all my heart – and I love you too.'

A few months later they met and a romance developed, one that she was careful to keep secret from her autocratic father. Browning later related that he gained great encouragement from an unusual source. One day in his library he asked himself, 'What will be the extent of my love for her?' and took a book at random. Only then did he see that it carried the unpromising title of *Cerutti's Italian Grammar*. He looked down to see what text would meet his eye, hoping for a positive word like 'together' or even just 'mine'. To his delighted surprise he found himself reading a sentence in a translation exercise, 'If we love in the other world as we do in this, I shall love thee to eternity.'

In September 1846 the couple married clandestinely, and a week later decamped for Italy, where they lived in genteel poverty, mostly in Florence, surrounded by ex-pat English and Americans, largely ignoring the Italians.

Although there is no doubt that Browning was devoted to her, Elizabeth must often have been a wearisome companion. In spite of her invalidity, she continued to write sentimental and successful poetry ('How do I love thee? Let me count the ways'). But she also became impassioned with Italian politics and devoted to the French Emperor Napoleon III, whom, despite all the evidence, she obstinately saw as a champion of democracy. She also turned to spiritualism and the occult under the guidance of an American named Daniel Home, whom Browning denounced as a fraud. Furthermore, she became addicted to laudanum, a habit her husband attempted to cure by persuading her to drink Chianti instead.

Nonetheless, the couple lived contentedly, he showing a continued tolerance and good humour towards his difficult wife and towards others as well. Once he was waylaid at a party by a guest who insisted on questioning him endlessly about his poems. Desperate to escape, Browning apologised to his interrogator. 'But my dear fellow, this is too bad', he said, turning away. 'I am monopolising you.'

In the summer of 1861 Elizabeth, still only 55, came down with something resembling the flu and died. Just before leaving for Italy sixteen years before, Browning had written one of his more famous lines, 'Oh, to be in England / now that April's there'. Now, with his wife gone, he returned there and a few years later produced his finest work, *The Ring and the Book*, a lengthy dramatic monologue based on a 17th-century Roman murder trial. He became even more celebrated than his wife had been and when he died was buried in Westminster Abbey.

Also on this day

1800: Washington DC is established as the capital of the United States * 1821: French novelist Gustave Flaubert is born in Rouen * 1863: Norwegian painter Edvard Munch is born * 1915: American crooner Frank Sinatra is born in Hoboken, New Jersey

13 December

Samuel Johnson dies in London

1784 'When a man is tired of London, he is tired of life; for there is in London all that life can afford.' So believed Samuel Johnson, the greatest conversationalist of the 18th century, who may himself have been tired of life when he died this evening at 7.15 in the city he loved.

Son of a bookseller, Johnson was considered both a leading literary figure and a formidable eccentric during his time. In his youth he had contracted scrofula, which left him scarred on the neck and face. A great, lumbering man with an erratic temper, he is unforgettably described by Macaulay: 'The gigantic body, the huge massy face, seamed with the scars of disease, the brown coat, the black worsted stockings, the grey wig with the scorched foretop, the dirty hands, the nails bitten and pared to the quick.'

Johnson's most famous work was his *Dictionary of the English Language*, which he published in 1755 after eight years of work. It contains some 40,000 entries, all articulate, many arresting and some amusing. With self-deprecating humour, he defined 'lexicographer' as 'a writer of dictionaries; a harmless drudge'. And surely he had his tongue firmly in his cheek with his definition of 'network':

'Anything reticulated or decussated at equal distances, with interstices between the intersections.' Because of the success of this work, he came to be known as 'Dictionary Johnson'. Ten years after the publication of his dictionary Johnson received an honorary Doctor of Laws degree from Trinity College, Dublin, thus gaining the title 'Dr'.

Although he maintained that 'no man but a blockhead ever wrote, except for money', Johnson achieved only moderate financial success, as his passion was literature rather than financial reward.

In spite of the admiration of his many literary friends, Johnson suffered from frequent depression, experiencing two nervous breakdowns. A religious man who nonetheless feared death, he had his watch engraved in Greek with the memento mori 'The night cometh'. He was also in severe physical discomfort for most of his life, plagued by a constant swelling of his legs and chronic bronchitis.

A year before his death Johnson suffered a stroke, while still in continual distress from his other illnesses. Depressed but determined to soldier on, he wrote to an acquaintance, 'I will be conquered [by death]; I will not capitulate.' Conquered he was at the end of 1784 at the age of 75. Here is the account given by his great biographer, James Boswell, of Johnson's last moments: 'Having, as has already been mentioned, made his will on the 8th and 9th of December, and settled all his worldly affairs, he languished till Monday, the 13th of that month, when he expired, about seven o'clock in the evening, with so little apparent pain that his attendants hardly perceived when his dissolution took place.' He is buried in Westminster Abbey.

Much of our knowledge of Johnson comes from Boswell's monumental biography. Published seven years after the good doctor's death, *The Life of Samuel Johnson LL.D.* recounts many of Johnson's pithy epigrams such as 'Patriotism is the last refuge of a scoundrel', and provides an imperishable portrait of a literary man whose work is now largely unread but whose personality fascinates us still.

The remarkable emperor, Frederick II

1250 Today Frederick II died of dysentery in Castel Fiorentino in southern Italy. He had been Holy Roman Emperor for 30 years, most of them spent vying with various popes for temporal power in Italy. Short, stout, bald and, according to a contemporary, not worth 200 dirhams on a Muslim slave market, he was nevertheless the most remarkable monarch of the Middle Ages.

Frederick was born in Palermo and learned to speak seven languages, including Arabic. At the age of two he was elected King of Germany by German princes and at 26 he was crowned Holy Roman Emperor.

Insatiably curious, he was both a patron of the arts and a scientist. In his most famed experiment he ordered some nurses to raise a group of foundlings without talking to them, to discover what language they would 'naturally' speak.

Sadly, according to a chronicle of the time, 'he laboured in vain, for the children all died, unable to live without the loving words of their mothers'.

On another occasion Frederick had two criminals fed identical large meals and sent one to run in the woods while the other slept. He then ordered both cut open to see which had better digested his food (the sleeper).

Frederick was a strong believer in education and founded the University of Naples. He was an expert on falconry and wrote a book on it, and was the father of Italian poetry, being the first to write love songs in the vernacular. His fondness for words extended even to spelling – so much so that, when a notary misspelled his name, Frederick had his thumb cut off.

Appropriately for a king, Frederick was royally lusty, keeping a large harem with him even when campaigning, but he preferred peace to war. During a crusade in the Holy Land, rather than attacking he negotiated the liberation of Jerusalem, Bethlehem and Nazareth without spilling a drop of Saracen blood. This so enraged Pope Gregory IX that thereafter he referred to Frederick as 'Christ's foe, the serpent'.

Frederick died thirteen days short of his 56th birthday. Although excommunicated at the time, on his deathbed he had himself dressed in the robes of a Cistercian monk, symbolising the relinquishment of all worldly goods. This final show of piety failed to placate the current pope, Innocent IV, whose comment on hearing of Frederick's death was, 'Let Heaven and Earth rejoice.'

Birth of France's first Bourbon king

1553 The town of Pau lies on the south-western edge of France, practically in Spain, and there on this cold December morning a baby boy was born to Jeanne d'Albret and her husband Antoine de Bourbon. Christened Henri, one day he would become one of his nation's greatest kings.

When Henri was born, he neither cried nor wailed, a sure sign that he was determined to enjoy life in spite of its occasional harshness. The infant's grandfather, Henri d'Albret, King of Navarre, attended the birth, and the moment young Henri saw the light of day the elder Henri seized him and rushed to the next room. There he held a cup of wine under the baby's nose and rubbed his lips with garlic. Henri clearly seemed to like both, accurately foretelling his love of food and drink throughout his life. Outside, bells pealed and all of Pau rejoiced at Henri's birth, for he was expected one day to become King of Navarre.

But fate had an even greater kingdom in store, for during the next 36 years France would be riven by religious wars as the Valois line of kings came to an end during the successive reigns of three weak, neurotic and childless brothers, François II, Charles IX and Henri III. When a deranged monk stabbed the last of these to death in 1589, the boy born this day in Pau would come to the throne as King Henri IV, the first of France's Bourbon kings.

Also on this day

1466: Florentine sculptor Donatello dies * 1642: Abel Tasman discovers New Zealand * 1944: Russian painter Wassily Kandinsky dies * 1961: American primitive painter Grandma Moses dies at the age of 101

14 December

George Washington dies hard

1799 Today at about ten in the evening George Washington, America's first president and its greatest 18th-century general, died quietly in his bed at the family home at Mount Vernon, the Virginia estate originally owned by his great-grandfather.

Washington was an active and robust man who delighted in the outdoors and horseback rides around his property. Two mornings earlier, after writing a reply to a letter from Alexander Hamilton on the subject of a military academy for the young republic, he rode for several hours in the damp cold of a snowy Virginia December, to return home frozen and exhausted. The next morning, suffering from a sore throat, he remained in the house to pursue farm business at his desk. Late in the afternoon, however, when the weather cleared, he went outside to mark trees for removal. At dinner he was hoarse and his cold had worsened, but he was cheerful and afterwards read aloud to his wife Martha from journals recently arrived. He refused the suggestion of medicine for his condition, preferring, he said, to 'let it go as it came'.

The next day he was unmistakably ill, suffering from fever and acute laryngitis, possibly with diphtheria. The local doctor James Craik ordered the former president to be bled and to gargle with a mixture of vinegar, butter and molasses.

By the morning of 14 December it was clear that Craik's prescriptions were ineffectual, for Washington was still in great pain and sinking fast. He knew his demise was imminent. For fear of being buried alive, he instructed his secretary, 'Do not let my body be put into the vault in less than three days after I am dead.'

Facing death with serenity, just before the end he murmured, 'I die hard, but I am not afraid to go.' His last words were, ''Tis well.' So departed the nation's Founding Father at the age of 67.

'I have no tenacity for life'

1861 An indefatigable worker, Queen Victoria's consort Prince Albert journeyed to Sandhurst to inspect some new buildings at the Military Academy there, in spite of the chill November damp. This was in character for the man who had created the Great Exhibition ten years before and who had become the Queen's chief advisor, obsessed with doing his duty.

Already feeling ill, Albert insisted on continuing his work and travelled on to Cambridge. Only then did he agree to return to Windsor Castle, tired and feverish.

Although Albert's condition worsened, the royal doctor, one James Clark, assured the Queen that he would soon be well. Albert himself was less sanguine, but had no fear of death. 'I have no tenacity for life', he told the doctor. At 10.45 on the evening of 14 December he breathed his last, an inconsolable Victoria at his bedside, holding his hand. He had succumbed to typhoid fever, probably contracted from the faulty drains at Windsor and totally undetected by Dr Clark. He was still only 42.

Victoria was prostrate with grief. 'My life as a happy one is ended!' she wrote to her uncle Leopold, King of Belgium. She never relinquished her widow's weeds in the 40 years that remained to her. In remembrance of her husband she ordered the construction in London of the Albert Memorial in Kensington Gardens, a 175-foot neo-Gothic spire decorated with mosaics and pinnacles. At its centre is a 14-foot bronze statue of a seated Albert looking rather like a deified Egyptian pharaoh. One guidebook today succinctly describes the memorial as 'the epitome of Victorian taste and sentiment'.

Now that Albert was dead, the British public, which for years had scorned him as a 'foreigner', also began to appreciate his many contributions to the nation. As the great British Prime Minister Benjamin Disraeli wrote, 'With Prince Albert, we have buried our sovereign. This German prince has governed England for twenty-one years with a wisdom and energy such as none of our kings have ever shown.'

Also on this day

1503: French astrologer and charlatan Nostradamus is born in Saint-Rémy * 1911: Norwegian Roald Amundsen and his expedition become the first to reach the South Pole, 35 days before Captain Scott

15 December

Napoleon divorces Joséphine

1809 Perhaps it was because she had bought 524 pairs of shoes that year alone. Or perhaps it was because she was 46 while he was still only 40 – and he thought that a delicious Austrian princess of eighteen was available. Or perhaps it was really because she had borne him no children in over thirteen years of marriage, he needed an heir and he now knew he could father one, having recently impregnated his mistress. Whatever the true reason, on this day the Emperor Napoleon divorced his wife Joséphine. 'I love you still,' he told her, 'but in politics there is no heart, only head.'

The ceremony took place in Napoleon's study in the Tuileries. First the

Emperor signed the decree, then Joséphine. As soon as the witnesses had added their signatures, Joséphine fled from the room in tears, leaning on the arm of Hortense de Beauharnais, her daughter by her first marriage.

Joséphine moved to Malmaison, still on cordial terms with her ex-husband, but she died there only five years later, while he was in exile on the Island of Elba. Sadly, she never knew that her grandson, not Napoleon's, would one day rule France, for Hortense had married Napoleon's brother Louis. Their son was Napoleon III.

Napoleon died in 1821, but his body was returned to Paris in 1840, where a great funeral was held on the exact anniversary of his divorce.

Also on this day

AD 37: Roman Emperor Nero is born * 1640: Portugal gains independence from Spain * 1675: Dutch painter Jan Vermeer dies * 1734: English painter George Romney is born * 1791: The Bill of Rights' ten amendments become part of the US Constitution * 1832: Engineer and tower builder Gustave Eiffel is born

16 December

The Boston Tea Party

1773 The colonial Americans had just about had enough. Restricted by British law from many types of manufacturing, the colonies' sole role had been arbitrarily defined by the Parliament in London as purchasers of British manufactured goods and suppliers of raw materials – except for some, like wool, in which the British had their own interest.

Britain had also given the foundering East India Company a monopoly of the colonial tea trade, including the sole right to transport the tea in its own ships. Worse, the tea was highly taxed – but only in America, not in Great Britain.

In early December 1773 the ships *Dartmouth*, *Eleanor* and *Beaver* of the East India Company reached Boston Harbor, but a furious populace refused to allow the tea to be landed. In retaliation, the British governor Thomas Hutchinson, already hugely unpopular because of his repressive measures, commanded the ships to remain in the harbour and posted two warships to enforce the order.

Led by the radical propagandist Samuel Adams, some 2,000 Americans gathered at the wharf on the afternoon of 16 December. Then a smaller group of about 60 protestors, some disguised as Mohawk Indians, boarded the three ships and flung the cargo of 342 cases of tea into Boston Harbor.

The incident at Griffin's Wharf was not the protest of a mob but a carefully organised political response, a true act of revolution. It provoked Governor Hutchinson to close Boston Harbor, caused much suffering among the citizens of Boston, and pushed the colonies one step closer to revolution. In time, however, it became remembered as a slightly comic affair, fondly celebrated as the Boston Tea Party. For its centennial observance in 1873 Oliver Wendell Holmes wrote 'The Ballad of the Tea Party', which hinted at the radical spirit of the original day with these splendid, mocking lines:

An evening party, – only that
No formal invitation,
No gold-laced coat, no stiff cravat,
No feast in contemplation,
No silk-robed dames, no fiddling band,
No flowers no songs no dancing –
A tribe of red men, axe in hand,
Behold the guests advancing.

The Battle of the Bulge – Hitler's last gamble

1944 At 5.30 this morning Operation Wacht am Rhein began its short but violent life with an intense artillery barrage. The German surprise attack, formally the Ardennes campaign but better known as the Battle of the Bulge, would last for six weeks of savage warfare.

For Hitler it was a last-ditch chance to turn the war around. He planned to send his panzer armies crashing through the weakest point in the Allied line, across the Meuse, on to Brussels, and thence Antwerp, the Allies' key supply point. Then, with the British–American coalition thoroughly disrupted, he could face eastward to concentrate his forces against the advancing Russians. His generals said the plan could never succeed, but they had told him exactly the same thing in 1940 and look what had happened then.

The surprise was, of course, an intelligence failure of the first magnitude. Viewed from Allied headquarters in Versailles, the war had looked close to being won. There were some indications of a build-up in the Ardennes, but few people read the signs to mean significant trouble. Codebreaking ULTRA gave no such warnings. No one among the top commanders – not Ike, not Monty, not Brad – believed that Hitler would mount such a desperate attempt to seize the initiative in the west. So, when it began this morning, they were caught flat-footed.

Remarkably, however, as the rampaging panzers broke through the line and two US divisions crumbled, the Allied commanders regrouped their forces and improvised to meet the threat. They threw reserve units into the line on either side of the Bulge and, with the help of courageous stands at places like St-Vith and Bastogne, slowed and constricted the German attack. When the weather mercifully cleared, Allied airpower joined the fray. By the 25th – Patton described it as 'a clear cold Christmas, lovely weather for killing Germans' – the offensive had been corralled, short of the Meuse.

Even so, much heavy fighting remained, and the cost was horrendous all around. By late January, when the Germans had been thrust back and the line restored, the Allies had lost an estimated 81,000 soldiers, killed, wounded or captured. For the Germans the comparable figure was well over 100,000, but, worse, they sustained absolutely crucial losses in tanks, planes and equipment. Now the war would resume its course, once again on Allied terms.

'It is not a disgrace to be defeated', Frederick the Great is supposed to have said. 'It is a disgrace to be surprised.' But the maxim doesn't fit the case of the Battle of the Bulge. Badly surprised though they were, the battlewise Allied forces recovered, fought back, and prevailed. At this stage in the war, defeat would have been the real disgrace.

Also on this day

1653: Oliver Cromwell is declared Lord Protector of England * 1689: The British Parliament enacts a Bill of Rights * 1770: German composer Ludwig van Beethoven is born

17 December

Henri IV divorces the notorious Reine Margot

1599 Today, after 27 years, three months and 29 days of marriage, King Henri IV of France was free at last of his scandalously unfaithful wife Marguerite de Valois. Not that he had been a saint – between the two of them they had bedded a full measure of France's nobility. But now Pope Clement VIII finally granted the annulment that, despite her infidelity, the Queen had so vigorously opposed.

From the very beginning the marriage seemed ill-omened. In 1572 Henri was a Protestant, King of Navarre but not yet King of France. Princess Marguerite – universally known as Margot – was a Catholic, daughter of French King Henri II (long dead) and Catherine de' Medici, and sister of Charles IX of France. The marriage was supposed to shore up the tenuous peace between France's Catholics and Protestants, but only five days after the wedding the Catholic League launched the Massacre of St Bartholomew against France's Protestant Huguenots. The leader of this bloodbath was Henri, duc de Guise, one of Margot's many former lovers. (Guise himself was murdered fifteen years later on orders from Margot's brother Henri.)

Although only nineteen at the time of her marriage, Margot was already renowned for her beauty and her licentiousness. Soon she was taking new lovers, the first of whom, Joseph Boniface de La Molle, was decapitated for plotting against Charles IX. (Legend has it that Margot had his head embalmed as a keepsake. Later this romance was idealised by Alexandre Dumas in his famous *La Reine Margot*.) After La Molle came liaisons with Bussy d'Amboise, de Saint-Luc, Champvallon, Aubiac (who was executed by another of Margot's brothers, Henri III, for more plotting), Vermont and Dat de Saint-Julien, who was murdered by Vermont.

625

In the meantime Margot's husband Henri acquired numerous mistresses for himself, and the couple lived largely apart. But in 1578 they were reunited, and a year later at Nérac they established a court that the French still remember for its gaiety and sophistication. Among those in attendance were the poet du Bastas and the essayist Montaigne, who was a particular favourite of Henri's. The court sparkled with parties, concerts, poetry reading and debates about love, all of which did not prevent more down-to-earth gallantries, to which both Margot and Henri turned a blind eye. Renowned throughout Europe, it became the setting for Shakespeare's *Love's Labour's Lost*.

But at length Henri tired of his faithless wife, and in 1586 he locked her up in gentle confinement in the Château d'Usson in the Auvergne, where she remained for the next eighteen years. During this period of semi-captivity she scandalised the local populace with her dissolute parties, heavy drinking and occasional trips through town riding a camel. But it was also at Usson that she wrote her famous *Mémoires*, full of anecdotal remembrances of her brothers Charles IX and Henri III and her husband, who in 1589 had become Henri IV of France.

While Margot was thus engaged, Henri found yet another glamorous mistress, Gabrielle d'Estrées, who bore him the children that Margot had failed to provide. There were many possible reasons for Henri to annul his marriage to Margot: consanguinity (they were cousins), duress and religious differences. But foremost in Henri's mind was his ardent desire to marry his mistress, legitimise their offspring, and put them in line for the throne of France. To this Margot swore she would never agree, and three-sided negotiations between Henri, Margot and the Pope dragged on until suddenly at Easter in 1599 Gabrielle died. Only then did Margot consent to an annulment. Pope Clement quickly invalidated their union, and Henri, with no Gabrielle to entice him, went on to marry the faithful but boring Marie de' Medici, whose enormous dowry would help resolve his debts. She also bore him six children to ensure the continuation of the House of Bourbon.

Free of her husband, Margot retained her title of Queen, was created Duchess of Valois and received large financial support from the King. In 1605 she returned to Paris, referred to herself as 'sister' to her ex-husband, and became a devoted friend to his new wife. There she lived for ten more years in ostentatious splendour in her *hôtel particulier* in the rue de Seine, still amorous but increasingly fat, a bizarre mixture of debauchery and piety, the subject of knowing snickers from Parisian society. Henri was assassinated in 1610, the fifth of her bed partners to have been either murdered or executed. Margot followed him to the grave on 27 March 1615 at the age of 61.

Also on this day

1830: South American liberator Símon Bolívar dies in Santa Marta, Colombia * 1843: Charles Dickens's *A Christmas Carol* is published * 1892: In St Petersburg the Russian Imperial Ballet performs Tchaikovsky's *The Nutcracker* for the first time * 1903: At Kitty Hawk, South Carolina, Wilbur and Orville Wright take man's first flight, lasting 59 seconds

18 December

A new bride in the White House

1915 This afternoon in Washington, DC, Edith Bolling Galt, a widow, married Woodrow Wilson, a recent widower and 28th President of the United States. Her presence in his life had rescued him from the acute depression he suffered after the death of his first wife in August 1914. With Edith at his side, a revitalised Wilson ran for re-election in 1916 and won a second term.

In 1919 she rescued him once again, with very different consequences. With the war in Europe over, President Wilson embarked on a strenuous nationwide campaign to raise public support for the Versailles Peace Treaty and the League of Nations. In late September he collapsed from exhaustion. Back in Washington a week later, he suffered a massive, near-fatal stroke that left him partly paralysed and incapacitated. It was then that Edith Wilson, at the head of a loyal inner circle that included his doctor and his press secretary, directed one of the most remarkable cover-ups in American history.

For a month Wilson lay in the White House, completely disabled. Edith was the buffer between him and the world outside his sickroom. Encouraging medical bulletins were issued to counter rumours about his condition. Few visitors were allowed. Trusted advisors were turned away. Messages for the President went mainly unanswered, or his replies were relayed by Edith. Slowly, Wilson made a limited recovery, but he had become in one observer's description, 'an emaciated old man with a white beard'. He was allowed on his first drive in January but didn't attend his first Cabinet meeting until mid-April. Legislation passed in the Congress became law without his signature. The business of government, insofar as it depended on the President, came to a standstill.

Edith's 'bedside presidency' was meant to keep the President at the helm. Personal loyalty was placed above the national interest. When his doctor refused to certify the President's incapacity, the question of resignation in favour of the Vice-President, as the Constitution provides, was avoided. Seventeen months after his stroke, Wilson was still not strong enough to attend the inaugural ceremony of his successor Warren G. Harding.

Besides the President himself, the greatest casualty of the episode may have been the League of Nations, whose establishment was contained in the Versailles Treaty. The League – and United States membership in it – was Wilson's great cause. It represented his vision of global peace ensured by America's involvement in world affairs. But to the Republicans in the Senate, where they held a majority, the League entailed a threat to American sovereignty and the unwelcome prospect of the nation's entanglement in international affairs. There was room for compromise in the wording of the Treaty, and many members of both parties were anxious for it, but Wilson, diminished in mental acuity and shielded from the political realities outside his sickroom, refused to budge, or allow his Democratic supporters to do so in his name.

Knowledgeable observers believed that if Vice-President Thomas Marshall had become President, a solution allowing ratification could have been found. Without compromise, however, the Treaty – and the League – went down to defeat in the Senate, first in December 1919, then a final time the following March. In later decades, as war clouds gathered, many people speculated on how the course of 20th-century history might have changed had the United States joined the League of Nations in 1920.

Woodrow Wilson died in 1924. Edith Wilson lived another 37 years, long enough for her to attend the inauguration of President John F. Kennedy in 1961.

The original Eminence Grise

1638 Today in the small town of Rueil about twelve miles west of Paris died 61-year-old Père Joseph, a Capuchin monk who, as secretary to Cardinal Richelieu, became one of the most powerful men in France.

While his master's great goal was to gain supremacy for France over Europe, Père Joseph's ambition was to convert Europe's Protestant heretics to Catholicism. To achieve his objective, Père Joseph, who was tantamount to Foreign Minister while Richelieu ran the country, followed a policy that placed France at the centre of the Thirty Years' War.

In a country where Louis XIII was, in theory, an absolute monarch, even Cardinal Richelieu's power came 'by the grace of the King', and he was known at the time as L'Eminence Rouge (The Red Eminence) due to the colour of his robes. Père Joseph had even less official power than Richelieu but became notorious as a shadowy figure behind the cardinal, dressed in Capuchin grey, thereby earning for himself the sobriquet of L'Eminence Grise (Grey Eminence), a phrase still with us today denoting hidden and unaccountable power behind the scenes.

Because of the horrors of the war in which he involved his country and his draconian attitude towards Protestants, Père Joseph lived feared by his countrymen and died despised by them.

Also on this day

1737: Violin maker Antonio Stradivari dies in Cremona * 1941: Six hundred and ten American defenders surrender to 5,000 attacking Japanese on the island of Guam after a three-hour battle

19 December

The coronation of Henry II

1154 Medieval chronicles tell us that this Sunday was brilliantly sunny despite the season, symbolic of the great occasion that took place today, the coronation of England's Henry II, who had inherited the throne on the death of King Stephen the previous October.

The place was London's Westminster Abbey, where a throng of commoners waited with anticipation in the road outside, and a few sanctuary seekers who had claimed refuge inside were locked up in a side chapel for the duration of the ceremony.

First entering the church were the realm's most eminent nobles, walking solemnly and bearing the royal crown and the ring of Edward the Confessor, miraculously retrieved from the Holy Land a century after it was lost. Then came the men of the cloth – bishops, abbots and priors, all in full vestment, followed by lesser persons of note, including simple knights and wealthy merchants. The Abbey was crammed with the great and good.

When all were in position, through the front door came Henry Plantagenet and his wife of eighteen months, the fiery Eleanor of Aquitaine. Still only 21, the King was sturdily built, with a leonine head of curly red hair cut short, a freckled face and blue eyes. He was dressed in a doublet and a short Angevin cloak, which would earn him the nickname of Henry Curtmantle. Eleanor wore white and gold, her head uncovered, her dark hair hanging in four plaits. Two pages carried her long train. Although eleven years older than her husband, she retained the beauty for which she was famed.

Henry would rule England for almost 35 years, during which time he would father five sons and three daughters, including two who would become kings of England, Richard the Lion-Heart and the conniving John.

His relations with Eleanor would be tempestuous, to say the least. She resented his string of mistresses, and the myth developed that she poisoned his favourite, Fair Rosamund Clifford. (No doubt she did resent her husband's inamorata, but Rosamund actually died in a convent.) She also foolishly schemed with her sons in their conflicts with their father. After encouraging a failed revolt in 1173, she tried to escape to France disguised as a nun, but on being apprehended, Henry locked her up in honourable and comfortable confinement at Woodstock.

Henry died in 1189, and Eleanor outlived him by fifteen years, but the Plantagenet dynasty they founded held the throne of England for 330 years, eight months and three days, until Richard III lay dead on Bosworth Field.

Poor Richard's Almanac *first appears*

1732 That almanacs have existed for centuries is shown by the origins of the word, which derives from *al manâkh*, meaning 'calendar of the heavens' in Spanish Arabic, probably coined before 1492 when the Spaniards completed their conquest of the Moors. But for most Americans the most famous almanac is *Poor Richard's*, which first appeared on this day, written, published and printed by that unique American polymath, Benjamin Franklin.

Franklin first published his famous almanac under the pen name of Richard

Saunders. In it the eponymous Poor Richard was portrayed as an earnest and somewhat pious farmer who spouts a seemingly unending stream of trenchant and witty aphorisms, to many of which we have become so accustomed that we no longer remember they were originally Franklin's.

Many were wise and rather worthy, such as:

Early to bed and early to rise, makes a man healthy, wealthy, and wise.
God helps those who help themselves.
Little strokes fell great oaks.

Occasionally Franklin penned a maxim that reflected his belief in America's principles of equality, such as 'A ploughman on his legs is higher than a gentleman on his knees.' But *Poor Richard's* was also peppered with more irreverent observations such as:

There's more old drunkards than old doctors.
A countryman between two lawyers is like a fish between two cats.
Neither a fortress nor a maid will hold out long after they begin to parley.
Three removes is as bad as a fire.
He's a fool that makes his doctor his heir.

Occasionally Franklin would include an aphoristic couplet:

You cannot pluck roses without fear of thorns
Nor enjoy a fair wife without danger of horns.

Some seem remarkably up to date, none more than 'There are no gains, without pains.'

Franklin published *Poor Richard's Almanac* until 1757.

Also on this day

1562: The Huguenots and the Catholics fight the first battle of the French Wars of Religion at the Battle of Dreux * 1783: William Pitt becomes the youngest British Prime Minister at the age of 24 * 1848: English novelist Emily Brontë dies * 1851: English painter Joseph Turner dies

20 December

Vespasian becomes Emperor when his predecessor is lynched

AD 69 Today one of Rome's worst emperors was killed with appalling brutality, leaving the Empire in the hands of one of the best.

It had been a horrendous eighteen months. In June 68 the atrocious Nero had escaped capture and execution only by suicide, plunging Rome into the calamitous Year of the Four Emperors. In January 69, Nero's successor Galba was brutally murdered in the Roman Forum by soldiers supporting Otho. But by April Otho was dead, another suicide after his defeat at Cremona by the army of the next claimant, Vitellius.

Vitellius was a cruel, vindictive man who was reputed to have had his own rebellious son put to death. Immensely fat, he often ate four times a day, while relieving himself with emetics between meals. According to Tacitus, 'He was the slave and chattel of luxury and gluttony.'

After only four months of power, Vitellius learned that the Roman legions in the eastern provinces had abandoned him, acclaiming their general Vespasian as Emperor. Soon an army supporting Vespasian was on the march towards Rome, although the general himself remained in the east for another year.

On this day the insurgents arrived at the gates of the city. Realising that his cause was hopeless, Vitellius hid himself in the janitor's quarters in the imperial palace, but Vespasian's marauding soldiers quickly discovered him. Frog-marching him to the Forum, they put him to the torture of the little cuts and then slit his throat and threw his body into the Tiber. Now Vespasian was the only would-be emperor left standing, and a fine ruler he turned out to be.

Already 60 when he took power, Vespasian was the son of a simple knight and had spent most of his life as a soldier. He was known for his bluff, straightforward style and infectious if sometimes coarse sense of humour. As Emperor he initiated a tax on public urinals, to the dismay of his son Titus, who believed it beneath imperial dignity. Holding out two gold coins, Vespasian asked, 'Do these smell bad?' Relaxed and down-to-earth, he dispensed with the usual bodyguard and mixed freely with Rome's citizens.

After nearly ten years in power, Vespasian was nearing 70 when he caught a fever while visiting Campania. He then made matters worse by retreating to his summer residence in Reate and bathing in cold water. Suspecting that the end was near, the old emperor wryly referred to Rome's habit of deifying dead emperors with the remark, 'Vae, puto deus fio.' (Oh dear, I think I'm becoming a god.)

Vespasian tried to soldier on with his imperial duties, but on 23 June 79 he was seized with violent diarrhoea. Almost fainting, he struggled to remain on his feet, murmuring, 'Decet imperatorem stantem mori.' (An emperor should die standing.) He then fell dead into the arms of his attendants.

During his ten years as Emperor Vespasian followed a practice of reconciliation, dispensing justice with mercy. According to Suetonius, 'No innocent party was ever punished during Vespasian's reign.' He ended the civil war and probably saved the Empire from dissolution. He also embarked on an ambitious reconstruction programme in a country torn by war. Now of course the Roman Empire is long gone, as are most of its buildings, but one of Vespasian's monuments is still with us, the Flavian Amphitheatre (Flavius was his original family name), which we call the Coliseum.

The Bonapartes are back

1848 Today in the 'Year of Revolution' in Europe Prince Louis Napoleon took his oath as President of France, restoring the Bonapartes to power after a hiatus of 33 years.

Louis had been born to the purple, son of Napoleon's brother, also named Louis, who at the time was King of Holland. But Napoleon's fall in 1815 had driven the family into exile, and young Louis had spent most of the next 30 years wandering around Europe, with periodic attempts to return to France.

At the beginning of 1848 Louis was a 39-year-old bachelor, a man of only medium height but with an imposing appearance: high, intellectual forehead, piercing eyes, a twirled and waxed moustache and a four-inch goatee. Something of a roué, he was highly intelligent and an accomplished linguist, speaking German, Spanish, English and Italian as well as the French which he pronounced with a slight German accent due to his early schooling in Augsberg. He was living in exile in England, as King Louis-Philippe wanted no Bonaparte threat in France.

But on 24 February a popular uprising forced Louis-Philippe to flee the country, bringing the monarchy to an end. Three days later Louis Napoleon made a brief foray to Paris, but the provisional government peremptorily ordered him to leave the country within 24 hours, so he scuttled back to London to wait for the next opportunity.

At the end of June Paris exploded into mayhem, as unemployed workers set up stone barricades in the streets and for four days fired on all who opposed them. Troops were soon in position, returning fire. Then first a general and next the Archbishop of Paris were shot and killed as they tried to arrange a compromise with the workers. Finally the rebellion was brutally suppressed by General Louis-Eugène Cavaignac, for which act he became known as 'the butcher of June'.

By-elections were scheduled for September, and Louis Napoleon, scenting new opportunity, put his name forward from his exile in England. Elected in five departments, he once again embarked for France, the government no longer able to force him to remain abroad. He immediately started campaigning for the presidential election scheduled for 10 December.

Louis was fortunate in that, while Louis-Philippe had permitted only a token 200,000 people to vote, the government that replaced him extended the franchise to some 8,000,000 citizens. Most of these knew little about politics and less about most of the candidates, but the one thing they recognised was the name Napoleon. Louis swept to victory with five and a half million votes versus one and a half million for his closest competitor. On this day ten days later he was sworn in as President of France.

Most men would see such an overwhelming triumph as the apogee of their careers. Not Louis Napoleon. Three years later he violated his presidential oath by staging a *coup d'état* and making himself dictator.

South Carolina's secession from the United States leads to the Civil War

1860 When the news of Abraham Lincoln's election reached the South, the Charleston *Mercury* wrote: 'The tea has been thrown overboard, the revolution of 1860 has been initiated.' Today, in Columbia, South Carolina, the state convention voted 160–0 in favour of dissolving 'the union now subsisting between South Carolina and the other states', beginning the Southern counter-revolution. Thus the United States was no longer united, and six more states would follow suit by February of the next year. Eventually eleven states would join the Confederacy.

Lincoln had been elected President of the United States even though his Republican Party had failed to win a single state in the entire south of the country. Certain that Northerners would soon destroy their way of life by freeing the South's 4 million black slaves, many Southerners saw secession from the nation as the only escape.

Southern fears were understandable. Their cotton industry alone accounted for more American exports than all other products combined, and America's slaves had a notional commercial value greater than the nation's railways, manufacturing and banks put together. And many Southerners had persuaded themselves that God had ordained the black man to remain in servitude to the white.

The Southerners' decision to abandon the Union remains in some ways unprecedented. No armies had invaded their territories, no laws had been passed limiting their freedom or interfering with their way of life. The secession came solely in reaction to a perceived threat that might or might not materialise sometime in the future. But once South Carolina had acted, the first inexorable step towards civil war had been taken.

Also on this day

1894: Australian Prime Minister Sir Robert Menzies is born in Jeporet, Victoria * 1915: The ANZACS, Australian and New Zealand forces with British troops, are evacuated from Gallipoli

21 December

King Richard the Lion-Heart is captured in Austria

1192 Returning from his famous crusade in the Holy Land, England's King Richard the Lion-Heart was sailing home through the Adriatic when a storm forced him ashore near Venice. He then made the foolish decision to continue his journey on land through Austria, even though he knew that its ruler Duke Leopold could be counted among his enemies. When the Crusaders had conquered Acre, Richard had refused to give Leopold his share of the booty and had ordered his standard thrown from the city's walls into the dirt below. Leopold left in cold fury, vowing revenge.

Richard's one precaution as he entered Leopold's domains was to travel disguised as a wealthy merchant. But nearing the Duke's capital in Vienna, Richard made two further mistakes. Exhausted from his time on the road, he remained in the town of Ganina for three days and sent one of his pages to purchase supplies with a pocket full of gold coins.

On this day, Richard's last in Ganina, the page ambled through the market dispensing his gold and with one of the King's gloves bearing the royal insignia carelessly tucked in his belt. Sharp-eyed agents of Duke Leopold spotted and seized the insouciant page and quickly forced him to reveal that Richard and the rest of his entourage were staying at a nearby inn.

Leopold's soldiers instantly surrounded the inn and had no trouble capturing the English King, despite his attempt to disguise himself yet again, this time as a cook in the kitchen.

For the next fourteen months Richard was held prisoner in Leopold's castle at Dürnstein on the Danube. Tradition has it that he was found by his faithful troubadour Blondel, who wandered through Europe singing a ballad that Richard and he had composed together. When Blondel passed before the castle, Richard heard his voice and responded by singing a verse of the same ballad so that Blondel would know he had found the King.

In all likelihood, however, Duke Leopold kept no secret of his royal prisoner since the King's primary value was his ransom. Richard was finally released on 3 February 1193 for a payment of 150,000 marks, equal to 34 tons in weight. In 2004 that would have been worth a paltry £3,500,000, but in 1192 it was truly a King's ransom, a price that virtually bankrupted England.

Also on this day

1375: Italian writer Giovanni Boccaccio dies in Certaldo * 1804: British Prime Minister Benjamin Disraeli is born * 1879: Russian tyrant Joseph Stalin (Dzhugashvili) is born in Gori, Georgia * 1940: American novelist F. Scott Fitzgerald dies

22 December

Napoleone becomes a general after the Siege of Toulon

1793 Today Captain of Artillery Napoleone Buonaparte was promoted to the rank of brigadier general at the tender age of 24, rewarded for his heroic achievements during Republican France's victorious Siege of Toulon.

In late August French royalist counter-revolutionaries had treacherously welcomed an enemy Anglo-Spanish fleet under the command of Admiral Hood into the key French naval base of Toulon, just down the Mediterranean coast from Marseille. There the English had seized over 70 vessels, including 30 ships of the line, over half the French fleet. For reasons of both political prestige and military necessity, the Revolutionary government in Paris had resolved to wrest back the base and ordered a siege.

The siege began on 28 August. After several months of mutual cannonading, French soldiers at length captured the forts overlooking the port. Then, on the afternoon of 18 December, Buonaparte, still an obscure captain in charge of the French artillery, focused withering fire from the secured forts directly on the English ships moored in the harbour. Forced to evacuate, the English burned more than half the French ships on their way out. In the evening the revolutionaries reoccupied the city and shot several hundred royalists who had not fled with the English.

Based on his successful use of artillery, Buonaparte became a hero and was jumped half a dozen ranks to brigadier general. With supreme confidence he wrote to the Committee of Public Safety in Paris, 'It is the artillery that takes places; the infantry can only aid it.' But, as remarkable as it was, his dizzying rise was a bit less spectacular in 1793 than it would be today, given that Buonaparte was a trained and professional soldier. During this self-same siege of Toulon the attacking French force was commanded by three successive generals, men who before the Revolution had been, respectively, a painter, a sugar planter and a dentist.

Also on this day

1858: Italian opera composer Giacomo Puccini is born in Lucca * 1894: French officer Alfred Dreyfus is convicted of espionage and sent to Devil's Island * 1895: German physicist Wilhelm Röntgen makes the first X-ray

23 December

Champollion and the Rosetta Stone

1790 Today in the picturesque town of Figeac in the Midi of France was born Jean-François Champollion, one of history's greatest archaeologists, the man who deciphered the Rosetta Stone and thus discovered the key to understanding Egyptian hieroglyphics.

From an early age it was clear that Champollion was a child of exceptional ability. By five he could read without help and started learning Latin. At eleven he entered the lycée at Grenoble, where he astounded his teachers by translating Virgil and Horace. There he also studied Hebrew, Arabic, Syrian and Aramaic. By the time he was fifteen he had also learned Coptic and Ethiopian. Four years later, in 1809, he moved to Paris to study Sanskrit, Chinese and Persian.

In 1799 Napoleon had invaded Egypt, and on 19 July of that year one of his retinue had been foraging near the town of Rosetta, 55 miles north-east of

Alexandria. There he had discovered an ancient slab of black basalt over three feet long and about two feet across commemorating the deeds of the thirteen-year-old boy Pharaoh Ptolemy V Epiphanes, which dated the stone to 196 BC. The stone was covered in Greek and Egyptian inscriptions with the same text in three writing systems, Greek, hieroglyphics and demotic script (a phonetic form of Egyptian writing). Two years later the British chased the French out of Egypt and captured the stone in the process, bringing it back to the British Museum in London, but fortunately paper copies of the writing became available for study.

In 1809 Champollion, still in Paris, began to study the Rosetta Stone texts. After thirteen years he finally deciphered the hieroglyphics, the first to see that they include alphabetic and syllabic signs as well as pictographs. On 27 September 1822, he presented his findings to a special meeting of the Académie des Sciences et des Arts and within the next two years published *Egyptian Pantheon* and *A Summary of the Hieroglyphic System of the Ancient Egyptians*. At last the world could read a system of writing that had served the Egyptians for 3,500 years.

Henri III *murders the duc de Guise*

1588 Cultivated and intelligent but weak, neurotic and effeminate, France's Henri III had spent most of his fourteen-year reign dominated by his appalling mother, Catherine de' Medici. The great issue of the day was France's Wars of Religion, which had festered since 1562 as fervent Catholics of the so-called Holy League had endeavoured to repress all Protestantism while French Huguenots bitterly fought back with no holds barred. Heading the Holy League was the country's most powerful noble, the muscular and athletic Henri, duc de Guise, whose face had been distinctively scarred by a war wound.

More interested in his *mignons* than in the subtleties of religious difference, the King had tried to soothe Catholics by cracking down on Protestantism, but his ineffectual efforts were taken by the Holy League to signify a lack of proper zeal, and in May 1588 they had tried to depose him, instigating an uprising in Paris that chased him from the city.

For Henri the situation was intolerable. He resolved to rid himself of the Holy League's leader, the duc de Guise, but Guise's position was so strong that he could not be arrested. The only solution was assassination.

In December the court was at the beautiful château of Blois on the Loire River, the meeting place for the Estates-General, the assembly of representatives of the French nobility, clergy and the so-called Third Estate, the ordinary people. The King knew the hated Guise was sure to attend. On the morning of the 23rd Henri summoned twenty hirelings to his bedroom, accompanied by two priests who were to pray for a successful murder. The King then sent word for Guise to join him and hid behind a curtain. When the

Duke entered the room, eight of the murderers threw themselves at him, swords drawn.

The immensely strong Guise threw off several assailants but at length fell to the floor, pierced by a dozen sword strokes. King Henri then stepped out from behind the curtain and kicked the dead duke in the face, exclaiming, 'My God, he's big! He looks even bigger dead than alive.'

Henri then rushed downstairs proudly to announce his deed to his mother, but she, only too conscious of her son's precarious hold on power, replied, 'God grant you have not made yourself king of nothing.' Ignoring her concern and untroubled by conscience, Henri left her to go to the Chapel of St Calais to hear Mass.

The following day Henri ordered the assassination of Guise's brother Louis, the Cardinal of Lorraine, had their bodies burnt and the ashes thrown into the Loire.

Also on this day

1834: English economist and demographer Robert Malthus dies * 1948: Japanese General Tojo and six other military leaders are hanged for crimes against humanity * 1953: Soviet secret police chief Lavrenti Beria is shot for treason

24 December

Van Gogh and his famous ear

1888 North-west of Marseille on the sunbaked Camargue Plain on the Rhône River lies the ancient town of Arles, a place of culture and beauty since it was settled by Greeks in the 6th century BC. With its 1st-century amphitheatre and 12th-century Romanesque church, it should be the perfect retreat for any sensitive artist.

In February 1888 a supersensitive artist arrived there: 35-year-old Vincent van Gogh. Worn out by the winter gloom of Paris, he was seeking to explore nature through the explosive colours that he saw in his mind. He hoped eventually to surround himself with other Impressionists such as Toulouse-Lautrec and Gauguin, perhaps to form a sub-group of 'Impressionists of the South'.

Van Gogh had long showed signs of instability, and his art dealer brother Theo was anxious to provide him with some sort of companionship and support. Theo approached Paul Gauguin and offered to foot the bill for the trip if he would join Vincent in Arles.

On 23 October Gauguin arrived at Arles and soon was living with van Gogh in the yellow house that van Gogh made famous in his paintings, a small, cosy establishment with green shutters and no indoor toilet.

The two painters worked together for two months, occasionally strolling to the Café de la Gare around the corner for a glass of Pernod or making a quick visit to one of the town's many *poules*. But as the days went by they discovered they were artistically and temperamentally incompatible.

By Christmas Eve the situation was unravelling fast. During the evening van Gogh attacked Gauguin with a razor but failed to wound him. He then returned to his little yellow house and hacked off his own left earlobe to give to a favourite prostitute, a certain Rachel.

Gauguin fled from Arles the following morning, never to see van Gogh again. He soon installed himself in Brittany and then moved on to Tahiti and the Marquesas Islands, where he died in 1903.

Van Gogh stayed at Arles for just four months after that fateful Christmas Eve and then committed himself to an asylum only a few miles away at Saint-Rémy-de-Provence. A year later he finally returned to Paris, ravaged by loneliness and tormented by failure. There, on 29 July 1890, he put a pistol to his breast.

The birth of England's worst king

1167 Today at Beaumont near Oxford was born John Plantagenet, son of England's King Henry II and his remarkable Queen, Eleanor of Aquitaine, who was 45 at John's birth. Although born in England, his first language was French. He grew up to be plump but strong, five feet six inches tall. While he was young he had curly dark hair, but later he went partially bald.

John was the fourth of four royal sons, the only one without an apanage (a grant of land from the king) in his parents' extensive territories in France. Hence he was dubbed Jean Sans Terre (John Lackland) by his father.

In 1199 John succeeded to the throne of England on the death of his brother Richard the Lion-Heart, but within seven years he lost Normandy, Maine, Anjou and parts of Poitou to Philip Augustus of France.

John's rule in England was no more successful than that in his French possessions, and still today he is considered England's worst king. 'Selfish, cruel, shameless, cynical, lustful, dishonourable, and utterly false', is the way Thomas Costain describes him. J.C. Holt calls him 'suspicious, vengeful, and treacherous'.

He betrayed his father when Richard the Lion-Heart rose against him, then conspired with Philip Augustus to keep Richard in prison when Richard had been captured in Austria returning from crusade. He murdered his nephew Arthur. He came into such bitter conflict with the Pope that all of England was placed under interdict for over five years. He is also notorious for plundering the Jews for their money, ordering their teeth extracted one by one until they revealed where they had hidden their hoarded gold.

Every cloud must have a silver lining, and in the case of John it was the Magna Carta, the great charter of civil liberties that John's rebellious barons forced him to sign in 1215.

John ruled England for seventeen years and died of dysentery at the age of 48.

The man who made Casablanca

1888 If you like movies then you should note that on this date Mihaly Kerstesz was born in Budapest.

Kerstesz started out directing films in Europe, then went to Hollywood in 1926 and found work with a small, under-financed studio called Warner Brothers. He changed his name to Michael Curtiz and helped put Warners on the map, staying with the studio for 28 years and directing over 80 movies that starred (and often helped launch) many of the greatest actors of the 1930s and 40s, among them Erroll Flynn (Curtiz's discovery), Bette Davis, Olivia de Havilland, Basil Rathbone, Claude Rains, Joan Crawford, William Powell, Edward G. Robinson, Humphrey Bogart, Laurence Olivier and Ingrid Bergman.

A critic said that Curtiz was to swashbucklers what John Ford was to Westerns, but in fact Curtiz's output covered almost every film genre, including historical dramas, film noir, westerns, horror films, mysteries and musicals. Here are a few of his most memorable: *Captain Blood, Charge of the Light Brigade, The Adventures of Robin Hood, Yankee Doodle Dandy, The Sea Wolf, Mildred Pierce, Life with Father* and *White Christmas.*

Actors detested Curtiz (Claude Rains was an exception) for his rude and arrogant dealings with them, and everyone else on the set. A Hungarian accent and an 'original' command of English did not soften the effect of his rages. He is reported to have called Bette Davis, in her presence, 'a goddamned nothing no-good sexless son of a bitch'. When angered by what he thought to be a prop man's mistake, he roared, 'Next time I send a damn fool, I go myself.'

Curtiz died in 1961, a few months after completing *The Comancheros,* starring John Wayne. For all his Hollywood success, he won only one Oscar for Best Director: it was for the 1943 film *Casablanca.* How could he miss?

Also on this day

1524: Portuguese explorer Vasco da Gama dies in Cochin, Kerala, India * 1822: English poet Matthew Arnold is born

25 December

Charlemagne is crowned Emperor

800 On Christmas Day Pope Leo III conducted the ceremonies in Rome. Charles, the great conqueror, devout Christian and King of the Franks, would be crowned Emperor with dominion over all the territories he had subjugated, which meant most of western Europe. Thus began a sort of revival of the Roman Empire that had lapsed in the 5th century. The new Emperor would be known in history as Carolus Magnus, Charles the Great, Charlemagne (or, if you're German, Karl der Grosse).

Charlemagne was the first Holy Roman Emperor to be crowned by the Pope. (Another Charles, the V, would be the last in 1530.) The empire he founded (or revived) would last over 1,000 years until the abdication of Franz II in 1806. His empire would first be described as 'Holy' by Emperor Frederick Barbarossa in 1157, and the full title, *Sacrum Romanum Imperium*, was first used in 1254. Even then it was a description, not a title, as the 'Holy Roman Empire' has in fact never existed as an institution but simply as a name used by historians.

Charlemagne was 48 at the time of his coronation, old for that time in history, but still the tall, athletic figure he had always been. Despite the French-sounding name by which he is known in the English-speaking world, his own language was German (although he had some Greek and Latin, too, and probably some of the Old French dialect spoken by his French subjects), and his capital was on the German side of the Rhine in Aachen, which the French persist in calling Aix-la-Chapelle.

As a ruler, Charlemagne was known for his personal leadership and excellent administration, and, although he could not write, his court was famed for the intellectuals it attracted from all over the world. Personally religious and a great supporter of the Church, he attempted to ban dancing throughout his empire because of its supposed pagan origins, but in this he was widely ignored.

Charlemagne also fiercely suppressed pagan German tribes, especially the Saxons, against whom he led his army into battle eighteen times over the years, but his conquests had more to do with building his empire than with promulgating his religion. In one rather unchristian moment, after a battle against the Saxons he ordered a mass beheading of 4,500 captured enemy warriors.

Charlemagne died in 814, leaving his empire to his son Louis I, but his Carolingian dynasty lasted only until 887.

And William the Conqueror is crowned King of England

1066 For his coronation today as King of the English William the Conqueror chose a new monastery church that had been consecrated only a year earlier – Westminster Abbey. William's saintly predecessor Edward the Confessor had built the great abbey, sensibly calling it West Minster (i.e. west monastery) as it was west of the royal palace.

There had long been a church on the site, as Saeberht, the first Christian king of the East Saxons, reputedly built one there at the end of the 6th century. So pleased was Heaven by this display of faith that St Peter miraculously came to consecrate it. Three and a half centuries later St Dunstan, the famously devout Archbishop of Canterbury, rebuilt and enlarged the monastery, but by Edward the Confessor's time it was falling into disrepair.

Edward was the first royal customer of his own new abbey, as he died only eight days after its consecration and was buried there. On the day of Edward's funeral Harold Godwine became the first king to be crowned there (as Harold II), but that very coronation impelled William to invade, as he claimed that Edward, his cousin, had promised him the throne.

Since this day in 1066 every British monarch has been crowned in Westminster Abbey except for two. One was Edward V, that unfortunate twelve-year-old whom Richard III treacherously locked up in the Tower of London and murdered before he could be crowned. The other was the feckless Edward VIII, who abdicated before his coronation, having served only eleven months as King.

The origins of some good old Christmas traditions

AD 336 (or thereabouts) There seems to be some considerable doubt concerning when Christmas was first celebrated on 25 December. Some sources put it at 336, others at 354, and yet others contend that the Pope and saint-to-be Julius I fixed the date, but his pontificate lasted from 337 to 352.

What all agree on is that the Church selected 25 December because, not knowing Jesus' actual birthday, it was canny enough to choose a time when pagans had traditionally celebrated the winter solstice.

In pagan Rome this meant the Saturnalia, a seven-day holiday starting on 17 December, when all business was suspended, executions postponed and gifts exchanged. During this *natalis solis invicti* (birthday of the unconquered sun) slaves were given temporary freedom and were served by their masters.

In Scandinavia the winter solstice holiday, the *midvinterblot* (midwinter blood), was a bit more grisly, as it featured animal and human sacrifices. In Scotland on the shortest day of the year the Druids worshipped the Sun God, hoping to ensure his return.

The word Christmas comes from the old English *Cristes maesse* (Christ's Mass). The Christmas tree originated in Germany, also derived from pagan winter festivals (although hagiographers credit it to Martin Luther), and was popularised in Great Britain by the German Prince Albert in 1841. German settlers had introduced it to America as early as the 17th century, but its popularity there blossomed when Albert made it fashionable in Great Britain. To the Scandinavians we owe one of Christmas's more pleasurable secular customs, kissing under the mistletoe, a plant that Norsemen thought special to Freya, the goddess of love.

Also on this day

AD 496: French King Clovis is converted to Christianity * 1642: English physicist and mathematician Isaac Newton is born in Woolsthorpe near Grantham * 1883: French painter Maurice Utrillo is born in Paris * 1899: American screen icon Humphrey Bogart is born * 1983: Spanish painter Joan Miró dies at the age of 90

26 December

Washington crosses the Delaware to surprise the Hessians

1776 Today, like Lazarus raised from the dead, the Continental army, widely dismissed as an effective fighting force after a series of defeats around New York, emerged from the early morning gloom in unexpected strength and total surprise to overwhelm the Hessian garrison at Trenton, New Jersey, and produce a timely and crucial victory in the American War of Independence, one of the most significant in the entire history of American arms.

Reports of the army's demise – from its friends as well as its foes – seemed well founded by the late autumn. As its columns retreated southward through New Jersey, they were harried by the pursuing British and their progress was marked by increasing desertions and near-mutinies from troops who were weary, underfed and defeated. It was a force reduced to 3,400 men, a 'shadow army' in the Commander-in-Chief's phrase, that Washington led across the Delaware River to Pennsylvania on 7 December.

Well satisfied with his own army's autumn operations, General Howe, the British Commander-in-Chief, went into winter quarters in New York City, leaving some 5,000 troops in forward positions in New Jersey, a force more than adequate, he thought, to keep the local population under control and deal with whatever attacks the rebel forces might mount.

At this blackest of times, with the enlistment periods of most of his regiments expiring at the end of the year, barely three weeks away, General Washington and his generals decided on a bold, do-or-die operation: they would lead the Continental Army back across the Delaware at night and attack the isolated British position at Trenton, held by three Hessian regiments.

From spies, deserters and British sympathisers, the British military expected American attacks against Trenton over Christmas, but assumed they would be no more than the usual patrol-sized, hit-and-run affairs. When, in fact, a rebel scouting party materialised and shots were exchanged on Christmas morning, Colonel Rall, the Hessian commander, supposed that he had met whatever the Americans intended. A raging northeaster bringing heavy snows that evening furthered the impression that the garrison was safe from raids, at least while the storm lasted.

On Christmas night, Washington and his regiments, numbering 2,400 men, began ferrying across the ice-swollen river nine miles above Trenton. It was slow, dangerous work, impeded by high winds, and the last of the artillery didn't get over until 3.00 a.m. The army marched over frozen roads in sleet, snow and freezing rain. The force divided at one point so that it would enter Trenton simultaneously from two directions. It was 8.00 when an outpost spotted the northern column advancing through the snow and shots were fired that roused the sleeping garrison.

It was a quick but bloody action as Washington's troops fought through the village of 100 houses. Captain Alexander Hamilton positioned the artillery pieces that enfiladed the streets in which the Hessians tried to form. Lieutenant James Monroe was wounded while leading a charge to capture Hessian cannon. By 9.30 the Hessians surrendered. American losses were light: four wounded, none killed. Of the Hessians, 106 were killed or wounded, and 918 taken prisoner. By noon the exhausted American army, with its large bag of prisoners, began returning to its positions across the river.

Washington's victory at Trenton – together with his brilliant follow-up successes a few days later at Assumpink Creek and Princeton – gave a tremendous boost to the American cause, breathing life into wavering patriots, restoring self-confidence to the army, and providing the Continental Congress with a glimpse of what its forces, poorly cared for as they had been, might after all accomplish.

Also on this day

1890: German archaeologist and finder of 'Troy' Heinrich Schliemann dies * 1891: American expatriate novelist Henry Miller is born * 1893: Dictator, mass murderer and founding father of the People's Republic of China Mao Tse-tung is born

27 December

Charles Darwin sets sail on the Beagle

1831 Today the refitted naval brig *Beagle* sailed from Plymouth on a voyage that would last five years and two days and change for ever our understanding of life on Earth. On board as an unpaid naturalist was Charles Darwin, not yet the balding, grey-bearded patriarch of later years but a clean-shaven 22 year old, cheerful and energetic, with an insatiable curiosity about the natural world.

Son of a wealthy doctor, Darwin showed little early indication of genius. He was so indifferent a student that his father once told him, 'You care for nothing but shooting, dogs, and rat-catching, and you will be a disgrace to yourself and all your family.' But after exposure at Cambridge to a circle of scientists and influenced by his beetle-collecting entomologist cousin, Darwin became fascinated by the natural world. Shortly after leaving university he accepted with alacrity the invitation to sail with the *Beagle* on an assignment to set up a series of time-keeping stations on the west coast of South America, the Galapagos Islands and in the Pacific.

During the next five years Darwin took every opportunity to go ashore wherever the *Beagle* docked. And every place he went he studied the flora, fauna, rocks, reefs and fossils, collecting specimens and assiduously taking notes. Particularly in the Galapagos Islands he noticed that birds seemed to have evolved differently to meet the varying conditions of each island. These observations would lead to his groundbreaking theory of evolution.

On returning to England, Darwin first published three books on geology. It was only seven years later, in 1838, that he began to complete his own evolutionary hypothesis on natural selection – the process by which 'favourable variations [in a species] would tend to be preserved, and unfavourable ones to be destroyed', leading to changes in the species.

As he refined his startling ideas, Darwin became increasingly aware of the hostile reactions most people would have to them, and so he continually deferred publication. Then, in June 1858, he received a letter from a younger colleague, Alfred Russel Wallace, which encapsulated in a single paper the principles that Darwin had been developing for the past two decades. Distraught, Darwin turned to his scientific friends for help.

Fortunately for Darwin, while Wallace's reasoning was correct, he lacked Darwin's extensive proof, and two friends arranged for a joint paper to be presented to the Linnaean Society of London on 1 July 1858. Darwin himself was not present at this first public unveiling of his earth-shattering theory, as he was attending the funeral of his youngest son, who had died of scarlet fever.

Sixteen months later, on 24 November 1859, Darwin at last published his great work defining the process of evolution, *On the Origin of Species by Means of Natural Selection, or The Preservation of Favoured Races in the Struggle for Life.* The book caused instant controversy, hailed by the scientific community and renounced by the powers of the Church. It has never since been out of print and is now recognised as one of the greatest and most influential scientific works ever written.

An attempt to kill a king

1594 Today King Henri IV's love of women almost cost him his life.

A seducer of accomplishment, Henri had numerous mistresses, but his favourite was the ravishing 21-year-old Gabrielle d'Estrées. Of noble birth, she had first been kept by Roger de Saint-Lary, who introduced her to the King. She became his paramour in 1591 when she was just nineteen. Henri fell deeply in love, but Gabrielle used her position to amass a fortune while occasionally taking less royal if younger lovers (Henri was twenty years her senior).

Returning to Paris from a royal tour of Normandy, today the King hurried impatiently to visit his beloved Gabrielle. He found her surrounded by a large group of courtiers, among whom was a young Catholic extremist named Jean Chastel, a teacher at the Jesuit college at Clermont. There other fanatical monks had persuaded him that, since the Pope had not yet recognised Henri's abjuration of Protestantism made seventeen months before, killing the King would be a service to God.

As the King entered the room, Chastel struck at him with a knife, wounding him in the lip. Henri leapt back, bleeding, and his bodyguards instantly dragged his assailant to the ground.

Henri soon recovered from the attack, and Gabrielle remained his adored mistress. The scheming Jesuits, however, fared less well, as Henri banished the entire order from France. A sterner fate awaited Jean Chastel, who was torn apart by four wild horses for his attempt to kill the King.

Also on this day

1822: French chemist and microbiologist Louis Pasteur is born * 1901: Singer and actress Marlene Dietrich is born in Berlin * 1927: Leon Trotsky is expelled from the Communist Party in Russia

28 December

The first true motion picture – cinema is born

1895 As you stroll up the boulevard des Capucines towards the Paris Opéra, you will pass the world-famous Café de la Paix, just a stone's throw from the spot where the Grand Café once stood. Here on this day Louis and Auguste Lumière demonstrated their new invention, the cinématographe, by projecting a short film clip that alarmed the café's customers with the image of an onrushing train as well as a longer film entitled *La Sortie des Usines Lumière* (Workers Leaving the Lumière Factory). It was the first true motion picture ever made and the birth of cinema.

Louis and Auguste had been born in Besançon in 1862 and 1864 respectively and brought up in Lyon. During their schooldays they exhibited both a taste and a talent for still photography, and when the elder brother was only eighteen he persuaded his father Antoine to bankroll him in establishing a photographic plate factory. It was such a runaway success that in a little over ten years the brothers were manufacturing 15 million plates a year.

Then, in 1894, father Antoine made a visit to Paris, where he saw a showing of Thomas Edison's Kinetoscope, a machine with which viewers could see a moving film, but only through an eyepiece. Returning to Lyon, he urged his sons to find a way to project a moving image.

Louis and Auguste combined two existing ideas, the projection of successive images, a concept already developed by Emile Reynaud, and Edison's use of sprocket-wound film. Their cinématographe was so successful that we have used its first three syllables – cinema – ever since. (The Lumières took their device's name from the Greek *kinema*, 'movement', which comes from *kinein*, 'to move'. Edison's 'Kinetoscope' derives from the same source. Although in English and all Latin languages the modern word starts with 'cine', the German word 'Kino' comes directly from Edison's contraption.)

The Lumières' machine had several clear advantages over Edison's apparatus: it could be used for both photographing and projecting, was quieter, smaller and lighter, and used less film. Furthermore, Edison's Kinetoscope showed images at 46 frames per second, but the Lumières understood that the human brain's illusion of continuous movement is created by images shown at any speed of more than 15 images per second. Therefore they reduced the rate of exposure to 16 frames a second, the rate still used in films today.

The brothers instantly patented their invention, and during the next four years made over 1,000 motion pictures. But, in spite of their technical brilliance, they proved less talented at predicting the future. Seeing their cinématographe as not much more than an oddity, they told a friend that it 'is an invention without a future'.

Also on this day

1065: Westminster Abbey is consecrated under King Edward the Confessor * 1734: Scottish freebooter and outlaw Rob Roy (Robert MacGregor) dies * 1836: Mexico's independence is recognised by Spain

29 December

Murder in the cathedral

1170 'What cowards have I about me', fumed an enraged King Henry II. 'Will no one rid me of this turbulent priest?' These hasty words spoken in anger triggered the most famous murder of the Middle Ages.

Henry Plantagenet had become King of England at only 21. Within a year he had appointed as Chancellor a tall, lean man with dark hair and a sallow complexion, fifteen years his senior. He was Thomas Becket.

The King and Becket were soon boon companions, perfectly complementing each other in court and enjoying each other's company while hunting or in the taverns of London. With his quick mind and astute understanding of Henry's will, Becket played a leading role in concentrating power in the King's hands at the cost of the feudal barons and the Church.

So pleased was Henry by Becket's performance that within seven years he appointed him Archbishop of Canterbury, second in power only to the King himself.

But then Becket began to change. His public style became more imperious, his arrogance more pronounced, his ostentation more insufferable. But privately he also changed, spending hours in prayer and becoming a vegetarian. Most critically, he increasingly came to support the old, medieval powers of the Church, especially when they ran counter to the claims of the crown.

The first signs of conflict came in January 1163 when Becket excommunicated one of Henry's senior barons. But the greatest dispute involved the trial of miscreant priests. Becket was adamant that all clerics suspected of crime be tried exclusively by canonical trial overseen by a bishop, but Henry insisted that they be subject to royal authority. The King also appropriated any income derived from vacant sees and banned the excommunication of court officials without royal consent.

So vehement were the arguments, so bitter the quarrel, that after Becket had been Archbishop for just over two years he fled to the continent when Henry bitterly denounced him.

Six years later an uneasy truce was arranged, and on 1 December 1170 the Archbishop returned to England, but he immediately rekindled the fire by excommunicating three bishops appointed by the King. Henry was in Bayeux when he heard the news. Incensed, he barked out his famous exhortation.

Henry had spoken in a moment of temper and had no intention of ordering a murder, but in court were four impatient barons, Reginald Fitzurse, Hugh de Moreville, William de Tracey and Richard le Breton. Immediately they were riding hard for England, and although Henry sent out orders to stop them, the messenger failed to catch up with them.

On the afternoon of 29 December the barons reached the Archbishop's palace at Canterbury. Dressed in white cloaks over chain mail, they confronted Becket and demanded that he abandon England for ever. Contemptuously he replied, 'Not for living man, not for the King, will I fly!'

At the hour of vespers the Archbishop went to his cathedral. As he stood in the north transept the four armed knights strode in, accompanied by another knight named de Brock, with whom they had stayed the previous night. Becket moved to the altar as the men approached, trying to take him prisoner. But Becket resisted, crying out, 'I am prepared to die for Christ and for His Church.' At these, his last words, de Tracey struck at him with his sword, wounding one of the few clerics supporting the Archbishop but only grazing Becket's forehead. Then de Tracey and le Breton both hacked at the Archbishop, knocking him down, and de Brock placed his foot on his neck and sliced through his skull so that his brains spread out on the stone floor.

The arrogant Archbishop was finally dead. After the barons had fled, cathedral priests recovered the corpse and discovered that under his robes Becket was clothed in sackcloth and his body was scourged with the marks of a penitent.

As was usual in medieval times on portentous occasions, directly after the murder a violent storm broke out and lightning filled the sky. Becket's tomb instantly became a place of worship, and in less than three years he was canonised. King Henry came to Canterbury to do penance and receive absolution.

For four centuries Becket's shrine remained a goal of pilgrimage for the faithful, but in the 16th century Henry VIII had it ripped from the cathedral and destroyed. He had no patience with the priest who would defy a king.

The Jameson raid on Johannesburg

1895 Towards sunset on this Sunday evening, Dr Leander Starr Jameson, right-hand man of the great British empire-builder Cecil Rhodes, led 600 armed and mounted men on a daring raid. Their destination was Johannesburg, 200 miles away in the Boer republic of Transvaal, their mission – a wild imperial gamble in the spirit of Wolfe, Clive or Gordon – to make Britain supreme in all of South Africa.

The Jameson raid was a disaster and failed utterly in its purpose of overthrowing the anti-British Boer government of President Paul Kruger. Jameson and his men were captured miles short of Johannesburg and carted away to jail. Found on them were incriminating copies of telegrams that linked the raiders with Rhodes, the Prime Minister of the Cape Colony, and with his superiors at the Colonial Office in London.

It was a terrible foreign policy embarrassment for Great Britain. In another age, CNN would have had a field day. In London and Cape Town, there were official investigations and public trials. The involvement of unnamed higher-ups was suspected. It was the Iran-Contra affair of its day: there was a cover-up and deals were made. A Colonel North figure in the Colonial Office was found who testified that he had never informed his chiefs of his dealings with the now thoroughly discredited Rhodes and the plotters of the raid. Rhodes was forced to resign.

Like John Brown's abortive 1859 raid on Harper's Ferry before the American Civil War, the Jameson raid succeeded in hastening conflict. Winston Churchill called it 'the herald, if not indeed the progenitor of the South African War'. War came in 1899 and lasted two and a half years at a frightful cost to Boers and Britons. It resulted in the Boer Republic's incorporation into the British Empire, Rhodes's intention from the beginning. Jameson spent fifteen months in a British jail for leading the raid, but after the war he got Rhodes's old job as Prime Minister of the Cape Colony. Cecil Rhodes died in 1902, reputation in ruins, but wealth intact. He is remembered today not for his imperial mischief in South Africa but for the scholarships that bear his name.

Also on this day

1809: British Prime Minister William Gladstone is born * 1825: French painter Jacques Louis David dies * 1890: The last major battle between American Indians and US troops takes place at Wounded Knee, South Dakota

30 December

Rasputin is murdered

1916 It was late in the evening of 29 December in St Petersburg when, accompanied by the jolly beat of *Yankee Doodle* playing on the gramophone, Prince Feliks Yusupov offered his guest two cakes laced with cyanide of potassium, along with a similarly doctored glass of Madeira. Yet despite a dosage theoretically 'enough to kill a horse', the intended murder victim, a bearded and brooding holy man, continued to chat calmly with his host.

After the clock chimed midnight Yusupov could wait no longer. Drawing a revolver, he shot his visitor in the back, knocking him to the ground. But instead of dying the victim rose to his feet and charged out into the garden. There another assassin waited. He shot the holy man twice, and then the two murderers rolled him up in a blue rug and pushed their grisly package through a hole they had carved through the frozen surface of the Moika Canal on the Neva River. When the body was recovered three days later, water was found in the lungs. The murdered man had finally drowned, after surviving both poison and bullets.

Such was the end of the sinister 'staretz', or self-styled mystic christened Grigory Yefimovich Novykh but universally known as Rasputin, Russian for 'debauched one'.

Rasputin had been born a peasant in Siberia in 1872. At eighteen he experienced a conversion to the Khlysty flagellant sect and developed the theory that he could achieve a state of grace through 'holy passionlessness', a condition best reached through the exhaustion of prolonged debauchery. Although illiterate, unkempt and unclean (he bathed but once a month), he found women susceptible to his sexually charged message from God.

For over a decade Rasputin wandered around Russia preaching and seducing and finally arrived in St Petersburg in 1903. There his reputation as a mystic grew until Tsar Nicholas and his neurotic wife Alexandra summoned him to attend their four-year-old son Aleksey, the Tsarevich, whose life was threatened by haemophilia. Miraculously, Rasputin seemed to help the boy, probably through his hypnotic powers, and his place at court was assured.

For the next ten years Rasputin continued his drunken orgies and faith-based seductions, claiming that any woman who had sex with him would purify her soul. But Nicholas and Alexandra refused to believe reports about him, considering them malicious and unfounded gossip, and his baleful influence grew, much to the distress of the country's nobility and even members of the imperial family. Then, in 1914, came war.

In August 1915 the feckless Tsar Nicholas decided to take personal command of his armies and left for the front, leaving the government in the hands of his wife Alexandra, whose spiritual and personal advisor Rasputin had become. Now the staretz could influence the choice of Cabinet ministers and even manipulate critical military decisions affecting the army.

This finally provoked Prince Yusupov and four other extreme conservatives to intervene to preserve the country, the monarchy and the power of the nobility. One, Vladimir Purishkevich, was a member of the Duma while another was the Tsar's cousin, Grand Duke Dmitry Pavlovish. Seeing the Tsar and Tsarina impervious to reason, they resolved to remove Rasputin by force and carried out the murder.

Hearing rumours of his impending assassination – the plotters were scarcely discreet about their intentions – Rasputin sent a last letter to the Tsar that may have proved him a psychic after all. 'I shall depart this life before the first of January', he wrote. 'If one of your relatives causes my death, then no one in your family, that is, none of your children or relations, will live for more than two years. They will be killed by the people of Russia.'

Just nineteen months later, on 16 July 1918, Communist insurgents shot Tsar Nicholas and Alexandra and their four children in a cellar at Ekaterinburg.

Also on this day
1865: British writer Rudyard Kipling is born * 1922: The USSR is established * 1924: American astronomer Edwin Hubble announces the existence of other galactic systems

31 December

Bonnie Prince Charlie

1720 Today Bonnie Prince Charlie, that quixotic Stuart prince who spent a lifetime in exile vainly trying to get his family and himself restored to the throne of England, was born in the Palazzo Muti in Rome.

Charlie was the grandson of the petulant and narrow-minded King James II, who in 1688 had been unceremoniously chased into exile for his fervent and unbending Catholicism. James had died in 1701, but his son, the unfortunate Old Pretender James Edward, twice tried and failed to invade the British Isles to regain the crown, resolutely refusing to convert to Protestantism for the chance to become the British heir. Then came the Bonnie Prince, a handsome, dashing young man who was determined to restore his father to the throne.

Charlie's first effort came when he was 24 and joined a French invasion fleet. But, just as it had with the Spanish Armada, a hurricane scattered the ships before they put the army ashore.

A year later Charlie mounted a second effort, this time on his own. In July 1745 he landed almost alone in the Hebrides. Reaching the mainland with only seven followers, he began rallying discontented Scots to his banner as he marched towards Edinburgh. By November he had attracted almost 6,000 supporters and headed for London. But soon a large English army was advancing towards him, and Charlie's officers and men started to trickle away, forcing him to retreat back across the border to Scotland.

In April 1746 the British army, now 9,000 strong, met Charlie's 5,000 men at Culloden Moor, six miles east of Inverness. The result was mass slaughter, as over 1,000 Highlanders perished during the battle to only 50 British.

What happened next is the stuff of legend. In a desperate attempt to escape his English pursuers, Charlie spent the next five months in what became celebrated as the 'flight through the heather'. In the Hebrides once again, he encountered Flora MacDonald, a brave young Jacobite sympathiser who disguised the prince as her serving maid and took him with her party across to the Isle of Skye. From there, still pursued, he wandered among the Highlands until he finally managed to get away to France. 'And so he left us,' wrote a bitter Scot, 'and he left us all in a worse state than he found us.'

Flora was temporarily incarcerated in the Tower of London for her treason but pardoned after a year. This adventurous tale became a popular classic after 1814 when Sir Walter Scott published *Waverley*, the account of Charlie's failed invasion and escape.

Bonnie Prince Charlie spent the next 42 years wandering around Europe, principally in Italy, gradually decaying into a drunken, self-indulgent wreck. Blindly committed to the theory of divine right, difficult and unapproachable, he styled himself Charles III of England. His wife, a woman 33 years his junior, called him 'the most insupportable man who ever lived, a man who combined the faults and failings of all classes, including the vice of lackeys, that of drink'. She went on to say that 'he rarely missed being drunk twice a day'. Such was the man who had once been the bonnie prince, who died one month after his 68th birthday in the Palazzo Muti, the palace where he had been born.

The birth of the first papal Borgia

1378 His father Domingo was a prosperous land holder and gentleman farmer who lived in the small town of Játiva, near Valencia in Catalonian Spain. It was there that Alfonso de Borja was born on the last day of 1378. Who would have predicted that he would be the first luminary in a famous dynasty of the Church?

In Spain Alfonso rose to the rank of Bishop of Valencia, hoping but not expecting to go further. But in 1455, when he was 77, the rivalry between the Orsini and Colonna families in Rome reached such a pitch that the College of Cardinals elected him Pope, expecting a short reign that could serve as a cooling-off period between the two Roman factions.

Indeed, Alfonso, or Pope Calixtus III as he now was, lived only another three years, his pontificate noted only for proclaiming the innocence of Joan of Arc, who had been burnt at the stake in 1431. But during his stay in the Vatican he brought large numbers of his Catalan relations to Rome, among whom was his nephew Roderigo, whom he created cardinal and named as generalissimo of the papal army.

Roderigo, who Italianised the family name to Borgia, rose to the papal throne in 1492. During his eleven years as pontiff he supported a series of mistresses, fathered the notorious Cesare and Lucrezia, and set new standards for nepotism.

Despite the corruption of Roderigo and his offspring, the Borgias continued to play a leading role in the Church. His great-grandson Francisco de Borjia became the third general of the Jesuits and eventually was canonised, while his great-great-grandson Giovanni Panfili became Pope Innocent X in 1644.

After Innocent, the Borgia religious bloodline seemed to be wearing thin, but in 1799 there was one last family thrust for Church prominence when Cardinal Stefano Borgia was very nearly elected Pope.

'I shall arrive in the other world in time to wish my friends
a Happy New Year'

1793 Armand-Louis de Gontaut, duc de Biron, was a noted sophisticate, an accomplished philanderer and one of France's most republican aristocrats. He fought under the comte de Rochambeau during the American Revolution and later commanded French republican troops in Belgium, but there and later in Italy he never saw action. Worse, he was an intimate friend of the duc d'Orléans (Philippe Egalité). That, combined with Biron's noble blood, was enough for the firebrand Robespierre to order his imprisonment and execution.

On the morning of the last day of 1793 Biron was in his cell breakfasting on oysters and white wine when an envoy from the Revolutionary Tribunal arrived to announce that he would be guillotined that very day. With exquisite *politesse* the Duke smilingly requested, 'Do permit me first to have another dozen oysters.' Permission was granted, and after Biron had finished his meal he was led to the place of execution.

Even at the end Biron never lost his sang-froid, remarking cheerily as he positioned himself beneath the blade, 'I shall arrive in the other world in time to wish my friends a Happy New Year.'

Also on this day
1869: French painter Henri Matisse is born in Le Cateau, Picardy * 1877: French painter Gustave Courbet dies at La Tour de Péliz, Switzerland * 1880 American general and father of the Marshall Plan George Marshall is born

And so, gentle reader, as we come to year's end we wish you, too,
a Happy New Year.

Bart Marsh and Bruce Carrick

Index

Ambrose, St 4 April 397
American Civil War 10 November 1775;
29 March 1790; 12 February 1809;
28 February 1854; 2 December 1859;
20 December 1860; 11 April 1861;
21 July 1861; 5 August 1861; 7 April
1862; 29 July 1862; 6 September 1862;
1 January 1863; 10 May 1863; 3 July
1863; 11 May 1864; 4 August 1864;
9 April 1865; 14 April 1865; 18 June
1867; 25 June 1876; 12 November 1880;
2 July 1881; 23 July 1885
American Revolution 30 October 1735;
10 January 1738; 13 April 1743; 16
December 1773; 18 April 1775;
19 April 1775; 17 June 1775; 10
November 1775; 4 July 1776; 22
September 1776; 26 December 1776;
20 March 1778; 23 September 1779;
14 June 1801
André, Major John 14 June 1801
Angelico, Fra (Guido di Pietro)
27 September 1389
Anna Karenina 20 November 1910
Anna, Empress of Russia 25 November
1741
Anne I of England (Stuart) 19 June 1566;
25 July 1603; 6 February 1665;
1 May 1707
**Anne of Austria (wife of Louis XIII of
France)** 5 September 1638; 9 March
1661; 27 July 1675
Anschluss 12 March 1938
Antarctica 18 November 1820
Antoninus Pius, Roman Emperor
8 August AD 117; 7 March AD 161
Anzio Landings 22 January 1944
Apollinaire, Guillaume 2 June 1740
Appomattox Courthouse 9 April 1865;
25 June 1876
Arbroath, Declaration of 6 April 1320
Aristotle 1 October 331 BC; 13 June 323
BC
Armada, Spanish 29 July 1588; 27 August
1635
Armistice (First World War)
11 November 1918
Arnald-Amaury, Papal legate
14 January 1208; 22 July 1208

Arnold, General Benedict 10 January
1738; 14 June 1801
Arnold, Matthew 20 November 1910
Artemisia, Queen of Helicarnassus
23 September 480 BC
Arthur, King 24 June 1348
Astor, 2nd Viscount Waldorf
1 December 1919
Astor, Jacob 1 December 1919
Astor, Viscountess Nancy 1 December
1919
Attila the Hun 20 June AD 451
Augerau, General 18 April 1802
Augustine, St 4 April AD 397; 24 August
AD 410
Augustus, Roman Emperor (Octavian)
13 June 323 BC; 8 December 65 BC;
23 September 63 BC; 29 February 45
BC; 2 September 31 BC; 30 August 30
BC; 19 August AD 14; 16 March AD
37; 18 July AD 64; 27 January AD 98;
4 September AD 476
Austerlitz, Battle of 2 December 1805;
23 January 1806; 21 August 1810

Babylonian Captivity 5 June 1305; 29
November 1314; 3 February 1377
Bach, Johann Sebastian 28 July 1750
Bacon, Roger 11 June 1292
Baden-Powell, Col. Robert 17 May 1900
Bakunin, Mikhail 17 May 1814
Balaclava, Battle of 4 October 1853;
25 October 1853
Balboa, Vasco Núñez de 26 September
1513
Baldwin IV of Jerusalem 2 October
1187
Baldwin, Stanley 10 December 1936
Ball, John 15 June 1381
Ballad of Reading Gaol, The 25 May
1895
Balloon, first flight (unmanned) 4 June
1783
Balue, Cardinal Jean 3 July 1423
Balzac, Honoré de 9 December 1565
Bannockburn, Battle of 23 August 1305;
23 June 1314; 6 April 1320
Barbarossa See Frederick I, Holy Roman
Emperor

654

Barbarossa, Khidr 4 July 1546; 20 January 1860

Barbarossa, Operation 10 June 1190; 23 August 1939; 31 January 1943

Barras, vicomte Paul 5 October 1795

Barry, Mme du (Marie-Jeanne Bécu) 13 May 1793

Bartholdi, Frédéric-Auguste 28 October 1886

Basil II, Byzantine Emperor 15 March 963; 16 November 1272

Bastille 17 March 1680; 2 January 1740; 14 July 1789; 21 September 1792; 20 May 1834; 13 November 1834; 13 July 1870

Bayezid I, Turkish Sultan 25 September 1396

Beagle 27 December 1831

Beatles 28 August 1206

Beauharnais, Empress Joséphine de (Joséphine Tascher de la Pagerie) (wife of Napoleon I) 5 October 1795; 9 March 1796; 2 December 1804; 20 April 1808; 5 July 1809; 15 December 1809; 5 May 1821

Beauharnais, Hortense de (Queen of Holland, wife of Louis Napoleon) 20 April 1808; 15 December 1809

Beauvais, siege of 27 June 1492

Becket, St Thomas 29 December 1170; 27 March 1204; 6 July 1762

Beethoven, Ludwig van 16 December 1770; 15 September 1814; 7 May 1824; 26 March 1827

Belgrade, Battle of 16 August 1717

Belisarius 17 January 532; 12 March 537; 1 November 565

Belleau Wood, Battle of 10 November 1775; 6 June 1918

Bellini, Gentile 3 May 1481

Bellow, Saul 10 December 1896

Ben-Hur 12 November 1880

Berengaria (queen of Richard I) 3 September 1189

Berenger, Raimond V, Count of Provence 4 January 1236

Bergman, Ingrid 24 December 1888; 21 October 1940

Berlin, Irving (Israel Baline) 11 May 1888

Bernadotte, Jean-Baptiste, Marshal and later King Charles John of Sweden 21 August 1810

Bernard, St 27 March 1204

Bernini, Gian Lorenzo 7 December 1598

Béziers, sack of 22 July 1208

Billy the Kid (William H. Bonney) 14 July 1881

Biron, Armand-Louis de Gontaut, duc de 31 December 1793

Bisceglie, Duke Alfonso di 11 March 1507; 23 June 1519

Bismarck, Prince Otto von 22 June 1527; 15 November 1684; 1 April 1815; 13 July 1870; 1 September 1870; 18 January 1871; 18 March 1890; 30 July 1898; 4 August 1914

Black Hand (Crna Ruka) 28 June 1914

Blake, William 14 September 1321

Blanche of Castile 27 March 1204; 25 April 1214; 6 August 1223; 29 November 1226; 26 May 1234; 26 November 1252; 25 August 1270

Blenheim, Battle of 10 June 1704; 13 August 1704

Bligh, Captain William 27 April 1521; 9 September 1754; 28 April 1789

Blondel 21 December 1192

Blücher, Field Marshal Prince Gebhard Leberecht von 18 June 1815

Boabdil, (Muhammad Abu 'Abd Allah), Sultan of Grenada 2 January 1492

Boccaccio, Giovanni 9 December 1565

Boer War 29 December 1895; 17 May 1900; 5 June 1916

Bohème, La 1 February 1896

Boleyn, Anne, wife of Henry VIII 25 January 1533; 7 September 1533; 6 July 1535; 7 January 1536; 29 January 1536; 19 May 1536; 17 November 1558

Bon Homme Richard 23 September 1779

Bonaparte, Joseph (Giuseppe Buonaparte) (King of Naples; King of Spain) 15 August 1769; 21 August 1810

Bonaparte, Louis (King of Holland) (Luigi Buonaparte) 20 April 1808; 15 December 1809

Cesena, destruction and massacre 3 February 1377
Cézanne, Paul 8 May 1903
Châlons, Battle of 20 June AD 451
Chamberlain, Neville 10 May 1940; 13 May 1940
Chambord, Château of 12 September 1494; 6 September 1519
Champollion, Jean François 23 December 1790
Champs Elysées 1 September 1715
Chancellorsville, Battle of 10 May 1863
Charing Cross 28 November 1290
Charlemagne, Holy Roman Emperor 10 October 732; 2 April 742; 25 December 800; 28 January 814; 27 September 1389; 23 October 1520; 2 December 1804; 6 August 1806; 26 July 1926
Charles I of England 23 April 1661; 11 December 1688
Charles I of Naples and Sicily (Charles of Anjou) 28 March 1285
Charles I of Spain See Charles V, Holy Roman Emperor
Charles II of England 2 February 1650; 23 April 1661; 6 February 1665; 24 September 1667; 4 November 1677; 6 February 1685; 15 July 1685; 11 December 1688
Charles II of Spain 18 September 1517; 1 November 1700; 4 December 1700
Charles II, duc de Bourbon 6 May 1527
Charles IV of France 23 June 1340
Charles V of France 22 February 1358; 31 July 1358; 12 September 1494
Charles V, Holy Roman Emperor (Charles I of Spain) 25 December 800; 19 June 1369; 22 June 1478; 10 November 1483; 12 September 1494; 24 February 1500; 18 September 1517; 12 January 1519; 23 October 1520; 18 April 1521; 27 April 1521; 11 October 1521; 19 November 1523; 24 February 1525; 6 May 1527; 24 February 1530; 29 November 1530; 4 July 1546; 24 April 1547; 27 October 1553; 13 April 1555; 31 July 1556; 3 February 1557; 14 March 1558; 21 September 1558; 17 November 1558; 13 February 1571; 13 September 1598; 7 June 1914
Charles VI of France 3 December 1368; 17 July 1388; 23 November 1407; 25 October 1415; 10 September 1419; 21 May 1420; 24 September 1435; 26 July 1926
Charles VII of France 6 August 1223; 10 September 1419; 31 August 1422; 6 March 1429; 17 July 1429; 24 September 1435; 20 September 1455
Charles VIII of France 7 July 1456; 30 June 1470; 9 November 1494; 7 April 1498; 23 May 1498; 1 November 1503
Charles IX of France 13 December 1553; 15 March 1560; 24 August 1572; 30 May 1574; 17 December 1599
Charles IX of Sweden 12 November 1611
Charles X of France 27 November 511; 13 July 1793; 4 October 1830; 13 November 1834
Charles XII of Sweden 30 November 1700; 8 July 1709; 30 November 1718
Charles John of Sweden See Bernadotte, Jean-Baptiste
Charles of Anjou 30 March 1282
Charles of Lorraine 12 September 1683
Charles the Bad, King of Navarre 28 May 1358
Charles the Bold, Duke of Burgundy (Charles le Téméraire) 3 July 1423; 20 September 1455; 15 June 1467; 7 August 1472; 2 March 1476; 5 January 1477; 1 February 1477; 19 August 1477; 30 August 1483; 27 June 1492
Charles von Habsburg, Austrian Emperor 9 May 1892
Charles, Prince of Wales 11 October 1521
Chartres Cathedral 6 August 1223
Chase, Salmon P. 5 August 1861
Chekhov, Anton 15 July 1904
Chenonceaux, Château of 28 October 1533
Cherry Orchard, The 15 July 1904
Chiang Kai-shek 20 October 1935; 7 July 1937
China Incident 7 July 1937
Chinon, Château of 6 July 1189; 6 March 1429

Cook, Captain James 9 September 1754; 18 January 1778; 17 April 1790

Coolidge, President Calvin 21 May 1927

Cooper, James Fenimore 9 August 1757

Copernicus (Mikotaj Kopérnik) 24 May 1543

Coral Sea, Battle of the 4 May 1942

Corday, Charlotte 13 May 1793; 13 July 1793

Corneille, Pierre 10 July 1099; 6 June 1606

Cornwallis, General Charles 19 October 1781

Corsica 15 May 1768

Cortés, Hernán 26 September 1513

Cranmer, Thomas (Archbishop of Canterbury) 21 March 1556; 17 November 1558

Creation 26 October 4004 BC

Crimean War 15 September 1814; 12 May 1820; 10 March 1831; 4 October 1853; 20 November 1910

Cromwell, Oliver 23 April 1661; 4 November 1677; 6 February 1685

Cromwell, Thomas 19 May 1536; 28 July 1540

Crown of Thorns 11 August 1239

Crusade, First 18 November 1095; 15 July 1099

Crusade, Second 11 June 1147

Crusade, Third 20 August 1191; 9 October 1192

Culloden Moor, Battle of 31 December 1720; 16 April 1746; 27 February 1776

Curtiz, Michael 24 December 1888

Custer, General George Armstrong 25 June 1876

Custer's Last Stand 25 June 1876

Daim, Olivier la 30 January 1278

Daly, Gunnery Sergeant Daniel 6 June 1918

Dante Alighieri 15 March 44 BC; 8 August AD 117; 1 May 1274, 1283; 28 March 1285; 25 August 1294; 23 January 1295; 5 June 1305; 14 September 1321

Danton, Jacques Georges 26 October 1759; 17 April 1790; 13 May 1793; 8 November 1793; 5 April 1794

Darius I (the Great), Persian Emperor 21 September 490 BC

Darius III, Persian Emperor 1 October 331 BC

Darnley, Lord (Henry Stewart) 6 March 1566; 19 June 1566; 9 February 1567; 15 May 1567; 10 June 1688

D'Artagnan 17 August 1661

Darwin, Charles 9 December 1565; 27 December 1831; 24 November 1859

Dauphin (origin of term) 22 August 1350

David, Jacques Louis 13 July 1793

Davis, Jefferson 12 February 1809

Davis, Richard Harding 22 June 1898

De Revolutionibus Orbium Coelestium (On the Revolutions of the Celestial Spheres) 24 May 1543

Decameron 9 December 1565

Declaration of Independence, US 30 October 1735; 4 July 1776

Decline and Fall of the Roman Empire 9 December 1565

Delacroix, Eugène 26 April 1798

Deladier, Edouard 10 March 1831

Descartes, René 9 December 1565

Descent of Man and Selection in Relation to Sex, The 24 November 1859

Dialogo Sopra I Due Massimi Sistemi del Mondo, Tolemaico e Copernicano 21 June 1633

Diane de Poitiers 28 October 1533; 30 June 1559

Dickens, Charles 7 February 1812; 3 June 1924

Diderot, Dennis 2 May 1729; 6 November 1796

Die Zauberflöte (The Magic Flute) 5 December 1791

Dien Bien Phu, fall of 7 May 1954

Dieppe, raid 19 August 1942

Dio Cassius 22 October 180

Diocletian, Roman Emperor (Gaius Aurelius Valerius Diocletianus) 23 February AD 303; 22 May AD 337; 3 February 1557

Disraeli, Benjamin 23 January 1806; 6 June 1861; 14 December 1861;

10 March 1872; 9 January 1878; 2 June 1882

Garnerin, Jacques 22 October 1797

Garrick, David 29 October 1740; 4 April 1774

Garter, Order of the 13 November 1312; 24 June 1348; 8 June 1376

Gaugamela, Battle of 1 October 331 BC

Gauguin, Paul 24 December 1888; 8 May 1903

Gaulle, General and President Charles de 3 July 1423; 19 July 1848; 21 February 1916; 26 October 1916; 3 July 1940; 23 July 1951

Gaveston, Piers 25 February 1309; 19 June 1312

Gelasius I, Pope 2 February AD 1

Geneviève, St (Genovefa) 20 June AD 451

Genghis Khan 18 August 1227; 1 September 1281

George I of England 18 September 1714

George II of England 6 November 1796

George III of England 16 November 1272; 13 November 1312; 24 June 1348; 4 July 1776; 8 April 1795; 23 January 1806

George IV of England 8 April 1795

George V of England 18 September 1714; 22 January 1901; 19 May 1935; 20 January 1936; 10 December 1936

Georgia, Sherman's march through 15 November 1864

Germanicus 31 August AD 12

Geronimo 3 September 1886

Gettysburg, Battle of 3 July 1863

Ghiberti, Lorenzo 27 September 1389

Ghirlandajo, Domenico 17 October 1483; 9 April 1492

Giap, General Vo Nguyen 7 May 1954

Gibbon, Edward 7 March AD 161; 23 February AD 303; 22 May AD 337; 24 August AD 410; 4 September AD 476; 15 March 963; 9 December 1565; 17 April 1790

Gibraltar 15 July 1212; 30 October 1340; 24 July 1704; 14 March 1757

Gilbert, William S. 25 March 1875

Gladstone, William 9 December 1868

Globe Theatre 29 June 1613

Godefroi de Bouillon 15 July 1099

Goebbels, Joseph 14 October 1944; 30 April 1945

Goethe, Johann Wolfgang 28 August 1749; 26 March 1827; 22 March 1832

Gogh, Theo van 24 December 1888; 8 May 1903

Gogh, Vincent van 24 December 1888

Gold Rush (California) 24 January 1848

Golden Hind 29 July 1588

Golden Spurs, Battle of 11 July 1302

Goldsmith, Oliver 4 April 1774

Gordon, General Charles 'Chinese' 26 January 1885

Göring, Reichsmarschall Hermann 27 February 1933; 10 July 1940; 14 October 1944

Goya, Francisco 3 May 1814

Gozzoli, Benozzo 27 September 1389

Grandson, Battle of 2 March 1476

Grant, President and General Ulysses S. 7 April 1862; 9 April 1865; 23 July 1885

Grape, Whiff of (Napoleon Bonaparte) 5 October 1795

Great Northern War 30 November 1700; 8 July 1709

Great Schism (Papal) 3 February 1337; 20 September 1378; 30 July 1419

Great Wall of China 20 June AD 451

Gregorian calendar 4 October 1582; 10 April 1585; 2 September 1751; 21 September 1792

Gregory I (Saint) 10 April 1585

Gregory VIII, Pope (Albert de Morra) 4 July 1187; 9 October 1192

Gregory IX (Ugo di Segni) 14 January 1208; 22 November 1220; 10 November 1241; 13 December 1250; 26 July 1826

Gregory XI, Pope 20 September 1378; 29 April 1380

Gregory XIII, Pope (Ugo Buoncompagni) 24 August 1572; 4 October 1582; 10 April 1585

Grenada, fall of 2 January 1492

Grey, Lady Jane 12 February 1554; 21 March 1556; 4 September 1588

João I of Portugal (John) 14 August 1385; 9 May 1386
João II of Portugal (John) 3 August 1492
Joffre, General Joseph-Jacques-Césaire 21 February 1916
John de Balliol, King of Scotland 23 August 1305
John III Sobieski of Poland 12 September 1683
John of England 25 March 1133; 1 August 1137; 18 May 1152; 19 December 1154; 24 December 1167; 6 July 1189; 27 May 1199; 24 August 1200; 3 April 1203; 6 March 1204; 27 March 1204; 23 June 1204; 28 August 1206; 23 March 1208; 15 June 1215; 19 October 1216; 14 July 1223; 17 June 1239
John of Gaunt 19 February 1377; 21 June 1377; 15 June 1381; 14 August 1385; 13 October 1399; 14 February 1400; 20 March 1413; 22 May 1455
John XXII (Jacques Duèse) 7 August 1316; 6 April 1320
John, 'Blind' King of Bohemia 26 August 1346
Johnson, Dr Samuel 29 October 1740; 4 April 1774; 13 December 1784
Johnson, President Andrew 28 February 1854
Johnston, General Joseph 23 July 1885
Jones, John Paul 23 September 1779; 17 April 1790
Josef II, Holy Roman Emperor 22 April 1787; 20 February 1790
Joyce, James 10 December 1896
Juan Carlos of Spain 31 May 1906
Juana la Loca (Crazy Joan) of Spain 22 June 1478; 24 February 1500; 18 September 1517; 12 January 1519; 23 October 1520; 13 April 1555
Juarez, Benito 19 June 1867; 19 January 1927
Judas (founder of Zealots) 15 April AD 73
Julian calendar 12 July 100 BC; 29 February 45 BC; 4 October 1582; 2 September 1751
Julius II, Pope (Giuliano della Rovere) 11 December 1475; 1 November 1503; 10 May 1508; 31 October 1517
Justin I, Byzantine Emperor 17 January 532
Justine 9 December 1565; 2 June 1740
Justinian, Byzantine Emperor 17 January 532; 12 March 537; 14 November 565; 2 February AD 1

Kafka, Franz 3 June 1924
Kamikaze 1 September 1281
Kanagawa, Treaty of 31 March 1854
Kappel, Battle of 11 October 1531
Keats, John 26 September 1513
Kenilworth 5 January 1585
Kennedy, President John F. 13 April 1743; 2 July 1881
Kerensky, Alexander Fyodorovich 7 November 1917
Kéroualle, Louise de, Duchess of Portsmouth 2 February 1650
Kershaw, Ian 20 April 1889; 27 February 1933
Key, Francis Scott 18 June 1814; 13 September 1814
Khartoum, Fall of 26 January 1885
King, Martin Luther 20 November 1910
Kipling, Rudyard 25 April 1895; 20 January 1936
Kitchener, Field Marshal Herbert Horatio 5 June 1916
Korean War 14 September 1950
Kossuth, Lajos 13 March 1848
Krakatoa, eruption of 27 August 1883
Kruger, President Paul 29 December 1895; 27 June 1898
Kublai Khan 1 September 1281
Kutuzov, General Prince Mikhail 7 September 1812

La Coruña, Battle of 16 January 1809
La Motte, Jeanne de 31 May 1785
La Rochefoucauld, François, duc de 17 March 1680
La Salle, Robert Cavelier, sieur de 19 March 1687
La Voisin, Mme 22 February 1680
Lady Chatterley's Lover 9 December 1565

Louis VI of France (the Fat) 1 August 1137

Louis VII of France 1 August 1137; 11 June 1147; 21 March 1152; 27 March 1204

Louis VIII of France (Coeur de Lion or Le Lion) 25 April 1214; 14 July 1223; 6 August 1223; 29 November 1226; 26 November 1252

Louis IX of France (St Louis) 25 March 1133; 24 August 1200; 27 March 1204; 25 April 1214; 29 November 1226; 26 May 1234; 4 January 1236; 11 August 1239; 26 November 1252; 25 August 1270; 30 January 1278; 30 March 1282; 28 March 1285; 23 January 1295; 29 November 1314

Louis X of France (the Quarreller – le Hutin) 5 June 1316; 2 January 1322

Louis XI of France 3 July 1423; 7 August 1472; 5 January 1477; 30 August 1483; 27 June 1492

Louis XII of France 12 September 1494; 12 May 1499; 1 November 1503

Louis XIII of France 29 January 1630; 11 November 1630; 5 September 1638; 4 December 1642; 14 May 1643; 27 July 1675; 6 November 1793

Louis XIV of France 6 September 1519; 13 August 1598; 11 November 1630; 5 September 1638; 13 April 1655; 14 June 1658; 9 March 1661; 17 August 1661; 24 September 1667; 17 February 1673; 27 July 1675; 4 November 1677; 22 February 1680; 17 March 1680; 6 May 1682; 26 July 1683; 18 November 1683; 15 November 1684; 11 December 1688; 1 November 1700; 4 December 1700; 19 March 1702; 24 July 1704; 13 August 1704; 30 March 1707; 26 April 1707; 11 September 1709; 1 September 1715

Louis XV of France 16 November 1272; 15 May 1768; 16 May 1770; 30 May 1778; 13 May 1793

Louis XVI of France 3 July 1423; 12 September 1683; 15 November 1684; 16 May 1770; 20 March 1778; 23 September 1779; 31 May 1785; 17 April 1790; 10 August 1792; 21 September 1792; 21 January 1793; 13 May 1793; 13 July 1793; 16 October 1793; 6 November 1793; 8 November 1793; 8 June 1795; 15 October 1795; 20 May 1834; 13 November 1834

Louis XVII of France 8 June 1795

Louis XVIII of France 26 February 1815; 6 December 1815; 13 November 1834; 17 May 1838

Louis-Philippe of France 6 November 1793; 10 March 1831; 17 May 1838; 28 September 1840; 8 October 1840; 24 February 1848; 13 March 1848; 20 December 1848

Louis, duc d'Orléans 23 November 1407

Louis, Joe 3 August 1936

Louisiana Purchase 30 April 1803

Love's Labour's Lost 17 December 1599

Low, David 23 August 1939

Loyola, St Ignatius (Ignacio de Loyola) 15 August 1534; 27 October 1553; 31 July 1556

Lubbe, Marinus van der 27 February 1933

Lucas, Major General John 22 January 1944

Ludendorff, General Erich 1 August 1934

Ludmila, St 28 September 929

Lumière, Louis, Auguste and Antoine 28 December 1895

Lupercalia 2 February AD 1

Lusitania 7 May 1915

Luther, Martin 25 December 366; 30 August 1483; 10 November 1483; 31 October 1517; 3 January 1521; 18 April 1521; 11 October 1521; 11 October 1531; 24 May 1543; 3 December 1545; 18 February 1546; 24 April 1547; 9 December 1565

Lützen, Battle of 12 November 1611; 16 November 1632

MacArthur, General Douglas 13 September 1759; 11 March 1942; 14 September 1950

Macaulay, 1st Baron Thomas Babington 15 March 44 BC; 13 December 1784

Mary I of England (Bloody Mary) (Tudor) 4 August 1347; 22 August 1485; 12 February 1554; 25 July 1554; 30 April 1555; 21 March 1556; 7 January 1558; 17 November 1558; 13 September 1598

Mary II of England (Stuart) 4 November 1677; 19 March 1702; 4 February 1716

Mary of Burgundy (wife of Maximilian I) 20 September 1455; 19 August 1477; 12 January 1519

Mary, Queen of Scots 24 November 1542; 15 March 1560; 6 March 1566; 19 June 1566; 9 February 1567; 15 May 1567; 8 February 1587; 25 July 1603; 10 June 1688; 4 February 1716

Masada, siege of 15 April AD 73

Mata Hari (Margaretha Zella) 13 March 1905

Matilda 5 August 1100; 25 March 1133; 1 December 1135

Matisse, Henri 20 January 1860

Matthias, Holy Roman Emperor 23 May 1618

Maximes 17 March 1860

Maximilian I, Holy Roman Emperor 20 September 1455; 19 August 1477; 12 January 1519; 23 October 1520; 4 October 1830

Maximilian of Mexico 2 December 1823; 19 June 1867; 19 January 1927

Mayerling (Prince Rudolf's suicide) 30 January 1889

Mazarin, Cardinal Giulio (Mazzarini) 29 January 1630; 4 December 1642; 9 March 1661; 17 August 1661; 17 March 1680; 26 July 1683

Mazzini, Giuseppe 10 March 1872

McHenry, Battle of Fort 13 September 1814

McKinley, President William 2 July 1881; 15 February 1898; 1 July 1898

Medici, Alessandro, Duke of Florence 9 July 1737

Medici, Cosimo de', Grand Duke of Florence 27 September 1389; 9 July 1737

Medici, Gian Gastone, Grand Duke of Tuscany 9 July 1737

Medici, Lorenzo de' (the Magnificent) 29 February 1468; 11 December 1475; 26 April 1478; 9 April 1492; 11 August 1492; 9 November 1494; 23 May 1498; 19 November 1523; 28 October 1533; 9 July 1737

Medici, Marie de', Queen of France (wife of Henri IV) 11 April 1599; 17 December 1599; 11 November 1630; 9 July 1737

Medici, Piero de' (son of Lorenzo) 9 November 1494

Meditations **(of Marcus Aurelius)** 7 March AD 161

Mehmed II (the Conqueror) 29 May 1453; 3 May 1481

Mein Kampf 12 March 1938

Mémoires de J. Casanova 9 December 1565

Mencken, H.L. 27 May 1564

Menelek, King of Ethiopia 1 March 1896

Mérimée, Prosper 10 March 1810

Merrimac 9 March 1862

Mers-el-Kebir 3 July 1940

Messalina 13 October AD 54

Metternich, Prince Klemens 15 September 1814; 12 August 1822; 2 March 1835; 13 March 1848; 10 March 1872

Mexican War 23 July 1885

Miani, Battle of 17 February 1843

Michelangelo Buonarroti 14 September 1321; 29 February 1468; 9 April 1492; 11 August 1492; 1 November 1503; 10 May 1508; 19 November 1523; 9 December 1565

Michelotto 11 March 1507

Middle Ages, Traditional end of 29 May 1453

Midway, Battle of 3 June 1942

Mill, John Stuart 19 July 1848

Milton, John 21 June 1633

Milvian Bridge, Battle of 27 October AD 312

Minuit, Peter 24 May 1626

Mirabeau, Honoré Gabriel Riqueti, comte de 5 December 1757; 6 May 1758; 17 April 1790; 2 April 1791

Mitterrand, François 26 October 1916

2 March 1835; 17 May 1838; 28 September 1840; 8 October 1840; 2 December 1851; 6 June 1861

Napoleon III of France (Louis Napoleon Bonaparte) 20 April 1808; 23 January 1832; 22 July 1832; 28 September 1840; 25 May 1846; 20 December 1848; 2 December 1851; 21 November 1852; 29 January 1853; 14 January 1858; 24 June 1859; 20 January 1860; 19 June 1867; 13 July 1870; 1 September 1870; 20 September 1870; 17 October 1870; 9 January 1873; 1 June 1879; 1 February 1896; 19 January 1927

Napoleon, Prince Louis (son of Napoleon III) 1 June 1879

Narva, Battle of 30 November 1700

Nasser, Gamal Abdel 17 November 1869; 25 November 1875

Naval Academy, US 23 September 1779; 2 November 1795; 1 June 1813

Navas de Tolosa (Las), Battle of 16 July 1212

Neipperg, Adam Adalbert, Count von 26 February 1815

Nelson, Admiral Horatio 4 October 1586; 27 November 1770; 24 July 1797; 1 August 1798; 21 October 1805; 15 January 1815

Nero, Roman Emperor (Nero Claudius Caesar Augustus Germanicus, original name Lucius Domitius Ahenobarbus) 13 October AD 54; 18 July AD 64; 9 June AD 68; 20 December AD 69

Nerva, Roman Emperor 27 January AD 98

Nesselrode, Count (Graf), Karl Vasilyevich 15 September 1814

Neue Zürcher Zeitung 12 January 1780

New Amsterdam 24 May 1626

New Orleans, Battle of 8 January 1815

Ney, Marshal Michel 6 December 1815

Nice, integration into France 24 June 1859; 20 January 1860

Nicholas I of Russia 7 September 1812; 4 October 1853

Nicholas II of Russia 30 December 1916; 20 January 1936

Nicholas V, Pope (Tommaso Parentucelli) 31 October 1517

Nicholas, St 6 December AD 343

Nicomedes, King of Bithynia 12 July 100 BC

Nicopolis, Battle of 25 September 1396

Nightingale, Florence 12 May 1820; 4 October 1853

Nika Revolt 17 January 532; 14 November 565

Nile, Battle of 1 August 1798

Nimitz, Admiral Chester 4 May 1942; 3 June 1942; 19 February 1945

Nineteenth Amendment (women's suffrage) 19 July 1848

Nobel, Alfred 10 December 1896

Nogaret, Guillaume de 6 February 1286; 8 September 1303

Nordhoff, Charles 9 September 1754

Numa Pompilius, King 29 February 45 BC

Octavian See Augustus, Roman Emperor

October Revolution 7 November 1917

Odoacer, King of Italy 4 September AD 476

Okinawa, Battle of 10 November 1775

Olivares, Gaspar de Guzmán y Pimental, Conde-Duque d' 17 September 1665

Olivier, Sir Laurence 24 December 1888

On the Origin of Species by Means of Natural Selection, or The Preservation of Favoured Races in the Struggle for Life 9 December 1565; 27 December 1831; 24 November 1859

O'Neil, Eugene 10 December 1896

Opium War 29 August 1842

Orlov, Grigory 2 May 1729; 28 June 1762; 6 July 1762; 12 April 1783

Orsini, Felice 14 January 1858

Orwell, George 3 June 1924

Otho, Marcus, Roman Emperor 9 June AD 68; 20 December AD 69

Otto I, Holy Roman Emperor 2 April 742; 6 August 1806

Otto IV, Holy Roman Emperor 27 July 1214; 14 July 1223

Philip II of Macedon 1 October 331 BC; 13 June 323 BC

Philip II of Spain 20 September 1455; 25 July 1554; 3 February 1557; 10 August 1557; 21 September 1558; 17 November 1558; 19 January 1568; 4 October 1586; 19 April 1587; 29 July 1588; 25 July 1593; 13 September 1598

Philip III (the Good), Duke of Burgundy 20 September 1455; 15 June 1467; 7 August 1472

Philip III of France 25 August 1270

Philip IV of Spain 17 September 1665

Philip IV the Fair of France (Philippe le Bel) 6 February 1286; 23 January 1295; 11 July 1302; 8 September 1303; 5 June 1305; 3 April 1312; 19 March 1314; 29 November 1314; 5 June 1316; 3 February 1377

Philip V of France 7 August 1316; 2 January 1322

Philip V of Spain 1 November 1700; 4 December 1700; 24 July 1704; 13 August 1704

Philip VI of France 23 June 1340; 26 August 1346; 22 August 1350

Philippa, Queen of England (wife of Edward III) 4 August 1347; 22 August 1485

Philippa, Queen of Portugal 14 August 1385

Philippe Egalité 13 May 1793; 6 November 1793; 31 December 1793

Picasso, Pablo 26 April 1937

Pied Piper 26 June 1284

Pirates of Penzance, The 25 March 1875

Pissarro, Camille 8 May 1903

Pitt, William (the Elder) 17 April 1790; 23 January 1806

Pitt, William (the Younger) 24 June 1348; 23 January 1806; 12 August 1822

Pius II, Pope (Enea Silvio Piccolomini) 27 September 1389; 14 August 1464

Pius IV, Pope (Giovanni Angelo de' Medici) 9 December 1565; 10 April 1585

Pius IX, Pope (Giovanni Mastai-Ferretti) 16 November 1272; 16 June 1846; 8 December 1854; 20 September 1870; 19 January 1927

Pius XII, Pope (Eugenio Maria Giuseppe Giovanni Pacelli) 18 July 1936; 26 April 1937

Pizarro, Francisco 26 September 1513; 18 July 1936; 26 April 1937

Plantagenet, Arthur 3 April 1203

Plantagenet, Count Geoffrey 5 August 1100

Plataea, Battle of 23 September 480 BC

Pliny the Elder 10 January 49 BC; 26 July 1926

Pliny the Younger 27 January AD 98

Plutarch 21 April 753 BC; 13 June 323 BC; 13 January 86 BC; 30 August 30 BC

Pocahontas 5 April 1614

Poincaré, President Henri 28 September 1841; 31 July 1914

Poitiers, Battle of 19 September 1356; 22 February 1358; 8 April 1364; 8 June 1376; 21 June 1377; 25 October 1415; 17 July 1453

Polish constitution 3 May 1791

Polk, President James Knox 2 November 1795; 2 December 1823

Poltava, Battle of 30 November 1700; 8 July 1709; 22 April 1787

Poltrot, Jean 18 February 1563

Polybius 2 August 216 BC

Pompey the Great 9 August 48 BC; 7 December 43 BC

Ponce de León, Juan 3 March 1513

Poor Richard's Almanac 19 December 1732

Portinari, Beatrice 1 May 1274, 1283

Potemkin villages 22 April 1787

Potemkin, Prince Grigory Alexandrovich 22 April 1787; 5 October 1791

Prague, First Defenestration of 30 July 1419

Prague, Second Defenestration of 23 May 1618; 8 November 1620

Presley, Elvis 6 November 1796

Priestley, Joseph 17 April 1790

Prince, The 22 June 1527

Princeton, Battle of 26 December 1776

Princip, Gavrilo 28 June 1914

1793; 8 November 1793; 31 December 1793; 28 July 1794; 8 June 1795

Rochambeau, comte Jean Baptiste de Vimeur de 19 October 1781

Röntgen, Wilhelm 10 December 1896

Rohan, Louis René Edouard, Cardinal de 31 May 1785

Roland, Mme Manon (Jeanne-Marie) 8 November 1793

Rolfe, John 5 April 1614

Roman Empire, end of 4 September 476

Rome, burning of 18 July AD 64

Rome, founding of 21 April 753 BC

Rome, fall to Visigoths 24 August AD 410

Rome, sack of 6 May 1527

Rommel, Field Marshal Erwin 24 October 1917; 4 November 1942; 20 July 1944; 14 October 1944

Romulus 21 April 753 BC; 29 February 45 BC; 4 September AD 476

Romulus Augustulus 4 September AD 476

Rooke, Sir George 24 July 1704

Roosevelt, President Franklin Delano 26 November 1789; 8 May 1884; 8 September 1935; 2 July 1937; 3 July 1940; 11 March 1942

Roosevelt, President Theodore 23 September 1779; 2 December 1823; 29 July 1862; 10 December 1896; 1 July 1898; 7 June 1914; 23 October 1917

Roquefort cheese 26 July 1926

Rosamund (Fair Rosamund Clifford) 19 December 1154

Rosenberg, Julius and Ethel 29 March 1951

Rosetta Stone 23 December 1790; 21 July 1798; 22 June 1815

Rossini, Gioacchino Antonio 14 September 1321

Rough Riders 1 July 1898

Rousseau, Jean-Jacques 9 December 1565; 29 October 1740

Roxelana 15 April 1558

Rozier, Jean-François Pilâtre de 21 November 1783; 22 October 1797

Rubicon (river), Caesar's crossing 10 January 49 BC

Rudolf I (The Founder), Holy Roman Emperor 26 August 1278; 6 August 1806

Rudolf von Habsburg, Prince and Archduke 24 April 1854; 30 January 1889

Sade, marquis Donatien Alphonse François de 9 December 1565; 2 June 1740; 3 June 1924

Sainte-Chapelle 25 April 1214; 6 August 1223; 11 August 1239; 25 August 1270

Saipan, Battle of 10 November 1775

Saladin (Salah Ad-Din Yusuf Ibn Ayyub – 'Righteousness of the Faith, Joseph, Son of Job') 18 November 1095; 4 July 1187; 2 October 1187; 20 August 1191; 9 October 1192; 4 March 1193

Salamis, Battle of 23 September 480 BC

Salic Law 2 January 1322; 23 June 1340

Salieri, Antonio 5 December 1791

San Francisco Earthquake 17 April 1906

San Juan Hill, Battle of 1 July 1898

Sancho II 16 February 1279

Sand, George (Aurore Dudevant, née Dupin) 10 March 1810; 17 October 1849

Sans Souci 17 August 1786

Santa Claus 6 December AD 343

Sardou, Victorien 14 June 1800

Sarto, Andrea del 9 April 1492; 12 September 1494

Sassoon, Siegfried 19 May 1935

Savonarola, Girolamo 9 November 1494; 23 May 1498

Schiller, Friedrich von 19 January 1568; 8 February 1587

Schism, Papal 3 February 1377; 20 September 1378; 30 July 1419

Schleswig-Holstein Question 1 April 1815

Schlieffen Plan 4 August 1914

Schlieffen, General Alfred von 4 August 1914

Schmeling, Max 3 August 1936

Schumann, Robert 14 September 1321

Schwerin, Field Marshal 10 February 1741

V-1 (doodlebug) 13 June 1944
V-2 13 June 1944
Valentinian III, Western Roman Emperor 20 June AD 451
Vanity Fair 15 June 1815
Vasari, Giorgio 9 April 1492
Vauban, Sébastien le Prestre, marquis de 30 March 1707
Vega Carpio, Lope Félix de 27 August 1635
Velázquez, Diego 17 September 1665
Venice, Republic of, end of 1 May 1797
Venus 12 July 100 BC
Verdi, Giuseppe 19 January 1568
Verdun, Battle of 21 February 1916
Vermeer, Jan 31 October 1632
Versailles, Palace of 17 August 1661; 6 May 1682; 15 November 1684
Versailles, Treaty of 15 November 1684
Verus, Roman Emperor 7 March AD 161
Vespasian, Roman Emperor (Titus Flavius Vespasianus) 20 December AD 69; 15 April AD 73; 18 September AD 96
Vetsera, Baroness Marie von 30 January 1889
Vicar of Wakefield, The 4 April 1774
Victor Emmanuel I of Italy 16 June 1846; 24 June 1859; 6 June 1861; 20 September 1870; 9 January 1878
Victor Emmanuel III of Italy 28 April 1945
Victoria Eugenia, Princess (wife of Alfonso XIII of Spain) 31 May 1906
Victoria of England 16 November 1272; 12 May 1820; 10 February 1840; 19 July 1848; 14 December 1861; 9 December 1868; 26 January 1885; 22 January 1901; 19 January 1927
Vienna Boys' Choir (Wiener Sängerknaben) 12 January 1519
Vienna, Congress of 4 January 1785; 15 September 1814; 13 November 1834; 2 March 1835
Vienna, Siege of 12 September 1683
Villa, Pancho 23 October 1917
Villars, Claude Louis Hector, duc de 11 September 1709

Villon, François (François de Montcorbier) 3 January 1463
Virgil (Publius Vergilius Maro) 21 April 753 BC; 8 December 65 BC; 14 August 1464
Virgin Mary 2 February AD 1
Vitellius, Roman Emperor 20 December AD 69; 15 April AD 73
Vivaldi, Antonio 14 September 1321; 28 July 1741
Voltaire (François-Marie Arouet) 9 December 1565; 27 July 1675; 2 May 1729; 31 May 1740; 29 October 1740; 14 March 1757; 30 May 1778; 6 November 1796

Wagram, Battle of 5 July 1809
Walewska, Marie 5 July 1809
Walküre (plot to assassinate Hitler) 20 July 1944
Wallace, Lew 12 November 1880
Wallace, William 17 June 1239; 23 August 1305; 27 November 1330; 7 November 1783
Wallenstein, Prince Albrecht von 12 November 1611; 16 November 1632
Walpole, Horace 17 April 1790
Walworth, William 15 June 1381
Wanamaker, Sam 29 June 1613
War and Peace 7 September 1812; 20 November 1910
Warbeck, Perkin 21 April 1509
Wars of the Roses 13 October 1399; 21 May 1420; 22 May 1455; 18 January 1476; 22 August 1485; 21 April 1509
Warwick the Kingmaker (Richard Neville) 21 May 1420; 22 November 1428; 22 May 1455
Washington, President and General George 30 October 1735; 5 March 1776; 22 September 1776; 26 December 1776; 19 October 1781; 26 November 1789; 29 March 1790; 14 December 1799; 20 May 1834
Waterloo, Battle of 2 December 1804; 15 June 1815; 18 June 1815; 6 December 1815
Webster, Daniel 29 March 1790